ENCYCLOPEDIA OF THE RECONSTRUCTION ERA

Greenwood Milestones in African American History

Encyclopedia of Antislavery and Abolition
Edited by Peter Hinks and John McKivigan

Encyclopedia of the Great Black Migration
Edited by Steven A. Reich

Encyclopedia of Slave Resistance and Rebellion
Edited by Junius P. Rodriguez

Encyclopedia of American Race Riots
Edited by Walter Rucker and James Nathaniel Upton

Encyclopedia of the Reconstruction Era
Edited by Richard Zuczek

ENCYCLOPEDIA OF
THE RECONSTRUCTION ERA

Volume 1: A–L

Edited by
Richard Zuczek

Foreword by
Eric Foner

Greenwood Milestones in African American History

GREENWOOD PRESS
Westport, Connecticut • London

To Etsuko, Les, Paul, Rob, and Anne,
five amazing people with one thing in common—faith in me

Library of Congress Cataloging-in-Publication Data

Encyclopedia of the Reconstruction era : Greenwood milestones in African American history / edited by Richard Zuczek ; foreword by Eric Foner.
    p. cm.
    Includes bibliographical references and index.
    ISBN 0-313-33073-5 ((set) : alk. paper)—ISBN 0-313-33074-3 ((vol. 1) : alk. paper)—ISBN 0-313-33075-1 ((vol. 2) : alk. paper)
    1. Reconstruction (U.S. history, 1865-1877)—Encyclopedias. I. Zuczek, Richard, 1966-
  E668.E53   2006
  973.803—dc22   2006010851

British Library Cataloging in Publication Data is available.

This book is included in the African American Experience database from Greenwood Electronic Media. For more information, visit www.africanamericanexperience.com.

Library of Congress Catalog Card Number: 2006010851
ISBN 0-313-33073-5 (set)
    0-313-33074-3 (vol. 1)
    0-313-33075-1 (vol. 2)

First published in 2006

Greenwood Press, 88 Post Road West, Westport, CT 06881
An imprint of Greenwood Publishing Group, Inc.
www.greenwood.com

Printed in the United States of America

The paper used in this book complies with the Permanent Paper Standard issued by the National Information Standards Organization (Z39.48-1984).

10 9 8 7 6 5 4 3 2 1

CONTENTS

LIST OF ENTRIES

LIST OF PRIMARY DOCUMENTS

GUIDE TO RELATED TOPICS

The categories listed below represent major themes and topics, and are not all-inclusive or all-encompassing. Please see the index for a further breakdown of related topics and associated terms.

African Americans

Abolitionists
Abolition of Slavery
African Americans
Agriculture
American Missionary Association (AMA)
Black Codes
Black Politicians
Black Suffrage
Black Troops (U.S.C.T.) in the Occupied South
Bloody Shirt
Bourbons
Bruce, Blanche Kelso
Bureau of Refugees, Freedmen, and Abandoned Lands
Cain, Richard Harvey
Carpetbaggers
Civil Rights
Civil Rights Act of 1866
Civil Rights Act of 1875
Compromise of 1877
Confiscation Acts
Congressional Reconstruction

Constitutional Conventions
Contraband, Slaves as
Contracts
Davis Bend, Mississippi
Delany, Martin R.
Disfranchisement
District of Columbia, Black Suffrage in
Douglass, Frederick
Dunn, Oscar James
Edisto Island, South Carolina
Education
Elliott, Robert B.
Emancipation
Enforcement Act (1875)
Enforcement Acts (1870, 1871)
Field Order No. 15
Fifteenth Amendment (1870)
Fourteenth Amendment (1868)
Freedman's Savings and Trust Company
Freedmen's Bureau Bills
Freedmen's Relief Societies
Garrison, William Lloyd
Gun Clubs
Hampton, Wade, III

Howard, Oliver Otis
Johnson, Andrew
Ku Klux Klan (KKK)
Labor Systems
Lincoln, Abraham
Lost Cause
Memphis Riot (1866)
Military Reconstruction Acts (1867–1868)
Militias
New Orleans Riot (1866)
New South
Phillips, Wendell
Pinchback, Pinckney Benton Stewart
Poll Tax
Port Royal Experiment
Presidential Reconstruction
Rainey, Joseph Hayne
Red Shirts
Redemption
Republicans, Radical
Revels, Hiram R.
Sharecropping
Sherman, William T.
Shotgun Plan

Federal Activism/Rights (Civil, Political, etc.)

Abolition of Slavery
Amnesty Proclamations
Black Suffrage
Chase, Salmon Portland
Civil Rights
Civil Rights Act of 1866
Civil Rights Act of 1875
Command of the Army Act
  (1867)
Confiscation Acts
Congressional Reconstruction
Disfranchisement
District of Columbia, Black
  Suffrage in
Electoral Commission of 1877
Emancipation
Enforcement Act (1875)
Enforcement Acts (1870, 1871)
Fifteenth Amendment (1870)
Fourteenth Amendment (1868)
Freedman's Savings and Trust
  Company
Freedmen's Bureau Bills
House Judiciary Committee
Joint Committee on
  Reconstruction
Military Reconstruction Acts
  (1867–1868)
Republicans, Moderate
Republicans, Radical
Southern Claims Commission
  (SCC)
Southern Homestead Act (1866)
Stevens, Thaddeus
Suffrage
Sumner, Charles
Supreme Court
Thirteenth Amendment (1865)
U.S. Army and Reconstruction
U.S. Constitution

Generals

Abolition of Slavery
Ames, Adelbert
Banks, Nathaniel P.
Black Troops (U.S.C.T.) in the
  Occupied South
Blair, Francis P., Jr.

Bureau of Refugees, Freedmen,
  and Abandoned Lands
Butler, Benjamin Franklin
Canby, Edward Richard
  Sprigg
Carpetbaggers
Command of the Army Act
  (1867)
Confiscation Acts
Congressional Reconstruction
Constitutional Conventions
Contraband, Slaves as
De Forest, John William
Emancipation
Field Order No. 15
Grant, Ulysses S.
Hancock, Winfield Scott
Howard, Oliver Otis
Joint Select Committee on the
  Conduct of the War
Lincoln, Abraham
McCardle, Ex parte (1868)
Milligan, Ex parte (1866)
Pope, John M.
Sheridan, Philip H.
Sherman, William T.
Sickles, Daniel E.
Stanton, Edwin M.
Tenure of Office Act (1867)
Thomas, Lorenzo
U.S. Army and Reconstruction
Violence

Jurisprudence, Laws, Courts, and Constitutions

Abolition of Slavery
Amnesty Proclamations
Black Codes
Black Suffrage
Chase, Salmon Portland
Civil Rights
Civil Rights Act of 1866
Civil Rights Act of 1875
Command of the Army Act
  (1867)
Confiscation Acts
Congressional Reconstruction
Constitutional Conventions
Contracts
Davis, David
Disfranchisement

District of Columbia, Black
  Suffrage in
Electoral Commission of 1877
Emancipation
Enforcement Act (1875)
Enforcement Acts (1870, 1871)
Fifteenth Amendment (1870)
Fourteenth Amendment
  (1868)
Freedman's Savings and Trust
  Company
Freedmen's Bureau Bills
House Judiciary Committee
Impeachment Managers
Impeachment of Andrew
  Johnson
Jim Crow Laws
Joint Committee on
  Reconstruction
Julian, George Washington
Loyalty Oaths
McCardle, Ex parte (1868)
Military Reconstruction Acts
  (1867–1868)
Milligan, Ex parte (1866)
Morrill, Justin Smith
Pardons
Poll Tax
Readmission
Republicans, Moderate
Republicans, Radical
Scandals
Sherman, John
Slaughterhouse Cases (1873)
Southern Claims Commission
  (SCC)
Southern Homestead Act
  (1866)
Stevens, Thaddeus
Suffrage
Sumner, Charles
Supreme Court
Tenure of Office Act (1867)
Texas v. White (1869)
Thirteenth Amendment (1865)
Trumbull, Lyman
Turner, In re (1867)
United States v. Cruikshank
  (1876)
U.S. Army and Reconstruction
U.S. Constitution
Vagrancy

Southern Politics and Politicians

FOREWORD

Nearly a century and a half after the nation's greatest crisis, the Civil War retains its fascination for millions of Americans, but the Reconstruction era that followed remains a much misunderstood period of American history. Reconstruction was both a specific time period, which began during the Civil War, and a prolonged and difficult process by which Americans sought to reunite the nation and come to terms with the destruction of slavery. As a time period, Reconstruction ended in 1877, when the federal government abandoned the policy of intervening in the South to protect the rights of black citizens. As a historical process, it lasted to the turn of the century, until new systems of labor and race relations and a new political order were entrenched in the South.

During Reconstruction, Congress engaged in a bitter struggle with President Andrew Johnson over the definition of American citizenship, culminating in the first impeachment of a president. The United States had its first confrontation with widespread terrorism in the form of the Ku Klux Klan. However, the era also produced enduring achievements, including the ratification of the Thirteenth, Fourteenth, and Fifteenth Amendments to the Constitution; the creation of religious, educational, and political institutions by the newly freed slaves; and their entrance onto the stage of American politics as voters and officeholders. At the dawn of the twenty-first century, the unresolved legacy of Reconstruction remains a part of our lives. In movements for social justice that have built on the legal and political accomplishments of Reconstruction, and in the racial tensions that still plague American society, the momentous events of Reconstruction reverberate in modern-day America.

As Richard Zuczek explains in the introduction to this volume, for many decades, Reconstruction was tragically misunderstood by both historians and the broader public. Academic monographs, popular books, and films portrayed Reconstruction as the lowest point in the entire American saga. According to this view, the vindictive Radical wing of the Republican Party, motivated by hatred of the South, overturned the lenient plans for national reunion designed by Abraham Lincoln and his successor, Andrew Johnson, and imposed black suffrage on the defeated Confederacy. A sordid period of corruption and misrule followed, presided over by unscrupulous political opportunists from the North (derisively termed "carpetbaggers"), southern whites who abandoned their racial and regional loyalties to cooperate with the Radical Republicans (the so-called "scalawags"), and the former slaves, who were allegedly unprepared for the freedom that had been thrust upon them and unfit to participate in government. Eventually, "patriotic" organizations like the Ku Klux Klan overthrew this "misgovernment" and restored "home rule" (a euphemism for white supremacy) to the South.

All history, the saying goes, is contemporary history, in the sense that historical interpretation both reflects and shapes the world in which the historian lives. No period in America's past better illustrates this idea than the era of Reconstruction. The portrait of Reconstruction that so long held sway originated in the contemporary propaganda of southern Democrats opposed to black suffrage and office holding after the Civil War. It gained national legitimacy when it became part of the overall process of reconciliation between North and South that gathered force in the 1880s and 1890s. The road to what the great black abolitionist Frederick Douglass derisively referred to as "peace among the whites" was paved with African Americans' broken dreams of genuine equality and full citizenship. The prevailing account of Reconstruction during the first half of the twentieth century formed an ideological pillar of the system of white supremacy. It provided justification for the white South's unalterable opposition to change in race relations, and for decades of northern indifference to the nullification of the Fourteenth and Fifteenth Amendments. Time and again, white southerners invoked the alleged horrors of Reconstruction to justify racial segregation and the disfranchisement of the region's black voters.

This image of Reconstruction did not go entirely unchallenged, but it was not until the civil rights revolution (sometimes called the Second Reconstruction) that it was finally abandoned by historians. Since 1960, scholars have overturned virtually every assumption of the traditional viewpoint, abandoning the racism at the base of that interpretation and presenting Reconstruction as a laudable attempt to put into effect the principle of equal citizenship for all Americans. In this scholarship, the reputations of Andrew Johnson, the Radicals, carpetbaggers, scalawags, and Klansmen have all been revised, but the most sweeping transformation has been the new emphasis on the centrality of the black experience to understanding the era. Rather than passive victims of the actions of others, a "problem" confronting white society, or an obstacle to reunion, blacks were active agents in overthrowing slavery, winning the Civil War, and shaping Reconstruction. Although thwarted in their quest for landownership, the former slaves' demands for civil and political rights and their efforts to create schools, churches, and other institutions of freedom proved crucial to establishing the social and political agenda of Reconstruction.

Today, the greatest obstacle to a broad appreciation of the history of Reconstruction and its centrality to the American experience is not so much misinformation as ignorance. A recent nationwide survey of college seniors found that fewer than 30 percent could identify Reconstruction. Nonetheless, important scholarship on Reconstruction continues to appear, adding further to our understanding of the era. Work on the development of new labor systems after the end of slavery, and on the legal and constitutional changes of Reconstruction, has continued to flourish. Scholars have examined the roots in slavery of black political mobilization during Reconstruction, and have devoted new attention to the experience of women, white and black, in the postwar South.

This encyclopedia is the first volume to offer a comprehensive portrait of Reconstruction, based on the most up-to-date scholarship. As such, it should be welcomed by professional historians and by a far broader audience of readers interested in gaining insight into this crucial era of the American past. Today, we still debate questions arising from Reconstruction: the rights of American citizens, the proper roles of the state and federal governments, the possibility of interracial political coalitions, affirmative action, reparations for slavery, the proper ways for the government to protect citizens against terrorist violence, and the relationship between political and economic democracy. These and other issues of our own time cannot be properly understood without knowledge of how they were debated during Reconstruction. As long as questions placed on the national agenda during Reconstruction remain unresolved, the era will remain relevant to modern-day America.

Eric Foner

PREFACE

The *Encyclopedia of the Reconstruction Era* represents a major reference work in the field of American Reconstruction. It is not the purpose of these volumes to explore all things American during this period, and the editor is aware that important people and events have been excluded. The focus is Reconstruction, as a period, a process, and a result. Even with that limited scope, the *Encyclopedia* cannot cover all people and occurrences relevant to Reconstruction; like the Civil War that preceded and produced it, Reconstruction occurred from Washington to Vermont to Texas; involved millions of politicians, soldiers, former slaves, and former confederates; had economic, religious, political, constitutional, and social dimensions; and encompassed different goals, agendas, and results, all depending on whom you asked and when you asked them. The editor, in consultation with the contributors and Greenwood Press, made conscious decisions about what to include and what not to include in the hopes of balancing girth with merit. The final entry list represents what we believe are the most important, useful, and pertinent elements of Reconstruction.

Intended for use by students, general readers, and researchers, the *Encyclopedia* is not without its idiosyncrasies, some due to the publisher's policy decisions, some stemming from choices of the editor, and some the natural result of a large work composed by several score of authors. The *Encyclopedia* has three main sections, in addition to the general front matter and back matter. More than 260 entries, many of which are illustrated, comprise the bulk of the volumes; the Primary Documents section provides twenty-six documentary materials from the Reconstruction period; and the three appendixes provide tables and lists of use to the Reconstruction researcher and of interest to the student and general reader. Appendix 1 lists the commanding generals of the five Reconstruction military districts; Appendix 2 lists all the Reconstruction governors in the former Confederate states; and

Appendix 3 supplies the dates of readmission, redemption, and passage of the Thirteenth and Fourteenth Amendments in all the former Confederate states.

The entries are arranged alphabetically, with biographical entries alphabetized by surname (**Ames, Adelbert**) and events by description, not by year (**Elections of 1866**). The entries themselves are structured to be user-friendly. Each has its headword, followed by the main text. Within the text, cross-references to other entries appear in **bold**, a device that also has been used in the Introduction. Longer entries are divided by subheads to allow readers to find pertinent sections more quickly. All entries have "See also" cross-references and "Further Reading" sections after the main text. The "See alsos" refer the reader to related items, but do not duplicate the internal cross-referencing within the entry itself. The "Further Reading" section presents the essentials for that topic—the best, most classic, or most recent works, rather than an exhaustive bibliography. A Bibliography of important general and classic works is also included in the back matter.

In most cases, the more formal labels for terms have been used, but, as with any encyclopedia, readers may need to be flexible and imaginative in locating an entry. For instance, readers seeking information on the economic depression of 1873 will not find the twentieth-century terms "depression" or "recession." Instead, that event is listed under its nineteenth-century name, **Panic of 1873**. Researchers interested in fraud and corruption will find such under **Scandals**. The Freedmen's Bureau is listed under its official name, the **Bureau of Refugees, Freedmen, and Abandoned Lands**, and so forth.

Those unfamiliar with Reconstruction may be perplexed by inconsistencies in some terms. For example, readers will see blacks, freedmen, freedpeople, and **African Americans** seemingly used interchangeably. While there is some latitude in Reconstruction studies, the switching is often deliberate, to either avoid constant repetition, avert an awkward phrasing ("white and black males" is simpler than "white and African American males"), or make a clear distinction. For example, "freedpeople" specifically refers to former slaves, not all African Americans in the country, or even in the South. Such distinctions may be important to the information at hand. Usage of "confederate" and "Confederate" may also pose problems. In most cases, lower-case confederate refers to an individual, whereas Confederate refers to the political entity ("former confederates" but the "former Confederate states").

The term "conservative" will also appear frequently, sometimes as a noun and sometimes as an adjective. The implication is the same, merely the part of speech has changed; both refer to those who seek stability and the status quo and reject sudden or significant changes in order or routine. As an adjective, conservative can be applied at any time, such as conservative Republicans who opposed support for black civil rights. As a noun, conservative commonly refers to white Democrats in the South, and is probably more synonymous with former confederates or Democrats. In Reconstruction writing, many authors use southern Democrats, former confederates, and conservatives almost interchangeably.

Users might find the lack of certain obvious entries confusing. There is no entry on the Republican Party, for example. For the Reconstruction period, the editor decided it was of greater benefit to discern between different types of Republicans. Thus, there are entries for **Republicans, Liberal**, **Republicans, Moderate**, and **Republicans, Radical**. Similarly, there is no entry for "Wartime Reconstruction." This phase, directed by President Abraham Lincoln, is included in the larger entry **Presidential Reconstruction**. Researchers can always consult the detailed subject index for aid in locating items.

The *Encyclopedia* also includes a Guide to Related Topics, which allows users to quickly and easily trace broad and important themes across the entries, and a Chronology, which lists the dates of the most important events of the period in a readable format. Finally, the *Encyclopedia* includes two maps, one showing the Reconstruction military districts and each state's date of readmission and redemption, and another showing the density of slave populations across the South.

Acknowledgments

It is fitting that Greenwood Press ask for an author's acknowledgments after he or she has nearly completed the project. Only then can the full measure of debt be calculated. I have written monographs, edited documentary editions, published essays and articles, and have even cowritten an encyclopedia, but this undertaking, begun in the summer of 2003, surpassed all those in complexity. True, the *Encyclopedia of the Reconstruction Era* is not a work of controversial interpretation, nor does it offer breathtaking new theories or research. Rather, it is a reference work, composed by the best of the best, offering what I hope is a thorough, balanced, and approachable guide to one of the most complex and fascinating chapters in our nation's history.

As such, this project brought all my abilities to bear, from an intellectual understanding of the material, to a need to "politik" the right people into participating. My logistical and administrative skills were as challenged as my writing and researching abilities. The undertaking proved far grander, more draining, and more rewarding than I ever conceived, but to paraphrase Abraham Lincoln while lauding the U.S. Navy in the Civil War, this project might never have been completed without the assistance I had, and without substantial aid certainly would not have been completed in the same time and manner. The team at Greenwood Press—Mike Hermann, John Wagner, Mariah Gumpert, Shana Grob, and Liz Kincaid, to name a few—has been patient yet attentive, and has gone beyond the call of duty. They provided just the right level of oversight, allowing me to call the shots when my expertise allowed, yet taking the lead on subjects when asked. My gratitude also goes to the contributors who composed most of this volume, from emeriti professors to overworked junior faculty, from freelance authors to editors; these folks are the ones really responsible for creating this work. I am especially grateful to Professor Eric Foner, not only for his Foreword and his graciousness, but also (rumor has it) for possibly being the reason Greenwood came to me with this opportunity.

I must also express my appreciation to the U.S. Coast Guard Academy and the Department of Humanities, for without their support, this book would never have seen the light of day. I am fully conscious of how lucky I am to be in my situation; I believe professional satisfaction comes from the convergence of three forces: You must find something you enjoy doing, something you are good at doing, and something you'll be paid to do. At the Coast Guard Academy, I have found all three, and will never take that for granted. My sincere thanks to the administration and the wonderful members of the Humanities Department, who, respectively, granted my sabbatical, and then found ways to cover my classes and my collateral assignments. I am grateful to Jon Russell, Dave Mazurek, and the Center for Advanced Studies for providing a summer fellowship. Special thanks to Captain Anne Flammang, who first as associate dean and now as my department head, has rendered unwavering support.

Finally, I recall the acknowledgments of my first book, published ten years ago, in which I predicted that the debt I owe my wife, Etsuko, would only continue to grow. I realize that so much of which I am proud, and so much that I adore, has been because of her. Fourteen years ago, it was she who told me to take a job at the University of Tennessee, a brilliant move on our part. Seven years ago, it was she who convinced me to apply to the Coast Guard Academy, and I landed a job I love. Two and a half years ago, it was she who advised me to take the Greenwood offer and edit this *Encyclopedia*. Her selfless support of my career and my goals has moved her from friends and jobs, and now, a woman who hates the cold shivers in New England, while I happily pursue my dream position. Her love, guidance, and understanding have brought me all that I have, including our wonderful boys, Nicholas and Alexander. They too look forward to the completion of this volume, and an end to my negative replies when they ask, "Daddy, can we play on the computer?"

INTRODUCTION

In American history, "Reconstruction" is the term generally applied to the period 1862–1877, during which the United States sought to bring order from the tremendous social, political, economic, physical, and constitutional changes wrought by secession and the Civil War. The decision by eleven southern states to attempt secession and reject the national government—and more important, the decision by the federal government under President **Abraham Lincoln** to deny that attempt and enforce federal law—unleashed forces that forever changed the American Republic. Some of these forces, and some of the changes that resulted, were confined to the war years. Others, once released, could not be contained. These included the **abolition of slavery**, the expansion of governmental power and constitutional jurisdiction, the rise of the Republican Party, the explosion of northern industry and the national market, and the appearance of a social dynamism that supported struggles by new social groups for political and civil equality.

Unfortunately, the drama of the Civil War often overshadows the importance of the Reconstruction period. In American history courses and Civil War classes and texts alike, Reconstruction is all too often summed up in nearly useless ways, or ignored altogether. The tendency to minimize the topic, or even avoid it when possible, certainly is not due to an historical emptiness, the reason perhaps why Americans can never name those evasive, forgettable presidents of the late nineteenth century. No, historians agree that Reconstruction was a period of immense importance for the nation. Perhaps instead it is the need for closure, for a clear ending. Appomattox (Virginia, where Lee surrendered to Grant) is far more satisfying for Americans, both then and now, than dates of **readmission**, nebulous court decisions, or controversial compromises.

Expanding on this, perhaps is it because when compared to the glorious, tangible, and rather straightforward years of the Civil War, Reconstruction seems an aimless denouement, a rambling collage of amendments and acts, generals and politicians, former slaves and former confederates, with constantly shifting historical views on who was right, who was wrong, who was important, who won, and who lost. The relatively one-dimensional clarity of the war, where such questions had clear answers, is more comfortable than the fuzzy, ambiguous nature of its aftermath.

Yet this ambiguity is necessary for an honest approach to Reconstruction. The confusion experienced by scholars for more than a century is easily understandable when we recognize that in the 1860s and 1870s, the nation itself could not fully understand Reconstruction. This "problem of Reconstruction" is not a creation of historians; it is an accurate portrayal of the anxieties and complexities that faced the nation at the time. Questions of the definition of Reconstruction, its process and direction, its scope and purpose, all perplexed contemporaries, just as they perplex us today. Debates over its goals, its fundamental players and drivers, and its successes, failures, and ultimate consequences are as vibrant and pertinent today as they were more than a century ago. Thus, the problem of Reconstruction is not new, not easily defined, and certainly not easily answered. This difficulty perhaps best explains our tendency to skirt the topic and move on.

For many reasons (some of which will be explored in these volumes), Reconstruction posed an insurmountable dilemma to its contemporaries, but two general issues comprised the heart of the problem. The first lay with the irony of the American Civil War. For both the Confederacy and the United States, Americans North and South fought to defend and thus preserve the nation as *they understood it should be*. Yet both sides, in fighting to preserve their vision of the nation, destroyed that society forever. As the war progressed, the United States of 1861 passed away into memory, and no one knew what would replace it. It seemed obvious that the victors might dictate the shape and direction of the new United States, but the essence of that shape and the goal of that direction were far from obvious when the war ended.

The second reason why Reconstruction posed such a dilemma is simply that no one expected it. For the most part, combatants and politicians, women and men, northerners and southerners, assumed the war would be short and reconciliation would be either brief (due to northern victory) or immaterial (because of a southern one). Instead, the war dragged on, and the costs—human, financial, and material—mounted month after month, year after year. As the illusions of a short war evaporated, the opposing governments resorted to more imaginative, more extreme, and ultimately more destructive means of prosecuting the war. First **emancipation** and then abolition, the vast physical devastation of the South, amendments to the national Constitution, even the victor's demands for contrition and cultural purging stemmed from the length, scope, and costs of the war. No one anticipated the totality, the viciousness, and the intensity of the struggle, and as a result, no one was prepared to deal with its consequences. Who should direct Reconstruction? How should the federal government treat the conquered states, their governments, and their soldiers? What would be the future of the freedpeople in the new republic? How would the war alter the Constitution, the party system, even the

American economy? These questions and others stymie us now just as they stymied Americans then, for no one foresaw a process or a result we call Reconstruction.

Reconstruction Historiography

Because of these complexities, Reconstruction has developed into a historical field with more than its share of trends, interpretations, and reinterpretations. In fact, the *historiography* of Reconstruction, the "history of the history," is so rich and contentious that its ebb and flow has garnered almost as much interest as the history itself.

There was a time when a consensus on the period did exist, at least among most scholars. In the late nineteenth and early twentieth centuries, when **Jim Crow laws** defined the American South and cultural anthropologists were busy defining human development based upon racist skin-colored levels, there seemed, in fact, little controversy. The overall perception regarding Reconstruction was pointedly negative. William Dunning's *Reconstruction, Political and Economic*, published in 1905, best epitomized the historical view of the period. The "Dunning School," as it came to be called, blamed white Republicans—and their ignorant tools, the barbaric former slaves—for the vicious, unwarranted retribution wreaked upon the beaten, downtrodden, and penitent South. Even the titles of the histories evoked a sense of doom and destruction: *The Tragic Era*, for instance, or *The Age of Hate*. The entire experiment was unnecessary, inhumane, unsuccessful, and, of course, un-American. Most of white America concurred; this was an age of national reconciliation and national forgetfulness, when northerners, southerners, and westerners alike embraced the **Lost Cause**, and applauded white progress and proficiency. At a time when Americans were conquering Cuba, Puerto Rico, Hawaii, and the Philippines, who was ready to interject the notion of racial equality? This was a time when the lynching of **African Americans** was too common, when a new generation of the **Ku Klux Klan** exploded in membership, when Thomas Dixon's racist *The Clansman* was translated into film as D. W. Griffith's epic *Birth of a Nation*, a film praised by such social progressives as President Woodrow Wilson himself. For the next several decades, historians such as John Burgess, Claude Bowers, Walter Fleming, and E. Merton Coulter painted Reconstruction as an abysmal failure, replete with corruption, **scandals**, debauchery, rape, murder, and a near-complete overthrow of civilization in the South.

As the United States took up the mantle of freedom and democracy in the middle of the twentieth century, historians began to see Reconstruction in a more favorable light. This was not surprising, given that events of that period stressed freedom, shamed tyranny and oppression, excoriated state-sponsored racism, and extolled the value of positive government activism in economic crisis and war. Certainly it did not require a crusade against fascism to motivate W.E.B. Du Bois, black activist and arguably the first African American Ph.D. from Harvard. In the mid-1930s, Du Bois seemed a lone voice calling for a reconsideration of the horribly skewed interpretation of Reconstruction. Du Bois began a personal crusade aimed at exposing the half-truths, deposing the conservative white saviors, and imposing the active and healthy role of blacks into the Reconstruction framework. By the 1940s, he was joined by other so-called "revisionists," including Howard K. Beale and another African American Ph.D. from Harvard, John Hope Franklin, scholars who approached the period in search of national themes, underlying motivations, and real, not romanticized, consequences. Soon these and other historians—C. Vann Woodward, David H. Donald, Kenneth Stampp, Joel Williamson, Vernon Lane Wharton, and Hans Trefousse, to name a few—reshaped Reconstruction historiography almost entirely. The freedpeople, the army, congressional Republicans, and even **carpetbaggers** became noble warriors in a valiant effort. In a reversal of fortune, figures such as **Andrew Johnson**, the old planter class, **Bourbons**, and Redeemers were cast as regressive, troublesome, racist guardians of a dying age. Although new in focus, the revisionists could not entirely escape certain established fundamentals: Some entrenched African American stereotypes remained, as did grudging acknowledgments that Reconstruction's accomplishments, while significant, were few and far between. Sadly, while the classic "Dunning" view of Reconstruction lay in the dust, it had taken new scholars, new techniques, new evidence, and decades of economic depression and global warfare to bring the misguided edifice down.

While the revisionists' views remain vibrant and meaningful to this day, they too have undergone challenges. By the latter 1960s and 1970s, the revisionists found themselves sharing the discipline with a new breed of investigators, the "neorevisionists," or "postrevisionists" (this editor prefers "postrevisionists" and often terms some of the more recent authors "neorevisionists," as discussed below). This historical trend argued that the moralities and virtues of either side meant little because, ultimately, Reconstruction's successes were minimal, and changes in the South cosmetic. To be sure, the Union was saved and slavery was abolished, *but these were results of the war, not of Reconstruction*; the postwar years were composed of grand promises, great expectations, and minimal results. The New South seemed to differ only superficially from the Old South. As this Introduction and the subsequent volumes will explore, even before Reconstruction ended, white conservatives—many of them former confederates—were back in power, former slaves were legally (and illegally) relegated to inferior status, and the southern economy was firmly in the hands of white landowners. A convergence of apathy and deliberation even undercut the possibilities inherent in the three Reconstruction amendments. Indeed, the work by such historians as Michael Les Benedict, William McFeely, Harold Hyman, and William Gillette paints a rather depressing picture, not just because postrevisionists argue that so little was accomplished, but also because some of them question how much was even possible. Harsh as it seems, this indictment of nineteenth-century activism made sense after the closing of the "Second Reconstruction," the **civil rights** era of the 1950s and 1960s. To men and women reared in the civil rights atmosphere, the successes, failures, and lessons of the 1860s and 1870s seemed particularly relevant a century later, as the nation again attempted to fulfill the promises of liberty and freedom, and again assessed why such spectacular opportunities produced such meager results.

Of course, the debate rages on as to how meager those results actually were and who was responsible for gaining—or preventing—them. More recently, Reconstruction historians have developed new strategies for dealing with these questions and controversies. Rather than a macro approach to winners and losers, change versus stasis, many scholars are following a more nuanced approach, by tackling specific slices of the Reconstruction era and southern society. After all, Reconstruction had many dimensions—regional, chronological, race-based, and even gender-based. State and local studies, for instance, have been popular as historians build a picture of Reconstruction from the ground up, rather than the top (federal level, for example) down. On a positive note, some researchers point to the South's progressive new state constitutions (some components of which survived **Redemption**); economic, financial, and urban expansion; and the appearance of a dynamic new capitalistic class that eagerly bonded with the North. New comparative methodologies also represent a fresh tack, such as in Peter Kolchin's examinations of American slavery and its abolition within an international framework, featuring other countries and other forced **labor systems** (such as serfdom).

As we have seen before, shifts in American society and trends in the historical profession often account for historiographic ebbs and tides. The "social history" surge has certainly influenced Reconstruction studies, so now politicians and white males must share the stage, as what I call "neorevisionists" tackle the problem of Reconstruction. A new focus on gender, family studies, and the African American community has reaped tremendous historical rewards. Asking heretofore unasked questions, and using evidence and a lens largely ignored, scholars are examining crucial aspects of the South's adjustment to war, defeat, occupation, and Reconstruction. In a region where the household was the basic unit of production and consumption, imagine the impact of devastation, emancipation, relocation, and military occupation. Add to that the loss of a third of the able-bodied white males, and the entire loss—from a property point of view—of nearly 4 million slaves. White and black, the growing recognition that *people*, as families and communities, passed through, changed, and were changed by war and Reconstruction has attracted unprecedented attention. Perhaps the grand ideals of Reconstruction—universal equality before the law, for instance—failed, but how can one disregard the incredible strides made during Reconstruction in black **education**, or in the development of black **churches**? Jacqueline Jones, George Rable, Catherine Clinton, Laura Edwards, Julie Saville, LeeAnn Whites, and Tera Hunter, coupled with the extensive and superb documentary publications under way at Ira Berlin's Freedmen's Project at the University of Maryland, have opened an entirely new subfield in Reconstruction historiography.

While many of these more recent studies seem desperate for a silver lining in the rain cloud, Reconstruction did, ultimately, fail. Just as this new generation has been asking new questions of new groups, so too researchers are revisiting such old questions as: Why did Reconstruction collapse? How did the New South develop? What role did the North play in this? Here, also, current dynamics of the historical profession have made inroads, as politics are now placed in context, alongside social movements, economic concerns, and even cultural attitudes. Edward Ayers, Gavin Wright, Gaines Foster, David W. Blight, Nina Silber, and Heather Cox Richardson have forayed into what once seemed bland territory, and have crafted stunning, even unsettling theories about the course, the results, and the ultimate significance of Reconstruction.

All of this brings us back to the following question: With all these dilemmas and controversies, trends and interpretations, on what can historians agree? In part, this *Encyclopedia of the Reconstruction Era* is an answer to that, an attempt to gather in one place the "fundamentals" of Reconstruction. The *Encyclopedia* attempts to identify, define, and place in historical context the major individuals, events, decisions, movements, and issues that, taken together, present a detailed overview of Reconstruction in the United States. The focus is Reconstruction, not the United States during Reconstruction, and thus the compilation found here is not a thorough study of the United States at the time. Many important, interesting, and even obvious events and developments are not included here if they are not relevant to Reconstruction. Readers will find little of the West and foreign policy, for instance, not because these topics are unimportant but because they do not fit the parameters of this encyclopedia.

So again we face a set of basic questions: What was Reconstruction? When did it occur? Simply put, Reconstruction represented an attempt to bring order out of the chaos wrought by secession and civil war. Thousands of players were involved, at scores of levels, possessing a variety of goals and interests. Everyone agreed that the disruption, dislocation, and devastation of war called for a response and created a need for order, but of what sort? A **Georgia** planter's view of bringing order certainly differed from that of a former slave, just as the goals of a Republican congressman from Ohio might differ from those of a Union general or a **scalawag** from **Virginia**. It is said that nature hates a vacuum, so the war and its aftermath saw a flurry of activity and a barrage of players trying their best to control their fate and their futures in the midst of unprecedented, unexpected change.

Reconstruction: An Overview

Perhaps it is uncommon for an encyclopedia to have such an elaborate introduction, but the *Encyclopedia of the Reconstruction Era* is unique. Unlike many reference works, which are purely topical or thematic in nature, this encyclopedia is also periodic in scope. It covers a relatively well-accepted time frame, and the relationships between actors and events—the various *streams of causation*, as historians say—are significant during that period. Therefore, an overview of the period is helpful to supply some general context to the corpus that follows.

Wartime and Early Presidential Reconstruction

The changes—and the controversies—that came to characterize Reconstruction began early in the Civil War. The ad hoc nature of these changes, their often dubious constitutional validity, and the varied and vocal responses they elicited, typified what historians call "wartime reconstruction."

Some of the great questions of Reconstruction—the status of freedpeople, the readmission of former Confederate states, the argument over who would control any reconciliation process—found expression well before any formal process began. In the summer of 1861, just as the war opened, Congress ended slavery in the U.S. territories. A year later, in April 1862, Congress abolished slavery in the nation's capital, and by July had moved to endorsing the backdoor emancipation espoused by a handful of aggressive Union generals; in the Second **Confiscation Act** of July 1862, Congress allowed federal troops to seize the personal property of those in rebellion. Whether interpreted as humanitarian efforts or simply necessary war measures, these acts carried huge ramifications, setting precedents for wartime actions that ignored peacetime consequences.

The president was not oblivious to the expanding nature of a war he tried so hard to control. By the spring of 1862, Abraham Lincoln had also taken the first steps toward political reconstruction (a word he avoided using) by setting up **military governors** and seeking out Unionist support to construct new southern state governments. By the summer of 1862, Lincoln privately professed to his **Cabinet** his desire for emancipation: Issued on September 22, the Preliminary Emancipation Proclamation declared that all slaves in areas still in rebellion, as of January 1, 1863, "shall be henceforth and forever free." Slavery was now directly linked to the fate of the rebellion, and the president had begun flexing his authority as commander in chief. Yet little thought was given to the potential outcomes of the proclamation—the peace itself, or the fate of African Americans who might become free.

In 1863, with the dual victories of Gettysburg and Vicksburg and more Confederate territory falling under federal control daily, Lincoln announced his program for "restoration," issuing his Proclamation of **Amnesty** and **Pardon** in December. The generous granting of pardons, open rejection of punitive or vengeful actions, and liberal view of allegiance (only 10 percent of 1860 voters needed to declare allegiance for a state to begin constituting a new government) represented another carrot-and-stick approach to ending the war and restoring the Union. Lincoln offered confederates a lenient alternative to continuing the war, while still hoping to safeguard his most precious gain—the acknowledgment of federal supremacy, including any federal measures relating to slavery (even including its possible abolition).

President Lincoln and Congress Lock Horns

Lincoln's plan pleased few in the North. **Abolitionists** and a growing pocket of aggressive Republicans in the army and Congress—**Radical Republicans** they would be called—wanted more change, more guarantees, and more punishment.

In July 1864, Congress responded to the presidential program by passing the **Wade-Davis Bill**. This proposal required a *majority* of eligible voters (not 10 percent) to take a **loyalty oath**, significantly restricted participation by former confederates in a new state government, and guaranteed some civil rights to freedpeople (former slaves). Lincoln refused to sign the bill into law, a so-called "pocket veto," so the initiative never went into effect. Yet, neither really did Lincoln's plan. Four states had begun reconstructing new governments under Lincoln's program—**Tennessee**, **Louisiana**, **Arkansas**, and Virginia—but Congress invoked its traditional prerogative of determining the validity of its members, and refused to admit the new representatives from the "Lincoln states." So as 1865 opened, the nation faced an odd dilemma. Although the war was drawing to a close with the U.S. government clearly triumphant, no one knew what would follow Union victory. Complexities that would plague Reconstruction were already in play—the gaps between federal policy and grassroots implementation, the uncertain status of the freedpeople, and the growing rift between the executive and legislative branches of government.

President Johnson Seizes the Initiative

In early spring 1865, discussions over the future of Reconstruction took a backseat to celebrations of the future of the Union; it had been preserved, and the rebellion had been crushed. Congress adjourned in March, its jubilant members eager to return home to their constituents. Abraham Lincoln, victorious war president, never saw home again. Shot by John Wilkes Booth on April 14, Lincoln died early the next morning, and the unprecedented task of rebuilding the country fell to Vice President Andrew Johnson, a Unionist Democrat from Tennessee. With Lincoln dead, anxiety over the war evaporating, and Congress adjourned, President Johnson seized the opportunity and embarked on a program to quickly bring former Confederate states back into the Union. Like his predecessor, Johnson stressed speed, reconciliation, and executive oversight.

Johnson rejoiced in the Union's preservation, but failed to realize that in winning the war, the federal government had accrued tremendous military, political, and financial powers that were problematic for his small-town version of America. And, of course, slavery had been abolished, but the wartime controversy over how to deal with the slaves mutated into a postwar controversy over how to deal with the freedpeople. This last question was not new, but it had never been adequately answered. The war had swept slavery away, but what would replace it? What new economy, new social order, new system of relationships would appear?

Such matters were of no concern to the federal government, according to Johnson, whose brash program ignored many of the realities of post–Civil War America: the former confederates' recalcitrance and animosity, the tenuous nature of the freedpeople's freedom, and—perhaps most significantly—the earnest desire among northerners for real change in the South. The war's end provided opportunities for multiple groups holding competing visions and interests; the president, former confederates, African Americans in the South, and northern Republicans all looked forward to "reconstruction" with a mixture of anxiety and hope.

Johnson's program was simple. Former confederates either needed to take a loyalty oath or petition the president directly for a presidential pardon. Then, these "loyal" white southerners would create new state governments, nullify and repudiate secession and confederate debts (in other words, affirm that neither ever existed or could exist), and draft new state constitutions that abolished slavery (emancipation was a personal manumission from slavery; abolition is the elimination of the system itself). Once complete, these states would be readmitted to Congress with all their rights and privileges intact. Johnson saw the war and the readmission process as vehicles for preserving the Union and humbling an oppressive planter elite, not for inciting economic, racial, or constitutional revolution. He believed that the traditional American system of state's rights federalism should reappear with the war's ending. So too should a new South, still a society ruled by local whites but one led by Unionists, merchants, and artisans; in other words, people like Johnson.

Through the summer of 1865, the former Confederate states elected new state governments, which, like Johnson himself, drastically misread the political and social atmosphere of the nation. Several states ignored some of Johnson's meager requirements, such as repudiating the Confederate debt, declaring secession null and void, and even ratifying the **Thirteenth Amendment**. Their most obnoxious blunder was passage of "**Black Codes**," laws crafted by the new southern state legislatures to regulate all aspects of black life in their respective states. To many white southerners, black codes created order out of chaos, stabilizing everything from labor needs to social relationships.

Many African Americans and northern Republicans believed differently, and saw the codes as an attempt to salvage a slave society. Some more radical individuals responded with demands for land confiscation, a total redistribution of southern land to secure economic power for blacks and punish former confederates. However, all agreed that the treatment of former slaves dredged up memories of the Old South, in total rejection of the spirit of emancipation and Confederate defeat. The losers were calling the shots, and the winners—or at least their southern allies—were subjected to their whims.

The final requirement facing Johnson's state governments, and their last collective misstep, was the election of new federal representatives. When the 1865 fall elections were over, half of the senators and representatives elected had served in either the Confederate Army or the Confederate government. This fact, added to the intransigence of the states toward Johnson's generous terms and the blatant arrogance apparent in the black codes, convinced northerners and their federal representatives gathering in Washington that the South seemed little, if at all, repentant.

Congressional Republicans Seek a Compromise

Reminiscent of the earlier clash between Lincoln and Congress, Republicans blocked part of the president's program, and then sought an alternative to it. When it convened in December 1865, Congress refused to seat the new southern members. Then Republicans created the **Joint Committee of Fifteen on Reconstruction**, and began congressionally sponsored investigations in the South itself. Republicans also set to work on a series of bills that would allow the federal government to intervene on behalf of the former slaves and protect them from the outlandish public and private treatment rampant in the South. In the spring of 1866, **Moderate Republicans** presented the **Freedmen's Bureau Bill** and the **Civil Rights Bill**, two measures attempting to bridge gaps between factions in the party, the Congress and the Executive, and the North and South.

In brief, while the measures could bolster federal oversight and clarify federal desires, they really sought to cajole the southern states into changing practices without fundamentally altering the Johnson governments. In March 1865, when abolition was imminent, the federal government had created the **Bureau of Refugees, Freedmen, and Abandoned Lands**. Usually called the Freedmen's Bureau, it provided support for the freedpeople as they transitioned from slave to free laborer. The Freedmen's Bureau established schools, oversaw and negotiated labor contracts, provided some rudimentary supplies and resources, and even operated land sales and rentals. The 1866 Freedmen's Bill extended the life of the agency, and infused new resources into it. The Civil Rights Bill was more significant; it directly affirmed black civil rights, made state-sponsored racial discrimination illegal, remanded certain violations to federal court jurisdiction, and overturned the black codes. While both assumed a more active and powerful federal presence, neither altered the political makeup of the southern governments or mentioned **black suffrage** (the right to vote).

Embarrassed by the de facto rejection of his program in December, President Johnson was in no mood to compromise. He vetoed both measures, and made his mistake worse by composing antagonistic veto messages. Johnson's vetoes so provoked Republicans that many Moderates grew exasperated with the president, and a unified front began to emerge. Republicans agreed that the South needed to accept defeat, federal supremacy, and some modicum of black rights, and if the Executive did not see to this, Congress would. In April 1866, the Republicans introduced the **Fourteenth Amendment**, passed the Civil Rights Act over Johnson's veto, and then proposed and passed a new Freedmen's Bureau Act in July.

The president sought alternate means of stabilizing the Union and protecting the Constitution. First, he tried to block implementation of the new program by urging the southern states not to ratify the Fourteenth Amendment. Second, he formally abandoned his wartime alliance with Republicans and created a new party, one opposed to African American rights, extensions of federal power, and modifications to the Constitution. Johnson believed his **National Union Movement** would attract anti-black northerners and win in the fall 1866 elections, ushering in a conservative, pro-Johnson Congress.

Again, the president was mistaken. Johnson and his alliance with white southerners had cost him dearly in the North, and this party only reaffirmed his leanings. Moreover, bloody summer clashes in the South between whites and African Americans and the president's ill-advised "**Swing Around the Circle**" campaign tour hardened northern hearts toward this new party while softening them toward the freedpeople. Although only a few northerners endorsed full equality or African American voting, when Republican newspapers and politicians depicted the choice as between innocent, helpless pro-Union former slaves, and vicious, belligerent former rebels, the groundswell of opposition could not be contained.

In many ways, the congressional **elections of 1866** served as a referendum on Reconstruction. The elections saw overwhelming Republican victories as President Johnson's National Union Party was trounced in a clear message about northern expectations for Reconstruction. The Congress-elect (which was scheduled to arrive in fall 1867) was so dominated by Republicans that it would be in effect "veto-proof," easily able to pass a measure with the requisite two-thirds majority to override a presidential veto. Yet, in the face of this message, the president stepped up his opposition to the Fourteenth Amendment, redoubling his efforts to have the southern governments derail its ratification. In the end, every former Confederate state save one—his own Tennessee—rejected the amendment (Tennessee was readmitted to Congress in the summer of 1866). Moderate Republicans watched in dismay as the last component of their compromise strategy collapsed.

Republican Theories of Reconstruction

Even more than the president's vetoes the previous spring, Johnson's actions in the summer and fall of 1866 brought a sense of unity and purpose to the Republican Party. With both Johnson's new party and his southern governments discredited, and a more moderate Republican alternative rejected, a golden opportunity appeared for real change in the South.

Republicans, however, were anxious about how to proceed, and what sort of constitutional authority the Congress actually held. If Republicans were right, and ten southern states were not in the Union, not really "states" at all, then what were they? Some described the former Confederate states as "conquered provinces," which placed them in a pseudo-territorial status, not unlike areas the United States had purchased (such as the Louisiana Territory) or conquered (such as in the Mexican War). Radicals such as **Charles Sumner**, **Thaddeus Stevens**, and **George Julian** favored this theory because it placed nearly unlimited—albeit temporary—authority in congressional hands. This authority could bring sweeping changes to these "territories," including the black suffrage long argued for by Sumner, confederate **disfranchisement**, even the redrawing of borders and renaming of states. Stevens, on the other hand, advocated for an economic revolution based upon confiscation and redistribution of confederates' landholdings among the freedpeople. Those most radical proponents of drastic change often coupled the "conquered provinces" theory with the "guarantee clause" of the Constitution, Article IV, Section 4, which reads, "The United States shall guarantee to every State in this Union a Republican Form of Government" (Republican meaning a representative governing system, *not* the party). Radicals were ready to interpret this to mean Congress could use its powers to establish new, fairer, more representative governments that held to national standards and national laws. This would bring only minor changes to the North, where the African American population was small, but could spell political revolution in the South. Invoking the clause would also represent a significant expansion in federal authority; the "territorial" argument only saw power *before* readmission, but the guarantee clause made no differentiation. Thus, it could be applied *after* readmission as well, if Congress believed an unrepublican system had emerged.

Some Radicals and Moderates alike espoused a "state suicide" model, which was not fundamentally different from another model, the "forfeited rights" idea. Both placed more direct blame on the South, and implied that the North had not so much dismantled the southern states as those states had plunged themselves into a constitutional void by their own action. Statelike entities still existed, with names and borders, but those entities had no governments, no leadership, and no rights or privileges that the federal government needed to recognize. Refusing to seat these states in Congress was an obvious example of this theory in action. The national government itself would bestow rights and privileges on the states, once the states were seen fit and ready to receive them.

But how would Congress determine when a state was fit and ready for readmission? This represented the greatest stumbling block toward Republican unity because critical differences existed between the most Radical designs—with black voting and land redistribution—and the more moderate approaches. Rather than arguing about the status of the states, lawyer Richard Henry Dana turned the question on its head. In a June 1865 speech, Dana predicted—and skirted—the "status" obstacle by merely insisting that the South and North had been "warring parties," and that, as such, they were governed by certain principles of war. Whether a conflict is of an internal nature, between nations, or even between individuals, "war is over when its purpose is secured . . . the conquering party may hold the other in the grasp of war until it has secured whatever it has a right to require." According to Dana, the North has a right to "hold the rebels in the grasp of war until we have obtained whatever the public safety and the public faith require." In other words, Dana's "grasp of war" approach focused on Reconstruction as a *result*, not merely as a process. His wonderfully vague euphemism nicely skirted much constitutional angst, and in many ways became an unofficial rationale for the congressional program.

The Alternative: Congressional ("Radical") Reconstruction

A Republican consensus was emerging on what that program should entail, and in March 1867, Republicans in control of Congress turned their considerable power toward instituting their version of Reconstruction.

That program was embodied in a series of measures called the **Military Reconstruction Acts**. Congress passed the first in March 1867, and followed with three supplements to fix loopholes that developed. Johnson vetoed them all, and saw each one become law over his opposition. On the surface, the measures did seem radical and unprecedented, and certain aspects were. Congress divided the South into five military districts, placed supervisory powers in the hands of army generals, and dictated the registration of all able-bodied, eligible males, as defined by the still-pending Fourteenth Amendment. Thus, in ten former Confederate states, African American men could now register to vote and hold political office, but many former confederates could not. This new electorate then voted for a **constitutional convention**, which drafted a new state constitution that provided for a new state government, which, finally, needed to ratify the Fourteenth Amendment. When all this had occurred, the state could present itself to Congress for readmission to the Union. In many ways, the Military Reconstruction Acts were a logical progression from the response to the Fourteenth Amendment, when the southern states rejected a compromise that balanced black political rights with white ones. Where negotiation left off, coercion began.

As we will see in the entries, this "Radical" Reconstruction was not as extreme as some made it sound. Republicans agreed that giving freedmen the vote was more important, more democratic, more American, and less controversial than giving them land. The acts only applied to the southern states still awaiting readmission, so African American males in the North, the border states, and even Tennessee were not affected.

Nonetheless, the Military Reconstruction Acts set in motion a political revolution in the South. Southern African Americans—male and female—fully understood the power of the ballot. Educated or illiterate, Free Black or former slave, urban or rural, upper South or delta, African American males eagerly registered under the provisions of the Reconstruction Acts—and the protective gaze of federal troops. Still, a fully developed Republican presence in the South required an alliance with whites. Although the Military Reconstruction Acts disfranchised many former confederates, Unionists could participate, and many did. Earning the pejorative label "scalawags," these southern whites brought an important local experience to southern politics, forging an at-times uneasy alliance with the black community. These two groups were joined by a third, which has traditionally borne the brunt of historical criticism: the "carpetbaggers," a derogative term applied to northerners who settled in the South after the war. While some members of these groups were merely opportunists, many were idealists who genuinely believed in Lincoln's "new birth of freedom" and hoped to play a part in a grand and exciting experiment.

That experiment began in late 1867 with eligible southerners, black and white, voting for delegates to state constitutional conventions. These conventions established—at least on paper—state governments and policies that represented incredible reforms; one could argue they collectively embodied a revolution. As a whole, the new state constitutions were as progressive as any in existence and what followed, for a few brief years, was an incredible experiment in democratic process and policy. Once the new state constitutions were complete, the new voters elected new governments, which were resoundingly Republican in makeup. Finally, these governments replaced the Johnson governments established during the **Presidential Reconstruction** phase.

Conservative myths notwithstanding, and excepting a few infamous individuals, these southern Republican governments did their best to bridge the gap between black hopes and former confederate demands. They pursued fairer taxation policies, public education, economic development, and did not disfranchise former confederates or confiscate land. At the national and state levels, one can argue that the halfway strategy of the Republicans—call it compromise, fairness, tepidness, practicality—left the southern Democrats humiliated and crippled, but not helpless or hopeless. They were out of power but not powerless, a dangerous combination.

Whatever unbiased reporting may say of the southern Republican governments, they could never change two simple facts: These structures were imposed from the outside, and they were comprised of scalawags, carpet-baggers, and blacks. Examining the long view of southern history, we see a steady and constant adherence to two principles: white supremacy and localism. These two characteristics dovetail together: The relations between the races—socially, politically, legally—should be determined by state or local authorities. The literature is vast on the various components of southern society, southern culture, and the so-called southern mind. Historically, southerners have defined and defended their rights to determine, decide, and dictate on affairs within their borders. Secession and the Civil War were results of this, when first a state (South Carolina) and then the region (the Confederacy) sought independence to control its own destiny.

Here then was the ultimate and fundamental flaw in Congressional Reconstruction—both white supremacy and regional autonomy were being swept away simultaneously. Andrew Johnson's initial policy and his reaction to Republican initiatives clearly demonstrated his adherence to traditional southern themes. In the South, the reaction from conservative southerners came in many forms, some legal, some illegal, some economic, some even literary. The response is best seen in two developments during this phase—the evolution of the agricultural labor system called **sharecropping**, and the rise of white **violence**. Both marked attempts by whites to regain control of elements within their society that had been traditionally theirs; the details of these developments are well captured in the entries in these volumes, but suffice it to say that in both cases the conservatives' drive to defend old ideas was greater than Republican willpower to protect new ones.

The Grant Administration: Climax and Denouement

Of course, the state of affairs in the South was partly dependent upon support from the North, be it public opinion or action by Republicans in Washington. For a time, that support was steady and strong, and embraced several far-reaching and unprecedented actions. But as Reconstruction wore on, two conflicting beliefs took on momentum and conspired to sap northern energy—a sense of success and accomplishment coupled with bewildering doubts about practicality and feasibility.

As with much of the Republican program, the achievements during this phase were not independent initiatives, but rather responses to threats from Democrats and President Johnson himself. Through 1867 and 1868, Congress passed the **Command of the Army Act** (as part of the 1867 Army Appropriations Act), the **Tenure of Office Act**, and supplements to the Military Reconstruction Act, all intended to strengthen the Reconstruction process and Republican positions in government. Ultimately, Johnson's obstinacy pushed Congress into entirely uncharted waters, and in 1868 resulted in the first **impeachment** of a president in American history. Again, divisions within the Republican Party brought about a moderate solution. The president was impeached and disgraced, but not convicted by the Senate or removed from office. The impeachment dealt a death blow to the national hopes of the **Democratic Party**, and allowed an easy victory for **Ulysses S. Grant** and the Republicans in the 1868 presidential contest. With the **Supreme Court**, for the time being, openly deciding not to rule on so-called "political matters" and thus abstaining from much of the Reconstruction debate, the Republican Party now firmly controlled the workings of the federal government.

The first few years of the Grant administration saw what many believe to be the climax of Reconstruction activism. In February 1869, Congress passed the **Fifteenth Amendment** and sent it forward to the states for ratification. A compromise, as usual, this measure offered hope to all—to those who believed it would enfranchise African American males nationwide, as well as those who preferred that blacks stay away from the ballot box. The amendment did not positively confer the right to vote; it merely prohibited voting restrictions that were based upon "race, color, or previous condition of servitude." Immediately in the North, and eventually in the South, this amendment led to a wide array of imaginative voting regulations and provisions designed to eliminate black voting without violating the letter of the law.

However, more immediate problems held the Grant administration's interest. Conservative Democrats in the South were already trying to dismantle the gains achieved via the Military Reconstruction Acts, as antiblack and anti-Republican violence expanded in scope and intensity with the coming of the Republican state governments. Such organizations as the Ku Klux Klan and the Knights of the White Camellia had appeared soon after the war to enforce classic values of white supremacy and black obedience. With the formation of new state governments, these and similar groups took on a more political aim and became terrorist agents of the Democratic Party in an attempt to demoralize Republican electoral majorities. Republicans in Washington fired back with three **Enforcement Acts**, passed in May 1870 and February and April 1871. Collectively, these acts extended federal jurisdiction over voting and voting practices, ensured that political rights were not being violated, outlawed organizations seeking to infringe on federally guaranteed rights, and allowed the president to suspend the writ of habeas corpus to enforce the laws. These measures would be the basis for the much-heralded federal crackdown on white supremacist groups in the early 1870s, when federal troops and Justice Department officials arrested thousands of whites accused of violating Republicans' civil rights.

Reconstruction Collapses

The flurry of Republican activity in Congress and across the South belied a growing exasperation with the entire Reconstruction program. On the one hand, Republican measures had been crafted to allow for local control—federalism, one might argue—as seen in granting African American suffrage. Its framers had intended that this burst of federal activity could then recede and southern Republicans could take care of themselves. That clearly was not the case because federal officials from the War and Justice Departments were constantly required to intervene in some southern dispute, riot, or electoral crisis. More than five years after the war, the former Confederate states seemed to be an endless sinkhole that demanded resources but produced no conclusive, stable results. That fact, added to the tales of political debauchery in the Reconstruction governments and the prevailing antiblack sentiment in the United States, began to erode support in the North.

On the other hand, some northerners argued that stable, tangible results had been achieved, and so it was time to move on. After all, slavery was abolished, African Americans were now citizens with civil and political rights (according to the Fourteenth and Fifteenth Amendments), states were being readmitted to Congress under new constitutions, and the southern economy—never a very progressive engine—seemed to be slowly making way. For many, it appeared as though the Union had been "reconstructed," and there was not much more to do. News of violence, economic coercion, and even political fraud constituted nothing more than general crime and interested few, especially in light of new issues making headlines. The presidential contest in 1872 captured this spirit, as many moderate Republicans and Democrats merged into the **Liberal Republican Party** to challenge Grant for reelection. Although unsuccessful, the Liberal Republican movement foreshadowed significant changes in northern priorities—the **Panic of 1873** (a recession), monetary policy, political corruption and civil service reform, westward expansion, and immigrant issues were becoming hot topics. The fate of African Americans in the South seemed like something from far away and long ago, perhaps best left to the states to deal with. The congressional elections of 1874 drove this home, as Democrats gained control of Congress for the first time since before the Civil War.

While some developments distracted northerners from their southern program, other forces worked deliberately and directly to undermine it. In the mid 1870s, the Supreme Court reentered the Reconstruction discussion and delivered several crippling blows to the Republican program. In the ***Slaughterhouse Cases*** (1873), *United States v. Reese* (1876), and ***United States v. Cruikshank*** (1876), the Court followed a conservative view of the Reconstruction amendments, limiting their scope and applicability. Even Republicans in Congress began to backpedal on federal activism; as early as 1872, Congress refused to extend President Grant's suspension of the habeas corpus in the South, and in 1875 a new enforcement bill, the Force Act, died in the Senate.

Of course, white violence in the South still comprised the greatest single threat to the Reconstruction governments. The hostility, shrewdness, and perseverance of southern Democrats became so organized by the middle 1870s that, without overt federal intervention, the "black and tan" governments in the South collapsed one by one. Republican divisions abetted conservative success, but it was the Democrat's clever balance that achieved the victory. Southern conservatives appealed to racism, applied economic and social coercion, developed mass intimidation techniques, and, when necessary, resorted to outright violence, kidnapping, and assassination. By the presidential **election of 1876**, all but three southern Reconstruction governments had toppled, and those three—**Florida**, Louisiana, and **South Carolina**—were precariously situated.

These two trends, apathy in the North and focused ruthlessness in the South, intersected in the 1876 election. The so-called **Compromise of 1877** allowed Republican **Rutherford B. Hayes** to become president, but signaled the overthrow of the last Republican governments in the South. Facing more-or-less formal abandonment by Washington, black and white Republicans in the South could only look to their local governments for help. Since these, in turn, relied on federal assistance, the last state regimes collapsed like a house of cards. The South had been "redeemed."

The effects were immediate, lasting, and predictable, since other states had returned to "home rule" earlier. Across the South, as had occurred under Andrew Johnson's restoration policy, many white southerners were ready to implement their own version of "reconstruction." Certainly, Reconstruction meant much more than just who governed, for it took into account the vast range of social, familial, legal, geographic, economic, even spiritual changes that were under way. Unfortunately, those who governed often dictated the scope and focus of those changes, opportunities, and initiatives. Soon the backlash began, with prosecutions of former Republican politicians; amendments to state constitutions regarding fiscal policies, education, and welfare; and, of course, clever articulations to legally restrict black male suffrage.

Again, this did not happen without northern consent, or at least northern indifference. The war had ended over a decade ago, and was already passing into a blur of glorious memories. White northerners and southerners sought to bury the contentious and divisive issues of the past and move forward together as one nation—into the West, into urbanization and the Second Industrial Revolution, and even abroad and into world affairs. Sectional reconciliation was in the air, and African Americans and their rights became victims of it. The South's "Lost Cause" mentality and the "Jim Crow" system of segregation were not out of place in the late nineteenth-century United States; in fact, they seem almost required, as American imperialists inspected other cultures and staked their claims of greatness upon white democracy and white development.

However, the slow and steady erosion of the promise of Reconstruction cannot erase its accomplishments. Some historians place among these abolition, the destruction of the planter aristocracy, and recognition of the Union as perpetual. Others disagree, noting these were products of the war, not its aftermath. Instead, they point to the social, religious, and economic achievements of the freedpeople; the genesis of southern economic reforms built upon diversification and northern capital; the progressive new state constitutions, parts of which outlived Redemption; the precedents set by the conscientious and subservient roles of the military during turbulent times; and, finally and perhaps most important, the three Reconstruction Amendments. While these represented expedient solutions at the time, they nonetheless placed before Americans a constant reminder that the nation still fell short of the ideals espoused in the Declaration of Independence. At least the pledge was now formal and official; it remains to be seen when and how that pledge will be fulfilled.

Although many of us will disagree, the consummate Southern historian, C. Vann Woodward, once wrote that American historians have only two great failures to explain: the failure of the Confederacy, and the failure of Reconstruction. Of course, these two questions—and their answers—are linked. The *Encyclopedia of the Reconstruction Era* is an important tool for those engaged in answering that second question.

CHRONOLOGY

1860

6 November   Abraham Lincoln becomes the first Republican elected president.

20 December   South Carolina secedes from the federal Union.

1861

January–June   Ten other slave states secede from the Union.

February   Confederate States of America established with its capital in Montgomery, Alabama.

25 May   General Benjamin Butler in Virginia declares runaway slaves "contraband of war."

22 June   House of Representatives passes John Crittenden's War Aims Resolution, declaring it the federal government's purpose to preserve the Union, not to interfere with the "internal affairs" of southern states.

25 July   Senate passes Andrew Johnson's War Aims Resolution, stating same as House version.

6 August   Congress passes the First Confiscation Act.

7 November   Union forces seize territory along the South Carolina coast, allowing first experiments with contrabands to begin.

December   Congress creates the Joint Committee on the Conduct of the War to push a more aggressive Radical agenda for prosecuting the war.

1862

2 March   Abraham Lincoln appoints Andrew Johnson military governor of occupied Tennessee.

16 April   Congress abolishes slavery in the District of Columbia and the federal territories.

1 May   In New Orleans, General Benjamin Butler begins informal reconstruction by coordinating Unionist elements in Louisiana.

19 May   President Lincoln appoints Edward Stanley as provisional governor of North Carolina.

20 May	Congress passes the Homestead Act.
19 June	President Lincoln appoints John Phelps provisional governor of Arkansas.
17 July	Congress passes the Second Confiscation Act, specifically allowing the seizure of slaves from those in rebellion. Act also authorizes president to "employ" freed slaves "as necessary and proper for the suppression of the rebellion," the first federal pronouncement mentioning the use of blacks in the service.
22 July	President Lincoln, at a cabinet meeting, declares his support for emancipation.
22 September	Following the battle of Antietam, Lincoln announces the Preliminary Emancipation Proclamation, giving Confederate states three months to end the rebellion or lose their slaves.
3 December	Election of first congressmen from Confederacy to the U.S. government, as Louisiana sends B. F. Flanders and Michael Hahn to serve in Congress until terms end in 1863.

1863

1 January	Promulgation of the Emancipation Proclamation, declaring free slaves in areas still under rebellion against the United States. Proclamation also calls for the enlistment of African Americans in the armed forces.
15 January	Governor Stanley of North Carolina resigns over the "radical" turn the Union war effort has taken.
20 April	West Virginia admitted to the Union.
20 June	Gradual emancipation begins under West Virginia's state constitution.
	President Lincoln appoints Francis H. Pierpont provisional governor of Virginia.
8 December	President Lincoln delivers his Proclamation of Amnesty and Reconstruction, also called the "Ten Percent Plan."

1864

4 January	Arkansas state constitutional convention opens under Lincoln's guidelines.
20 January	Isaac Murphy selected as provisional governor of Arkansas under Ten Percent Plan.
18 April	Isaac Murphy inaugurated as governor of Arkansas.
21 May	Congressmen from Arkansas denied admittance to federal legislature; breach between executive and Congress evident.
2 July	Congress passes Wade-Davis Bill as a more stringent alternative to Lincoln's Reconstruction plan.
8 July	Lincoln pocket-vetoes the Wade-Davis Bill.
	Republican National Convention in Baltimore nominates Abraham Lincoln on a "National Union Party" platform of Union, victory, and reconciliation. Andrew Johnson, War Democrat from Tennessee, is chosen as his running mate.
5 August	Release of the Wade-Davis Manifesto, criticizing Lincoln's veto of the Wade-Davis Bill.
29 August	Democratic National Convention meets in Chicago and nominates ticket of General George B. McClellan and George Pendleton.
5 October	Louisiana convenes its constitutional convention as per Lincoln's Ten Percent Plan.
29 October	Maryland adopts new constitution, abolishing slavery.
8 November	Abraham Lincoln reelected president, receiving nearly 75 percent of the Union soldier vote; Democrat/Union Party Andrew Johnson elected vice president.

6 December	Salmon P. Chase, Lincoln's secretary of the treasury, becomes Chief Justice of the United States.

1865

11 January	Missouri, a "border state," emancipates its slaves.
16 January	In Savannah, Union General William T. Sherman issues Special Field Order No. 15, setting aside abandoned coastal lands for use by freed slaves; the mythical federal grant of "forty acres and a mule" is born.
31 January	Congress passes the Thirteenth Amendment, which will formally abolish slavery in the United States. It is sent to the states for ratification.
13 February	Virginia convenes its constitutional convention as per Lincoln's Ten Percent Plan.
22 February	Tennessee emancipates its slaves.
3 March	Congress creates, within the War Department, the Bureau of Refugees, Freedmen, and Abandoned Lands to help blacks in their transition from slavery to freedom.
4 March	Abraham Lincoln is inaugurated a second time as president. His address reflects his Reconstruction policy with the immortal "with malice toward none; with charity for all."
11 March	Lincoln delivers speech encouraging Louisiana to investigate possibilities for limited black suffrage.
5 April	William G. Brownlow elected governor of Tennessee.
9 April	Confederate General Robert E. Lee surrenders the Army of Northern Virginia to Ulysses S. Grant at Appomattox Court House, Virginia.
14 April	President Lincoln is shot while watching a play at Ford's Theater in Washington, D.C.
15 April	Lincoln dies; Andrew Johnson is sworn is as president at the Kirkwood House.
1 May	President Johnson authorizes military trials for the Lincoln assassins.
29 May	Johnson issues his First Amnesty Proclamation, which includes a liberal amnesty but requires many to appeal for a special presidential pardon.
	Johnson initiates his Reconstruction program with his Proclamation for North Carolina, appointing William W. Holden provisional governor.
13 June	Johnson appoints Benjamin F. Perry and William H. Sharkey provisional governors of South Carolina and Mississippi, respectively.
17 June	Johnson appoints James Johnson and Andrew J. Hamilton provisional governors of Georgia and Texas, respectively.
21 June	Johnson appoints Lewis Parsons provisional governor of Alabama.
13 July	Johnson appoints William Marvin provisional governor of Florida.
14 August	First constitutional convention to be held under Johnson's program opens in Mississippi; others follow through fall.
2 October	In Mississippi, Benjamin Humphries becomes the first governor elected under Johnson's Reconstruction plan.
18 October	In South Carolina, James L. Orr is elected governor.
November–December	Official fact-finding tour of the former Confederate states by Carl Schurz and Ulysses S. Grant.
6 November	In Louisiana, James Madison Wells is elected governor.
9 November	In North Carolina, Jonathan Worth is elected governor.

15 November	In Georgia, Charles M. Jenkins is elected governor.
29 November	In Florida, David S. Walker is elected governor.
2 December	New Mississippi legislature passes "black codes" to regulate freedpeople; other former Confederate states follow.
3 December	Thirty-Ninth Congress reconvenes and refuses to seat representatives and senators elected under Johnson's program.
13 December	Congress creates the Joint Committee of Fifteen on Reconstruction.
	In Alabama, Robert M. Patton inaugurated as governor.
18 December	Thirteenth Amendment gains ratification and becomes part of the U.S. Constitution.

1866

19 February	Johnson vetoes the Freedmen's Bureau Bill.
22 February	Johnson's antagonistic Washington's Birthday Address.
27 March	Johnson vetoes the Civil Rights Bill.
April	Ku Klux (from Greek "kuklos" or circle) founded in Pulaski, Tennessee (the "Klan" was added much later).
2 April	Johnson issues proclamation formally declaring the "insurrection" at an end.
9 April	Congress passes the Civil Rights Act over Johnson's veto, the first significant piece of legislation passed over an executive veto.
30 April/1 May	Race riot in Memphis, Tennessee.
13 June	Congress passes the Fourteenth Amendment and sends it to the states for ratification.
21 June	Congress passes the Southern Homestead Act.
16 July	Johnson vetoes second Freedmen's Bureau Bill.
	Congress overrides Johnson's veto and passes the Freedmen's Bureau Renewal Act.
24 July	Tennessee, after ratifying the Fourteenth Amendment, becomes the first former Confederate state readmitted to the Union.
30 July	Race riot in New Orleans, Louisiana.
13 August	In Texas, James W. Throckmorton becomes governor.
14–15 August	National Union Movement holds its convention in Philadelphia.
20 August	Johnson issues second proclamation declaring insurrection over and peace restored.
28 August–5 September	Johnson's "Swing Around the Circle" takes him on a speaking tour from Washington to Illinois.
October–November	Republicans are successful in congressional elections, trouncing Johnson's conservative National Union Movement.
20 November	First convention of the Grand Army of the Republic, a formal organization merging together many satellite Union veterans' groups.
17 December	Supreme Court delivers *Ex parte Milligan*.

1867

5 January	Johnson vetoes bill to enfranchise blacks in the District of Columbia.
8 January	Congress overrides Johnson's veto; black male suffrage begins in D.C.
14 January	The Supreme Court renders decisions in the "Test Oath Cases," restricting the use and limiting the effectiveness of loyalty oaths.

2 March	Congress passes First Military Reconstruction Act, Tenure of Office Act, Army Appropriations Act, and Fortieth Congress Act.
	Johnson vetoes Military Reconstruction Act, Tenure of Office Act, and Fortieth Congress Act; approves but submits formal protest to Army Appropriations Act.
	Congress overrides presidential vetoes and passes into law Military Reconstruction, Tenure, and Fortieth Congress Acts.
11 March	President Johnson appoints five generals to command the five military districts in the South.
22 March	Congress passes, and Johnson vetoes, the Second Military Reconstruction Act.
23 March	Second Military Reconstruction Act becomes law.
13 July	Congress passes the Third Military Reconstruction Act.
19 July	Johnson vetoes Third Military Reconstruction Act; Congress overrides veto the same day.
12 August	Johnson suspends Secretary of War Edwin M. Stanton and appoints General Ulysses S. Grant secretary ad interim.
17 August	Johnson removes General Philip Sheridan from command of the Fifth Military District.
26 August	Johnson removes General Daniel Sickles from command of the Second Military District.
7 September	Johnson issues Second Amnesty Proclamation.
23 September	In Louisiana, the first state constitutional convention under Congressional Reconstruction begins.
October– November	Democrats score sweeping surprise victories in state contests across the North.
7 December	First vote on impeachment fails in House of Representatives.
28 December	Johnson removes General John Pope as commander of the Third Military District.
1868	
9 January	Johnson removes General E.O.C. Ord as commander of the Fourth Military District.
13 January	Senate reconvenes and refuses to consent to Johnson's suspension of Secretary Stanton and appointment of Ulysses S. Grant.
4 February	William H. Smith of Alabama becomes the first governor elected under Congressional Reconstruction and the Military Reconstruction Acts.
21 February	Johnson formally removes Stanton as secretary of war; appoints General Lorenzo Thomas.
24 February	House of Representatives votes to impeach President Johnson.
2–3 March	House adopts eleven Articles of Impeachment and names impeachment managers for the Senate trial.
11 March	Congress passes the Fourth Military Reconstruction Act.
27 March	Supreme Court rules in *Ex parte McCardle* that Congress can restrict the Court's jurisdiction relating to "political issues."
30 March	Senate convenes as High Court of Impeachment as the president's trial opens.
16 April	Republican Robert K. Scott, a carpetbagger from Ohio, is elected governor of South Carolina under the Congressional Reconstruction constitution.

20 April	Georgia elects carpetbagger Rufus Bullock governor under the Congressional Reconstruction program.
23 April	William W. Holden elected governor of North Carolina under the Congressional Reconstruction program.
16 May	Senate votes on Article Eleven, finding Johnson "not guilty" by a vote of 35 to 19, one shy of conviction.
20 May	Republican National Convention nominates Ulysses S. Grant for president, Speaker of the House Schuyler Colfax as vice president.
26 May	Senate votes on Article Two, finding Johnson "not guilty" by a vote of 35 to 19, one shy of conviction; Senate adjourns as High Court.
30 May	First official Memorial Day, established by the Grand Army of the Republic (GAR) across the North to remember Union dead.
22 June	Congress readmits Arkansas to the Union as the first state readmitted under the Republican's plan of Reconstruction.
25 June	Johnson vetoes bill readmitting Florida, North Carolina, South Carolina, Georgia, Alabama, and Louisiana to the federal Union; veto will be overridden and all six are readmitted over the next four weeks.
1 July	Republican carpetbagger Harrison Reed becomes governor of Florida.
2 July	Republican carpetbagger Powell Clayton becomes governor of Arkansas.
4 July	Johnson's Third Amnesty Proclamation.
9 July	Democratic National Convention nominates ticket of Horatio Seymour of New York and Francis P. Blair, Jr.
13 July	Carpetbagger Henry C. Warmoth inaugurated as governor of Louisiana.
25 July	Congress passes bill dismantling the Freedmen's Bureau; all operations other than education will cease as of January 1, 1869.
28 July	Fourteenth Amendment ratified and added to the U.S. Constitution.
September	Georgia legislature expels black members and regresses on fulfilling Military Reconstruction Act requirements; congressional/military investigation begins.
3 November	Ulysses S. Grant elected president.
1 December	Georgia remanded to military supervision for violating Reconstruction acts.
25 December	Johnson issues his Fourth Amnesty Proclamation, a general amnesty covering nearly all former confederates.

1869

25 February	Congress passes the Fifteenth Amendment and sends it to the states for ratification.
4 March	Ulysses S. Grant inaugurated as president.
5 March	President Grant removes E.R.S. Canby from command of the Fifth Military District; reappoints Joseph Reynolds.
12 April	Supreme Court upholds constitutionality of the Military Reconstruction Acts in *Texas v. White*.
4 October	Tennessee, the first state readmitted, becomes the first state "redeemed" by conservatives as DeWitt Senter wins governorship.
5 October	Virginia "redeemed" as elections result in a conservative legislature that will join conservative governor Gilbert C. Walker, elected in July; Virginia is the only state redeemed before readmission.

| 30 November | Republican James L. Alcorn elected governor of Mississippi under Congressional Reconstruction. |
| 22 December | Georgia directed to reconvene the 1868 legislature, which includes blacks, before Congress will consider readmission. |

1870

18 January	Edmund J. Davis inaugurated as governor of Texas under the Military Reconstruction Acts.
26 January	Despite its conservative government, Virginia is readmitted to the Union.
23 February	Congress readmits Mississippi to the Union.
25 February	Hiram R. Revels, Senate-elect from Mississippi, becomes the first black U.S. senator.
30 March	Upon ratification, the Fifteenth Amendment becomes part of the U.S. Constitution. Congress readmits Texas to the Union.
31 May	Congress passes the First Enforcement Act, placing certain forms of voting harassment under federal jurisdiction.
June–August	In North Carolina, the "Kirk-Holden War" begins, pitting state forces against the Ku Klux Klan.
15 July	Congress readmits Georgia to the federal Union for the second time.
19 October	Republican carpetbagger Robert K. Scott reelected governor of South Carolina.
4 November	Conservative legislature convenes, "redeeming" North Carolina.
12 December	Joseph H. Rainey, the first African American to serve in the House of Representatives, takes his seat in Washington; he will serve until 1879.
19 December	Lower house of North Carolina legislature passes formal Articles of Impeachment against Republican governor William W. Holden.

1871

28 February	Congress passes the Second Enforcement Act.
3 March	Congress creates the Southern Claims Commission, which will operate until 1880.
22 March	William W. Holden is convicted and removed by the North Carolina Senate, the first governor in American history thus removed.
20 April	Faced with growing evidence of well-organized terrorist challenges to the southern Republican governments, Congress passes the Third Enforcement Act (also called the Ku Klux Act; later generations added the "Klan" portion of the title).
17 October	Citing the Ku Klux Act, President Grant suspends the writ of habeas corpus in portions of up-country South Carolina and orders military/Justice Department intervention.
1 November	After second readmission, Georgia is again "redeemed" with ascension of James M. Smith as governor.

1872

3 May	"Liberal Republicans" bolt Grant's Republican Party and hold convention in Cincinnati; *New York Tribune* owner Horace Greeley nominated for president.
22 May	Congress passes the Amnesty Act, clearing nearly all former confederates from political liabilities imposed under the Military Reconstruction Acts and Fourteenth Amendment.
5–6 June	Republican National Convention nominates Ulysses S. Grant for reelection.

9–10 July	Democratic National Convention backs the Liberal Republicans and their candidate, Horace Greeley.
September	Evidence breaks about federal fraud and corruption surrounding the transcontinental railroad, ultimately leading to the "Credit Mobilier" scandal.
16 October	Republican Franklin J. Moses elected governor of South Carolina.
5 November	Ulysses S. Grant reelected president.
30 November	Liberal Republican nominee Greeley dies.
9 December	Division among Republicans in Louisiana leads the Republican legislature to impeach Republican governor Henry Clay Warmoth; although he is not removed, the governorship falls to P.B.S. Pinchback, making him the first black governor in U.S. history.

1873

9 January	Republican divisions in Louisiana result in disputed election and dual governments: Republicans assemble under William P. Kellogg, and conservatives under John McEnery.
14 January	Redemption of Texas as conservative Richard Coke becomes governor.
12 February	Known as the so-called "Crime of '73," the Silver Coinage Act takes silver out of circulation, marking a victory for fiscal contractionists and spurring a political debate for the next generation.
13 April	White vigilantes murder black and white Republicans in the Colfax Massacre in Louisiana.
14 April	Supreme Court, in the *Slaughterhouse Cases,* renders very narrow interpretation of the scope of the Fourteenth Amendment.
May	Grant administration recognizes Kellogg government in Louisiana; orders McEnery to desist or face federal intervention.
18 September	Panic of 1873 begins with the failure of Jay Cooke's investment house.

1874

21 January	Morrison R. Waite succeeds Salmon P. Chase as Chief Justice of the United States.
22 January	Republican carpetbagger and former Union general Adelbert Ames becomes governor of Mississippi.
March–May	In the Brooks-Baxter War, Republican infighting in Arkansas moves from political disputes into court fights, and finally erupts in bloodshed.
16 May	Grant recognizes Elisha Baxter as governor of Arkansas, ending Brooks-Baxter War.
June	Appearance of White League in Louisiana, terrorist organization aimed at overthrowing Republican Kellogg.
30 August	White League murders Republicans in the Coushatta Massacre.
16 September	White League battles police in New Orleans; Kellogg temporarily overthrown; Grant sends federal troops to reinstate Kellogg.
October–November	Democrats score sweeping victories in congressional elections; the next House of Representatives, set to convene fall 1875, will be under Democratic control.
15 October	Carpetbag Republican Daniel H. Chamberlain elected in South Carolina.
10 November	Arkansas is "redeemed" with the election of conservative Augustus H. Garland as governor.
14 November	Redemption in Alabama as George Houston becomes governor.

| December | Race riots and violence across Mississippi, as white conservatives embark on a violent, terror-based campaign to seize control at the next election. Across the South, whites adopt the term "Mississippi Plan" when referring to brutal, overt tactics. |

1875

14 January	Congress passes the Specie Resumption Act to ease the recession; act temporarily releases greenbacks and silver into circulation.
26 January	Andrew Johnson becomes the only president elected to the U.S. Senate after leaving executive office.
1 March	Congress passes the Civil Rights Act of 1875.
May	Federal officials are implicated in the "whisky ring," a collage of importers, distillers, and wholesalers based in New York and operating to defraud the government of taxes.
16 April	Wheeler Compromise produces armistice in Louisiana by dividing the legislature between houses and parties: Democrats control the assembly, while Republicans control the Senate.
September	Widespread assaults and rioting by "white liners" across Mississippi as part of an organized reign of terror for the upcoming election.
3 November	Violence and fraud result in the redemption of Mississippi; conservative whites regain control of the state legislature.

1876

4 January	Conservative legislature convenes in Mississippi.
March	Federal investigation into financial dealings of Secretary of War William Belknap lead to his impeachment; Belknap resigns.
2 March	Mississippi legislature impeaches Republican governor Ames.
27 March	Supreme Court, in *U.S. v. Cruikshank* and *U.S. v. Reese*, restricts scope and use of Enforcement Acts.
15–17 June	In Cincinnati, Republican National Convention nominates Rutherford B. Hayes of Ohio for president.
27–29 June	In St. Louis, Democratic National Convention nominates New Yorker Samuel Tilden for president.
7 July	Hamburg Massacre in South Carolina, as election campaigning pits Republican black militiamen against white conservative gun clubs.
6 September	King Street Riot in Charleston, as conservatives and Republicans continue to battle in South Carolina.
16–19 September	In South Carolina a three day, countywide killing spree conducted by white gun clubs earns the name the Ellenton Riot; ends with direct intervention by U.S. infantry units.
16–17 October	White attack on a Republican meeting, called the Cainhoy Riot, leads Grant to send more federal troops to South Carolina for the election.
8 November	Presidential and state elections disputed; state gubernatorial elections in South Carolina and Louisiana result in dual governments for both, while improprieties in state electoral returns deadlock the presidential decision.
28–30 November	Democrats and Republicans establish rival legislatures in South Carolina.
6 December	Republican legislature elects Daniel H. Chamberlain governor of South Carolina.

14 December	South Carolina Supreme Court and Democrat legislature declare Wade Hampton III governor of South Carolina.

1877

1 January	Democrat Zebulon Vance, governor of North Carolina during the Confederacy, is sworn in as governor once again.
2 January	Florida Democrats "redeem" the state by contesting their gubernatorial election, but not the national one; Democrat Charles F. Drew becomes governor over Republican Marcellus Stearns, but electoral votes all go to Hayes.
8 January	In Louisiana, rival governors are sworn in: Stephen B. Packard has Republican (and federal) support, while Francis T. Nicholls is backed by Democrats.
20 January	The Federal Electoral Commission is established to decide the presidential contest.
February	Discussion, rumors, and trips North and South occur as commission debates presidential decision.
26 February	Wormley House "deal" negotiates a complex series of trade-offs to settle the presidential controversy.
2 March	Disputed electoral votes go to Rutherford B. Hayes.
4 March	Hayes inaugurated as president.
3 April	Hayes tells cabinet that federal troops must be withdrawn from state capitals, and must cease to interfere in state political disputes.
10 April	Federal troops leave Columbia; Hampton becomes governor and South Carolina is formally "redeemed."
24 April	Federal troops withdraw from Baton Rouge; Nicholls becomes governor of a "redeemed" Louisiana.

1878

18 June	Congress passes the Posse Comitatus Act, severely restricting the use of federal military forces as agents of law and order in civilian society.

1883

15 October	Supreme Court, in the *Civil Rights Cases*, overturns the Civil Rights Act of 1875 and declares that the Fourteenth Amendment only covers government action. Segregation by private individuals in privately owned establishments is legal, as Court creates difference between "civil rights" and "social rights"; federal condoning of Jim Crow laws fully under way.

1887

July	First major reunion between Union and Confederate veterans takes place at Gettysburg Battlefield in Pennsylvania.

1889

10 June	United Confederate Veterans formally chartered.

1890

1 November	Mississippi becomes first southern state to alter its state constitution to legally disfranchise blacks, using loopholes in the Fifteenth Amendment. Other southern states follow over the next decade.

1892

April
In response to antiblack violence and the rise of lynchings across the South, African American journalist Ida B. Wells begins an antilynching crusade that grows to international dimensions.

1895

18 September
Booker T. Washington, founder of the Tuskegee Institute, offers the "Atlanta Compromise" at the Cotton States Exposition, telling African Americans they should concentrate on economic development and self-improvement instead of demanding political equality.

1896

18 May
Supreme Court rules in *Plessy v. Ferguson* that accommodations that are separate but equal do not violate the Fourteenth Amendment.

1898

25 April
Supreme Court rules in *Williams v. Mississippi* that the states can use poll taxes and literacy tests to determine voter qualification, as these do not violate the race injunction in the Fifteenth Amendment.

1899

18 December
Supreme Court, in *Cummings v. Georgia*, declares segregation in the schools is legal under the Fourteenth Amendment.

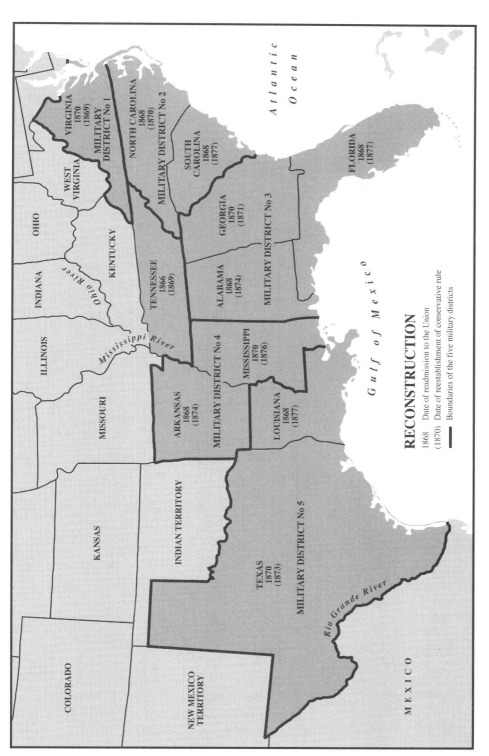

Reconstruction military districts and dates of readmission and redemption. (Courtesy of the author.)

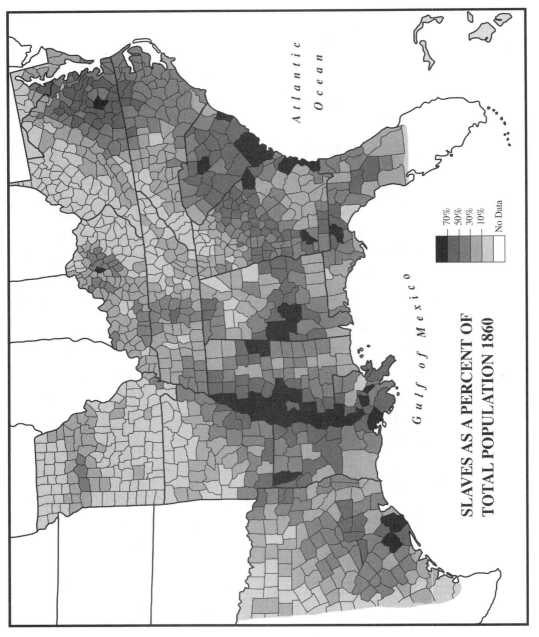

**SLAVES AS A PERCENT OF
TOTAL POPULATION 1860**

70%
50%
30%
10%
No Data

*Atlantic
Ocean*

Gulf of Mexico

Slaves as a percent of total population 1860. (Reprinted by permission of Louisiana State University Press from *Atlas of Antebellum Southern Agriculture* by Sam Bowers Hilliard. Copyright © 1984 by Louisiana State University Press.)

ENCYCLOPEDIA OF
THE RECONSTRUCTION ERA

A

Abolitionists

Abolitionists advocated ending slavery and emancipating slaves. African American and white American abolitionists were part of an antislavery movement that spanned the Atlantic world during the eighteenth and nineteenth centuries. Prior to 1830, most of them favored gradual elimination of slavery, but by the early 1830s, abolitionists became influential by supporting immediate general emancipation through their words and deeds. During the Civil War, they pressed the Lincoln administration to make emancipation a Union war aim. During Reconstruction, they advocated national protection of black rights and promotion of black advancement.

When people used the term *abolitionist* during the era of the Civil War and Reconstruction, they usually meant the immediatists—small radical groups of agitators, political activists, Underground Railroad leaders, and freedom fighters. Historians distinguish between these abolitionists and a larger, less radical, group of journalists and politicians who, to varying degrees, opposed the territorial expansion of slavery and the influence slaveholders exercised on the U.S. government. During the Civil War and Reconstruction, Radical Republicans constituted the majority of this larger group, which became less distinguishable from abolitionists as time passed.

Early American Abolitionists

As soon as slavery came into existence in Great Britain's North American colonies during the seventeenth century, enslaved people of African descent sought freedom. They purchased freedom, sued for it, escaped, and—on rarer occasions—took up arms. During the 1690s, a few Quakers began to contend that slavery was sinful and dangerous, but natural rights doctrines and evangelical Christianity did not begin to spread antislavery sentiment beyond

African Americans and Quakers until the era of the American Revolution. During the 1780s, white rationalists and evangelicals began to exercise considerable influence. These early abolitionists contributed to the decisions between 1783 and 1804 on the part of all the states north of Delaware to end slavery or provide for its gradual abolition. In 1787, Congress adopted the Northwest Ordinance banning slavery in the Northwest Territory. By the 1790s, small gradual abolition societies had spread to Delaware, **Maryland**, and **Virginia**.

Early abolitionism peaked during the 1780s. During the following decades, the spread of cotton cultivation into the Old Southwest created a market for slaves that ended the southward spread of antislavery sentiment. Meanwhile white northerners increasingly interpreted social status in racial terms and restricted black access to schools, **churches**, and jobs. In 1800, the Virginia slave Gabriel organized a revolt conspiracy that—when revealed to white authorities and crushed—intensified an anti-abolitionist reaction. As whites became convinced that free blacks encouraged slave revolt and constituted a dependent and criminal class, antislavery societies in Delaware, Maryland, and Virginia disbanded, became inactive, or declined. White abolitionists gradually accepted the contention that emancipation must be linked with expatriation of former slaves. For a time, black abolitionists, aware of the limits on their freedom in the United States, agreed.

The American Colonization Society (ACS), organized in Washington, D.C., in 1816, epitomized the linkage of gradual emancipation and expatriation. In 1821, the ACS established a colony for free African Americans at Liberia in West Africa. During the society's early years, it enjoyed the support of black and white abolitionists who later became immediatists. Yet, from its beginning, many African Americans were suspicious of the ACS. They feared that its real goal was to strengthen slavery by removing all free black people from the United States.

Immediatism during the Late 1820s and 1830s

Black opposition to the ACS contributed to the rise of immediatism. In 1829, black abolitionist David Walker published in Boston his *Appeal to the Colored Citizens of the World*. He denounced the ACS, asserted the right of African Americans to U.S. citizenship, and suggested that black men must fight for freedom. Although most early immediatists, both black and white, rejected violent means, Walker's opposition to colonization and his demand for action helped shape the movement.

Several developments led a few young white men and women to become immediate abolitionists. The emergence in the North of factory production and wage labor made slave labor seem outmoded and barbaric. As middle-class family life developed in the North, the disruption slavery imposed on black families appeared increasingly reprehensible. The religious revival known as the Second Great Awakening encouraged evangelical northerners to establish benevolent organizations designed to fight a variety of sins. Meanwhile, contact with African Americans and observation of slavery had an enormous impact on white reformers who became immediatists.

More than any other individual, white abolitionist **William Lloyd Garrison** spread immediatism during the 1830s. Influenced by black abolitionists, Garrison began publishing his weekly newspaper, *The Liberator*, in January 1831. Like Walker, Garrison rejected gradualism and colonization. He demanded immediate general emancipation without expatriation and equal rights for African Americans. In late 1833, Garrison brought together a diverse group, including a few black men and a few white women, to form the American Anti-Slavery Society (AASS). Rejecting the violent abolitionist tactics endorsed by Walker and put into practice by slave rebel Nat Turner in his failed Virginia slave revolt of August 1831, the AASS pledged to use peaceful moral means to promote immediatism and convince masters to free their slaves. Although immediate abolitionists remained a tiny, despised minority, AASS affiliates spread across the North. In 1835 and 1836, the organization sent thousands of antislavery petitions to Congress and stacks of abolitionist propaganda into the South. These efforts produced another antiabolitionist and anti-black reaction, which strengthened proslavery sentiment in the South and encouraged mob violence against abolitionists and black communities in the North.

Rise of a More Aggressive Abolitionism

The anti-abolitionist reaction and the failure of peaceful agitation to weaken slavery led immediatists in new directions. Garrison and his associates centered in New England became social perfectionists, feminists, and anarchists. They denounced violence, human government, and organized religion. They embraced dissolution of the Union as the only way to save the North from the sin of slavery and force the South to abolish it. The great majority of immediate abolitionists (both black and white), however, believed that church and government action could be effective against slavery. They became more willing to consider violent means and rejected radical assertions of women's rights.

At its 1840 annual meeting, the AASS split apart on these issues. The Garrisonian minority retained control of what became known as the "Old Organization," while the great majority of immediatists launched new organizations. Until the Civil War, the AASS concentrated on agitation in the North; the new organizations were more aggressive. The American and Foreign Anti-Slavery Society (AFASS), led by New York City businessman Lewis Tappan, sought to convert the nation's churches to immediatism and sent antislavery propaganda into the South. The Liberty Party employed a variety of political strategies to fight slavery. The more radical Liberty abolitionists, centered in upstate New York and led by Gerrit Smith, maintained that slavery was illegal and that immediatists had an obligation to go south to help slaves escape. The more conservative Liberty faction, centered in Cincinnati and led by Gamaliel Bailey and **Salmon P. Chase**, accepted the legality of slavery in the South. It rejected abolitionist aid to slave escape, and sought to build a mass political party in the South as well as the North on a platform calling not for abolition but "denationalization" of slavery. The breakup of the AASS also encouraged autonomous organization among black abolitionists, who led in forming local vigilance associations designed to protect fugitive slaves, but most black abolitionists also supported the AFASS and the Liberty Party. In 1846, black abolitionists joined church-oriented white abolitionists in the **American Missionary Association (AMA)**, an outgrowth of the AFASS that sent antislavery missionaries into the South.

In 1848, the conservative wing of the Liberty Party merged into the Free Soil Party and its members, for all intents and purposes, ceased to be immediatists. They, nevertheless, had an enormous impact on those who by the Civil War were called **Radical Republicans**. The more radical members of the Liberty Party, known as radical political abolitionists, maintained their organization under a variety of names into the Civil War. They excelled in underground railroad efforts and in resistance to the Fugitive Slave Law of 1850. More than any other immediatist faction, the radical political abolitionists supported John Brown's raid at Harpers Ferry in 1859.

Abolitionists during Civil War and Reconstruction

White southerners anticipated that the victory of Republican candidate Abraham Lincoln in the presidential election of 1860 would encourage underground-railroad activity, abolitionist politics in the upper South, and slave revolt. Such fears had an important role in the secession movement that led to the Civil War in April 1861. Lincoln, who was not an immediate abolitionist, hoped for the "ultimate extinction" of slavery and the colonization of African Americans outside of the United States, but as the war began, he promised not to interfere with slavery in the South. He believed that abolitionism of any sort would alienate southern Unionists and weaken support of the war in the North.

Immediate abolitionists, nevertheless, almost universally supported the war as a means of ending slavery. By the late 1850s, Garrison and his associates had become less committed to nonviolence. When the Civil War began, they dropped their opposition to forceful means. Church-oriented and radical political abolitionists rejoined the AASS, and the organization's membership and influence grew. AASS leader **Wendell Phillips** emerged as the North's most popular public speaker. Well aware of their new standing, immediatists in alliance with Radical Republicans lobbied Lincoln to make emancipation and racial justice Union war aims. Phillips, **Frederick Douglass**, Sojourner Truth, and others called on Lincoln at the White House to make their points. Immediatists—especially black immediatists—led in urging the president to enlist black troops.

Immediatists realized that strategic considerations were more important than their influence on Lincoln's decision to issue his Emancipation Proclamation in January 1863. They worried that, by resting emancipation on military necessity rather than racial justice, Lincoln had laid an unsound basis for permanent black freedom, but they also recognized the Proclamation's significance, particularly its endorsement of enlisting black troops. Douglass, for example, declared it to be "the greatest event" in American history, and worked tirelessly to recruit black soldiers to fight for freedom. Younger white immediatists became officers in the otherwise segregated black Union regiments. Phillips, a few other immediatists, and a similarly small group of Radical Republicans attempted to block Lincoln's renomination for the presidency in 1864, but Garrison, Douglass, and most other immediatists enthusiastically supported him.

Meanwhile, immediatists led in wartime reconstruction efforts in the South. During the summer of 1861, the AMA and many smaller abolitionist organizations began sending missionaries and teachers into war zones to minister to the physical, spiritual, and educational needs of the former slaves. Women predominated, in part because younger immediatist men had enrolled in Union armies. The most ambitious abolitionist effort occurred in the South Carolina Sea Islands centered on Port Royal, which Union forces captured in 1861. With organizational and financial backing from Lewis Tappan and support from former immediatist Secretary of the Treasury Salmon P. Chase, younger abolitionists, who called themselves "Gideonites," launched the Port Royal Experiment in 1862. They provided medical care, taught school, and helped former slaves purchase land. At Port Royal and in a similar undertaking in southern Louisiana, immediatists attempted to transform an oppressed people into independent proprietors and wage laborers. Immediatist men and women also worked in black refugee camps in the Chesapeake and **Kentucky**. In addition to providing clothing, food, medical care, and educational services, they lobbied for rent control, and helped former slaves find jobs locally and in the North. These efforts had numerous shortcomings. Northern immediatists had little understanding of slave culture, tended toward bureaucratic solutions, and patronized the freedpeople. Both black and white immediatists put too much emphasis on wage labor as a social cure and too little emphasis on establishing economic independence for the former slaves.

The front page of *The Liberator* from July 16, 1862. (Courtesy of the Library of Congress.)

When the freedpeople did not progress under these circumstances, immediatists tended to blame the victims.

In 1863, antislavery organizations began petitioning Congress in support of a constitutional amendment to prohibit forever slavery in the United States. When the ratification of the **Thirteenth Amendment** achieved this goal in December 1865, Garrison and his closest associates declared that their efforts had succeeded. Garrison ceased publication of *The Liberator* and urged the AASS to disband. He and those who agreed with him believed the Republican Party could best protect black rights and interests. However, a majority of immediatists, including Douglass, Phillips, and Smith, disagreed; they kept the AASS in existence until 1870. This division and the advancing age of most immediatist leaders signaled the movement's rapid decline. Immediatists, nevertheless, continued to participate in Reconstruction and in the debate over its character.

Early in the Civil War, immediate abolitionists advocated the right of black men to vote as a means of protecting their freedom. Immediatists favored land redistribution and advocated creating a federal agency to provide food and medical care to freedpeople, find jobs for them, and defend their civil and political rights. In December 1863, when Lincoln announced a mild Reconstruction plan that would leave former masters in control of the status of their former slaves, many immediatists criticized it as insufficient. They supported voting rights, education, and land for African Americans as recompense for generations of unrequited labor and as essential for black economic and political independence. In these things, immediatists were similar to Radical Republicans, but much more insistent on involving African Americans in the reconstruction process. The immediatist missionaries who went South worked with and on behalf of the former slaves. In 1863 and 1864, other immediatists pressured the Lincoln administration to sell lands confiscated from southern planters to former slaves. When Congress created the **Freedmen's Bureau** in 1865, it provided for this, but the effort failed.

As the war ended, most immediatists believed that Lincoln's policy of reconciliation with former rebels threatened the rights of former slaves. After Lincoln's **assassination**, immediatists mistakenly anticipated that his presidential successor, **Andrew Johnson**, would be more active in establishing black rights in the South, but by the fall of 1865, they had become very critical of Johnson. Black abolitionists in particular lobbied in Washington on behalf of the freedpeople. Following Johnson's veto of the **Civil Rights Act** in Februrary 1866, immediatists began calling for his **impeachment**. They were disappointed when Congress failed to remove Johnson from office in 1868.

Immediatist influence increased after the congressional **election of 1866** in which their Radical Republican allies made impressive gains. Unlike the Radicals, however, most immediatists opposed the ratification of the **Fourteenth Amendment**, contending that its threat to reduce the representation in Congress of states that denied black men the right to vote was by no means a guarantee of **black suffrage**. Instead, immediatists advocated a revolutionary reordering of southern society that would provide justice and full citizenship for African Americans. They supported the Reconstruction Acts passed by

Congress in February 1867, which established military rule in the former Confederate states. With the exception of some feminists led by **Elizabeth Cady Stanton**, who believed that the right of white women to vote was more important than that of black men, immediatists supported the **Fifteenth Amendment** guaranteeing that the right to vote would not be denied to black men. With the ratification of this amendment in 1870, Douglass, Phillips, and Theodore Tilton declared that the immediatists had achieved their ultimate objective. Other abolitionists were not so sure, but the rump of the AASS voted to disband.

Four years later at a reunion in Chicago, aging immediatists acknowledged that they had been too hasty as northern politicians and opinion shapers sought reconciliation with the white South at the cost of black rights. They recalled their warning that northern support for black rights based on wartime expediency rather than morality was unsound. The immediatists themselves bore some responsibility. Once it became clear that there would be no extensive land redistribution, they placed too much hope in the ballot and left black southerners to fend for themselves in an increasingly hostile environment. Nevertheless, immediatists played a crucial role in ending slavery, in creating black institutions in the postwar South, and in placing protections for minority rights in the **U.S. Constitution**.

Further Reading: Curry, Richard O. "The Abolitionists and Reconstruction: A Critical Appraisal." *Journal of Southern History* 54 (1968): 529–32; Fredrickson, George. *The Inner Civil War: Northern Intellectuals and the Crisis of the Union*. New York: Harper and Row, 1968; Friedman, Lawrence J. *Gregarious Saints: Self and Community in American Abolitionism, 1830–1870*. New York: Cambridge University Press, 1982; Gara, Larry. "A Glorious Time: The 1874 Abolitionist Reunion in Chicago." *Journal of the Illinois State Historical Society* 65 (1972): 280–92; Harrold, Stanley. *American Abolitionists*. Harlow, U.K.: Longman, 2001; McPherson, James M. *The Struggle for Equality: Abolitionists and the Negro in the Civil War and Reconstruction*. 1964; reprint, Princeton, NJ: Princeton University Press, 1992; Rose, Willie Lee. *Rehearsal for Reconstruction: The Port Royal Experiment*. Indianapolis: Bobbs-Merrill, 1964; Stewart, James Brewer. *Holy Warriors: The Abolitionists and American Slavery*. 2nd ed. New York: Hill and Wang, 1997.

Stanley Harrold

Abolition of Slavery

The abolition of slavery is usually associated with the Civil War. Certainly it is true that this conflict made **emancipation** possible. However, slavery's end arguably is the most important event associated with wartime Reconstruction. That is, many phenomena associated with Reconstruction—the reorganization of the southern economy, biracial politics in the southern states, and the social and cultural upheavals associated with this period—started during the Civil War, including the abolition of slavery. However, none of these developments was as revolutionary as emancipation. Indeed, without freedom for the slaves, all the rest would have been moot.

From Slave to Contraband

Freedom for the slaves did not appear likely in the early months of the Civil War. Both Unionists and Confederates denied slavery was a cause for the war. White southerners claimed they were fighting for independence, states' rights, and to defend their homes against northern aggression. White northerners asserted they fought to suppress a rebellion against the legitimate national government and to preserve the Union. Both groups disavowed slavery as irrelevant in a "white man's war" and rebuffed attempts early in the war by free black men to enlist in the North and South.

Significantly, it was the slaves themselves who demonstrated their own relevance. From the earliest days of the conflict, men and women in bondage never doubted the war was about them. Likewise, they constantly sought ways to transform it into a war of liberation. Even before the start of hostilities at Fort Sumter, **South Carolina**, in April 1861, slaves escaped their plantations seeking refuge from northern troops. These early escapees were rebuffed, but that policy soon began to change. Union soldiers found it hard to turn away slaves in the face of their horrid stories, often made believable by the all too visible scars of past whippings. For many northern troops, it was their first personal encounter with the "peculiar institution," and they did not like what they saw. Union officers also quickly realized that slaves were a military asset for the Confederacy. Slaves could dig entrenchments, deliver supplies, and provide personal service to the southern army, as well as keep the plantation system functioning despite the absence of so many white men who had gone off to war. Therefore, giving refuge to escaped slaves was a double gain for the Union; it deprived the Confederacy of their services while at the same time making their labor available to northern forces.

It took the crafty administrative brain of General **Benjamin F. Butler**, though, to formalize what quickly became an informal policy of giving sanctuary to escaped slaves. Butler had been a Democratic member of Congress from Massachusetts prior to the war. Once hostilities commenced, he accepted a commission as a general in the Union **army** and was initially assigned to oversee the occupation of Union-controlled areas in coastal **Virginia**. Like other northern officers, he soon realized the slaves' military value. Yet, like many white northerners in the early days of the Civil War, he also did not want to confront the institution of slavery itself. So Butler needed a way to justify legally holding onto slaves without challenging slavery's legality. What he devised was to declare slaves entering Union lines to be "**contraband** of war." In other words, because they likely would be used to support a rebellion against the legal government of the United States, the duly authorized agent of that government—the Union army—could seize the slaves as contraband (i.e., illicit property) and refuse to return them to their disloyal owners.

The First and Second Confiscation Acts

Other Union commanders quickly copied Benjamin Butler's contraband policy and it became the basis for the First **Confiscation Act** passed by the U.S. Congress in the summer of 1861. This legislation made slaves used in support of the Confederacy subject to seizure. Federal officials quickly interpreted the

First Confiscation Act to mean that not only did federal officials in the rebellious states have the authority to confiscate the slaves of disloyal owners, but also that those slaves could be put to work for wages in support of the Union.

The First Confiscation Act also was evidence of growing sentiment in the North in favor of ending slavery. Certainly, black people and their white **abolitionist** allies had been in favor of emancipation at the beginning of the war and were eager to transform the conflict into a war of liberation. Some abolitionists were in positions of considerable authority and used their power to alter Union war aims to include the end of slavery. For example, in August 1861, General John C. Frémont declared the slaves free in Missouri by virtue of his authority as Union military commander in the state. However, Frémont's emancipation order never went into effect because President **Abraham Lincoln** forced him to rescind it.

Lincoln's decision showed his unwillingness to embrace abolition early in the Civil War. Although he personally hated slavery, Lincoln did not support abolitionism before the Civil War. Like most Republicans, he merely wanted slavery confined to the states where it already existed, with no possibility for its expansion into the western territories—the Free Soil position. Lincoln was loath to abandon this stance early in the Civil War because he feared alienating the four remaining Union slave states: **Maryland**, Delaware, **Kentucky**, and Missouri. Lincoln also hoped that if his government did not embrace emancipation, he might encourage the rebellious states to end their insurrection by showing them slavery would be safe within the Union if they returned to it.

Yet, as the war dragged on through the remainder of 1861 and into 1862, events increasingly made Abraham Lincoln's position untenable. The trickle of contraband slaves into Union lines in 1862 became a torrent as northern forces occupied increasingly large amounts of the South. Congress responded to the growing numbers of contraband slaves in the South by passing the Second Confiscation Act in July 1862. This law built on the First Confiscation Act by actually freeing the slaves of disloyal owners. So no longer were slaves that reached Union-controlled territory from the Confederacy in limbo merely as confiscated property—under this law, they became free.

In passing the Second Confiscation Act, Congress also was responding to increasing sentiment in the North in favor of emancipation. As the casualties and costs mounted from the fighting, conciliatory sentiments toward the Confederacy evaporated and the significance of slavery in the war became increasingly apparent. Many people in the North came to believe that if the Union was ever to be restored, to be truly healed, it must be as a nation without slavery. That is, emancipation was more and more perceived as the only result that would justify the horrendous number of dead, wounded, and missing men. While Union remained a northern war aim, it was increasingly seen as insufficient by itself to validate the tremendous human and financial sacrifice of the war.

The Emancipation Proclamation

The Second Confiscation Act also was passed by Republicans in Congress to pressure President Lincoln, whom the **Radical Republicans** in particular saw as lagging behind his party in embracing emancipation. What they did not know was that during the summer of 1862, Lincoln's position on this issue was changing. By spring of 1862, he had already proposed federal support for the state-implemented emancipation in the border states, which would be gradual and where loyal slaveholders would be compensated. Lincoln also stated that he thought the emigration of emancipated slaves from the United States would be a good idea (although he quickly abandoned this position when it appeared impractical). Neither Delaware, Kentucky, Maryland, nor Missouri accepted in 1862 the idea of gradual compensated emancipation. Lincoln was reluctant to pressure these states because he feared they would leave the Union, especially Maryland—a state that surrounded the national capital, Washington, D.C., on three sides. So in May 1862, when another Union general, David Hunter, again tried to abolish slavery by military decree—this time in South Carolina, **Georgia**, and **Florida**—it is not surprising that Lincoln reversed Hunter's order, as he had done with John Frémont the year before.

Yet, by the summer of 1862, with pressure from Congress and a growing segment of the northern public, Lincoln realized how untenable his position on slavery was becoming. Hence, it is not surprising that by July, he told his cabinet privately that he planned to issue a proclamation freeing the slaves in the rebellious states. However, he also took their advice to delay a public announcement until the Union won a significant victory on the battlefield, so that the pronouncement would not appear as a desperate, last-ditch measure meant to stave off northern defeat.

This victory finally came on September 17, 1862, at the Battle of Antietam, when Union forces stopped a Confederate invasion of Maryland. Shortly thereafter, on September 22, Lincoln issued what became known as the Preliminary Emancipation Proclamation. This proclamation threatened that unless the seceded states rejoined the Union by the end of 1862, Lincoln would issue a decree freeing the slaves in those states. He also renewed his call for gradual and compensated emancipation in the border states. In neither case was there a positive response.

Abraham Lincoln's threat was serious. On January 1, 1863, he signed the final Emancipation Proclamation. As critics have pointed out, this pronouncement did not immediately free a single slave. It exempted not only the loyal slave states, but also those areas of the Confederacy then under Union occupation (a gesture by Lincoln to encourage Union sentiments). It is also true that Lincoln embraced emancipation more from expediency than principle. His main aim continued to be to save the Union and as far as slavery was concerned, he was prepared to do whatever it took to achieve that goal. As Lincoln famously wrote to **Horace Greeley**, editor of the *New York Tribune*, in August 1862, he was ready to preserve slavery if that would save the Union, and free some slaves while keeping others as slaves, to accomplish the same goal. The fact remains, however, that Lincoln chose to embrace both Union and freedom for the slaves, and once he did so, he never abandoned his support for emancipation. Lincoln famously reiterated his belief that the Union and emancipation had become inseparably intertwined in November 1863, when he spoke during the Gettysburg Address of a "new birth of freedom."

Black Military Service

The commitment of the Union to emancipation was further bolstered by the recruitment of black men into the Union army. The recruitment of black soldiers began in a limited fashion in late 1862 and accelerated considerably after Lincoln signed the final Emancipation Proclamation. From 1863 on, the Union army became an army of liberation, and freedom for the slaves became inexorably tied to Union success on the battlefield.

Not only did the nearly 179,000 black soldiers who served bolster the Union cause, but also their very existence undermined slavery. The most common excuse for excluding black men from military service before the Civil War was that they were not citizens. When military necessity for the Union prompted their recruitment, reversing the logic gave all black men a powerful claim to both freedom and citizenship. When blacks later claimed **suffrage** and other citizenship rights, they often cited the service of black soldiers in the Union army to strengthen their case. Indeed, black soldiers still in the army and recently discharged veterans played a prominent part in the black political conventions of 1865 and 1866 agitating for suffrage rights.

The Thirteenth Amendment

The widespread recruitment of black soldiers in the border states undermined slavery there by taking away many prime fieldhands from plantations. Slaveholders understood this and consistently opposed the military service of their property, but their opposition was eventually overwhelmed by the insatiable manpower needs of the Union army. Maryland and Missouri ultimately bowed to this reality, emancipating slaves on their own in late 1864 and early 1865, respectively. (Unionist governments in **Arkansas**, **Louisiana**, and the new state of West Virginia also freed their slaves by the end of 1864.) Delaware and Kentucky, however, stubbornly clung to slavery even after the final Confederate surrender in the spring of 1865.

It was the resistance of Delaware and Kentucky, plus uncertainty that statutory law or executive orders concerning emancipation were beyond reversal that prompted the **Thirteenth Amendment** to the **U.S. Constitution**. The amendment simply stated, "Neither slavery nor involuntary servitude, except as a punishment for crime whereof the party shall have been duly convicted, shall exist within the United States, or any place subject to their jurisdiction." The amendment passed the U.S. Senate with the required two-thirds majority in April 1864, but was unable to pass the House of Representatives due to lack of Democratic support. After key Union victories in the fall of 1864 and Lincoln's reelection in November of that year, the House finally approved the amendment in January 1865, and by the end of the year, it had been ratified by the states. The year's delay in the Thirteenth Amendment passing Congress, though, is indicative that as late as 1864 there was still significant opposition or indifference to emancipation in the North. (The racism that underlay this sentiment would manifest itself again in the mid-1870s and prove instrumental in bringing Reconstruction to an end.) The resistance also probably explains the decision of Congress in March 1865 to free the families of black soldiers (a move that strongly undermined slavery in

Kentucky by stimulating the enlistment of slaves into the Union army), and to found the **Bureau of Refugees, Freedmen, and Abandoned Lands**—the Freedmen's Bureau—an agency meant to guide former slaves in the transition to freedom.

Liquidation of Slavery

Still, the fact was that by early 1865, slavery on the ground in the U.S. South was rapidly on its way to extinction. The actual end of slavery in particular locales varied from place to place. In some locations, owners bowed to the inevitable and freed their slaves with the arrival of the Union army. In other places, it was necessary for army officers or agents of the Freedmen's Bureau to inform slaves of their liberation. Some slaveholders, especially on isolated plantations, tried as long as possible to hide the news. This proved difficult to accomplish, however, especially as the prospect of their liberation long preceded the arrival of Union forces, and slaves determinedly sought out any news that might herald approaching freedom. With the prospect of freedom, slaveholders often were forced to bargain with their slaves to retain their labor, even before northern troops actually reached their locale.

The end of slavery, of course, begged the question of what would replace it. It was here that the work of Reconstruction began in earnest. Wartime Reconstruction occurred mostly on an improvised basis, which should not be surprising, given the fact that a **labor system** that had dominated a vast region for centuries was eliminated in the midst of huge and tumultuous civil war. The slaves themselves seemed content, when allowed, to cease the production of staple crops—such as cotton—in favor of food crops like corn that always had been central to the private plots owners often allowed them to grow. Abolitionists and other philanthropic northerners organized **Freedmen's Relief Societies** to assist and guide newly liberated slaves, most famously in the so-called **Port Royal Experiment** in South Carolina. Northern entrepreneurs eager to prove that cotton could be produced more profitably using free labor than it had been under slavery joined them at Port Royal and other locations. Treasury Department agents eager to unload property they had confiscated from rebel slaveholders supported both groups. The efforts of the northern activists and budding cotton planters in South Carolina, Louisiana, and other locations was often undermined by their own ideological rigidity and inexperience, Confederate raids, and the recruitment of black men in the Union army and as military laborers. More realistic and lasting alternatives to slavery would have to wait for the end of the Civil War, when peace would allow for a more stable reorganization of a society turned upside down. *See also* Confiscation Acts; Howard, Oliver Otis.

Further Reading: Berlin, Ira et al., eds. *Free at Last: A Documentary History of Slavery, Freedom, and the Civil War.* New York: The New Press, 1992; *Slaves No More: Three Essays on Emancipation and the Civil War.* Cambridge: Cambridge University Press, 1992; Guelzo, Allen C. *Lincoln's Emancipation Proclamation: The End of Slavery in America.* New York: Simon and Schuster, 2004; Klingaman, William K. *Abraham Lincoln and the Road to Emancipation, 1861–1865.* New York: Viking,

2001; Vorenberg, Michael. *Final Freedom: The Civil War, the Abolition of Slavery, and the Thirteenth Amendment.* Cambridge: Cambridge University Press, 2001.

Donald R. Shaffer

Adams, Charles Francis, Jr. (1835–1915)

The direct descendant of two presidents (John Adams and John Quincy Adams), the son of a distinguished politician and diplomat (**Charles Francis Adams, Sr.**), and the brother of perhaps the deftest ironist America ever produced (Henry Brooks Adams), Charles Francis Adams, Jr., inevitably bore the peculiar burdens of his prominent surname. A soldier in the Civil War, a sometime lawyer, journalist, railroad reformer, and historian, he also shared his younger brother Henry's eclectic tastes, as well as the latter's talent for self-deprecation. Unfortunately, given the historical record, this shared fraternal gift lacked a certain zest in Charles's case.

In nearly all things political, Charles was a moderate, a tendency that manifested itself in a streak of independence, especially given the conflicted times in which he came to maturity. As a Civil War officer, for a short time he led the Fifth Massachusetts, a largely **African American** regiment. He consistently doubted the intellectual capabilities of his charges, but believed that military life could have an overwhelmingly positive influence on the African race. At war's end, he expressed dismay at the radical disposition of his home state of Massachusetts, preferring easier terms for southern reconstruction.

After 1865, this independence took the form of faith in scientific methods and ideas, particularly of a Comtean stripe, which made him somewhat of an iconoclast in his newly chosen field of interest, the burgeoning **railroad** industry. Admittedly naïve, he thought he could be useful to the industry by offering his services as a reformer. In 1869, he gained some prominence by exposing the corrupt, cutthroat practices of railway competitors in an article entitled "A Chapter of Erie." "Chapter" is more distinguished for its attention to detail and aloof patrician sensibility than for any radical indignation. True to his Adams birthright, Charles ironically condemned the dealings of Vanderbilt, **Gould**, and Fisk as vulgar and ungentlemanly. More than a few observers agreed, giving Adams a reputation as a trenchant critic and industry insider. In a freewheeling age, Adams believed that ordered, rational regulation of railroads was possible, and he dedicated the next two decades of his life to this philosophy, particularly as the dominating mind in the Massachusetts Railroad Commission, established in 1869, which he lobbied to create, arguably a statewide predecessor to the Interstate Commerce Commission (ICC).

In tune with his independently genteel proclivities, he was among that group of New England intellectuals who sought political reform of the Republican Party in the mid-1870s, particularly in the troubled 1876 election (an effort that met with obvious failure). After a decidedly mixed tenure as president of the Union Pacific Railroad, ending in 1890, Adams left the industry for good. Over the rest of his life, he wrote numerous well-regarded histories, including two prominent biographies, of Richard Henry Dana and his father. He died in Massachusetts in 1915.

Further Reading: Adams, Charles Francis, Jr. *Charles Francis Adams 1835-1915, an Autobiography*. Boston and New York: Houghton Mifflin, 1916; Adams, Charles Francis, Jr., and Henry Adams. *Chapters of Erie and Other Essays*. Boston: Osgood and Company, 1871; reprint, New York: A. M. Kelley, 1967; Ford, Worthington Chauncey, ed. *A Cycle of Adams Letters, 1861-1865*. 2 vols. Boston and New York: Houghton Mifflin, 1920; Kirkland, Edward Chase. *Charles Francis Adams, Jr., 1835-1915: The Patrician at Bay*. Cambridge, MA: Harvard University Press, 1965.

Peter A. Kuryla

Adams, Charles Francis, Sr. (1807–1886)

The son of John Q. Adams and the grandson of John Adams, Charles Francis had a distinguished political and diplomatic career. He was destined for governmental service. After graduating from Harvard in 1827, he read law with Daniel Webster. While practicing law in Boston, Adams devoted himself to scholarly activities, particularly U.S. history. He edited the letters of his grandmother, Abigail Adams, and undertook the lifelong task of editing the papers of his grandfather, John.

His successful marriage to a wealthy daughter of a Boston merchant allowed him to continue his gentlemanly activities and later to engage in political and diplomatic affairs. First active with the Anti-Masonic Party, Adams supported Martin Van Buren for president. He supported the **Democratic Party** because the Whigs had been so unkind to his father. By the mid-1830s, Adams's political activities changed along with many of his contemporaries.

Adams became a conscience Whig committed to antislavery and against the annexation of **Texas**. He served in the Massachusetts House and the U.S. Congress. Later, in the 1840s, he began his political pilgrimage that led to the Republican Party. In the decade before the Civil War, he sought the restriction of slavery and the slave interests. In 1858, he was elected to the House of Representatives. Adams believed that **Lincoln** was a weak candidate and therefore supported **William Henry Seward** in his push to the White House. In the days before the firing on Fort Sumter, Adams worked for compromise, but his efforts failed.

After Seward was appointed secretary of state, Adams accepted the position as America's representative to Great Britain. It was his greatest contribution to the Union war effort. He effectively protested the cozy relationship of Great Britain to the rebel states and worked to end the utilization of Great Britain (and France) as a source of supplies. His son, Henry Adams, ably helped him in the diplomacy of the situation. It was close, but Adams realized his goal. England did not support the rebel states in any significant manner.

He resigned in 1868 and retired from active political and policy activity since he was a strong critic of Radical Reconstruction both in theory and practice. He helped settle the Alabama Claims. Active in the **Liberal Republican** revolt in 1872-1873, he nearly won the presidential nomination. Defeated, he returned to publishing the Adams family papers, an activity that stood the test of time until well into the twentieth century. His last campaign was a defeat for the governorship of Massachusetts. By the late 1870s, his mind began to wander and his health declined.

His efforts at the Court of St. James were his greatest contribution to the creation of a new nation after 1865. A gentleman scholar, his conservative manner and desire to uphold his family's ethical standards meant he made an invaluable contribution to the nation.

Further Reading: Adams, Charles Francis, Jr. *Charles Francis Adams, by His Son Charles Francis Adams*. Boston: Houghton Mifflin, 1900; Brookhiser, Richard. *America's First Dynasty: The Adamses, 1735–1918*. New York: The Free Press, 2002; Duberman, Martin B. *Charles Francis Adams, 1807–1886*. Boston: Houghton Mifflin, 1960; Shepherd, Jack. *The Adams Chronicles: Four Generations of Greatness*. Boston: Little, Brown, 1975.

Donald K. Pickens

African Americans

The place of African Americans in Reconstruction was central. The emancipation of slaves during the Civil War, after centuries in bondage, initiated a world-shattering transformation in the political, economic, and social order of the American South. Yet black freedom also was revolutionary because former slaves played an unusually active role in bringing it to fruition. Likewise, in few other places in the Americas after slavery's end did people of African descent achieve real power and influence so quickly and so widely.

Nowhere is this last fact as apparent as in African American involvement in Reconstruction politics. At least 1,465 black men served in elected and appointive political office in the U.S. South between 1867 and 1877. Some of the men who served literally had been slaves only a few years before. Black office holding resulted from the genuine aspirations of African Americans themselves; the political idealism of the **Radical Republicans**, who genuinely believed in racial equality; and the practical calculations of **Moderate Republicans**, who realized that only the participation of black men would make a successful party organization possible in the South.

African Americans greatly desired political involvement to promote the needs and aspirations of their race. An active political role for them was made possible by the Reconstruction Act of 1867, which dissolved the state governments in the South constituted by **Andrew Johnson**, and provided for the formation of new state governments on the basis of universal manhood **suffrage**. Not only could black men vote for delegates to the **constitutional conventions** that would organize the new governments, but also they could run for election as delegates themselves. Nearly 150 black men were elected as delegates to the state constitutional conventions in 1867, and many more would serve in political office at the local, state, and federal level in the years to come. (In fact, sixteen black men served in Congress during Reconstruction.)

The black political agenda in Reconstruction stemmed in part from aspirations of the former slaves. Freedom was not an abstract concept for African Americans, but one with tangible, achievable meanings. For example, many ex-slaves in the wake of emancipation sought to rid themselves of "badges of servitude," which consisted of the restrictions on how slaves could dress, their proper behavior vis-à-vis whites, and what they were allowed by their owners to possess in the way of petty property. Naturally, emancipated slaves sought to free themselves from these limitations. They dressed nicer, refused to act subserviently to whites, and began to acquire such heretofore banned possessions as firearms, liquor, and pet animals.

During Reconstruction, African Americans also asserted their freedom of movement. The most telling restriction placed on slaves was that they could not leave their owner's plantation without permission. Often, the earliest action of black people in asserting their freedom was to depart the plantation where they had been enslaved. Many left seeking better living conditions and some ended up in southern cities that quickly gained a reputation of being places where "freedom was freer."

Another reason to exercise their new freedom of movement was for ex-slaves to go in search of lost loved ones. Family members found themselves separated from each other all too often during slavery due to sale, estate division, and other causes. Black people sometimes traveled long distances in an attempt to find family members they had been separated from under slavery. Some of these people knew where to go, others did not. Hence, it was not unusual in black newspapers during Reconstruction, and for decades thereafter, to find advertisements from former slaves seeking information on the whereabouts of lost family members.

For those black families who remained together or who proved able to reunite with their loved ones, Reconstruction was a time to strengthen family ties. Couples in "abroad" marriages (where a couple had different owners during slavery and was forced to live apart on separate plantations) were able to set up full-time housekeeping together. Countless couples married

African American teamsters near a signal tower in Bermuda Hundred, Virginia, 1864. (Courtesy of the Library of Congress.)

in slavery reaffirmed their bonds by entering a legal marriage once that right came during **Presidential Reconstruction**. It was also common for black men to take the surname they associated with their father to assert patriarchal family connections. In some cases, black men also removed their wives and children from fieldwork as another way to assert their patriarchy and bring their families closer to respectable Victorian norms. Not all women supported this move toward greater patriarchy in the black community, though.

Just as many African Americans thirsted for a more stable and secure family life during Reconstruction, they also yearned for **education**—to learn how to read and write. Learning, like freedom of movement, had been denied to slaves as yet another badge of servitude. Owners feared educated slaves would become discontented and be better able to resist bondage. Once freedom came, many former slaves naturally desired an education, not only to avail themselves of a once-denied opportunity, but also from the recognition that they would not be able to take advantage of the possibilities of freedom as fully as they might without it. No formal education system existed in the South at the beginning of Reconstruction that ex-slaves could turn to. However, **Freedmen's Relief Societies**, the **Freedmen's Bureau**, and other organizations took an interest in educating former slaves, and numerous small schoolhouses appeared all over the South. Observers there often could witness the curious spectacle of children beside their parents, both learning how to read and write.

Yet, perhaps the most fervent desire of the black masses in Reconstruction was landownership. African Americans understood that to be fully independent from whites, it would be necessary to own land; otherwise, they would continue to be dependent on their former owners, and subject to economic pressure and other forms of intimidation. Many former slaves believed they were entitled to receive the land of their former owners, both as compensation for their years of uncompensated toil and as a reward for their loyalty to the federal government during the war (particularly the service of nearly 200,000 black men in the Union army and navy).

The federal government did take some tentative steps in the direction of promoting landownership among former slaves. In early 1865, Union general **William T. Sherman** issued **Field Order No. 15**, setting aside land in coastal **South Carolina** and **Georgia** for the settlement of African Americans. Each black family was eligible to occupy up to forty acres and receive the loan of army mules to cultivate the land—most probably the origin of the phrase "forty acres and a mule." Likewise, Congress passed the **Southern Homestead Act (1866)**, which gave former slaves priority over most white southerners in claiming up to eighty acres of federal land in **Arkansas**, **Alabama**, **Florida**, **Louisiana**, and **Mississippi**. However, Field Order No. 15 was nullified by the **Amnesty Proclamations** of Johnson, which restored the lands of ex-Confederates and ended any realistic hope that former slaves might have of land redistribution. Andrew Johnson also implemented the Southern Homestead Act so that black applicants received no particular preference under the law contrary to its intent (which effectively put them at a disadvantage compared to whites).

The fact was, however, that not all African Americans were enthusiastic about land redistribution. The black elite in the South, which disproportionately consisted of those who had been free before the war and the light-skinned, tended to emphasize suffrage and equal rights over economic issues. Consisting of property owners, or men who realistically aspired to buy property one day, these black men tended to oppose land confiscation and redistribution. They made common cause with white Republicans on this issue, few of whom supported confiscating land from ex-Confederates—even among the Radical Republicans. The fact that members of the elite predominated among black officeholders during Reconstruction also meant they rarely pushed this issue in Congress or state legislatures (not that it had much chance of passing even if they had, due to white majorities in these bodies).

Hence, most African Americans during Reconstruction did not achieve the dramatic economic progress comparable to that demonstrated by their race in politics. However, neither were white southerners successful in coercing them into the quasi-slavery of **contract** labor in **agriculture**, which was the point of the **Black Codes**. Instead, former slaves found themselves participating in new **labor systems** based on a compromise between landowners and laborers. The most notable new arrangement, of course, was **sharecropping**. Under this system, in return for the use of land, the farmer (which could be white as well as black) would give the landowner a quarter to a third of the final crop. Plantation owners could not as tightly control black laborers under this system as they had under slavery, but found they could obtain a reliable workforce. Former slaves did not achieve landownership under sharecropping, but it gave them considerable day-to-day freedom from supervision. Not all former slaves participated in sharecropping. Some rented land paying cash rather than a share of the crop; others worked for cash wages as agricultural laborers. It is also significant that the 1880 census, the first after the end of Reconstruction, found that about 20 percent of black farmers actually owned the land they cultivated.

Hence, some African Americans achieved a significant degree of independence during Reconstruction. Yet, for the black masses, institutions rather than property tended to underlay it; therefore, to the degree that they achieved autonomy during Reconstruction, it was more as a people than individually.

No institution embodied an independent existence for African Americans during Reconstruction like black **churches**. This period saw the emergence of denominations organized by and catering to former slaves in the South. There was a mass departure of black people from white-controlled churches into the African Methodist Episcopal (A.M.E.) Church, and other Protestant denominations, such as numerous black Baptist groups. These churches became far more than simply places of worship. Clergymen became the most important source of leadership in the black community, helping to shape the political beliefs of their parishioners. As many former slaves could not read, in church they learned from their minister who to vote for, which issues to support, and who their friends and enemies were. Some black ministers went as far as to run for political office themselves.

The church, though critical, was not the only independent institution for African Americans. While many of churches had existed prior to the Civil War among free people of color, Reconstruction allowed these institutions to develop more fully as they gained more freedom from white interference. Fraternal organizations and women's clubs multiplied to satisfy the need for sociability, assistance to members, and as centers for community action. Mutual aid societies and insurance companies catering to the black community developed to help people cope with the vicissitudes of life. Black-owned businesses sprung up, especially those serving the special needs of the community, such as barbershops, beauticians, undertakers, and the like. Black newspapers also commenced publication, especially in the major cities. Likewise, many black institutions of higher education sprung up during this period.

Still, the critical focus on African Americans during Reconstruction must remain on politics. Blacks achieved a degree of success during this period that would not again be repeated until the post–World War II **civil rights** revolution. Yet their success was not simply in electoral politics. Both white and black politicians realized the untapped potential of the black population in the South and sought to utilize it. In the wake of the Civil War, the Republicans moved south with the **Union Leagues**. While the purpose of this organization was ostensibly to promote loyalty to the Union, the real purpose of this grassroots political club was to draw black men into the Republican Party. The Union League proved enormously successful at this task, making African Americans in the South loyal Republicans until the arrival of the New Deal in the 1930s.

African Americans also engaged in mass political organizing on their own during Reconstruction. Early in this period, blacks in the North as well as in the South held a series of local and regional political conventions. While the conventions addressed many issues, their main focus was on achieving suffrage and other citizenship rights for black men. The delegates to the conventions saw it as essential that blacks enjoy the same rights as whites to successfully function and compete as free people. The conventions achieved considerable success in this goal—at least in the short run. Citizenship rights initially came to black Americans with the **Civil Rights Act (1866)** and more substantially with the ratification of the **Fourteenth Amendment** to the **U.S. Constitution** in 1868. As noted, they also achieved suffrage rights in the South with the Reconstruction Act of 1867 and nationally with the ratification of the **Fifteenth Amendment** in 1870.

The tragedy of Reconstruction for African Americans was that the revolution for them during these years was not immune to counterrevolution. Most white southerners came to resent greatly the advances of black people, correctly seeing it as a threat to white supremacy. They responded with passionate resistance, most famously through the **Ku Klux Klan**. Through fraud, intimidation, and **violence**, the Klan and other so-called "regulator" groups slowly ground down the determination of northerners to remake southern society until white Republicans openly abandoned their black allies in the wake of the **election of 1876**. Murders, beatings, arson, and other forms of terrorism also slowly sapped, if never completely extinguished the resolve of blacks in the South. They proved unable to resist the efforts of white southerners to roll back their political gains in Reconstruction through **disfranchisement** and the rise of segregation.

However, African Americans never saw their gains from Reconstruction entirely extinguished either. Many of the independent institutions they established during this period survived and even flourished, remaining a source of strength and succor even in the darkest days of **Jim Crow**. Likewise, they maintained the gains made in law in terms of family and marriage. Finally, Reconstruction was never forgotten by the black community, and became a source of example and inspiration when the second Reconstruction of the U.S. South began in the 1950s. *See also* American Missionary Association (AMA); Black Politicians; Black Suffrage; Black Troops (U.S.C.T.) in the Occupied South; Bruce, Blanche Kelso; Bureau of Refugees, Freedmen, and Abandoned Lands; Civil Rights Act of 1875; Davis Bend, Mississippi; Delany, Martin R.; Lynch, John R.; Military Reconstruction Acts; Revels, Hiram R.; Union League of America.

Further Reading: Foner, Eric: *Freedom's Lawmakers: A Directory of Black Officeholders during Reconstruction*. New York: Oxford University Press, 1993; *Reconstruction: America's Unfinished Revolution, 1863–1877*. New York: Harper and Row, 1988; Foner, Philip S., and George E. Walker, eds. *Proceedings of the Black National and State Conventions, 1865–1900*. Vol. 1. Philadelphia: Temple University Press, 1986; Franklin, John Hope, and Alfred A. Moss, Jr. *From Slavery to Freedom: A History of African Americans*. 8th ed. New York: McGraw-Hill, 2000; Schwalm, Leslie Ann. *A Hard Fight for We: Women's Transition from Slavery in South Carolina*. Urbana: University of Illinois Press, 1997.

Donald R. Shaffer

Agriculture

The Civil War exerted a profound impact on the agricultural system of the United States. Northern agriculture received a boost during the war years, while southern agriculture was dealt a severe blow. Because the country remained primarily an agricultural nation after the war, reviving the farming system in places where it had been damaged stood out as a significant but difficult goal for American leaders, especially those in the South. Hindrances to recovery were related not only to farming practices, but also sectional animosities and racial attitudes. The farming system eventually stabilized, and while it retained many prewar aspects, it also reflected new realities.

The Impact of War and Reconstruction

Most of the fighting during the Civil War took place in the South, wreaking havoc on the region's agricultural system. Both Union and Confederate armies destroyed fields in their wake; the **emancipation** of slaves disrupted the **labor system**; manpower dwindled because of the large number of casualties in Confederate ranks; and even farm animals were scarce as a result of the war's carnage. Complicating matters was the destruction of the South's communication and transportation network, especially **railroads**, and the worthlessness of Confederate money. One of the most famous anecdotal allusions to the desperate situation comes from the surrender at Appomattox

Court House in **Virginia**. There, Confederate general Robert E. Lee, aware of the coming difficulties his soldiers would face in reviving their farms after the war, asked Union general **Ulysses S. Grant** that his men be allowed to keep their horses; Grant acquiesced. In some cases, the farms and plantations to which Lee's soldiers and other ex-Confederates returned had become dilapidated. New realities concerning race also confronted them on their return home.

The passage of the **Thirteenth Amendment** in 1865 officially ended slavery in the United States. President **Abraham Lincoln** had issued the Emancipation Proclamation during the war, on January 1, 1863, freeing **African American** slaves in certain areas of the South. Most of these "freedmen," or "freedpeople" as ex-slaves were sometimes called during Reconstruction and later by historians, remained in the South after the war. Recent historians have increasingly emphasized the freedmen's role in Reconstruction, while granting less attention than earlier scholars to political events unfolding in Washington. The **impeachment** trial of President **Andrew Johnson**, for example, received a great deal of attention from historians until the late twentieth century, when the racial issues of Reconstruction grew in importance.

Trained in farmwork and restricted from seeking employment in other fields, blacks played a major role in rebuilding the agricultural system after the war. However, immediately after the war they found themselves in conditions strangely similar to slavery. The **Black Codes**, laws that conservative white leaders implemented in the southern states after the war, denied many basic **civil rights** to blacks. Among the restrictions included in the codes were prohibitions against interracial marriage and liquor distillery ownership. The codes also prevented blacks from starting businesses or making a living as skilled craftsmen without first paying for expensive licenses and obtaining court permissions. In the opinion of many southern whites, the Black Codes provided the edifice upon which black subordination would be maintained in the postwar period. The attitude that the ex-slaves were fit only for manual labor—especially fieldwork—endured well into the twentieth century.

Readjusting to a New World

Officials of the U.S. government attempted to aid the freedmen in their attempt to adjust to freedom. Established by a March 1865 act of Congress, the **Bureau of Refugees, Freedmen, and Abandoned Lands** provided important services to blacks. For example, it offered advice concerning labor **contracts** and provided **education** in Freedmen's Bureau schools. Nevertheless, in 1872, federal officials shut down the Freedmen's Bureau, an agency that, it could be argued, had provided the first large-scale social programs in the United States.

Aid from the Freedmen's Bureau notwithstanding, the freedmen strove for as much independence as possible in an agricultural system, which, like slavery, was tilted heavily against them. Black landownership was nearly nonexistent, so their nominal freedom did not translate into economic liberty.

For blacks toiling on plantations, many of which were still intact after the war, working and living patterns did change during the Reconstruction era. Gang and squad systems were employed as work patterns immediately after the war, but, because they were reminiscent of the systems used under slavery, new forms of labor arose, which blacks found more agreeable. One of these new forms was **sharecropping**. A landlord provided sharecroppers with land and farming tools, and, in return, sharecroppers surrendered to the landlord a percentage (a "share") of their crop.

Sharecropping allowed black laborers to escape the old slave quarters, often built close together and within easy view of the landowner's home, and to escape old work patterns, especially the direct supervision under the old gang and squad systems. Consequently, they gained a degree of independence from whites, while distancing themselves from their former status as slaves. Not all whites grasped the symbolic nature of black sharecroppers' desire to abandon these old patterns of living to farm small patches of land located farther away from the landlord's home than the slave quarters had been situated.

The once-vast plantations were split into a number of small units farmed by poor sharecroppers. Over time, developments occurred in the sharecropping system, which trapped many blacks and poor whites alike. Perpetual debt often hounded sharecroppers, and landlords sometimes offered them unfair contracts. Abuse and exploitation became the shameful hallmarks of a system once welcomed by the freedmen as a more appealing alternative to previous work arrangements. This system of subjugation, with sharecroppers ever more in debt and eventually becoming tied to the land, had its roots in the Reconstruction era. In many places across the former Confederacy, sharecropping remained intact until as late as the 1950s and 1960s.

Although certain aspects of southern agriculture, such as the cotton industry, rebounded from the shock of war, others struggled to regain their prewar vitality during the Reconstruction era. While working and living patterns changed dramatically, cotton continued to be the dominant crop grown on southern plantations, especially those in the Deep South. The increased use of fertilizers during Reconstruction enabled agriculturalists to grow the crop in regions of the South that had known little or no cotton production. Tobacco farming, most of which was carried out in the upper South, reestablished itself after the war, but continued to struggle. Growing bright and white Burley tobacco proved to be profitable ventures for farmers, while the production of dark tobacco brought fewer financial rewards. The other two major southern crops prior to the Civil War, hemp and sugarcane, never recovered from the carnage of the war. Rice replaced sugarcane on many **Louisiana** plantations, a switch that tended to pay off for rice growers. In coastal **South Carolina** and **Georgia**, however, the rice industry suffered decline, as black workers increasingly turned to other industries for their livelihood.

Agriculture in the North, Midwest, and West during Reconstruction

Agriculture in the North fared far better during the Reconstruction period than it did in the South. Many of the ills that afflicted southern agriculture, such as labor system breakdown, wartime destruction, and economic ruin, did not apply in the North. In fact, the opposite was quite the case, with the war providing a boom for northern markets and producers. Northern farmers benefited from the Union army's demand for food, as well as continued demand from European markets. New technologies, such as reapers, mowers, and other advances enabled northern farms to increase production and meet this demand. Milk proved to be an especially valuable farm product for the Union army. As in the South, agricultural production also benefited from the use of fertilizers. Growing urban markets (largely due to immigration) affected farmers in other regions of the North, providing a boost to commercial farming. In many cases, the value of a northern farmer's land increased as a result of the war.

The Reconstruction era, however, was not all positive for northern farmers. After the war, the once-profitable sheep raising industry in New England declined significantly. Farmers in this industry felt the impact of several factors: lack of tariff protection, opening of western lands, and the expansion of the **railroad** system. With heavier competition from foreign countries and midwestern farmers, sheep farming in New England became less profitable. Northern agriculturalists also felt the impact of impersonal economic forces influencing their occupation during the Reconstruction era. Distant markets, expanded railroads, new technologies, and other developments of the Reconstruction era—an intensification of the so-called Market Revolution that began before the war—would later prompt the populist movement, characterized by widespread agrarian unrest in the South and the West.

Another issue related to agricultural developments was westward expansion. During the Civil War and Reconstruction eras, emigration to the midwestern and western section resumed its frantic pace. One motivation for westward migration was the availability of public lands. Settlers even received free land in the West through the provisions of the 1862 Homestead Act, which required a five-year residence on the land to establish ownership. Through the provisions of the Timber Culture Act and the Desert Land Act, territory also became available for free or at affordable prices, in exchange for making "improvements" in the land. Another motivation for westward migration was the growing lure of the cattle industry. A surge in European immigration, especially from Germany, helped fuel the populating of the West. With improved transportation, in particular the completion of the transcontinental railroad in 1869, access to the West was quicker, safer, and cheaper than ever before. This opened up western lands for development, benefiting many who went westward and having an array of effects on the rest of the nation's economic picture.

Conclusion

During Reconstruction, the American agricultural system had to adjust from the trauma of the Civil War. Agriculturalists in the South faced the most daunting challenge, reviving the region's devastated farming system. New labor systems, sharecropping, and tenant farming aided their efforts and initially benefited blacks and poor whites. In the final analysis, although the agricultural system had been somewhat altered after the Civil War, prejudice against these oppressed groups remained deeply imbedded in white southern racial and class ideology. Other areas of the country, while having to deal less intensely with the issue of race, contended against economic and technological changes, which proved both a blessing and a curse. Woven deeply into the fabric of national existence, the agricultural system in the United States maintained itself in the face of challenges and calamities during the war and Reconstruction, and served a vital role in the nation's recovery. *See also* Abolition of Slavery; Fourteenth Amendment; Freedmen's Relief Societies; Vagrancy.

Further Reading: Aiken, Charles S. *The Cotton Plantation South since the Civil War*. Baltimore: The Johns Hopkins University Press, 1998; Foner, Eric. *Reconstruction: America's Unfinished Revolution, 1863–1877*. New York: Harper and Row, 1988; Hurt, R. Douglas. *American Agriculture: A Brief History*. Rev. ed. West Lafayette, IN: Purdue University Press, 2002; Otto, John Solomon. *Southern Agriculture during the Civil War Era, 1860–1880*. Westport, CT: Greenwood Press, 1994.

James S. Humphreys

Aiken, D. Wyatt (1828–1887)

Although remembered as a **Democratic** politician during later Reconstruction, David Wyatt Aiken of **South Carolina** was also one of the leading agricultural reformers of his day. Aiken was born in Winnsboro, South Carolina, on March 17, 1828, to two immigrants from County Antrim, Ireland, David Aiken and Nancy Kerr. He graduated from South Carolina College in 1849 and began farming near Winnsboro in 1852. Aiken immediately became interested in agricultural improvement, and in 1855, he was one of the founding members of the State Agricultural Society. Aiken became involved in Democratic politics the next year, attending the Democratic National Convention as a delegate. In 1858, he attended the Southern Commercial Convention in Mobile and began to make speeches in favor of secession. Serving with the Seventh South Carolina Regiment during the Civil War, Aiken was severely wounded at Sharpsburg.

During Reconstruction, Aiken continued his antebellum efforts to cultivate agricultural practices in the South and thus improve the lot of the white farmer. For Aiken, this required finding a means to control black labor in the absence of slavery. Aiken warned against overreliance on cotton, and turned to growing small grains, clover, and other crops at his "Coronaca" plantation in Abbeville County. In 1869, Aiken helped reorganize the old State Agricultural Society into the State Agricultural and Mechanical Society and encouraged the new body to do more to educate farmers. As part of that effort, he became a correspondent, and later editor and owner, of the *Rural Carolinian* from 1869 to 1877. Aiken's most significant work for agricultural improvement was his role as an organizer for the Patrons of Husbandry (the Grange), a fraternal organization for white farmers. In 1872, Aiken organized at least seventy-six subordinate Granges across South Carolina. He joined the Grange's

National Executive Committee in 1873 and served as head of the South Carolina Grange from 1875 to 1877.

Aiken had never left politics, serving as a representative in the South Carolina House of Representatives from 1864 to 1866. When the new state constitution was implemented in 1868, he canvassed the state for the Democratic Party. When Republican politician B. F. Randolph was assassinated in Abbeville County, authorities charged Aiken with the murder, but the charges were eventually dropped. Aiken stood as a candidate for Congress in the upstate's Third District in 1876. One observer noted that the local Granges often formed the backbone of the Democratic **Red Shirt** clubs that provided the muscle for the victorious white supremacy campaign that gave Democrats control of South Carolina and Aiken a seat in the U.S. House of Representatives. Once in Congress, Aiken served until 1887. "I speak for those who feed the cotton-gin and the grain-thresher and walk between the plough handles," he announced, and his greatest legacy was his ultimately successful fight to get the Bureau of Agriculture raised to a cabinet-level department. While that occurred in 1889, Aiken was not around to celebrate it; he died

D. Wyatt Aiken, c. 1870. (Courtesy of the Library of Congress.)

on April 6, 1887, of complications arising from a fall a year earlier. D. Wyatt Aiken's son, Wyatt Aiken, served in the U.S. House of Representatives from 1903 to 1917. *See also* Labor Systems; Redemption.

Further Reading: Pritchard, Claudius Hornby, Jr. *Colonel D. Wyatt Aiken, 1828–1887: South Carolina's Militant Agrarian.* Hampden-Sydney, VA: privately printed, 1970.

Bruce E. Baker

Akerman, Amos Tappan (1821–1880)

A lawyer from **Georgia** and U.S. attorney general during the presidency of **Ulysses S. Grant**, Amos Tappan Akerman used his federal office to aggressively prosecute members of the **Ku Klux Klan** and to protect the **civil rights** of **African Americans** in the South.

Akerman was born February 23, 1821, in Portsmouth, New Hampshire. One of twelve children, he attended Philips Exeter Academy and graduated Phi Beta Kappa from Dartmouth College. To pay for his **education** he relocated to the South, teaching school in several locations before moving to Savannah, Georgia, to tutor the children of Judge John M. Berrien, U.S. senator and former U.S. attorney general. Akerman studied law with Berrien and became a member of the Georgia bar in 1850. He set up law practices in Clarkesville and

Elberton. A devout Presbyterian, Akerman married Martha Rebecca Galloway in 1864; the couple produced seven children.

Although opposed to secession, Akerman joined the Georgia State Guard in 1863 and was called into active service in 1864 as **Sherman**'s troops moved through Georgia. He joined the Republican Party after the war and served as a delegate to the 1868 Georgia state **constitutional convention**, where he authored much of the document's judiciary section. In 1869, President Ulysses S. Grant appointed him federal district attorney for the state, and a year later, to the surprise of many, Akerman was offered the job of U.S. attorney general. Akerman's relative obscurity may have helped him secure the cabinet position; his nomination also reflected political maneuvers to secure the annexation of the Dominican Republic.

Along with his new position, Akerman assumed charge of the newly created Justice Department. He rigorously regulated government contracts with **railroads**, demanding that corporations fulfill all contractual agreements before receiving lucrative land subsidies. Akerman reserved his greatest efforts, however, to destroying the political force of the Ku Klux Klan in the South. In 1871, upon Akerman's recommendation, President Grant suspended the writ of habeas corpus in nine counties in Piedmont, **South Carolina**. Federal marshals arrested numerous suspected members of the vigilante organization, and Akerman's legal team helped to decrease the strength of the South Carolina Klan by prosecuting many of its leaders in federal court.

Akerman's dedication toward apprehending Klan members attracted criticism from some of Grant's cabinet members, who felt he had become overzealous in his cause. Corporate railroad interests also lobbied against him, leading President Grant to request his resignation in December 1871. Akerman returned to Cartersville, Georgia, where he had resettled his family in early 1871. He continued to practice law until his death from rheumatic fever on December 21, 1880.

Further Reading: Akerman, Robert H. "Amos Tappan Akerman." In Kenneth Coleman and Charles Stephen Gurr, eds., *Dictionary of Georgia Biography*. Vol. 1. Athens: University of Georgia Press, 1983, pp. 8–10; McFeeley, William S. "Amos T. Akerman: The Lawyer and Racial Justice." In Morgan J. Kousser and James M. McPherson, eds., *Region, Race, and Reconstruction: Essays in Honor of C. Vann Woodward*. New York: Oxford University Press, 1982, pp. 395–415.

Kimberly R. Kellison

Alabama

Alabama rejoined the Union on June 25, 1868 after opting for secession in January 1861. Although the Reconstruction period allowed Alabama to rectify its state constitution, harsh injustices toward **African Americans** remained an unsolved problem.

Emancipation and the African American Population

Southern whites believed that newly emancipated slaves would remain compliant to antebellum social codes. Newly freed blacks instead turned riotous toward white power. Many southerners attested that the new generation of blacks was an agitated and troublesome group who would not submit to old labor laws. One of Alabama's Reconstruction governors, **Robert M. Patton**, noted a marked difference in the approach that blacks took toward **education** after the Civil War. Alabama blacks who were raised and educated before the **Emancipation** Proclamation were considered good students who were more capable of learning than postbellum African Americans. Patton continued by stating that young blacks roamed the streets day and night, especially on Saturdays when crowds of young people could be seen throughout the city. The young generation of freed slaves refused to obey their employer's demands because they felt that subservience to white industrialists would be the equivalent of submitting to bondage.

Freed slaves no longer wanted to work on plantations and therefore chose to labor on **railroads**, in coal mines, and other fields. A major reason why Alabama blacks were capable of manipulating white planters was the shortage of labor in industries that supported the South's economy prior to the Civil War. African Americans under plantation domination rebelled by rejecting work for white field owners. As an alternative, freed blacks bought or rented terrains to gain a livelihood and remain as far removed as possible from slavery.

Many regard the Reconstruction era as the first black renaissance. James K. Green was a prominent African American politician who later turned to carpentry. Green remembers that at the Civil War's end, he had no other aptitude except that of obeying his master. Postbellum blacks unrelentingly stressed the significance of education. The Alabama Senate Committee found startling results when they inspected a freedpeople's school in Opelika. Among the usual black children, the Alabama Senate Committee discovered three adults following courses. The adult students claimed that the ability to read and write would surely provide them with the necessary tools to someday act independently. Freed African Americans intended to use education as a means of communicating their views across the United States. Only after an effective rhetorical voice was established among African Americans could they truly fight for equal rights. The correlation between literacy and black identity was not a novel one developed exclusively during Reconstruction. Antebellum authors like **Frederick Douglass**, Harriet Jacobs, and Joshua Henson had established a pattern in African American education that lasted well into the twentieth century.

The Freedmen's Bureau

The **Bureau of Refugees, Freedmen, and Abandoned Lands** (Freedmen's Bureau) was chartered by an act of Congress on March 3, 1865, to assist emancipated slaves in adjusting to new living conditions. Major Brigadier General Wager Swayne was assigned the post of assistant commissioner for Alabama. Swayne's tenure was rigorous from the start because he was responsible for an estimated 430,000 emancipated slaves who became dependent on the state when General Richard Taylor surrendered his Confederacy troops. The principal function of the Freedmen's Bureau was to relieve newly freed African Americans by using funds accumulated by the **U.S. Army**.

Alabama's Freedmen's Bureau consisted of five departments: Department of Abandoned and Confiscated Lands, Department of Records (Labor, Schools, and Supplies), Department of Finance, the Medical Department, and the Bounty Department. The state was split into five sections, with Freedmen's offices in Mobile, Selma, Montgomery, Troy, and Demopolis. Twelve northern Alabama counties were under the control of the assistant commissioner for Tennessee, General Clinton B. Fisk. A majority of Freedmen's Bureau offices were members of the Veterans Reserve Corps.

The Freedmen's Bureau and the **Union League of America** occasionally merged once **Congressional Reconstruction** was fully applied throughout Alabama. The Union League was a political group that attempted to educate and prompt African Americans to support the Republican Party. When Wager Swayne arrived in Alabama, he found that whites were apprehensive and blacks uncertain of their new freedom. Swayne resolved the dilemma by having the Freedmen's Bureau perform similar duties for emancipated Alabama blacks that plantation owners had before the Emancipation Proclamation; such functions included the distribution of clothing and food rations. Swayne's goal was to mold current institutions to post–Civil War standards instead of implementing an aggressive military stance. Alabama law courts remained closed to freed slaves until Wager Swayne appointed judges and magistrates to work as administrators of justice for the bureau. Reconstruction therefore amended the American Civil Code at both the state and federal levels since blacks now had equal representation before the law across the country. Judges and magistrates who contravened Swayne's assignment were revoked from office and replaced with administrators who would accept the Freedmen's Bureau's demands. One example of Swayne's determination was the resignation of Mayor Stough. Stough refused to allow the use of African American evidence against white defendants. The Freedmen's Bureau replaced Stough with John Forsythe.

Oath of Allegiance

Abraham Lincoln's Amnesty Proclamation granted amnesty to any former Confederate individual willing to pledge allegiance to the United States of America. Representatives from Alabama signed the Oath of Allegiance on June 25, 1868. A great percentage of Alabamans signed because four years of warfare had left many poor and homeless. **Lewis E. Parsons**, a Talladega lawyer, was chosen as the **provisional governor** of Alabama by President **Andrew Johnson** on June 21, 1865. Governor Parson's tenure would last until a civilian government was ordained. Parson's responsibilities as state governor included registering citizens willing to pledge allegiance, holding a delegate convention for the drafting of a new constitution that guaranteed an end to rebellion, voiding Alabama's Civil War debt, and enacting the complete **abolition of slavery**. The oath of allegiance read as follows:

I ——— of the County of ———, State of Alabama, do solemnly swear, in the presence of Almighty God, that I will henceforth faithfully support, protect and defend the Constitution of the United States and the union of the states there under; and that I will, in the like manner, abide by and faithfully support all laws and proclamations which have been made during the existing rebellion with reference to the emancipation of slaves; so help me God. Subscribed and sworn before me, this ———. (Griffith, 447)

Leading Confederate representatives, former southern governors, high-ranking army and naval officers, and southern citizens owning property evaluated at $20,000 or more were obligated to apply directly to the president for official **pardon**. The latter type of citizens were asked to sign an oath of allegiance that stipulated their rank, monetary worth, and their ties to the Confederate government. Alabama's media praised Parson's impartiality, moderation, and familiarity with the state.

The Alabama State Convention

The Alabama State Convention was held in Montgomery on September 15, 1865. **Constitutional convention** delegates included Mr. Stanford, whose ordinance reduced the size of counties from 900 to 600 square miles. Mr. Webb proposed that all laws passed by the legislature on and after January 11, 1861, that were contradictions to the Constitution and laws of the United States be amended. The leader of the Alabama State Convention was former governor Benjamin Fitzpatrick of Wetumpka. Assisting Fitzpatrick was Tuscumbia delegate J. B. Moore.

Alabama's state constitution underwent four principal changes. One ordinance repealed the January 11, 1861, amendment to Alabama's state constitution so that it would recognize the immediate **abolition of slavery**. The convention decreed that Alabama would never allow the practice of slavery within its state boundaries. Alabama also recognized **black suffrage**, stating that security and protection of emancipated slaves would be ensured. Alabama would therefore accept responsibility for all desolate African Americans. Furthermore, Alabama nullified and voided all laws that were not in concordance with the **U.S. Constitution**. The Alabama State Convention eliminated any possibility that Alabama would ever again claim republic status. Moreover, Alabama resolved to aid the deserted families of Civil War soldiers and distribute veterans' annuities accordingly.

Alabama voters were asked to elect a new state governor on November 6, 1865. Three representatives were nominated: Robert M. Patton (Lauderdale County), M. J. Bulger (Tallapoosa), and **William H. Smith** (Tuscaloosa). Robert M. Patton ultimately won the election, collecting 21,442 popular votes. Alabama believed that presidential Reconstruction was not effective enough, and therefore rejected sending any delegates to Congress for three years, until the signing of the new 1868 constitution.

Alabama Blacks and Republicanism

Republicans won the favor of Alabamans with the help of southern blacks who rallied en masse under the Republican banner. Blacks also enjoyed a new constitution and the right to purchase land as a direct result of Republican pressure. Black opposition toward the **Democratic Party** stemmed from the fact that Democrats were anxious to forget the past and consequently unsympathetic to

African American suffrage. Alabama's black community wanted their dilemmas treated before supporting any one party.

The 1868 Convention

By 1867, Republicans in Congress had seized control of Reconstruction policy away from President Johnson. Ten southern states, including Alabama, would be placed under military supervision until new state constitutions were written and new federal officers elected.

Although the Confederate government no longer existed, its voice still remained fairly prominent in constitutional debates. Confederate advocates utilized newspapers as their primary source of communication. The February 2, 1868, edition of the Selma *Times and Messenger* stressed that no honest white civilian residing north or south of the Mason-Dixon Line should concur with an electoral testament of oath that advanced the idea of allotting the ballot to an illiterate and unintelligent race. In fact, former Confederates advocated that most blacks were unable to read the same constitution that gave them the right to vote. Alabama's conservative media attacked sections of the constitution that allowed interracial marriage, the admission of black children into public schools, and the banishment of more than 40,000 Confederate leaders.

The *Nationalist*, a radical newspaper, demanded that American whites contemplate voting against adopting a constitution that would force them to protect themselves from newly emancipated blacks. The fears were that African Americans would eventually reduce the number of powerful whites and subsequently weaken their stranglehold on America's public sphere. Republicans eventually lost the Alabama state election, regardless of their large following. Robert M. Patton attributed the disappointing loss to a lack of quality Republican representation and on constitutional amendments that explained how Radical Reconstruction would function instead of clarifying why it was necessary. According to the U.S. Constitution, Reconstruction was already a process in motion that would best suit the needs of all Americans.

The new constitution of Alabama was one based on defining the role that the state would play in the upcoming industrial age. Article 11 predetermined the new form of education that Alabama was to follow. Section 14 ensured state funding for state colleges and the University of Alabama. Institutions of higher learning financed by the state government were to receive large amounts of grants in order to develop excellent instruction in **agriculture**. Farming and horticulture would then form the basis of Alabama's postbellum economy. Article 12 outlined the new laws for Alabama's industrial resources. Annual reports were compiled noting the agriculture and geology of Alabama. These reports were designed to gauge the effectiveness of scientific development; based on their findings, the state of Alabama would decide whether or not more research in agriculture was needed. The commissioner of industrial resources submitted yearly evaluations of Alabama's machinery and production so that other states and foreign countries could decide if they wanted to invest in Alabama's economy. Such measures also encouraged the immigration and emigration of potential workers to Alabama, who would naturally increase the state's revenue through tax dollars.

The Ku Klux Klan

The **Ku Klux Klan** countered Radical Reconstruction via terrorism across the southern United States. Klan members wanted a restoration of pre–Civil War race constraints that assured the white race of absolute power in the southern states. Congress's approval of the **Thirteenth Amendment** caused great apprehension among white supremacists. Scores of hate crimes including lynching, rape, and arson ensued against Alabama's black community. However, the acts were not merely driven by cultural and social need to subjugate blacks; white supremacists were deeply concerned about the voting power of African American males, granted under the **Military Reconstruction Acts** of 1867.

General George G. Meade addressed the various incidences of Klan aggression in the spring of 1868. The Anti-Kuklux Statute defined the Ku Klux Klan as an immediate threat against Alabama civilians that undermined the civil authority of Alabama's state government. Sections 1 and 2 of the Anti-Kuklux Statute stipulated that anyone seen masked or disguised in a Klan uniform would be fined or imprisoned. The Anti-Kuklux laws also applied to anyone seen in the presence of the latter persons. Section 5 tried to eliminated any possibility of racism in Alabama's judicial system for the reason that it obliged all magistrates, sheriffs, or other officials to act in accordance with the Anti-Kuklux Statute. Any official who refused to comply with Section 5 would be terminated immediately. Klan **violence** persisted despite the efforts of the state government, forcing the national government to intervene. Congress investigated the racial tension in Huntsville, Demopolis, Montgomery, Livingston, and Columbus from June to August 1871. The findings were filled with testimonials by freed slaves stating their fear that the Klan would soon reinstate the Confederacy. African Americans who benefited from equal **civil rights** or spoke against white supremacy were typically beaten or became victims of arson. Several whites who assisted Alabama blacks were also terrorized by the Ku Klux Klan. *See also* Amnesty Proclamations; Black Codes; Black Politicians; Bourbons; Carpetbaggers; Congressional Reconstruction; Disfranchisement; Enforcement Act (1875); Enforcement Acts (1870, 1871); Fourteenth Amendment; Labor Systems; Presidential Reconstruction; Readmission; Redemption.

Further Reading: Bailey, Richard. *Neither Carpetbaggers nor Scalawags: Black Office Holders during the Reconstruction of Alabama*. Montgomery, AL: R. Bailey Publishers, 1991; Feldman, Glenn. *Reading Southern History*. Tuscaloosa: University of Alabama Press, 2001; Gilmour, Arthur. *The Other Emancipation: Studies in the Society and Economy of Alabama*. Baltimore: The Johns Hopkins University Press, 1972; Griffith, Lucille. *Alabama: A Documentary History to 1900*. Revised and Enlarged Edition. University: University of Alabama Press, 1968; Kolchin, Peter. *First Freedom: The Responses of Alabama's Blacks to Emancipation and Reconstruction*. Westport, CT: Greenwood Press, 1972.

Gerardo Del Guercio

Alcorn, James Lusk (1816–1894)

James Lusk Alcorn was a Republican governor of **Mississippi** and a U.S. senator during Reconstruction. Though born in Illinois, his family moved to

Kentucky soon after his birth. Admitted to the Kentucky bar in 1836, Alcorn practiced law for six years before moving to Coahoma County in the rich alluvial Mississippi Delta. There he became a wealthy lawyer-planter; by 1860, he owned ninety-three slaves. During the late 1840s and 1850s, Alcorn served as a Whig in the state legislature, where he devoted most of his time to the creation of a makeshift levee system to protect the frequently flooded Delta counties. After **Abraham Lincoln** won the presidential election of 1860, Alcorn served as a Union delegate in the state convention called to consider the question of secession. When it became clear that Mississippi would leave the Union, he announced that he would vote for the secession ordinance. The convention later appointed Alcorn a brigadier general of state troops, but after a brief army service, he resigned and went home to manage his plantations.

After the Civil War, Alcorn was elected to the U.S. Senate by the state legislature under President **Andrew Johnson**'s plan of Reconstruction. The Republican Congress, however, refused to seat Alcorn and the other representatives from the former Confederate states. When Congress assumed control of Reconstruction policy and enacted **black suffrage**, Alcorn announced his support for black political equality and led in the organization of the state's Republican Party. Unlike other southern states under military rule, Mississippi voters in 1868 rejected the new state constitution because it contained clauses politically proscribing many whites. The failure of the federal military forces to prevent the intimidation of black voters also contributed to the defeat of the constitution. In 1869, another vote occurred on the constitution, and, shorn of the proscriptive clauses, it was approved. In the same election, Alcorn easily won the governorship because he was supported overwhelmingly by black voters and a few thousand whites.

Alcorn as Governor

In his inaugural address, Alcorn promised to protect black rights and to provide public **education** for both races. The school system that he helped to establish was racially segregated. His appointments to office reflected a strong prejudice against northern newcomers, known as **carpetbaggers**, and especially those who supported Senator **Adelbert Ames**, a **Radical Republican**. Alcorn believed that by appointing former Union Whigs to judicial position whites would be encouraged to support his administration and his party. In view of the poor condition of the state's finances, Alcorn, unlike several southern Reconstruction governors, warned against hasty schemes for **railroad** development.

Despite his moderate policies, Alcorn failed to obtain a broadly based following for the Republican Party. Most of the old citizens never recognized the legitimacy of the new political order. Opposition to Alcorn's party became clear by late 1870 with the rise of the **Ku Klux Klan**. Operating throughout most of the state, the Klan used both intimidation and **violence** in an attempt to overthrow Republican rule and suppress black rights. Senator **Adelbert Ames** and other Radicals demanded that Governor Alcorn seek federal intervention to put down the Klan. The governor, however, believed that state law enforcement resources should be fully utilized before calling on President **Ulysses S. Grant** for federal troops. He asked the legislature for the authority and funds to raise an elite, white cavalry regiment that would be able to act swiftly wherever the Klan threatened a community. By a strange combination of Radicals, who had no confidence in Alcorn's plan, and Conservatives, who opposed any military force organized by "black Republicans," the legislature rejected the proposal. Only after the terror became endemic in the South did the Republican Congress, at President Grant's urging, pass legislation to suppress the Klan, although it did not completely end intimidation and violence in Mississippi.

In the U.S. Senate

Meanwhile, Alcorn was elected to the U.S. Senate, and he resigned as governor to take his seat in late 1871. His main effort in the Senate was toward obtaining federal aid for the rebuilding of the Delta levees. He failed despite almost obtaining congressional approval of a $3.4 million appropriation for the purpose. When his rival, Ames, won the Republican nomination for governor in 1873, Alcorn returned home, bolted the regular state party, and announced that he would run as a reform Republican. His effort to gain the support of conservative **Democrats**, who did not nominate a candidate, backfired. Most black voters as well as many whites refused to support him, and Ames won the election by a vote of 69,870 to 50,490. Alcorn continued in the Senate until 1877, after which he returned to his plantations in the Mississippi Delta. In 1879, President **Rutherford B. Hayes** briefly considered him for a position in his cabinet, but the post went instead to a midwesterner. Like many southern Republicans by the 1890s, Alcorn had succumbed to the hardening racism of the age. In 1890, he served as a delegate to a state constitutional convention and supported the adoption of a clause **disfranchising** blacks and making possible the passage of rigid segregation laws for the state. He died in 1894 at his home in the Delta. *See also* Carpetbaggers; Civil Rights; Congressional Reconstruction; Disfranchisement; Enforcement Acts; Jim Crow Laws; Presidential Reconstruction; U.S. Army and Reconstruction.

Further Reading: Harris, William C. *The Day of the Carpetbagger: Republican Reconstruction in Mississippi*. Baton Rouge: Louisiana State University Press, 1979; Pereyra, Lillian A. *James Lusk Alcorn: Persistent Whig*. Baton Rouge: Louisiana State University Press, 1966; Sansing, David G. "Congressional Reconstruction." In Richard Aubrey McLemore, ed., *A History of Mississippi*. Vol. 1. Hattiesburg: University and College Press of Mississippi, 1973.

William C. Harris

AMA. *See* American Missionary Association.

Amendments, Constitutional, Proposed by Andrew Johnson

President **Andrew Johnson** had a generally conservative view of the **U.S. Constitution**. However, in a message to Congress of July 18, 1868, he proposed four constitutional amendments to provide certain reforms that he believed to be necessary. An advocate of direct democracy, opponent of elite politicians, and ardent follower of the late Andrew Jackson, President Johnson hoped his measures would bolster and sustain white man's democracy in the United States.

First, Johnson wanted to eliminate the Electoral College so that the president and vice president would be elected directly by the people. He favored limiting the president to a single term of four or six years. However, mainly, he wanted to insure that the people would not be deprived of their choice, either by the electors or the House of Representatives, in case no candidate received a majority in the Electoral College. Johnson supported his proposal by citing an amendment sponsored by President Andrew Jackson beginning in 1829. Johnson also proposed an amendment detailing the succession to the presidency in case of the death or disability of both the president and vice president. This was an issue particularly on Johnson's mind because of the **assassination of Abraham Lincoln** and Johnson's own near removal through the **impeachment** process. Johnson believed that the successor should be someone in the executive department, such as a cabinet member, rather than the president pro tempore of the Senate or the Chief Justice. Both of these men would be leaders in the process of removing an official from office, and thus might have a vested interest in doing so. Johnson's third proposed amendment would allow the people to directly elect senators rather than having them elected by the state legislature. Finally, Johnson proposed that judges should have term limits, rather than serving for life or good behavior.

Although Johnson's **cabinet** members objected to his proposed amendments for a variety of reasons, Johnson submitted them to Congress anyway. He had previously proposed similar amendments in 1851, when he was a member of the House of Representatives, and in 1860, when he was in the Senate, but they had not passed. In 1868, both houses of Congress politely printed the president's recommendation and submitted it to their respective judiciary committees, where these proposals died.

Johnson was still advocating these amendments in 1873, after he had left the presidency. Congress took no action on any of these issues until the twentieth century. The Seventeenth Amendment, providing for the direct election of senators, became law in 1913. In 1967, the Twenty-fifth Amendment partially clarified the presidential succession by permitting the president to nominate a vice president if the office were to become vacant. In addition, a law passed in 1979 lists the other successors in order as the Speaker of the House of Representatives, the president pro tempore of the Senate, and then the cabinet members, beginning with the secretary of state. Elimination of the Electoral College and various term limits still generate controversy at times.

Further Reading: Graf, LeRoy P., Ralph W. Haskins, and Paul H. Bergeron, eds. *The Papers of Andrew Johnson.* Vols. 4, 14. Knoxville: University of Tennessee Press, 1967–2000.

Glenna R. Schroeder-Lein

American Indians

Because the Civil War divided all Native American tribes in the Southeast and the Oklahoma Indian Territory into pro-Confederate and pro-Union factions, the U.S. government reconstructed the tribes at the end of the war, declaring that they had forfeited their rights by aiding the Confederacy. The Choctaw, Chickasaw, Creek, and Cherokee Indian tribes, which had been living in Oklahoma since their forced removal from the Southeast in the 1830s, divided over whether to fight for the Confederacy or the Union in 1861. Although the Choctaws and Chickasaws generally joined the Confederate cause, all tribes in the area provided some support to the southern rebellion. A massive exodus of population occurred as Union sympathizers moved out of their homelands. By 1862, Confederate Indian allies had been defeated and the region faced **violence** and terror from Union and rebel guerillas, lawlessness, hunger, and destruction of homes and livestock. The status of freedmen, nearly 30 percent of the population of the region, had to be determined.

Tribal leaders assembled at Fort Smith, **Arkansas**, on May 15, 1865, to deliberate with U.S. officials. Dennis Cooley, Elijah Sells, Thomas Wistar, Brigadier General W. S. Harney, and Colonel Ely S. Parker led the U.S. delegation and hoped to negotiate land cessions for the Comanche, Caddo, Osage, Cheyenne, Kiowa, Arapahoe, Lipan, North Caddo, and Anadarko Indians. Tribes that had divided during the Civil War had to be reconstituted. They also wanted to establish an orderly, new civil government for the entire region that would facilitate the American push westward. Indian leaders of each nation insisted that they were not sanctioned to sign any treaty, so each delegation received proposed treaties and promised to send representatives to Washington, D.C., in January 1866.

The Washington treaties of 1866 placed the Choctaw, Creek, Chickasaw, and Cherokee nations in the eastern half of Oklahoma and divided the western half into cessions for the Cheyenne, Arapaho, Iowa, Sac, Fox, Kickapoo, Pottawatomie, Shawnee, Seminole, Comanche, Kiowa, and Apache tribes. Each tribe established their own variants of republican government, created law codes and judicial systems, and abolished slavery. The freedmen proved an intractable problem for Indians since the status of mixed bloods made a clear demarcation between freed and subservient difficult. The U.S. government purchased Indian land for redistribution to Indian tribes as it saw fit. Funds received by tribes helped build schools and provided funds to care for orphans.

Many Seminole left **Florida** for Oklahoma in the 1860s as the Civil War raged. In 1866, they agreed to sell their land in eastern Oklahoma to the U.S. government for 15 cents an acre and in return purchased land in western Oklahoma for 50 cents an acre. Their reconstructed government consisted of two principal chiefs and a legislative body that served as both Congress and court. Full **civil rights** were granted to all persons regardless of their race or color, making the emancipation of slaves a less volatile issue.

The Creeks divided into a conservative, traditional faction and a more pro-United States group. The freedmen faced less prejudice than many had predicted, and the tribe voted to remunerate blacks as well as Creeks from land sales. Schools flourished for both blacks and Creeks.

Understanding the mechanisms of U.S. government better than the Seminole or Creeks, the Choctaw and Chickasaw negotiated very favorable treaties with the U.S. government. Although agreeing to abolish slavery, they did not grant freedmen civil rights until the 1880s. After the Civil War, each tribe patterned their governments after the United States and included a written constitution, written law codes, and a bicameral legislature. They established schools for tribal members and mixed bloods, but did not include provisions for schools for blacks until the 1870s.

The Cherokee, the most divided tribe during the Civil War, continued to face serious internal dissension. They continued to use a constitution and government institutions patterned after the United States as they had done since the 1830s. Although unpopular among the Cherokee masses, blacks, Shawnees, and Delawares were granted all the civil rights of residents.

A general council of all tribes in Indian Territory was established in 1870. Although no individual tribe ever relinquished sovereignty to this organization, the council did serve as a successful conduit between Indian tribes and the U.S. government, especially when dealing with **railroad** and land negotiations. The council was abolished in 1878.

Reconstruction provided a means for the federal government to gain more power within Indian Territory. Insisting that new Indian governing institutions be patterned after those used by the United States and that land boundaries be refashioned to facilitate sale to U.S. citizens and railroad companies, the Reconstruction policies of the 1860s and 1870s helped the U.S. government gain an even stronger hold over Native American peoples, institutions, and culture.

Further Reading: Abel, Annie Heloise. *The American Indian and the End of the Confederacy, 1863–1866*. New York: Arthur H. Clark, Co., 1925; Bailey, M. Thomas. *Reconstruction in Indian Territory: A History of Avarice, Discrimination, and Opportunism*. Port Washington, NY: Kennikat Press, 1972; Littlefield, Daniel: *Africans and Seminoles: From Removal to Emancipation*. Jackson: University Press of Mississippi, 1977; *The Cherokee Freedmen: From Emancipation to American Citizenship*. Westport, CT: Greenwood Press, 1978; Perdue, Theda. *Slavery and the Evolution of Cherokee Society, 1540–1866*. Knoxville: University of Tennessee Press, 1987; Saunt, Claudio. "The Paradox of Freedom: Tribal Sovereignty and Emancipation during the Reconstruction of Indian Territory." *Journal of Southern History* 70 (2004): 63–94.

Randy Finley

American Missionary Association (AMA)

The American Missionary Association, founded in September 1846 as a merger of the Union Missionary Society, the Committee for West Indian Missions, and the Western Evangelical Missionary Society, supported the **abolition of slavery**. Led by Lewis Tappan, Simeon Jocelyn, Gerrit Smith, Joshua Leavitt, George Whipple, and William Jackson, the association sent missionaries to Africa, Egypt, Hawaii, Ireland, Jamaica, the Sandwich Islands, and Siam to monitor living conditions. In the United States, missionaries labored in **Kentucky**, Missouri, **North Carolina**, and the Northwest and often faced beatings and ostracism in their communities. Channeling the impulses of humanitarianism and romanticism that surged throughout American and European culture in the 1840s, the missionaries sought to better the world in practical ways.

In the early years of the Civil War, the AMA collected and distributed clothing, food, and medicine to southern slaves in areas liberated by the Union army. They also sought homes for scores of black orphans that followed the Yankees. As northern blacks volunteered to join the army after the **Emancipation** Proclamation made the destruction of slavery an integral war aim, AMA missionaries volunteered to serve in black regiments as they journeyed southward to fight. They often upbraided both black and white Yankee soldiers for their sexual abuse and manipulation of freedwomen.

From the beginning, AMA laborers pushed **education**, as when Reverend Lewis C. Lockwood conducted schools in the **Virginia** war zone in late 1861. By 1863, schools had been established in the **District of Columbia**, Virginia, **South Carolina**, the Sea Islands, and Memphis, **Tennessee**. Focusing on **Port Royal**, South Carolina, as an early showplace of what could be achieved, thirty-one AMA teachers labored in fourteen schools with more than 1,000 students in the state. Not only interested in teaching basic literacy and mathematical skills, the missionaries hoped to spread Christianity as they defined it, inculcate middle-class values and morality, instill patriotism toward the United States, encourage a strong work ethic, and stimulate civic virtue and citizenship.

Complex and conflicting motives drove northern AMA missionaries to Dixie. Many insisted that their religion had to be practically applied; and what better place than in one's own backyard, the war-torn American South? Paternalism often tinged missionaries' behavior as they demanded that blacks assimilate their bourgeois values about work, sexuality, gender, and the family. They also encouraged blacks to pattern their religious practices after northern Protestant **churches** and become less emotional and more formalized. The missionaries pushed southward to bring schools to the South, believing that education would ensure real freedom for the freedpeople and to make white southerners less barbaric. As with many American reformers, they often viewed schools as a panacea for all societal woes.

As the war ended in April 1865, many northern benevolent societies competed against each other instead of uniting to help the freedpeople. The **Bureau of Refugees, Freedmen, and Abandoned Lands** Freedmen's Bureau, established in March 1865, attempted to unite and direct the efforts of organizations such as the National Freedmen's Relief Association, the Freewill Baptist and Boston Education Commission, Iowa Quakers, and the African Civilization Association. Although **Oliver Otis Howard**, Freedmen's Bureau head, could not persuade the AMA to let him coordinate their activities with his newly formed American Freedmen's Union Commission, he still used AMA workers as teachers in many Freedmen's Bureau schools. By 1871, he had appropriated more than $4 million to schools led by AMA associates.

AMA workers faced enormous challenges as they tried to remake the South into the North while helping blacks become good Christian citizens. Mistrust and misunderstanding festered in almost all relationships. The AMA missionaries feared other white benevolent organizations that competed against them. Their regional bias made them haughty and condescending toward most white southerners. They not only alienated southern whites, but many southern blacks as well. Their middle-class worldview made them constantly harp about blacks' lying, stealing, sexuality, drinking, smoking, gambling, and cursing. Female teachers faced unusual challenges as they altered the Victorian cult of domesticity while performing many "masculine" tasks in the classroom and community.

In attempting to open schools in southern communities, AMA laborers often encountered **violence**, intimidation, and ostracism by local whites who considered them meddlesome and self-righteous. Schoolhouses were often burned and teachers were unable to secure lodging. School funding always proved problematic, with AMA speakers canvassing the North and England for donations.

Freedpeople diligently tried to collect enough money to buy the land for the schools so they could own it. They also continually petitioned the AMA and Freedmen's Bureau to send black teachers when possible, disdaining the paternalism that sometimes slipped into racism of many white instructors.

Although the AMA faced gargantuan problems during Reconstruction, their most significant and lasting contribution occurred in the creation of a southern school network. Early difficulties included procuring a location for a school and then building it, overcrowding, inadequate lighting and heating in the schoolroom, the endemic poverty of southerners that made purchasing school supplies or paying teachers difficult, and constant disruption in the school calendar during crop planting, cultivating, and harvesting time. By 1867, more than 400 AMA teachers labored in the South, teaching nearly 40,000 students in day and night schools and more than 18,000 students in Sabbath schools. A constant shortage of properly qualified teachers spawned creation of secondary and teacher training schools that included Fisk University in Nashville, **Tennessee**; Hampton Institute in Richmond, Virginia; Atlanta University in Atlanta, **Georgia**; Tougaloo University in **Mississippi**; Avery Institute in Charleston; Berea College in Berea, Ohio; Dillard University in New Orleans, **Louisiana**; Howard University in Washington, D.C.; Huston-Tillotson College in Austin, **Texas**; and Talladega Institute in Talladega, **Alabama**. Students studied the typical classical curriculum that included Latin, Greek, mathematics, science, philosophy, and history.

AMA officials innovatively raised funds. Black students who had been former slaves journeyed north to scour the region for donations. Their emotional stories pulled at both northern hearts and purse strings. A periodical of the organization, *The American Missionary*, pulled in more than half of the association's yearly funds and emphasized the successes, hopes, and fears of the freedpeople and of laboring missionaries. In 1871, the Fisk Jubilee Singers began touring the United States and Europe, singing African American spirituals and folk songs. Within their first fifty years of existence, they contributed more than $150,000 to Fisk University, allowing it to become a preeminent African American university.

Further Reading: "The American Missionary Association and the Promise of a Multicultural America: 1839–1954." http://www.amistadresearchcenter.org; DeBoer, Clara Merritt. *His Truth Is Marching On: African Americans Who Taught the Freedmen for the American Missionary Association, 1861–1877.* New York: Garland Publishers, 1995; Jones, Jacqueline. *Soldiers of Light and Love: Northern Teachers and Georgia Blacks, 1865–1873.* Athens: University of Georgia Press, 1992; McFeely, William S. *Yankee Stepfather: General Oliver Otis Howard and the Freedmen.* New Haven, CT: Yale University Press, 1968; McPherson, James M. *The Abolitionist Legacy: From Reconstruction to the NAACP.* Princeton, NJ: Princeton University Press, 1975; Richardson, Joe M. *Christian Reconstruction: The American Missionary Association and Southern Blacks, 1861–1890.* Athens: University of Georgia Press, 1986.

Randy Finley

Ames, Adelbert (1835–1933)

Adelbert Ames, Union general, Reconstruction senator, and governor of **Mississippi**, was born October 21, 1835, in Rockland, Maine, to Captain Jesse Ames and his wife, Martha. As a youth, Adelbert and his older brother, John, sailed with their father, a sea captain, on numerous voyages. A strong student, Ames received an appointment to the U.S. Military Academy at West Point in 1856. He graduated fifth in a class of forty-five from West Point in May 1861. Commissioned a second lieutenant upon graduation, Ames soon received a promotion to first lieutenant of Griffin's Battery of the Fifth U.S. Artillery. At the First Battle of Bull Run, Ames received a leg injury. Refusing to leave his battery, he continued to issue orders until he collapsed. A promotion followed, and years later, in 1893, his actions at First Bull Run earned him the Congressional Medal of Honor. Ames fought in numerous battles in the eastern theater, including the Peninsula Campaign, Antietam, Fredericksburg, Chancellorsville, Gettysburg, Petersburg, and Fort Fisher. By the end of the war, Ames had been brevetted to major general in the volunteer army.

Weighing options for his postwar career that included studying law and working in his father's flour-milling business, Ames chose to remain in the regular army with the rank of lieutenant colonel. In spring 1865 he served with occupation forces in **North Carolina**, and later in the summer was transferred to **South Carolina**, where he remained until 1866. In North and South Carolina, Ames observed white reactions to **emancipation** and became increasingly sympathetic to the plight of the freedpeople. He received a year-long leave of absence from the army and traveled throughout Europe, returning to the United States in June 1867. After a visit to his parents, who had moved to Minnesota, Ames reported to his new command in Mississippi.

Enforcing Congressional Reconstruction

The **Military Reconstruction Acts** of 1867 divided the Confederate South into five military districts, and Ames was assigned to the Fourth Military District covering Mississippi and **Arkansas**. He arrived in the district headquarters of Vicksburg in August 1867. In June 1868, President **Ulysses S. Grant** appointed Ames **provisional governor** of Mississippi; in early 1869, Ames accepted a second appointment as military commander of the Fourth Military

District. In his governing capacity, Ames used federal troops to protect the rights of **African Americans**. He removed numerous Democrats from state offices, replacing them with both white and African American Republicans. Other measures included a reduction of the **poll tax**, the repeal of a special clause allowing disabled Confederate veterans to waive the poll tax, and an executive order allowing African Americans to serve on juries. White Democrats fiercely opposed Ames's policies, as did some native white Republicans who criticized the governor for failing to establish legal residence in the state.

Mississippi completed its reconstruction process in 1870, with Radical Republicans capturing control of the state legislature. Republican legislators proceeded to elect two U.S. senators: **Hiram R. Revels**, the first African American seated in the U.S. Senate, and Adelbert Ames. Ames resigned from the army and left for Washington, where he faced a Senate investigation over the legitimacy of his candidacy. Senators debated whether a military governor with dubious claim to Mississippi citizenship could hold office; they also addressed the problem that Military Commander Ames's signature appeared on his own senatorial credentials. Ultimately, the Senate seated Ames, who during this period had met and fallen in love with Blanche Butler, daughter of Union general and Massachusetts congressman **Benjamin F. Butler**. The two married in July 1870 in Lowell, Massachusetts.

Union Soldier Turned Mississippi Politician

In 1871, the Mississippi legislature elected former Republican governor **James L. Alcorn** to succeed Hiram R. Revels as U.S. senator. A native Mississippian, Alcorn drew political support from Conservative Republicans and some white Democrats. Alcorn and Ames soon clashed over a variety of issues. In the Senate, they publicly debated the extension of the **Enforcement Acts**. Alcorn disclaimed the need for military intervention to break the power of the **Ku Klux Klan**, while Ames, who also supported the integration of the **U.S. Army**, demanded greater federal assistance. In Mississippi, both Alcorn and his ally, Ridgley C. Powers, the current governor, continued to criticize Ames for failing to establish full residence in the state. To answer his critics, Ames purchased a home in Natchez and traveled to Mississippi in 1871 and 1872 to promote the Radical Republicans who supported him; he also voted for the first time in his life in the election of 1872.

In 1873, both Alcorn and Ames sought the Republican nomination for governor. Ames secured the nomination, leading Alcorn to run as an Independent. Both men canvassed the state seeking support, but Radical Republicans carried the election for Ames. Inaugurated in January 1874, the governor promoted compulsory public **education**, cuts in state funding for **railroads**, more equitable codes of taxation, and agricultural diversification. Although Ames publicly criticized the inequities of land ownership and rates of tenancy, he did not endorse land redistribution.

Ames had always been unpopular with most white Mississippians, some of whom increasingly resorted to **violence** to reassert political control from Republicans. Vigilantism became especially rampant during the elections of 1875. In what became known as the Mississippi Plan, whites formed **gun**

clubs and used violence to keep Republicans from the polls. In Vicksburg, a full-scale **race riot** ensued, forcing many African Americans to flee the city. Ames appealed to the president for troops and began to organize an African American **militia**, but his efforts failed when election returns revealed that Democrats had captured the state legislature. Ames addressed the new legislature in January 1876, labeling them an illegitimate body elected through fraudulent means. Democrats responded by drafting eleven impeachment charges against the governor. Principal charges alleged that Ames did not truly reside in the state and accused the governor of pardoning accused criminals but did not claim political corruption. Ames adamantly denied the allegations but, upon consultation with his wife, offered to resign his office in return for the dismissal of all charges. Both sides agreed to the compromise, and on March 29, 1876, Ames resigned from his position as governor of Mississippi.

Abandoning Mississippi

The Ames family permanently left Mississippi in 1876. Ames traveled to Northfield, Minnesota, to help run his father's flour-milling business. The family then moved to New York and New Jersey before relocating to Tewksbury, Massachusetts, close to Lowell. In Massachusetts the former politician flourished as a businessman, investing in textile mills and real estate as well as dabbling in minor inventions. The family vacationed in Italy, where Ames purchased a home, as well as **Florida**, California, and several European locales. An avid golfer, Ames spent leisure time with business magnates including John D. Rockefeller.

When the Spanish-American War began in 1898, Ames returned to his military roots by volunteering for the U.S. Army. As brigadier general he participated in the siege of Santiago, Cuba. Ames also spent parts of his later life attempting to dispel accusations that he had dramatically increased the state debt as governor of Mississippi. On April 12, 1933, at the age of 97, he died at his winter home in Ormand, marking the death of the last surviving Civil War general. *See also* Congressional Reconstruction; Pardons; Redemption; Republicans, Radical; Scandals.

Further Reading: Ames, Blanche. *Adelbert Ames, 1835–1933: General, Senator, Governor.* New York: Argosy-Antiquarian Ltd., 1964; Current, Richard. *Three Carpetbag Governors.* Baton Rouge: Louisiana State University Press, 1967; King, Benson Harry. "The Public Career of Adelbert Ames, 1861–1876." Ph.D. dissertation, University of Virginia, 1975.

Kimberly R. Kellison

Amnesty Proclamations

Several amnesty proclamations were issued during the Civil War and Reconstruction. The first one, **Abraham Lincoln**'s Proclamation of Amnesty and Reconstruction, was published on December 8, 1863, and clarified on March 26, 1864. The second, **Andrew Johnson**'s, was promulgated on May 29, 1865. Johnson issued a third on September 7, 1867, a fourth, on July 4,

1868, and a fifth on December 25 of that year. Congress also passed several declarations of amnesty, the first as part of the **Confiscation Act** of July 16, 1862, the second, of the **Fourteenth Amendment**, and a third specific Amnesty Act in 1872. Not until 1896 were all restrictions on former Confederate leaders removed.

Lincoln and Amnesty

Though Lincoln's and Johnson's proclamations have often been compared, they were very different. Also called the Ten Percent Plan, Lincoln's was a wartime measure, designed to bring about the return to loyalty of as many Confederates as possible. Relying on the presidential pardoning power authorized by the **U.S. Constitution** as well as congressional legislation for the same purpose, he provided for full **pardon** for all persons who had participated in the rebellion,

> with restoration of all rights of property, except as to slaves, and in property cases where rights of third parties shall have intervened for all insurgents willing to take an oath of allegiance to support the Constitution, the Union, and all acts of Congress passed during the existing rebellion with reference to slaves, and in property case, so long and so far as not repealed, modified or held void by Congress or by decision of the Supreme Court.

Six exceptions to this amnesty consisted of all who had been civil or diplomatic agents of the Confederacy, all who had left judicial positions in the United States to aid the Confederacy, all Confederate officers above the rank of colonel in the army or lieutenant in the navy, all who left seats in Congress to join the Confederacy, all who resigned commissions in the federal army or navy, and all who had mistreated black soldiers or their officers in U.S. service. As soon as 10 percent of the voters of the seceded states in 1860 had taken the oath, they could reestablish a state government, which would receive the benefits of the constitutional provision declaring that "the United States shall guarantee to every State a republican form of government," and the representatives of which were to be readmitted to Congress subject to the agreement of that body. On March 26, 1864, Lincoln further explained the proclamation by exempting from it all those who were prisoners at the time they took the oath and authorized civil and military officers to register the oath.

Lincoln had long considered an amnesty policy as a solution for the war. When in December 1862, the New York Democrat Fernando Wood wrote him that he had been advised by reliable authorities that southern states would send representatives to the next Congress, provided that a full and general amnesty would permit them to do so, he replied favorably. Although Lincoln believed the information to be groundless, if this meant that the southerners would cease resistance and submit to the national authority, "a full and general amnesty" would not be withheld. By December, he was ready to publish his proclamation.

At first, the proclamation appealed to both Conservatives and Radicals. The conservatives liked it because it suggested keeping state boundaries and state laws not relating to slavery inviolate. The Radicals were pleased because of its insistence upon **emancipation**. To some degree, it showed that Lincoln had

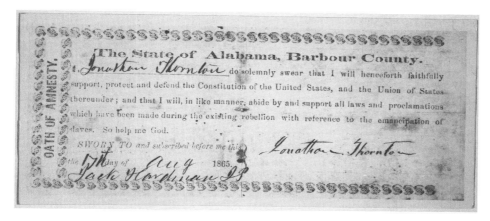

Oath of amnesty for Jonathan Thornton, c. 1938. (Courtesy of the Library of Congress.)

changed his original idea that the rebellion was an individual affair, and that there was a large number of Unionists in the South.

Radical Opposition to Amnesty

In spite of its original popularity, the proclamation soon ran into opposition, especially among the **Radical Republicans**. As early as December 15, 1863, Henry Winter Davis, the radical **Maryland** representative, moved that so much of the president's message as referred to the duty of the United States to guarantee a republican form of government be referred to a select committee. The 10 percent provision and the alleged failure to provide for complete emancipation came in for particular criticism, and on May 1, the committee reported a bill authorizing the president to appoint **provisional governors** for each of the insurgent states and providing that as soon as 50 percent of the whites had taken a **loyalty oath**, or oath of allegiance, they could elect delegates to a **constitutional convention** to set up a new government. The Senate added a provision to eliminate the word "white," but the House refused to accept it and in July, Congress passed the **Wade-Davis Bill** offering a more stringent plan of Reconstruction to be administered by Congress. It, too, required an oath of 50 percent of the voters of 1860 before a state could be restored, but it admitted only those able to take an ironclad oath to the following elections, and it abolished slavery. Lincoln's pocket veto of the measure led to the Wade-Davis Manifesto, which accused the president of seeking reelection by means of pocket boroughs and admonished him to execute, not to make the laws. His reelection followed, but the amnesty and Reconstruction issue was not settled prior to his **assassination**, although both **Louisiana** and **Arkansas** had reestablished governments under his policy without being recognized by Congress.

Johnson's Amnesty Program

Because the war was over when **Andrew Johnson** issued his proclamation, he did not need to woo insurgents, and it was necessarily different.

Believing as he did that the states had never left the Union, despite their secession, he was anxious to restore them as quickly as possible. In addition, he wanted to keep the South a "white man's country." Thus, the proclamation offered full pardon to all insurgents willing to take an oath of loyalty to support the Constitution and the Union and the wartime proclamations concerning slavery, much in the same manner as his predecessor, but there was no provision for any percentage necessary to reestablish a state. There were fourteen exemptions, including all those who were covered by the previous proclamation, as well as all Confederate governors, all who left the United States to help the Confederacy abroad, all who engaged in the destruction of U.S. commerce on the high seas or from Canada, all who violated their oath of amnesty in accordance with the proclamation of December 8, 1863, and all those whose property was worth more than $20,000, as Johnson considered the conflict to have been "a rich man's war and a poor man's fight." Special application for pardon, however, might be made by any of the exempted persons. This proclamation was joined with one appointing a provisional governor for **North Carolina** (and later for other states) whose duty it was to convene conventions to reestablish the commonwealths. Further proclamations of September 7, 1865, July 4, 1868, and December 25, 1868, diminished the list of exemptions and finally ended them altogether, although this proclamation was ineffectual because of the provisions of the **Fourteenth Amendment**.

As Congress was not in session at the time of Johnson's original proclamation, its provisions were speedily carried out, so that by December, all southern states except **Texas** had completed the Johnson process of Reconstruction. The president had freely granted pardons to the exempt classes, so that any number of leading former confederates, including Vice President **Alexander H. Stephens**, were elected to prominent positions, including membership in Congress. Moreover, the Johnson legislatures passed stringent **Black Codes**, virtually remanding the blacks to a status similar to slavery.

Coming of Congressional Reconstruction

That the congressional Republicans would not agree with this policy was not surprising. Not only the Radicals, unhappy with the president's failure to protect the freed persons, but also **Moderate Republicans** could hardly sanction measures as conservative as these. Not only did Johnson's plan seem to undo most of the gains of the Civil War, but the dominance of the Republican Party itself appeared to be in danger. Should the southerners, now almost all members of the **Democratic Party** or conservatives, be admitted to Congress, they could combine with their northern confreres and seize control of the government. Consequently, Congress appointed a **Joint Committee on Reconstruction** to which all questions pertaining to the Southern states were to be referred and refused to admit any of the southern representatives and senators-elect. Nevertheless, hoping still to make common cause with the president, the Moderates sought to win him over, but he remained adamant and vetoed the **Freedmen's Bureau Bill** and **Civil Rights Bill**. Thereupon, Congress enacted the Fourteenth Amendment, which **disfranchised** and disbarred from office all former officers of the United States who had joined the Confederacy but provided for a possible amnesty for them by a vote of two-thirds of both houses.

Congress, too, made provisions for amnesty. The Second **Confiscation Act** of July 2, 1862, provided that the president was authorized to extend pardons to the insurgents, and it exercised the pardon specified in the Fourteenth Amendment in a special Amnesty Act of May 22, 1872, which left only members of the 36th and 37th Congress, military, naval, and judicial officers, as well as heads of departments and foreign ministers of the Confederacy, still barred from office holding. During the next decades, individual pardons were extended to most of these, until Congress finally repealed the restrictions altogether in 1896.

Considering the overall effect of the amnesty policy after the Civil War, it is evident that federal treatment of former adversaries was comparatively mild. The only persons executed were the commandant of Andersonville prison and those implicated in the assassination of Abraham Lincoln; even **Jefferson Davis**, the Confederate president, was allowed to resume his writing after a short prison term. In comparison with the punishments meted out by other countries after victory in civil wars, the United States comes off very well indeed. *See also* Congressional Reconstruction; Presidential Reconstruction; Readmission; Republicans, Radical.

Further Reading: Belz, Herman. *Reconstructing the Union: Theory and Policy during the Civil War.* Ithaca, NY: Cornell University Press, 1969; Dorris, Jonathan T. *Pardon and Amnesty under Lincoln and Johnson.* Chapel Hill: University of North Carolina Press, 1953; Hesseltine, William B. *Lincoln's Plan of Reconstruction.* Chicago: Quadrangle Books, 1967; McKitrick, Eric. L. *Andrew Johnson and Reconstruction.* Chicago: University of Chicago Press, 1960; Trefousse, Hans L. *Andrew Johnson: A Biography.* New York: W. W. Norton, 1989.

Hans L. Trefousse

Annual Messages of the President

The presidential annual message in the nineteenth century was the forerunner of today's State of the Union address. Both carry out the instructions in Article II, Section 3 of the **U.S. Constitution** that the president "shall from time to time give to the Congress Information of the State of the Union." In the nineteenth century, the annual message was not a speech but a lengthy written document, read by a clerk to the members of Congress in early December, just after Congress assembled for its session.

A substantial part of each message consisted of material from the annual reports of the various government departments, including information on military activities, the postal department, Indian affairs, foreign treaties and disputes, the financial condition of the country, and similar matters. Each president also discussed various situations that particularly concerned him and suggested solutions to problems. At some point, each of the four Reconstruction presidents also discussed issues relating to the aftermath of the Civil War.

In his first two annual messages, **Abraham Lincoln** mentioned several items related to the return of peace. However, his third annual message was sent to Congress on December 8, 1863, the date on which he issued his "Proclamation of **Amnesty** and Reconstruction," (also known as the "Ten Percent Plan"). He discussed the proclamation at some length, particularly his reasons for issuing the proclamation and the timing of its release. Lincoln wanted southerners to understand that he would not retract the **Emancipation** Proclamation and wanted to have a plan in place for any states that were ready to begin the reconstruction process. The following year, in his fourth annual message, Lincoln reported that some people had taken advantage of the amnesty plan and urged others to do so before something with more stringent requirements went into effect (such as the proposed **Wade-Davis Bill**).

With the end of the Civil War, President **Andrew Johnson** found Reconstruction to be not just a theoretical matter, but a problem that was critical and controversial. In his first message (1865), Johnson explained how his perspective on the perpetual nature of the Union and his desire to reincorporate the South as rapidly as possible, led him to avoid treating the South as a conquered territory. Instead, he took the steps of reconstructing the states by appointing **provisional governors**, having the states elect **constitutional conventions** and new officeholders, and restoring government services such as courts, customs houses, and post offices. In 1866, Johnson reported that civil governments had been restored in all of the former Confederate states. However, he lamented that Congress refused to seat the senators and representatives elected from any of those states except **Tennessee**, thus depriving the states of their constitutional right to representation.

The following year, Johnson complained that "there is no Union as our fathers understood the term" because all the states still were not represented in both houses of Congress. He saw an important tie between obedience to the Constitution and preservation of the Union. He believed that the **Military Reconstruction Acts** passed by Congress conflicted with prohibitions in the Constitution and should be repealed. In addition, **Congressional Reconstruction** provisions were expensive and would lead to heavy taxation. Johnson opposed **black suffrage** and the **Tenure of Office Act**. The latter act prevented him from carrying out some of his executive duties, Johnson stated, because he could not remove, or even threaten to remove, corrupt Treasury Department officials.

By the time of Johnson's final annual message in 1868, he had survived **impeachment** and failed to be nominated for another term as president. He saw no reason to be polite to Congress and, in fact, criticized them resoundingly for creating great trouble by passing the Reconstruction acts, which "have substantially failed and proved pernicious in their results." States were prevented from being governed by their constitutionally elected officials, and Johnson believed the national situation was actually worse than when Congressional Reconstruction began.

Ulysses S. Grant, president from 1869 to 1877, prepared eight annual messages, mentioning Reconstruction issues in the first through fourth and the sixth messages. In 1869, Grant indicated that seven former Confederate states had been properly reconstructed, and three others were in the process of electing their officials. **Georgia** had gone through all the proper procedures, but then had unseated its black legislators and replaced them with men disqualified by the **Fourteenth Amendment**. Grant recommended measures to restore properly qualified legislators to office.

The following year, Grant mentioned that certain former Confederate states had experienced **violence** and intimidation during elections, and Georgia still had no representatives in Congress. In 1871, Grant suggested that the provisions of the Fourteenth Amendment, which disqualified certain former Confederates from holding office but not from voting, could be repealed. In 1871 and 1872, Congress passed a series of **Enforcement Acts** to enforce the provisions of the Fourteenth Amendment. In his annual message of 1872, Grant deplored the actions which made it necessary to pass such acts, but affirmed his commitment to enforce them, while urging the populace to behave with good order rather than violence. Grant's sixth annual message in 1874 dealt with Reconstruction matters most extensively. Because of considerable politically motivated violence in the southern states, Grant had been called upon to send troops to protect both governments and citizens. This had been true particularly in **Louisiana** and **Arkansas**. Grant reiterated his commitment to enforcing the provisions of the **Fourteenth** and **Fifteenth Amendments**, particularly protecting the freedmen in their right to vote, while deploring the need to take special measures to do so.

Rutherford B. Hayes, who succeeded Grant, explained in his first annual message (1877) why he had taken certain actions to promote the restoration of peace in the southern states, particularly by removing **U.S. Army** forces stationed there. Hayes believed that these actions had produced good results. Hayes also emphasized the need to be sure that the freedmen were not restricted in their **civil rights**. In his second annual message, the last one in which he mentioned Reconstruction issues, Hayes deplored the violence and intimidation against black voters in Louisiana, **South Carolina**, and, to a lesser extent, other states during the 1878 congressional elections. He insisted that the authorities must punish the perpetrators of these offenses and seek to prevent them in the future.

Taken together, these four presidents' annual messages—Lincoln, Johnson, Grant, and Hayes—provide a useful window into events relating to Reconstruction, the executives' perceptions of the process, and their opinions on causes, possible actions, and potential solutions. *See also* African Americans; Amnesty Proclamations; Compromise of 1877; Presidential Reconstruction; Readmission; Scandals.

Further Reading: Basler, Roy P., ed. *The Collected Works of Abraham Lincoln.* Vols. 5, 7, 8. New Brunswick, NJ: Rutgers University Press, 1953; Graf, LeRoy P., Ralph W. Haskins, and Paul H. Bergeron, eds. *The Papers of Andrew Johnson.* Vols. 9, 11, 13, 15. Knoxville: University of Tennessee Press, 1967–2000; Richardson, James D., comp. *A Compilation of the Messages and Papers of the Presidents, 1789–1897.* Vols. 6, 7. Washington, DC: Bureau of National Literature, 1896–1899.

Glenna R. Schroeder-Lein

Arkansas

At the end of the Civil War—in which more than 5,000 Arkansans died, 110,000 slaves gained their freedom, and more than $30,000,000 worth of property was destroyed—the state faced staggering political, economic, and social challenges. State officials had to renegotiate **readmission** into the Union with the federal government. Planters clashed with newly empowered politicians, many from the North and now including **African Americans**, to see who regained political mastery. Economically, planters wondered how to regain their labor supply, while others sought to diversify the Arkansas economy by making it less dependent on cotton. Socially, whites and blacks and men and women reconstructed new identities that reflected the **emancipation** of former slaves and Confederate defeat. As Reconstruction ended in 1877, it could be argued that not much had changed; but no one knew that when Reconstruction began in 1863.

Political Reconstruction

By the end of 1863, the Union army controlled almost all of the strategically important points in Arkansas. President **Abraham Lincoln** recommended leniency for readmission to the Union with his Ten Percent Plan. Excluding high-ranking civil and military Confederate officers, the proposal created a new state government when 10 percent of those who voted in 1860 swore allegiance to the Union and agreed to abolish slavery. By January 1864, 10 percent had met the requirements; so delegates met in Little Rock to draft a new constitution. Similar to the former 1836 constitution with the exception of the mandatory **abolition of slavery**, a small percentage (12 percent) of eligible voters approved the new constitution and elected Isaac Murphy, an opponent of secession in 1860 and 1861, as the new governor. The newly elected legislature chose Elisha Baxter and William Fishback as U.S. senators. Although Lincoln accepted the new regime as legitimate, **Radical Republicans** in Congress refused to recognize the two senators.

President Lincoln's **assassination** on April 14, 1865, forever changed Reconstruction in Arkansas and throughout the South. Replaced by the far less able **Andrew Johnson**, many Confederate Arkansans felt that the prerequisites for reentry into the Union would be much less harsh. The legislature in April 1865 approved the **Thirteenth Amendment**, but did little else. Hoping to disfranchise many returning Confederate veterans, the legislature imposed a second **loyalty oath** that required voters to prove their loyalty to the new government since its inception in March 1864. Believing they could maintain political power, the Murphy government called for congressional elections in October 1865. Although voters elected Unionist congressmen, only 7,000 Arkansans participated. Anti-Murphyites, calling themselves Conservatives, made an impressive showing. Congressional refusal to seat the new delegation and the state Supreme Court voiding the second loyalty oath also troubled Unionists.

Many Conservatives gained seats in the new state legislature elected in August 1866. Meeting in November, they tested the perimeters of Presidential Reconstruction by refusing to allow blacks to vote, run for office, serve on juries, marry whites, or receive state funds for schools. Although not as harsh as **Black Codes**, the legislature ensured that newly freed slaves gained no political, economic, or social power. They also, along with all southern states except **Tennessee**, rejected the **Fourteenth Amendment**.

Conservative dreams of restoring the antebellum world evaporated in 1866, as Radical Republicans gained control of Congress. They attacked President Johnson's leniency in granting **pardons** to nearly all Confederate officers and they lambasted his laissez-faire policy toward Black Codes and race riots in **Memphis** and New Orleans. With Johnson embroiled in an **impeachment** controversy with Congress, Radicals in Congress decided to redirect Reconstruction. Insisting that the white South attempted to return blacks to slavery, Radicals in Congress passed three Reconstruction acts from May to July 1867 that put Arkansas in the Fourth Military District to be supervised by army personnel, required states to ratify the Fourteenth Amendment, and mandated universal male **suffrage** in new state constitutions.

E.O.C. Ord, commander of the Fourth Military District that included Arkansas and **Mississippi**, disbanded the state legislature and restricted state courts. Supported by Governor Murphy, Ord called for a November 1867 referendum to decide whether Arkansas approved a new **constitutional convention**. Having broad powers to disfranchise voters under the Fourteenth Amendment or any voter considered disloyal, Ord and Arkansas Unionists encouraged more than 21,000 African American men to register. In the November 1867 elections, 27,576 Arkansans favored a constitutional convention, while 13,558 opposed it.

The constitutional convention convened on January 7, 1868, in Little Rock. Seventy-five delegates, including eight African Americans, debated voting qualifications, interracial marriages, equality before the law, educational reform, and gubernatorial powers. By a vote of 46 to 20 on February 1, 1868, the convention passed the new constitution that afforded male suffrage to all men over 21 years of age regardless of race; opposed interracial marriages; allowed blacks to serve in government offices, on juries, and in the **militia**; ordered the legislature to fund school systems for students regardless of race; established a state university; and created a strong executive elected to a four-year term. Democrats loathed this new constitution and intimidated black and white Unionists from voter registration. The **Ku Klux Klan**, a paramilitary organization appearing in Arkansas in late 1867 to deter black registration and voting, whipped, shot, and killed political enemies and often burned their homes and churches. Withstanding **violence** and intimidation, voters ratified the new constitution in April 1868, chose **Powell Clayton** as the new governor, and elected Republicans to Congress and state offices. When the newly elected radical legislature ratified the Fourteenth Amendment, Congress officially readmitted Arkansas to the Union on June 22, 1868.

Inaugurated on July 2, 1868, Republican governor Powell Clayton, a Union cavalry officer from Pennsylvania who fought in Arkansas during the Civil War, intended to restore law and order to Arkansas. Facing the violence spurred by the Ku Klux Klan, by white militias in much of the state, and by renegade bands of reconstructed veterans and sociopathic hooligans such as Cullen Montgomery Baker in southwestern Arkansas, Clayton tried to reconcile the disparate factions throughout the presidential campaign in Arkansas in 1868. Violence escalated as more than 200 blacks and Unionists were murdered on the eve of the election. Preparing to end the anarchy, Clayton purchased guns and ammunition from Detroit that the Klan captured and destroyed. In the Presidential election, **Ulysses Grant** received 22,112 Arkansas votes to 19,079 votes for Democratic contender **Horatio Seymour**. Arkansans also elected a Republican congressional delegation.

On November 4, 1868, the day after the presidential election, Clayton imposed martial law and quartered Arkansas into four military districts. He used Union troops and black Arkansas militiamen to restore order. Although both pro-Unionists and anti-Unionist forces committed atrocities against civilians living in southwestern and eastern Arkansas, by early 1869, the Klan had been suppressed and desperadoes such as Baker had been killed.

In April 1869, a group of Republican insurgents, calling themselves "liberals" and led by Lieutenant Governor James Johnson, opposed Clayton. They accused him of abuse of power during martial law, mismanagement, and corruption. Although Clayton expertly defused the situation, he recognized that his power base drastically diminished with the enfranchisement of former Confederates in 1872. In January 1871, the state legislature selected him to the U.S. Senate, but he refused to surrender the governorship to Lieutenant Governor Johnson. A stalemate ensued between the two factions as the House impeached Governor Clayton. Absentee pro-Clayton senators denied a quorum for the trial. Inexplicably, Johnson resigned to become secretary of state, a blunder that allowed Ozra Hadley, president of the Senate and a Clayton ally, to become the new governor. Clayton entered the U.S. Senate in March 1871.

Republican Joseph Brooks, an Iowa Methodist minister, replaced Johnson as the leader of the anti-Clayton insurgents. Supported by blacks and by white Democrats and Conservatives who applauded his integrity and his opposition to Clayton, he opposed Elisha Baxter, a North Carolinian who had served on the state Supreme Court and as a federal district court judge. Marred by electoral fraud, Baxter received 41,681 votes to 38,415 votes for Brooks. Supporters of Brooks insisted the election was a sham and began their judicial redress. Inaugurated on January 6, 1873, Baxter appointed liberals and insurgents to state office to broaden his power base. On April 15, 1874, a Pulaski County circuit judge overturned the election and certified Brooks the winner. Sworn in by Chief Justice John McClure, Brooks and a score of armed men marched to the statehouse and forced Baxter out of the governor's office. Each faction quickly assembled a militia that congregated in Little Rock. Fearing imminent bloodshed, President Grant ordered Brooks's forces to disband, reinstated Baxter as governor, and selected Brooks as postmaster of Little Rock.

In June 1874, voters approved the calling of a new constitutional convention by a margin of 80,259 to 8,547. Conservative Democrats won over 75 percent of the convention seats and met in Little Rock from July until September 1874. The new constitution curtailed the executive's power and limited the state's taxation power. Arkansans ratified the new constitution on October 13, 1874. Conservatives also gained control of the state legislature and elected Augustus H. Garland as governor. The election ended political Reconstruction in Arkansas.

Economic Reconstruction

As in all the rebellious southern states, the Civil War destroyed much of the Arkansas economic infrastructure. Farm animals had been stolen or killed;

fences, roads, and bridges lay in disrepair; and unpaid taxes levied during the war years made landownership uncertain. Equally tentative was the labor status of Arkansas' 110,000 freedpeople, freed incrementally from 1863 to 1865 as the Union army secured the area. Rumors of "forty acres and a mule" and Confederate fears that the federal government would confiscate their property made 1865 an uncertain year for all.

Those who had stayed at home during the war planted the 1865 cotton crop as veterans returned throughout the spring. Back taxes often had to be paid before the former owner secured the land title, but creditors supplied the necessary means for this. Large-scale planters especially worried about where to find laborers for their cotton crop. Local **Freedmen's Bureau** agents arrived in twenty-four Arkansas locations throughout 1865 and immediately surveyed the labor supply. Promoting the free labor ideology many brought with them from the North, agents met individually with planters and freedpersons to arbitrate **contracts**. They received no preset guidelines from national headquarters on the type of contract most beneficial to freedpersons, hence they approved various arrangements. Some contracts reinstituted slavery by providing only food, clothing, and medical aid; but most contracts provided for either monthly wages or a share of the crop. Monthly wages for males ranged from $5 to $60 per month, while females received from $5 to $40 per month. Men earned an average of $17.25 per month, while females received an average $12 per month. Shares of the finished crop varied contractually, ranging from one-eighth to three-quarters of the crop going to the laborer. Although neither the price nor the amount baled equaled prewar quantities, cotton seemed to both blacks and whites their best bet to gain economic security. Throughout 1865, black parents complained to the local Freedmen's Bureau agency that local judges declared their children "orphans" and gave "apprenticeships" to planters where they were bound to work until their twenty-first birthday; receiving only food, medical supplies, clothing, and housing.

Eighteen sixty-six seemed a promising year as the cottonseed was planted in March. Factors predicted prices would approach 40 cents a pound. Freedmen's Bureau agents moved to seven new posts (thirty-one total in 1866) and supervised contracts. Agreements became more streamlined in 1866 and established the system of **sharecropping** as landowners and laborers each received half of the crop at harvest. Bankers extended credit to both landowners and tenants, as all expected great profits from the 1866 crop, but heavy spring flooding and a subsequent summer drought caused less than half of the cotton crop to be baled in October. This economic catastrophe hit freedpeople and small-scale white farmers especially hard.

Creditors continued to offer loans to planters and yeomen, still believing the cotton crop would yield lucrative profits, but nature once again intervened with an unusually cool spring that retarded plant growth, followed by torrential downpours throughout the summer that flooded low-lying fields. The price of cotton plummeted to 17 cents a pound in October 1867. The fall harvest produced less than two-thirds of the crop anticipated in the spring.

Increasingly mired in debt, large-scale planters borrowed large sums of money in 1868 from northern capitalists. With each year, farmers sank deeper in debt, becoming more dependent on cotton. By 1874, the price of cotton had fallen to 11 cents per pound. Both whites and blacks plunged into a perennial debt that lasted, with few exceptions, until World War II.

Beginning in 1867, Radical Reconstruction created new economic opportunities for blacks and whites. Leaders such as scalawag Edward Gantt and **carpetbagger** governor Powell Clayton hoped to induce industries to the region by building state-funded **railroads** to lure textile mills, but the low-lying terrain of much of the state made laying track difficult. Railroad bonds depreciated to 40 percent of their face value by 1871. During Reconstruction, workers laid more than 600 miles of track. Radicals also hoped to lure immigrants to Arkansas by offering 160-acre farms to anyone who paid a nominal filing fee. Although more than 30,000 immigrants moved into Arkansas during Reconstruction, most stayed for only a brief time and soon moved to **Texas**.

In 1866, President Johnson signed the **Southern Homestead Act**, which opened up 46,000,000 acres of land in **Alabama**, **Florida**, **Louisiana**, **Mississippi**, and Arkansas. Blacks inundated Freedmen's Bureau offices with requests for information about the land deals in Arkansas. Dr. W. W. Granger, Freedmen's Bureau surveyor, discovered that three-quarters of the nine million acres open in Arkansas could not be farmed, yet he still exhorted blacks to purchase land whenever they could. Of the 16,395 claims made in Arkansas under the Southern Homestead Act, only 44 percent (10,807) were completed. African Americans in Arkansas entered approximately 1,000 of these original claims, with 25 percent completing their entries. By the end of Reconstruction, more African Americans had moved to Arkansas than to any other southern state.

To enact the Radical agenda of better schools, roads, and hospitals, the state legislature raised property taxes and ordered a reassessment of real estate values. Although historians debate whether these higher tax rates were exorbitant, they were unprecedented for Arkansas at a time when many eked out a mere subsistence and provided political fuel for conservatives who promised lower taxes during campaigns.

By the end of Radical Reconstruction in 1875, Arkansas stayed yoked to the erratic ups and downs of the cotton market. Vibrant urban areas and industrial smokestacks remained rarities. In many areas, prewar planters regained political and economic hegemony. To the degree that freedom hinged on economic success and opportunities, most Arkansas blacks and whites remained slaves to poverty and debt.

Social Reconstruction

Nearly all antebellum structures and institutions were contested after the bloody Civil War had unmoored previous understandings of self, family, race, gender, class, education, and religion. Arkansas' 110,000 former slaves created and re-created new identities as they asserted their freedom and independence. For many, registration at the local Freedmen's Bureau office allowed them to publicly and legally proclaim their new names. They constantly sought lost family members. Freedmen's Bureau agents often served as contacts for blacks who searched for lost spouses, children, parents, and grandparents. Black parents protected their children from apprenticeships and from harsh working conditions. Hoping to instill monogamy, Freedmen's Bureau agents solemnized black marriages in mass wedding ceremonies conducted by religious leaders. Black husbands and wives and Freedmen's Bureau officers continually upheld the sanctity of marriage and repeatedly protected black women from the sexual abuse endured during the antebellum era.

Reconstruction empowered many white and black women to assert themselves into new areas unavailable to them before the Civil War. White women who had managed farms and plantations while their absent husbands fought demanded new respect from their husbands and asserted themselves into myriad economic decisions. Black women pushed their husbands to become politically active and often played major roles in deciding where to live and when to move. Both black men and women demanded that black women be given more time away from the cotton fields to spend in household work. A typical contract mediated by a Freedmen's Bureau agent stipulated that the black wife would "do all the housework such as cooking, working, and scouring, after which she is to make a hand in the field."

Whites also reconstructed their new identities and quickly tried to reinstitute white supremacy. Confederate defeat contorted many white men and women's spirits. Debt and poverty constantly reminded many of their defeat; they regained some sense of worth by restoring their racial dominance. Race and skin color consciousness became critical, but prewar miscegenation made demarcation between whites and blacks problematical. An Arkansas Freedmen's Bureau agent, for example, recorded race by using the shades of black, dark, brown, light, white, medium, and yellow. The 1868 state constitutional convention seriously debated miscegenation, and delegates recommended that the legislature oppose any "amalgamation of the races."

Whites attempted to restore white supremacy by reinstituting prewar racial mores. Titles of address, sidewalk etiquette, and clothing worn became contested areas between whites and blacks as each tried to assert dominance or equality. Repeated altercations between whites and blacks occurred over who yielded the sidewalk, who tipped their hat as a sign of deference, or who was called "mister" or "missus."

Freedpersons quickly recognized that **education** would help them realize their dreams of freedom. One Freedmen's Bureau agent observed the desire for schools by blacks amounted "almost to a passion." Blacks demanded schools so they could appraise their contracts for themselves, calculate their debt or profits at harvest time, vote intelligently, and move up in the social hierarchy. At one plantation, for example, blacks spent their lunch break in school. Although more than one-third of the funding for black schools in 1868 came from blacks, the Freedmen's Bureau and northern benevolent agencies such as the **American Missionary Association** aided them. Surprisingly, many of the local white elite such as planters, clergymen, sheriffs, judges, and newspaper editors encouraged educational improvement. More than sixty teachers (about five-sixths of them black) labored in Arkansas in 1868–1869. Although the desire for schools was great, the problems faced were enormous. Money for school buildings and for teachers was always needed. The cotton crop—which had to be planted, chopped, and picked—impeded schoolwork. Many whites, abhorring the idea of a school for blacks, intimidated teachers, parents, and students with violence and arson. In the end, approximately 40,000 blacks gained literacy and basic math skills to help them live as freedpeople.

Freedpersons also pursued new identities in **churches** they established. Baptist and Methodist congregations attracted most black Arkansans. Preachers emphasized morality, "uplifting of the race," education, political activism, and community formation. In many black communities, the preacher became the conduit between blacks and the white elite.

Conclusion

As Reconstruction ended, much in Arkansas returned to prewar patterns: planter hegemony, dependency on cotton, white supremacy, male dominance, and poverty for the masses of whites and blacks. However, many fundamental changes had occurred. No longer could whites whip or rape blacks. Black families could no longer be torn apart and became significant psychological and economic resources for freedpeople. Schools and churches for blacks now appeared frequently throughout Arkansas. Although it was not—as blacks had dreamed—the Day of Jubilee, it was a beginning of freedom and an end to slavery. *See also* Assassination of Abraham Lincoln; Bureau of Refugees, Freedmen, and Abandoned Lands.

Further Reading: Crouch, Barry, and Donaly E. Brice. *Cullen Montgomery Baker: Reconstruction Desperado.* Baton Rouge: Louisiana State University Press, 1997; De-Black, Thomas A. *With Fire and Sword: Arkansas, 1861–1874.* Fayetteville: University of Arkansas Press, 2003; Finley, Randy. *From Slavery to Uncertain Freedom: The Freedmen's Bureau in Arkansas, 1865–1869.* Fayetteville: University of Arkansas Press, 1996; "Freedmen's Bureau Online." http://www.freedmensbureau.com/arkansas/; Moneyhon, Carl H. *The Impact of the Civil War and Reconstruction in Arkansas: Persistence in the Midst of Ruin.* Baton Rouge: Louisiana State University Press, 1994; "Persistence of the Spirit: African-American Experiences in Arkansas." http://www2/aristotle.net/persistence/.

Randy Finley

Army. *See* U.S. Army and Reconstruction.

Ashley, James M. (1824–1896)

James Ashley was born in Pittsburgh, Pennsylvania, on November 14, 1824. During his early twenties, Ashley worked as a boat clerk for ships sailing the Ohio and Mississippi Rivers. Law was a passion of Ashley's, and he was admitted to the bar in 1849. Ashley moved to Toledo, Ohio, where the Republican Party elected him into the 36th Congress on March 4, 1859. A vocal **abolitionist**, Ashley became a guiding force in the Republican camp. He played a significant part in the passing of the **Thirteenth Amendment** of the **U.S. Constitution** in 1865. A major feature of Ashley's political career was his opposition to **Andrew Johnson**'s presidency, which he countered with his Radical Reconstruction agenda.

Ashley's Ideal American Nation and Reconstruction Agenda

The ideal American nation that Ashley proposed was one based on absolute racial equality. Ashley advocated that **African Americans** share access to the same educational system with white children because both races would inherently benefit from the others' experiences (see **Education**). When J. W. Chandler asked Ashley whether or not he would support a state composed entirely of African Americans, Ashley responded that any state, regardless of racial makeup, would be granted **suffrage** and protected by the U.S. federal government. Furthermore, Ashley's Reconstruction agenda ensured the complete amnesty of all members of any former Confederate state without taking skin color into consideration.

Andrew Johnson's Reconstruction program ignored the notion of territorialization. There was also no stipulation assuring blacks access to public schools. According to Ashley, the term "Radical Reconstruction" was an obsolete one that simply maintained antebellum race rights. The sole variant between Johnson's perception of antebellum and postbellum America was that African Americans would no longer be enslaved. Once Ohio ratified the **Fourteenth Amendment**, the state government fought to eliminate the word "white" from its constitution. Ashley argued in favor of the proposal since the original statement claimed that black Americans had no constitutional rights in postslavery United States.

To Ashley, **Congressional Reconstruction** was severely flawed. First, according to Ashley, his Republican colleagues were wrong when they argued that the **Military Reconstruction Act** guaranteed that newly emancipated slaves were to have all the necessary rights to lead productive and economically independent lives. What made black independence impossible was that African Americans still had no power rooted in landownership. Black Americans therefore remained dependent on either renting land owned by whites or working for their former masters. Both scenarios connoted a restoration of antebellum **labor system** and labor code founded on white racial superiority.

Ashley's Political Motives

To create a more equal society, James Ashley openly sought the **impeachment** of President Andrew Johnson, on the grounds that Johnson abused his presidential powers by refusing to provide black Americans with decent **civil rights** and political access—what Ashley called a bill of rights. When more moderate Republicans were lukewarm on impeachment, arguing that no actual crime had been committed, Ashley claimed that narrow constraints for impeachment guaranteed that the president could never be forced from office. To Ashley, abuse of power, violation of public trust, and neglect of duty should constitute the right of Congress to overthrow the president. James Ashley considered Johnson's reluctance to give African Americans absolute inalienable rights an "undetectable crime" that defined a presidential abuse of power, violation of public trust, and neglect of duty. The latter assertion claimed that Johnson purposely violated the Fourteenth Amendment of the U.S. Constitution. Ashley alleged that maintaining Johnson's strict, racist view of the Constitution would inevitably impede America's development. Creating racial equality was one measure that Ashley considered primordial for the United States to secure a strong economic future. Only once equal social and labor rights were established could African Americans fully participate in the booming American market economy and pay tax dollars to provide every U.S. citizen with greater social benefits.

Ashley's Contributions

Ashley's contributions to American history were significant because they ensured that African Americans would always have a political voice in U.S. politics. Many black Americans, especially those residing in **Kentucky**, vowed to vote in block fashion for the political party that promised them the right to vote. Block fashion voting meant that blacks in a particular region would vote for the political candidate that provided them with the ballot. Republican members like Ashley forecasted the affect that black political participation would later have on American elections and therefore maintained that blacks be given the vote. Another contribution that Ashley made to American history was his relentless struggle to oppose what he believed was tyrannical leadership. The United States, in Ashley's estimation, was a nation founded on the belief that every citizen must have equal representation and power. Allowing a president or a member of Congress to devise racially restrictive laws implied a contradiction to Thomas Jefferson's statement that all Americans are allowed to life, liberty, and the pursuit of happiness. Giving African Americans the right to vote provided the United States with a novel political perspective that helped the nation better adapt to the national policies of the rest of the world because America would no longer be known as the only nation left that practiced slavery. Instead, the equal racial representation that figures like James M. Ashley fought for throughout their entire careers proved that America was capable of following an emerging political trend. African Americans could then practice American lifestyle and have the chance to prosper economically on an even arena with whites. Irresponsible American politicians who followed Ashley's tenure purposely acted to make certain that blacks did not receive proper civil rights protection until the second half of the twentieth century. *See also* Amnesty Proclamations; Black Suffrage; Disfranchisement; Field Order No. 15; Joint Committee on Reconstruction; Presidential Reconstruction; Stevens, Thaddeus.

Further Reading: Foner, Eric. *Free Soil, Free Labor, Free Men: The Ideology of the Republican Party before the Civil War*. New York: Oxford University Press, 1970; Horowitz, Robert F. *Great Impeacher: A Political Biography of James M. Ashley*. New York: Brooklyn College Press, 1979; Kahn, Maxine B. "Congressman Ashley in the Post-Civil War Years." *Northwest Ohio Quarterly* 36 (Summer, Autumn 1964): 116-33, 194-210.

Gerardo Del Guercio

Assassination of Abraham Lincoln (1865)

John Wilkes Booth shot President **Abraham Lincoln** on Good Friday, April 14, 1865. Vice President **Andrew Johnson** and Secretary of State **William H. Seward** were supposed to be assassinated at the same time; Seward was severely wounded, but Booth's accomplice who was to kill Johnson, George A. Atzerodt, lost his nerve. The death of Lincoln and the survival of Johnson affected Reconstruction in profound ways.

The conspirators' original plot involved kidnapping Lincoln and taking him south to be held for a ransom advantageous to the Confederacy. The conspirators included Booth, an actor; Atzerodt, a carriage painter and ferryman; John H. Surratt, Jr., a Confederate courier; David E. Herold, a pharmacist's clerk; Lewis Paine (or Payne, who also used the alias Lewis Thornton Powell) and Samuel Arnold, former Confederate soldiers; and Michael O'Laughlin, a feed-store clerk. The group met at the Washington, D.C., boardinghouse of **Mary Surratt**, John's mother. When the kidnapping attempt failed, Arnold, O'Laughlin, and probably John Surratt left the group.

After the fall of Richmond and the surrender of Robert E. Lee's army, the kidnap plot was no longer viable. Booth's decision to assassinate Lincoln was evidently a last-minute development, possibly even determined as late as the morning of the fourteenth when Booth learned that Lincoln would be attending the play *Our American Cousin* at Ford's Theatre that evening. Thanks to a few advance preparations and his reputation within the acting profession, Booth was able to enter the presidential box during the performance. He shot Lincoln in the head and jumped over the railing onto the stage, shouting "Sic semper tyrannis" ("thus ever to tyrants," the motto of **Virginia**). He made his way to a waiting horse, despite a broken leg caused by catching his spur in a flag draped near the president's box. President Lincoln, mortally wounded, was taken across the street to the Peterson house, where he died at 7:22 the following morning.

Booth fled Washington and joined up with David Herold, but they stopped near Bryantown, **Maryland**, where Dr. Samuel A. Mudd set Booth's broken bone; it is possible that the two were previously acquainted. The War Department conducted a massive manhunt for Booth and Herold, which ended on April 26, when they were cornered in a Virginia tobacco barn. Herold surrendered, but Booth was shot and died shortly after.

Agents of the federal government rounded up hundreds of assassination conspiracy suspects, but finally focused on eight: Herold, Atzerodt, Paine (who had seriously wounded Secretary of State Seward), Mary Surratt, Mudd, Arnold, O'Laughlin, and Edman (or Edward) Spangler, a Ford's Theatre handyman and friend of Booth who was in the wrong place at the wrong time (John Surratt had fled the country). These eight were tried before a military commission May 9–June 30, 1865, and this controversial process found all eight guilty. Herold, Atzerodt, Paine, and Mary Surratt were hanged on July 7, while the other four were sentenced to life imprisonment at Fort Jefferson in the Dry Tortugas, off the coast of **Florida**. O'Laughlin died in 1867 during a yellow fever epidemic, and Johnson ordered the others freed in early 1869.

A broadside advertising a reward for the capture of the Lincoln assassination conspirators, illustrated with photographic prints of John H. Surratt, John Wilkes Booth, and David E. Herold. (Courtesy of the Library of Congress.)

John Surratt was arrested in Egypt, extradited to the United States, and tried in 1867. The jury could not agree on a finding, and so he too was freed.

Lincoln's assassination affected Reconstruction in several ways. It immediately caused a tremendous cry for vengeance against the South in general and against the conspirators in particular, resulting in a trial of questionable fairness. The hanging of Mary Surratt was especially controversial, partly because she was a woman, and partly because she had not participated in the plot in any significant way; evidence implicating her was circumstantial at best. Her death haunted Andrew Johnson politically, because as president he had approved the sentence and not granted her a reprieve. It also led to a war of words between Johnson and Judge Advocate General Joseph Holt, who had prosecuted the conspirators. Also, Johnson's ascendancy to the position of executive brought a president far more rigid in his beliefs and opinions than Lincoln had been. In addition, and despite early indications, Johnson approached the South leniently; with the exception of Unionism, his principles were in line with the **Democratic Party**, not the Republican Party, and so he had no interest or sympathy for the freedpeople. These factors combined to have significant effects on the course and results of Reconstruction. While no one knows what would have followed the Civil War had Lincoln lived, in all probability Lincoln would have dealt with southern—and northern—opposition more flexibly, and would have shown greater concern for the plight of former slaves. *See also* Democratic Party; Johnson, Andrew; Lincoln, Abraham; Republicans, Radical; Seward, William H.; Surratt, Mary (Elizabeth) Eugenia.

Further Reading: Hanchett, William. *The Lincoln Murder Conspiracies*. Urbana: University of Illinois Press, 1983; Leonard, Elizabeth D. *Lincoln's Avengers: Justice, Revenge, and Reunion after the Civil War*. New York: W. W. Norton, 2004; Turner, Thomas Reed. *Beware the People Weeping: Public Opinion and the Assassination of Abraham Lincoln*. Baton Rouge: Louisiana State University Press, 1982.

Glenna R. Schroeder-Lein

Atkinson, Edward (1827–1905)

A New England cotton manufacturer and unofficial adviser to several presidential administrations during the late nineteenth century, Edward Atkinson was best known as a frequent commentator on the great socioeconomic questions of his day—what might today be termed a pundit. Born to an old merchant family of Boston, by the 1850s, Atkinson had become the manager of several regional textile mills. An **abolitionist** and a supporter of the Republican Party upon its founding in 1854, the young Atkinson began to publicly advocate reforms that struck an angry chord among many of his fellow manufacturers. His ardent free-trade principles, for example, made him hostile to the tariffs that many northerners saw as providing vital support to nascent American industries. After the war, his antitariff efforts in Washington, D.C., brought him into conflict with the powerful protectionist lobby that centered around Pennsylvania iron and steel interests, their congressional representatives, and their famous spokesman, the economist Henry C. Carey.

For a textile manufacturer, just as exceptional as his free trade principles were the opinions Atkinson first expressed in his widely circulated 1861 pamphlet, *Cheap Cotton by Free Labor*, which garnered international attention. In it, he argued—contrary to conventional wisdom—that the mercantile and manufacturing classes of the North had nothing to fear from slave **emancipation** in the South; Atkinson maintained that a regime constituted of free laborers could grow the staple more plentifully and efficiently. Though the **sharecropping** system that soon dominated the South after emancipation did not provide the region's farmers with the general prosperity he hoped for, Atkinson did correctly forecast the postwar demise of the gang-based plantation system in favor of thousands of individuated small farms—composed of both black and white households—whose collective production of cotton would exceed that of the antebellum era by the 1880s.

On economic matters, Atkinson was long a staunch supporter of the various principles that underlay the emergent orthodoxy of laissez-faire economics: low tariffs, minimal government intervention, and most of all, hard money (that is, currency redeemable in precious metals, especially gold). Atkinson was also long regarded as an ideological enemy of the organized-labor movement, and he rejected as fundamentally socialist the very associationist principles that made trade unionism possible. Politically, Atkinson was closely associated with the independent, reform-minded wing of Republican Party intellectuals that emerged in the early 1870s, but his disillusionment with the **Grant** administration, along with his new business interests in the fire insurance industry, led him to briefly withdraw from public political engagement after the end of Reconstruction. He reemerged in the mid-1880s, however, as a prominent opponent of the burgeoning free-silver movement, a "Mugwump" supporter of Democratic president Grover Cleveland in 1884 and 1892, and a vociferous critic of American imperialism toward the end of the century. Atkinson's oft-demonstrated talent for articulating his convictions in clear if often strident prose left a lasting imprint on Reconstruction and Gilded Age political culture.

Further Reading: Cohen, Nancy. *The Reconstruction of American Liberalism, 1865–1914*. Chapel Hill: University of North Carolina Press, 2002; Williamson, Harold Francis. *Edward Atkinson: The Biography of an American Liberal, 1827–1905*. Boston: Old Corner Book Store, 1934.

Scott P. Marler

B

Banks, Nathaniel P. (1816–1894)

Nathaniel P. Banks was a central figure in **Abraham Lincoln**'s plans for Reconstruction. A politician's politician, Banks developed the reputation before the Civil War as a master parliamentarian, someone who could harness the energies of a fractious assembly and coax it to consensus. He first demonstrated these talents as Speaker of the House in the Massachusetts legislature and later as president of a convention to rewrite the state's constitution. Elected as a representative to the U.S. Congress in 1853, Banks moved skillfully to gain election as Speaker of that body in 1855. His elevation to Speaker of the House in the U.S. Congress was notable because it represented the first political victory on a national level for the newly formed, antislavery Republican Party.

Returning to Massachusetts to serve as governor in 1858, Banks was a politician to be reckoned with when war broke out in 1861. On May 16, Lincoln appointed Banks major general of U.S. volunteers to consolidate political support in the Northeast. Although Banks was clearly ill-prepared to assume such a lofty rank so early in the war, he quickly proved his worth by successfully implementing Lincoln's strategy in **Maryland** to keep that state from seceding.

Banks was given a chance to display his martial talent in February 1862, when he was ordered to occupy the Shenandoah Valley. Neither he nor Lincoln could have predicted that an unknown Confederate general, Thomas J. Jackson, would take advantage of Banks's inexperience to make him a scapegoat for the defeat that followed. Whipping Banks soundly at Winchester, Jackson did it again at Cedar Mountain in August, at which point it became apparent to Lincoln that Banks's usefulness as a political general might find a more suitable application in a geographic location of less-strategic importance.

The opportunity for a new assignment with an expanded role in Lincoln's plans to reunite the country occurred when another political general from Massachusetts, **Benjamin F. Butler**, created problems for Lincoln in **Louisiana**. Butler had encouraged the formation of Union clubs in New Orleans when he arrived, but had offended many of its citizens with his iron-fisted rule. Lincoln needed someone who could demonstrate more finesse in working with people whom he counted on to reestablish loyalty to the Union. Banks's success in handling a touchy political situation in Maryland made him the obvious choice to replace Butler. As one of Banks's aides explained, "There had been harsh measures enough in this department, and since Butler had stroked the cat from the tail to head, and found her full of yawl and scratch, [Banks] was determined to stroke her from head to tail, and see if she would hide her claws, and commence to purr" (Hepworth, 27–28).

Despite Banks's skills as a politician, the good citizens of New Orleans did not commence to purr. Both Banks and Lincoln tended to underestimate the strength of secessionist sentiment in the Crescent City and were surprised that people who had many personal ties to the North and who depended on commerce with the Midwest for their economic survival would be so resistant to the notion that they should proclaim their loyalty to the Union. Undeterred by the resistance, Banks began compiling a list of voters who had taken an oath that would qualify them to vote in state and municipal elections. The number of voters on Banks's list was not large, but he did not need many because Lincoln had announced a plan to reconstruct the southern states in his annual address to Congress on December 9, 1863. According to his plan, Lincoln would recognize the legitimacy of a state government when the number of persons taking an oath of loyalty and voting in a state election exceeded 10 percent of the number of votes cast in the presidential election of 1860.

Nathaniel P. Banks, c. 1870. (Courtesy of the Library of Congress.)

Believing that Banks had the political skill to make his plan work, Lincoln gave Banks absolute authority to direct the effort for Reconstruction in Louisiana. Reacting swiftly to Lincoln's vote of confidence, Banks ordered two elections in parts of the state that were under Union control. The first election scheduled for February 22, 1864, was for governor, lieutenant governor, and several other state offices. A second election on March 28 would select delegates to a **constitutional convention**. Together, the two elections formed the basis for a new state government, the Free State of Louisiana, which both Banks and Lincoln hoped would gain the approval of the U.S. Congress for **readmission** to the Union.

Both elections took place as scheduled, but the number of voters was not large. Nevertheless,

Georg Michael Hahn, a Banks supporter born in Switzerland who had immigrated as a child to New Orleans, was elected governor. Elections for the constitutional convention one month later seated ninety-five delegates, who convened in April to rewrite the state's constitution. The document they adopted in July was forward-looking, given the standards of the day. It abolished slavery, recognized the rights of the working man to a degree that had not occurred previously in Louisiana, and left the door open for extending the vote to **African Americans**, especially those who "by military service, by taxation to support the government, or by intellectual fitness, may be deemed entitled thereto" (*Debates*, 237).

Banks worked behind the scenes to make the Free State a success but was distracted by his campaign up the Red River toward Shreveport during the spring of 1864. Committing the same errors he had made two years before in **Virginia**, Banks was soundly thrashed at Mansfield (Sabine Crossroads) and retreated to Simmesport. Lincoln could no longer ignore Banks's shortcomings as a general and reluctantly agreed to set him aside. To that end, Lincoln kept Banks in place, but he appointed another man, **Edward R. S. Canby**, to command a larger department that superceded Banks's command.

Stripped of his military authority but with the Free State of Louisiana still in place, Banks was summoned back to Washington to lobby for its admission to the Union. He spent the fall and winter of 1864–1865 doing his best to persuade the members of Congress to accept the Free State as the legitimate voice of a pro-Union Louisiana, but with the end of the war in sight, congressional leaders had no interest in letting Louisiana slip in before the broader issues regarding the readmission of all of the states that had seceded were settled.

Disappointed at having the admission of the Free State of Louisiana blocked in Congress, Banks started back to Louisiana on April 5, 1865. He heard about Lincoln's assassination in Cairo, Illinois, and proceeded to New Orleans, intent on doing what he could to bolster Unionist spirits, particularly now that the war was over. It was clear, however, that Banks's future did not lie in the Crescent City. Learning that the congressional seat in his home district was up for grabs, Banks said good-bye to his friends in Louisiana and headed home to Massachusetts. His departure from New Orleans marked the end of Nathaniel P. Banks's involvement in Reconstruction. Although he was elected and went on to serve six terms, Banks's postwar career in the U.S. House of Representatives was remarkable for its lack of distinction.

The Free State of Louisiana, minus Banks's leadership or support from Washington, quickly gave way to the reemergence of former secessionists, who captured the legislature in the fall of 1865, thanks to President **Andrew Johnson**'s lenient policy in regard to former rebels. The window of opportunity for the peaceful transformation of Louisiana from a slave to a free society that opened with elections in the spring of 1864 soon closed. *See also* Amnesty Proclamations; Presidential Reconstruction; Republicans, Moderate.

Further Reading: *Debates in the Convention for the Revision and Amendment of the Constitution of the State of Louisiana.* New Orleans, LA: W. R. Fish, 1864; Harrington, Fred Harvey. *Fighting Politician: Major General N. P. Banks.* Philadelphia:

University of Pennsylvania Press, 1948; Hepworth, George H. *The Whip, Hoe, and Sword: The Gulf-Department in '63*. Boston: Walker, Wise & Co., 1864; Hollandsworth, James G. *Pretense of Glory: The Life of General Nathaniel P. Banks*. Baton Rouge: Louisiana State University Press, 1998; McCrary, Peyton. *Abraham Lincoln and Reconstruction: The Louisiana Experiment*. Princeton, NJ: Princeton University Press, 1978.

James G. Hollandsworth, Jr.

Belmont, August (1813–1890)

An influential New York investment banker and well-connected power broker, August Belmont was an important figure in the **Democratic Party** during the Civil War and Reconstruction era, as well as a significant presence in New York cultural life. Belmont was born to Jewish parents in the village of Alzey in the Rhenish Palatinate (now the German state of Rhineland Palatinate), where his father was a landowner and prominent citizen. He grew up in Frankfurt, where he was educated and as a teen began working for the Rothschild financial house. After a stint in Italy and on the way to a banking post in Cuba in 1837, Belmont stopped in New York during a financial panic and decided to remain. He set up August Belmont & Company to act as the Rothschilds' agent in the United States and successfully capitalized on the financial opportunities available in New York. Within a few years of his arrival, Belmont was among New York's richest citizens and most prominent bankers.

Belmont continued to climb socially and became involved in politics. In 1844, he was naturalized as an American citizen, worked for President James K. Polk, and was appointed Austrian consul general in New York from 1844, a post he held until 1850. In 1849, Belmont married Caroline Slidell Perry, daughter of Commodore Matthew Perry and niece of **Louisiana** politician John Slidell. In 1853, Belmont was named U.S. charge d'affaires at the Hague. Belmont was an instrumental fundraiser and advocate in various political campaigns in the 1850s and was a key supporter of Stephen A. Douglas in the 1860 presidential campaign. Belmont served as chairman of the Democratic National Committee from 1860 until 1872 and after a hiatus remained active in party politics. He passed away in 1890, an elder statesman of the Democratic Party and a milestone in the economic and cultural history of New York. *See also* Democratic National Convention; Elections of 1864; Elections of 1868; Nast, Thomas; Tilden, Samuel J.; Tweed, William M.

Further Reading: Black, David. *The King of Fifth Avenue: The Fortunes of August Belmont*. New York: Dial Press, 1981; Katz, Irving. *August Belmont: A Political Biography*. New York: Columbia University Press, 1968.

Alex Feerst

Bennett, James Gordon, Jr. (1841–1918)

James Gordon Bennett, Jr., was a newspaper proprietor, sponsor of expeditions, and benefactor of several sports. A millionaire's son, he was known for his wild lifestyle, erratic behavior, and extravagant spending. His father (1795–1872) was a Scottish immigrant who founded in 1835 the *New York Herald*, a highly successful four-page penny paper. A leading figure in early American journalism, Bennett, Sr., was a hardworking, heavy-handed manager who pursued sensational news stories and invented many innovative reporting methods such as the use of the transatlantic cables and of Civil War correspondents.

Bennett, Jr., was born in New York City on May 10, 1841, and was educated mostly in France. A sailing enthusiast, he participated in the Civil War as a U.S. revenue marine third lieutenant, commanding his 170-ton schooner yacht *Henrieta* while she was in federal service (1861–1862). In 1866, he also won the first transoceanic boat race.

In 1867, he took charge of his father's newspaper publishing business. In an effort to increase the circulation of the already commercially successful paper, he funded the 1869 expedition by British explorer Henry Morton Stanley into Africa to find the missing Scottish missionary Dr. David Livingstone. The search continued for two years until November 10, 1871, all the while providing the *Herald* exclusive coverage of exotic stories from Africa. In 1874–1877, Bennett's paper cosponsored—along with Britain's *Daily Telegraph*—Stanley's African transcontinental journey from Zanzibar, Tanzania, to the mouth of the Congo River. The 1879–1881 North Pole expedition of the steamer *Jeannette* was also funded by the *Herald*; although this voyage ended in the deaths of twenty crew members, the tragic event nevertheless boosted the paper's circulation. A sports enthusiast, Bennett funded several highly popular sporting events such as polo, international yachting, automobile racing, a gas balloon competition, and airplane racing.

Bennett left New York in 1877 and spent the last four decades of his life mainly in France. The departure followed a **scandal** that terminated his engagement to the rich socialite Caroline May. Arriving late and drunk at the mansion of her family in New York, he urinated into the living room fireplace in the presence of his hosts. This incident is recorded in the *Guinness Book of World Records* under "Greatest Engagement Faux Pas" and is considered the origin of "Gordon Bennett" as a British expression of disbelief.

Residing in France, Bennett continued to manage the *Herald* via telegraph communications, and, in 1887, launched the Paris edition of the paper, a notable English language daily that is still published as the *International Herald*

A caricature of James Gordon Bennett, Jr., from the *New York Herald*, 1884. (Courtesy of the Library of Congress.)

Tribune. He remained single until the age of seventy-three, when he married Baroness de Reuter, a daughter of the founder of the Reuters news agency. Bennett died at Beaulieu, France, on May 14, 1918. After his death, the *New York Herald* was merged with the *New York Sun* (1920) and the *New York Tribune* (1924) to become the *New York Herald Tribune*, a Republican daily newspaper that existed until 1966. *See also* Greeley, Horace; Johnson, Andrew; Nast, Thomas.

Further Reading: Crockett, Albert Stevens. *When James Gordon Bennett Was Caliph of Baghdad*. New York: Funk & Wagnalls, 1926; Laney, Al. *Paris Herald: The Incredible Newspaper*. New York: Greenwood Press, 1968; O'Connor, Richard. *The Scandalous Mr. Bennett*. Garden City, NY: Doubleday, 1962; Seitz, Don Carlos. *The James Gordon Bennetts: Father and Son, Proprietors of the New York Herald*. New York: Beekman, 1974; Villard, Oswald Garrison. *Some Newspapers and Newspaper-Men*. Freeport, NY: Books for Libraries Press, 1971.

John J. Han

Bingham, John A. (1815–1900)

John Armor Bingham, congressman, leader of **Moderate Republicans** during Reconstruction, and author of the key phrases of Article 1 of the **Fourteenth Amendment**, was born in Mercer, Pennsylvania, on January 21, 1815. John was the eldest of the five children of Hugh and Esther Bailey Bingham, devout Presbyterians whose ancestors came to America during the colonial era and served in the American Revolution.

Antebellum Whig to Civil War Republican

After his mother died in 1827, Bingham went to live with his father's brother, Thomas Bingham, in Cadiz, Ohio, a strong antislavery area. Four years later, after his father remarried, Bingham returned to Mercer where he was apprenticed to the publisher of *The Mercer Luminary*, an anti-Masonic newspaper that opposed slavery and supported temperance and internal improvements. He then entered Mercer Academy where, from 1833 to 1835, he received a classical **education**. In 1835, Bingham returned to Cadiz, and for two years he attended Franklin College in New Athens, six miles from his uncle's home. His education at Franklin served to enforce the antislavery influences that had already shaped his early life. After teaching for a term, Bingham returned to Pennsylvania, read law with John J. Pearson and William Stewart, and was admitted to the Pennsylvania bar. He then returned to Cadiz, read law with Chauncey Dewey, was admitted to the Ohio bar, and, in 1841, established a law practice with Josiah Scott, one of his uncle's sons-in-law. At the same time, he launched his political career, stumping for William Henry Harrison, the Whig presidential candidate. In June 1844, he married Amanda Bingham, one of his uncle's daughters, and settled in nearby New Philadelphia. In the fall of 1846, he won his first election, gaining the office of prosecuting attorney for Tuscarawas County, a post he held for two terms. He also served as a delegate to state and national Whig conventions and campaigned for the Whig tickets. Bingham returned to Cadiz, and in the mid-1850s, along with other antislavery Whigs and Democrats, he took an active role in forming the new Republican Party in Ohio, as the Whig Party disintegrated over the issue of the extension of slavery into the territories. In 1854, he won election to Congress, where he earned a reputation as a skilled orator and debater. He continued to serve as Ohio's representative from the Twenty-first Congressional District until his defeat in 1862, when his district was eliminated and his county placed in the Sixteenth District. He quickly became a leader in the House, speaking forcefully against admitting Kansas as a slave state, for high tariffs, and against the **Supreme Court**'s Dred Scott decision.

During the Civil War, Bingham joined the **Radical Republicans**, pushing for the confiscation of property owned by those who aided the Confederacy, advocating that the army not return slaves who had fled to their lines, and urging the expansion of federal power to prosecute the war. Economically, he favored the issuance of greenbacks and more taxes, homestead and soldier bounty bills, and a protective tariff. As a member of the **House Judiciary Committee**, he vigorously advocated the **emancipation** of all slaves, supported **Lincoln**'s suspension of the writ of habeas corpus, and managed the bill to admit the western counties of **Virginia** into the Union as the new state of **West Virginia**.

Elected as the representative of the Sixteenth Congressional District in 1864, recovering from his 1862 defeat, Bingham continued in Congress until 1872. From 1869 to 1873, he chaired the House Judiciary Committee. Also, in late April 1865, Secretary of War **Edwin Stanton** appointed him chief investigator into the **assassination of Abraham Lincoln**. President **Andrew Johnson** then appointed him as special judge advocate in the trial of the conspirators. At the trial, which lasted from May 9 through June 10, 1865, Bingham worked to prove that Confederate president **Jefferson Davis** worked with the conspirators, but he failed to convince the military tribunal hearing the case. However, that tribunal did convict the eight men and women Bingham prosecuted.

A Moderate in Reconstruction

During Reconstruction, Bingham emerged as one of the leading members of Congress and the moderate wing of the Republican Party, playing an influential role on the **Joint Committee on Reconstruction**, the committee Congress created in 1865 to recommend legislation needed to complete the restoration process. Believing Radical Republicans to be impractical ideologues, Bingham attempted to work with President Andrew Johnson and southern whites until it became apparent that southern whites could not be trusted to respect black freedom and that Johnson would not compromise with those who believed legislation was needed to protect the freed people before the southern states could be readmitted. Having voted to sustain Johnson's veto of the **Civil Rights** bill because he believed that the **U.S. Constitution** did not permit such legislation, he proposed, instead, a constitutional amendment to ensure that all citizens had federal protections for their inalienable rights. According to Supreme Court Justice Hugo Black, Bingham's campaign earned him the title of "the Madison of the Fourteenth Amendment." Bingham's initial proposal would have empowered Congress to enact all laws necessary to secure to all citizens equal protection in their rights to life, liberty, and property. Although the committee rejected such nationalist language, Bingham continued to work on the project and eventually authored the version of the first section of the amendment (except for the first sentence defining citizenship) accepted by Congress and the nation. In speeches before the House and in correspondence with friends and political associates, Bingham made clear that what he intended by his words was to enable Congress to enforce the Bill of Rights against state action. In addition to working for the adoption of the Fourteenth Amendment, Bingham supported **Tennessee**'s readmission to the Union after it ratified the amendment, initially opposed military reconstruction until it became apparent that no other choice was available, supported the **Enforcement Acts**, and opposed civil service. Economically, Bingham continued to support high tariffs. However, despite his work to ensure rights for blacks, Bingham opposed efforts on behalf of female **suffrage**.

By late 1867, Bingham had joined the radical forces, supporting expansion of military reconstruction. Still, he opposed Johnson's **impeachment** on solely political grounds. Only after Johnson fired Secretary of War Stanton in violation of the **Tenure of Office Act** did Bingham reluctantly join those supporting impeachment. In 1868, he served as a member of the committee to draw up the articles of impeachment and, after a power struggle with the radicals on the committee, he served as chairman of the **impeachment managers** for the House of Representatives at Johnson's impeachment trial before the Senate. As chairman, he read the articles of impeachment to the Senate and made the closing arguments in the case. Congressman **Benjamin F. Butler**, however, served as chief counsel, making the opening statement and examining the witnesses.

In 1872, after eight terms in Congress, Bingham failed to gain his party's renomination, losing to a **Liberal Republican**, Lorenzo Danford, amid charges of corruption, favoritism, and involvement with the Credit Mobilier **scandal**. In 1873, President **Ulysses S. Grant** appointed him U.S. minister plenipotentiary to Japan. He served in that capacity until 1885, and in 1894, Bingham helped end the treaties inflicted on Japan by the leading European nations that infringed on Japan's sovereignty, while also working to maintain America's diplomatic independence from Europe. Bingham also promoted peace between Japan and China over the question of Formosa, protested the British opium trade, and defended American commercial interests in Japan. After being recalled by Democratic president Grover Cleveland, he retired to Cadiz.

Bingham and his wife, Amanda, had three sons and four daughters. All the sons and two of the daughters died of diseases in their childhood. Another daughter died in her thirties. Bingham died March 19, 1900, and was buried at the Cadiz Union cemetery. *See also* Congressional Reconstruction; Presidential Reconstruction; Republicans, Moderate; Scandals; Trumbull, Lyman.

Further Reading: Aynes, Richard L. "The Continuing Importance of Congressman John A. Bingham and the Fourteenth Amendment." *Akron Law Review* 36 (2003): 589–616; Beauregard, Erving. *Bingham of the Hills: Politician and Diplomat Extraordinary*. New York: Peter Lang, 1989; Benedict, Michael Les. *The Impeachment *and Trial of Andrew Johnson*. New York: Norton & Company, 1973; Curtis, Michael Kent. "John A. Bingham and the Story of American Liberty: The Lost Cause Meets the 'Lost Clause.'" *Akron Law Review* 36 (2003): 617–70; Riggs, C. Russell. "The Ante-Bellum Career of John A. Bingham: A Case Study in the Coming of the Civil War." Ph.D. dissertation, New York University, 1958; TenBroek, Jacobus. *Equal under Law*. Berkeley: University of California Press, 1951.

Roberta Sue Alexander

Black, Jeremiah Sullivan (1810–1883)

Jeremiah S. Black, lawyer, U.S. attorney general, and political advisor, was born near Stony Creek, Pennsylvania. After attending several schools and studying on his own, Black read law with Chauncey Forward in Somerset, Pennsylvania, and was admitted to the bar on December 3, 1830. Black married Forward's oldest daughter, Mary, in 1836. The couple had five children between 1837 and 1852.

Black was judge of the court of common pleas for Pennsylvania's Sixteenth Judicial District (1842–1851) and on the Pennsylvania Supreme Court (1851–1857) before President James Buchanan selected him to serve as attorney general. In this capacity, Black oversaw the settlement of some controversial land titles in California and attempted to enforce unpopular laws relating to the slave trade and the return of fugitive slaves. Black defended the Buchanan administration in a pamphlet war with Illinois senator Stephen A. Douglas, who favored popular sovereignty and criticized Buchanan.

After **Abraham Lincoln**'s election as president in the fall of 1860, the southern states threatened to secede. In Black's legal opinion, the states could not do this, but neither could Buchanan "coerce" or force a state to stay in the Union. However, it was Buchanan's responsibility, Black said, to uphold the laws and protect federal property. Black also urged Buchanan to garrison southern forts more strongly, which the president did not do. In December 1860, Buchanan made Black secretary of state when Lewis Cass resigned.

In poor physical and financial health, he left office on March 4, 1861, but soon took a position as **Supreme Court** reporter and assembled two volumes of case accounts. Black's legal practice also grew. Politically, he opposed Abraham Lincoln's alleged "unconstitutional" violations of **civil rights** in the North during the war, but he supported the war effort generally.

After the war, Black served as a leading defense attorney for confederates **Jefferson Davis** and Clement C. Clay (whose cases never came to trial), as well as Lambdin P. Milligan and

Jeremiah Sullivan Black, c. 1859. (Courtesy of the Library of Congress.)

William H. McCardle. The Supreme Court cases *Ex parte Milligan* and *Ex parte McCardle* involved the issue of whether a civilian could be tried and convicted by a military commission in a state not actively threatened by war.

For a time, Black played an important role as an advisor to President **Andrew Johnson** on **patronage** and political issues. He helped Johnson to write his vetoes of the First and Second **Military Reconstruction Acts** as well as Johnson's Third **Annual Message**. As a result, the **House Judiciary Committee** questioned Black as part of its efforts to impeach Johnson. Black broke with Johnson because the president failed to act on behalf of two of Black's clients in a dispute over rights to mine guano on the island of Alta Vela in the Caribbean near Santo Domingo. Because of this, Black declined to be part of Johnson's defense team during his **impeachment** trial.

Black's right arm was crushed in a **railroad** accident in May 1869, but he learned to write left-handed. An unusual and eccentric character, Black continued to practice law and write controversial articles until the end of his life. *See also* Cabinets, Executive; Recusants.

Further Reading: Brigance, William Norwood. *Jeremiah Sullivan Black: A Defender of the Constitution and the Ten Commandments.* Philadelphia: University of Pennsylvania Press, 1934; Graf, LeRoy P., Ralph W. Haskins, and Paul H. Bergeron, eds. *The Papers of Andrew Johnson.* Vols. 3, 8, 12–15. Knoxville: University of Tennessee Press, 1967–2000.

Glenna R. Schroeder-Lein

Black Codes

The Black Codes, passed by the former Confederate states during **Presidential Reconstruction**, were part of a complex web of postwar economic, legal, and extralegal restraints designed by white conservatives to maintain broad control over the freedpeople.

The Black Codes originated in 1865 and 1866, as southern lawmakers met to bring their state constitutions in line with President **Andrew Johnson**'s Reconstruction program. **Mississippi** legislators passed the first Black Code in November 1865; this became the prototype for similar legislation throughout the South.

Whites insisted that the Black Codes recognized the blacks' freedom and extended to them rights accorded antebellum whites: The freedmen could own property, testify in courts, and sue and be sued. Their marriages were recognized by law and their children were deemed legal heirs. In fact, though, white politicians fashioned both state Black Codes and local proscriptive ordinances in order to keep the former slaves at work and tied to the land—in a condition as close to bondage as possible.

Mississippi's Black Code mandated that the freedpeople "have lawful home or employment," but stipulated that they could not lease or rent land outside towns or cities. It required them to sign labor **contracts**, and those who broke their contracts "without good cause" were liable to arrest. It empowered probate courts to apprentice black children "whose parent or parents have not the means, or who refuse to provide and support said minors." The courts were instructed to award first preference to "the former owner of said minors."

Mississippi's "Act to Amend the **Vagrant** Laws of the State" defined "vagrants" broadly—to include idle blacks and whites who associated with them "on terms of equality" or with whom they were proven to have had sexual relations. Vagrants of both races received fines, but whites could circumvent the fines by taking a pauper's oath. Blacks who failed to pay their fines after five days were hired out at auction to recoup the fine and court costs.

In a broadly discriminatory supplementary act, Mississippi's Black Code forbade freedmen, with exceptions, from carrying "firearms of any kind, or any ammunition, dirk or bowie knife." The act further prohibited people of color from

> committing riots, routs, affrays, trespasses, malicious mischief, cruel treatment to animals, seditious speeches, insulting gestures, language or acts, or assaults on any person, disturbance of the peace, exercising the function of a minister of the Gospel, without a license from some regularly organized church, vending spirituous or intoxicating liquors, or committing any other misdemeanor, the punishment of which is not specifically provided for by law.

Persons who violated this act were subject to fines and possible imprisonment.

Though each southern state modeled its Black Codes after Mississippi's, one state after another applied special racial proscriptions to its freedpeople. **South Carolina**, for example, included among vagrants "those who are engaged in representing publicly or privately, for fee or award, without license, any tragedy, interlude, comedy, farce, play, or similar entertainment, exhibition of the circus, sleight-of-hand, wax-works, or the like." South Carolina's Black Code authorized the master of an apprentice "to inflict moderate chastisement and impose reasonable restraint upon his apprentice, and to recapture him if he depart from his service."

A police ordinance in St. Landry Parish, **Louisiana**, was designed to maintain the public order, "comfort and correct deportment" of the freedpeople. Blacks required passes to enter the parish; they could not be absent from their employers after ten o'clock at night. In St. Landry, freedpeople were prohibited from renting or owning land. Blacks residing there were "required to be in the regular service of some white person, or former owner, who shall be held responsible for the conduct of said negro."

While the **Texas** Black Code guaranteed the freedpeople the right to choose their employers, it stipulated "but when once chosen, they shall not be allowed to leave their place of employment, until the fulfillment of their contract, unless by consent of their employer, or on account of harsh treatment or breach of contract on the part of the employer." Black Texans did possess a lien of one-half of the crop to guarantee their payment, and their employers were to be fined double the amount due the laborer should they default on payment or treat their employees inhumanly. Texas law, however, required the black employee to "obey all proper orders of his employer," and he or she was liable for fines if proven disobedient. Talking back, swearing, neglecting duty, leaving the farm without permission, entertaining visitors during work hours—such infractions might be tolerated on the part of white workers, but they were strictly forbidden in the case of the freedpeople.

Such provisions, not surprisingly, led to a firestorm of protest in the North. The Black Codes outraged **Radical Republicans** and moderate northerners alike who interpreted them accurately as evidence of white southerners' unwillingness to accept **emancipation**'s full meaning.

Upon returning from his 1865 fact-finding tour of the South, for example, General **Carl Schurz** denounced the Black Codes as mere extensions of the old slave codes. The new codes bound the freedpeople to their employers, Schurz charged, much as under slavery. Employers conspired to keep wages low and placed the freedpeople under vigilante-like law. The Black Codes subjected the blacks to the control of men who, Schurz explained, were "hardly fit to control themselves." Commenting on South Carolina's Black Code, the editor of the *New York Tribune* remarked that under it "involuntary servitude will exist for the punishment of no crime except the old crime of having a black skin."

While white southerners acknowledged begrudgingly the freedom of their former slaves, the Black Codes proved that they nonetheless refused to recognize the blacks' citizenship and to bestow upon them social or political equality. Unwilling to subject the freedpeople to their provisions, federal army commanders, agents from the **Bureau of Refugees, Freedmen, and Abandoned Lands**, and **provisional governors** prevented the Black Codes' enforcement.

The Black Codes nevertheless signified white southerners' ongoing commitment to slavery, to white supremacy, and their determination to circumscribe the legal status of the freedpeople. Confident that Johnson and the U.S. Congress would allow them to retain racial control over the blacks, during the first months of Reconstruction, whites brazenly passed laws designed to keep their former bondspeople separate and unequal, to limit severely their behavior and mobility, and to tie them to the land as a perpetual peasant class. In 1866, Congress passed the **Civil Rights Act** and the **Fourteenth Amendment** in part to protect the freedpeople from the neoslavery captured in the spirit and the letter of the notorious Black Codes. These laws nevertheless provided the ideological and legal foundation for the labor contracts, vagrancy legislation, lien laws, convict labor statutes, enticement laws, and debt peonage laws enacted by the southern states following Radical Reconstruction's demise. *See also* Abolition of Slavery; African Americans; Congressional Reconstruction; Labor Systems.

Further Reading: Fleming, Walter L. *Documentary History of Reconstruction.* 2 vols. 1906-1907; reprint, New York: McGraw-Hill, 1966; Harris, William C. *Presidential Reconstruction in Mississippi.* Baton Rouge: Louisiana State University Press, 1967; Mecklin, John M. "The Black Codes." *South Atlantic Quarterly* 16 (1917): 248-59; Smith, John David. *An Old Creed for the New South: Proslavery Ideology and Historiography, 1865-1918.* Westport, CT: Greenwood Press, 1985; Wilson, Theodore B. *The Black Codes of the South.* University: University of Alabama Press, 1965.

John David Smith

Black Politicians

For the purpose of Reconstruction, these are **African Americans** who, to foreground and advance the objectives and interests of the black community, act in a leadership role, inspire others to take action toward a specific political goal, and actively seek or are elected to legislative offices. During the Reconstruction era, the activities of black politicians encouraged Congress to ratify Constitutional Amendments that would offer **suffrage** for black men and provide equal protection for all American citizens.

Suffrage: Legislative Victory

Prior to the **Military Reconstruction Acts**, African Americans as a group were in a precarious social and economic state. The successful ratification of the **Thirteenth Amendment** in 1865, which legislatively abolished slavery, did not sufficiently quell racial **violence** against African Americans, nor did it protect them from de facto slavery and political **disfranchisement**. After Congress overrode **Andrew Johnson**'s veto, the **Civil Rights Act of 1866** yielded a modest return and little protection for blacks from vigilante whites and economic depression. Shortly after the bill was passed, Memphis, **Tennessee** witnessed the massacre of at least forty-six African Americans, while a police raid of a Republican meeting in New Orleans, **Louisiana** resulted in the murder of at least forty blacks and whites and left more than 140 wounded. Eighteen sixty-six also marked the establishment of the **Ku Klux Klan**, a white terrorist group whose sole purpose was to re-create the economic and social conditions of slavery. Many blacks and whites, including senator **Charles Sumner**, believed black political power was necessitated by the violence and political disempowerment of all African Americans. Before March 1867, blacks were not permitted to vote or hold public office. When **Congressional Reconstruction** enfranchised southern black men via the Military Reconstruction Acts, all of that changed swiftly. Between 1868 and 1876, more than 250 black men were elected to federal and state offices in **South Carolina** alone. (The Acts, however, only applied to the ten former Confederate states still not readmitted to Congress. Black voting and office holding in the rest of the nation had to wait until state reforms and, most important, the passage and ratification of the **Fifteenth Amendment** in 1870.)

Prominent Politicians

From 1867 on, the political interests of African Americans were significantly advanced in government and the southern states, where black political activity was concentrated. Many black politicians became participants in the national political process, or were elected to various legislative offices. **Pinckney Benton Stewart Pinchback** of Louisiana, James H. Harris of **North Carolina**, H. E. Hayne of South Carolina, and G. T. Ruby of **Texas** became the first black delegates to participate in a Republican convention in May 1868. Reflective of their population size, black delegates also held the majority of seats at the South Carolina **constitutional convention** that year, and likewise, maintained those seats in the first assembly of the state's Reconstruction government.

However, the political movement of African Americans in general and black politicians in particular motivated more racial violence. Possibly in response to the ratification of the **Fourteenth Amendment** on July 21, 1868, and the election of **Oscar J. Dunn**, a former slave, as lieutenant governor of Louisiana, in September of that year, at least 250 African Americans were murdered in the Opelousas Massacre in Louisiana's Opelousas and Saint Bernard parishes.

Between 1869 and 1872, the activities of black politicians contributed to securing more political, civil, economic, and educational rights for African Americans. In 1869, the Colored National Labor Union convened to campaign for the equal distribution of land, and **Hiram Revels**, a pastor, was elected to the **Mississippi** State Senate. In 1870, Congress ratified the Fifteenth Amendment; **Joseph Hayne Rainey** was elected to the U.S. Congress representing South Carolina; **Robert Smalls**, who had been a member of the South Carolina House of Representatives in 1868, became a member of the State Senate; and **Robert Brown Elliott** (R-SC) and Benjamin S. Turner (R-AL) were elected to the U.S. Congress. In Louisville, **Kentucky**, a campaign to integrate public transportation began, when black men refused to disembark a streetcar, leading to a suit against the Central Passenger Company, in which the U.S. District Court ruled to integrate in 1871. In 1872, Pinchback became the first American elected to two public offices simultaneously, the House of Representatives and the Senate; however, he was not officially seated to either position, as his election was deemed suspicious, but never proven fraudulent.

Black women were rendered voiceless and invisible in the political process during the nineteenth century. However, taking their lead from Maria Stewart, a political speaker and friend of David Walker, black women would make their political marks during the Reconstruction era. During the many state constitutional conventions being held throughout the South in the 1870s, black women, despite gender restrictive participation, voiced their opposition to segregation, and argued for blacks' equal access to **education** and the vote. When black men began to exercise their Fifteenth Amendment rights, black women were directly involved not only in getting black men to vote, but also in deciding which platforms African American voters should support. Teaching was the first professional position widely held by black women; therefore, they used their standing as educators to further the black agenda. Because of black women politicians such as Fanny Jackson Coppin, the first black woman to head an American educational institution; Louisa Rollin and Mary Ann Shadd Cary, who spoke to Congress regarding women's suffrage in 1869 and 1871, respectively; and Harriet Purvis, the first African American to hold the vice presidential seat with the National Women's Suffrage Association, black women were able to sway the political process toward increasing the upward mobility of African Americans, even if, as in 1875, they had to arm themselves to secure the voting process for black men. Although most of their names have fallen into historical obscurity, their presence in the political process during Reconstruction was acknowledged by leading politicians such as **Frederick Douglass**, who is noted as being the first black male feminist.

Between 1872 and the end of Reconstruction, hundreds of black men served as delegates to Republican conventions, were elected to myriad political offices, advanced the passing of a supplementary civil rights bill written by Charles Sumner, as well as Constitutional Amendments, and pushed the political envelope to its limit to equalize African Americans' standing as American citizens. However, southern whites argued that blacks—regardless of their background as slaves or freeborn men—were inadequate and sometimes blatantly irresponsible at their posts, and black politicians were ridiculed by the mainstream press. As a result, many of the positions to which black men were elected were rescinded under the auspices of white ideological belief of their inferiority.

One anecdote is metaphorical for the incredible rise, and then decline of black political activity. The first black man to serve a full term in the U.S. Senate (1875–1881) **Blanche Kelso Bruce** (R-MS) was a former slave from **Virginia**. He was even considered for a presidential cabinet post, under the McKinley administration. Not until 1966 would another African American serve a full term in the Senate. *See also* Abolitionists; Abolition of Slavery; Black Suffrage; Civil Rights; Congressional Reconstruction; Emancipation; Jim Crow Laws; Johnson, Andrew; New South; Redemption; Republicans, Radical; Women's Movement. See also the individual southern state entries.

Further Reading: Foner, Eric. *Freedom's Lawmakers: A Directory of Black Officeholders during Reconstruction*. New York: Oxford University Press, 1993; Hine, Darlene Clark, and Kathleen Thompson. *Shining Thread of Hope: The History of Black Women in America*. New York: Broadway Books, 1998; Holt, Thomas. *Black over White: Negro Political Leadership in South Carolina during Reconstruction*. Urbana: University of Illinois Press, 1977; Litwack, Leon, and August Meier, eds. *Black Leaders of the Nineteenth Century*. Urbana: University of Illinois Press, 1988; Rabinowitz, Howard, ed. *Southern Black Leaders of the Reconstruction Era*. Urbana: University of Illinois Press, 1982; Middleton, Stephen, ed. *Black Congressmen during Reconstruction: A Documentary Sourcebook*. Westport, CT: Greenwood Press, 2002; Sterling, Dorothy, ed. *The Trouble They Seen: The Story of Reconstruction in the Words of African Americans*. New York: Da Capo Press, 1994.

Ellesia A. Blaque

Black Suffrage

First implemented by congressional legislations in 1867 and then nationalized by the **Fifteenth Amendment** in 1870, the enfranchisement of **African American** men in the wake of the Civil War represented the most revolutionary reform in American political and constitutional orders of the Reconstruction era. It was the possession of voting rights by the freedmen that separated African Americans' postemancipation experience from their counterparts in most Latin American nations in the nineteenth century. Black suffrage, however, should not be seen as an inevitable result of the destruction of slavery and black **emancipation**, neither of which was actually the original goal of the Civil War. Instead, it was achieved only through constant contests between the inspirations for constructing a new American democracy and the desires for retaining the old one that tolerated slavery and encouraged exclusions.

Black Suffrage before the Civil War

Since the beginning of the nation, African Americans had been generally denied the right to vote, even though more than 5,000 of them had fought for the nation's independence. In their first constitutions, half of the original states specifically limited **suffrage** to "whites" or "freemen," while the other half practically excluded the majority of blacks from voting with property, literacy, and other requirements. When suffrage was extended to all adult white males in the early nineteenth century, a notable development of the "Jacksonian Democracy," a number of the original states that had not explicitly excluded blacks in their first constitutions added racial qualification for their voters. Pennsylvania, for example, took voting rights away from its black citizens in 1838, fearing the growing black population in Philadelphia might eventually exert some decisive influence in the state's politics. New York removed property qualifications for white voters, but required the possession of a freehold worth of $250 for a black man to take part in casting a ballot. Most of the new states that joined the Union between the ratification of the **U.S. Constitution** and the Civil War had explicitly limited suffrage to white males. On the eve of the Civil War, only in New England states, where less than 7 percent of the northern black population lived, could blacks vote as whites without additional discriminatory qualifications. African Americans in the North had consistently protested against voting discriminations. Northern black newspapers constantly published petitions from ordinary folks demanding suffrage. Black leaders also held regional and state conventions to put pressure on state legislatures, but most of the efforts ended without success.

Emancipation and Wartime Demand for Suffrage

The Civil War proved to be pivotal in abolishing slavery and subsequently creating the opportunity for blacks to win voting rights, but the Republican Party had envisioned neither black emancipation nor black enfranchisement as the outcomes of the Civil War when it began in April 1861. The party confined its political objective to stopping the expansion of slavery into unorganized federal territories and refused to be recognized as a pro-black-rights party, much less to advocate political equality between blacks. Slaves in the South and free blacks in the North saw the impending war not as a struggle to preserve the old Union, but as a godsend opportunity to win freedom. When the first group of fugitive slaves (later known as "**contrabands**") voluntarily entered the Union army line in **Virginia** in early 1861, they were actually freeing themselves from slavery. Their action of self-emancipation had compelled the federal government to face the issue of their ultimate emancipation. In two **confiscation acts**, respectively passed in 1861 and 1862, Congress declared freedom for those slaves who had been used by the Confederacy for military purposes. The Emancipation Proclamation, initially issued by

President **Abraham Lincoln** on September 22, 1862, was intended to be a military measure and "an act of justice." It declared freedom for all slaves still living in the Confederate-controlled areas and called the freedmen to join the Union army. Even before the Emancipation Proclamation took effect on January 1, 1863, African Americans, free and enslaved, had begun to enlist in the Union army. Eventually, about 200,000 African American men served in the Union army and navy between 1863 and 1865. Another 300,000 served as laborers for the Union throughout the war. Black soldiers' participation laid the foundation for their demand for suffrage after the war, but for some Republican leaders, the commitment to liberty and the Union made the freedpeople the only loyal population that the Republican Party could rely on for postwar Reconstruction.

As a people long deprived of political rights, African Americans were among those who first seized the opportunity of the Civil War to demand a re-definition of their political status in America. Northern black leaders urged blacks to join the Union army and to embrace the American nation, but at the same time they demanded that black soldiers be rewarded with equal citizenship and rights, including political rights. When Lincoln, in his Get-tysburg Address (November 19, 1863), predicted "a new birth of freedom" after the Civil War, black abolitionist **Frederick Douglass** responded that the new American freedom should make "every slave free, and every freeman a voter."

Presidential Reconstruction

In the first phase of Reconstruction—the **Presidential Reconstruction** between 1863 and 1866—however, black suffrage was not on the agenda. Lincoln's first Reconstruction plan, known as the "Ten Percent Plan," was issued in December 1863, when the war was still going on. The plan instructed a southern state to reestablish its new state government after 10 percent of its registered voters in 1860 had taken the required oath of allegiance to the Union. Since no southern blacks could vote before the Civil War, African Americans had been excluded from the process of Reconstruction. Lincoln's policy was shaped by his view of Reconstruction, which he believed should not overthrow the original constitutional framework of federalism that gave states the exclusive power to prescribe qualifications for voters.

African Americans protested against Lincoln's white-only Reconstruction plan. Black leaders held a national convention in Syracuse, New York, in 1864 to demand suffrage. African Americans in New Orleans sent two of their representatives—Jean-Baptiste Roudanez and Arnold Bertonneau—to Washington, D.C., in early 1864, to lobby Congress and Lincoln for making black suffrage a national requirement for Reconstruction. After meeting the black representatives in the White House, Lincoln wrote to the **military governor of Louisiana** to privately suggest that the state consider enfranchising black soldiers and "intelligent" blacks because these people could help the Union "to keep the jewel of liberty within the family of freedom." In his last public speech on April 11, 1865, Lincoln openly expressed the same wishes, but he did not intend to invoke the power of federal government to enfranchise the freedmen.

Andrew Johnson, Lincoln's successor, continued to pursue the white-only Reconstruction policy, although he increased the oath-taking white voters in a southern state to 50 percent. Johnson might have shared Lincoln's concerns about retaining the original constitutionalism, but his Reconstruction plan, issued in May 1865 when the war was already over, also reflected his refusal to recognize the changed circumstances and the need for a different plan. Lincoln's Reconstruction program contained an obviously expedient wartime objective—to establish a pro-Union state government in the Union-occupied regions to politically dismantle the Confederacy. However, Johnson was facing a different situation: Ex-Confederates were hoping to restore the prewar political order and had no intention to make ex-slaves their political equals during and after the process of Reconstruction.

Initial Congressional Reactions

Congress attempted to shape presidential Reconstruction from early on. The **Wade-Davis Bill**, which required a southern state to have at least 50 percent of its prewar voters to take the allegiance oath, was a response to Lincoln's Ten Percent Plan. Even though the bill never intended to enfranchise the freedmen, Lincoln still pocket vetoed it. Congress's limited role during this period was in part due to the internal division of the Republicans— the majority party in both houses—over such questions as what would be the objectives of Reconstruction and how they would be achieved. Conservatives were in line with the Presidential Reconstruction plan and saw Reconstruction as no more than the restoration of the original constitutional framework without slavery. Moderates, who comprised the majority of the party, would not oppose limited national protections for the basic rights of the freedmen, but they were reluctant to enfranchise ex-slaves, fearing that such policy would backfire and hurt the party in northern and western states, many of which still disfranchised free blacks. Many of them, too, did not think freedmen would be able to understand the political process that quickly. Radical Republicans saw Reconstruction as an opportunity to uproot the southern ruling elite, who were responsible for starting the war, and to build a new South ruled by the free labor Republicanism and market economy. They saw the freedmen as the party's only trustworthy ally in promoting such reforms. Black enfranchisement was a necessity to protect and strengthen the shared interests of freedmen, the Republican Party, and the nation. Thus, they demanded that black suffrage be made a prerequisite for the **readmission** of the ex-Confederate states. The Radicals, who were a minority within the party, made several attempts to insert black suffrage into various Reconstruction policies or legislations, including the proposed **Thirteenth Amendment**, but none of such efforts were successful. The Thirteenth Amendment, ratified in December 1865, abolished slavery in the United States, but said nothing about black rights.

The enactment of a series of state laws, known as **Black Codes**, in 1865–1866 by reconstructed southern states changed the course of history. In the name of establishing and maintaining social order, Black Codes set up various legal barriers for freedmen to enjoy equal rights and freedom. For some Republicans, Black Codes represented a political comeback of the defeated planter politicians who wanted to resume slavery in a different format. To counter the Black Codes, Congress moved to enact a **Freedmen's Bureau bill** and a **Civil Rights** bill in early 1866. The former would empower the federal agency to assist and protect freedmen in the South and the latter would confer national citizenship on all freedmen and guarantee them a number of essential civil and economic rights, including the right to own property, make **contracts**, and sue. Neither of the bills mentioned black political rights. **Moderate Republicans** had hoped that President Johnson would approve these bills, which they regarded as supplementary to Johnson's own Reconstruction plan, but Johnson vetoed both bills, citing that these laws had extended federal powers beyond the limits of the original Constitution.

In response, the enraged and frustrated Moderate Republicans joined the Radicals in early 1866 to repass both bills over Johnson's vetoes and, subsequently, to enact the **Fourteenth Amendment**. The second section of the Fourteenth Amendment stipulated that if a state denied its male citizens of twenty-one years or older the right to vote, the number of its representatives to the House of Representatives would be reduced in proportion. The wording of the section reflected a carefully constructed compromise between different factions of the Republicans in Congress. Since 90 percent of four million blacks lived in the South, southern states would be heavily punished by losing representation in the House for withholding suffrage of freedmen; but northern states could continue to **disfranchise** their black citizens with little impunity since the northern black population was too small to make a real difference in the proportionate calculation of a state's representation in the House. The rationale as embedded in the section was similar to that of presidential Reconstruction plans, namely, to let individual states grant suffrage to their freedmen. The difference is that the Fourteenth Amendment did imply a new national power to punish states for denying voting rights to U.S. citizens. Although the section was never enforced, Republicans quickly applied the new national power of regulating suffrage to several other occasions. Between December 1866 and February 1867, Congress succeeded, over Johnson's vetoes, in enfranchising black men in the District of Columbia and unorganized federal territories, and made impartial suffrage—equal voting rights for adult male citizens regardless of color—a precondition for the admission of Nebraska and Colorado.

Congressional (Radical) Reconstruction

Johnson's obstruction and southern states' resistance made the prospect of ratifying the Fourteenth Amendment very dim. When the midterm elections of 1866 gave a two-thirds majority for Republicans in both houses of Congress, a united front of Moderate and Radical Republicans began to initiate a congressional Reconstruction program to replace Presidential Reconstruction. Proclaimed in March 1867, **Congressional Reconstruction** repealed

A woodcut of freedmen casting their ballots, 1868. (Courtesy of the Library of Congress.)

Presidential Reconstruction and ordered the making of new state constitutions in ten former Confederate states (**Tennessee** was exempted from the process). Congress mandated that freedmen be allowed to elect delegates to state **constitutional conventions** and universal manhood suffrage be made a permanent provision of new state constitutions. Under the congressional program, about 735,000 blacks and 635,000 whites were registered in the ten unreconstructed states, and blacks constituted a majority of voters in five states. Blacks were also majorities in the state constitutional conventions in **Louisiana** and **South Carolina**. The new state constitutional conventions produced the most democratic state constitutions since the founding of the nation as they adopted universal suffrage, public schools for both blacks and whites, and state-funded services for the poor and disabled. African Americans' participation in Congressional Reconstruction was instrumental in the South's adoption of the Fourteenth Amendment, a requirement by Congress. With the ratification of the Fourteenth Amendment in 1868, seven states including **Alabama**, **Arkansas**, South Carolina, **North Carolina**, **Georgia**, and Louisiana were readmitted into Congress. **Virginia**, **Mississippi**, and **Texas** were readmitted respectively in 1869 and 1870. In 1870, **Hiram Revels** of Mississippi was seated in the Senate as the nation's first black senator. In the next thirty years, altogether twenty-two African American men were elected to Congress from the South. Another 1,400 held public offices at the state and local governments during Reconstruction. For the period between 1867 and the early 1870s, interracial democracy was an American reality.

The Making of the Fifteenth Amendment

Black enfranchisement in the South inevitably raised the issue of black disfranchisement in the North. It also intensified the debate on women's suffrage. Northern states, however, continued to vote down black suffrage reform proposals in Ohio, Minnesota, Kansas, and Michigan in 1867 and 1868. **Ulysses S. Grant**'s slim victory (a plurality of 300,000 out of 5.7 million votes) and the Democrats' victories in three northern states (Oregon, New Jersey, and New York) and three border states (Delaware, **Maryland**, and **Kentucky**) alarmed Republicans about losing their backyard in the near future to Democrats. The party's double standard on treating black suffrage in the South and North also made its ideological commitment to black equality look hollow and hypocritical. Furthermore, Republicans felt it necessary to secure black voting rights on a more permanent basis as they saw former Confederate states returning to Congress. Because of these concerns, Republicans proposed the Fifteenth Amendment in early 1869.

Out of a host of proposals emerged three versions of the would-be Fifteenth Amendment: The first simply forbade states to deny citizens the right to vote on grounds of race, color, or previous condition of servitude; the second further forbade states to impose literacy, property, or nativity qualifications for voting in addition to racial qualification; and the third simply declared that the voting right was a universal entitlement to all adult male citizens. Fearing a more stringent version would lead to the defeat of the amendment, moderates adopted, on February 26, 1869, the first and most conservative version, an action that outraged Radical Republicans who had preferred the third version. Ratification of the amendment went rather quickly. Seventeen Republican-controlled state legislatures then in session ratified the amendment. Four southern states—Virginia, Mississippi, Texas, and Georgia—were required to ratify it to fulfill the additional prerequisite for readmission. By March 30, 1870, the Fifteenth Amendment became part of the Constitution.

The Fifteenth Amendment was largely a work of the Moderate Republicans. It did not affirmatively confer voting rights on African Americans and simply prohibited states to deny voting rights for racial reasons. It did not grant voting rights to women, still a taboo subject even for many Radical Republicans. It continued to allow wide latitudes for states to disfranchise citizens with literacy, residence, and nativity qualifications, but the amendment recognized political equality between blacks and whites as a new fundamental constitutional principle in American democracy. It affirmed and nationalized the practice of black voting as first implemented in 1867, effectively overrode northern and western states' power to exclude blacks from political process, and gave Congress the power to enforce black suffrage in the years to come.

Enforcing the Fifteenth Amendment

The ratification of the Fifteenth Amendment did not, as President Grant predicted, take the issue of black suffrage "out of politics." The rising and widespread **violence** as conducted by the **Ku Klux Klan** and similar organizations posed foremost challenges for freedmen to freely exercise voting rights in the South. Southern states either had no resources or willingness to enforce their anti-Klan laws. In the meantime, Republicans confronted unchecked election frauds, occurring nationwide, which they believed particularly helped strengthen the Democrats in northern cities where noncitizen immigrants were organized to cast votes. To guarantee southern blacks' right to vote and to establish a uniform federal mechanism of election supervision, the Republican Congress launched an enforcement campaign. Within a year, between May 1870 and April 1871, Congress enacted three laws to enforce the Fifteenth Amendments. Among other things, these laws put the exercise of voting rights by U.S. citizens (as defined by the Fourteenth Amendment) under the protection of federal government and provided severe penalties against state officials, as well as private citizens, for using force, bribery, threats, or intimidation to obstruct citizens from registering or voting. These laws also established federal mechanisms for enforcement, including authority for federal district courts to hear enforcement cases and federal district attorneys and marshals to investigate violations of the Fifteenth Amendment and make arrests. Under these laws, the president was empowered to use military forces to guarantee "free election and fair count."

Federal courts and the newly created Department of Justice (founded in 1870) shouldered the bulk of enforcement work. In 1871, a total of 314 cases under the **enforcement acts** were reported, and 128 of the 206 cases from the South that year ended in convictions. The number of enforcement cases tripled in 1872; 456 of the 603 cases coming from the South ended in convictions. This demonstrated the enormous power of the national government in enforcing the Reconstruction amendments and also brought peace to the polls nationwide. The presidential election of 1872, at which Grant was reelected with a landslide victory, was the most peaceful one in the nineteenth century.

The vigor of enforcement began to decline after the 1872 elections. Short of funding, the removal of able leadership from the federal department of justice, the shift of national attention to economic issues (a result of the 1873 economic panic), and the waning of northern interest as demonstrated in the rise of the **Liberal Republicans**, all contributed to the ultimate decline of enforcement. The **Supreme Court** in deciding *United States v. Reese* (1876), which involved a state official refusing the registration of a black voter in Kentucky, declared two sections of a major enforcement act (May 31, 1870) "insufficient." In ***United States v. Cruikshank*** (1876), the Court deemed another six of the same enforcement laws defective. Although the Court did not invalidate the enforcement law, its rulings substantively diluted the law's power, as well as the entire cause of enforcement. In the midterm elections of 1874, the Democrats regained the House and vowed to block any further legislation of enforcement. Under such circumstances, federal enforcement continued to decline. In 1873, 36 percent of 1,304 enforcement cases ended in convictions, but in 1874, the conviction rate dropped to 10 percent, with 102 of 966 reported enforcement cases ending in convictions. In 1876, the total number of the enforcement cases dropped to 149, of which only three resulted in convictions.

The Coming of Disfranchisement

The final blow upon enforcement came from the disputed 1876 presidential elections. As part of the "bargain" struck by Democrats and Republicans behind the scenes, Republican candidate **Rutherford B. Hayes** received the disputed electoral votes, but promised to restore "home rule" in the South.

After the withdrawal of federal troops from the statehouses in Louisiana and South Carolina in April 1877, the Republican governments in those two states collapsed, completing the process of Democrats' recapture of all southern states. Systematic disfranchisement of African Americans in the South began as early as 1874 (as carried out by the notorious **Mississippi** Plan), proceeded through the 1880s, and reached a peak in the 1890s. Elaborate voting restrictions, such as a **poll tax** and literacy test, substantively disfranchised African Americans throughout the South at the turn of the twentieth century. Blacks who managed to register to vote were further curtailed by the white primary, a mechanism that restricted the participation of Democratic Party primary elections only to whites (in the South, the Democratic Party was virtually the only party). Republicans made attempts to reinforce the Fifteenth Amendment in 1890–1891, but the party's fight ended with a fiasco. In 1894, after a Democratic Congress repealed federal enforcement laws, the Fifteenth Amendment remained virtually unenforced by the federal government until the passage of the Voting Rights Act of 1965. The implementation of black suffrage during Reconstruction, however, remained a powerful memory of interracial democracy that inspired new generations of blacks and whites in their fights for black re-enfranchisement in the twentieth century. *See also* Compromise of 1877; Elections of 1876; Redemption.

Further Reading: Benedict, Michael Les. *A Compromise of Principle: Congressional Republicans and Reconstruction, 1863–1869*. New York: W. W. Norton, 1974; Finkelman, Paul, ed., *African Americans and the Right to Vote*. New York: Garland, 1992; Foner, Eric. *Reconstruction: America's Unfinished Revolution, 1863–1877*. New York: Harper and Row, 1988; Gillette, William. *The Right to Vote: Politics and the Passage of the Fifteenth Amendment*. Baltimore: The Johns Hopkins University Press, 1965; Goldman, Robert M.: *"A Free Ballot and a Fair Count": The Department of Justice and the Enforcement of Voting Rights in the South, 1877–1893*. New York: Fordham University Press, 2001; *Reconstruction and Black Suffrage: Losing the Vote in Reese & Cruikshank*. Lawrence: University Press of Kansas, 2001; Holt, Thomas. *Black over White: Negro Political Leadership in South Carolina during Reconstruction*. Urbana: University of Illinois Press, 1977; Kaczorowski, Robert J. *The Politics of Judicial Interpretation: The Federal Courts, Department of Justice, and Civil Rights, 1866–1876*. 1985; reprint, New York: Fordham University Press, 2005; Keyssar, Alexander. *The Right to Vote: The Contested History of Democracy in the United States*. New York: Basic Books, 2000; Kousser, J. Morgan: *Colorblind Injustice: Minority Voting Rights and the Undoing of the Second Reconstruction*. Chapel Hill: University of North Carolina Press, 1999; *The Shaping of Southern Politics: Suffrage Restriction and the Establishment of the One-Party South, 1880–1910*. New Haven, CT: Yale University Press, 1974; Perman, Michael. *Struggle for Mastery: Disfranchisement in the South, 1888–1908*. Chapel Hill: University of North Carolina Press, 2001; Tergorg-Penn, Rosalyn. *African American Women in the Struggle for the Vote, 1850–1920*. Bloomington: Indiana University Press, 1998; Upchurch, Thomas Adams. *Legislating Racism: The Billion Dollar Congress and the Birth of Jim Crow*. Lexington: University Press of Kentucky, 2004, especially chapters 4–7; Wang, Xi. *The Trial of Democracy: Black Suffrage and Northern Republicans, 1860–1910*. Athens: University of Georgia Press, 1997; Woodward, C. Vann. *The Strange Career of Jim Crow*. 3rd rev. ed. New York: Oxford University Press, 1974.

Xi Wang

Black Troops (U.S.C.T.) in the Occupied South

The U.S. Colored Troops (U.S.C.T.), part of the volunteer Union army amassed during the Civil War, consisted of black troops who served during the war and in the early part of Reconstruction. Former slaves as well as free black men from the North and South served in all theaters of the Civil War. After the war, black troops served as occupation forces in all parts of the South, although after 1865 they were concentrated in coastal forts and in **Texas**. The service of black troops in the war and Reconstruction influenced Reconstruction in both practical and symbolic ways.

Approximately 180,000 black men served as soldiers in the Union army during the Civil War. While black men were not admitted into the Union army in the war's first year, they were accepted in 1862, and were actively recruited from 1863 through the end of the war. Although many black men eagerly sought the opportunity to enlist and fight against secession and slavery, they faced obstacles in the Union army. Black soldiers served in segregated units under white officers, and could not become officers until late in the war. Initially, they were paid less than white troops. U.S. Colored Troops often received inferior food, equipment, and medical care, and at first they were confined to noncombat tasks such as laboring and guard duty. Black troops also faced greater risks than white troops: If captured by Confederates, they could be sold into slavery, tried for insurrection and executed, or killed. Black troops overcame a number of the disadvantages they faced. They won the right to fight, and key 1863 battles such as Port Hudson and Fort Wagner proved black troops' effectiveness and bravery in combat, which modified many white northerners' assumptions of black inferiority. In June 1864, black troops won another critical victory when the U.S. Congress equalized pay between black and white soldiers. The experiences men gained as soldiers equipped many for leadership roles in equal rights conventions, **suffrage** leagues, and other forms of grassroots political activism during Reconstruction. For all, serving as soldiers who helped to save the Union laid claim to full citizenship rights in the reconstructed nation.

During Reconstruction, the Union army (including the U.S. Colored Troops) served as an army of occupation in the South. Although demobilization happened quickly once the Civil War ended, white regiments were often mustered out faster than black regiments, because white regiments had been formed earlier in the war. Therefore, nearly 85,000 black soldiers remained in the Union army at war's end, comprising more than one-third of the federal occupying force. In the immediate aftermath of the Civil War, the Union army provided the only source of order in the war-torn South; one major role played by black troops was keeping the peace. U.S. Colored Troops also helped to distribute rations to needy civilians, clear away rubble, and begin rebuilding the South. The presence of black Union soldiers often inspired former slaves, and black soldiers working in cooperation with the **Bureau of Refugees, Freedmen, and Abandoned Lands** (the Freedmen's Bureau) encouraged local freedpeople in the formation of civic organizations, mutual assistance societies, schools, and political leagues to press for **civil rights** and **black suffrage**. Black troops also protected communities of former slaves, discouraging white southerners from attacking blacks or coercing them into conditions that resembled slavery. By their very presence in southern towns and throughout the countryside, black troops signified that the weight of the U.S. government backed freedpeople's safety and exercise of their rights. Meanwhile, black soldiers who had themselves been slaves before the war often took advantage of their army service as an opportunity to learn to read and write.

Yet, just as army service during the war often proved full of disappointments for black soldiers, serving in the U.S. Colored Troops during Reconstruction fell short of black soldiers' aspirations in many ways. During the war, service in a shared cause helped unite white and black Union troops, and even began to erode some white northerners' racist attitudes. Once victory made that common cause obsolete, many white soldiers who were impatient to get home reverted to earlier prejudices. In Charleston, **South Carolina**, a riot erupted between white and black Union troops in 1865. Alliances between white officers and black soldiers began to break down, sometimes leading black troops to revolt

Unidentified African American soldier on horseback, c. 1865. (Courtesy of the Library of Congress.)

against their officers. In October 1865, one regiment even mutinied in Jacksonville, **Florida**, when an officer tied a soldier up by his thumbs; in response, military authorities executed five enlisted men. Such incidents were rare, but the fact they occurred at all indicated that the equality and civil rights that black troops felt they had earned remained elusive, even within the army.

Black troops faced even more trouble in their interactions with hostile white southerners. To former Confederates, black Union troops as occupying forces symbolized the complete destruction of the southern social order, and utter defeat of the Confederate cause. Plantation owners often felt that the presence of black soldiers disrupted the black labor force by giving black workers ideas about rights and equality. Some responded by trying to discredit black troops as disorderly, vicious, or incompetent, and called on army officials to remove black troops. Others harassed U.S. Colored Troops outright, which led to **violence**. In Augusta, **Georgia**, a city policeman murdered a black private. Whites in Raymond, **Mississippi**, fired on three black soldiers, killing one. In Baton Rouge, a brawl broke out when a white bartender refused to serve six enlisted soldiers. One of the worst occurrences took place in Memphis, **Tennessee**, where the general persecution of black troops by white residents led to the **Memphis Riot (1866)**, a race riot that resulted in the deaths of forty-six blacks, most of them civilians.

The mounting violence became intolerable to Union authorities. In 1865 and 1866, ranking Union army general **Ulysses S. Grant** toured the South, and decided that the persistent hostilities must be stopped. While Grant believed that freedpeople deserved the protection of the U.S. government, he also decided that removing black soldiers might ease tensions. Most black regiments were relocated to coastal forts where they interacted with few civilians, or were sent to western posts. The Twenty-fifth Corps, for instance, was shipped to Texas; France had invaded Mexico, and black soldiers now patrolled the Mexican border to ensure that the French did not invade the United States. For black southerners, the transfer of black troops removed a crucial source of protection from white aggression. For black soldiers, the change often meant more unpleasant duty and unwelcome distance from home and loved ones. Inadequate food, water shortages, and bad weather conditions in Texas led to health problems. As black troops waited out the expiration of their enlistments, much of the early promise of the army seemed to fade.

While the volunteer U.S. Colored Troops eventually mustered out at the end of their enlistments, the worthy service of black soldiers during the Civil War and Reconstruction ensured a place for black troops in the regular U.S. Army. In July 1866, the U.S. Congress reorganized the regular army by passing "An Act to Increase and Fix the Military Peace Establishment of the United States." The Act created two black cavalry regiments, the Ninth and Tenth Cavalry, and four black infantry regiments, which were later consolidated into two black infantry regiments, the Twenty-fourth and Twenty-fifth Infantry. The black regular army regiments served mainly in the West, where they became known as Buffalo Soldiers. Ironically, black soldiers continued to strive for recognition of their full citizenship rights by fighting in the Indian Wars against **American Indians** who resisted the federal government's attempts to turn them into U.S. citizens. At the end of the century, Buffalo Soldiers participated in the Spanish-American War and Philippine Insurrection.

The experiences of black soldiers in the U.S. Colored Troops influenced Reconstruction in several ways. In practical terms, black troops performed critical duties in the immediate aftermath of the war. By guarding, patrolling, cleaning up the rubble of war, and helping to reassert law and order in the defeated South, black troops did much of the day-to-day work of early Reconstruction. To former slaves, black soldiers symbolized liberation and a new relationship between blacks and the U.S. government. To southern whites, black soldiers emphasized the complete destruction of the old social order. For black soldiers themselves, army service staked a claim to full equality that could hardly have been imagined before the Civil War began. Yet, the reality of the army also reflected many of the disappointments blacks confronted in the aftermath of the Civil War, as black troops in Reconstruction continued to face discrimination and hostility. Like Reconstruction itself, service in the U.S. Colored Troops was full of both great promise and tragically unfulfilled hopes for many black Americans. *See also* U.S. Army and Reconstruction.

Further Reading: Berlin, Ira, Joseph P. Reidy, and Leslie S. Rowland, eds. *Freedom: A Documentary History of Emancipation, 1861–1867.* Series II. *The Black Military Experience.* New York: Cambridge University Press, 1982; Glatthaar, Joseph T. *Forged in Battle: The Civil War Alliance of Black Soldiers and White Officers.* New York: The Free Press, 1990; Hahn, Steven. *A Nation under Our Feet: Black Political Struggles in the Rural South from Slavery to the Great Migration.* Cambridge, MA: Harvard

University Press, 2003; McRae, Bennie J., Jr. *Freedom Fighters: United States Colored Troops*. Website [Online July 2004] http://www.coax.net/people/lwf/data.htm; Miller, Steven F. *Freedmen and Southern Society Project*. Website [Online July 2004] http://www.history.umd.edu/Freedmen/home.html; Smith, John David, ed. *Black Soldiers in Blue: African American Troops in the Civil War Era*. Chapel Hill: University of North Carolina Press, 2002.

Chandra Miller Manning

Blaine, James G. (1830–1893)

James Gillespie Blaine, "the continental liar from the State of Maine," was one of the most prominent politicians of the postwar era. His agenda mixed ideology with economics, blunt party power with morality and human values. His career before, during, and after Reconstruction provides a window into the complex men and motives of such a chaotic age.

Early Life and Motivating Forces

Born in Pennsylvania in 1830, he established his political career in Maine, where he relocated in 1854 to edit the influential *Kennebec Journal*. Joining the Republican Party soon after its inception, Blaine was elected to the Maine legislature in 1859, where he quickly became Speaker. His election to the 38th Congress elevated him to the national stage he craved. Serving in the house from March 4, 1863, until July 10, 1876, when he resigned to enter the Senate as a replacement for the retiring Lot M. Morrill, Blaine held the post of Speaker from the 41st through 43rd Congresses. Serving in the Senate from July 10, 1876, to March 5, 1881, Blaine's power was almost unequalled. In 1881, he left the Senate to become secretary of state under President **James Garfield**; Garfield's death in July cut short Blaine's tenure, and he resigned from President Chester Arthur's cabinet on December 12, 1881. Under President Benjamin Harrison, Blaine became secretary of state once again, and served from 1889 until 1892, when ill health forced him to resign.

Blaine's consuming drive for power was based more on his determination to promote the Republican vision of a great and rich nation than on his principled support for **African American** rights in the face of southern Democrat hostility. During the Civil War years, Blaine hitched his star to the Washburn brothers, who controlled Republican politics in Maine, but after the war, while they stayed mired in principles of equality, he turned quickly to consolidating Republican power to guarantee that the **Democratic Party** would not gain national influence. Supporting **black suffrage** on the one hand, while supporting legislation to develop business and overlooking corruption on the other, Blaine represented the contradictions of post–Civil War Republicanism.

For the Good of the Nation and the Party

For Blaine, economics and financial demands held center stage and unified his many goals for the nation. He insisted on federal protection of southern

African American voters, determined that their votes must be counted to offset the votes of the southern Democrats. Opposition by such Conservatives, who cheated black laborers, interfered with Blaine's desire to guarantee Republican plans for a unified, progressive nation based on free labor. At the same time, Blaine stood firmly in the probusiness wing of the Republican Party, championing the hard money businessmen despite demands of farmers, laborers, and miners for the greenbacks or silver coinage that would expand the currency. An adamant supporter of a tariff to protect American manufacturers, Blaine drew the wrath of consumers saddled with the high prices that protected businesses could charge for their products. Courting the votes of those who disliked the increasingly foreign-born American workforce, Blaine backed in the mid-1870s a constitutional amendment prohibiting the use of tax dollars to support religious schools. Aimed at new Catholic immigrants, this amendment did not pass Congress, but many states adopted "Blaine amendments," which remain in effect today. While supporting Republican probusiness economic politics at home, he also worked to expand economic American power abroad, trying to establish a Pan-American Congress to endorse free trade, negotiating reciprocity treaties, and insisting on American control of the immensely valuable Bering Sea seal fisheries (a battle the United States ultimately lost in international arbitration).

Letting others worry about principles and rhetorical effect, Blaine counted votes, plotted election strategies, and used his familiarity with the newspaper business to cozy up to reporters. Using the **patronage** system of political appointment to his best advantage, Blaine built a powerful machine of "Half-Breed" Republicans that rivaled the organization of his personal enemy, Republican **Roscoe Conkling** of New York, leader of the "**Stalwarts**." Blaine was a consummate political insider, central to party politics, but unable to win the popular approval that would carry him to the presidency he wanted so badly.

Fall from Power

Already known as a wheeler and dealer by the early 1870s, Blaine's reputation took a hit with the exposure of the Credit Mobilier **scandal**, which revealed that **railroad** lobbyists had apparently distributed stock to various politicians—including Republican vice president **Schuyler Colfax** and Speaker of the House Blaine—in exchange for favorable legislation. Blaine used his press connections to protest his innocence, reading edited selections from letters between him and a railroad executive about the relevant financial transactions (these letters were known as the "Mulligan letters," after the bookkeeper who produced them, James Mulligan). Convincing enough to hang onto the Speakership, Blaine's performance did not change the growing public perception that he was willing to do almost anything to keep himself and his party in power. His stand against Catholic schools was often interpreted as a sop to racist whites; his determination to protect southern black voting looked to many observers like a desire to use the federal army to control the southern polls and guarantee that the Republicans could not lose an election. When, eager to win the presidential nomination that had passed him by in 1876 and

1880, Blaine endorsed the Chinese Restriction movement that had gained popularity in the West, eastern Republicans dismissed him as pandering to labor. Nominated for president by the Republicans in 1884, with infamous spoilsman John A. Logan as second on the ticket, Blaine represented to many the worst of the Republican Party; he seemed to be a corrupt politician willing to do anything to retain power. Blaine himself sought to counter this impression with the first volume of his masterful *Twenty Years of Congress*, a history of the Civil War era that defended Republican policy as the true policy of the country.

In the vicious campaign of 1884, Blaine and Logan ran against Democratic reformer Grover Cleveland. Hit with the publication of the unedited "Mulligan letters," one of which had an incriminating "Burn this letter" at its conclusion, the Blaine camp responded both with the information that Cleveland had fathered an illegitimate child and with the accusation that Cleveland would enact a Confederate agenda. However, Blaine's "waving the **bloody shirt**" served only to convince voters that he would do anything to win. Democratic rallies dubbed him "the continental liar from the State of Maine." Unable to stomach Blaine, reform Republicans bolted the party and endorsed Cleveland. The votes of these "mugwumps" were critical, and Cleveland won the election, becoming the first Democrat to hold the presidency since the Civil War.

Battered by the campaign, Blaine retired to finish the second volume of *Twenty Years of Congress*, which was published in 1886. Refusing to run for office in 1888, he became Republican president-elect Benjamin Harrison's secretary of state in 1889. Bouts with ill health meant he spent much time away from Washington trying to recuperate, and in 1892, he resigned his post. He died in Washington on January 27, 1893, and was buried in Oak Hill Cemetery. In June 1920, the state of Maine requested his reburial in Augusta, Maine, at the Blaine Memorial Park. *See also* Compromise of 1877; Elections of 1876; Greeley, Horace; House Judiciary Committee; Joint Select Committee on the Conduct of the War; Julian, George Washington; New Departure; Panic of 1873; Redemption; U.S. Army and Reconstruction.

Further Reading: Blaine, James G. *Twenty Years of Congress*. Norwich, CT: The Henry Bill Publishing Company, 1884–1886; Crapol, Edward P. *James G. Blaine: Architect of Empire*. Wilmington, DE: Scholarly Resources, 2000; Healy, David. *James G. Blaine and Latin America*. Columbia: University of Missouri Press, 2001; Muzzey, David Saville. *James G. Blaine: A Political Idol of Other Days*. New York: Dodd, Mead & Company, 1934; Volwiler, Albert T., ed. *The Correspondence between Benjamin Harrison and James G. Blaine, 1882–1893*. Philadelphia: The American Philosophical Society, 1940.

Heather Cox Richardson

Blair, Francis P., Jr. (1821–1875)

A representative and senator from Missouri and a military leader, Francis Preston Blair played a crucial role in keeping Missouri in the Union. As a congressman, he vigorously defended President **Abraham Lincoln**'s early war programs. During the Civil War, he distinguished himself as a divisional and corps commander in several key campaigns.

Francis Preston Blair, Jr.—better known as "Frank" Blair—was born in Lexington, **Kentucky**, on February 19, 1821. His father of the same name (1791–1876), a journalist and politician, was an ardent supporter of Presidents Jackson and Lincoln, and was one of the founders of the Republican Party. Frank's brother, Montgomery **Blair (1813–1883)**, was a lawyer and politician who defended Dred Scott before the **Supreme Court** in 1857 and served as President Lincoln's first postmaster general (1861–1864). After the war, in 1866, the Blair family joined the **Democratic Party** in protest against the **Radical Republicans** and their Reconstruction policy.

As a child, Frank Blair attended private schools in Washington, D.C., where his father edited the influential pro-Jackson *Washington Globe*. After attending the University of North Carolina at Chapel Hill, he graduated from the College of New Jersey (now Princeton University) in 1841. After earning a law degree at Transylvania University in Lexington, Kentucky, he was admitted to the bar in Lexington in 1842. He and his brother then moved to St. Louis, Missouri, and commenced legal practice in 1843.

Blair participated in the Mexican War as an enlisted private, serving briefly as attorney general of the New Mexico Territory in 1847. After the war, he returned to St. Louis to resume law practice, but soon entered into politics as a leader of the Missouri Free-Soil movement. In 1848, he founded the *Barnburner*, a Free-Soil newspaper. Although a slave owner himself, Blair opposed slavery on both moral and economic grounds, advocating gradual **emancipation** of blacks. He was a member of the State House of Representatives in 1852–1856 and served as a congressman in 1857–1859, the only Free-Soiler out of the fifteen slave states. He lost his reelection bid in 1858, but returned to Congress as a Republican in 1860, serving his term in 1861–1862.

A firm antisecessionist, Blair campaigned on behalf of the Union during the Civil War. Immediately after **South Carolina** seceded from the Union to found the Confederate States of America, Blair organized the St. Louis chapter of the pro-Union Wide Awakes, a secret paramilitary force. In May 1861, he teamed up with Captain (later Brigadier General) Nathaniel Lyon to remove full arming in the U.S. arsenal in the southern part of St. Louis from the secessionist militiamen at Camp Jackson. The stolen guns and munitions were then transferred across the Mississippi River to Alton, Illinois, under cover of darkness. This action gave the Union cause a vital boost in Missouri, but it also led to the St. Louis Massacre and intensified the intrastate conflict between Unionists and the southern sympathizers.

Francis P. Blair, Jr., c. 1873. (Courtesy of the Library of Congress.)

Blair recruited seven regiments and was commissioned a brigadier general of volunteers in the **U.S. Army** on August 7, 1862. A major general by November 29 of that year, he commanded Missouri troops in the Vicksburg Campaign, winning the praise from Major General **William T. Sherman** for his military success. Blair also led the Fifteenth Corps at the Battle of Chattanooga, which was the turning point in the Civil War, and commanded the Seventeenth Corps in fierce combat during Sherman's march toward Atlanta. After the fall of Atlanta, Blair led his corps in the "March to the Sea," the Civil War's most destructive campaign against civilians.

In 1866, Blair was appointed collector of customs in St. Louis and commissioner of the Pacific **Railroad**. Two years later, he unsuccessfully ran for vice president of the United States as a Democrat with **Horatio Seymour** as his running mate. After working as a member of the State House of Representatives, he was appointed in 1871 to the U.S. Senate to fill the position vacated by the resignation of Charles D. Drake. Blair retained the seat until 1873, when his bid for a full term failed. In 1874, he suffered an unrecoverable paralytic stroke and died on July 9, 1875. He was interred at Bellefontaine Cemetery in St. Louis. In 1899, the state of Missouri donated a statue of Blair—alongside one of Thomas Hart Benton (1782–1858)—to the National Statuary Hall Collection in the U.S. Capitol. *See also* Blair, Francis P., Sr.; Cabinets, Executive.

Further Reading: Croly, David Goodman. *Seymour and Blair, Their Lives and Services with an Appendix Containing a History of Reconstruction.* New York: Richardson & Co., 1868; Parrish, William E. *Frank Blair: Lincoln's Conservative.* Columbia: University of Missouri Press, 1998; Phillips, Christopher. "The Radical Crusade: Blair, Lyon, and the Advent of the Civil War in Missouri." *Gateway Heritage* 10 (Spring 1990): 22–43; Smith, William Ernest. *The Francis Preston Blair Family in Politics.* 2 vols. 1933; reprint, New York: Da Capo Press, 1969; Wurthman, Leonard B., Jr. "Frank Blair: Lincoln's Congressional Spokesman." *Missouri Historical Review* 64 (April 1970): 263–88.

John J. Han

Blair, Francis P., Sr. (1791–1876)

Patriarch of the powerful Blair family of Missouri, Francis Preston Blair participated in the rise of the Democratic and Republican parties, served as advisor to three presidents, and witnessed the decline of his—and his family's—power and influence.

Born in Abingdon, **Virginia**, Blair moved to **Kentucky** while still quite young. At first attracted to law, he met and married Violet Gist while still in school; the couple had five children, including Montgomery (1813–1883) and Francis Jr. (1821–1875), both of whom became prominent national figures. By the 1820s, Blair had largely abandoned law in favor of journalism and banking. He supported the Henry Clay faction of the National Republicans, but by the end of the decade, he embraced Andrew Jackson and the message of the embryonic **Democratic Party**. Blair's conservatism led him to oppose the tariff, the national bank, and internal improvements, while his understanding of finances, law, and communication made him a national spokesperson for the new party.

Blair moved to Washington with the Jackson administration, and built his estate, "Silver Spring" outside the capital (the genesis of the modern city there). In 1830, he started the *Washington Globe* as the administration's official mouthpiece. Blair was a member of Jackson's unofficial "kitchen cabinet," and helped establish the *Congressional Globe* (now the *Congressional Record*), which reports the debates of Congress.

By the 1850s, as sectional interests and the spread of slavery took center stage, Blair's affiliation with the Democratic Party began to fray. Since the mid-1830s, the family officially hailed from Missouri, when Montgomery moved there to begin his law practice. As a western state, the issue of slavery and westward expansion held more significance for Blair. With the passage of the Kansas-Nebraska Act in 1854, Blair led the charge to create the Missouri Republican Party, and backed the relatively unknown **Abraham Lincoln** in the 1860 election. In the secession crisis of 1861, Missouri—which allowed slavery—teetered on the edge. Blair and his sons played critical roles in keeping the state in the Union, and were rewarded accordingly: Montgomery became postmaster general, Francis Jr. ("Frank") became a Union general, and their father again assumed the role of unofficial advisor to the president.

As the war ground to a close and Lincoln announced his Reconstruction intentions, Blair supported the executive completely. Blair believed the war was to secure the Union and, perhaps, to decide the issue of slavery; those who sought black equality or Confederate retribution were "extremists." Despite his admiration of Lincoln and his sadness at his **assassination**, Blair was not distressed by the rise of **Andrew Johnson** to the presidency.

Blair knew Johnson, as the Tennessean had been in the Senate when Montgomery was in the House of Representatives, plus both sons had dealings with Johnson when he was **military governor** of **Tennessee** during the war. In fact, Johnson rested at Silver Spring after his disastrous vice presidential inauguration speech on March 4, 1865, and both Blair and his son, Montgomery, were witnesses when Johnson was sworn in at the Kirkwood House on April 15.

By the summer of 1865, therefore, Blair found himself the confidant of a third president. As with his other executives, the timing placed him with a man he related to: Both men hailed from slave states, both were staunch Unionists, both were originally Democrats, and both believed the ending of the war had settled the most pertinent issues. Like Lincoln, Johnson approached Reconstruction as reconciliation, a period of transition back to state's rights, a small federal presence, and a white man's society. Blair agreed completely, and his advice ranged from the ridiculous (deporting former slaves to Mexico) to the prophetic (ousting Secretary of State **William Seward** and Secretary of War **Edwin Stanton**, two powerful Republicans). Johnson also often turned to Blair for advice on **patronage** appointments. As **Radical Republicans** grew in numbers and presence, Blair retreated back into the regular Democratic fold and his former conservatism; a vicious cycle developed, for as the president's behavior emboldened the Radicals and alienated Moderates, their responses made many moderate-conservatives become more conservative. Such was the case with Blair and his sons.

During Reconstruction, Blair had three interrelated goals: to help Johnson protect his Reconstruction agenda, help rebuild the northern Democratic Party, and push the favorite son, Frank, into national greatness (many, in and out of the family, looked toward Frank to become president one day). In 1866, Blair was a driving force behind the **National Union Movement**, and used his considerable political influence to urge moderates to join the new party. Deeply disappointed by the losses in the **elections of 1866**, Blair continued his organizing and tried to rebuild the Democratic Party structure in the North. He allied with New Yorker **Horatio Seymour**, and this led to the selection of Frank as Seymour's running mate for the 1868 election. Ironically, this turn of events did more harm than good. It hurt his relationship with Johnson (who naively sought the nomination), and Frank's lack of discretion with his hostile, venomous attacks on **Congressional Reconstruction** earned the party more enemies than friends.

Blair's hopes collapsed with the victory of **Ulysses S. Grant** and the Republicans in 1868. When Johnson left the White House in March 1869, Blair and his sons found themselves without influence and without position. Despondent over the fate of the Democratic Party and the white South, Blair's greatest regret was more personal: his failure to further promote his son Frank's career. Blair straddled homes in Missouri and Maryland, but after Frank suffered a stroke, the father's health declined as well. Frank never fully recovered, and died from an accident in 1875. The blow caused Blair great mental anguish, and his health deteriorated rapidly; he died the following year, in 1876. *See also* Amnesty Proclamations; Black Suffrage; Blair, Francis P., Jr.; Blair, Montgomery; Cabinets, Executive; Democratic National Convention; Elections of 1864; Elections of 1868; Presidential Reconstruction; U.S. Army and Reconstruction.

Further Reading: Parrish, William E. *Frank Blair: Lincoln's Conservative*. Columbia: University of Missouri Press, 1998; Schroeder-Lein, Glenna, and Richard Zuczek. *Andrew Johnson: A Biographical Companion*. Santa Barbara, CA: ABC-CLIO, 2001; Smith, Elbert B. *Francis Preston Blair*. New York: Free Press, 1980; Smith, William Ernest. *The Francis Preston Blair Family in Politics*. 2 vols. 1933; reprint, New York: Da Capo Press, 1969.

Richard Zuczek

Blair, Montgomery (1813–1883)

Montgomery Blair was born in Franklin County, **Kentucky**, the eldest son of **Francis P. Blair, Sr.**, one of the state's leading political figures and founder of the *Washington Globe*. After graduating from West Point in 1836, Montgomery served as a first lieutenant during the Seminole War in **Florida**, but soon resigned his commission to study law and to work under the tutelage of Thomas Hart Benton, a Democratic senator from Missouri. Blair moved to St. Louis in 1839, where he served as U.S. district attorney for Missouri, mayor of St. Louis, and judge of the Court of Common Pleas during the 1840s.

In 1853, Montgomery relocated to Washington, D.C., where he ran a lucrative law practice and, unwilling to accept the expansion of slavery into the territories, began to support the Republican Party. Blair gained national notoriety in 1857, when he unsuccessfully defended Dred Scott, a Missouri slave who sued for his freedom on the ground that his temporary stay in the free

Montgomery Blair, c. 1877. (Courtesy of the Library of Congress.)

state of Illinois had made him a free man. Following the Dred Scott case, Blair encouraged former Jacksonian Democrats to join the Republican Party.

Blair's pronounced Unionism and family connections paid off when President **Abraham Lincoln** appointed him postmaster general in 1861. As a cabinet member, Blair sided with moderates and attacked **Radical Republicans** like Secretary of the Treasury **Salmon P. Chase** for supporting immediate **emancipation**. In the summer of 1862, he warned Lincoln not to issue the Emancipation Proclamation, fearing that it would drive border-state elements to the South. Blair, under pressure from Radical Republicans, resigned from his cabinet position in 1864.

During Reconstruction, Blair left the Republican Party and supported **Andrew Johnson**, a war Democrat who had become president after Lincoln's **assassination** in April 1865. He, along with his father and brother, **Francis P. ("Frank") Blair, Jr.**, exerted great influence upon the president. They advised Johnson to gain the support of border-state Unionists by not giving in to Radical Republicans' demand for harsher measures against the South. Montgomery, like his father, feared that **black suffrage** would lead to racial amalgamation, and wanted Democrats to use the issue of race, not slavery, as a means of garnering political support. "If we can dispose of the slave question," he reasoned, "we shall have the miscegenationists [his term for anyone favoring black voting] in a party to themselves and can beat then easily." Not surprisingly, Montgomery endorsed Johnson's intention to leave **suffrage** in the hands of southern whites.

Blair remained active in politics during the 1870s. In 1874, he attempted to become the **Democratic Party**'s nominee for Congress in the Sixth District of **Maryland** (where he had lived since the late 1850s), but lost because of his associations with the Republicans during the Civil War. He also worked with middle-of-the-road Democrats and Republicans to develop a moderate policy toward the South based on the opposition to **African American** political equality. Blair denounced Republican **Rutherford B. Hayes**'s victory in the controversial presidential **election of 1876**, believing that the **Electoral Commission** had legally elected Democrat **Samuel J. Tilden**. Seven years later, Montgomery died at his estate near Silver Spring, Maryland.

Further Reading: Monroney, Rita. *Montgomery Blair: Postmaster General.* Washington, DC: U.S. Government Printing Office, 1963; Smith, William E. *The Francis Preston Blair Family in Politics.* New York: The Macmillan Company, 1933.

Bruce E. Stewart

Bloody Shirt

Worn with pride by an endless parade of northern politicians, the "bloody shirt" was a rhetorical garment, the inspiring of resentments between North and South for political gain. Republicans used it especially, although occasionally Democrats could use it—and indirectly acknowledged its force whenever they tried to lessen its impact by nominating former Union soldiers for office (which happened regularly, and was one reason why in 1880 the four major parties all chose generals as their standard-bearers). Republican orators like Senator **Oliver P. Morton** of Indiana reminded voters that Democrats had been responsible for the war, or warned them that a change in parties would bring old Confederates back to power, perhaps with the same old designs against the Union. Just after the war, newspapers saw plots by Confederates to build new armies that, working hand in glove with the president, would oust a Republican Congress and install one of their own. Other orators spoke of the atrocities against black former slaves, and Republican voters of both races in the ex-Confederacy, as the "Redeemer" Democrats threatened, whipped, and killed their way toward creating a "Solid South."

As fears of a renewed Civil War faded, the rhetoric changed: former rebels meant to force the North to pay the rebel war debt or "southern claims," or to enact a low tariff as their vengeance against the industrial North. No southerner had a chance of being nominated for president—unless from the border South, and then the chance was a slim one. However, this offered Democrats little real protection. Democratic presidential candidate **Horatio Seymour**, who as governor of New York had protested the stretching of the Constitution to win the war, was portrayed as the friend of draft-resisting rioters; editor **Horace Greeley** was shown clasping hands with the ghost of John Wilkes Booth over the grave of Lincoln; and New York reformer **Samuel J. Tilden**, whose wartime record had been noncommittal, was branded "a demurrer filed by the Confederate Congress against the amendments to the Constitution of the United States." At every election, listeners were urged to vote as they had shot. Veterans organizations like the Boys in Blue marched in Republican parades, to make the point that true loyalty strode to one party's beat; Democratic White Boys in Blue clubs offered only a pale alternative. Former Union soldiers in the Grand Army of the Republic turned Memorial Day into a celebration of the national struggle and eventually into a national holiday, though in the first years, they used the occasion to remind stay-at-homes of who the enemy was; a guard was put around the Confederate gravesites in Arlington to make sure that no traitor decorated *them*.

Historians long dismissed the bloody shirt as cynical rhetoric, a sucker's game of capture the flag. They ascribe the phrase itself to that scapegrace Massachusetts congressman, **Benjamin F. Butler**, who supposedly waved the tattered, blood-spattered shirt of a minister flogged by the **Ku Klux Klan** during one debate in 1871. (There is no record of him doing so, and the phrase dates at least back to 1867, when a newspaper took the image from legends about the Presbyterian Scots Covenanters of the seventeenth century.) In fact, as later scholarship emphasized, the blood was very real, and the fears that the South might rise in war again were sincerely held, sometimes even by reasonable people. Blacks were being killed; the polls in **Alabama** and **Louisiana** were being carried by fraud and **violence**, and "bulldozing," as this muscling out of the Republican vote was called, created a Democratic South by making real democracy practically impossible. Without strong-arm tactics and manipulation of election laws, many southern states would have gone Republican in the 1880s and 1890s, and quite possibly several close presidential elections would have been easy victories for the Grand Old Party (GOP).

The South had its own bloody shirt, as well. Inventing a history of Reconstruction as base tyranny, describing white southerners as enslaved and under "negro rule," Democrats would use fictive and distorted memories to undo every challenge to their rule and warn that any lessening of white supremacy's controls would lead to that perished barbarism. There was no chance of a Union soldier attaining state office in "redeemed" **Tennessee**, and **Kentucky** and Missouri, which never joined the Confederacy, elected a spate of former Confederate governors and senators, in large part because of where they had stood in wartime. No less than in the North, a war record became the easiest way to elected office, and as late as the early 1900s, Jeff Davis, candidate for governor of **Arkansas**, dressed in grey suits with the half-hope that his youth might be overlooked and his name might connect him to Confederate president **Jefferson Davis** himself. (A few voters actually assumed that they were one and the same.) Indeed, the last veteran to hold a seat in Congress died only in 1932—and he was a former Confederate.

Further Reading: Blight, David W. *Race and Reunion: The Civil War in American Society*. Cambridge, MA: Harvard University Press, Belknap Press, 2001; Buck, Paul H. *The Road to Reunion, 1865–1900*. New York: Alfred A. Knopf, 1937.

Mark W. Summers

Bourbons

The term Bourbons refers to a political group comprised of white southerners, who overthrew their respective state's Reconstruction governments during the 1870s to reestablish the racial and social hierarchy of the antebellum South. They are also responsible for the **Redemption** movement in the post-Reconstruction South. As such, they are also commonly referred to as Redeemers.

"Bourbons" began as a derogatory term, which opponents used to parallel the reactionary and vengeful spirit of the white southerners and the Bourbon kings of France, who many scholars characterize in the same way. The term was particularly appropriate in the later 1870s, as antebellum families—or those of that same ilk—returned to power across the southern states, mirroring the return to power of the reactionary, conservative Bourbon family following the defeat of Napoleon in 1815. Comprised of southern Democrats, 90 percent of the group's membership included former Confederate government workers and veterans, but scholars do debate their socioeconomic origins, with some arguing that members represented the antebellum southern elite, and others that most members were simply hungry economic opportunists interested in bringing industrialization to the **New South**. No matter their origins, the Bourbons were united in purpose. Their core message centered around resurrecting the social hierarchy of the antebellum South and wresting political control from the newly freed slaves and the Republican Party.

The Bourbons' desire to reentrench the South in its antebellum social politics was largely a reaction to the social and political policies implemented by Reconstruction governments. These policies gave former slaves unprecedented political power in the former white hegemony. Outnumbering their white counterparts in some states, **African Americans** became a valuable and influential group in the American political process. The results of the presidential **election of 1868** testify to this fact. **Ulysses S. Grant** only won the popular vote with a little more than 300,000 votes, a slim victory. The black vote comprised approximately 500,000 votes in that election, and it is these votes that are credited as being responsible for Grant's victory.

Recognizing the power of **black suffrage** and the threatening political gains being made by the freedmen and the Republican Party, the white conservative Bourbons sought to regain political control by coercively instituting policies and practices that undermined the social and political gains made possible by Reconstruction policies. Such coercive practices successfully reduced the number of former slaves who voted and registered. The Bourbons passed legislation in their respective states that derailed Republican agendas and eviscerated freedmen's newfound **civil rights**.

The Bourbons also sought to cripple the former slaves by sabotaging their opportunities to become financially independent. The Bourbons enacted legislation to heighten the obligations of black tenant farmers and **sharecroppers** to the white landowners. These political efforts proved successful. The political group quickly garnered local support, and eventually remained in control of their respective southern states until the 1890s. During their two decades of power, they regained political and social control of all of the southern states, held one-third of the seats in Congress, and facilitated the introduction of industrialization into the New South.

Though they achieved many of their objectives, the group was criticized for its attitude toward public services. In **Texas**, for example, free public **education** was ended, and in many other states, state governments insisted that local governments shoulder the burden of paying for public education. The Bourbons' disregard for basic public services had a negative effect on the greater population of the South. In some states, illiteracy rates actually went up as a result of Bourbon policies. Historians and contemporary critics use the Bourbons' neglect of public services as a way to illustrate the group's economic greed. Although they are largely regarded as a political group that stood for the return of a white supremacist hegemony in the South, they are also sometimes regarded as economic opportunists, who simply preyed upon the political disarray of the South after the Civil War, and really only sought to exploit the burgeoning economic opportunities in the region. *See also* Compromise of 1877; Democratic Party; Gun Clubs; Jim Crow Laws; Ku Klux Klan; Labor Systems; Readmission; Red Shirts; Violence; White League.

Further Reading: Hart, Roger. *Redeemers, Bourbons, and Populists*. Baton Rouge: Louisiana State University Press, 1975; Richter, William L. *The ABC-CLIO Companion to American Reconstruction, 1862–1877*. Santa Barbara, CA: ABC-CLIO, 1996; Trefousse, Hans L. *Historical Dictionary of Reconstruction*. Westport, CT: Greenwood Press, 1991; Woodward, C. Vann. *The Origins of the New South, 1877–1913*. Baton Rouge: Louisiana State University Press, 1971.

Jennifer Coates

Boutwell, George S. (1818–1905)

Statesman, lawyer, and memoirist, George Sewall Boutwell distinguished himself with sixty years of political service on local, state, and federal levels. Boutwell's political alliances and practices were strongly aligned with the principles of the **Radical Republicans**, and at times his political views were thought extreme.

Boutwell, the son of a farmer, was born in Brookline, Massachusetts. During his teenage years, he worked in a store in Lunenberg and attended local schools. He took an early interest in politics and gained notoriety as a young man by writing newspaper commentaries that fostered collaboration between antislavery Democrats and Free Soilers. His political organizing helped to end the dominance of the Whig Party in Massachusetts and nurtured the fledgling Republican Party in the state's politics. In 1842, he was elected to the Massachusetts State House of Representatives and served there until he was elected governor of the state in 1850. He was a member of the Republican national convention that nominated **Abraham Lincoln** to the presidency. Shortly after Boutwell was admitted to the bar in 1861, Lincoln appointed him the first commissioner of internal revenue.

Radical in War and Reconstruction

In 1863, Boutwell was elected to represent Massachusetts in the U.S. House of Representatives, where he served until 1869. As a congressman, Boutwell became a leader among Radical Republicans, standing alongside more high-profile men such as **Thaddeus Stevens**. Boutwell's commitment to freedmen's **civil rights** and universal **suffrage** compelled him to become one of the primary voices to guide drafts of the **Fourteenth** and **Fifteenth Amendments** to the **U.S. Constitution** and early drafts of plans that would later form the basis of congressional strategies for southern Reconstruction. He was a guiding member of the **House Judiciary Committee**, and in 1867, fearing that President **Andrew Johnson**'s policies would lead to the destruction of the U.S. government and once more bring the country to civil war, Boutwell drafted and submitted the first report that attempted to initiate **impeachment** hearings against the president. When impeachment finally came in early 1868, Boutwell briefly served as chairman of the impeachment managers for the trial, before a strategic move gave the position to a more moderate representative, **John A. Bingham**.

In Grant's Cabinet

President **Ulysses S. Grant** appointed Boutwell secretary of the treasury in 1869. In this capacity, Boutwell took measures to cut the enormous postwar debt, but also overhauled the department's collection procedures and personnel. On September 24, 1869—a date referred to by the popular press of the time as "Black Friday"—Boutwell followed orders from President Grant to release $4 million into the gold market in order to block speculator-conspirators **Jay Gould** and James Fisk from cornering the gold market. Boutwell's unquestioning support for the gold standard later contributed to the temporary demonetization of silver or the "Crime of 1873." Many businesspeople claimed to have been ruined by the ensuing panic, and these affairs cast the administration in an unfavorable light, as it was thought that the presidential administration could have acted more quickly and decisively. Like many politicians of the time, while Boutwell disliked "corruption," political expediency moved him to make practical decisions over purely ideological ones.

Boutwell may be best remembered for his chairmanship of the committee that investigated the suppression of **African American** votes in **Mississippi** in the elections of 1875. The brutality of the events outraged Boutwell, whose dedication to universal suffrage persisted even after he failed in bids for reelection. Boutwell's memoirs of his years in office were completed and released in 1902. He died in Groton, Massachusetts, in 1905. *See also* Ames, Adelbert; Cabinets, Executive; Congressional Reconstruction; McCulloch, Hugh; Panic of 1873; Presidential Reconstruction; Scandals; Sherman, John; White League.

Further Reading: Benedict, Michael Les. *A Compromise of Principle: Congressional Republicans and Reconstruction, 1863–1869*. New York: W. W. Norton & Co., 1974; Bogue, Allan G. *The Earnest Men: Republicans of the Civil War Senate*. Ithaca, NY: Cornell University Press, 1981; Boutwell, George S. *Reminiscences of Sixty Years in Public Affairs*. New York: McClure, Phillips and Co., 1902; Trefousse, Hans L. *The Radical Republicans: Lincoln's Vanguard for Racial Justice*. New York: Knopf, 1969.

Michelle LaFrance

Bristow, Benjamin (1832–1896)

A **Kentucky** Unionist who served as secretary of the treasury in the administration of **Ulysses S. Grant**, Bristow was born in Elkton, Kentucky, the son of Francis Bristow, a prominent lawyer, and his wife, formerly Emily Edwards Helm, a frontier aristocrat. Bristow's paternal grandfather freed his slaves on his deathbed, and his father gradually freed those acquired through his wife. After Bristow graduated from Jefferson College in Canonsburg, Pennsylvania (1851), he studied law in his father's office where he acquired Whig political views that carried over into opposition to secession.

When war came, the Bristows stood firm. The senior Bristows fled to Indiana, while their son responded to a threat of disinheritance from his father-in-law by saying, "you may take your property and go to hell." By the end of 1861, Bristow was lieutenant colonel of the Twenty-fifth Kentucky. Later, he commanded the Eighth Kentucky Cavalry, a regiment involved in the capture of Confederate John Hunt Morgan.

In August 1863, Bristow was elected to the state senate, where he became active in a party of "Unconditional Unionists," who reluctantly supported the enlistment of Kentucky blacks and ratification of the **Thirteenth Amendment**.

Bristow and his allies had formed the nucleus of the Republican Party in Kentucky. After the war, Bristow served as assistant U.S. district attorney for Kentucky, advancing to full district attorney. There he established a commendable record in protecting black **civil rights**, prosecuting vigilantes and **Ku Klux Klansmen**. In addition, the upright Bristow took on evaders of taxes on both tobacco and whiskey.

Bristow's appointment as the first solicitor general of the Department of Justice in 1870 reflected Grant administration hopes for more effective law enforcement and recognition of the chronically weak Republican party of Kentucky. Bristow defended the seizure of rebel property under the **Confiscation Acts** and rebuffed assaults on the Thirteenth, **Fourteenth**, and **Fifteenth Amendments**. Unlike other reformers, who called themselves "**Liberal Republicans**," Bristow loyally supported Grant for a second term. With hopes for appointment as attorney general, Bristow resigned as solicitor general in 1872, but George H. Williams obstructed his advancement. Instead, Bristow began a successful and lucrative practice in corporate law. In 1873, Grant nominated Williams as chief justice, Bristow as attorney general. Williams's unsavory reputation torpedoed both nominations.

In need of reform and honesty, Grant appointed Bristow as secretary of the treasury in 1874. Bristow delivered beyond Grant's hopes and his tolerance. Bristow dismissed the corrupt chief of the treasury's secret service, negotiated lower fees for sales of government bonds, pressed **railroads** for repayment of government subsidies, and attempted to control customhouse corruption. Despite evidence of an increase in government revenues and more responsible administration, such policies roused enemies who whispered that Bristow's motives embraced the 1876 Republican presidential nomination.

Bristow's assault on the Whiskey Ring proved the last straw. For many years, corrupt government officials connived at evasion of legitimate federal taxes on whiskey, with proceeds divided between swindlers and the Republican Party. "Let no guilty man escape," wrote Grant before the investigation of St. Louis frauds exposed his personal secretary, Orville E. Babcock. Unwilling to believe in Babcock's guilt, Grant prepared a deposition in his defense that led to Babcock's acquittal. By the time the trial ended, Grant knew that Babcock had betrayed him, and Bristow had embarrassed him. In 1876, Grant used his influence to deny Bristow the presidential nomination. In 1877, President **Rutherford B. Hayes**'s appointment of Bristow's close associate, John Marshall Harlan, to the **Supreme Court** denied Bristow the only appointment he ever wanted.

The remainder of Bristow's long life was an affluent anticlimax. His support of the Democratic presidential candidate in 1884 against the corrupt Republican **James G. Blaine** demonstrated the response of a dedicated Kentucky Unionist far better qualified for the White House. *See also* Enforcement Acts (1870, 1871); Scandals.

Further Reading: Nevins, Allan. *Hamilton Fish: The Inner History of the Grant Administration.* New York: Dodd, Mead, 1936; Webb, Ross A. *Benjamin Helm Bristow: Border State Politician.* Lexington: University Press of Kentucky, 1969.

John Y. Simon

Brooks-Baxter War (Arkansas)

This 1874 clash between two contending Republican governors effectively ended Reconstruction in **Arkansas**. Republicans came to power in Arkansas following the adoption of the Constitution of 1868, whose ironclad oath denied the franchise to ex-Confederates. In the first state elections, former Union brigadier general **Powell Clayton** was elected governor. Those styled Conservatives declined to participate in politics, but Democrats organized the paramilitary **Ku Klux Klan** to carry on the fight. In what was called the **Militia War**, Clayton not only survived an assassination attempt but also forced the Klan to back down. Meanwhile, Republicans pursued their agendas of economic development through **railroad** construction and **education** creating both a public school system and a state university.

Clayton had trouble holding the various elements of his party together. Mountain Unionists ("**scalawags**") were not enthusiastic about higher taxes or railroads they would never see, and blacks felt they had not received enough in the way of **patronage**. In response both to national and state problems of corruption, a group called **Liberal Republicans** challenged the governor. Liberals called for universal amnesty, which meant giving the vote to ex-Confederates. Powell Clayton managed to remove himself from the direct fray by becoming a U.S. senator in 1871, but only after insuring that Ozra A. Hadley would be his handpicked successor. By the time of the gubernatorial election of 1872, Republicans were divided into two camps, both denominated by nicknames. The "Minstrel" faction—so named because Republican editor John G. Price was a former musician—consisted primarily of northern businessmen ("**carpetbaggers**"). Senator Powell Clayton still led this group. The second set of Republicans were called "Brindletails" because their leader, former Methodist minister Joseph Brooks, had a voice that sounded like a brindle-tail bull. Brooks, a passionate supporter of **civil rights** for the former slaves, also endorsed the program of the national Liberal Republican movement by calling for restoring voting rights to ex-Confederates and ending corruption in office.

In the 1872 gubernatorial election, the Minstrels cunningly nominated native Unionist Elisha Baxter of Batesville to oppose carpetbagger Brooks. A Batesville merchant and lawyer before the Civil War, Baxter had thrown his support to the Union when General Samuel Curtis's army occupied the town in 1862. Forced to flee after Curtis left, Baxter was tracked down in Missouri, brought back to Arkansas, and charged with treason. Little Rock friends engineered his escape, and he then joined the Union army. In 1864, he was rejected by the U.S. Senate along with William M. Fishback when sent to Washington to fill the state's empty senate seats. Baxter had been quietly laboring as a circuit judge prior to his nomination. Succinctly put by the author of this sketch in an earlier publication, "The November 1872 election was a masterpiece of confusion. That carpetbagger Brooks ran with Democratic support against a scalawag nominated by a party composed almost exclusively of carpetbaggers was enough to bewilder most voters as well as the modern student" (Dougan, 258). After massive voting fraud mostly committed by the Minstrels, Baxter was declared the winner.

Brooks then turned to the courts, but made little headway until March 1874, when Baxter vetoed a railroad bond request, thereby questioning whether any of the railroad grants—the economic centerpiece of Republican Reconstruction—were legal. Senator Clayton then decided that Baxter had to go, and, forming an alliance with Brooks, who agreed to support the bond program, he engineered Baxter's removal. A circuit court judge without warning called up Brooks's long dormant case, and without Baxter's attorney even being present, removed Baxter from office. Chief Justice John McClure, who earlier had sworn in Baxter, then administered the oath to Brooks as governor, and on April 15, Brooks, accompanied by an armed force of about twenty men, seized the state house and expelled Baxter. Baxter soon made the nearby Anthony House (and its famous bar) his headquarters.

Abandoned by most Republicans, Baxter was embraced by his antebellum colleagues, the Democrats. Some Democrats who had earlier supported Brooks continued their allegiance, but most gathered around Baxter. Both sides recruited militias, and **African Americans** were divided as well. Ex-Confederates commanded both forces: General Robert C. Newton for Baxter and General James F. Fagan for Brooks. Baxter proclaimed martial law under his "private seal," and even more important, seized Little Rock's telegraph office. To prevent **violence**, two companies of U.S. infantry were stationed between the contesting parties. Both sides issued calls for volunteers. Generally, the railroad depot was in Brooks's hands; the steamboat landing in Baxter's. Both sides composed songs and fired them at each other. Various individuals, including a large number from the press, were taken into custody by both sides at various times. From Washington, Postmaster General John A. J. Creswell ordered the Little Rock postmaster to deliver Baxter's mail to Baxter and Brooks's mail to Brooks, but to hold all letters addressed to "governor of Arkansas." On April 20, following much marching around by Baxter's forces, an accidental gunshot ignited indiscriminate firing, resulting in the death of Little Rock businessman David F. Shall. Seriously wounded in both legs was newspaperman Dan O'Sullivan, later a noted Chicago drama critic. Federal troops responded by using the fire company's hook and ladder wagons to form a barricade supported by pieces of artillery. To the Baxter party, it appeared that the Brooks forces were being protected by the military, but despite high tensions, no attack followed. No federal intervening forces existed elsewhere, and extensive fighting between the partisans developed around the state, costing perhaps as many as 300 lives, the most violent single episode being the Brooks forces attack on Baxter militia aboard the steamer *Hallie*.

Politically, the state's Washington delegation supported Brooks and urged Grant to recognize that government. Baxter, too, had plenty of political support, especially because of the devious way he had been removed from office. Grant, who had greater problems of this sort in **Louisiana**, hesitated to act, and Baxter responded by suggesting that the legislature resolve the matter.

Grant's equivocal response prompted Baxter then to call the legislature into session in May. Secretary of State James M. Johnson countersigned the order, but the state seal was still in Brooks's possession. Both sides continued to collect soldiers, and the Baxter forces repaired an abandoned Confederate eight-inch naval colombiad cannon they christened "Lady Baxter." [This cannon has remained on the grounds of the Old State House (to use the current name) to the present day.] Anxious to prevent the state supreme court from ruling on behalf of Brooks, Baxter supporters stopped the Memphis train and kidnapped judges John E. Bennett and E. J. Searle. Federal authorities began a search for the missing justices, who had been carried off to Benton. An attempt by partisans to hand over the judges to the U.S. military collapsed when Bennett mistook the U.S. soldiers for hostile forces and fled into woods. Only Searle was turned over; Bennett, though, made his way safely to Little Rock.

Meanwhile, legal maneuvering continued. Baxter engaged U. M. Rose, Arkansas' premiere lawyer and founder of the still prominent Rose law firm. Baxter's calling the legislature into special session, a move President Grant finally supported and Brooks opposed, set in motion the events that ended the crisis. Implicit in this move was the calling for another convention to write Arkansas a new constitution. On May 13, 1874, the legislature assembled; on May 15, President Grant came down in support of Baxter; and on May 16, Generals Newton and Fagan negotiated an armistice that ended the "war."

During the summer, the convention wrote the easily adopted Constitution of 1874 that restored voting rights to ex-Confederates and seriously weakened the powers of the governor. Congress, heretofore inactive, now belatedly entered the fray, as Congressman Luke P. Poland and his committee revisited the legal and constitutional issues. Although a majority supported Baxter, President Grant now embraced the minority report. Former lieutenant governor Volney Voltaire Smith then claimed to be the real governor. Newly elected governor Augustus H. Garland proclaimed him a traitor, and Grant, unable at this late date to find meaningful support, relented. After Congress accepted the majority report on March 2, 1875, the end of Republican Reconstruction in Arkansas became final.

Joseph Brooks was paid off by being appointed U.S. postmaster in Little Rock, but died in 1877. Elisha Baxter declined the gubernatorial nomination under the new constitution, hoping instead to get a Senate seat. This never materialized. He died in 1899, and a proposed monument to mark his role in returning Arkansas to the Democrats was never erected.

Further Reading: Dougan, Michael B. *Arkansas Odyssey: The Saga of Arkansas from Prehistoric Times to Present.* Little Rock: Rose Publishing Co., 1994; Harrell, John M. *The Brooks and Baxter War: History of the Reconstruction Period in Arkansas.* St. Louis, MO: Slawson Printing Co., 1893; Moneyhon, Carl. *The Impact of the Civil War and Reconstruction on Arkansas: Persistence in the Midst of Ruin.* Fayetteville: University of Arkansas Press, 2002; Woodward, Earl F. "The Brooks and Baxter War in Arkansas, 1872–1874," *Arkansas Historical Quarterly* 30 (1971): 315–36. See also http://www.oldstatehouse.com.

Michael B. Dougan

Brown, Joseph Emerson (1821–1894)

Joseph Brown, Civil War governor, Reconstruction **scalawag**, and U.S. senator, was born in **South Carolina** on April 15, 1821, to Scotch-Irish parents.

He attended Yale University Law School for one year and began his legal career in Canton, **Georgia**, in 1847, the same year he married Elizabeth Grisham. The couple had eight children.

Elected to the state Senate in 1849, Brown emerged as a Democratic leader. His legislative contacts helped him invest in real estate, mineral rights, and **railroads** that soon made him very wealthy. When the Democratic Convention in 1857 deadlocked over a choice for governor, they nominated Brown. He defeated Benjamin H. Hill, a Know-Nothing candidate, by more than 10,000 votes. A Jacksonian Democrat, Governor Brown refused to give special privileges to banks during the Panic of 1857 and replaced officials of the Western and Atlantic Railroad, the state's richest company, with his cronies. Reelected in 1859, he clamored about the miscegenation that would result if slavery ended. Believing that **Lincoln**'s election meant the end of the southern way of life, he urged secession in January 1861.

As the Confederate government formed and the Civil War began, Governor Brown constantly opposed interference by Confederate officials with the Georgia **militia**. Inaugurated for a third term in November 1861, he tried to control the Georgia home front by monitoring troop movements, distributing salt and food, and providing relief for soldiers and their families. Elected for a fourth term in 1863, he tried to bolster state morale as the Yankees approached from **Tennessee**. By the summer of 1864, as the fall of Atlanta neared, Brown denounced the tyranny and incompetence of Confederate president **Jefferson Davis**. In late 1864, as General **William T. Sherman** moved steadily toward the sea, the governor called for a national peace convention to end the war. In February 1865, he furloughed the state militia and awaited his fate as a defeated Confederate governor.

On May 7, 1865, President **Andrew Johnson** ordered the arrest of Governor Brown and seizure of his papers. Incarcerated at Carroll Prison in Washington, D.C., the president pardoned him in September. He journeyed throughout the nation and urged acceptance of the end of slavery and applauded Johnson's moderate Reconstruction policies. Believing that southern whites momentarily must accept their defeat, he urged that blacks be granted legal rights. He favored the **Fourteenth** and **Fifteenth Amendments**. Throughout 1866 and 1867, he effectively lobbied in Washington, D.C. on behalf of Georgia railroads. By 1867, he approved moving the state capital to Atlanta, where he represented scores of prominent businessmen. During Radical Reconstruction, he encouraged conservative whites to accept the inevitable changes that the end of slavery brought and he urged blacks not to push too fast for radical change. By 1868, he openly embraced Republicans and received **patronage** from Republican governor **Rufus Bullock**, including his appointment as the prosecutor in a prominent case of the assassination of a local scalawag. He stumped the state during the 1868 presidential campaign in favor of Republican **Ulysses Grant**. In return for his support, Brown was appointed chief justice of the State Supreme Court in August 1868. As Radicals prohibited Confederates from holding office and elected black legislators, white conservatives seethed. They returned to power in 1870, as Radicals overextended their power through electoral fraud and corruption.

By 1872, many Democrats saw the wisdom of Brown's counsel of momentarily accepting change and they urged him to rejoin the Democratic Party. Supported by *Atlanta Constitution* editor Henry Grady, he replaced Senator John Gordon in the U.S. Senate in May 1880. Serving in Washington until 1890, he continued to control Georgia's railroads and amass an ever larger fortune. He died on November 30, 1898. *See also* Scandals.

Further Reading: Cimbala, Paul. *Under the Guardianship of the Nation: The Freedmen's Bureau and the Reconstruction of Georgia*. Athens: University of Georgia Press, 1997; Davis, William C. *The Union That Shaped the Confederacy: Robert Toombs and Alexander Stephens*. Lawrence: University of Kansas Press, 2001; Parks, Joseph H. *Joseph E. Brown of Georgia*. Baton Rouge: Louisiana State University Press, 1977; Roberts, Derrell C. *Joseph E. Brown and the Politics of Reconstruction*. University: University of Alabama Press, 1973. See also "Reconstruction in Georgia" at http://www.sosu.edu/lib/subh1865.htm.

Randy Finley

Browning, Orville Hickman (1806–1881)

Orville Hickman Browning, Illinois lawyer and politician, served as secretary of the interior and interim attorney general under **Andrew Johnson**. Born near Cynthiana, **Kentucky**, Browning attended Augusta College in Augusta, Kentucky (1826–1829), but had to leave before graduating because of family financial difficulties. He read law with his uncle, William Brown, in Cynthiana, and after being admitted to the bar in 1831, Browning moved to Quincy, Illinois.

In addition to practicing law, Browning became involved in politics as a Whig. An opponent of costly internal improvement plans, Browning served a term in the state senate (1836–1840) and the state house of representatives (1842–1844). After a vigorous contest in 1843, Browning lost the race for a congressional seat to Democrat Stephen A. Douglas. Browning was later defeated for the same seat by Democrat William A. Richardson in 1850 and 1852.

When the Whig Party died in the early 1850s, Browning, who opposed slavery and its extension into the territories, helped to organize the Republican Party in Illinois in 1856. Although well-acquainted with **Abraham Lincoln** from years of law practice on the circuit, Browning favored Edward Bates of Missouri for the Republican presidential nomination in 1860. However, as an Illinois delegate to the nominating convention, Browning pledged to support Lincoln and campaigned for his election.

Although Browning did not receive any **cabinet** or court appointment from Lincoln, on June 12, 1861, Illinois governor Richard Yates appointed Browning to the U.S. Senate as an interim replacement for the deceased Stephen A. Douglas. Browning voted as a conservative Republican on the various measures before that chamber until January 30, 1863, when he was succeeded by the choice of the Illinois General Assembly, William A. Richardson. After a few months in Quincy, Browning returned to Washington, D.C., as a lawyer and a lobbyist.

After Lincoln's **assassination**, Browning became a strong supporter of Andrew Johnson's Reconstruction policy. Browning favored conciliating the South and opposed extending the **Bureau of Refugees, Freedmen, and**

Abandoned Lands. When Secretary of the Interior James Harlan resigned from the cabinet because he disagreed with Johnson's policies, the president nominated Browning as Harlan's replacement in July 1866. Browning helped to plan and also attended the **National Union Party** convention in Philadelphia in August. Browning was one of several who urged Johnson not to make impromptu speeches on his **Swing Around the Circle** in August–September 1866, advice the president ignored.

As secretary of the interior, Browning dealt with land cessions, public lands, the transcontinental **railroad**, pensions, patents, **American Indian** affairs, and **patronage** matters for Indian agencies and land offices. From March 31 to July 20, 1868, Browning also served as interim attorney general when **Henry Stanbery** resigned the office in order to join Johnson's defense team during the **impeachment** crisis.

After Johnson's presidential term ended in March 1869, Browning returned to Quincy. He played a role in the Illinois state **constitutional convention** of 1869–1870, but held no further political offices. Instead he practiced law, frequently representing the Chicago, Burlington, and Quincy Railroad. *See also* Presidential Reconstruction; Republicans, Moderate.

Further Reading: Baxter, Maurice G. *Orville H. Browning: Lincoln's Friend and Critic*. Bloomington: Indiana University Press, 1957; Randall, James G., ed. *The Diary of Orville Hickman Browning*. 2 vols. Springfield: Illinois State Historical Library, 1925–1933.

Glenna R. Schroeder-Lein

Brownlow, William G. ("Parson") (1805–1877)

William Gannaway Brownlow, Methodist preacher, Whig newspaper editor, southern Unionist, and Reconstruction governor of **Tennessee**, was born in 1805 in Wythe County, **Virginia**. Orphaned at age eleven, he was subsequently raised by relatives and apprenticed as a carpenter. He experienced conversion at a camp meeting in 1825 and later became a Methodist minister. In 1836, after a decade on the preaching circuit in southern Appalachia, he married, gave up the ministry, and settled in East Tennessee. Drawn to politics and idolizing Henry Clay, Brownlow became editor of a Whig newspaper in Elizabethton in 1839, moved it to Jonesboro two years later, and in 1849 moved it to Knoxville, which became his permanent home.

As a child of poverty and of the semifrontier environment of the early nineteenth-century southern mountain region, Brownlow had little formal schooling. Although he educated himself to a remarkable level of literacy, he could never boast of great learning or refinement; his language and manners reflected the rough culture he grew up in. As a preacher and editor, and later as a politician, his style was no-holds-barred. On the masthead of his newspaper (*The Whig*) was the motto he lived by: "Cry Aloud and Spare Not." He defended his causes and denounced his enemies with great vehemence and sarcastic wit. In his eyes, those enemies were many, including Presbyterians, Baptists, Catholics, Democrats, immigrants, drinkers, **abolitionists**, and secessionists above all. Many of them responded in kind: During his lifetime, Parson Brownlow (as he was generally known) was often assaulted rhetorically and several times physically. Even his opponents, however, had to admit that the private Brownlow contrasted starkly with the public man, for he was unfailingly kind and generous in his personal relations.

Brownlow and the Sectional Crisis

As the North-South dispute heated up in the 1850s, Brownlow, like most of his fellow southern mountaineers, rejected secession and vowed fidelity to the Union. His Unionism was not based on any antislavery principles, for he was an outspoken defender of slavery. In his view, the sectional troubles had been stirred up by extremists on both sides—scheming, self-interested southern politicians and fanatical northern abolitionists. Through his widely read newspaper, Brownlow gained a reputation as an uncompromising southern loyalist and won a large following.

Like the other states of the Upper South, Tennessee remained predominantly Unionist even after **Abraham Lincoln**'s election to the presidency in 1860, which provoked the Deep South to secede and form the Confederate States of America. With the outbreak of war in April 1861, however, public sentiment in Middle and West Tennessee (where slavery and plantations were more prevalent than in East Tennessee) went over to secession. East Tennessee held firm, however.

Brownlow played a leading role in the Unionist convention held in Greeneville, Tennessee, in June 1861, following Tennessee's secession. The convention petitioned the state legislature to allow East Tennessee to break off as a separate state. The petition got nowhere, but the East Tennessee Unionist movement remained strong and became a thorn in the side of the state and Confederate governments.

Those governments at first tried to conciliate the disaffected East Tennesseans. Brownlow was even permitted to go on publishing his antisecession editorials (the only editor in the Confederacy to do so after the war began). Conciliation failed to win over the Unionists, however, and the authorities cracked down in late 1861. Brownlow's press was seized, and he was imprisoned in Knoxville. Charged with treason but offered leniency if he disavowed his Unionism, he stubbornly refused and prepared stoically for the hanging he expected. The authorities eventually decided to banish rather than hang him, and in March 1862, he was permitted to travel to the North, where he

William G. Brownlow. (Courtesy of the Library of Congress.)

promptly went on the lecture circuit and published a best-selling book about his experiences in the Confederacy.

When a Union army invaded East Tennessee in the fall of 1863, Brownlow returned to Knoxville, reestablished his newspaper, and resumed his anti-Confederate editorial diatribes. He also served as a U.S. Treasury agent and helped raise money for the relief of impoverished Tennessee loyalists. He quickly emerged as a leader of the state's Radical Unionists, who favored dealing harshly with secessionists and abolishing slavery. (Brownlow's about-face on slavery was spurred not by any sympathy for the slaves but by his desire to punish secessionists.) Conservative Unionists took issue with the Radicals on these points but were overpowered politically.

In January 1865, with Tennessee firmly under Union army control, a Radical-dominated Unionist convention met in Nashville and set in motion the state's political restoration. In an election held in March 1865, in which only Unionists could vote, Brownlow was elected governor of Tennessee. He assumed office on April 5, just before the Confederacy collapsed and the war ended.

Brownlow and Reconstruction

Tennessee had a distinctive Reconstruction experience under the Brownlow administration. As a fully functioning loyalist entity in operation when the war ended, the state government played no part in the **Presidential Reconstruction** program instituted in the late spring of 1865 by **Andrew Johnson**. Moreover, in July 1866, the Tennessee legislature ratified the **Fourteenth Amendment** to the **U.S. Constitution**, whereupon Congress readmitted the state to the Union. Tennessee was the only former Confederate state readmitted before **Congressional Reconstruction** was imposed in 1867, and thus the only one exempted from it.

Brownlow's tenure as governor was controversial from the start. The main point of contention was the franchise. The legislature elected along with Brownlow was solidly Radical, and one of its early actions, taken at the governor's urging, was to deny the vote to all who had supported the Confederacy. The governor was not content with this proscription, however, because it allowed Conservative Unionists (by now reconciled to **emancipation** but still advocating leniency to Confederates) to vote. In the August 1865 Tennessee congressional elections, the Conservatives won four of eight seats, alarming Brownlow. Reacting forcefully but with questionable legality, the governor invalidated enough Conservative votes to give one of those four seats to the Radical candidate. Nevertheless, he remained fearful of Conservative strength. In 1866, the legislature gave Brownlow control over voter registration, which he deviously used to keep many Conservative Unionists as well as ex-Confederates from the ballot box. In early 1867, he made his most controversial move yet, calling for (and securing from his compliant legislature) **black suffrage**, a measure bitterly opposed by Conservative Unionists and ex-Confederates. Brownlow, who remained a devout white supremacist at heart, took this step for purely partisan reasons, knowing that the blacks would vote Radical. Tennessee thus became the first southern state to fully enfranchise black men. That same month (February 1867), in order to help ensure Radical control of the polling places at election time, the legislature created the State Guard, a **militia** composed of soldiers (black and white) loyal to Brownlow.

These measures assured Brownlow an easy reelection in August 1867 and another Radical-dominated legislature for his second term, but they also alienated many of his followers and provoked fierce resistance from his enemies. By mid-1867, there was widespread **violence** in opposition to Radical rule in Tennessee, notably that carried out by the **Ku Klux Klan**. To counter it, Brownlow mobilized the State Guard and cracked down using state acts that outlawed political terrorism and gave the governor power to impose martial law in unruly districts. Anti-Radical violence continued despite Brownlow's counterattack, although it was insufficient to prevent Tennessee from going Republican in the 1868 presidential election.

End of the Brownlow Regime

As early as 1867, Brownlow had let it be known that he wanted a U.S. Senate seat. In February 1869, when one became vacant, the legislature gave it to him and he resigned the governorship. Not long after he departed for Washington, the Radical party in Tennessee succumbed to factionalism, violence, and election fraud. In the August state elections it was swept from power and Tennessee's Reconstruction period came to an end.

Brownlow, by now in poor health, managed to serve out his term in the Senate but kept a low profile, focusing mainly on securing federal compensation for Tennessee Unionists' wartime losses. He retired to Knoxville in 1875, where he continued to live until his death in 1877.

Few historians have had much good to say about Brownlow's governorship. Certainly his vitriolic rhetoric and uncompromising partisanship were inappropriate for an American political leader, even in the extreme conditions of Reconstruction; and his manipulation of ballots and voter registration was indefensible, to say the least. In addition, although he was personally untainted by corruption, the government Brownlow presided over was riddled with it, especially in connection with state underwriting of **railroad** construction. Nevertheless, his administration did have some laudable achievements: a modernized public school system that provided for black **education**, laws that gave blacks **civil rights** and legal protection, and of course **black suffrage**. Although Brownlow supported most of these measures for less than idealistic reasons (the public education act was an exception), and although all were soon gutted by the "redeemers" after the Radicals' downfall, Brownlow's four-year rule should be remembered as a time of unparalleled progress for black Tennesseans. *See also* Disfranchisement; Scandals.

Further Reading: Ash, Stephen V., ed. *Secessionists and Other Scoundrels: Selections from Parson Brownlow's Book.* Baton Rouge: Louisiana State University Press, 1999; Coulter, E. Merton. *William G. Brownlow: Fighting Parson of the Southern Highlands.* Knoxville: University of Tennessee Press, 1999; Kelly, James C. "William Gannaway Brownlow." *Tennessee Historical Quarterly* 43 (1984): 25–43, 155–72.

Stephen V. Ash

Bruce, Blanche Kelso (1841–1898)

Blanche K. Bruce was a black political leader and the first **African American** to serve a full term in the U.S. Senate. Born a slave in Farmville, **Virginia**, in Prince Edward County, he may have been the son of his owner. He was comparatively well treated as a youngster and was taught to read and write by the same tutor who instructed his master's white son. Bruce was taken briefly to **Mississippi** and then to Missouri where he learned the printing trade. His beneficent treatment notwithstanding, he escaped to Kansas in 1861. He subsequently returned to Missouri and opened a school for black children in Hannibal. He may have attended Oberlin College briefly before becoming a porter on a Mississippi River steamboat.

In 1867, Bruce settled in Mississippi and became active in Republican politics. He served as an election commissioner and then sergeant at arms for the state senate. Well-spoken, charming, and unfailingly courteous, he became a skilled politician with a reputation for moderation that garnered him the respect and support of blacks and whites. He was on compatible terms with many Democrats, including L.Q.C. Lamar. He emerged as Bolivar County's chief power broker, where he served as sheriff, superintendent of education, tax collector, and editor of the Foreyville *Star*. He also acquired a 1,000-acre plantation. In 1873, he declined Republican suggestions that he run for lieutenant governor.

With the support of Governor **Adelbert Ames**, the Mississippi legislature elected Bruce to the U.S. Senate in 1874, and he served from 1875 to 1881. He supported federal aid for **railroads** and opposed the Chinese Exclusion Act of 1878. He called for a more just policy toward **American Indians**. He spoke out in opposition to the exodus of African Americans from the South to Kansas in 1879, and he counseled black people not to fall prey to Back-to-Africa movements. His efforts to gain legislation to reimburse depositors in the bankrupt **Freedmen's Savings Bank** failed. He worked diligently to secure federal **patronage** for Republicans in Mississippi. Although genteel and circumspect, he spoke bluntly and vainly in opposition to white **violence** as Democrats sought to redeem Mississippi in 1875.

Bruce remained in Washington after his term expired. He served as register for the U.S. Treasury from 1881 to 1885 and 1897 to 1898. There was an unsuccessful effort to promote Bruce for a **cabinet** position in the McKinley administration in 1897. By the 1890s, Bruce was a strong advocate for Tuskegee Institute president Booker T. Washington and his benign racial policies.

Blanche Kelso Bruce, c. 1877. (Courtesy of the Library of Congress.)

In 1878, Bruce married Josephine B. Wilson, the daughter of a well-to-do dentist from Cleveland. They had one son. At the time of his death, Bruce was reportedly worth $100,000. He was buried in Washington, D.C.

Further Reading: Harris, William C. "Blanche K. Bruce of Mississippi: Conservative Assimilationist." In Howard N. Rabinowitz, ed., *Southern Black Leaders of the Reconstruction Era*. Urbana: University of Illinois Press, 1982; Gatewood, Willard B. *Aristocrats of Color: The Black Elite, 1880–1920*. Bloomington: Indiana University Press, 1990; Urofsky, Melvyn. "Blanche K. Bruce: United States Senator, 1875–1881." *Journal of Mississippi History* 29 (1967): 118–41; Wharton, Vernon Lane. *The Negro in Mississippi 1865–1890*. Chapel Hill: University of North Carolina Press, 1947.

William C. Hine

Bullock, Rufus B. (1834–1907)

The only Republican governor of **Georgia** until 2002, New York–born Rufus Brown Bullock's short political career brought into sharp contrast the complexities facing the South after the war. Bullock's saga is one of opportunism and opportunity, morality and malignance. Known to many only through the vindictive portrait found in Margaret Mitchell's *Gone with the Wind*, Bullock was actually a well-intentioned, if egotistical, northern proponent of a **new South**.

Bullock was born in 1834 in Bethlehem, New York, but grew up in Albion. Educated at the Albion Academy, Bullock soaked up the progressive local environment and developed a taste for **abolition** and technological experimentation. By the early 1850s, he had married Rhode Island native Elizabeth Salisbury and moved to Philadelphia to work for the American Telegraph Company. In 1856 or 1857, he moved to Augusta, Georgia, to take advantage of the burgeoning telegraph and **railroad** business developing in the South.

When the secession crisis struck Georgia, Bullock remained a staunch Unionist but was unable to cut ties to his adopted state. He stayed in Georgia when the state seceded, and—perhaps to avoid persecution or a combat assignment—accepted a position in the Confederate army's quartermaster corps. His technical and business skills made him valuable, and they also made him a lieutenant colonel supervising various railroad and telegraph operations.

A Yankee Scalawag

When the war ended, Bullock, like many whites in the South, felt little beyond defeat and dismay. However, the northerner had no deep association with slavery, the Confederate cause, or state's rights idolatry, so he was able to quickly see opportunity in the mayhem. He was dubious about President **Andrew Johnson**'s rapid restoration program, and his Yankee upbringing questioned the morality and practicality of ignoring the freedpeople's needs. Bullock was no radical reformer, but he was a progressive thinker, and he calculated that a prosperous new Georgia—and a new South—could rise from the ashes of the Confederacy. Building this new Georgia would require spectacular social, political, and economic changes, and he could not see how former confederates, or Andrew Johnson, would allow this to happen.

Therefore, as congressional Republicans gradually wrestled control of Reconstruction policy from the president, Bullock migrated into politics. Following the passage of the **Military Reconstruction Acts** in 1867, Bullock was elected to serve in the state's **constitutional convention** that convened in December. Along with a liberal new constitution, the convention also proposed another initiative, moving the state capital to Atlanta. The vote on that issue, as well as the state offices and constitution itself, was set for the next spring.

Establishing a new state government would not be easy. In December, General George Gordon Meade became the new Third District commander, and ordered the state to pay the costs associated with the convention. Governor **Charles Jenkins**, elected under Johnson's Reconstruction program, refused to release the funds, and instead removed them and escaped to New York, where he deposited them in a bank. Meade removed Jenkins from office, made General Thomas H. Ruger provisional military governor, and proceeded with the elections in April. Rufus Bullock was the Republican gubernatorial candidate, opposing former Confederate general **John B. Gordon**. Bullock won the close election, but had nary a mandate; because of Republican factions and infighting, control of the legislature was not as clear. Nonetheless, Bullock proceeded to do his duty.

As governor, Bullock saw two priorities: fulfill the necessary requirements for Georgia's **readmission** to the Union, and rebuild the state's shattered economy. He was ultimately successful at both, yet the paths taken were arduous and meandering, with Bullock serving as more or less a martyr to both causes. He quickly embarked on an expansive—and expensive—series of loans and borrowing to begin rebuilding the state's infrastructure and communications network. His business contacts crossed party and regional lines, and brought a great deal of money into the state—money for erecting a new capital city, rebuilding railroads, laying telegraphs, and constructing bridges and canals. These improvements opened the door for other investments, such as for schools and factories. Of course, the money also brought **scandal** and accusations, and certainly there were those who benefited personally from the spending. Margaret Mitchell's prejudiced portrait of Bullock in her novel *Gone with the Wind* pays particular attention to alleged nefarious dealings by the governor, but the momentum he initiated, merging public and private interests into a common progressive venture, far outlived his tenure as governor.

Problems of Readmission

Success with many long-term business enterprises seemed overshadowed by Governor Bullock's problems returning Georgia to the Union. At first, prospects seemed good; the constitution and the **Fourteenth Amendment** were ratified in the April election, and in June, Congress readmitted Georgia to the Union. But the summer witnessed a backlash, with the appearance of **Ku Klux Klan** cells (many tied to John B. Gordon) and a rise in **violence** against black and white Republicans. The 1868 presidential campaign increased tensions, and the inflammatory statements made by Democratic vice presidential nominee **Francis P. Blair Jr.** encouraged opposition to Congress's Reconstruction measures. In September 1868, conservatives and some moderates in the new legislature joined forces to declare black membership illegal; they nullified the election of twenty-eight **African American** members, and against Bullock's exhortations, expelled the men. Already admitted and now under control of conservatives, the legislature refused to ratify the **Fifteenth Amendment** the following spring.

Sincerely believing in political rights for blacks, and knowing that a hostile legislature would spell doom for his plans, Bullock risked his political and financial fortunes and traveled to Washington to see the new president. Bullock had an unusual request of President Grant—that Georgia be remanded to military supervision, effectively kicked back out of the Union. The Grant administration eventually concurred, and in December 1869, placed Georgia back under military supervision and ordered Third District Commander Alfred Terry to reassemble the original 1868 legislature. In January 1870, Terry and Bullock formed a committee to inspect legislators' credentials, and the general removed many conservatives from the assembly. The following month, Bullock's new legislature ratified the Fifteenth Amendment and reapplied for readmission. In July, Congress readmitted Georgia to the Union, again.

However, Bullock's success was short-lived. Although he had been elected to a four-year term, the legislature only sat for two. So, since this was the 1868 body, new elections were called in December 1870, which resulted in a Democratic victory. Many say that Bullock's gamble—placing the state back under military control—backfired; in any case, the incoming legislature that following autumn was a hostile one.

Outcast and Insider: Life after the Governorship

Even before the incoming legislature convened in November 1871, reports were circulating about plans to impeach Bullock. For reasons no one knows clearly, Bullock decided not to risk the fight. In October, he quietly pulled up stakes and moved the family back north. The democratic legislature met in November, and held a special election in December; conservative James M. Smith was elected governor.

Bullock and his family remained in the North until he was located and arrested in 1876. Despite nebulous charges of malfeasance and chicanery, he returned to Georgia for trial, and was acquitted of any wrongdoing. Strangely, given the circumstances of his departure and his return, Bullock opted to stay in Atlanta. He became one of the city's most prominent citizens, a veritable symbol of the trials, tribulation, and finally the rise of a new Georgia. Bullock became president of the city's first cotton mill, president of a loan company, served on many public and industrial boards, and was twice president of the Atlanta Chamber of Commerce.

In declining health, Bullock and his wife returned to Albion, New York, in 1903, and he died there in 1907. His vision for a new Georgia was only half realized; Atlanta's symbol, the Phoenix, certainly captures the spirit of the city's entrepreneurial success, but unfortunately Georgia's social progress took far longer to materialize. *See also* Akerman, Amos T.; Black Politicians; Congressional Reconstruction; Elections of 1868; Presidential Reconstruction; Provisional Governors; Redemption; U.S. Army and Reconstruction.

Further Reading: Drago, Edmund L. *Black Politicians and Reconstruction in Georgia: A Splendid Failure*. Baton Rouge: Louisiana State University Press, 1982; Duncan, Russell. *Entrepreneur for Equality: Governor Rufus Bullock, Commerce, and Race in Post–Civil War Georgia*. Athens: University of Georgia Press, 1994; Nathans, Elizabeth Studley. *Losing the Peace: Georgia Republicans and Reconstruction, 1865–1871*. Baton Rouge: Louisiana State University Press, 1969.

Richard Zuczek

Bureau of Refugees, Freedmen, and Abandoned Lands

The Bureau of Refugees, Freedmen, and Abandoned Lands, commonly known as the Freedmen's Bureau, was a branch of the U.S. War Department created near the end of the Civil War to oversee the South's transition from slavery to freedom. Often considered the first federal social welfare agency in American history, the bureau was involved in a vast array of activities from the Confederate surrender through the end of 1868, when its responsibilities were significantly curtailed, until its June 1872 closing. The Freedmen's Bureau never received the resources sufficient to fulfill its broad mandate, and although it represented an unprecedented expansion of federal authority and involvement in everyday life, it was nonetheless envisioned as a temporary expedient rather than a long-term solution to the challenge of reconstructing southern society. Former slaves viewed the bureau as their main ally in the postwar South, but the bureau confronted the animosity of most white southerners, the opposition of President **Andrew Johnson** and other Democrats, and even the reservations of many of its Republican supporters over increasing federal power. All of these factors undermined the bureau's effectiveness and contributed to its mixed legacy. While the bureau dramatically improved the lives of thousands of freedmen and indigent whites during the immediate postwar years, it could not fulfill all the responsibilities with which it was entrusted, nor could it realize the hopes that freedmen and their advocates had invested in it.

Background and Establishment

The origins of the Freedmen's Bureau lay in the efforts of the War Department, Treasury Department, and various northern benevolent organizations to address the disruption of southern civilian life during the Civil War. Fugitive slaves who had fled to federal lines—as the Union army gained Confederate territory—required humanitarian aid, as did white southern Unionists driven from their homes. Throughout the Union-held South, thousands of former slaves worked under federally sponsored free-labor arrangements on abandoned and confiscated plantations, while thousands more, especially the families of black soldiers and military laborers, lived and worked within the confines of **contraband** camps, "freedmen's villages," or "home colonies." Along the Atlantic coast, in parts of the Upper South, and throughout the Mississippi Valley, federal authorities worked with philanthropic organizations and private individuals to provide relief and assist former slaves in making the transition to freedom.

Even before Union victory was assured, congressional Republicans considered the need for a federal agency to oversee the process of transition throughout the South. In December 1863, a bill calling for a federal "bureau of **emancipation**" was introduced in the U.S. House of Representatives. It passed the following March but stalled in the Senate for a year owing to Democratic charges that the proposed bureau was unconstitutional and to Republican disagreement over whether the agency should be part of the War Department or Treasury Department. Republican senatorial debate reflected ongoing conflicts in the South between officials of these two executive departments over control of abandoned and confiscated plantations and their lucrative crops. Not until early 1865, with Union victory imminent, did Republicans agree to locate the bureau within the War Department. On March 3, Congress passed a bill, which president **Abraham Lincoln** immediately signed, creating the Freedmen's Bureau.

The 1865 Freedmen's Bureau bill established within the War Department—for the remainder of the war and for one year thereafter—a "bureau of refugees, freedmen, and abandoned lands" that was charged with the supervision and management of abandoned lands and "the control of all subjects relating to refugees and freedmen from rebel states." The bureau was to be headed by a commissioner appointed by the president, who was also authorized to appoint up to ten assistant commissioners to head the bureau in the ex-Confederate states. The legislation empowered the secretary of war to issue provisions, clothing, and fuel for the relief of destitute refugees and freedmen. It also authorized the commissioner, under the president's direction, "to set apart, for the use of loyal refugees and freedmen," abandoned and confiscated land within the insurrectionary states, stipulating that "every male citizen" could rent up to forty acres of such land for three years with an option to purchase at any time during this period.

Commissioner Howard and the Bureau

The first and only Freedmen's Bureau commissioner was General **Oliver Otis Howard**, a graduate of Bowdoin College and the U.S. Military Academy at West Point and a distinguished Civil War veteran who had lost his right arm in battle. An avowed Christian, Howard's missionary zeal and connections to **Freedmen's Relief Societies** earned him the moniker "Christian General" and, along with his war record, made him a leading candidate for the position. Howard's first task was to assemble a staff, including members of his Washington, D.C., headquarters as well as assistant commissioners for the southern states. Since Congress made no separate appropriation for the bureau, while also authorizing the detailing of military officers for bureau duty, Howard relied mostly upon army personnel in staffing the bureau. For the original assistant commissioners, he nominated men who had served with him or who had been involved in freedmen's affairs during the war.

While the racial and political views of individual assistant commissioners and other bureau personnel varied widely, most bureau officials saw themselves as engaged in the mission to remake the South upon a free-labor basis. Given time and guidance, they believed, former slaveholders and freedmen would come to see the benefits of a **labor system** predicated upon mutual consent and the freedom to **contract** rather than upon coercion. Since most bureau officials hailed from middle-class backgrounds and were well educated, they articulated commonly held northern assumptions about the moral superiority and greater efficiency of voluntary over involuntary labor and about the supremacy of the marketplace. Although prevailing white attitudes on race led most bureau officials to conclude that it would take longer for blacks to internalize the values of the marketplace than it would for whites, many also demonstrated an almost naive belief that freedmen and their former masters would soon overcome slavery's bitter legacy.

The Freedmen's Bureau was involved in a program of social change, but its organizational structure was military in nature. Howard's Washington headquarters initially included an assistant adjutant general, a chief disbursing officer, a chief medical officer, and a head of the Land Division. In 1866, he added a superintendent of **education**, a chief quartermaster, and a head of the Claim Division, which assisted black veterans in filing and collecting claims for bounties, pay, and pensions. The staffs of the assistant commissioners in the states were arranged similarly. Although the administrative structure of the bureau varied from state to state and underwent periodic reorganizations, the states were generally divided into districts and subdistricts and were administered by a hierarchy of officials that included subassistant and assistant subassistant commissioners, civilian and military superintendents, and agents. In addition to drawing upon army personnel, the bureau in several states, especially **Georgia**, employed white southerners—either civilian officials or private citizens—as agents. Nonetheless, the bureau was chronically understaffed. No more than 900 men ever served at any one time, and individual agents were sometimes responsible for thousands of square miles of territory. Frequent turnover of personnel and the unfitness, incompetence, or prejudices of particular agents also hampered the bureau's effectiveness.

Freedmen's Bureau Activities

Because the Freedmen's Bureau had been charged with responsibility for "all subjects" relating to freedmen and refugees, little lay beyond its scope. In establishing a workable system of free labor for the South, bureau agents oversaw the signing of labor contracts between employers and freedmen, ensuring that such contracts were equitable and voluntary. They also mediated labor disputes and saw that freedmen received their due compensation at year's end. They established systems of public health and provided medical care. They supplied transportation to former slaves trying to reunite families or seeking employment. They dispensed aid to those incapable of self-support and furnished temporary relief to the indigent; in fact, more than a quarter of the approximately twenty million rations that the bureau issued went to whites. Bureau agents validated the marriages of former slaves, whose unions had no legal basis, and they were frequently called upon to mediate domestic disputes among members of freed families. Despite the importance of these activities, bureau officials were as much concerned with maintaining the

American tradition of limited government, and with preventing the creation of a permanent class of dependents, as they were with the relief of suffering.

Two particularly important bureau functions involved law enforcement and education. Commissioner Howard and most bureau agents were firmly committed to the principle of equality before the law. Throughout the South, however, freedmen not only found themselves subject to **violence** by whites, but they were also denied redress by the southern state governments created under **Presidential Reconstruction**. In response, the bureau instituted a system of courts that adjudicated all manner of cases and that varied in structure from state to state. Freedmen saw the bureau courts as their only means of securing impartial justice, and Howard estimated that bureau courts annually heard more than 100,000 complaints. Nonetheless, doubts about the constitutionality of military tribunals in the southern states—especially after the U.S. **Supreme Court**'s decision in the 1866 *Milligan* case—caused bureau officials to lessen their reliance on bureau courts and to focus their efforts on securing freedmen justice in civilian courts.

For Howard and many other bureau officials, education was central to the goal of racial uplift. The bureau established and maintained its own system of schools, and it worked in conjunction with the host of missionary societies involved in freedmen's education, especially the **American Missionary Association (AMA)**. Bureau officials were motivated by a combination of paternalism and a genuine commitment to the freedmen's advancement. They and the many white, female teachers sent South by the missionary societies saw it as their duty to teach freedmen basic literacy and to instill in them the values—such as frugality, punctuality, sobriety, and the dignity of labor—essential for competing in the capitalist marketplace. Moreover, education was also seen as part of the larger mission to remake southern society upon the principles of equality before the law and **black suffrage**. By 1869, the bureau administered some 3,000 schools, with a total enrollment of more than 150,000 pupils, and by doing so, it helped lay the foundations of public education in the South, perhaps its most important long-term accomplishment.

Just as the Freedmen's Bureau worked with the AMA and other missionary societies, it was involved with a number of other organizations that, while not officially affiliated with the bureau, also assisted former slaves. Several "normal" (teacher training) schools and universities—such as the Hampton Normal and Industrial Institute at Hampton, Virginia, and Howard University in Washington, D.C. (which was named after the commissioner)—received bureau assistance and established the foundations of the historically black colleges. Some bureau officials also worked with the **Freedman's Savings and Trust Company**, a private savings bank established in 1865 for the benefit of former slaves. In the Barry Farm project, bureau funds were used to purchase a Washington, D.C., farm that was divided into one- or two-acre plots on which small houses were built. The homesteads were then sold on easy terms to some 260 black families.

The Bureau and Land

Perhaps the bureau's most important assignment, and its greatest failure, involved land redistribution. Congress charged the bureau with managing

"A peep at the Freedmen's Bureau office of Lieut. S. Merrill, Superintendent Third District (15 people in office)." Illustration from *Frank Leslie's Newspaper*, 1867. (Courtesy of the Library of Congress.)

abandoned and confiscated land in the South, and it directed the president and the commissioner to make such land available to freedmen. Land redistribution was intended, especially by the **Radical Republicans** in Congress, to achieve the larger objective of reconstructing southern society by dismantling the plantation system and providing at least some freedmen with the property that was deemed essential to economic independence. Owing to the wartime abandonment of farms, plantations, and city lots, and to the various confiscation and direct-tax measures enacted by Congress, by war's end, the federal government controlled some 900,000 acres of land and 5,000 town lots, almost all of which were transferred to the Freedmen's Bureau. Because the bureau had received no appropriation, Howard intended to use revenue from property sale and rental to subsidize the bureau.

In attempting to undertake land redistribution, Howard and the bureau faced the opposition of Andrew Johnson, whose conservative vision of Reconstruction did not include fundamentally overturning southern society. Johnson especially objected to the bureau's mandate to make land available to freedmen, and his **amnesty proclamation** of May 1865 restored property rights to pardoned ex-Confederates. During the late spring and early summer of 1865, ex-Confederate landowners petitioned Johnson for **pardons** and for the return of their property, while freedmen refused to surrender land on which they had been working and raising crops. Although the legal status of this land remained uncertain, Howard drafted an order in late July, Circular No. 13, instructing bureau agents not to return abandoned land to former owners, even to those who had secured presidential pardons. This order was never officially promulgated, but Johnson objected to it and directed Howard in September to issue a second order, Circular No. 15, rescinding the earlier one and specifying that all land still controlled by the bureau be returned to pardoned ex-Confederates. Only the small amount of confiscated land that had already been sold under court decree would not be restored. Johnson further instructed Howard to inform the assistant commissioners to comply strictly with the new circular.

As broad as Circular No. 15 was, it did not apply to land that fell under General **William T. Sherman**'s Special **Field Order No. 15**—a January 1865 directive that had conditionally granted freedmen forty-acre plots along coastal **South Carolina** and Georgia. By mid-1865, some 40,000 freedmen had gained possessory title to almost a half-million acres, and others were flocking to the "Sherman lands" in hopes of receiving what they believed were the promised forty acres. Johnson, however, decided that Circular 15 also applied to this land, and in October, he ordered Howard to oversee personally the restoration of this land and to convince freedmen there to sign labor contracts for 1866. Restoration of the Sherman lands was met by freedmen with much discontent and some resistance, but Johnson's wishes were eventually carried out. Although a small number of freedmen in this and other parts of the South gained land, and although the 1866 Freedmen's Bureau bills attempted to address the plight of dispossessed freedmen on the Sherman lands, the main function of the bureau's Land Division after Circular 15 involved the restoration of property to former owners.

The Bureau and the Politics of Reconstruction

Because the Freedmen's Bureau was entrusted with affecting social change, it inevitably became embroiled in Reconstruction politics. Radical Republicans saw the bureau as the linchpin to remaking southern society. **Moderate Republicans** recognized the need for the bureau but expressed reservations over increasing federal authority. Members of the **Democratic Party**, North and South, likewise objected to the expansion of federal power that the bureau represented. Freedmen regarded the bureau as their ally in fending off white violence and hostile southern state governments. White southerners protested its very existence, and they took special umbrage at being hauled into bureau courts and at bureau agents intervening in labor disputes. Moreover, because the bureau was originally intended to last for only one year after the war, and because of unsettled conditions in the South into 1866, political conflict arose over continuing the bureau's existence.

Having concluded by early 1866 that Johnson's Reconstruction policy required modification, congressional Republicans passed a **Civil Rights Act** and a **Freedmen's Bureau bill** that continued the bureau and expanded its powers. Despite his land restoration policy, and despite his having pressured Howard to relieve several radical assistant commissioners, Johnson had expressed no overt hostility to the bureau, and he was expected to approve the Freedmen's Bureau bill, which had received overwhelming majorities in Congress. Instead, not only did Johnson veto the bill, but he also issued a scathing veto message that condemned the bureau as an unconstitutional expansion of federal authority. When an attempt to override Johnson failed, congressional Republicans focused on drafting another bill that could survive a veto.

To counter this effort Johnson undertook a number of measures to weaken or undermine the bureau. In April 1866, he officially declared the rebellion ended, casting further doubt on the bureau courts' legality. That same month, he commissioned two conservative army generals, James B. Steedman and Joseph S. Fullerton, to make an official investigation of the bureau that, while ostensibly for the purpose of rooting out corruption and mismanagement, was clearly intended to discredit the bureau and any attempt to extend its life. Nonetheless, in July 1866, Congress enacted legislation over a second veto that continued the bureau for two more years, while another law provided the bureau its first separate appropriation.

The End of the Bureau

With passage of the 1867 **Military Reconstruction Acts**, the bureau lost much of its separate identity to the military districts. The 1868 **readmission** of several southern states resulted in the further relinquishing of many bureau responsibilities to civilian governments. Nonetheless, the bureau had been instrumental in implementing **Congressional Reconstruction**, assisting the process of black political mobilization, and electing Republican candidates. In order to keep the bureau in place through the **elections of 1868**, Congress enacted a law in July 1868 extending it until January 1, 1869, after which date all bureau operations ceased except for the education and claim divisions.

In 1870, educational activities were terminated, and in a June 1872 appropriation bill, Congress discontinued the bureau entirely. Between 1872 and 1879, black veterans' bounty claims and pensions were administered by the Freedmen's branch in the office of the adjutant general. The 1870s also witnessed several **scandals** that clouded the reputations of the bureau and Howard, and provided political ammunition to opponents of governmental assistance to the freedmen. An 1870 congressional investigation uncovered considerable mismanagement and misappropriation of bureau funds, but exonerated Howard. Irregularities surrounding the paying of veterans' bounties led to a military court of inquiry in 1874 that again absolved Howard. That same year the Freedman's Bank failed, a victim of poor oversight and the financial **Panic of 1873**. After the Freedmen's Branch was discontinued in 1879, black Civil War veterans' affairs were administered by the Colored Troops Division in the adjutant general's office. *See also* Abolitionists; Abolition of Slavery; African Americans; Agriculture; Atkinson, Edward; Black Codes; Black Troops (U.S.C.T.) in the Occupied South; Canby, Edward Richard Sprigg; Carpetbaggers; Chase, Salmon Portland; Churches; Civil Rights; Confiscation Acts; Contraband, Slaves as; Davis Bend, Mississippi; De Forest, John William; Delany, Martin R.; Dunn, Oscar James; Eaton, John; Edisto Island, South Carolina; Elections of 1866; Grant, Ulysses S.; Hancock, Winfield Scott; Joint Committee on Reconstruction; Julian, George Washington; Ku Klux Klan; Labor Systems; McCulloch, Hugh; Pope, John M.; Port Royal Experiment; Reynolds, Joseph J.; Saxton, Rufus; Schofield, John M.; Schurz, Carl; Scott, Robert K.; Sharecropping; Sheridan, Philip H.; Sickles, Daniel E.; Southern

Homestead Act; Stanton, Edwin M.; Stevens, Thaddeus; Sumner, Charles; Thomas, Lorenzo; Trumbull, Lyman; Twitchell, Marshall, H.; U.S. Army and Reconstruction; Vagrancy; Washington's Birthday Speech.

Further Reading: Bentley, George R. *A History of the Freedmen's Bureau.* Philadelphia: University of Pennsylvania Press, 1955; Carpenter, John A. *Sword and Olive Branch: Oliver Otis Howard.* Pittsburgh, PA: University of Pittsburgh Press, 1964; Cimbala, Paul A. *Under the Guardianship of the Nation: The Freedmen's Bureau and the Reconstruction of Georgia, 1865–1870.* Athens: University of Georgia Press, 1997; Cimbala, Paul A., and Randall M. Miller, eds. *The Freedmen's Bureau and Reconstruction: Reconsiderations.* New York: Fordham University Press, 1999; Howard, Oliver Otis. *Autobiography of Oliver Otis Howard.* 2 vols. New York: The Baker & Taylor Company, 1908; McFeely, William S. *Yankee Stepfather: General O. O. Howard and the Freedmen.* New Haven, CT: Yale University Press, 1968.

John C. Rodrigue

Butler, Benjamin Franklin (1818–1893)

Congressman, federal volunteer general, and Reconstruction commander, Benjamin Butler was born in Deerfield, New Hampshire, and matriculated at Waterville (renamed Colby) College, Waterville, Maine, graduating in 1838. Moving to Massachusetts, he set up a law practice in Lowell. Butler dabbled in the **militia**, but politics became his passion. As a Democrat, he was elected to the state house and the state senate in the 1850s. He served as a delegate to the **Democratic Party**'s national convention in 1860, endorsing the nomination of a southern slave owner, **Jefferson Davis** of **Mississippi**. Devoted to the Union, Butler sought a high command in the federal volunteer army when the Civil War began. Based on the policy of President **Abraham Lincoln**, who wanted support for the war across party lines, Butler gained the president's appointment as a volunteer major general in 1861. His appointment as a volunteer general began a transition, taking Butler from the Democrats to the Republicans in the next four years.

Throughout the war, Butler held a series of assignments, most relating more to politics than to combat. After an initial posting in Baltimore, **Maryland**, Butler was sent to the coast of **Virginia** and at Fort Monroe he enunciated an important policy. Declaring slaves to be **contraband** of war—property to be confiscated—Butler intensified the debate over slavery and provided a way to strip Confederates of their slaves. The nickname "contrabands" became a common phrase for confiscated or escaped slaves. In 1861, Butler led Union forces in two engagements—Big Bethel, Virginia, in June and Hatteras Inlet, **North Carolina**, in August—the first a defeat but the second a handsome victory (won by the navy) that boosted his recognition. This led to his most important assignment of the war—commanding the army expedition intended to occupy New Orleans and to begin Reconstruction in **Louisiana**.

Following in the wake of the victory by Flag Officer David G. Farragut's naval squadron over Confederate forts and ships, Butler's army of 10,000 soldiers occupied New Orleans in May 1862. Southern sensibilities were tender, but the general was determined to reestablish Louisiana's ties with the

"Bluebeard of New Orleans." A caricature of Benjamin Franklin Butler's behavior as military governor of New Orleans, May–December 1862. (Courtesy of the Library of Congress.)

Union and replace Confederate with federal governance. Symbols were important in this transition. Butler would not abide civilians insulting his soldiers or the U.S. flag, ordering the execution of William Mumford, a local gambler who had torn the flag from atop a federal building. Furthermore, Butler ordered that any woman who insulted Union soldiers would be arrested and treated as a prostitute—the infamous "woman order." The general also got into a contretemps with consuls posted in New Orleans to represent other nations, due to their supporting or appearing to side with the Confederacy. Confederate president Jefferson Davis and others condemned Butler and his actions, but any general reinstituting federal authority would have met with criticism and opposition. That Butler's policies of Reconstruction were stern and not gentle intensified the shrillness of southerners' criticism. Louisians and political opponents added to the volatile situation by accusing the general and his brother, Andrew, of various illegalities, including trading with Confederates as well as stealing personal belongings, including silverware. None of the charges were proven against the general, but the accusations cast a shadow over his time in New Orleans.

Controversies almost canceled out Butler's social, economic, and political accomplishments related to this early phase of Reconstruction. Confederates and some northerners (including fellow Democrats) castigated Butler for his policies, even the ones necessary if Louisiana would be restored to the Union. Meanwhile, the general took steps to clean up the city streets and reduce diseases. He inaugurated programs to feed the destitute and replaced Confederate currency with federal money in business and government transactions. He shut down pro-Confederate newspapers and supervised all **churches**, closing some houses of worship until their ministers no longer used their pulpits to deliver pro-Confederate sermons. Butler replaced pro-Confederate politicians with pro-Union office holders, including the mayor of New Orleans. Everyone appearing in federal courts was required to swear loyalty to the Union. Many southerners and northerners thought that Butler appeared to shift to the Radical Republicans because the general considered how former slaves could be allowed to serve in Union military units. The general arranged Louisiana's first electoral steps under federal control, including elections for seats in Congress, won by Michael Hahn and Benjamin Flanders, both longtime Louisiana residents now supporting the Republican Party.

Recognizing that pressure had built up against Butler due to the general's many controversies, President Lincoln reassigned him in December 1862. Replacing Butler was Major General **Nathaniel P. Banks**, another Massachusetts politician holding a volunteer general's commission. Subsequently, Butler remained controversial, militarily and politically. He commanded the Army of the James in 1864 in a campaign near Richmond, where he lacked aggressiveness and declined to bring pressure against Confederate defenses.

After the war, Butler was elected to four terms in Congress as a Republican. In 1882, he switched back to the Democrats to be elected governor of Massachusetts.

Further Reading: Dawson, Joseph G., III. *Army Generals and Reconstruction, Louisiana 1862–1877*. Baton Rouge: Louisiana State University Press, 1982; Hearn, Chester. *When the Devil Came Down to Dixie: Ben Butler in New Orleans*. Baton Rouge: Louisiana State University Press, 1998; Trefousse, Hans L. *Ben Butler: The South Called Him Beast!* New York: Twayne, 1957.

Joseph G. Dawson III

C

Cabinets, Executive

The cabinet members of each of the four Reconstruction presidents—**Abraham Lincoln**, **Andrew Johnson**, **Ulysses S. Grant**, and **Rutherford B. Hayes**—assisted the president with developing and carrying out Reconstruction policy.

Lincoln chose his cabinet members primarily from among the Republican Party leadership, especially his greatest political rivals. He tried to balance party factions by including both former Whigs and former Democrats from a variety of geographical locations.

Lincoln's Cabinet

Secretary of State: **William H. Seward** (1861–1865)

Secretary of the Treasury: **Salmon P. Chase** (1861–1864); **William P. Fessenden** (1864–1865); **Hugh McCulloch** (1865)

Secretary of War: Simon Cameron (1861–1862); **Edwin M. Stanton** (1862–1865)

Secretary of the Navy: **Gideon Welles** (1861–1865)

Attorney General: Edward Bates (1861–1864); James Speed (1864–1865)

Secretary of the Interior: Caleb B. Smith (1861–1863); John P. Usher (1863–1865)

Postmaster General: **Montgomery Blair** (1861–1864); William Dennison (1864–1865)

When Andrew Johnson suddenly assumed the presidency upon Lincoln's **assassination**, Johnson decided to retain Lincoln's cabinet. However, due to political disagreements, several cabinet members eventually resigned. Johnson's **impeachment** resulted from his attempts to remove Edwin M. Stanton, who refused to resign.

Johnson's Cabinet

Secretary of State: William H. Seward (1865–1869)

Secretary of the Treasury: Hugh McCulloch (1865–1869)

Secretary of War: Edwin M. Stanton (1865–1868); Ulysses S. Grant (1867–1868); **Lorenzo Thomas** (1868); **John M. Schofield** (1868–1869)

Secretary of the Navy: Gideon Welles (1865–1869)

Attorney General: James Speed (1865–1866); **Henry Stanbery** (1866–1868); **Orville H. Browning** (1868); William M. Evarts (1868–1869)

Secretary of the Interior: John P. Usher (1865); James Harlan (1865–1866); Orville H. Browning (1866–1869)

Postmaster General: William Dennison (1865–1866); Alexander W. Randall (1866–1869)

Ulysses S. Grant tended to choose friends and acquaintances for cabinet posts, many of whom had little qualification for the position. A number of the appointees became involved in corruption and **scandals**, resulting in a considerable turnover of officeholders.

Grant's Cabinet

Secretary of State: Elihu B. Washburne (1869); **Hamilton Fish** (1869–1877)

Secretary of the Treasury: **George S. Boutwell** (1869–1873); William A. Richardson (1873–1874); **Benjamin H. Bristow** (1874–1876); Lot M. Morrill (1876–1877)

Secretary of War: John A. Rawlins (1869); **William T. Sherman** (1869); William W. Belknap (1869–1876); Alphonso Taft (1876); James D. Cameron (1876–1877)

Secretary of the Navy: Adolph E. Bone (1869); George M. Robeson (1869–1877)

Attorney General: Ebenezer R. Hoar (1869–1870); **Amos T. Akerman** (1870–1871); George H. Williams (1871–1875); Edwards Pierrepont (1875–1876); Alphonso Taft (1876–1877)

Secretary of the Interior: **Jacob D. Cox** (1869–1870); Columbus Delano (1870–1875); **Zachariah Chandler** (1875–1877)

Postmaster General: John A. J. Creswell (1869–1874); James W. Marshall (1874); Marshall Jewell (1874–1876); James N. Tyner (1876–1877)

Rutherford B. Hayes determined to be independent in his cabinet choices and not to include either members of the previous administration or his rivals for the presidency. This stance offended leaders of the Republican Party factions, but Hayes's cabinet is considered the strongest of the late nineteenth century.

Hayes's Cabinet

Secretary of State: Hamilton Fish (1877); William M. Evarts (1877–1881)

Secretary of the Treasury: **John Sherman** (1877–1881)

Secretary of War: George W. McCrary (1877–1879); Alexander Ramsey (1879–1881)

Secretary of the Navy: Richard W. Thompson (1877–1881); Nathan Goff, Jr. (1881)

Attorney General: Charles Devens (1877–1881)

Secretary of the Interior: **Carl Schurz** (1877–1881)

Postmaster General: David M. Key (1877–1880); Horace Maynard (1880–1881)

Glenna R. Schroeder-Lein

Cain, Richard Harvey (1825–1887)

Richard Harvey Cain was a black **abolitionist**, minister, editor, Republican state senator, and congressman from **South Carolina**. Born free in Greenbriar County, **Virginia**, Cain grew up in Ohio to become an African Methodist Episcopal (A.M.E.) minister in the Midwest. Between 1859 and 1861, he attended Wilberforce University in Ohio before relocating to a church in Brooklyn for the duration of the Civil War. As an abolitionist, Cain worked with prominent leaders such as **Frederick Douglass** and **Martin R. Delany**. He collaborated with Delany through the African Colonization Society to promote emigration to Africa in the late 1850s. Once the Civil War began, Reverend Cain and the African Civilization Society focused on domestic matters such as **freedmen's relief** and promoting literacy among black soldiers. In 1864, as the organization's assistant superintendent of **education**, Cain established freedmen's schools in Washington, D.C.

In May 1865, Reverend Cain was transferred to Charleston, South Carolina, as superintendent of the A.M.E. Church missionary activities there. Through his efforts, the A.M.E. Church became the largest black Methodist denomination in the state by 1877. Cain deemed the spread of African Methodism especially important because as a racial enterprise, it gave blacks control of their religious lives for the first time and because its representatives were inculcating the values among the former slaves, which would secure the future success of the race. In 1866, Cain purchased a Republican newspaper, the *South Carolina Leader*, to become editor of the state's first black newspaper. Renamed the *Missionary Record*, Cain's newspaper covered a variety of topics including religion and contemporary affairs; his became a clarion voice promoting freedmen's interests.

Reverend Cain is often considered the consummate preacher-politician. He participated in the November 1865 Colored Peoples Convention in Charleston, where blacks protested against racial strictures in the 1865 South Carolina Constitution and demanded equal civic rights. In early 1867, Cain was a founder of the state Republican Party and was elected a delegate to the 1868 state **constitutional convention**. He persuaded that body to reject efforts to restrict the franchise by **poll taxes** or educational requirements. He led an effort to secure a loan from the **Bureau of Refugees, Freedmen, and Abandoned Lands** (Freedmen's Bureau) to be used by the state to assist freedmen to acquire land. When Congress proved unsympathetic, Cain's efforts led the constitutional convention to provide for creation of a state land commission to assist small farmers and the landless to acquire realty in small plots. South Carolina was the only state to create such an agency, and Cain later served as one of its members. Reverend Cain served a term in the state senate (1868–1870) and two terms in Congress (1873–1875 and 1877–1879).

In state politics, he was a frequent critic of corruption among Republicans. As a state senator, Cain was initially skeptical about the efficacy of laws to end discrimination in public places but as a congressman, he proved a staunch supporter of the **Civil Rights Act of 1875**, the nation's first federal public accommodations law.

After Reconstruction, Reverend Cain encouraged black Carolinians to seek a future in Africa and he assumed a leadership role in the Liberian Exodus Movement 1877–1878, based in Charleston. In 1880, he was elected an A.M.E. bishop with responsibility for **Louisiana** and **Texas**, where he founded Paul Quinn College. He died on January 18, 1887, in Washington, D.C.

Further Reading: Foner, Eric. *Freedom's Lawmakers: A Directory of Black Officeholders during Reconstruction*. New York: Oxford University Press, 1993; Hildebrand, Reginald. *The Times Were Strange and Stirring: Methodist Preachers and the Crisis of Emancipation*. Durham, NC: Duke University Press, 1995; Holt, Thomas. *Black over White: Negro Political Leadership in South Carolina during Reconstruction*. Urbana: University of Illinois Press, 1977; Powers, Bernard E. " 'I Go to Set the Captives Free': The Activism of Richard Harvey Cain, Nationalist Churchman and Reconstruction-Era Leader." In Randy Finley and Thomas A. DeBlack, eds., *The Southern Elite and Social Change*. Fayetteville: University of Arkansas Press, 2002.

Bernard E. Powers, Jr.

Canby, Edward Richard Sprigg (1817–1873)

A professional army officer, Edward Canby was one of the most important army commanders during postwar Reconstruction, serving in three districts during the 1860s and 1870s. Canby was born in Piatt's Landing, **Kentucky**, but his family moved to Crawfordsville, Indiana, where he attended Wabash College before transferring to the U.S. Military Academy. Graduating in 1839, Canby ranked only thirtieth of thirty-one cadets. He served on the frontier and in the Mexican War prior to the Civil War.

In the Civil War, Canby's command of federal troops in New Mexico held the territory for the Union and his victory at Glorieta Pass in March 1862 blocked Confederate expansion toward California. The campaign earned Canby promotion to brigadier general. In July 1863, he supervised troops in putting down the controversial draft riots in New York City. Following promotion to major general, Canby directed a campaign in **Alabama**, leading federal forces that captured the port of Mobile and the state capital of Montgomery by April 1865.

After the war, Canby ranked ninth on the list of only ten brigadier generals in the regular army in July 1866. Unlike some leading federal generals, such as Republicans **John Pope** and **Philip H. Sheridan** or Democrats George G. Meade and **Winfield S. Hancock**, Canby displayed no identifiable political leanings. Most northern and southern politicians acknowledged that he was fair-minded.

Starting out in **Louisiana** in 1866, Canby irritated Sheridan, who sought more ideological officers. In August 1867, on orders of President **Andrew Johnson**, Canby replaced General **Daniel Sickles** in command of the Second Military District (**North Carolina** and **South Carolina**). Suffering from no visible ill effects on his career by serving in **Louisiana**, Canby scrupulously adhered to the terms of the congressional **Military Reconstruction Acts**, causing North Carolina governor **Jonathan Worth** to condemn him for establishing a "military despotism." Canby ordered army officers to register black men to vote and supervised an election in the Second District. Obtaining fair trials was difficult for blacks, and therefore the general ordered some cases handed to military judges. Canby also served simultaneously as assistant commissioner of the Freedmen's Bureau for the Second Military District, encouraging the bureau's agents, active duty and former army officers, to provide assistance to blacks. Furthermore, he required that black men serve on juries. Former Confederates grew more distressed when Canby used his authority under the Reconstruction Acts to remove civil officials whom he considered "impediments to Reconstruction," including city councilmen and mayors in Charleston and Columbia, South Carolina. The general replaced some of those officials with **African Americans**. In elections held under Canby's supervision, voters in the Carolinas approved new state constitutions, elected state officeholders, including legislators and governors, and ratified the **Fourteenth Amendment** to the **U.S. Constitution**. All of these accomplishments were carried out with minor problems and little **violence**. Fulfilling these steps enabled Congress to declare that North Carolina and South Carolina were readmitted to the Union in June 1868, terminating the existence of the Second Military District. Canby and the army had fulfilled a difficult and nearly thankless task in an exemplary fashion.

In November, President Johnson called on Canby again, posting him to **Texas**, where Canby removed a few state officials who he deemed "impediments to Reconstruction" and carefully oversaw the steps leading to the **election of 1868** when the voters ratified the new state constitution giving African American men the right to vote. While some Democrats criticized Canby, most observers believed that he had been fair to both parties in Texas. Soon after **Ulysses S. Grant** took the oath as president, he ordered Canby to California, where the general was killed by Modoc Indians in April 1873. *See also* Bureau of Refugees, Freedmen, and Abandoned Lands; Readmission.

Further Reading: Dawson, Joseph G., III. *Army Generals and Reconstruction: Louisiana, 1862–1877.* Baton Rouge: Louisiana State University Press, 1982; Heyman, Max L. *Prudent Soldier: A Biography of Major General E.H.S. Canby, 1817–1873.* Glendale, CA: Clarke Co., 1959; Sefton, James E. *The United States Army and Reconstruction, 1865–1877.* Baton Rouge: Louisiana State University Press, 1967.

Joseph G. Dawson III

Cardoza, Francis L. (1837–1903)

Francis L. Cardoza was a black minister, educator, Republican secretary of state, and state treasurer in Reconstruction **South Carolina**. Born free in Charleston to a wealthy Jewish merchant and a free black woman, as a youth, Cardoza was trained as a carpenter and attended private schools for free blacks. In 1858, he enrolled at the University of Glasgow to pursue a ministerial **education**. Graduating with a distinguished record for classical scholarship, he subsequently studied in Presbyterian seminaries in London and Edinburgh. In 1864, he returned to the United States, was ordained a congregational minister, and accepted a pastorate in New Haven, Connecticut. Cardoza represented Hartford as a delegate to the 1864 Syracuse, New York, National Convention of Colored Men, convened to promote the civic and social interests of black Americans. In June 1865, Cardoza accepted a position with the **American Missionary Association (AMA)**, which was promoting freedmen's education. He returned to Charleston to become founding principal of the Avery Normal Institute, a prestigious private school for black Charlestonians. Under Cardoza's leadership, which continued until 1868, Avery developed a classical curriculum and produced students who pursued careers as teachers and in other professions.

The political character of freedmen's education during Reconstruction drew Francis Cardoza into the political arena. In November 1865, he participated in the Colored Peoples Convention of South Carolina in Charleston, to protest the discriminatory South Carolina Constitution of 1865 and to demand equal educational and political rights. In March 1867, Cardoza helped found the state Republican Party and subsequently served in party leadership roles and as president of the **Union League**. He was later elected to the **Constitutional Convention** of 1868, serving as chairman of the education committee. In that capacity, he oversaw provisions creating the state's first publicly financed statewide school system. When educational and **poll tax** qualifications were proposed for the franchise, Cardoza vociferously opposed such measures until they were defeated. In April 1868, he was elected secretary of state to become the first black elected to statewide office in South Carolina. In 1872, he was elected state treasurer and held the position until 1877. During Reconstruction, Cardoza's actions established his reputation as a conservative reform-minded politician. Rather than tolerate corruption on the state land commission, he resigned from its advisory board. As secretary of state, he investigated widespread mismanagement at the land commission and reorganized this agency to establish a reputation for efficient and honest operations. As state treasurer, he garnered a reputation for fiscal integrity and on one occasion so offended a group of legislators that some initiated impeachment proceedings against him. The attempt was thwarted by a coalition of reform Republicans and Democrats in the legislature. Cardoza was the staunch ally and close advisor to **Daniel Chamberlain**, the reform Republican governor elected in 1872. In 1874 for example, Cardoza cooperated with

Francis L. Cardoza, c. 1877. (Courtesy of the Library of Congress.)

Governor Chamberlain, independent Republicans, and Democrats to prevent the election of **William Whipper** as a circuit court judge because of the legislator's reputation for corruption.

Despite Republican reformers' best efforts, the **Compromise of 1877** abruptly ended Reconstruction in South Carolina. In the Redeemers' politically motivated campaign against Reconstruction-era officials, ironically Cardoza was convicted of corruption while treasurer. He was subsequently pardoned in 1879. After Reconstruction, Francis Cardoza lived out his life in Washington, D.C., working for the Treasury Department and as a high school principal. He died on July 22, 1903.

Further Reading: Bleser, Carol K. *The Promised Land: The History of the South Carolina Land Commission, 1869–1890*. Columbia: University of South Carolina Press, 1969; Foner, Eric. *Freedom's Lawmakers: A Directory of Black Officeholders during Reconstruction*. Oxford: Oxford University Press, 1993; Holt, Thomas. *Black over White: Negro Political Leadership in South Carolina during Reconstruction*. Urbana: University of Illinois Press, 1977; Powers, Bernard E., Jr. "Francis L. Cardoza: An Early African American Urban Educator." In Roger Biles, ed., *The Human Tradition in Urban America*. Wilmington, DE: Scholarly Resources, 2002; Underwood, James L., and W. Lewis Burke. *At Freedom's Door: African American Founding Fathers and Lawyers in Reconstruction South Carolina*. Columbia: University of South Carolina Press, 2000.

Bernard E. Powers, Jr.

Carpetbaggers

"Carpetbagger" was a pejorative epithet applied to white northerners who moved South during or shortly after the Civil War and became Republicans. The term first appeared in **Alabama** newspapers in late 1867, and by mid-1868 was coming into general usage throughout the country. The epithet was vital in the white South's morality play version of Reconstruction. This sordid melodrama depicted carpetbaggers as the dregs of northern society, swarming the South like hungry locusts after Appomattox, their meager belongings stuffed in woolen carpetbags. Corrupt and vindictive, these loathsome adventurers established "Negro-Carpetbag rule," robbing virtuous whites, looting public treasuries, and sowing decades of racial discord. This hoary legend has long since been debunked by professional historians; still, it remains embedded in popular culture, in large part due to Hollywood films such as *Birth of a Nation* (1915) and *Gone with the Wind* (1939).

While some carpetbaggers were corrupt, as a group they were no more venal than their Democratic enemies or politicians in other parts of the country. Carpetbaggers such as **Mississippi** governor **Adelbert Ames** and **South Carolina** governor **Daniel H. Chamberlain** earned reputations for honesty. In **North Carolina**, even Judge **Albion W. Tourgée**'s Democratic enemies conceded that the jurist from Ohio was fair, honest, and able. On the other hand, George E. Spencer, U.S. senator from Alabama, and **Louisiana** governor **Henry Clay Warmoth** had shady reputations. Spencer's alleged misdeeds consisted mainly of liberal cash donations to Alabama lawmakers, combined with job favors and ample free food and drink, widespread practices in Gilded Age America. As to Warmoth, "I don't pretend to be honest," he said. "I only pretend to be as honest as *anybody in politics*." Louisiana was a notoriously corrupt state, and Warmoth at least was no hypocrite. On the one hand, he observed, wealthy New Orleans Democrats tirelessly complained about corrupt lawmakers while, on the other hand, buying their votes at every opportunity. (Although his enemies never admitted it, Louisiana's other carpetbag governor, **William Pitt Kellogg**, was an honest man.)

In the main, the carpetbaggers' real story stands "Tragic Era" legend on its head. Most northern migrants in the postwar South were young men in their twenties and thirties who had served in the Union army during the Civil War, many as officers in the U.S. Colored Troops. The great majority settled in the South before **Congressional Reconstruction**, with little thought of political careers. They came as cotton planters, businessmen, lawyers, physicians, Freedmen's Bureau agents, treasury officials, and so on. They were well educated, many with college backgrounds. They relocated in the South in search of opportunity, bringing with them, as a rule, scarce capital and business know-how. At first, most southern whites welcomed their arrival, recognizing the region's need for talent and capital. Significantly, northerner newcomers who joined the southern **Democratic Party** were not called carpetbaggers. The word carpetbagger, like the word **scalawag**, is basic to the lexicon of the era, but modern historians use it neutrally.

Most carpetbaggers settled in plantation districts with large black populations and few scalawags. After the enfranchisement of southern blacks under **Congressional Reconstruction**, the northerners' **education**, experience as soldiers (especially leading **black troops**), service in the Freedmen's Bureau, and general concern for improving freedmen's lives marked them as natural leaders of black-belt Republicans. Though they numbered no more than a few hundred active men in any state, between 1867 and 1877 carpetbaggers held public offices of every description in the eleven states of the former Confederacy. They comprised about one-sixth of the delegates in the **constitutional conventions** of 1867–1869; hundreds more served as state legislators, judges, sheriffs, and in other state and county offices; still others held key posts in federal post offices and customhouses and served as U.S. marshals. Overall, carpetbaggers held about one-fourth of public offices in most of the Reconstruction states; in Louisiana, **Arkansas**, and **Florida**, the northerners held a third or more of public offices. Ten governors were carpetbaggers; indeed, the northerners largely dominated the executive office in Louisiana, Mississippi, Arkansas, South Carolina, and Florida. Seventeen carpetbaggers served in the U.S. Senate and forty-four in the U.S. House of Representatives.

As a group, carpetbaggers were practical men of affairs who combined self-interest with reform. Inspired by northern state constitutions and legal codes, they were a modernizing, progressive influence in the southern states. They helped establish state-supported free public schools and pushed the creation of penitentiaries, insane asylums, and other public institutions. They promoted **railroads**, canals, and harbor clearance. They helped rid the South of whipping posts, imprisonment for debt, and other outdated, inhumane

Caricature of Carl Schurz carrying bags labeled "carpet bag" and "carpet bagger South," 1872. (Courtesy of the Library of Congress.)

practices. They backed liberalized divorce laws and separate property rights for married women. Above all, they supported basic civil and political rights for blacks. While only a minority truly accepted blacks as equals, far more than most white Americans, carpetbaggers accorded blacks respect, dignity, and legal protection.

The carpetbaggers' moment was brief. With their Republican allies, blacks and scalawags, they battled enemies who challenged their very political existence. Viewing a party based on black votes as illegitimate, southern Democrats sought not merely to vote Republicans from office; they sought to destroy the Republican Party and expunge it from the polity. To this end, they freely employed fraud, assassination, and mass murder. In 1874–1876, white liners (conservative southern whites who drew a "line" between whites and blacks) terrorized carpetbaggers, scalawags, and blacks (the chief victims) in the Deep South. In one particularly egregious case, the **White League** murdered six carpetbaggers in Red River Parish, Louisiana—four of the victims were members of the Twitchell family from Vermont. Although shot six times, the head of the family, **Marshall H. Twitchell**, survived after the amputation of both arms.

In overwhelming degree, moreover, Democrats controlled the private wealth of the southern states—the plantations, banks, and businesses—and employed that economic power against the radical party. Whites also ostracized carpetbaggers socially. Faced with unyielding opposition—political, economic, and social—neither the carpetbaggers nor the allies managed to mold a political culture that stressed Republican unity. In the 1870s, the surviving Republican regimes splintered into factions pitting scalawags against carpetbaggers, blacks against whites, and carpetbaggers against carpetbaggers. In Louisiana and Arkansas, this internecine feuding bordered on opéra bouffe, with carpetbag officials arresting one another and armed **militias** parading the streets of Little Rock and New Orleans.

Carpetbaggers generally had their greatest influence in states with majority or near-majority black populations. For this reason, regimes dominated by carpetbag governors outlasted those dominated by scalawag executives. Hence, Congressional Reconstruction in Mississippi lasted until 1875, and the Republican regimes in Louisiana, South Carolina, and Florida lasted two years longer. Indeed, carpetbag officials in the latter three states were key players in the disputed election crisis of 1876–1877. Without the electoral votes of South Carolina, Louisiana, and Florida—awarded by carpetbag regimes—**Rutherford B. Hayes** could not have become president.

When Reconstruction ended, many carpetbaggers returned North. Former Mississippi governor **Adelbert Ames** made a fortune in Massachusetts through business investments and mechanical inventions (notably pencil sharpeners and fire-engine ladders). A general in the Civil War, Ames reentered the army in the Spanish-American War as a brigadier general of volunteers. At his death in 1933, the press eulogized him as the last surviving general of the Civil War. Former South Carolina governor **Daniel H. Chamberlain** became a prominent member of the New York City bar and wrote a series of articles about Reconstruction for *North American Review* and *Atlantic Monthly*. **Albion W. Tourgée** also settled in New York City and wrote a best-selling novel, *A Fool's Errand* (1879), about a North Carolina carpetbagger who closely resembled the author. He later acted as lawyer without pay in the landmark *Plessy v. Ferguson* case (1896), unsuccessfully challenging segregation on Louisiana passenger trains. Driven out of Louisiana by the White League, Marshall H. Twitchell became American consul in Kingston, Canada. Still at his post in the Spanish-American War, he helped bust a Spanish spy ring operating in Montreal. His unpublished autobiography remained in storage in Vermont for more than half a century, eventually being published as *Carpetbagger from Vermont: The Autobiography of Marshall Harvey Twitchell* (1989). Albert T. Morgan accepted a clerkship in Washington, D.C., and wrote an excellent account of his Reconstruction experience in Mississippi, *Yazoo: Or, On the Pickitt Line of Freedom in the South* (1884).

Powell Clayton and **Henry Clay Warmoth**, on the other hand, along with many others, remained in the South after 1877. Clayton became an Arkansas railroad president, a business promoter, and the owner of a 40,000-acre plantation on the Arkansas River. He wrote about his Reconstruction experience in *The Aftermath of the Civil War in Arkansas* (1915). Warmoth remained active in Louisiana business and politics for decades. He ran for governor in 1888 and, from 1890 to 1893, was collector of the Port of New

Orleans. The owner of a large sugar plantation, in the mid-1890s, he was a lobbyist for Louisiana sugar planters. His *War, Politics and Reconstruction: Stormy Days in Louisiana* (1930), published just before his death, is one of the best political memoirs of the period.

Further Reading: Current, Richard N.: "Carpetbaggers Reconsidered." In David H. Pinckney and Theodore Ropp, eds., *A Festschrift for Frederick B. Artz*. Durham, NC: Duke University Press, 1964; *Those Terrible Carpetbaggers*. New York: Oxford University Press, 1988; Foner, Eric. *Reconstruction: America's Unfinished Revolution, 1863–1877*. New York: Harper and Row, 1988; Hume, Richard L. "Carpetbaggers in the Reconstruction South: A Group Portrait of Outside Whites in the 'Black and Tan' Constitutional Conventions." *Journal of American History* 64 (1977): 313–30; Powell, Lawrence N. "The Politics of Livelihood: Carpetbaggers in the Deep South." In J. Morgan Kousser and James M. McPherson, eds., *Region, Race, and Reconstruction*. New York: Oxford University Press, 1982; Tunnell, Ted: *Crucible of Reconstruction: War, Radicalism and Race in Louisiana, 1862–1877*. Baton Rouge: Louisiana State University Press, 1984; *Edge of the Sword: The Ordeal of Carpetbagger Marshall H. Twitchell in the Civil War and Reconstruction*. Baton Rouge: Louisiana State University Press, 2001.

Ted Tunnell

Chamberlain, Daniel Henry (1835–1907)

Governor of **South Carolina** from 1874 to 1877, Daniel Chamberlain was the ninth of ten children born to Eli Chamberlain, a farmer in West Brookfield, Massachusetts. An accomplished student, he entered Yale College in 1859. When the Civil War broke out in 1861, he was torn between finishing college, thus fulfilling his duty to those who had paid for his **education**, and the duty he felt as a Republican and **abolitionist** to "bear a hand in this life-or-death struggle for the Union and for Freedom." He remained at Yale, graduating fourth in his class in 1862, then entered the Harvard Law School, but he withdrew after only one year to serve in the army, writing to a friend that he "ought to have gone in '61." Thus, he joined the Fifth Massachusetts Cavalry, a black regiment, as a lieutenant. Soon after his service ended in December 1865, he moved to Charleston, South Carolina, to settle the affairs of a friend; there he engaged unsuccessfully in cotton planting for two years. In 1867, he married Alice Ingersoll of Bangor, Maine.

While Chamberlain was setting down roots in the state, South Carolina's political system was undergoing dramatic change. The 1867 **Military Reconstruction Act** required the southern states to call new **constitutional conventions** with delegates elected by universal manhood **suffrage**. With blacks now comprising 60 percent of South Carolina's voters, the state's electorate was now overwhelmingly Republican. Few men in the state possessed both the markers of education and intelligence, and the unassailable Republican credentials that Chamberlain possessed. He was therefore elected to represent Berkeley District in the 1868 constitutional convention, where he impressed his colleagues and even the Democratic press with his intelligence and ability.

After his work in the convention, Chamberlain was elected state attorney general, in which capacity he served from 1868 to 1872. This position also made him, ex officio, a member of the three-person state financial board, which was his most controversial role during Reconstruction. He was deeply implicated in the board's overissue of state bonds and in its failure to control the state's financial agent, who was corrupt. It is somewhat less clear whether Chamberlain himself benefited from any of the frauds practiced by the state government; he denied it and called for reform, but many Democrats considered him part of the "bond ring." Defeated in the Republican caucus for governor in 1872 by **Franklin J. Moses**, Chamberlain then pursued the private practice of law.

In 1874, the national Republican Party and President **Grant** demanded that the southern governments, and South Carolina's especially, reform their ways. In the intervening two years, the state had acquired national notoriety as the "Prostrate State," a sink of corruption. Chamberlain again ran for governor as a reform candidate and won election. As governor, Chamberlain exceeded the expectations of all those who wanted reform. He replaced incompetent officeholders, vetoed spending bills, and spoke frequently and passionately about the need to reform. In so doing, he increasingly won praise from moderates of both parties and condemnation from hardliners of his own party. In 1875, when he used extralegal means to prevent the legislature's choices for three judgeships from receiving the offices, he was fiercely criticized by many Republicans.

The true threat to Chamberlain's regime, however, was not hardline Republicans but hardline Democrats. In July 1876, white Democrats (organized in "**gun clubs**") provoked a confrontation with black **militias**, captured them, and murdered several in cold blood. Chamberlain responded with outrage to the "Hamburg Massacre" and asked the Grant administration to send more U.S. troops to the state. While this action unified the Republican Party behind Chamberlain, it alienated the moderate Democrats he had been courting. The **Democratic Party**, therefore, was also united in support of former Confederate General **Wade Hampton III**. During the 1876 campaign, Democratic "**Red Shirts**" rode around the state, harassing leading Republicans and breaking up Republican meetings. In some instances, they went further; the "Ellenton Massacre" saw thirty blacks killed by Red Shirts.

Because the election was marred by fraud on a massive scale, both parties were able to claim victory, and for several months both Chamberlain and Hampton claimed to be governor and attempted to exercise the powers of the office. In April 1877, however, newly elected President **Rutherford B. Hayes** abandoned his predecessor's activist southern policy, and with it, his support of Chamberlain. Without the support of federal troops, Chamberlain had no choice but to resign, telling his Republican supporters, "To-day—April 10, 1877—by the order of the President whom your votes alone rescued from overwhelming defeat, the Government of the United States abandons you, deliberately withdraws from you its support, with the full knowledge that the lawful government of the State will be speedily overthrown."

After the defeat of Reconstruction, Chamberlain left South Carolina for New York, where he prospered as a lawyer and, later, a scholar. At first he defended Reconstruction and the policy of universal male suffrage, but later he came to accept the scientific racism of the times. In 1904, he was ready to conclude that it had all been a mistake, that "with a preponderating electorate of ne- groes, it was never within the bounds of possibility to keep up a bearable government." By the end of his life, he was more comfortable in the Demo- cratic Party than the Republican, and more comfortable with white su- premacists than **abolitionists**. South Carolina Democrat Alfred B. Williams congratulated Chamberlain on being "so fortunate as to live long enough to allow his natural character and clarity of judgment to prevail." It might better be said that Chamberlain was so unfortunate as to trust social science in an age when it provided more folly than wisdom.

Further Reading: Allen, Walter. *Governor Chamberlain's Administration in South Carolina*. New York: G. P. Putnam's Sons, 1888; Current, Richard N. *Those Terrible Carpetbaggers*. New York: Oxford University Press, 1988; Fowler, Wilton B. "A Car- petbagger's Conversion to White Supremacy." *North Carolina Historical Review* 43, no. 3 (1966): 286–304; Simkins, Francis B., and Robert H. Woody. *South Carolina during Reconstruction*. Chapel Hill: University of North Carolina Press, 1932; Zuczek, Richard. *State of Rebellion: Reconstruction in South Carolina*. Columbia: University of South Carolina Press, 1996.

Hyman Rubin III

Chandler, Zachariah (1813–1879)

A leading **Radical Republican** and U.S. senator from Michigan, Chandler significantly contributed to Reconstruction policy during and after the Civil War. Chandler was born in Bedford, New Hampshire, to farming parents. After being educated in local schools and working at various jobs, he migrated to Michigan in 1833. In Detroit, he established a successful dry goods store and developed toll roads in the area. Married in 1844, he and his wife, Letitia Grace Douglass, had one child. Politics, however, was his major career interest.

Chandler possessed an affectionate personality, quick temper, and high ideals of public service. As a Whig in 1851, he became mayor of Detroit, but he lost the governor's race the following year. Committed to the Under- ground Railroad and **abolition**, his opposition to the Kansas-Nebraska Act of 1854 placed him in a leadership position in the newly created Republican Party. By 1857, he was elected to the U.S. Senate, a position he did not leave until 1875.

As a senator during the Civil War, he opposed secession and constantly encouraged Union generals to take the offensive to the rebels. Creator and a leading member of the **Joint Select Committee on the Conduct of the War**, he was a strong critic of General George McClellan's military activities. As a leading radical, he recognized early that the destruction of slavery and saving the Union were one and the same policy. Viewing President **Abraham Lincoln**'s Reconstruction policy as inadequate, Chandler supported a wide range of policies such as **suffrage** for **African American** males and a material stake for them in society, popularly known as "40 acres and a mule." He also wanted the Confederate leadership punished by confiscating their property, and voted "yea" in the unsuccessful conviction effort following **the im- peachment of Andrew Johnson**.

Significant as he was during Reconstruction, Chandler's political career involved far more. As chairman of the Committee on Commerce from 1861 to 1875, Chandler did not neglect the economic interests of Michigan. He supported higher tariffs, the creation of national banks, and hard money. Chandler believed that federal aid to economic growth was not only desirable but necessary. His foreign policy was a simple one of expansion. At various times he wanted to annex Canada and Santo Domingo, and resist Great Britain's expansionism. In the 1874 election, he lost his Senate seat, but President **Ulysses S. Grant** appointed him secretary of the interior. He was an effective secretary, and has been praised highly for his reforms within the Bureau of Indian Affairs.

In 1876, Chandler managed Republican **Rutherford B. Hayes**'s campaign for the presidency. He later broke with Hayes over the latter's policy toward the former Confederate states. By 1879, he had returned to the U.S. Senate, where, not surprisingly, he opposed a pension for former Confederate president **Jefferson Davis**. Always a loyal party man, he died in Chicago campaigning for the Republicans. A successful businessman—his estate exceeded $2 million—he also possessed high ideals, as expressed in his abolitionism and nationalism. He believed that **civil rights**, federal authority, moral force, and economic nationalism all worked for the greater good. This perspective made the end of Reconstruction an especially bitter disappointment for him. *See also* Congressional Reconstruction; Field Order No. 15; Johnson, Andrew; Presidential Reconstruction.

Further Reading: Harris, Wilmer C. *Public Life of Zachariah Chandler, 1851–1875*. Lansing: Michigan Historical Commission, 1917; Williams, T. Harry. *Lincoln and the Radicals*. Madison: University of Wisconsin Press, 1941; [No Author.] *Zachariah Chandler: An Outline Sketch of his Life and Public Services*. Detroit: Post and Tribune Co., 1880.

Donald K. Pickens

Chase, Salmon Portland (1808–1873)

According to William Herndon, **Abraham Lincoln**'s ambition was a little engine that knew no rest. If that judgment is true, then Chase's ambition was a dynamo of the first order. His achievements were many, but he undoubtedly found no relief from his presidential ambitions. His life and honors covered before and after the Civil War and, with many of his contemporaries, he had his opinions regarding Reconstruction.

Born in Cornish, New Hampshire, the eighth child in a family of eleven, Chase's parents, Ithamar, a glassmaker, and Janette, also ran a tavern. Life was difficult. His father died when Chase was nine and for economic security the family moved to Ohio. In the Buckeye state, Chase lived with his uncle, Philander Chase, an Episcopal bishop. It was the defining moment in Chase's life; he developed a strong sense of self-discipline and awareness with a concern for his religious and social obligations. Chase's faith sustained his ambition to do something of large import. The work ethic and stewardship were cornerstones in his character.

When he enrolled at Dartmouth in 1824, he participated in the religious revival sweeping the campus. His ambition matched his Christian desire to perform mighty deeds of goodness. After his graduation in 1826, he moved to Washington, D.C., and studied law with William Wirt, the U.S. attorney general. He also opened a school for well-to-do children of the city. Within a few years, he decided that his future was in the West and so he moved to Ohio in pursuit of a golden reputation. His success—financial, political, and social—was great in Cincinnati.

In 1834, he married Catherine Jane Garniss, who soon died in childbirth. Five years later, he married Sarah Bella Dunlop; she died in 1852. Four of his six children died young. In all these sad circumstances, his first wife's death continually haunted him. It provoked in him a desire to engage in good works that would demonstrate his religious faith. His dedication provided a full and successful career in politics.

Beginning with his efforts on behalf of the American Sunday School Union in 1837, Chase soon became a vital part of the antislavery crusade. That same year, Chase defended Matilda, a slave whose master brought her into Ohio; she sued for her freedom. Chase and James G. Birney argued that local law was the sole enforcement of slavery in the States. His argument was that slavery was "denaturalized" by the Constitution. State law enslaved people; freedom territory restored their freedom. Chase's argument was that the Constitution, an antislavery document, was constitutionally and historically incorrect. Nevertheless, he continued to use the thesis in several cases dealing with fugitive slaves.

His legal career led to his joining the Liberty Party in 1841, and he pushed to reduce slavery's influence by ending slavery in the **District of Columbia** and stopping the interstate tariff in slavery. Because the antislavery forces held the balance of power in the state, in 1849, Chase became a U.S. senator, thanks in part to his leadership in the Free Soil Party. His fight to repeal the Black Laws in Ohio also contributed to his political success. Ambitious, yes, but he worked hard in building political coalitions that moved in his desired direction. He was quite artful in the matter.

In the Senate, he desired a coalition between the Democratic and Free Soil forces; on sectional issues, he maintained his antislavery position. He led the fight against the Kansas-Nebraska Act of Stephen A. Douglas. Dealing carefully with nativist elements in the state, Chase was elected governor in 1855. He continued to gaze toward the White House; maybe the Republican Party nomination would be his in 1856. In fact, he did a great deal of organizational work for the young party. Rejected by the Republicans for John C. Fremont's candidacy, Chase returned to the U.S. Senate in 1860; his greatest triumphs were ahead.

In the Senate, he defended the **Lincoln** administration by attacking the Crittenden Compromise. He urged Lincoln to resupply Fort Sumter. He recognized that war was close at hand. "The truth," he remarked, "is that God seems to be punishing [us] for our sins—among the greatest I believe [is] that of complicity with slavery." It was a sentiment echoed by many of his fellow citizens, including Lincoln.

Appointed secretary of the treasury in 1861, Chase's contributions were considerable. In fact, Chase ranks second to Alexander Hamilton in creating a significant public fiscal policy. He started slow in reforming the policy, believing that the war would be brief. It was not. He shaped the bureaucracy and improved collection of taxes. By 1862, it was clear that the war and all of its revolutionary consequences would endure for some time. Working with Jay Cooke, a leading Philadelphia banker and family friend, the financial situation improved. Chase carefully kept **scandal** away from the department. He forced paper money as legal tender through Congress and in 1863, he established a national banking system. It was a remarkable change in public attitude and policy.

In addition, he handled confiscated and abandoned Confederate property. He used such power to help the **Port Royal Experiment** to allow the freedmen to work for wages and their own land. He was ahead of Lincoln in moving toward freeing the slaves and thereby changing the dynamic of the Civil War. Chase desired **emancipation** without reference to colonization or compensation. Always mindful of religious context for human action, Chase placed "In God we trust" on the new greenbacks and encouraged Lincoln to close the Emancipation Proclamation with a phrase to invoke the "gracious favor of Almighty God." He supported the freedmen as soldiers and as landowners.

Because of his presidential aspirations, Chase's relationship with Lincoln suffered over time. His behavior prior to the 1864 nomination was a disaster. The result was that Lincoln forced Chase out of the cabinet. The use and abuse of **patronage** broke the relationship; in June 1864, Chase left the Lincoln administration.

Within six months, Lincoln appointed Chase chief justice of the U.S. **Supreme Court**. It was a critical appointment, and illustrated the centrality of Chase's contributions to the events and policies of the day. In 1866, in *Ex parte Milligan*, he upheld that civil courts when open could conduct legal business instead of military courts, the institutional means to Radical Reconstruction. Speaking for the majority in the *Texas v. White* case in 1869, he ruled that the Union was inviolable, upholding the view that the rebel states never left the Union.

In other matters before the court, he and the majority ruled that wartime paper money was unconstitutional in *Hepburn v. Griswold*. He dissented in the *Slaughterhouse Cases* in 1873. He also saw the future in claiming that the **Fourteenth Amendment** allowed federal authorities to protect individuals from unjust state actions.

Chase was a fascinating combination of ambition, talent, and political enterprise. He combined and maintained his youthful religious idealism with cold ambition to have a tremendous impact on the nation. Aside from Lincoln, Chase was a very major player in the events of his day. He died in New York City on May 7, 1873. *See also* Recusants.

Further Reading: Blue, Frederick J. *Salmon P. Chase: A Life in Politics.* Kent, OH: Kent State University Press, 1987; Chase, Salmon P. *Diary and Correspondence of Salmon P. Chase.* New York: Da Capo Press, 1971; Hart, A. B. *Salmon Portland Chase.* Boston: Houghton Mifflin, 1909; Niven, John. *Salmon P. Chase: A Biography.* New York: Oxford University Press, 1995; Smith, Donnal V. *Chase and Civil War Politics.* Columbus, OH: The F. J. Heer Publishing Co., 1931.

Donald K. Pickens

Churches

Churches played a central role in explaining and realizing the meaning of the Civil War to victor and vanquished alike. They provided organized relief to rebuild the South and, in the case of northern denominations, extended missionary aid to the freedpeople. Northern churches emerged from the war triumphant in proclaiming the United States a redeemer nation and insisting that Reconstruction policies respect the Union victory by supporting the veterans and the families of those who had fallen and by arguing for a "just peace." White southern churches became rallying points for a defeated people needing to reclaim a sense of common purpose. White southern ministers figured prominently in the cult of the "**Lost Cause**," which cast the Confederacy as a noble enterprise and the Confederate soldier as the embodiment of Christian character. Blacks, meanwhile, left biracial churches in the South to create their own churches, which became the foundations of black political leadership and community. The major Protestant denominations (Baptists, Methodists, and Presbyterians) that had split before the war over slavery and related theological issues remained divided during, and in part because of, Reconstruction. Other "national" churches stayed united by letting clergy follow local political practices, as long as they did not conflict with church doctrine and purpose. Churches' involvement in, and effects on, Reconstruction thus varied according to place and interest.

During and after the war, northern churches linked religion with relief. The U.S. Sanitary Commission and the Christian Commission—the principal Union agencies developed during the war to provide support for war widows and orphans and succor to wounded soldiers—grew out of and relied on Protestant churches for resources and recruits. The networks of associations they created continued as a nexus of reform-minded effort during Reconstruction, and for some individuals laid the foundation of the Social Gospel later in the century. So, too, the millions of Bibles, religious tracts, pamphlets, and newspapers they distributed to soldiers and civilians during the war put a religious stamp on the war that informed understandings of what peace demanded after it. If the war was a test of faith as well as national purpose, the arguments went, so too must be the efforts to bind up the nation's wounds.

The northern churches' special interest was promoting Reconstruction through **education**. During and after the war, the Protestant religious press called for educational and other aid to the freedpeople, and individual churches and denominations sponsored schools, supplied and paid teachers, and distributed countless Christian reading materials to evangelize among whites and blacks, but also to make possible organized religious life in the postwar South. Northern missionaries in the South also established Sunday schools to save the region through Christian nurture and education. White southerners, who were otherwise suspicious of northern "intrusions" into local affairs and resentful of northern missionaries' presumptions of moral superiority and Republican politics, welcomed the Sunday school initiatives, which included teaching materials and Bibles supplied by northern churches. The war had torn families apart, challenged parental authority, encouraged lawlessness, and left many women alone to raise their children. Sunday schools promised a useful corrective. Southern white churches soon adopted and adapted Sunday schools on their own account to instill respect for authority in their youth and to revitalize their communities with their own lessons in morality, Christian discipline, catechism, and the three Rs.

Northern churches invested most heavily in education for the freedpeople. Best known among such ministries were the Quaker-run freedmen's schools in the **South Carolina** sea islands, some of which continued well into the twentieth century. Virtually all Protestant denominations made some attempt at setting up schools. The United Presbyterian Church in North America, for example, established a Freedmen's Mission in 1863, and the U.S. Presbyterian Church appointed a Committee for Freedmen in 1865—organizations from which Presbyterians founded and maintained industrial and teacher training schools for the freedpeople in several southern states. Especially active was the **American Missionary Association (AMA)**, which carried its antebellum and wartime antislavery witness into Reconstruction. The AMA first did so as part of the **Port Royal Experiment** in South Carolina, but its principal and most enduring contributions were establishing more than 500 schools for blacks in every former Confederate state, as well as in Missouri, Illinois, **Kentucky**, **Maryland**, and the **District of Columbia**. The AMA also chartered nine historically black colleges, most of which survive today. Northern churches and the AMA often worked in hand with the **Freedmen's Bureau**, which, under the leadership of General **Oliver O. Howard**, a devout Congregationalist who believed black uplift depended on Christian principles and education, combined free labor ideology with evangelical interest in setting up, staffing, and supplying schools. Howard and other Freedmen's Bureau officers appealed to northern churches for support, and the bureau in turn supported the missionary teachers, many of them white women recruited directly from northern churches. At the Second Plenary Council of Baltimore (1866), the Catholic Church also promised educational and material assistance to the freedpeople, but preoccupation with assimilating a swelling tide of diverse Catholic immigrants coming to the United States from the 1870s on diverted the church's attention from the Reconstruction South to northern cities. Still, through the Josephites and black orders of religious women, especially, the church did attempt a ministry to blacks, and by the 1880s, it ran segregated schools for blacks in most southern dioceses.

The freedpeople did not wait on white churches in asserting their own ideas on the meaning of freedom. In a mass exodus, blacks left biracial Baptist and Methodist congregations to form their churches free of any white oversight. The African Methodist Episcopal Church (A.M.E. Church), the largest and most powerful black denomination, evangelized vigorously among the freedpeople, encouraged and underwrote church foundings, and attracted a large following, but in their quest for autonomy, most southern blacks preferred starting up independent congregations rather than affiliating with the northern-based A.M.E. Church. Black churches provided spiritual and practical benefits of worship and fellowship. As the black population spread out geographically in taking up tenancy on individual plots, black churches cropped up across the Reconstruction South and literally became the meeting place for the black community in every locale. Churches ran schools, sponsored social events, and established mutual aid associations, burial societies, temperance clubs, and literary organizations. Churches gave blacks a sense of collective mission. The ministers preached self-reliance and moral probity as the path to spiritual and temporal salvation, and cast the now-free black community as "children of Zion" through whom God would reveal His true purposes.

That powerful messianic message echoed in black politics. Churches served as the venues for political debate and mobilizing, and ministers pounded home the duty to vote as the best way to save the republic and for the freedpeople to help themselves. Some ministers complained that politics threatened to crowd out church building, but no black minister could avoid preaching politics in the hothouse of Reconstruction. Ministers used their speaking and organizational skills, and their stature in the black community, to enter politics directly. **Richard H. Cain** in South Carolina, Henry M. Turner and Tunis G. Campbell in **Georgia**, and **James D. Lynch** in **Mississippi** were the most prominent minister-politicians among the more than 100 black ministers who won election to southern legislatures.

The political association of black, and white, congregations with the Republican Party made them targets of white **violence**. The **Ku Klux Klan** and other vigilante groups sought to silence the black vote by silencing black ministers, several of whom suffered beatings and worse because of their political activism. White Unionist churches suffered a similar fate, especially those aligned with the northern-based Methodist Episcopal Church, which in conservative white southerners' eyes was singularly obnoxious for its support of black rights and protection for white southern Unionists, now reviled as "**scalawags**."

White southern churches, meanwhile, were most intent on rebuilding the physical structures damaged or destroyed during the war, while also rebuilding the shattered spiritual and social lives. Men crippled by wartime injuries and disease found it hard to reclaim their manly station in a still largely agrarian culture where men worked with their hands, and women left widowed or abandoned during the war doubted the old truths about God as a protecting father and their men as Christian patriarchs. The white churches responded by restoring community through worship, a full array of social services, Sunday schools, and programs to bring families together in the church. Women especially gained new authority by engaging in church-sponsored reform efforts, such as temperance and orphan relief, and running fund drives to support church building.

White southern churches also entered politics. Ministers called for a public morality that rejected the supposed corruption of Republican-controlled "black and tan" legislatures and insisted on a racial order consistent with biblical "truths." Most important, white churches explained southern military defeat and Republican-imposed Reconstruction in scriptural terms that made resistance to Reconstruction almost a divine command. Many white southern clergymen took up the Lost Cause by arguing that the Confederacy was Christian and constitutional in purpose. God had not forsaken the South in allowing northern victory; rather, the argument went, He was chastising the South for its sins of selfishness that had undercut the noble Confederate experiment. In doing so, the ministers likened the South to the Israel of old, thereby encouraging white southerners that, as God's "chosen people," they would escape their own exile in Reconstruction by getting right with God and acting right in politics and public life. Central to this theme was the deification of the Confederate soldier, especially Robert E. Lee, and the construction and consecration of monuments, gravesites, and other public reminders of what Christian duty demanded. The public involvement of ministers and prominent church club women in rituals celebrating the Lost Cause ideology, such as Confederate Memorial Day, bound church and state in "redeeming" the South from Republican rule. They also further convinced blacks that white churches had no place for them.

Protestant churches reflected three visions of Reconstruction and spiritual and moral renewal for the South, and the nation rooted in a common theological core of providential history but revealed variously in differing sectional, racial, and social identities and interests. By the end of the century, northern white churches had retreated from Reconstruction and many had taken up the "white man's burden" in endorsing expansionism and arguing for immigration restrictions. They also joined in rituals of sectional reconciliation that emphasized the nobility of the Civil War soldier, ignored slavery as the cause of the war, and denigrated Reconstruction as a fool's errand. The distinctions among the white and black churches that informed Reconstruction, however, did not wholly disappear. They persisted into the twentieth century to reemerge in public consciousness during the modern **civil rights** movement. *See also* Bureau of Refugees, Freedmen, and Abandoned Lands; Redemption; Women's Movement.

Further Reading: Blum, Edward J. *Reforging the White Republic: Race, Religion, and American Nationalism, 1865–1898.* Baton Rouge: Louisiana State University Press, 2005; Cimbala, Paul A., and Randall M. Miller, eds. *The Freedmen's Bureau and Reconstruction: Reconsiderations.* New York: Fordham University Press, 1999; Dvorak, Katharine L. *An African American Exodus: The Segregation of Southern Churches.* Brooklyn, NY: Carlson Publishing, 1991; Friedman, Jean E. *The Enclosed Garden: Women and Community in the Evangelical South, 1830–1900.* Chapel Hill: University of North Carolina Press, 1985; Howard, Victor B. *Religion and the Radical Republican Movement 1860–1870.* Lexington: University Press of Kentucky, 1990; Jacoway, Elizabeth. *Yankee Missionaries in the South: The Penn School Experiment.* Baton Rouge: Louisiana State University Press, 1980; McMillen, Sally G. *To Raise Up the South: Sunday Schools in Black and White Churches, 1865–1915.* Baton Rouge: Louisiana State University Press, 2001; Miller, Randall M., Harry S. Stout, and Charles Reagan Wilson, eds. *Religion and the American Civil War.* New York: Oxford University Press, 1998; Stowell, Daniel W. *Rebuilding Zion: The Religious Reconstruction of the South, 1863–1877.* New York: Oxford University Press, 1998; Walker, Clarence E. *A Rock in a Weary Land: The African Methodist Episcopal Church during the Civil War and Reconstruction.* Baton Rouge: Louisiana State University Press, 1982; Wilson, Charles Reagan. *Baptized in Blood: The Religion of the Lost Cause, 1865–1920.* Athens: University of Georgia Press, 1980.

Randall M. Miller

Cincinnati Convention (1872)

In three short days, the Cincinnati Convention saw both the birth and death of the hopes of liberal reformers that they could create a viable new political party that would change what they believed was the course of the United States in the late nineteenth century.

In the early 1870s, Republicans disgruntled with their party's increasing corruption and unhappy with President **Ulysses S. Grant**'s attempts to annex Santo Domingo (the Dominican Republic) joined with **New Departure** Democrats who were anxious to distance themselves from their own party's southern extremists to create a new, national political party that would appeal to moderates across the nation. Meeting in Cincinnati, Ohio, on May 1, 1872, the **Liberal Republicans** adopted a platform that was designed to reclaim the government from the politicians who stayed in power by using corporate or tax money to create pork-barrel projects that provided jobs to constituents. The platform called for recognition of the Reconstruction Amendments, for an end to the political disabilities of former confederates, and for an end to the corruption of modern politics by reducing the power of both organized labor and big business. While the new party was designed to move the country past the issues of the war years, it was not progressive. Emphasizing their essential conservatism, Liberal Republicans at the convention refused to allow female delegates and silenced female protesters from the floor.

The father of the Liberal Republican movement, Senator **Carl Schurz** of Missouri, hoped to see the convention nominate Missouri's Liberal Republican governor B. Gratz Brown for president. Others hoped that reformers **Charles Francis Adams** or **David Davis** would take the nomination. Instead, a series of political maneuvers by protariff forces meant that the convention's endorsement went to the eccentric and comical **Horace Greeley**, editor of the *New York Tribune*, who was well-known as a staunch supporter of protective tariffs. Even more well-known than his hatred of free trade, though, were Greeley's diatribes against Democrats and southerners. Greeley's nomination meant that the Liberal Republican Party would be unable to mount any serious challenge to the dominant Republicans. Antitariff northern Democrats could not be mustered to his standard; disgusted southern Democrats simply refused to vote in the election; and most Republican reformers washed their hands of the ridiculous candidate. By the time the convention adjourned on May 3, prescient observers had already declared the Liberal Republican movement dead.

Although the election of 1872 offered no serious threat to the regular Republicans and Grant, the issues that arose did not fade. The succeeding years would keep the South, **African Americans**, and the problems of corruption at the forefront of the party's concerns. *See also* Bennett, James Gordon, Jr.; Blair, Francis P., Sr.; Bloody Shirt; Democratic Party; Pendleton, George Hunt; Readmission; Republicans, Moderate; Scandals; Stalwarts; U.S. Army and Reconstruction.

Further Reading: Chamberlin, Everett. *The Struggle of '72: The Issues and Candidates of the Present Political Campaign.* Chicago: Union Publishing Company,

1872, available at http://www.hti.umich.edu/m/moagrp/; Ross, Earle Dudley. *The Liberal Republican Movement*. New York: Henry Holt & Company, 1919.

Heather Cox Richardson

Civil Rights

In light of rather loose, present-day, commonplace usage, civil rights is a somewhat murky concept. The term might refer to the modern movement that bore its name, aimed at eliminating **Jim Crow laws** and customs in the South, a second Reconstruction completing the work began during the first Reconstruction. It may refer to a constitutionally guaranteed set of powers a person, as a member of a civil society, has or can claim from the state against others who might incur upon those powers. Thus, one might distinguish such rights from political rights, in that they refer to the rights a citizen bears or can claim beyond or outside those of basic political participation, as in disputes involving private parties. In some cases, it evokes a species of rights derived from nature, from a transcendent moral order, or from the fact of being human, a use to which many **Radical Republicans** and civil rights movement activists lent the term. In nearly every case, overlapping with all such definitions, the idea involves the problem of racial and ethnic inequality in America and the persistent struggle of various actors to combat such inequities. Today, the historical trajectory of the black freedom struggle and the idea of civil rights are inextricably linked. The Reconstruction era was the historical moment when the term civil rights, for the first time nationally, acquired this modern meaning.

Antebellum Assumptions

From its founding, the United States has always been a culture of rights. Such language, in the European natural law tradition, informs our founding documents, especially the Declaration of Independence and the Bill of Rights in the **U.S. Constitution**. Prior to the Civil War and Reconstruction, the individual states were the keepers of the large share of these oft-celebrated civil liberties. The national government did not often incur in the states' sovereign doings in civil matters. In other words, our modern conception of civil rights, which includes the active national protection of, and the ability of groups to claim, such rights in the event of their violation by states or by private parties, did not exist. The Bill of Rights was thus a very limited set of guarantees, having little to do with how people experienced their daily lives. (It is this antebellum conception that comprises our contemporary legal understanding of *civil liberties*, particularly as distinct from *civil rights*.) Before the prerequisites for our modern understanding of civil rights could be met then, this antebellum state of affairs had to change. The Civil War partly fulfilled such a requirement. Reconstruction completed the transformation, in theory if not always in practice.

More specifically, the end of slavery and the clear resolution of the constitutional conflict between the national government and the states in favor of the Union did the job. But in order for civil rights to acquire the meaning it did during the Reconstruction, the idea that a group of people, namely **African Americans**, could even claim rights, particularly from the national government, needed legitimizing. In antebellum America, such notions existed in astonishingly few quarters. The Fugitive Slave Law of 1850 and chief justice Roger Taney's decision in the 1857 case *Dred Scott v. Sanford* expressed in national, legal-juridical terms what northern and southern social practice had already made abundantly clear: Ostracized and unrecognized by civil society, black people had little or no status whatsoever as rights-bearers in the minds of the vast majority of white Americans.

Republican Congress, War, and the Creation of Civil Rights

So concomitant with the bloodshed of the war and the coming of Reconstruction was an intellectual revolution, one that transformed America's existing culture of rights in such a way that civil rights, as a cipher for the fortunes of African Americans, became a legitimate, supportable issue in more than merely radical (most notably **abolitionist**) arenas of public discourse. The startling shift in thinking about slavery within the national Republican Party between 1861 and 1865 was an especially telling example of this phenomenon. In early 1861, Congress, with widespread Republican support, approved a constitutional amendment to protect slavery in perpetuity where it already existed. After Fort Sumter, such legislation faded from public view, and Congress began to undermine the peculiar institution. Still, action in this vein was conceptually uneven. Congress passed legislation in 1862 to repeal the Fugitive Slave Law and eliminate slavery in the **District of Columbia**, yet **confiscation** laws enacted that same year against white southerners operated in such a way as to acknowledge the legitimacy of slaves as property, as objects capable of seizure. As for presidential politics, the **Emancipation** Proclamation, effective January 1, 1863, was immensely important in symbolic terms while limited in actual scope, a martial statement made by President **Abraham Lincoln** in his capacity as commander in chief, applying only narrowly to those states in rebellion, merely confirming a process that many slaves had initiated in practice well before 1863. That by 1865 so many whites would support a constitutional amendment (the **Thirteenth Amendment**) outlawing slavery speaks to a substantial shift in thought and in America's culture of rights, precipitated by the experience of civil war and the revolutionary actions of African Americans, slave and free. So it bears mention that African American soldiers who fought capably for the Union certainly played a significant role in this remarkable change in thinking, as they proved their capacity to act politically and even heroically as members in a civil society. Too, the public pronouncements of Abraham Lincoln later in the war had an immense impact, as the president led the Union cause in clear reference to the Declaration of Independence, interpreting its invocation of the self-evident truth that all men were created equal in more inclusive terms. By war's end, the elimination of slavery became a moral necessity crucial to most every Republican vision for national Reconstruction, whether moderate or radical.

The Thirteenth Amendment

Perhaps more important to the creation of the modern concept of civil rights, though, were the theoretical implications of this vision when made law, namely in the Thirteenth Amendment, ratified in 1865. The notion that civil rights might be something African Americans could claim now became a distinct possibility. The second article of the amendment clearly stated that "Congress shall have the power to enforce this legislation by appropriate legislation." Congress, supported by the national Constitution, would provide the necessary protections for the right of African Americans to be free against those who would deny such rights. The point at which the Constitution definitively enabled the national government to enter the space of civil concerns was the point at which it unequivocally outlawed slavery, which in the United States applied to African Americans. Race, civil rights, and an assertive national government were now indelibly connected.

The Civil Rights Act of 1866

Congressional action during the Reconstruction would complete the task of binding the term civil rights to the fortunes of African Americans, all the while making the national government, at least in theory, the guarantor of those rights, thus creating our modern understanding of the concept. In 1866, Congress passed, over President **Andrew Johnson**'s veto, the first congressional action to deal with the status of free African Americans following the Civil War—the **Civil Rights Act of 1866**. Language transformed conceptual connections, making the association explicit. The act for the first time defined citizenship in national terms, applying it to all those born in the United States "of every race and color, without regard to previous condition of slavery or involuntary servitude," entitling them to certain rights. Among the most significant of these rights was the ability to make and enforce contracts; to bring lawsuits in court; and to hold, conduct, and defend personal property in terms equal to white citizens. The act also gave those denied of their rights under the new law the opportunity, in federal court, to prosecute those who refused to uphold its provisions. The law was passed in response to the many **Black Codes** that emerged in the South at the end of the Civil War, where newly free African Americans were often forced into a legal position not far removed from slavery. It was the first real effort following the Civil War, after having recognized freedom in the Thirteenth Amendment, to define it in legislative terms. While symbolically important, its impact proved minimal in practice.

The Act banned certain public acts of injustice against African Americans, but failed to curb the widespread acts of **violence** against African Americans in the aftermath of the Civil War. Also, the states had the primary responsibility to enforce the law, and few did. Federal courts could only enforce the law if the states violated it explicitly. In the years that followed, according to a pattern that would become very familiar, many southern states passed fiendishly sophisticated legislation that effectively circumvented the language of federal laws. Most often, states enacted laws that made no mention of color or race, while at the same time excluding African Americans from the benefits of citizenship. In the final analysis, the Civil Rights Act of 1866 was a prelude to the more substantial congressional measures passed in the years that followed, in particular the **Fourteenth Amendment**.

The Fourteenth Amendment

Ratified in 1868, the Fourteenth Amendment was a piece of legislation made necessary at least in part by many Republicans' belief that the 1866 act, if subjected to scrutiny, would be found unconstitutional, particularly in light of the 1857 *Dred Scott* decision, in which the court ruled that African Americans had no legal standing to pursue rights claims. Moreover, President Andrew Johnson's veto of the 1866 bill, and reports of white southern resistance made it clear to many Republicans that the civil rights of African Americans must be protected to guard against the lingering forces of rebellion. In effect, the Fourteenth Amendment overturned the *Scott* decision, expanding the reach of citizenship to far more people. The amendment challenged the traditional relationship between the national government, the states, and individuals in a way crucial to the creation of civil rights that took place during the period.

Yet the language of this challenge revealed exploitable limitations. The first clause, for example, was both potentially revolutionary and fatally ambiguous. Clearly making citizenship a dual proposition (of nation and of individual states), the document maintained that

> No State shall make or enforce any law which shall abridge the privileges and immunities of citizens of the United States; nor shall any state deprive any person of life, liberty or property, without due process of law; nor deny any person within its jurisdiction equal protection of the laws.

Though the amendment paved the way for the process of incorporation, whereby the national government would assume primary authority in the defense of civil rights, thus opening conceptual doors, tricky terms like "privileges and immunities" proved subject to broad reaches of interpretation. Republican supporters believed that the amendment gave Congress the right to ensure the civil rights of American citizens, supplanting duties formerly under state jurisdiction given the existence of certain natural laws, thus the Lockean "life, liberty, and property." In short, the amendment changed the nature of American federalism, embracing a strong national perspective. Others of a more contrary bent, especially in the judiciary, contended that the Fourteenth Amendment merely reinforced the traditional authority of the states to determine the conditions by which citizens could exercise their civil rights.

Enforcement Acts and the Courts

While many Republicans contended that Congress had the power to protect the civil rights of African Americans, widespread instances in which recalcitrant white southerners repeatedly violated such rights through fraud, violence, and intimidation led to more legislation, the series of **Enforcement Acts**, enacted in 1870 and 1871. The acts, supported by then president **Ulysses S. Grant**, were especially designed to stop **Ku Klux Klan** terrorism, which they accomplished with some success. The 1870 acts dealt primarily with the protection of **suffrage** as guaranteed by the **Fifteenth Amendment**, ratified in early 1870. The 1871 Ku Klux Klan Act more explicitly enforced the provisions of the 1866 Civil Rights Act. Dealing a mortal blow to Klan vigilantism, the legislation made individual acts of violence and conspiracy federally prosecutable crimes. In this, it made more definite the modern meaning of civil rights. The national government would now guarantee that even private individuals could not deny the relevance and efficacy of African American claims to civil rights.

As quickly as Congress helped to create modern civil rights, many politicians would increasingly sense and respond positively to a national mood set against their practice. For its part, the **Supreme Court** would undermine the revolutionary implications of civil rights legislation in a series of decisions that reoriented American federalism much closer to the antebellum constitutional universe. In the *Slaughterhouse* decision of 1873, disastrous for the fortunes of African Americans, the court ruled that the Fourteenth Amendment, while specifically intended for black people, protected only those rights specifically emanating from constitutionally narrow national, rather than state, citizenship. In other words, the states retained their authority over the vast majority of civil rights that African Americans might enjoy in their daily lives. In 1876, based upon the limited definition of citizenship proposed in *Slaughterhouse*, the court ruled in *United States v. Cruikshank* that the Fourteenth Amendment authorization of congressional enforcement applied only to violations of African American civil rights by states, not by individuals. Contending that it was the responsibility of the states to prosecute individual violations, the court effectively rendered the national government powerless to protect black civil rights.

The Civil Rights Act of 1875

With the revolutionary meaning of Reconstruction largely compromised, Congress enacted potentially one of the most far-reaching pieces of civil rights legislation in U.S. history, though in practice, it would prove anything but. It would take nearly nine decades for the legislative body to pass anything close in intent, namely the Civil Rights Act of 1964. The **Civil Rights Act of 1875**, passed largely in homage to Senator **Charles Sumner**, who vigorously shepherded and defended the legislation before his death in 1874, made racial discrimination and exclusion in several public accommodations illegal, providing for "full and equal" use of inns, theaters, and public transportation. The act also made clear that race should not be a factor in jury selection. (Sumner, a stubborn, uncompromising supporter of racial equality before the law, favored even more expansive provisions that would have made enforced separation in **churches** and schools illegal, ideas that the vast majority of his peers knew to be untenable. Sumner's notion of "before the law" employed a rather generously narrow and confusing definition of the social realm.)

In any case, African Americans shouldered the large share of the burden for enforcement of the Civil Rights Act of 1875. Blacks could seek redress for violations of their civil rights in the federal courts. Few tried; those who did found the wheels of court bureaucracy trammeled by heavy caseloads.

Following an all-too-familiar pattern, the Supreme Court in the *Civil Rights Cases* of 1883 struck down nearly all aspects of the act, leaving only the jury section.

Conclusions

Though Republican legislation occurred well in advance of changes in white popular opinion about the rightful status of black people in the United States (opinion confirmed by the Supreme Court), the conception of civil rights created during the Reconstruction era largely endures to this day. For many white southerners, and more than a few northerners, the term civil rights came to signify the injustices of Reconstruction, particularly decisions made in favor of the black race and at the apparent expense of whites. On the other hand, northern and southern black folk, by creating and sustaining vibrant institutions during the period, blurred the traditional distinctions between the civil and the political, in some cases actively fighting racial discrimination under the banner of civil rights—a concept now peculiarly attached to (and even conflated with) the black freedom struggle in the United States. By the end of Reconstruction, as formal recourse for their grievances and claims evaporated, African American activists kept the idea alive, while the masses of black folk (North and South) maintained the social institutions so crucial to the practice of Reconstruction politics. That the modern civil rights (or freedom) movement (1954–1965) emanated from black social institutions on the local level should come as no surprise—in many cases, the creation and cultivation of those institutions coincided with the intellectual construction of civil rights in America, an innovative way of thinking and speaking about African Americans and their relation to the national government that was fashioned during the Reconstruction era.

Further Reading: Cortner, Richard C. *The Supreme Court and the Second Bill of Rights: The Fourteenth Amendment and the Nationalization of Civil Liberties.* Madison: University of Wisconsin, 1981; Du Bois, W.E.B. *Black Reconstruction: An Essay toward the Part Which Black Folk Played in the Attempt to Reconstruct Democracy in America, 1860–1880.* New York: S. A. Russell, 1956; Dworkin, Ronald. *Taking Rights Seriously.* Cambridge, MA: Harvard University Press, 1977; Fleming, Walter L. *Documentary History of the Reconstruction: Political, Military, Social, Religious, Educational, and Industrial 1865 to the Present Time.* 2 vols. Cleveland: Arthur H. Clark, 1906–1907; Foner, Eric. *Reconstruction: America's Unfinished Revolution, 1863–1877.* New York: Harper and Row, 1988; Green, Robert P., ed. *Equal Protection and the African American Constitutional Experience: A Documentary History.* Westport, CT: Greenwood Press, 2000; Hahn, Steven. *A Nation Under Our Feet: Black Political Struggles in the Rural South from Slavery to the Great Migration.* Cambridge, MA: Harvard Belknap, 2003; Hyman, Harold. *A More Perfect Union: The Impact of the Civil War and Reconstruction on the Constitution.* New York: Knopf, 1973; Kaczorowski, Robert: *The Politics of Judicial Interpretation: The Federal Courts, Department of Justice, and Civil Rights, 1866–1876.* Dobbs Ferry, NY: Oceana, 1985; "To Begin the Nation Anew: Congress, Citizenship, and Civil Rights after the Civil War." *The American Historical Review* 92 (February 1987): 45–68; Litwack, Leon. *Been in the Storm So Long: The Aftermath of Slavery.* New York: Vintage, 1980.

Peter A. Kuryla

Civil Rights Act of 1866

In the aftermath of the American Civil War, emancipated slaves in the South faced an uncertain future and occupied an uncertain status. Presidents **Abraham Lincoln** and then **Andrew Johnson** believed that the defeated Confederate states would make some reasonable attempt to integrate **African Americans** into southern society as free persons. When white southerners failed to do so, Congress attempted to secure basic civil and legal rights for the millions of emancipated slaves in the South. The earliest of these efforts was the Civil Rights Act of 1866.

In December 1865, Republicans in control of the U.S. Congress created a fifteen-member **Joint Committee on Reconstruction**, which was made up of six senators and nine representatives. This committee drafted the Civil Rights Act of 1866, which, for the first time, defined national citizenship and provided citizenship to anyone born or naturalized in the United States. The act did not apply to nontaxed Native Americans. Prior to the law, defining the rights of citizenship was the sole prerogative of the states. The act was part of a congressional effort to combat the **Black Codes** put in place by several southern states after the war. These codes severely limited the legal and economic freedom of blacks after the Civil War, and included limits on the ability to make contracts, to own property, and, in some instances, even to marry. The act was also a direct repudiation of the holding in the 1857 case of *Dred Scott v. Sanford*, which denied citizenship to blacks, both slave and free. The legislation defined certain minimum legal rights of citizenship, including the right to serve on juries, to sue, to give evidence at trial, to make **contracts**, to serve as a witness, and to own private property, as well as provided a right to due process. Congress passed the act in March 1866, with unanimous Republican support in the House of Representatives and the support of all but three Republican senators. Later **civil rights** legislation was also passed in the **Civil Rights Act of 1875** and the **Enforcement Acts** of 1870 and 1871.

In political terms, the act was evidence of growing tension between **Moderate** and **Radical Republicans** and President Andrew Johnson, Lincoln's vice president and a former senator from **Tennessee**. Johnson never accepted the idea of providing full citizenship to African Americans and vetoed the Civil Rights Act of 1866. His hostile veto message first confused and then energized the Republicans, many of whom found the act to be a reasonable, even conservative, answer to the dilemma of the freedpeople. The Republican factions came together and enacted the law over the president's veto on April 9, 1866, the first significant piece of legislation passed over a presidential veto in American history. The concern over future battles with the president over the question of national citizenship for freed slaves, and the threat of repeal by a later Congress, led in large part to the inclusion of similar citizenship provisions in the **Fourteenth Amendment**. The amendment was adopted by the Congress and sent to the states for ratification two months after the Civil Rights Act, on June 13, 1866.

The Civil Rights Act not only defined basic civil and legal rights but also provided for federal enforcement of those rights. Under the legislation, Congress gave the states concurrent jurisdiction over civil rights, except for the power to regulate the rights named in the act on the basis of race, color, or previous condition of servitude. Those found violating the law were subject to fines and imprisonment in federal court. Moreover, the army and navy were given the power to enforce the act.

After his veto was overturned, President Johnson remained openly opposed to the act. As a result, the executive branch did not vigorously enforce the legislation during his term. Moreover, federal efforts at enforcement were often powerless in the face of organized campaigns of **violence** directed by the **Ku Klux Klan** and other organizations that relied on physical and economic intimidation to deprive free blacks of their new legal and constitutional rights. *See also* Abolition of Slavery; Congressional Reconstruction; Emancipation; Freedmen's Bureau Bills; Presidential Reconstruction; Supreme Court; U.S. Constitution.

Further Reading: Symposium: "Theories of Taking the Constitution Seriously Outside the Courts." *Fordham Law Review* 73: 1415.

Daniel W. Hamilton

Civil Rights Act of 1875

Coming only nine years after the nation's first experiment with **civil rights** legislation, the Civil Rights Act of 1875 was the last civil rights statute of the Reconstruction period. Before its enactment, the country had added three amendments to the **U.S. Constitution** and passed several **enforcement** statutes as it sought to eliminate the discrimination that limited the freedom of black Americans. This act was both a logical and a threatening next step.

The statute was first proposed by **Charles Sumner**, whose death in March 1874 prompted some to see the enacting of his bill as a form of tribute to the influential Radical Republican senator from Massachusetts. In unsuccessfully proposing the bill in 1870, 1871, 1872, and 1873, Sumner had argued that both the **Thirteenth** and **Fourteenth Amendments** supported the providing of federal protection for blacks denied access to such public, quasi-public, and private accommodations as schools, inns and theaters, **churches**, and cemeteries. The bill that he proposed in 1871 and 1872 was, he said, merely a supplement to the **Civil Rights Act of 1866**, which required equal civil (economic) rights for blacks and whites; the rights were necessary if Americans were to be free rather than slaves. Sumner believed that private racial discrimination was a badge of slavery and thus was prohibited by the Thirteenth Amendment. With the **Supreme Court**'s decision in the *Slaughterhouse Cases* in 1873, the focus of the bill's constitutionality shifted to the Fourteenth Amendment. With Sumner's death, the overall focus of the debate shifted to the coverage of schools, a provision excluded from the final version of the bill.

By the mid-1870s, the country was tired of Reconstruction and had developed no real commitment to black rights, much less to racial equality. Nevertheless, thanks in part to Republicans' desire to appeal to black voters after the Democratic victories in the 1874 state and congressional elections, a version of Sumner's public accommodations bill was passed in 1875 during the lame duck session. The new law fell short of Sumner's goals, excluding such especially controversial areas as schools and cemeteries. Instead of the comprehensive coverage envisioned by Sumner, the statute, entitled "An act to protect all citizens in their civil and legal rights," stipulated that all Americans should have equal access to such public accommodations as inns and theaters, public conveyances on land or water, and places of amusement in general. It also prohibited racial discrimination in the selection of federal and state juries. The law gave the federal courts exclusive jurisdiction over both civil and criminal cases arising under the law and made these cases reviewable by the Supreme Court.

During the bill's consideration by Congress, many Americans in both the North and South opposed it as a dangerous expansion of federal power and intrusion into private affairs. The bill's provisions, they argued, took the national government into the sensitive and personal area of social equality at a time when most Americans accepted government efforts only on behalf of economic rights and, to a degree, political rights.

In 1880 in *Ex parte Virginia* and *Strauder v. West Virginia*, the U.S. Supreme Court upheld the jury section, but sections 1 and 2 dealing with public accommodations were voided in 1883 in the *Civil Rights Cases*. The last, a collection of five cases from California, Kansas, Missouri, New Jersey, and **Tennessee** testing the application of section 5 of the Fourteenth Amendment, involved innkeepers, theater owners, and a **railroad**. By an 8 to 1 vote, the Court declared that the Fourteenth Amendment limited only official state action. Hotel and theater owners and railroad conductors were private individuals, according to the majority opinion delivered by Justice Joseph P. Bradley, even if they operated as a result of state-issued licenses and franchises. As a result of being private, these businessmen's actions were not covered by the prohibitions of the Fourteenth Amendment.

In addition, although the Thirteenth Amendment prohibited slavery and its "badges," denial of access to a hotel, restaurant, or railroad car was not a reinstitution of slavery. In lone dissent, Justice John Marshall Harlan supported the argument that private racial discrimination was a badge of slavery prohibited by the Thirteenth Amendment.

The Court's narrow interpretation of the Fourteenth Amendment's reach into state and private action severely limited the provision's usefulness in battling racial discrimination over the next 100 years. As a result, Congress did not pass another public accommodations bill until 1964, this time framed on Congress's Commerce Power. *See also* Jim Crow Laws.

Further Reading: Donald, David. *Charles Sumner and the Rights of Man*. New York: Knopf, 1970; Gillette, William. *Retreat from Reconstruction, 1869–1879*. Baton Rouge: Louisiana State University Press, 1979.

Claudine L. Ferrell

Clayton, Powell (1833–1914)

Union brigadier general and ninth governor of **Arkansas** (1868–1871), Powell Clayton was born on August 7, 1833, in Bethel County, Pennsylvania, to John and Ann (Clarke) Clayton. He attended Partridge Military Academy in

Bristol, Pennsylvania, and then studied civil engineering before moving to Leavenworth, Kansas, in 1855. A Douglas Democrat in the election of 1860, he was elected lieutenant of the Leavenworth Light Infantry (U.S.) and rose to the rank of brigadier general by the Civil War's end. He participated in the Battle of Wilson Creek. Especially notable was his defense of Pine Bluff (October 25, 1863), in which he repulsed a much larger Confederate force commanded by John S. Marmaduke.

After the war, he stayed in Arkansas and settled on a plantation near Pine Bluff. He married Adaline McGraw, the daughter of a Confederate major. Clayton did not enter politics until the beginning of **Congressional Reconstruction**. Under the **Radical Republican**'s program, the state held a convention, dominated by Unionist "**scalawags**" and so-called **carpetbaggers**, which drew up a new constitution to enfranchise blacks, **disfranchise** former confederates, and recognize the **Thirteenth Amendment** to the **U.S. Constitution**. New state elections were held under this constitution, and Clayton was elected governor in 1868.

The next three years saw Clayton attempt to restore law and order, only to be met by resistance from the **Democratic Party**, whose political action arm was the **Ku Klux Klan**. Building on his base of loyal mountain residents and newly enfranchised freedmen, Clayton fought the Klan to a standstill. He also survived an assassination attempt.

Other parts of Clayton's agenda included establishing for the first time in Arkansas a public **education** system, refinancing Arkansas's enormous antebellum state debt, and funding **railroad** construction. In trying to accomplish these ends, he erected a formidable **patronage** machine but still could not satisfy all the elements within his own party. By the late 1860s, state **Liberal Republicans** in Arkansas repudiated both President **Ulysses S. Grant** and Governor Clayton and allied themselves with the Democrats in trying to wrest control away from the governor. Clayton in turn decided to move his power base to Washington by becoming a U.S. senator. His enemies were even anxious to help in this, but Clayton would not leave until he had arranged for his own supporters to retain control of the statehouse. Once this was accomplished by means of some timely resignations, Clayton moved on to Washington in 1871.

Although the system he left collapsed in the **Brooks-Baxter War** in 1874 and he served only one Senate term, incredibly Clayton remained in charge of federal patronage in Arkansas until his retirement in 1912. His most important reward was appointment as ambassador to Mexico, serving from 1897 to 1905. He retained an interest in Arkansas and was one of the principal investors in the spa town of Eureka Springs. His name, along with other Republican Reconstruction officials, is engraved in stone inside The Crescent, the town's crowning grand hotel.

Clayton was by far one of the ablest and most effective of the Republican Reconstruction governors. His memoir, *The Aftermath of the Civil War in Arkansas* (1915), is a straightforward defense of his actions, based on research from documents and newspapers. Although all the usual Democratic charges about corruption were cast at him, and his infamy was such that his portrait was not allowed to grace the state capitol until 1976, his efficiency as a leader cannot be questioned, even if his skills were more of a military order than those of a consensus builder. *See also* Black Suffrage; Constitutional Conventions; Military Reconstruction Acts; Scandals; Union League of America; U.S. Army and Reconstruction; Violence.

Further Reading: Burnside, William H. *The Honorable Powell Clayton.* Conway: University of Central Arkansas Press, 1991; Clayton, Powell. *The Aftermath of the Civil War in Arkansas.* New York: Neale, 1915; Donovan, Timothy P., Willard B. Gatewood, Jr., and Jeannie M. Whayne, eds. *The Governors of Arkansas: Essays in Political Biography.* Fayetteville: University of Arkansas Press, 1995. See also http:// www.oldstatehousemuseum.com/ for a multipart biography with photo illustrations.

Michael B. Dougan

Colfax, Schuyler (1823–1885)

Congressman and later vice president of the United States, Colfax brought little leadership and much questionable behavior to his political career. Born on March 23, 1823, to working-class parents in New York City, Colfax's father died when Schuyler was a young boy. He entered the workforce as a clerk. His mother remarried and the family moved to New Carlisle, Indiana. A bit of an indifferent student, his main interest was politics—Whig and then Republican. Elected county auditor in 1841–1849, he moved to South Bend. He also worked as a journalist reporting on the state legislature.

His marriage in 1844 to Evelyn Clark was childless. For nearly twenty years, he owned and operated a newspaper that turned into an effective instrument for Whigs and, later, Republicans. Always a strong and loyal party man, his views developed after he took the "pulse" of the voters. By 1854, he recognized the political significance of the Kansas-Nebraska Act. Creating a coalition with nativist groups, he was elected to the House of Representatives. He served from 1855 to 1869.

He was Speaker of the House for nine years. He developed no major legislation, but backed his supporters. His role as chair of the post office and Post Roads Committee allowed him to take advantage of **patronage** opportunities. Colfax was quick to support Republican candidates. In this effort, he cultivated newspaper reporters and held informal press conferences.

Colfax was a safe addition to the **Grant** ticket in 1868. After the election, the widowed vice president married Ellen Wade; they had one child. As his private life became dull and routine, his last years in politics turned on issues of ethics and corruption.

Always open about his financial support from **railroads**, he used a railroad pass as a natural benefit of his position. He and Jay Cooke were

Schulyer Colfax, c. 1877. (Courtesy of the Library of Congress.)

close business and social friends. A fellow member of the House, Oakes Ames drew Colfax into the Credit Mobilier **scandal**. His congressional salary never covered his expenses, so he felt no shame in accepting the kindness of lobbyists and railroad interests.

Without being indicted or even charged, Colfax left government service in 1873. Primarily, he was mad at lack of defense from his friends and the lack of their gratitude for his services over the years. In Indiana, he remained popular and had a good living lecturing on various topics throughout the Midwest. He was a successful orator. He died on January 13, 1885, during a speaking tour. Never a reformer, never a Radical, he was a typical example of the Gilded Age politician as spoilsman.

Further Reading: Morgan, H. Wayne. *The Gilded Age*. Syracuse, NY: Syracuse University Press, 1963; Smith, Willard H. *Schuyler Colfax: The Changing Fortunes of a Political Idol*. Indianapolis: Indiana Historical Bureau, 1952; Summers, Mark W. *Party Games: Getting, Keeping, and Using Power in Gilded Age Politics*. Chapel Hill: University of North Carolina Press, 2004.

Donald K. Pickens

Command of the Army Act (1867)

The fight to control Reconstruction policies prompted Congress to take matters into its own hands. In 1867, Congress passed a series of acts to wrangle power out of the hands of President **Andrew Johnson**. The main premise of the Command of the Army Act required that any order issued to the **U.S. Army** be done only through the general in chief. The validity of this act would be tested with the **impeachment** trial of the president.

Background

Members of Congress and President Johnson found themselves at odds over the handling of Reconstruction policies. Congress challenged Johnson's sympathetic program toward the former Confederate states and people, thus commencing action to strip the president of his authority over Reconstruction. Contending that the army followed congressional directives only since it was dissatisfied with the operations conducted under the president's initiative, members of Congress began their efforts to wrestle control of Reconstruction through various acts of legislation.

Reconstruction

In 1867, ascertaining that the army sought direction from Congress and not President Johnson, Congress began taking steps to initiate its own Reconstruction policies. In *Acts and Resolutions, 39 Congress, 2 Session*, thus deemed the Command of the Army Act, dated March 2, 1867, Congress passed an additional provision to the Army Appropriations Act. The first stipulation enacted through this legislation defined the residence of the general of the army. Henceforth, the general was to establish his headquarters in the nation's capital—a minor condition, but one that would put the general of the army in close proximity to the workings of the government, specifically Congress.

This piece of legislation further stipulated that operations of the military would solely be delivered through the general of the army. With this condition, the president, who was the commander in chief, was denied his right to issue commands directly to the nation's military. The secretary of war also was denied this authority.

In order to further strip the president of his powers, the Command of the Army Act also specified that the general in chief could not be taken out of office temporarily or permanently by presidential initiative alone. Henceforth, the Senate had to approve any such changes in the holder of this office. The general in chief could only be reassigned or removed if it was done at his own initiative.

In addition to these major limitations placed upon presidential authority, Congress also required that any **militia** that was in existence in the former Confederate states, with the exception of **Arkansas** and **Tennessee**, be immediately dispersed. Also, all military and Freedmen's Bureau officers were delegated the duty of preventing the implementation of violent punishments rendered by any illegitimate judicial body in these states.

In 1868, when President Johnson found himself before impeachment hearings, the ninth item of impeachment incorporated his violation of the Command of the Army Act by his action of conversing with a military officer. *See also* Bureau of Refugees, Freedmen, and Abandoned Lands; Congressional Reconstruction; Stanton, Edwin M.

Further Reading: Chambers, John Whiteclay, III. "The Military and Civil Authority." In John E. Jessup and Louise B. Ketz, eds., *Encyclopedia of the American Military.* Vol. 3. New York: Charles Scribner's Sons, 1994; Craven, Avery. *Reconstruction: The Ending of the Civil War.* New York: Holt, Rinehart and Winston, 1969; Dawson, Joseph G., III. "Reconstruction and American Imperialism." In John E. Jessup and Louise B. Ketz, eds., *Encyclopedia of the American Military.* Vol. 2. New York: Charles Scribner's Sons, 1994; Fleming, Walter L. *Documentary History of Reconstruction.* Vol. 1. Cleveland, OH: The Arthur H. Clark Company, 1906; Schieps, Paul T. "Darkness and Light: The Interwar Years 1865–1898." In Maurice Matloff, ed., *American Military History.* Washington, DC: Office of the Chief of Military History, 1969.

Heidi Amelia-Anne Weber

Compromise of 1877

The Compromise of 1877, generally cited as the concluding event of the Reconstruction period, is draped in myth and legend, centering on a February 26, 1877, meeting in the Wormley House hotel in Washington, D.C. There the Republicans allegedly promised the end of Reconstruction efforts if southern Democrats cooperated in the election of **Rutherford B. Hayes**. The truth was both more and less complicated.

The Compromise of 1877 grew out of the presidential **election of 1876** and the Democrats' attempt to wrest control from the Republicans in the three southern states still in Republican hands: **Florida**, **Louisiana**, and **South Carolina**. Democrat **Samuel J. Tilden**, the governor of New York, won the popular vote, but when uncontested state electoral votes were counted, Tilden had received 184 votes, one short of election. Republican rival Rutherford B. Hayes, the governor of Ohio, needed all of the disputed votes from four states: Oregon (one vote) and the three southern states (Florida, four; Louisiana, eight; and South Carolina, seven) still in Republican hands.

Democrats and Republicans in the three states leveled charges and countercharges of intimidation, corruption, and **violence**. White terrorists had prevented thousands of blacks from voting, and both ballots and ballot boxes were stolen. It was unclear to whom the states' electoral votes should go, and the Republican Senate and Democratic House could not reach an agreement on how to determine which votes should be counted. The nation had no precedent for handling a disputed presidential election. As a result, on January 29, 1877, Congress created a special **Electoral Commission** to investigate the situation in each state and determine which candidate should receive its electoral votes. The commission included five members of the House of Representatives, five of the Senate, and five of the **Supreme Court**. By party, the breakdown was seven Republicans, seven Democrats, and one neutral, the nonpartisan Justice David Davis of the Supreme Court. The independent Davis, who leaned toward Tilden's election, soon accepted election to the U.S. Senate from Illinois, a step unwisely supported by that state's Democrats; his removal from the commission put Justice Joseph P. Bradley in the fifteenth and deciding seat and turned the election to Hayes.

When Congress counted the electoral votes in February 1877, the first disputed state to have its vote counted was Florida. The Electoral Commission announced, in an 8 to 7 decision, that Florida's votes should go to the Republican Hayes. It reached the same conclusion for both Louisiana and

"A truce—not a compromise, but a chance for high-toned gentlemen to retire gracefully from their very civil declarations of war." Thomas Nast cartoon, 1877. (Courtesy of the Library of Congress.)

South Carolina. Unable to get the single vote needed by Tilden, the Democrats sought to delay the count with a filibuster.

Some prominent Democrats, assured by the Republicans that Hayes would not use federal power to support Republican governments in Louisiana and South Carolina (Florida had returned to Democratic control) and would support the return of "home rule" to that region's states, were not inclined to cooperate and were in negotiations with Hayes's advisors from December to March. During the campaign, Hayes had indicated his desire to see the end of federally enforced Reconstruction and the protection of black rights. Now he and the Republicans promised to support a southern-based transcontinental **railroad**, federal funds for the rebuilding of levees on the Mississippi River, and the appointment of a southerner as postmaster general, a position with extensive **patronage** powers. Allegedly negotiating these terms at the Wormley House hotel, the Democrats agreed in return to obey the three new constitutional amendments and to help in the election of **James A. Garfield**, an Ohio Republican, as Speaker of the House. As a result, the Democrats' filibuster strategy failed, and on March 2, 1877, the electoral count was complete, with Hayes winning by a 185 to 184 vote. He was sworn in as president on March 3. Tilden accepted the election results despite the lack of constitutional basis for an Electoral Commission and the commission's failure to investigate charges of corruption in the Republican-certified election results in the disputed states.

The Compromise and Hayes's presidency were the culmination of the North's growing disinterest in the continuing violence and political wrangling in the former Confederate states. Despite periodic attempts, the goal of equal citizenship for black Americans had to wait until the middle of the next century for renewed federal support. Political Reconstruction was over. *See also* Redemption.

Further Reading: Polakoff, Keith Ian. *The Politics of Inertia: The Election of 1876 and the End of Reconstruction*. Baton Rouge: Louisiana State University Press, 1973; Roseboom, Eugene H., and Alfred E. Eckes, Jr. *A History of Presidential Elections: From George Washington to Jimmy Carter*. 4th ed. New York: Macmillan, 1979; Simpson, Brooks D. *The Reconstruction Presidents*. Lawrence: University Press of Kansas, 1998; Woodward, C. Vann. *Reunion and Reaction: The Compromise of 1877 and the End of Reconstruction*. Boston: Little, Brown, 1951.

Claudine L. Ferrell

Confiscation Acts

During the Civil War, the U.S. Congress, in the First and Second Confiscation Acts, put in place sweeping confiscation programs designed to seize the private property of enemy citizens on a massive scale. These measures demonstrated two significant shifts on the part of the federal government and the North in general: a growing recognition regarding the expanding totality of the war effort, and an increasing understanding of the centrality of slavery to the Confederate war effort and the war itself.

Meeting in special session in August 1861, the U.S. Congress passed the First Confiscation Act, authorizing the federal government to seize the property of those participating directly in the rebellion. Ten months later, in July 1862, the burgeoning faction that came to be called **Radical Republicans** pushed Congress into passing the much broader Second Confiscation Act. This expansive law permitted the Union government to seize all the real and personal property of anyone taking up arms against the government, anyone aiding the rebellion directly, anyone offering aid or comfort to the rebellion, or any property being used to support the war effort. This effectively meant that U.S. forces could legally seize any and all property of all those who recognized or supported the legitimacy of the Confederacy.

These acts revealed contradictory attitudes within the North. First, the idea of confiscation itself reflected a developing radicalism in the North. Although the seizing of Confederate property was not surprising or new, the intended nature of the property was: slaves. Since Confederates were quite fixed on considering the southern **African American** population as property, Radicals in Congress decided to turn the tables and used their definitions against them. Thousands of slaves had already self-**emancipated** themselves, fleeing plantations and towns and heading toward the invading Union armies. Some generals embraced these "**contrabands**" as a form of proper moral retribution for slavery, while others saw it merely as a practical way of damaging the South. After all, with such a large portion of the white male population under arms, the Confederacy depended on the labor of slaves. Although primarily involved in **agriculture**, slaves also worked in the mines, built roads, **railroads**, and bridges, and even constructed forts and defensive systems. Defining them as "property" used to aid in the rebellion allowed federal officers to seize them and argue—a bit disingenuously—that they were not freeing slaves, but merely attacking the Confederate war machine. With the coming of the Emancipation Proclamation on January 1, 1863, federal officials no longer needed any pretense or subterfuge.

Yet, in other ways, federal confiscation policy showed a conservative side of Union efforts. The Civil War represented, after the American Revolution, the second great American experiment with broad legislative confiscation during wartime. The Civil War is justly described as America's second revolution, yet the Civil War experience with confiscation reveals the extent to which—when it came to the relationship of property and the state—the country had changed from the time of the first revolution to the second. The outcomes of these two wartime experiments with confiscation were nearly opposite. Revolutionary confiscation was marked by the quick, decisive, vigorous pursuit of disloyal property. A great deal of Loyalist (or Tory) property was seized permanently, without compensation or recourse to the courts (the 1783 Treaty of Paris did address this, but colonists-turned-Americans never fully made amends).

Eighty years later, confiscation met quite a different fate. During the Civil War, Union confiscation was marked by an agonized, intractable, ideological impasse. Union confiscation defied legislative consensus and mostly failed in practice as a result. Relatively little property was in fact confiscated, and—with the exception of slaves—the Second Confiscation Act was more or less ignored by President **Abraham Lincoln** and the executive branch during the war. It then languished in the federal courts for decades afterward. No one can accurately account for the private, unofficial acts of confiscation attributed to Union troops in the South, but the official acts of confiscation were carefully registered, bureaucratically handled, and even frequently compensated. The grandest threat of confiscation never came to fruition—the Radical's demand that plantations be taken from Confederates and divided among the freed-people. Even such obvious actions as seizing abandoned homesteads were only temporary; nearly all lands and homes were returned to their former owners in the years after the war. The Revolutionary precedent of zealous confiscation had met its inverse in Civil War paralysis.

In both sections, the constitutionality and legal legitimacy of confiscation produced fierce, explicit, and sustained debate. This debate was not primarily between academics, but among legislators and lawyers, with the property of millions at stake. Legislators were thrown back upon first principles, forced to articulate their vision of property, and just as important, to attempt to turn that vision into law and into policy. Congress came to a nearly paralyzing stalemate when it came to confiscating rebel property. In the end, Congress did produce a bill, but an internally divided one that seemed at once to promote widespread confiscation, while at the same time providing for a painstaking method of enforcement that made widespread confiscation nearly impossible. This internally inconsistent law was not the result of incompetence, or loss of focus, or due to the fact that confiscation was considered relatively unimportant. Instead, months of debate in the midst of war revealed that confiscation was fundamentally divisive along ideological lines and so defied legislative consensus.

This ideological deadlock is the most interesting aspect of the Union confiscation debates. In a time of exuberant and transformative change, when it came to the confiscation of enemy property, Congress, surprisingly, restrained itself. Confiscation revealed, as it almost necessarily must, core conceptual differences surrounding the competing rights of property, the demands of citizenship, and the prerogatives of sovereign power. Even as war raged, the making of confiscation policy prompted fundamental questions about the basis of private property, the nature of the **U.S. Constitution**, and the relationship of individual property rights to the needs of the state. Together, Civil War sequestration and confiscation belong within the context of landmark American debates over property. They were legislative programs that tested, and ultimately changed, the extent of sovereign power over property at mid-century. *See also* Abolition of Slavery; Amnesty Proclamations; Bureau of Refugees, Freedmen, and Abandoned Lands; Edisto Island, South Carolina; Field Order No. 15; Howard, Oliver Otis; Loyalty Oaths; Pardons; Port Royal Experiment; Southern Claims Commission (SCC); Stevens, Thaddeus; U.S. Army and Reconstruction.

Further Reading: *An Act to Confiscate Property Used for Insurrectionary Purposes. U.S. Statutes at Large 319 (1861): 12; An Act to Suppress Insurrection, to Punish Treason and Rebellion, to Seize and Confiscate the Property of Rebels, and for Other Purposes. U.S. Statutes at Large 589 (1862): 12;* Grimsley, Mark. *The Hard Hand of War: Union Military Policy towards Southern Civilians, 1861-1865.* New

York: Cambridge University Press, 1995; McPherson, James M. *Abraham Lincoln and the Second American Revolution.* New York: Oxford University Press, 1991.

Daniel W. Hamilton

Congressional Reconstruction

Reconstruction, the process of restoring the Confederacy to the Union following the Civil War, proceeded in two distinct phases—**Presidential Reconstruction** and Congressional Reconstruction. Congressional Reconstruction refers to the stage of that process when Congress, rather than Presidents **Abraham Lincoln** and **Andrew Johnson**, took the initiative in determining policy.

Presidential Efforts

Even as the Civil War raged, northerners debated the future of the seceded states. In 1863, Lincoln outlined his plan for restoring the former Confederate states to the Union. He offered a general **amnesty** to all Confederates, except prominent political and military leaders, and a restoration of property, except slaves. His plan specified that the southern states could create new state governments once 10 percent of the eligible white male voters pledged an oath of allegiance to the Constitution. Many **Moderate Republicans**, who also favored lenient terms and a quick restoration, supported Lincoln's Ten Percent Plan. The **Radical Republicans**, however, were anxious to punish white southerners with **disfranchisement** and loss of property. They lobbied for full **civil rights** for blacks, including the right to vote, and hoped to give them lands confiscated from the ex-Confederates.

While Moderates and Republicans disagreed on Reconstruction policy, they did agree that Congress should play a role in the process. Therefore, they rejected Lincoln's lenient plan in favor of the **Wade-Davis Bill**, which required a majority of the white males, not 10 percent, to swear an oath to the Constitution and barred ex-Confederates from voting for delegates to a **constitutional convention** that would establish a new state government. Lincoln used a pocket veto to kill the measure, sparking an angry response from Congress. It became obvious that the Republicans could not reach a consensus, and Reconstruction became an improvised process of compromise that evolved as circumstances dictated. When the war ended in the spring of 1865, the debate continued, and key questions remained unanswered. Who would control Reconstruction? What would happen to the former slaves? What would be the terms for the southern states' **readmission**? An assassin's bullet prevented Lincoln from fulfilling his dream of seeing the United States restored. Now that challenge belonged to Andrew Johnson.

Like Lincoln, Johnson favored a quick restoration with lenient terms. In May 1865, he outlined a plan that restored civil and political rights to all ex-rebels, except fourteen exempt groups such as prominent political and military leaders and those with more than $20,000 in taxable property. Johnson required these men to apply to him for **pardons**. He recognized the Lincoln-sponsored governments of **Arkansas**, **Louisiana**, **Tennessee**, and **Virginia**, and he appointed **provisional governors** in the remaining seven unreconstructed states. These governors were to organize state conventions that drafted new constitutions abolishing slavery, repudiate state debts incurred under the Confederacy, and nullify ordinances of secession. Elections could then be held for state and federal officials. Once the new state legislatures endorsed the **Thirteenth Amendment**, martial law would end, federal troops would be withdrawn, and the states could resume their place in the Union.

From the outset, white southerners defied Johnson's program. Some states refused to ratify the Thirteenth Amendment, others repealed rather than nullified their secession ordinances, and many balked at repudiating the Confederate debt. The new state legislatures also passed a series of laws known as the **Black Codes** to restrict black civil rights. Most brazen of all, the states elected high-ranking Confederate civil and military officials as convention delegates, state legislators, and congressmen. Although irritated, Johnson ignored such actions because he hoped to woo white southerners into a coalition with northern Democrats and Conservative Republicans. This new Conservative Party, with Johnson as its leader, would then dominate national politics.

Congress Asserts Itself

In December 1865, Congress refused to seat the new southern delegates and insisted on major revisions to Johnson's program. To supervise these revisions, Congress created a **Joint Committee on Reconstruction** to examine all future resolutions on restoration. While the Radicals continued to push for Confederate disfranchisement and full civil rights for the freedmen, the Moderates objected to the Radical agenda. They merely wanted to secure basic civil rights for the blacks (not including the right to vote) and to prevent prominent ex-rebels from reasserting control of the South. The Moderates courted Johnson's approval of a new **Freedmen's Bureau Bill** and a **Civil Rights Act**. Although both measures passed easily, the president shocked the Republicans by vetoing both. In retaliation, Moderate and Radical Republicans united to override the veto of the Civil Rights Act and to pass a new Freedmen's Bureau bill.

Congressional Reconstruction: First Phase

Republicans soon acknowledged that Johnson would never acquiesce to their objectives regarding Reconstruction. Therefore, the Joint Committee on Reconstruction proposed an amendment to the Constitution. In June 1866, after months of deliberation, the **Fourteenth Amendment** passed both houses of Congress with the necessary two-thirds majority. The result was an awkward compromise between the Radicals and Moderates. The amendment essentially became the Republican peace treaty for the Confederacy.

To protect blacks, it defined all native-born and naturalized persons as citizens and prohibited states from denying any person equal protection under the law. Also, while blacks were not granted **suffrage**, any state that withheld the vote from its adult male citizens would have its congressional representation reduced proportionally. This allowed the Republicans to prevent the former Confederate states from increasing their congressional representation in the absence of the Three-Fifths Compromise. The Confederate debt was voided, and the amendment stipulated that any person who had sworn to uphold the Constitution and then supported the rebellion was now disqualified from federal and state offices (although a two-thirds vote by Congress could remove the disability).

For the amendment to become part of the Constitution, it needed a three-fourths vote of approval from the states, including some former Confederate states. Johnson discouraged the southern states from approving the amendment, claiming that it was unconstitutional since Congress had no right to submit an amendment without the southern states being represented in Congress. Johnson's home state of Tennessee ratified it in July 1866, and became the first Confederate state to reenter the Union.

Undaunted, Johnson embarked on a speaking tour of the northeastern and midwestern states to drum up support for his policies. Although his so-called **Swing Around the Circle** began favorably, hostile crowds soon challenged his depiction of the Republicans as traitors. Johnson often bantered with the hecklers, adding fuel to the fire. Reporters criticized his undignified emotional displays, and Radicals portrayed him and his supporters as the true traitors to the Union.

Johnson's antics and his resistance to the Fourteenth Amendment, coupled with **race riots** in Memphis and New Orleans, convinced northern voters that the president's policies had failed. The Republicans swept the **elections of 1866**, gaining a huge majority in Congress, winning all northern gubernatorial contests, and controlling every northern state's legislature. Johnson's bid for a new conservative coalition collapsed, and Republicans believed they could now force a recalcitrant South into submission.

Congressional Reconstruction: Second Phase

Before the Fourteenth Amendment could be adopted, at least some of the unreconstructed states had to ratify it. The first step toward this goal required Congress to force compliance with the **Military Reconstruction Act**. Passed in March 1867 over the president's veto, the law declared that the ten Johnson-supported state governments were provisional and divided them into five military districts, each commanded by a major general. Congress granted the army authority to supervise the registration of all male voters, including blacks but excluding whites who were barred by the Fourteenth Amendment. Once registered, voters would elect delegates to participate in state conventions where they would frame new constitutions providing for **black suffrage** and barring prominent ex-rebels from holding state and federal offices. Once Congress approved the new constitutions, elections for state and national office would follow, and the new legislatures would be required to ratify the Fourteenth Amendment. Reconstruction would then end. Although the provisions of the Military Reconstruction Act fell far short of the restructuring of southern society sought by the Radicals, they did secure the Moderates' two key requirements of protecting black rights and preventing the former Confederates from returning to power.

To curtail the president's power, Congress passed two statutes of questionable constitutionality. The **Command of the Army Act**, a provision of the 1867 Army Appropriations Act, required Johnson to issue all orders to subordinate army commanders through the general in chief of the army, **Ulysses S. Grant**. The Radicals hoped thereby that Grant could control Johnson's actions. The most direct challenge to presidential authority, however, was the **Tenure of Office Act**, which authorized an official appointed with the Senate's consent to remain in office until that body approved a successor. Ostensibly intended to protect **patronage** offices, in reality, the law was designed to prevent the removal of Secretary of War **Edwin Stanton**, a Radical in Johnson's inherited cabinet. Although Johnson vetoed the Tenure of Office Act, he signed the Military Appropriations Bill in order to fund the army. However, he strongly protested its command provisions.

Meanwhile, white southerners refused to succumb to congressional demands and fought to delay the registration of voters indefinitely. Congress passed a Second Military Reconstruction Act in March 1867, authorizing district military commanders to initiate the process of voter registration, convene the conventions, and schedule the elections. Again, Johnson vetoed the bill, and again, Congress overrode the veto. When Johnson authorized Attorney General **Henry Stanbery** to issue a ruling that limited military authority in the South to policing duties and prevented commanders from removing civilian officials, Congress passed yet another Military Reconstruction Act in July 1867, declaring the army's supremacy over southern civilian governments.

White southerners discovered a loophole in the original Reconstruction Act. Since it mandated that a majority of registered voters was needed to affirm the new constitutions, they thought that by persuading or coercing enough voters to stay home, passage of the constitutions could be prevented. Congress quickly closed the loophole, however, by passing the Fourth Military Reconstruction Act in March 1868. This one required ratification of the constitutions by only a majority of those actually voting. By June 1868, six states—**Alabama**, **North Carolina**, **South Carolina**, Arkansas, Louisiana, and **Florida**—had approved constitutions, elected government officials, ratified the Fourteenth Amendment, and rejoined the Union.

Impeachment of Johnson

Johnson was appalled at congressional efforts to enfranchise blacks while disfranchising the very southern whites he hoped to entice into a conservative coalition for the **election of 1868**. While he could not prevent the Republican majority from legislating their program, he planned to impede its progress. Despite attempts to restrict Johnson's authority and power, the president retained a considerable capacity to obstruct congressional efforts. As commander in chief, he could appoint conservative generals to administer the five military districts, and as chief executive, he could interpret the Reconstruction Act narrowly in terms of its enforcement. Radicals recognized Johnson's intent and advocated his removal from office. Their first attempt occurred in January 1867, when the House authorized the Judiciary Committee to investigate the possibility of **impeachment**. However, Moderates dominated the committee and saw no reason to take such an extreme step. While Radicals claimed that the president's thwarting of congressional legislation constituted a misuse of power and grounds for impeachment, Moderates insisted that officials could only be removed from office for indictable crimes.

The Radicals launched another impeachment effort after Johnson suspended Secretary of War Edwin Stanton in August 1867 and began to replace generals such as **Philip H. Sheridan** and **Daniel E. Sickles**, who had energetically enforced the Reconstruction Acts. However, Moderates again stood by the president. Johnson's suspension of Stanton occurred when Congress was in recess; therefore, it technically did not violate the Tenure of Office Act, provided Congress agreed with the suspension when it reconvened. Moreover, Democrats had gained ground on the Republicans in the 1867 elections. Black suffrage and the continued occupation of the southern states were unpopular issues in the North, and the Moderates feared Johnson would become a martyr. The Radicals forced a House vote on impeachment, but without Moderate support, the resolution failed, 108 to 57. Johnson's subsequent actions, however, resurrected the specter of impeachment one last time.

Determined to rid himself of Stanton, the president replaced him in February 1868, this time with Adjutant General **Lorenzo Thomas**. Since the Senate was in session, Johnson's actions allegedly violated the Tenure of Office Act and prompted another outcry for his impeachment. This time, the Moderates voted with the Radicals, and the president was impeached by a party-line vote of 126 to 47 on February 24, 1868. House prosecutors, known as managers, proffered eleven charges against the president. Eight dealt with his apparent violation of the Tenure of Office Act, while one accused the president of attempting to circumvent the army's chain of command in violation of the rider to the Army Appropriations Bill of 1867. The tenth article accused Johnson of bringing Congress into disrepute with his public pronouncements, and the final article drew together charges from the previous ten. Johnson's able legal team claimed that he had committed no crime in testing the constitutionality of the Tenure of Office Act, and they argued that even if the act were constitutional, it did not apply to Stanton, who had been appointed by Lincoln.

Although Moderate Republicans abhorred Johnson, many feared his removal would pave the way for future Congresses with a two-thirds majority to remove any president who disagreed with their proposals. The constitutional balance of power would be destroyed. Moderates also distrusted radical **Benjamin Wade**, president pro tem of the Senate and next in line to the presidency. Using intermediaries, Johnson and the Moderates worked toward a compromise. The president gave no more speeches or interviews denouncing Congress, and he promised to enforce Reconstruction Acts. Johnson also appointed the well respected General **John M. Schofield** as secretary of war. On May 16, 1868, the Senate voted on the eleventh article of impeachment, 35 to 19. All twelve Democrats and seven Moderate Republicans voted against removal. With a two-thirds majority (thirty-six votes) needed to remove the president from office, Johnson had been saved by one single vote. Votes on articles 2 and 3 on May 26 had the same result, forcing the **impeachment managers** to concede defeat.

During his final months in office, Johnson continued to defy Congress by vetoing Reconstruction bills that the Republicans easily overrode and delivering speeches critical of the Radicals. Naively, he clung to the hope that the **Democratic Party** would nominate him for president in 1868. However, the party threw its support behind New York Governor **Horatio Seymour**, leaving Johnson to be a president without a party and with no influence on national policy.

Congressional Reconstruction: Third Phase

While the nation focused on the duel between Johnson and Congress, Reconstruction marched forward. Hundreds of thousands of black southerners registered to vote, while many whites refused to participate. A coalition of blacks, southern white Republicans (known to their Confederate neighbors as "**scalawags**"), and recent northern transplants or "**carpetbaggers**" united to direct the proceedings at the conventions. The progressive constitutions produced there granted universal manhood suffrage and provided for statewide public schools. Many also disqualified a small percentage of ex-Confederates from voting and participating in the political process. By 1872, however, those disqualifications were removed, and all former rebels could vote and hold office.

By mid-1868, North Carolina, South Carolina, Florida, Alabama, Arkansas, and Louisiana had ratified new constitutions and elected new officials. Not surprisingly, the Republican coalition won control of the states. The new legislatures promptly ratified the Fourteenth Amendment, and the states rejoined the Union. **Georgia**, **Texas**, **Virginia**, and **Mississippi** would follow by 1870.

The **election of 1868** served as a referendum on Republican Reconstruction policy. Republican **Ulysses S. Grant** easily defeated his Democratic challenger, **Horatio Seymour**, in the Electoral College vote. Had it not been for black votes in the South, however, Grant would have lost the popular vote. The results of the 1868 election, along with the northern state elections in 1867, demonstrated that Democrats had gained ground in the North by campaigning against governmental activism, black suffrage, and the so-called bayonet rule in the South.

Republicans scrambled to strengthen the party. They passed the **Fifteenth Amendment** to the Constitution in February 1869, nationalizing black voting rights. Despite the unpopularity of black suffrage in the North, Republicans reasoned that their survival, especially in the South, depended on increasing their voter base. While Republicans focused their attention on securing the votes of southern blacks, they lost support in the North. Their reformist coalition splintered because of the issue of black suffrage and the increasing probusiness policies of the party. Therefore, securing votes from southern blacks became even more crucial to the party's control of the federal government.

In the South, however, conditions worked against the Republicans. Tensions between northerners and southerners and between blacks and whites, together with the extreme hostility toward the Republicans among white southerners, fractured the party in various elections. Between 1869 and 1874, seven states returned to white Democratic control: Virginia, North Carolina, Tennessee, Alabama, Georgia, Texas, and Arkansas.

The growth of the **Ku Klux Klan** and similar groups accelerated the collapse of the southern Republican coalition. These organizations waged a successful guerrilla war against Republicans across the South. Using intimidation and **violence**, these groups prevented southern Republicans, especially blacks, from voting. Except in Arkansas, North Carolina, and Tennessee, the state **militias** were incapable of controlling the insurgents. Republican governments turned to Washington for help, and Congress responded with the **Enforcement Acts** in 1870–1871. These acts protected a citizen's right to vote and outlawed groups such as the Klan. Using provisions that allowed the president to suspend the writ of habeas corpus in areas he deemed to be in a state of insurrection, the Grant administration drove the Klan underground in time for the election of 1872.

This election presented another serious challenge to the Republicans, however. Tired of the **scandal** and corruption that had plagued the Grant administration, a splinter group known as the **Liberal Republicans** allied with the Democrats. Rallying behind presidential candidate **Horace Greeley**, the parties promised to clean up the corruption rampant in American society and to end Reconstruction once and for all.

Despite the efforts of his adversaries, Grant won an impressive reelection. Almost immediately afterward, however, the party's momentum began to lag. In 1873, a depression swept the nation. Northern voters registered their dissatisfaction with Republican economic policies by giving the Democrats control of Congress. Many Republicans remained committed to black rights and pushed through Congress the **Civil Rights Act of 1875**, which outlawed segregation. This was the last piece of Reconstruction legislation. That same year, Democrats in Mississippi used economic and social pressure along with violence to win control of the state from the Republicans. The North had grown tired of the ongoing struggle in the South. Most northern whites believed that the three amendments to the Constitution were enough because blacks now had legal equality.

The presidential **election of 1876** brought down the final curtain on Reconstruction. Republican candidate **Rutherford B. Hayes** ran against Democratic hopeful **Samuel Tilden** of New York. Although Tilden won the popular vote, the electoral votes of South Carolina, Florida, and Louisiana were disputed. If Hayes won all three states, he would win the presidency. The Republicans struck a deal. Known as the **Compromise of 1877**, the informal pact stipulated that if the Democrats agreed not to challenge Hayes's claim to the presidency, the Republicans would remove the remaining federal troops from the South and not oppose new Democratic state governments.

Without federal support, the remaining Republican state governments in the South collapsed, and Democrats gained control of the southern political process. White southerners gradually established laws to segregate the black population and disenfranchise them through **poll taxes**, literacy tests, intimidation, and violence. The U.S. **Supreme Court** supported their efforts by issuing conservative rulings. An 1883 decision, for example, declared the Civil Rights Act of 1875 unconstitutional except in cases of juries, and the landmark 1896 *Plessy v. Ferguson* decision sanctioned segregation through the doctrine of separate but equal. The two Republican goals following the Civil War of protecting black civil rights and preventing the ex-Confederates from regaining power had failed. During the first half of the twentieth century, the South became a rigidly segregated society dominated by an all-white Democratic Party.

Historians continue to debate the success of Reconstruction. The effort to transform the South and turn the freedpeople into citizens was not entirely successful, yet considering the prevailing racism of the time, much was accomplished. Reconstruction left the important legacy of the federal government's commitment to equality under the law. Unfortunately, it would take another century, until the civil rights movement, before blacks would enjoy the promises of the Fourteenth and Fifteenth Amendments. *See also* Abolition of Slavery; Bureau of Refugees, Freedmen, and Abandoned Lands; Memphis Riot; New Orleans Riot; Recusants; Redemption; Scandals; U.S. Army and Reconstruction.

Further Reading: Belz, Herman. *Reconstructing the Union: Theory and Policy during the Civil War*. Ithaca, NY: Cornell University Press, 1969; Foner, Eric. *Reconstruction: America's Unfinished Revolution, 1863-1877*. New York: Harper & Row, 1988; Gillette, William. *Retreat from Reconstruction: A Political History, 1867-1878*. Baton Rouge: Louisiana State University Press, 1979; Perman, Michael. *The Road to Redemption: Southern Politics, 1869-1879*. Chapel Hill: University of North Carolina Press, 1984; Rable, George C. *But There Was No Peace: The Role of Violence in the Politics of Reconstruction*. Athens: University of Georgia Press, 1984; Richardson, Heather Cox. *The Death of Reconstruction: Race, Labor, and Politics in the Post-Civil War North, 1865-1901*. Cambridge, MA: Harvard University Press, 2001; Stampp, Kenneth M. *The Era of Reconstruction, 1865-1877*. New York: Vintage Books, 1965; Trelease, Allen W. *White Terror: The Ku Klux Klan Conspiracy and Southern Reconstruction*. New York: Harper & Row, 1971.

John D. Fowler

Conkling, Roscoe (1829–1888)

Roscoe Conkling was the ideal target for reformer's criticism. Vain and simply cocky, Conkling worried not about the issues of the day but directed his talent toward **patronage** and related matters. He supported **Radical Reconstruction**, which, in some political circles, did more harm than good.

Born in Albany, New York, on October 30, 1829, Roscoe was the son of Eliza Cockburn and Alfred Conkling, a leading Whig congressman. With no formal training, Conkling became a lawyer in Utica and quickly became district attorney in 1850. The nuts and bolts of politics attracted him. Four years later, he helped in the creation of the New York State Republican Party. Even his marriage had political overtones. His bride, Jane Seymour, was the sister of **Horatio Seymour**, New York's Democratic governor and a political force in the Empire State for years.

After serving as mayor of Utica, Conkling was elected to the U.S. House of Representatives where he served, except for the years 1863 to 1865. He became the senator from New York in 1867. Upset over patronage issues, he resigned his office in 1881. The New York legislature rejected his efforts to return.

An advocate of physical exercise and moderate in his personal habits, Conkling's hair was the talk of town with its spit curls and shoulder length. He was always dressed to the nines. Distant with both friend and foe, his savage wit (and political office) kept his political friends and foes in order. He clashed with **Rutherford B. Hayes** over patronage, claiming "senatorial courtesy."

Retired from office in 1881, he rejected an appointment to the **Supreme Court**. In his last years, he practiced law. *San Mateo County v. Southern Pacific Railroad Company* (1885) was his famous case in which he argued a most dubious point. Along with his fellow lawyers, Conkling argued for a "conspiracy theory" in regard to the creation of the **Fourteenth Amendment**. He claimed that the amendment's objective was the protection of corporate property from state and federal regulation and supervision. Due process and civil liberties were apparently a sideshow for the authors of the amendment. Until the 1930s, this conspiracy theory held sway in scholarly and reform circles.

His personal vanity contributed to his death. Caught in a snowstorm in March 1888, he walked home. He collapsed at his doorstep and died on April 18, 1888. No great achievement is connected to his name; only his life and career were upheld as ripe examples of the political culture of the Gilded Age, which hastened the demise of Reconstruction in all of its various forms.

Further Reading: Chidsey, Donald Barr. *The Gentleman from New York: A Life of Roscoe Conkling*. New Haven, CT: Yale University Press, 1935; Hoogenboom, Ari Arthur. *Outlawing the Spoils: A History of the Civil Service Reform Movement, 1865–1883*. Urbana: University of Illinois Press, 1961; Jordan, David M. *Roscoe Conkling of New York: Voice in the Senate*. Ithaca, NY: Cornell University Press, 1971; Morgan, H. Wayne. *From Hayes to McKinley: National Party Politics, 1877–1896*. Syracuse, NY: Syracuse University Press, 1969.

Donald K. Pickens

Constitution. *See* U.S. Constitution.

Constitutional Conventions

The **Military Reconstruction Acts**, passed by the U.S. Congress in early 1867, required that southern states revise their constitutions before they would be readmitted into the full privileges of statehood. Delegates to the conventions that rewrote southern state constitutions were elected in late 1867, in elections supervised by the **military governors** appointed to run southern states under the auspices of the Reconstruction Acts. Black voters turned out and supported Republican candidates for these conventions in huge numbers. In many places, their conservative opponents boycotted the elections entirely. As a result, these political bodies were typically controlled by Radicals and they included significant, though by no means overwhelming, representation from the **African American** community. White northerners comprised about one-sixth of the delegates, white southerners the majority, and southern blacks the rest. Only in **South Carolina** and **Louisiana** did blacks make up a majority of members.

Despite the condemnation heaped upon the conventions and the resulting constitutions by white conservatives, most of the changes made to state constitutions were well within the contemporary traditions of state governance. The most important and radical change enshrined in the new constitutions was equality before the law for all citizens, but none of the constitutions mandated social integration, nor did any enact land redistribution. White critics in the South relied on bigotry and fear to spur opposition, but they were ultimately unsuccessful at blocking passage of the new rules. Even in South Carolina, where conservatives possessed deep strength, the constitution passed by a majority of three to one. After the constitutions were passed, new elections were held, Congress confirmed the constitutions, and power was restored from military to civil officials.

The constitutional conventions addressed three major areas of state administration: voting regulations, rules regarding office holding, and general social policies. Foremost among the changes insisted upon by Congress was the enfranchisement of black men. As a result, Republican delegates in all the southern states devised methods of opening the vote to all men. In some places, black voting was expressly sanctioned, while in others, universal **suffrage** was established. Up-country Republicans, mostly white, who had opposed secession and the Confederacy through the war, argued for extensive **disfranchisement** of ex-Confederates, but this was not widely supported by black delegates. African American delegates advocated full access to the vote on principle and were generally reluctant to institutionalize restrictions on suffrage. As a result, only a few states expressly disfranchised ex-Confederates.

In several states, Republican delegates enacted changes to the structure of state government that both increased popular access and helped diminish the power of prewar political elites. One important change was to repeal the remaining qualifications for office holding, mostly property owning thresholds, that remained in many southern states. This helped lay the groundwork for Republican governments to assume power in the South since many of their white and black southern delegates were substantially less wealthy than prewar legislators had been. For the most part, the qualifications were undemocratic provisions that had angered white yeomen in the antebellum period. In **Virginia**, for instance, western residents had long complained about the state apportionment system that favored large landholders in the East. South Carolina—where delegates abolished property qualifications for office holding and gave voters the power to elect the governor, state officers, and presidential electors—saw the first truly democratic charter in that state's history.

Convention delegates also empowered state governments to address some of the multitude of social problems that confronted the postbellum South. Of paramount importance was establishing school systems to educate former slaves. Southern states did not maintain systems of public **education** in the antebellum period, so this marked a sharp divergence in public policy. All the former Confederate states provided for free education of all persons age five to twenty-one. Opposition to public education came from three directions. Social conservatives had long viewed education as a privilege belonging only to those who could afford it, fiscal conservatives objected on the grounds that the system would prove ruinously costly, and whites predicted that a public system would bring integrated schools and massive social disorder. Republican delegates argued that education formed the only sound basis for an informed citizenry. African Americans had already demonstrated an insatiable demand for schooling and most saw education as the only reliable path for the upward mobility of their children. Though unpopular, these delegates endorsed new taxes and land sales in order to generate the revenue for schools. Integrated schools proved to be one of the many red herring arguments adopted by conservatives. Only in New Orleans and parts of South Carolina were integrated schools established. In all other states, African Americans were so eager for education that the issue of segregation did not diminish the importance of establishing the system.

Outside of their policy initiatives, the constitutional conventions provided a mobilization point for African Americans and Republicans. The process of forging the coalitions that would lead southern Republican governments for the next decade began in the halls of these conventions. Hindsight also allows us to identify the fault lines hidden in these coalitions from their very inception. Black delegates focused on **civil rights**, access to the vote, land, and fair labor policies. Northern white Republicans looked ahead to economic development, and southern white Republicans sought moderate change and the racial status quo. The conventions also helped focus white opposition to black and Republican political activism. Conservative delegates opposed the new constitutions from within the conventions themselves, while white conservatives worked to defeat them at the polls. Boycotts of the ratification elections worked in **Alabama** because Congress had initially required that a majority of registered voters needed to approve the new constitution. The opposition was strident and blatantly racist in its tactics, particularly in accusing Republican delegates of promoting social equality between the races, an issue most of the conventions avoided entirely.

Like most of Reconstruction, assessing the character of the constitutional conventions depends on the perspective that historians adopt. White conservatives saw the new constitutions as radical documents destined to destroy the South. Black Republicans regarded them as not radical enough, especially with regard to their hopes for land redistribution. Ultimately, the constitutions can be regarded as progressive but not revolutionary. Despite the intensity of opposition from conservative whites, most of the constitutions lasted a full generation, testimony to their effectiveness and to their essentially moderate nature. *See also* Black Suffrage; Readmission.

Further Reading: Franklin, John Hope. *Reconstruction after the Civil War*. Chicago: University of Chicago Press, 1964.

Aaron Sheehan-Dean

Contraband, Slaves as

By fleeing bondage during the Civil War, slaves began the process of Reconstruction; fugitives seeking freedom behind Union army lines were known as contrabands. The name arose from the phrase "contraband of war," or enemy property confiscated during wartime. Defining slaves as contraband allowed army officers to **emancipate** without undermining the premise that slaves were property. Classifying slaves as contraband influenced Reconstruction by implanting ambiguity within Union policy toward former slaves.

In May 1861, three slaves fled to Union general **Benjamin Butler**'s lines at Fortress Monroe, **Virginia**. The runaways' owner, a Confederate officer, demanded their return. Butler refused: The slaves had been building fortifications for the Confederacy, and were contraband of war, subject to confiscation by the Union army. Congress validated Butler's actions with the **Confiscation Acts**. The First Confiscation Act (August 1861) allowed army officers to divest slaveholders of slaves used to aid the Confederacy. The Second Confiscation Act (July 1862) authorized the confiscation of rebels' property (including slaves), whether or not that property assisted the Confederacy. Contrabands provided invaluable services to the Union army, including military intelligence and camp labor. After 1862, many became Union soldiers. To many Union officials, the purpose of defining slaves as contraband was to deprive the Confederacy of labor while gaining labor for the Union. To former slaves, contraband status represented one step toward full freedom. These goals sometimes clashed.

By late 1862, fugitives were directed into contraband camps run by the Union army, often with the assistance of philanthropic organizations like the **American Missionary Association (AMA)**. Later, the **Bureau of Refugees, Freedmen, and Abandoned Lands** (the Freedmen's Bureau) became involved. In camps, former slaves worshipped, founded schools and organizations, and labored for the army and themselves; however, overcrowding led to shortages, unsanitary conditions, and disease. In many areas, the only pieces of land large enough to accommodate contrabands were confiscated plantations. Northern investors often leased these plantations and impressed contrabands to work on them to demonstrate the profitability of free labor. Wage-**labor systems** on government-leased plantations did not re-create slavery, but they fell far short of former slaves' hopes for freedom. Instances in which slaves leased land, such as **Davis Bend, Mississippi**, delivered more promising results, but advances evaporated when President **Andrew Johnson** later returned land to former Confederates.

The impact of defining slaves as contraband was mixed. Since it pragmatically allowed army officers to free slaves while sidestepping moral questions, contraband policy emancipated many slaves earlier than otherwise would have been the case, because even northerners wary of **abolition** acknowledged the benefits of depriving Confederates of slave labor. Contraband policy also created opportunities, which slaves eagerly seized, to play active roles in the war. Afterward, freedpeople could assert full membership in the Union they helped to save. Yet, by confiscating slaves as property, contraband policy perpetuated tensions in slaves' status and rights, which shaped Reconstruction. Further, the narrow practical rationale behind contraband policy robbed emancipation of an expansive ideological foundation capable of supporting racial progress, and limited the responsibility that white northerners felt toward freedpeople during and after Reconstruction. *See also* Agriculture; Sharecropping.

Contrabands accompanying the line of William T. Sherman's march through Georgia, 1864. (Courtesy of the Library of Congress.)

Further Reading: Berlin, Ira, Barbara J. Fields, Thavolia Glymph, Joseph P. Reidy, and Leslie S. Rowland, eds. *Freedom: A Documentary History of Emancipation, 1861–1867*. Series I, Volume 1. *The Destruction of Slavery*. New York: Cambridge University Press, 1985; Gerteis, Louis S. *From Contraband to Freedman: Federal Policy toward Southern Blacks 1861–1865*. Westport, CT: Greenwood Press, 1973; Hahn, Steven. *A Nation under Our Feet: Black Political Struggles in the Rural South from Slavery to the Great Migration*. Cambridge, MA: Harvard University Press, 2003.

Chandra Miller Manning

Contracts

The end of the American Civil War brought a sea change of alterations to the South and the nation. The imposition of free labor ideology on the South by the victorious North dictated the type of transformations that would be expected. Passage of the **Thirteenth Amendment** ended the institution of slavery that had helped to sustain large-scale **agricultural** production in the region since its introduction into Colonial Virginia. Such changes affected virtually every facet of labor relations between those who had been masters and those who had been slaves.

Freedom also brought new opportunities and responsibilities for the former slaves. In relatively short order, blacks left the slave quarters and the gang labor of the antebellum period to live as tenants responsible for working a portion of the land for the maintenance of themselves and their families and the profit of the landowners. This decentralization of the plantation represented the most significant physical alteration of the system, but others, like the introduction of contracts, proved to be important developments in the lives of the former slaves as well.

In order to return plantation lands to productivity, landowners and laborers had to reach new accommodations. Planters sought the security of a stable workforce that would continue to function, while former slaves desired to create conditions reflective of their newfound freedom. As slaves, they had been commodities themselves, to be bought and sold or used as chattel or property. As free persons, former slaves entered the economic sphere as individuals who, theoretically at least, had choices about where and for whom they would work.

Profits and paternalism had shaped the "peculiar institution" prior to the war and established the parameters for those working under it. Masters accepted the obligation of providing the basic needs for enslaved people as an essential element of the sustaining notion that those individuals could not care for themselves without the masters' supervision. Inherent in this mentality was the sense that the support and protection of their charges would produce a reciprocal sense of loyalty and affection; while firmness and coercion would create docility and obedience.

The transition to a free **labor system** meant an end to that sense of obligation. Former slaves would now be expected to fend for themselves, using the fruits of their labor for their own sustenance. Contracts for these freed laborers in this transitional period were supposed to protect both parties to the agreement by requiring that duties be carried out while ensuring the basic rights of the workers. Abuses were virtually inevitable.

Powerful legacies of slavery persisted, including limited **education** that made it difficult for former slaves to read and understand the contracts they were now expected to negotiate and enter into with their former masters. Agents of the **Bureau of Refugees, Freedmen, and Abandoned Lands** hoped to assist the freed laborers in making the transition from slavery to freedom. The bureau performed a balancing act between the competing interests of the planter and the worker that sought to create a favorable condition for both parties, but often varied according to the inclinations of the agents who supervised the specifications of each contract. Tied as it was to the most conservative of institutions—the army—the Freedmen's Bureau established a priority of returning workers to the plantation.

The contracts the planters and workers entered into in the immediate aftermath of the war were often very basic documents. They specified wages, usually to be held until the crop was sold or the end of the year, and required little more in return than faithful and diligent service. Increasingly, these contracts also stipulated behaviors and restrictions on free men and women that were reminiscent of slavery. They became more elaborate with sets of rules that implemented deductions for various offenses, such as time lost from work or broken and misplaced tools that had to be replaced. In such instances, the planter or designated representative determined compliance, with enforcement consisting of deduction or forfeiture of wages by the worker. Clearly, these contracts left the power in the hands of the landowners in much the same way it had existed under slavery and by people who maintained the same type of expectations they had formerly held of their slaves.

Yet, with **emancipation**, and without an abundance of working capital, planters could not completely replicate a slave system. They had to adjust to the new conditions themselves, and did so relatively quickly; first with "share wages," paid collectively, and then **sharecropping** arrangements, worked out individually with the former slaves.

The "share wage" system proved short-lived because it provided the least disruption to the old patterns of slavery. Under this system, planters used a portion of the crop to compensate their workers, in lieu of cash, but made arrangements with gangs of laborers, not with individuals. These gangs would continue to operate as they had previously, with whites determining the tasks to be accomplished and supervising their working activities. Naturally, ex-slaves viewed this expedient as nothing more than a return to the prewar status quo and balked at adhering to it.

For this reason, sharecropping proved the most effective device for estab-lishing working relationships between landowners and laborers. This type of agreement involved splitting the proceeds from the sale of the crop upon harvest between the parties. The planter's share came from providing the land itself, while the laborer's was based on the work, minus the cost of items provided by the landowner, such as farming implements, seed, and work an-imals. Sharecroppers often raised subsistence crops on a small scale for their own use, but the market required that most of the production be in cash crops. In any case, the sharecropping arrangement allowed the hands a greater amount of autonomy and a degree of separation from the institution of slavery.

Merchants also became involved in the process when they provided goods to workers on credit. Since capital was in such short supply, this type of credit came in the form of crop liens that offered a measure of protection for the lender and access for cash-strapped borrowers. It also allowed for fraud and abuse on a broad scale, as workers purchased items on credit at higher initial prices than those paid by cash customers and then labored mightily under the burden of exorbitant interest rates that drove up the amount of the loan to be repaid.

These measures created a system of debt peonage, as well as free labor. Landowners quickly learned that by providing the basic necessities that had previously been part of their obligation as slave owners, they could deduct those charges from the compensation set in the contracts. When the debts accumulated exceeded the amount of money that the sale of crops entitled the workers, that debt "rolled over" or continued into the next year. Thus, cycle after cycle, year after year, the indebtedness of the workers grew. With laws that required such debts to be discharged before an individual could leave the plantation, workers became tied legally to the plantation. In a real sense, this meant that the immobility of slavery had been reinstituted.

States that established **Black Codes** placed themselves in a position to enforce contracts. **Vagrancy** laws and other devices ensured that workers who refused to sign them or left before their obligations under them were satisfied could be arrested and forced back onto the plantation. Even when the U.S. Congress took measures to combat these laws, the states found the means to continue them in general terms or everyday practice.

White planters and merchants who understood the new state of affairs could benefit greatly. Confederate general **Nathan Bedford Forrest**, a former slave trader, plantation and slave owner, acquired a reputation for offering good contracts for his hands built on higher wages than others could or wanted to pay in order to induce them to work for him. Such activities helped to encourage antienticement laws that would make it more difficult for one landowner to lure workers from another.

Taken as a whole, the implementation of contracts for the former slaves helped to institutionalize the theories of free labor ideology in the South. White southerners worked to shape the contracts in a manner that reflected their best interests, while former slaves used them as a means of gaining greater control over their lives and the fruit of their labor. These contracts were part of an exploitative system that kept power in the hands of land-owners and were susceptible to abuse. Yet, the fraud that was so often evident does not negate the fact that planters who had once demanded work without monetary compensation from the laborers as slaves, now had to at least appear to pay them for it. *See also* U.S. Army and Reconstruction.

Further Reading: Foner, Eric. *Reconstruction: America's Unfinished Revolution, 1863–1877*. New York: Harper & Row, 1988; McFeely, William S. *Yankee Stepfather: General O. O. Howard and the Freedmen*. New Haven, CT: Yale University Press, 1968; Wiener, Jonathan M. *Social Origins of the New South: Alabama, 1860–1865*. Baton Rouge: Louisiana State University Press, 1978.

Brian S. Wills

Cox, Jacob Dolson (1828–1900)

The arc of Jacob Cox's life is instructive regarding the historic trends of the time. Born on October 27, 1828, in Montreal, Canada, his parents were Jacob Dolson Cox, Sr., and Thedia Redelia Kenyon. The elder Cox supervised the construction of the Basilica of Notre Dame in the Canadian city. The family returned to New York City, but the Depression of 1837 meant young Cox's formal **education** was terminated, for a while. He clerked for several lawyers and followed a strong program of self-study.

By 1846, he attended Oberlin College where Charles G. Finney was a major influence on his life. Three years later, he married Helen Finney Cochran, Finney's recently widowed daughter. They had seven children. When Cox became superintendent of schools in Warren, Ohio, Finney was disappointed.

At Warren, he studied for the Ohio bar and helped organize the state's Republican Party. He was elected to the Ohio senate in 1859 and began his lifelong social and political relationship with **James A. Garfield**. They were strong foes of slavery's expansion. When the Civil War came, Cox became a Union officer, a brigadier general in May 1861.

His military career was active. He experienced combat at South Mountain, Antietam, and Burnside Bridge after serving in **West Virginia**, in **Sherman**'s Atlanta campaign and Sherman's march to the sea. By December 1864, he was promoted to major general. His military career gave him entry into a successful political career.

In June 1865, he was nominated and elected governor of Ohio on the Union Party ticket. In his Oberlin letter, he rejected **suffrage** for the freedmen and supported racial segregation. Despite the uproar, he took office and had an uneventful governorship. Choosing not to run again, Cox moved to Cincinnati to practice law, but President **Ulysses S. Grant** selected him to be secretary of the interior. Compared to the other questionable characters in the Grant cabinet, Cox was an effective secretary, following Grant's policy of eventual assimilation for **American Indians**.

Despite the opposition of powerful Republican senators, Cox endorsed civil service. Believing that Grant was behind the attacks, Cox resigned on October 5, 1870. Because of his disdain for **Horace Greeley**, Cox did not support the **Liberal Republican** Revolt of 1872. He served one term as a congressman from 1877 to 1879. Retiring from politics, he was president of the Toledo & Wabash & Western **Railroad**. He was dean of the Cincinnati Law School for sixteen years, and for four of those years, he served as president of the University of Cincinnati.

Rejecting an opportunity to serve as U.S. minister to Spain, in 1897, Cox retired to follow scientific and literary interests. A student of European cathedrals, he also studied microscopy and photo microscopy, winning a gold medal at the Antwerp Exposition of 1891. He reviewed Civil War books for *The Nation* and published his two-volume account of *Military Reminiscences of the Civil War* in 1900. He died on August 8, 1900. Cox was a fascinating figure, very much a part of his time, yet his various interests and achievements set him apart from his contemporaries.

Further Reading: Amazingly, there is no published biography of Jacob D. Cox. The papers of James A. Garfield and John M. Schofield contain many of his letters. Two comprehensive dissertations exist: Eugene D. Schmeil, *The Career of Jacob Dolson Cox* (Ohio State University, 1969); and Jerry Lee Bower, *The Civil War Career of Jacob Dolson Cox* (Michigan State University, 1970).

Donald K. Pickens

D

Davis, David (1815–1886)

Davis's career was significant for two major reasons. First, he was a close personal and political friend of **Abraham Lincoln** and second, he served on the **Supreme Court** during Reconstruction. Born in **Maryland** to Ann Mercer and David Davis, a physician, Davis completed a course of study at Kenyon College in Ohio and later read law in Massachusetts. His father-in-law, Judge William P. Walker, greatly influenced him. After a year at the New Haven Law School, Davis moved to Illinois and began the practice of law. In 1838, he married Sarah Woodruff, and had two surviving children. Sarah died in 1879, and Davis married Adeline Burr in 1883. He moved to Bloomington, Illinois, where he remained until his death.

A Whig, Davis failed election to the state legislature in 1840, but won five years later. In 1847, he was selected to be a member of the **constitutional convention** for Illinois, and he successfully lobbied for the popular election of state court judges. Davis became judge in the Eighth Judicial District of Illinois in 1848, a post he held for fourteen years.

During this time, he became a close friend and legal associate of Abraham Lincoln. Lincoln appeared more than ninety times in Davis's court room. They both joined the Republican Party in 1856, and Davis supported Lincoln in his unsuccessful bid to unseat Senator Stephen A. Douglas in 1858. In 1860 Chicago, Davis's role was vital in Lincoln's acquiring the Republican nomination, and as a result, Davis went to Washington when Lincoln won the presidency.

Davis desired a federal judgeship in the Midwest, but instead Lincoln appointed him to the Supreme Court. Davis worried over his ability to meet the task, yet at the same time, worked on politics and **patronage**. Despite being a close friend and adviser to Lincoln (he later served as the administrator for

Lincoln's estate), Davis served as an objective Justice, maintaining his own understanding of the issues before the court. ***Ex parte Milligan*** serves as a good example. Davis and the majority ruled that Lincoln had exceeded his authority in suspending the writ of habeas corpus and the army should be used only in extreme situations, and never when civil courts remained functioning.

Also important were the *Prize Cases* (1863) and *Georgia v. Stanton* (1867). In the former, the court held that citizens of the rebel states were wartime belligerents; in the latter, the court upheld military Reconstruction and use of **loyalty oaths**. In the *Legal Tender Cases* (1870–1871), Davis and the court endorsed paper notes as legal currency. While he supported business interests, he voted with the majority in the landmark case *Munn v. Illinois*, which addressed state authority to regulate **railroads** and other institutions doing business with the public.

Frustrated by the **Radical Republican** program and disappointed in the **impeachment of Andrew Johnson**, Davis left the Republican Party and briefly dallied with the Labor Reform Convention and the **Liberal Republican** movement. When he was appointed to the **Electoral Commission** created to solve the issues in the disputed **election of 1876**, he resigned his seat on the Supreme Court.

Davis's political work on Lincoln's behalf, and his service on the Supreme Court places him in a secondary but significant place in the Republican Party and the development of Reconstruction policy. *See also* Compromise of 1877; U.S. Army and Reconstruction; U.S. Constitution.

Further Reading: Fairman, Charles: *Five Justices and the Electoral Commission of 1877*. New York: Macmillan, 1988; *Mr. Justice Miller and the Supreme Court, 1862–1890*. Cambridge, MA: Harvard University Press, 1939; *Reconstruction and Reunion, 1864–1888*. New York: Macmillan, 1971–1987; King, Willard L. *Lincoln's Manager*. Cambridge, MA: Harvard University Press, 1960; Silver, David Myer. *Lincoln's Supreme Court*. Urbana: University of Illinois Press, 1956.

Donald K. Pickens

Davis, Edmund J. (1827–1883)

Davis, Reconstruction governor of **Texas**, was born in St. Augustine, **Florida**, on October 2, 1826. His family moved to Texas in the 1840s. Davis practiced law and served as a district court judge prior to the Civil War. A Unionist, he opposed secession in 1860–1861 and ran unsuccessfully for the state's secession convention. He refused to swear the oath of allegiance to the Confederacy required of all public officials, so in the spring of 1862, he left the state to avoid persecution. He visited Washington, D.C., and received permission from the War Department to raise a cavalry regiment from among Texas refugees. He organized the First Texas Cavalry, U.S., at New Orleans and became the unit's first commander. He saw service with his unit during General **Nathaniel Banks**'s Rio Grande expedition, and quickly rose to the rank of brigadier general. General **Edward R. S. Canby** sent Davis to Galveston to receive the surrender of Confederate forces in Texas on June 12, 1865.

Davis ran for the state's **constitutional convention** of 1866 as a Unionist. His private communications indicated that by this time he had come to oppose President **Andrew Johnson**'s program of Reconstruction and believed that only **black suffrage** would make possible the creation of loyal governments in the South. The triumph of the Conservatives, a loose coalition of former secessionists and Unionists who supported the president, relegated Davis and others of like mind to insignificant roles in the convention. The actions of the majority convinced Davis that former confederates had regained control of the state. Although he ran unsuccessfully for a seat in the state senate in the subsequent election, he hoped to undo the work of the convention and actively encouraged congressional intervention in the South.

The beginning of **Congressional Reconstruction** in the spring of 1867 led Davis back into politics. He joined the state's Republican Party that summer, ran successfully for the constitutional convention of 1868–1869, and became its president. In the convention, he became associated with the group that came to be known as the **Radical Republicans**. The Texas Radicals supported black suffrage and the extension of **civil rights** to the **African American** freedmen and favored restricting the political rights of secessionists like Radicals elsewhere. Their backing of a declaration nullifying from the beginning all laws passed between secession and the convention (the so-called *ab initio* controversy) was a more important issue than in other states. Texas Radicals also desired a division of the state that would create a haven for loyalists in the South. The Radical program confronted a hostile majority, composed of a coalition of Conservatives and Conservative Republicans led by Johnson's **provisional governor**, Andrew J. Hamilton, and they failed in all goals but the guaranteeing of **suffrage** and a minimum of civil rights for blacks.

Davis ran for governor against Andrew J. Hamilton in the election that followed the convention. Davis narrowly won in a closely contested race that saw **violence** at the polls in numerous counties. Hamilton disputed the results when the local military commander, General **Joseph J. Reynolds**, discarded some returns. Claiming that Reynolds had counted Davis in, Hamilton tried unsuccessfully to have officials in Washington negate the outcome. Later scholarship has shown that Hamilton's claims were fallacious, but the charge that military officials had given him the election haunted Davis while governor, and provided another issue for his opponents to use in disputing the legitimacy of his government.

Davis took office as governor in March 1870. He successfully moved a progressive program through the legislature. His plan included the creation of a state police force, which secured greater control over the **militia** as an instrument of law and order. The legislature also created more state courts. Davis considered all of this necessary, not just to suppress normal lawlessness, but also to protect the freedmen in their new situation. Davis also obtained a public school system, a measure he considered critical to helping the freedmen and poor whites of the state as well as facilitating economic growth. The governor also supported state aid to **railroad** construction, although he believed the state possessed the resources to subsidize only one road, a major trunk line from the state's northeastern border to Laredo on the Rio Grande. Implementing this conservative approach to internal improvements proved difficult, and members of his own party joined with Democrats to pass numerous railroad subsidies and then override his veto.

Davis's legislative program had little chance to prove itself successful. Conservative Republicans and Democrats joined together after the passage of the militia measures to charge the governor with tyranny and suppressing the will of the majority, accusations they used over and over during his administration. Their claim that Davis's government did not represent the majority lent support to their assertion that its taxes were unjust and everything from the schools to the courts were nothing more than means to create a massive government bureaucracy to keep Davis in power. As with many Reconstruction governments, expenses did increase, but largely due to an increase in services; Davis's administration successfully avoided, except in one case, the fraud associated with Republican regimes elsewhere. Nonetheless, Davis's opponents used their claims to foster a **Taxpayers' Convention** and revolt that produced court challenges to state taxes and a denial of revenue that caused operational problems across the state.

The tax issue stood in the way of all of Davis's efforts to attract wider support for his administration. At the same time, a steady immigration of people from other former Confederate states created an expanding electorate hostile to any Republican regime. By the time Davis ran for reelection in 1873, the **Democratic Party** essentially had reestablished its power in the state. Republicans already had lost their majorities in the state legislature, and all of the seats in the national House of Representatives had fallen into Democratic hands. In the 1873 gubernatorial election, Davis's Democratic opponent, Richard Coke, handily defeated the governor. Davis had no intention of remaining in power, but Republican leaders in Houston challenged that election's constitutionality on a technicality, and the state Supreme Court declared the results void in a decision known as the *Semicolon Case*. Reflecting Davis's concept of duty, he concluded that he had to sustain the court, even though the successful Democrats refused to accept its decision. Davis's stand produced a crisis in January 1874, when the legislature reassembled. After the governor refused to recognize the legislature, it met anyway and then inaugurated Coke, even though Davis's term officially extended until the next March. Davis tried to obtain the intervention of federal troops, but with no support coming from President **Grant** or Congress, and recognizing his own supporters would be crushed quickly in a confrontation, he stepped down.

Davis continued to be active in the state's Republican Party after 1874. He chaired the state executive committee, participated in national campaigns, ran for governor again in 1880, and then for Congress in 1882. He never held another elected office, however. He stayed true to his basic principles, such as when he refused an appointment as collector of customs at Galveston during the administration of President **Rutherford B. Hayes**, because he opposed the president's policy of reconciliation with the existing southern governments and abandonment of blacks. Davis supported himself through these years by practicing law in Austin. He died there on February 7, 1883, and is buried in the state cemetery. *See also* Compromise of 1877; Education; Military Reconstruction Acts; Presidential Reconstruction; Redemption; Scandals; U.S. Army and Reconstruction.

Further Reading: Gray, Ronald Norman. "Edmund J. Davis: Radical Republican and Reconstruction Governor of Texas." Ph.D. dissertation, Texas Tech University, 1976; Moneyhon, Carl H. "Edmund J. Davis in the Coke-Davis Election Dispute of 1874: A Reassessment of Character." *Southwestern Historical Quarterly* 100 (1996): 131–45.

Carl H. Moneyhon

Davis, Jefferson Finis (1808–1889)

Jefferson Davis, the future Confederate president, was born in **Kentucky**, the tenth and last child in his family. When Jefferson was quite young, the Davis family moved to **Mississippi**. He developed a close relationship with his oldest brother, Joseph Emory Davis, who functioned as a father figure for Jefferson for many years. Davis attended schools in Kentucky and Mississippi, then Transylvania University, and finally West Point, where he graduated twenty-third of thirty-three in the class of 1828.

Davis served in isolated Wisconsin and Illinois forts for seven years as an infantry lieutenant. He resigned from the **U.S. Army** in 1835, and married Sarah Knox Taylor, the daughter of his commanding officer, Zachary Taylor. They moved to Davis's new plantation, "Brierfield," in Mississippi where Sarah soon died, probably of malaria, and Davis suffered aftereffects of the illness for the rest of his life. He married Varina Howell in 1845; the couple eventually had six children.

About 1840, Davis became interested in politics and was elected to Congress as a Democrat in 1845. On July 4, 1846, Davis resigned his seat to serve as colonel of the First Mississippi Volunteers in the Mexican-American War. He distinguished himself in the battles of Monterrey and Buena Vista, where he was wounded in the foot. As a war hero, Davis was elected to the U.S. Senate from Mississippi, taking his seat in December 1847. He favored slavery expansion and vigorously opposed the Compromise of 1850. After the death of John C. Calhoun, Davis became the leading Senate defender of southern views. He resigned his seat to run for governor of Mississippi, unsuccessfully, in 1851. However, in 1853, Franklin Pierce selected Davis as his secretary of war. In 1857, Davis was again elected to the Senate, where he served until Mississippi seceded in January 1861.

In February 1861, representatives of the six seceded states chose Davis as the provisional president of the new Confederacy. Davis was soon elected to a six-year term. While he may have been the best person available to serve as president, he personally would have preferred to be general in chief of the Confederate armies or secretary of war. He was not good at dealing with people with whom he disagreed, he showed favoritism and excessive loyalty to friends, was extremely inflexible, and found it nearly impossible to admit error. Davis also tended to focus too much on relatively minute details and suffered from poor health, which often made him ill-tempered. Nevertheless, he did a creditable job of overseeing the Confederate administration in the face of tremendous obstacles.

Captured on May 10, 1865, Davis spent two years imprisoned at Fortress Monroe, **Virginia**, part of this time in close confinement. Many southerners who had been highly critical of Davis as president, came to regard him as a hero during his imprisonment. Secretary of War **Edwin M. Stanton** and Judge Advocate General Joseph Holt tried to prove that Davis was implicated in the **assassination of Abraham Lincoln** and attempted to bring him to trial. When it became evident that the testimony against Davis was perjured, and that the postassassination excitement had died down, Davis was allowed to live in more comfortable quarters at the fort with his family. Because it was difficult to determine a realistic charge on which to try Davis and to decide in what court he should be tried, the indictment against him was dropped in December 1868.

After his release, Davis tried his hand at several business ventures, but these were unsuccessful and his family lived in genteel poverty, eventually at "Beauvoir," a home in Biloxi, Mississippi, given to him by a friend. He wrote his memoirs, the two-volume *Rise and Fall of the Confederate Government* (1881), but it was not a financial success. He died in New Orleans of pneumonia on December 6, 1889. *See also* Amnesty Proclamations; Republicans, Radical; Surratt, Mary (Elizabeth) Eugenia.

Further Reading: Cooper, William J., Jr. *Jefferson Davis, American*. New York: Vintage, 2000; Davis, William C. *Jefferson Davis: The Man and His Hour*. New York: HarperCollins, 1991.

Glenna R. Schroeder-Lein

Davis Bend, Mississippi

Located on a peninsula formed by the meandering **Mississippi** River about thirty miles southwest of Vicksburg, Davis Bend was home to several thriving cotton plantations in the antebellum era, most prominently Hurricane and Brierfield, which belonged, respectively, to Joseph Davis and his younger brother, the Mississippi senator and soon-to-be Confederate president **Jefferson Davis**. The elder Davis was a slaveholder of relatively enlightened views, who organized these plantations according to cooperativist principles derived from the Owenite utopian-community movement: generous incentives and benign regulations were the hallmarks of his paternalist regime. Joseph Davis even helped one talented black bondsman, Benjamin Montgomery, to establish and run a successful general store and forwarding depot on the river landing, and he also allowed Montgomery to ease his two sons, William T. and Isaiah, into the business.

After the Union army assumed control of the region in early 1863, General **Ulysses S. Grant** took heed of the numbers of newly freed slaves who flocked to the area, and he gave orders that it be turned into a showcase for free labor—a "Negro paradise," he called it. Davis Bend gained national notoriety too: "Jeff Davis's plantation a **contraband** camp," the *New York Times* noted gleefully. Inexperienced military officers, however, often created more problems than they solved; for example, their **confiscations** of livestock and tools from freedpeople sowed distrust and anger. The Montgomerys returned to Davis Bend in 1865, and with Joseph Davis's encouragement, tried to mediate between federal officials and the nearly 2,000 freedpeople gathered there in order to get the various plantations running profitably again. Perhaps due to Davis's frequent interventions, though, the Montgomerys were unfairly perceived by the newly organized **Bureau of Refugees, Freedmen, and Abandoned Lands** as merely interested in self-aggrandizement. The Montgomerys would later encounter further, more predictable resistance from the estate of Joseph Davis after his demise in 1870. Davis had sold his plantations to the Montgomerys on credit in the fall of 1866, but his heirs—including brother Jefferson—proved less forgiving of the debt that rapidly accrued during the difficult economic times that followed.

Though a similar experiment on a grander scale in the Sea Islands off the Atlantic coast is better known, Davis Bend is notable in part as the site of one of the Freedmen's Bureau's few sustained attempts to assist recently **emancipated** slaves in readjusting to a free-labor regime. More noteworthy than the bureau's temporary, often ambivalent, and sometimes counterproductive efforts, however, was the long-term, proactive role played by the freedpeople of Davis Bend, especially under the Montgomerys' multigenerational leadership, in seeking to establish a local, relatively autonomous, and economically viable society on something approximating their own terms. Although the revived plantations of Davis Bend were quite successful in some respects, especially during the early 1870s, the unrelenting hostility of local whites and depressed late nineteenth-century cotton markets ultimately doomed the freedpeople's wider ambitions. They nevertheless left behind a substantial legacy of communitarian self-help that would linger in the area, especially in the nearby all-black town of Mound Bayou, well into the twentieth century. *See also* Agriculture; Contracts; Edisto Island, South Carolina; Port Royal Experiment; U.S. Army and Reconstruction.

Further Reading: Hermann, Janet Sharp. *The Pursuit of a Dream.* New York: Oxford University Press, 1981.

Scott P. Marler

Dawes, Henry Laurens (1816–1903)

The author of the Indian **Emancipation** Act of 1887, Henry Laurens Dawes was a prime example of a reformer in the Gilded Age. Born in Massachusetts to a farming family, Dawes attended local schools and received private instruction before entering college. He graduated from Yale in 1839. After a brief period of schoolteaching and journalism, he studied law in New York State and was admitted to the Massachusetts bar in 1842. He combined his law practice with teaching. In 1844, he married Electa Allen Sanderson, with whom he had three children.

Politics, particularly reform politics, was his main interest and life's work. Beginning as a Whig, he served four years in the Massachusetts House and one term in the state senate. He served in the state **constitutional convention** of 1853 and was U.S. district attorney for four years. He was also one of the founders of the Republican Party in Massachusetts. By 1857, he was elected to the U.S. House of Representatives, where he served for eighteen years.

In the House, he demonstrated legislative leadership and attention to detail. He defended President **Lincoln**'s war policy and often visited Union hospitals and camps. He was chairman of the Committee on Appropriations (1869) and the Committee on Ways and Means (1871). From 1861 to 1869, he was chairman of the Committee on Elections. He was a party stalwart, but events often moved him toward the Radicals despite his natural inclination to seek a moderate course and uphold party unity. Like many of his contemporaries, he believed that the fate of the Union and enduring electoral success of the Republican Party were one and the same.

Dawes's relationship with President **Andrew Johnson** was a prime example of Dawes's political and policy troubles. When Johnson came to the White House, Dawes urged cooperation and unity, believing that Johnson's policies were the same as Lincoln's. With the veto of the **Freedmen's Bureau Bill** in 1866, Dawes broke with President Johnson, although he greatly disliked the Radical leadership. Dawes wanted stronger evidence of southern loyalty and obedience to the federal Union.

He was an activist in other ways as well. As with any Republicans, he supported a strong tariff policy. He also championed the National College for Deaf Mutes, and in 1869, with the help of Cleveland Abbe, a noted meteorologist, Dawes supported the issuance of daily weather statements; this led in time to the establishment of the National Weather Service.

In 1875, Dawes became a member of the U.S. Senate, where he remained until he retired in 1893. His major achievement in these years was the Indian Emancipation Act of 1887 or the Dawes General Allotment (Severalty) Act. As the author of the act, Dawes wanted the total assimilation of the Indians into the culture. By abolishing the tribal form of government and culture, and dividing land among individual tribal members, the act sought to transform the Indians into farmers. A probationary twenty-five-year period was included, to protect the individual new landowners from speculators. Full landownership could also mean full U.S. citizenship.

The act's fate was complex. On the one hand, it represented a link to Reconstruction thinking, a certain trust that legislation could change culture, and those changes were just and equitable. Desiring to end government dependence by Indians, the act only increased the connection. It was not administered well, corruption was common, and the reservation system endured in squalor and neglect. The Indian Reorganization Act of 1934 replaced the Dawes Act. Despite the act's record and its obvious white paternalism and ethnocentrism, Dawes tried to be a friend of the Native Americans. After he retired, he continued to operate on behalf of Native Americans, and he passed away highly respected by two cultures. *See also* American Indians.

Further Reading: Arcanti, Steven J. "To Secure the Party: Henry L. Dawes and the Politics of Reconstruction." *Historical Journal of Western Massachusetts* 5 (1977): 33–45; Nicklason, Fred H. "Early Career of Henry L. Dawes, 1816–1871." Ph.D. dissertation, Yale University, 1967; Priest, Loring Benson. *Uncle Sam's Stepchildren: The Reformation of United States Indian Policy, 1865–1887.* 1942; reprint, New York: Octagon Books, 1969.

Donald K. Pickens

De Forest, John William (1826–1906)

Best known for his novels about the Old South and Reconstruction, John William De Forest was born in Humphreysville, Connecticut, on March 31, 1826. Plagued by poor health throughout most of his life, he spent much of his early adulthood traveling abroad. At the age of twenty, he visited his eldest brother, a missionary, in Syria, and then spent the next two years touring and writing about the Middle East. In 1850, he returned to Connecticut, where he began researching his first book, *History of the Indians of Connecticut from the Earliest Known Period to 1850*, published in 1850. That same year, De Forest again left America, living and traveling for four years in England, France, Germany, and Switzerland. He initially hoped to train as a historian or biographer, but while abroad became fascinated with French realism and other forms of literature. Upon his return to America (1855), he settled into a serious writing career, publishing two travel books about his trips abroad. His first novel, *Witching Times*, initially appeared in *Putnam's Monthly Magazine* in 1856 and 1857. A second novel, *Seacliff*, followed in 1859.

In the fall of 1855, De Forest journeyed with his soon-to-be wife, Harriet Silliman Shepard, to Charleston, **South Carolina**. Shepard's father, a professor of chemistry and natural history, divided his teaching between Amherst College and the Medical College in Charleston. John and Harriet married in Connecticut in 1856, but spent much of their time in Charleston in the years preceding the Civil War. Their only child, Louis Shepard De Forest, was born in Charleston in 1857, and the De Forests sailed out of the city shortly before the firing on Fort Sumter.

During the Civil War, De Forest organized and served as captain in a company of volunteers for the Twelfth Connecticut Volunteers (also called the Charter Oak Regiment). The regiment participated in action in **Louisiana** in 1862 and in the Shenandoah Valley campaign of 1864. Discharged in 1864 because of poor health, De Forest joined the Veteran Reserve Corps in 1865; later that year, he was transferred to the **Bureau of Refugees, Freedmen, and Abandoned Lands**, where he served as field officer in Greenville, South Carolina until 1867. He recorded many of his observations about war and Reconstruction in letters and magazine articles, and in the mid-1880s, attempted to publish his collective recollections as a two-volume work entitled "Military Life." No publisher accepted the project at the time, but in the late 1940s, Yale University Press published De Forest's manuscript as two separate works, *A Volunteer's Adventures* and *A Union Officer in the Reconstruction*, both of which offer firsthand insights into social relations and local life in the South.

In the years after the war, De Forest continued to write serialized articles and books, some of which, such as his best-known novel *Miss Ravenel's Conversion from Secession to Loyalty* (1867) and *Kate Beaumont* (1872), presented critiques of southern slaveholding society. De Forest failed to achieve significant literary popularity during his lifetime, however. He died in New Haven, Connecticut, on July 17, 1906, of heart disease. *See also* Tourgée, Albion Winegar; Trowbridge, John T.; U.S. Army and Reconstruction.

Further Reading: De Forest, John. *A Union Officer in the Reconstruction*. New Haven, CT: Yale University Press, 1948; Light, James F. *John William De Forest*. New York: Twayne Publishers, 1965; Woodward, Robert H. "John William De Forest." *Dictionary of Literary Biography*. Volume 12: *American Realists and Naturalists*. Detroit: Gale, 1982, pp. 129–37; Tabor, Carole Sims. "John William De Forest." *Dictionary of Literary Biography*. Volume 189: *American Travel Writers, 1850–1915*. Detroit: Gale, 1998, pp. 99–108.

Kimberly R. Kellison

Delany, Martin R. (1812–1885)

Martin R. Delany was a black **abolitionist**, Union army recruiter, and political activist in Reconstruction **South Carolina**. Born free in Charles Town, **Virginia**, Delany grew to manhood in Pittsburgh, Pennsylvania, and in 1850, briefly undertook medical studies at Harvard University. As an abolitionist, in the 1840s, Delany published *The Mystery*, the first black newspaper west of the Alleghenies and coedited *The North Star*, with **Frederick Douglass**. As a black nationalist, Delany believed that **African Americans** possessed a unique destiny and ought to identify with Africans worldwide. His 1852 treatise, "The Condition Elevation Emigration and Destiny of the Colored People of the United States," refers to black Americans as a "nation within a nation" and promoted emigration to Africa. In 1854, Delany convened the first emigration convention and in 1859–1860, his Niger Valley Exploring Party traveled to Yorubaland (southwest Nigeria today) and arranged for black Americans to emigrate there. The Civil War transformed Delany's activism, as he began recruiting blacks for the famous Massachusetts Fifty-Fourth and Fifty-Fifth Regiments. He was commissioned a major in the **U.S. Army** and was its first black commissioned officer. During 1865–1868, Delany worked as a **Freedmen's Bureau** agent on Hilton Head and other sea islands, and his greatest disappointment as a black nationalist was that most confiscated planter land was restored, leaving the former slaves landless.

Although he never held a major political office, Martin Delany was politically active and his efforts reflect the difficult choices faced by Reconstruction's black politicians. Following the **Military Reconstruction Acts**, Delany joined several other black leaders who cautioned blacks against aggressively pursuing statewide and national offices under the new 1868 state constitution, hoping to avoid alienating whites. When nominated for a congressional seat, he declined to run, for this reason. There was only one black candidate for statewide office that year, and no black congressional candidates. By 1870, Delany accused white Republicans, so-called **scalawags** and **carpetbaggers**, of unfairly dominating appointive and elective positions and urged black men to pursue their fair share of offices, proclaiming that black people required their own leaders. Delany helped write a new chapter in Reconstruction politics, as three blacks were elected congressmen, one as lieutenant governor, and one to the state supreme court. Delany remained a critic of white Republicans, many of whom he claimed were corrupt and only interested in profiting from black votes, while sowing dissension and conflict. Thus, he became a political maverick in the 1870s, supporting reform Republicans and growing less hostile to Democrats. In 1874, he ran unsuccessfully for lieutenant governor on the Independent Republican ticket, headed by a Democrat. In the **election of 1876**, Delany supported **Wade Hampton**, the Democratic candidate for governor, having concluded that black rights could best be preserved by southern aristocrats, rather than by white Republicans who faced a limited future in the South. Conservative whites praised Delany, but this position branded him an apostate among black Carolinians.

Delany's hopes were ultimately dashed with **Redemption** and the end of Reconstruction, and he returned to his earlier strategy for race liberation: African emigration. In 1877–1878 he was a leader in the Charleston-based Liberian Exodus Movement, which promised blacks a better future in West Africa. Financial difficulties ended this effort after the organization sponsored a single voyage in 1878. Martin Delany eventually left South Carolina for Wilberforce, Ohio, where he resided until his death on January 24, 1885. *See also* Bureau of Refugees, Freedmen, and Abandoned Lands; Stevens, Thaddeus.

Further Reading: Foner, Eric. *Freedom's Lawmakers: A Directory of Black Officeholders during Reconstruction*. New York: Oxford University Press, 1993; Holt, Thomas. *Black over White: Negro Political Leadership in South Carolina during Reconstruction*. Urbana: University of Illinois Press, 1977; Painter, Nell I. "Martin R. Delany: Elitism and Black Nationalism." In Leon Litwack and August Meier, eds., *Black Leaders of the Nineteenth Century*. Urbana: University of Illinois Press, 1991; Ullman, Victor. *Martin R. Delany: The Beginnings of Black Nationalism*. Boston: Beacon Press, 1971.

Bernard E. Powers, Jr.

Democratic National Convention (1868)

Called to order by the party's national chairman, **August Belmont**, the **Democratic Party**'s tenth national convention convened in the newly built Tammany Hall in New York City on a very hot July 4, 1868. Not for the first time, the Democrats came together in some disarray. Internal disagreements stretching back to the Civil War still plagued them as they faced a presidential election. They were firm in their opposition to Republican reconstruction policies in the South but uncertain about their candidate, and, most critically, they were divided over the emerging issue of paper money. Many western Democrats favored the continued circulation of the paper greenbacks that the government had issued during the war. They demanded that a law be passed mandating the repayment of government bonds in these greenbacks, not solely in gold, as banks and bondholders wanted. Such would benefit all Americans, they argued, as it was fairer, and legal tender paper money would stimulate a lagging economy. A conservative hard money bloc of mostly eastern Democrats strongly disagreed. They believed that specie was the only proper medium of commercial activity. To them, greenbacks were inflationary and threatening to a prosperous economy.

Still, there was much confidence among the party members gathering in New York. The 781 accredited delegates on the scene were optimistic that their meeting would give the party a fresh start after their failures in the

elections of 1864 and **1866**. Their Republican opponents were in turmoil, split over the future direction of Reconstruction policy; they had tried and failed to oust President **Andrew Johnson** through **impeachment** proceedings, and, the year before, the Democrats had won a number of important state elections and come close in others, suggesting they were well on their way back from their low point in the mid-1860s. They were meeting at the same time as the "Conservative Soldiers and Sailors Convention," who joined them in denouncing **Radical Republican** extremism and concurred in the need to elect Democrats to office—demonstrating, party leaders hoped, that they too had support from veterans of the late war, which could be a significant electoral boost. Finally, the appearance of delegates from the readmitted southern states offered promise of electoral gains in the former Confederacy.

On the opening day, the delegates chose **Horatio Seymour**, the former governor of New York, as the convention's permanent chairman. Committees were quickly organized and the meeting turned to address its two main tasks: the party's platform, and selecting candidates for president and vice president. The platform came first. Despite the differences in the party, the Resolutions Committee found common ground, demanding the restoration to the Union of those southern states still being held down by a radical dominated Congress; **amnesty** for political offenses, that is, holding high office in the Confederate States during the war; the **abolition** of the **Bureau of Refugees, Freedman, and Abandoned Lands**; and generally haranguing the Republicans for all of their sins over the past years, in particular their policies of "military despotism and negro supremacy." On monetary matters, the committee called for paying off the public debt "in the lawful money of the United States," including, it was clear, if not directly stated, the government-issued greenbacks.

Balloting for candidates for president and vice president began on July 7. The convention adopted the party's traditional two-thirds rule, the vote of 205 of the delegates present (not only those voting) would be necessary for a successful nomination. From the beginning, **George Pendleton** of Ohio, once a Peace Democrat, now the leader of the soft money forces, led the field, but his vote totals never approached the needed two-thirds mark. The conservative wing had not settled on any one candidate and supported several different possibilities—Senator Thomas Hendricks of Indiana, General **Winfield Scott Hancock**, President Andrew Johnson, and **Supreme Court** Chief Justice **Salmon P. Chase**—but no one had the necessary strength. A few delegates began to push Seymour forward, but he adamantly refused to be considered.

The convention settled into a repetitive cycle of voting, trying different candidates, and delegates switching from one name to another. After three days, and eighteen ballots, the party was still unable to agree. Then, Ohio withdrew Pendleton's name and on the twenty-second ballot, Ohio swung its votes from Pendleton to Seymour. The ex-governor continued to protest, but the delegates were not dissuaded. The other candidates fell into line, and Seymour was unanimously nominated on that ballot. The convention then finished its work by choosing as the vice presidential nominee **Francis P. Blair, Jr.**, a former Republican, Civil War general, and scion of an old Democratic family. Now living in Missouri, he was strongly supported by southern delegates for his outspoken stance against Reconstruction and apparent willingness to allow white southern conservatives to oppose policies enacted by the Republican Congress.

The convention adjourned on July 9. Despite the usual grumbling from the dissatisfied, the party mainstream remained optimistic that their convention promised victory, through their platform and the candidates chosen. The stakes were high: The country's monetary policy, the fate of Reconstruction, and the future of **African Americans** hung in the balance. *See also* Congressional Reconstruction; Elections of 1868; Grant, Ulysses S.; McCulloch, Hugh; Military Reconstruction Acts; Recusants.

Further Reading: Franklin, John Hope. "Election of 1868." In Arthur M. Schlesinger, Jr., ed., *History of American Presidential Elections, 1789-1968*. New York: Chelsea House, 1971; Mitchell, Stewart. *Horatio Seymour of New York*. Cambridge, MA: Harvard University Press, 1938; Silbey, Joel H. *A Respectable Minority: The Democratic Party in the Civil War Era*. New York: W. W. Norton, 1977; Unger, Irwin. *The Greenback Era: A Social and Political History of American Finance, 1865-1879*. Princeton, NJ: Princeton University Press, 1964.

Joel H. Silbey

Democratic Party

Democratic Party leaders displayed great confidence as the Civil War ended in 1865, believing that the time was ripe for their party's resurgence. What they saw as the **Lincoln** administration's aggressive centralization policies and social experimentation had provoked party members from the first days of the conflict and reinforced their determination to carry on against their political enemies even during wartime. Since their original coming together in the 1820s, Democrats had carved out an ideological focus that stressed limited federal government intervention in economic affairs and into the lives of American citizens. Their strict view of the **U.S. Constitution** and laissez faire approach had characterized their public persona as they fought to win and retain power. As they did so, they drew popular support from the lower Midwest's southern-born citizens, from growing urban centers where Irish Catholics were becoming a significant electoral force as they faced intense Republican hostility, and from traditionally antigovernment farmers and shopkeepers elsewhere in the North.

Democrats during the Civil War

Although many equated Democrats with southerners and secessionists (since the Democratic Party dominated the South), the party's appeal in the North remained cogent even after the war began, but the war caused great strain among them despite their common ideological perspective. A small group of War Democrats, arguing that Americans had to rise above partisan differences in the emergency they faced, actively supported the Lincoln administration. Peace Democrats ("Copperheads" to their enemies) challenged the war and its costs, and—to them—its unacceptable disruption of American society. The largest group of party supporters rejected both extremes and tried to mark out a position as legitimate critics of Republican policies while declaring their support for restoring the Union by military action. At the same time, while bitterly fighting each other in party councils over whether to support the war, the Peace faction and the legitimists argued that wartime exigencies should not allow the federal government to assume too much power, change accepted social realities, regulate and control the way the nation went about its business, or force adherence to its dictates. They also pursued a racist, antiblack strategy as the war developed, arguing that the United States was a white man's country and government authority could not be used to uplift blacks as the Lincoln administration was doing.

The Republicans successfully resisted the Democratic challenge with great skill. They took advantage of their opponents' divisions, labeled all Democrats as treasonous, cowardly Copperheads, indifferent to the Union's survival, and successfully held off the party in a series of wartime elections culminating in the reelection of Lincoln in 1864. By the end of the war, the Democracy, although still enjoying a great deal of voter support, had only occasionally demonstrated enough electoral vigor to threaten Republican dominance of the political world.

Early Reconstruction: Hope and Despair

As Reconstruction began, however, optimistic party leaders believed the worst was behind them. Americans had, said former New York governor **Horatio Seymour** in late 1865, "closed our lips upon the questions of the past." The issues of wartime were no longer relevant, the Democrat Party was united and "confident that their policy commands the approval of a large majority of the people." The Democracy was "the party of the future." Congress's passage of the **Thirteenth Amendment** in 1865, which abolished slavery (with some Democratic support) provided the opportunity for party leaders to announce that the debate about such matters was now over. They accepted that slavery was dead. It was time to focus elsewhere, to take advantage of new conditions and draw back to them former Democrats and disaffected **Moderate Republicans**.

That hopeful outcome was not to be. The Republicans continued to denounce the stance of the Democracy in the harshest terms they could, focusing particularly on the attitude and behavior of the Peace Democrats during the battle to save the Union. As a result, and despite their electoral potential, the latter made little headway. Republicans' waving of the "**bloody shirt**" of Democratic treason, and the white South's refusal to accept the results of the war, cost the party dearly. Southern white resistance to **African American** rights and the too-easy Reconstruction policy of **Andrew Johnson** caused a reaction against the Democrats in the early postwar years. There was a strong reaction at the polls against the Democrats in state and congressional elections in the northern states in 1865 and 1866.

Democratic leaders realized that they needed additional strength, but how were they to find it? **Radical Republicans**, and their determination to suppress white citizens and to impose black **civil rights** and **black suffrage**, provided the opportunity. The party set its face resolutely against **Congressional Reconstruction**, focusing on the un-American aspects of military control and black dominance. In short, after 1865, while paying some regard to the changes the war had wrought in the South, Democratic strategy was the same as during the war. They still stood by their strict constitutional conservatism and refusal to accept the changes demanded by Republicans and the newly freed blacks. "The Constitution as it is," they continued to chant, "the Union as it was."

Still, their significant electoral support occasionally led to Democratic victories and encouraged the hopes of party members. After 1865, they increased their vote in the South over prewar levels, as former Democrats came to the polls once more, while also drawing support from people there who had voted against the party in the years before the war. In 1867, they made significant gains due to Republican overreach on the black suffrage issue in several northern states. The Democrats' resistance to that proved quite potent as they won a number of statewide elections, came very close in others, and mobilized voters to defeat Republican-backed black suffrage amendments to state constitutions. Their success once again led to a resurgence of their hopes.

The Republican response to these Democratic gains continued to be as harsh as it always was when their opponents threatened them at the polls. Their leaders moved to impeach the president (who was now working closely with the Democrats) and replace him with someone from their own ranks to prevent interference in the Reconstruction program, but Republicans failed to convict (and remove) Johnson in a close vote in the Senate. Radical failures gave moderate party leaders an opportunity: Fearing the growing Democratic vote and the increasing disillusionment within the Republican Party, they nominated **Ulysses S. Grant**, the nation's greatest war hero. Although determined to continue to protect African American rights, there were insinuations that the party was going to ease up in its aggressive policies in the South and its pro-black initiatives there and elsewhere. Their electoral strategy also continued their decade-long assault on the Democrats for their wartime behavior and support for unrepentant southern whites.

The Democrats made a powerful effort in the presidential **election of 1868** behind former Governor Horatio Seymour of New York, but lost once again. Despite their differences over an emerging issue regarding the nation's currency—a significant soft money faction wanted the party to support legislation to continue war-issued greenback notes in circulation as legal tender in commercial transactions—the Democrats remained united, and once more challenged Republican excesses in the South. Their opponents, in response, again raised Democratic wartime behavior and, behind Grant, held them off, although with reduced majorities from Republican totals in recent national elections. Clearly, waving the bloody shirt remained a powerful barrier to Democratic resurgence, despite growing popular resistance to some of the Republican's programs and activities.

A New Departure

After the election of 1868, the Democratic Party was in angry confusion. Strong as it was, it continued to be the nation's minority party, unable to wrest control from its opponents. The party made some gains in congressional elections in 1870, but still seemed very far from power. How could they overcome this? Some of their leaders argued more strongly than ever for changed directions and a different focus in their efforts on policies, which came to be called a "**New Departure**." In other words, they should, while still hostile to Reconstruction in their public stance, focus more and more on issues of government corruption and federal monetary policy. The final ratification of the **Fifteenth Amendment** in 1870 seemed to be a coda for much that they had contended against. The issue of black voting was now settled by constitutional amendment. Occasionally, events would reignite Reconstruction issues: renewed white intransigence and **violence** in the South, particularly with the growth of the **Ku Klux Klan** in the early seventies, for one prominent example. However, other issues were also growing in importance, including the revival of cultural tensions, which had played a significant role in voter choice since the 1840s. In the early 1870s, Republicans at the state level were pushing for the prohibition of alcohol, and instituting school curricula reforms and demanding religious instruction that Catholics considered hostile to their values. The Democrats strongly resisted what they argued was nothing more than cultural and religious bias.

New Departurism was also a quest for new allies, particularly from a growing, vocal band of dissident Republicans emerging as the **Liberal Republican** movement. The Grant administration had been beset by inept appointments, **scandals**, and controversial policies in the South and in foreign affairs. Many from the Republican Party assailed what they called Grantism: the corruption, waste, and **patronage**, that amounted to a general sense of the failure of the Republican-controlled national government. The Republican Party no longer served the public good. These Liberal Republican "bolters" argued that new men and new ideas, such as civil service reform, were necessary. Their critique led to political action. For the election of 1872, they formed a third party to contest the presidential race. The Democrats (with a small minority vigorously dissenting) went along with them since most party leaders believed they had no other choice but to fuse with other opponents of the Grant administration if they hoped to win. In a national convention that lasted only six hours, the party threw in its lot with the Liberal Republicans, adopted its platform, and supported its eccentric presidential candidate, the long time Democratic hater, **Horace Greeley**.

Despite Greeley's vigorous campaign, the effort at fusion was a failure and the election a fiasco for the Democratic Party. Turnout sagged as some party loyalists stayed home in protest against the new strategy and the party's strange allies. At the same time, the Republicans once again kindled the bloody shirt, and war-induced anger and the distrust of the white South's postwar intransigence once again demonstrated their potency among northern voters. As a result, the Democratic-Liberal Republican movement attracted even less support than the Democrats had received in 1868 and 1870. The party seemed to be going backward.

Democratic Resurgence amid Republican Turmoil

Developments in 1873 at last provided an opportunity for the Democrats to improve their political fortunes. Grant's second term provided a fertile field for Democratic resurgence as the nation plunged into a recession; the country's faltering economic condition came to the center of the stage. The **Panic of 1873** began with thousands of **railroad** workers being thrown out of their jobs. A severe stock market downturn added to the chaos, followed by still other workers being laid off as the crisis percolated throughout the economy. The situation offered new opportunities beyond the Reconstruction issues that had not led to party victory. Hard times brought the currency issue to prominence once again. This was, many (but not all) Democrats argued, not the time to fall back on sole reliance on hard money. An inflationary policy was necessary to stimulate the economy. The "Crime of '73," Congress's passage of a law that had ended the coinage of silver, had to be reversed and that metal made legal tender once again. At the same time, soft money advocates argued that the federal government had to continue to use greenbacks in the economy.

Significant economic difficulties had a crucial political impact, allowing the Democrats to make strong gains in 1874 against a confused Republican Party. In the House of Representatives, with 169 Democrat seats—up from only 88, a massive gain in a single election—they would control the House for the first time in fifteen years. They added ten additional Democratic senators, also a substantial gain, if not yet enough to give them control of the upper house of Congress.

As the presidential **election of 1876** approached, Democrats believed that they had finally gained advantages over their opponents: cries of Grantism and a failing economy. Plus, they offered a unifying candidate of great experience and charisma, rare for them in recent years. Their nominee for president, **Samuel J. Tilden**, stood in a long line of Democratic leaders going back more than forty years. Originally a protege of Martin Van Buren, always a loyal party man, part of the legitimist group during the war, Tilden was deeply committed to a conservative social and political perspective. Furthermore, Tilden had made his mark as a reformer. He had prosecuted the corrupt **Tweed** ring in New York City and brought it down, a perfect symbol to combat Grantism and its depredations of the government purse.

It looked for a time like Tilden would defeat his opponent, **Rutherford B. Hayes** of Ohio. Despite Republicans waving the bloody shirt and advertising their anti-Catholicism (which continued to be a useful issue for them against the Democrats in the North), Democrats came extraordinarily close to winning the election. However, victory slipped away due to their own blunders and the shrewdness of the Republican leadership. Tilden arguably won a majority of the popular vote and the largest number of electoral votes the Democratic Party had ever received, but the close, confused, questionable results from several southern states, and political sleight of hand as they were counted, at first gave neither candidate victory. The Democrats' harsh anger about what was happening in the count gave way first to wavering about how far they should go in contesting the outcome, and, then, an agreement to abide by the decisions of an **electoral commission**. There, they lost out one more time.

The Republicans retained the presidency. Nevertheless, a new, post-Reconstruction political era was dawning. Whatever the final outcome of the

1876 election, the Democratic Party had bounced back, at last, into electoral equilibrium with the Republicans for the first time since the 1850s. Even more important, they had not lost their ideological soul as they did so. Somewhat delayed, "the party of the future" would, the faithful believed, soon return to power. *See also* Black Codes; Cincinnati Convention; Compromise of 1877; Democratic National Convention; Disfranchisement; Elections of 1864; Elections of 1866; National Union Movement; Recusants; Redemption; Scandals; Suffrage; U.S. Army and Reconstruction.

Further Reading: Flick, Alexander. *Samuel Jones Tilden: A Study in Political Sagacity.* New York: Dodd, Mead, 1939; Gambill, Edward. *Conservative Ordeal: Northern Democrats and Reconstruction, 1865–1868.* Ames: Iowa State University Press, 1981; Gillette, William. *Retreat from Reconstruction, 1868–1879.* Baton Rouge: Louisiana State University Press, 1979; Mitchell, Stewart. *Horatio Seymour of New York.* Cambridge, MA: Harvard University Press, 1938; Polakoff, Keith I. *The Politics of Inertia: The Election of 1876 and the End of Reconstruction.* Baton Rouge: Louisiana State University Press, 1973.

Joel H. Silbey

Disfranchisement

Disfranchisement generally means depriving a person of his or her vote. In the context of the history of Reconstruction, the term refers to the political movement between 1890 and 1910 by which southern states set up voting barriers to effectively remove **African Americans** from the political process. Together with the implementation of **Jim Crow laws**, which took place during the same time, disfranchisement represented a counterrevolutionary response to, and a devastating regression of, the constitutional and democratic reforms introduced during **Congressional Reconstruction**.

Background: Black Enfranchisement during Reconstruction

Black enfranchisement, or **black suffrage**, was a result of the Civil War, which had brought the nation the opportunity not only to end slavery but also to reform its democracy. When the wartime Reconstruction began in late 1863, however, black suffrage was not included in President **Abraham Lincoln**'s Reconstruction program. President **Andrew Johnson**, who succeeded Lincoln, continued to ignore black leaders' pleas for **suffrage** and pursued a white (male)-only Reconstruction policy. When southern states implemented "**Black Codes**" in 1865–1866 and later refused to ratify the **Fourteenth Amendment**, the Congress was convinced that, unless the freedmen were enabled with the vote and made a political ally, the party would have little chance to secure the outcomes of the Civil War. In early 1867, Congress took over the leadership of Reconstruction from President Johnson and passed legislation that enfranchised African Americans in the **District of Columbia** and unorganized federal territories and, most important, all freedmen in former Confederate states. Between 1867 and 1868, about 735,000 southern blacks took part in voting. Black votes helped to secure the ratification of the Fourteenth

Amendment, to rewrite southern state constitutions to recognize universal male suffrage, and to elect **Ulysses S. Grant** to the White House in 1868.

Black voting in the South paved the way for the enfranchisement of African Americans in northern and western states, where most were still denied the vote. In 1869, Congress proposed to adopt the **Fifteenth Amendment** to nationalize black suffrage. The amendment did not directly confer upon African Americans the right to vote. Instead it conferred upon them a constitutional right of not being denied voting rights purely "on the account of race, color, or the previous condition of servitude." The ratification of the amendment in 1870 nonetheless affirmed the new constitutional principle of racial political equality. The election of **Hiram Revels**, a former slave from **Mississippi**, to the U.S. Senate in the same year marked the beginning of a new American democracy at the national level. In the meantime, about 1,400 African Americans were elected to offices at both state and local levels throughout the era of Reconstruction, and twenty-two African Americans were elected to Congress between 1870 and 1901.

However, the struggle for establishing black suffrage did not end in 1870. To meet the challenge of growing **violence** and outright political terrorism—as conducted by the **Ku Klux Klan**, an organization determined to prevent blacks from voting—Congress passed three laws in 1870–1871 to enforce the Fifteenth Amendment. These federal laws penalized both state officials and individuals who obstructed or prevented freedmen's exercise of the vote by intimidation, conspiracy, or violence. Congress authorized the appointment of federal election supervisors to challenge election irregularities, inspect registration, and certify election results. Federal courts were empowered to hear all the cases arising under the **Enforcement Acts**. Congress also authorized the president to use military force to keep peace at the polls if necessary. The Department of Justice, which was created in 1870, prosecuted a large number of Klansmen and members of similar groups who were involved in preventing blacks from voting.

Federal enforcement, however, began to wane after 1873. A major economic panic of the year had shifted northern attention to economic and labor issues. The lack of adequate funding, insufficient quality of enforcement personnel, and the opposition from within by the **Liberal Republicans** had all contributed to the decline of northern support of enforcement. More detrimental were the **Supreme Court**'s opinions in *United States v. Cruikshank* and *U.S. v. Reese*, both rendered in 1876, which declared several sections of a major enforcement law "defective." Federal enforcement never regained its vitality after these rulings and subsequently there was a sharp decline in convictions from enforcement cases.

The judicial conservatism reflected the growing northern weariness of the southern problem. In the meantime, the Republican Party, which had dominated both houses of Congress since 1859, lost the House of Representatives to Democrats in the 1874 midterm elections. Republicans also lost control of a number of southern states by 1875, including **Tennessee**, **Arkansas**, **Alabama**, **North Carolina**, and Mississippi. The overthrow of the Republican government in Mississippi was achieved in 1875 through the implementation of the notorious "Mississippi Plan," which featured a combination of threats, intimidation, and obstruction to stop black votes at the local level.

Against such a backdrop began the bitterly contested presidential **election of 1876**, which eventually ended in a deadlock between the Republican candidate, **Rutherford B. Hayes**, and his Democratic opponent, **Samuel Tilden**. Neither candidate had won the majority of the electoral votes, but the allocation of the disputed electoral votes in **South Carolina**, **Louisiana**, and **Florida** would determine the result. Ultimately, the deadlock was broken with a special commission awarding Hayes the disputed votes; he subsequently became president. In return, Hayes promised to withdraw the federal troops guarding the Republican-controlled state governments in South Carolina and Louisiana and allowed the South to restore "home rule." The withdrawal of federal troops in April 1877 was quickly followed by a return to control by Democrats in all southern state governments, which was referred to as "**Redemption**," meaning the restoration of home rule and white supremacy. The decline of federal enforcement and the discontinuation of using federal troops to enforce the law left black voters unprotected. Black disfranchisement thus began.

Phase I: Early Disfranchisement

Black disfranchisement was not pursued or implemented in a uniform manner or timetable, at least not in the period of achieving Redemption in the late 1870s and early 1880s. There were two distinctively different periods of black disfranchisement in the post-Reconstruction era. The first period, running from the mid-1870s through the late 1880s, was marked by southern Democrats' employment of various means, including gerrymandering election districts, manipulating the balloting system, controlling the supervision of elections, and engaging in outright fraud at the ballot box. The goal for this period was to topple the Republican governments that had the support of the majority of African American voters. The second period, running from the late 1880s through the early twentieth century, was marked by the use of constitutional or statutory mechanisms to deprive African Americans of their vote. What distinguished the two periods, as historian Michael Perman puts it, was that the first aimed at diminishing blacks' voting ability at the polling places, while the second aimed at entirely eliminating blacks' right to vote, long before they had a chance to reach the polling place (Perman, 14–15).

Mississippi took the lead during the first period. In 1875, the state's Democrats used various methods to threaten the Republican Party's black supporters, ranging from verbal and physical threats to threats of unemployment. The Democrats' strategy contained two parts: to galvanize all whites into the **Democratic Party** and to intimidate black voters into voting Democratic— or keep them from voting at all. Blacks who voted Republican often were dismissed from their jobs. Bribery purchased black votes in some places. Violence was frequently applied. The sweeping door-to-door campaign was very effective, and ultimately responsible for overthrowing the Republican government. Other southern states quickly copied the method.

South Carolina's 1882 law best demonstrated the manipulation of the election system. The law created a complex registration procedure that required voters to enroll between May and June of that year or to risk permanent exclusion from the suffrage list. Voters were required to register each time they moved, a measure to penalize transient and migrant **sharecroppers** and workers, many of whom were African Americans. The law also established eight categories of national, state, and local elections with separate ballot boxes for each. The measure, later known as "Eight Box Law," was designed to confuse illiterate voters. As executed, the law permitted election officials to assist whites and obstruct blacks at polling places.

In the late 1880s, states began to adopt the secret ballot, known as "The Australian Ballot" system. The new ballot system used state-prepared, uniform ballots to replace the previously colored ballots prepared by political parties. Although a reform for the American balloting system, it often disfranchised those blacks who could not read or write, and undermined the effect of party organization and mobilization. In addition to these legally permissible methods, ex-Confederate states still resorted to intimidation and fraud.

In spite of these disfranchising efforts, blacks were not completely removed from the political process. Even in Mississippi, as late as 1888, seven blacks sat in the state legislature, and in the 1890s, Congress admitted black representatives from North Carolina, South Carolina, and **Virginia**. This had a lot to do with socioeconomic structure and the class-based power relations in the post-Reconstruction South. In the late 1870s and throughout the 1880s, biracial political coalitions formed in several southern states, including Virginia and North Carolina. Blacks pledged their support for white political groups in exchange for a share of the minor offices and variable protections of their voting rights. So while white conservatives restrained black voting and prevented federal interference, African Americans used the opportunity to advocate and advance their own economic interests. Indeed, their alignment with different white interests sometimes remained a crucial determinant of a local or state election.

Phase II: Complete Disfranchisement

For southern Democrats, the destruction of the Republican Party in the South was simply not enough. The constitutional framework as introduced by Radical Reconstruction and the Fifteenth Amendment continued to allow the existence of the so-called "negro domination"—a term used by white disfranchisers in the 1890s to refer to the political viability of southern black voters to determine the result of competitions between different white groups. Thus, the complete denial of blacks' exercise of the vote emerged as the principal goal for the second period of disfranchisement. Although Democratic disfranchisers like Ernest B. Kruttschnitt claimed that disfranchisement meant to eliminate "mass of corrupt and illiterate voters" who had "degraded our politics" since Radical Reconstruction, the movement was really meant to replace so-called "negro domination" with "white supremacy." Race, as historian Michael Perman points out, was "the driving force behind disfranchisement" (quoted in Perman, 27).

Nonetheless, race was not alone. Disfranchisement was also motivated by some other contemporaneous developments within each state, the region, and the nation. For instance, dissenting farmers in Mississippi and South

Carolina began a movement to challenge the dominance of state political power by the conservatives and their sometime alliance with the blacks. Federal government activity, especially the congressional debate over a new federal enforcement law, the so-called "Lodge Force Bill," in 1889–1891, also rendered some impact. Electoral reform, a nationwide movement of the emerging Progressive Movement, and the rise of the Populist Movement all in one way or another mingled with the upsurge of the disfranchisement movement in the South. In South Carolina, the notorious governor Benjamin Tillman spearheaded the movement. He took disfranchisement as a major component of his mission to reform the state's Democratic Party. In short, southern states' disfranchisement might begin with diverse purposes, but all moved toward one direction—eliminating black votes.

Disfranchisers, however, had to carefully maneuver their policies through practical and legal minefields to be successful. For instance, disfranchisers might use the loopholes of the Fifteenth Amendment to dismantle its effect, but they could not overtly challenge the amendment. In other words, a race-neutral scheme had to be employed instead of laws like the previous "**Black Codes**." Also, whatever new conditions a state intended to prescribe to eliminate black voters had to be accompanied by certain not-so-racially neutral mechanisms, to exempt whites (who might also be poor, or illiterate) from being subject to the eliminating conditions. Otherwise, disfranchisement would not have the popular support from the whites. Thus, disfranchisement was not merely a movement to remove blacks from political process, but also to construct—or reconstruct—a racial hierarchy in the South on a permanent and political basis.

Both **constitutional conventions** and state legislation played a role in designing and implementing disfranchisement. Between 1889 and 1908, most southern states held constitutional conventions to revise the chapters on voting. At the conventions, special parliamentary procedures were introduced to prevent black delegates to exert leverage. In South Carolina's 1895 convention, for instance, at least ten delegates had to call for a vote on a motion, a device that prevented the six African American delegates from exerting leverage on the conventional proceedings. Methods of disfranchisement adopted by these state conventions include **poll taxes**, literacy tests, complicated registration systems, and residence requirements. In addition, states adopted secret ballot laws, developed elaborate and complicated registration systems, reapportioned representation, and moved to the election of state officials by an electoral college.

Poll taxes had actually been used by at least two southern states in the 1870s, but not as a voting requirement. When Florida and Tennessee required it as a voting qualification in 1889, the poll tax became a ready device to get rid of poor voters, black and white. The scheme required a voter to present the receipt of a tax payment when he tried to register to vote. The time for paying the tax was rather cumbersome and usually long before the registration. The amount of poll tax varied from one to two dollars, but represented a burden to many poor sharecroppers. Those who could not produce their tax receipts were effectively disfranchised. A cumulative poll tax was even more effective since it required voters to produce consistent receipts of tax payments over several years.

Literacy tests, like poll taxes, were universally adopted by southern states. These required voters to read or interpret a certain passage of the state constitution in front of a state election supervisor. To protect illiterate white voters who might otherwise fail the test like illiterate black voters, in its 1890 constitution, Mississippi adopted the "understanding" clause to be attached to administration of the literacy test. Via the "understanding" clause, state officers who administered the test were given the power to judge the result of the test, and thus spare whites. The "grandfather" clause, first adopted in South Carolina in 1890, was another device to exempt whites from the literacy test. It allowed those to vote whose grandfathers, fathers, or themselves were voters before implementation of black suffrage in 1867.

The final disfranchising scheme was the white primary, adopted by southern states during the first decade of the twentieth century. This occurred during the rise of the Progressive Movement, as party primaries were introduced to reform the party nomination systems. Ironically a "progressive" scheme, this was intended to destroy the monopoly power held by party elites, who controlled nominations. However, this device was introduced to the South at the time when the region was completing its movements to disfranchise blacks and to eliminate the Republicans and Populists as viable opponents to the Democrats. Party primaries, instead of general elections, offered the only meaningful opportunities for contested elections, but when Democratic primaries barred blacks from taking part in the process, it rendered them completely powerless in southern politics.

To be sure, many disfranchising mechanisms met strong opposition from white groups, which were divided by regional and economic interests. (Recent studies, however, challenged the traditional "myth" that poor whites had forged a formidable opposition against disfranchisement.) Black disfranchisement was orchestrated and engineered by Democratic Party leaders at various states between 1888 and 1908, while the rank and file of the party and electorate were not involved. The Democratic leaders, however, manipulated the prevalent racist sentiment, sectional animosity toward Radical Reconstruction, and socioeconomic conditions to engineer the political "coup d'état," a phrase used by political scientist V. O. Kay.

Impact

The implementation of these disfranchising mechanisms had an obvious impact on southern politics. In the first congressional election (1892) after Mississippi's disfranchising convention, only 9,036 from a total of 147,000 voting-age blacks were registered to vote. In Louisiana, 130,000 blacks had been registered to vote in 1896, but after the state's new registration law took effect by December 1897, black votes dropped sharply. In 1900, only 5,320 African Americans were registered, a mere 4.1 percent of the total registration and just 3.6 percent of eligible African Americans. In 1904, only 1,342 were able to vote. In Alabama, after it adopted a grandfather clause in 1901, all but 1,081 of the 79,311 blacks formerly on the rolls in fourteen black-belt counties disappeared.

These new registration laws also discouraged white voters, albeit to a lesser extent. In Texas, for instance, after the implementation of the state's election bills of 1903, voter turnout dropped to 46 percent of eligible males, and black turnout fell to 15 percent and in a few years, to 2 percent. In Georgia, white registration fell by 122,000 from a total of 273,000 in 1904, while only one out of every six black voters registered during the same period.

The federal government did very little to stop disfranchisement. After the failure of the Lodge Bill in 1891, Republicans failed to stop the Democrats' repeal of federal enforcement laws in 1894. Even after the party regained the control of the national government between 1897 and 1910, the party made no effort to challenge disfranchisement or reinforce the Fifteenth Amendment. The Supreme Court in its *Williams v. Mississippi* ruling (1898) gave a green light to the use of "grandfather" clauses. In *Giles v. Harris* (1901), the Court used a technical issue to avoid challenging the disfranchising provisions in Alabama's state constitution. Not until 1915 did the Court invalidate the grandfather clause, in the *Guinn and Beal v. United States* ruling. The white primary was challenged by the National Association for the Advancement of Colored People (NAACP) in the 1920s, but the Supreme Court did not declare it a violation of the Fifteenth Amendment until *Smith v. Allwright* in 1944. Other disfranchising schemes, like poll taxes and literacy tests, remained effective until the passage of the Voting Rights Act of 1965 during the Civil Rights Movement, under a different President Johnson. *See also* Black Politicians; Bloody Shirt; Cincinnati Convention; Civil Rights Act of 1866; Compromise of 1877; Gun Clubs; Military Reconstruction Acts; Red Shirts; Republicans, Moderate; Republicans, Radical; U.S. Army and Reconstruction; U.S. Constitution; White Leagues.

Further Reading: Feldman, Glenn. *The Disfranchisement Myth: Poor Whites and Suffrage Restriction in Alabama*. Athens: University of Georgia Press, 2004; Hine, Darlene Clark. *Black Victory: The Rise and Fall of the White Primary in Texas*. Millwood, NY: Kraus-Thomson Organization, 1979; Key, V. O., Jr. *Southern Politics in State and Nation*. 1949; reprint, Knoxville: University of Tennessee, 1984; Kousser, J. Morgan. *The Shaping of Southern Politics: Suffrage Restriction and the Establishment of the One-Party South, 1880–1910*. New Haven, CT: Yale University Press, 1974; Perman, Michael. *Struggle for Mastery: Disfranchisement in the South, 1888–1908*. Chapel Hill: University of North Carolina Press, 2001; Smith, John David, ed. *Disfranchisement Proposals and the Ku Klux Klan Solutions to "The Negro Problem," Part I*. New York: Garland Publishing, 1993; Upchurch, Thomas Adams. *Legislating Racism: The Billion Dollar Congress and the Birth of Jim Crow*. Lexington: University Press of Kentucky, 2004; Wang, Xi. *The Trial of Democracy: Black Suffrage and Northern Republicans, 1860–1910*. Athens: University of Georgia Press, 1997; Woodward, C. Vann. *The Strange Career of Jim Crow*. 3rd rev. ed. New York: Oxford University Press, 1974; Zelden, Charles. *The Battle for the Black Ballot: Smith v. Allwright and the Defeat of the Texas All-White Primary*. Lawrence: University Press of Kansas, 2004.

Xi Wang

District of Columbia, Black Suffrage in

After the Civil War, a substantial minority of Americans, particularly **Radical Republicans**, believed that at least some **African American** males should be granted the right to vote (**suffrage**, or be enfranchised). However, when such proposals appeared on the ballots in several northern states, they were defeated. In December 1865, voters in Washington and Georgetown, District of Columbia, also defeated an enfranchisement proposal by an overwhelming 7,369 opposed to 36 in favor of **black suffrage**.

Despite this referendum, the U.S. Senate and House of Representatives, as the legislative body for the district, passed a suffrage act in mid-December 1866. This act gave the vote to all males over the age of twenty-one who were citizens, had lived in the district for at least a year, had no criminal conviction, and had not willingly supported the Confederacy. The act thus permitted blacks to vote while **disfranchising** white former confederates.

President **Andrew Johnson** vetoed this legislation on January 5, 1867. Although Johnson believed that educated or property-owning blacks should be able to vote when given that right by their state, he opposed any sort of federal enforcement of suffrage in places which were unwilling to extend the vote themselves. Although Congress had the right to legislate for the district, it should not go against the wishes of residents who had already declined to grant black suffrage. Johnson further opposed Congress using the district for an experiment. Because blacks had so recently been slaves, they were not ready to be informed voters or hold office. Johnson believed that black suffrage in the nation's capital would lead to an influx of other blacks into the city, who would exacerbate current unemployment problems. Forcing black suffrage on Washington would be seen as a prelude to enforced suffrage elsewhere, provoking race hatred. Blacks in Washington did not need special protection, in Johnson's opinion, nor were their votes required to retain a loyal government. In fact, these uninformed voters might be subject to corrupt influences and weaken the government.

Not surprisingly, many members of Congress were unsympathetic to Johnson's views. The Senate overrode his veto on January 7, 1867, and the House followed on January 8. As a result, black suffrage went into effect in the District of Columbia. *See also* Congressional Reconstruction; Emancipation; Fifteenth Amendment; Fourteenth Amendment; Military Reconstruction Acts.

Further Reading: Graf, LeRoy P., Ralph W. Haskins, and Paul H. Bergeron, eds. *The Papers of Andrew Johnson.* Vol. 11. Knoxville: University of Tennessee Press, 1994.

Glenna R. Schroeder-Lein

Doolittle, James R. (1815–1897)

Conservative statesman, lawyer, and senator, James Rood Doolittle's political career spanned the era in which the United States fell into Civil War and passed into and through the era of Reconstruction.

Doolittle was born in Wyoming County, New York. He graduated from Geneva College (now Hobart Smith College) in 1834, and studied law in Rochester. After passing the bar, he returned to Wyoming County, was elected county district attorney as a Democrat, and at the 1848 New York State Democratic convention, introduced the "Corner Stone Resolution" against extending slavery to new states. This resolution demonstrated Doolitte's commitment to what would shortly be called the "Free Soil" Party.

As a Moderate Republican

In 1851, Doolittle moved to Racine, Wisconsin, and became a circuit judge two years later. The repeal of the Missouri Compromise via the Kansas-Nebraska Act of 1854 moved Doolittle to become a member of the Republican Party; he was elected a U.S. senator in 1857. Though ardently opposed to the expansion of slavery, he was a reserved **abolitionist**; throughout his political career, Doolittle would consider supporting **emancipation** legislation only if proposals included financial support for black recolonization, or if proposals supported nonslaveholding whites over treasonous plantation owners. Doolittle feared that economic and political competition would arise if true emancipation for blacks occurred. Like many prominent prewar Republicans, including **Abraham Lincoln**, Doolittle believed that "colonization" or the planned relocation of freedmen to a U.S. colony established in the Caribbean or Africa was the only effective resolution to the "Negro question."

Reconstruction and a Return to the Democracy

A devout Unionist and dedicated supporter of the Lincoln administration during the Civil War, Doolittle's **moderate Republicanism** transformed into support for **Andrew Johnson** when the latter became president in 1865. Like Johnson, he supported the **abolition of slavery**, but he also opposed extending significant rights to the freedpeople; in 1865, Doolittle blocked the Wisconsin Union Convention from adopting a plank of **black suffrage**. By 1866, Senator Doolittle had moved formally back into the **Democratic Party**, driven away by what he saw as government extremism on the part of the **Radical Republicans** in general and fellow senator **Charles Sumner** in particular. Johnson came to rely on Doolittle as a sounding board, and he was ready and willing to offer the executive advice and political comment. Not surprisingly, Doolittle supported the 1866 **National Union Movement**, and was one of the most vocal defenders of Johnson in Congress. His loyalty drove the Wisconsin State Legislature to call for his resignation in 1867, but he ignored the assault. He stood by the president through all the opposition and considered himself proud to cast a "not guilty" vote for Johnson at the president's **impeachment** trial in 1868.

Doolittle's impact was sizeable in other areas as well. His beliefs in the possibilities of colonization made him especially suited to participate in the reform of the Indian Affairs Bureau that also took place in the years shortly after the Civil War ended. Doolittle's work as the chairman of the Senate Committee on Indian Affairs not only complemented his activities and philosophies during Reconstruction, but laid the groundwork for the **Grant** administration's large-scale removal of **American Indian** tribes to reservations along the Western Frontier.

After an unsuccessful bid for governor of Wisconsin in 1871, Doolittle largely withdrew from public service. He practiced law in Chicago and taught at the University of Chicago. In 1872, he served as chairman of the Baltimore Democratic convention. He died in Edgewood, Rhode Island, on July 27, 1897. *See also* African Americans; Amnesty Proclamations; Blair, Francis P., Sr.; Civil Rights; Congressional Reconstruction; Elections of 1866; Presidential Reconstruction; Readmission; Swing Around the Circle.

Further Reading: Benedict, Michael Les. *A Compromise of Principle: Congressional Republicans and Reconstruction, 1863–1869.* New York: W. W. Norton & Co., 1974; Mowry, Duane. *An Appreciation of James Rood Doolittle.* Proceedings of the State Historical Society of Wisconsin, 1909; Trefousse, Hans L. *The Radical Republicans: Lincoln's Vanguard for Racial Justice.* New York: Knopf, 1969; Yerger, Bessie Pearl. *Certain Aspects of the Congressional Career of Senator James Rood Doolittle.* Master's thesis, University of Washington, 1921.

Michelle LaFrance

Douglass, Frederick (c. 1818–1895)

Frederick Douglass, former slave, **abolitionist**, and orator, was born into slavery along the shores of **Maryland**. He was the son of a white man, of whom he knew nothing, and a slave woman, who died when he was a child. Relatives reared him, until he was sold as a child to the Auld family of Baltimore. It was in the Auld home that he enjoyed freedoms that many other slaves did not know; however, upon discovering that his wife was teaching Douglass to write, Hugh Auld demanded her to stop. Douglass secretly continued to pursue reading and writing by bribing other white children with food. Douglass used *The Columbian Orator*, which contained a collection of speeches on democracy and freedom, to study and shape his personal beliefs.

As a teenager, Douglass was sold to a brutal plantation owner who whipped and barely fed him. In 1838, while working on the Baltimore shipyards, he escaped to the North and arrived in New York City. Shortly thereafter, Douglass changed his last name from Baily to Douglass so that he might avoid being taken by slave catchers. Within a month, Douglass married Anna Murray, who was a freed slave he had met in Baltimore. They had five children, four of whom survived to adulthood.

He settled in New Bedford, Massachusetts, and began participating in abolitionist activities and became well known through his slave narratives. He also contributed to abolitionist newspapers, the *Liberator* and *Anti-Slavery Standard*. Prominent abolitionists **William Lloyd Garrison**, **Wendell Phillips**, and William Collins heard Douglass tell his story and encouraged him to take to the abolitionist speaking circuit. In 1841, Douglass heard William Lloyd Garrison speak at an antislavery meeting and adopted his method of oratory. Douglass became involved in the American Massachusetts Anti-Slavery Society, which sent him on speaking tours across the United States and Great Britain.

Shortly after beginning his speaking tour, Douglass wrote his *Narrative of the Life of Frederick Douglass, an American Slave, Written by Himself.*

Completed in 1845, this was one of the first narratives written by a slave rather than a white abolitionist, and he asked William Lloyd Garrison and Wendell Phillips to write introductions to the book. Douglass primarily wrote the novel in response to individuals who believed that he was using other slaves' stories. Since he spoke and wrote in such an educated way, many had difficulty believing he had been a slave. Yet his popularity brought risks: he had to flee to Great Britain to avoid capture, since his book made him well recognized throughout the country. Finally, in 1846, two friends from England raised more than $700 to pay Hugh Auld for Douglass's freedom; he returned to the United States shortly thereafter. Unfortunately, Douglass would flee again, this time to Canada, when documents found among John Brown's possessions implicated him in planning the attack on Harper's Ferry. He was exonerated, and he later returned to the United States permanently.

Douglass became very involved in **civil rights** and the **women's movement**. By 1848, he had begun publishing his own antislavery newspaper, *The North Star*, which was later renamed *Frederick Douglass' Paper*. He also attended the first women's rights convention in Seneca Falls, New York. In 1855, he wrote an account of his slavery days in *My Bondage and My Freedom*, which gave gruesome details of brutality suffered by himself and other slaves.

It was during the Civil War that President **Abraham Lincoln** consulted Douglass regarding options for slaves in assimilating them into the mainstream population. As a result, Douglass became one of Lincoln's trusted advisors, and he assisted in helping recruit **African Americans** for regiments in Massachusetts. Throughout the war, he campaigned tirelessly for the rights of blacks to enlist in the Union army and for **emancipation** and abolition.

Douglass approached politics as a way to further the independence and rights of African Americans. In 1870, he became editor of *The New National Era*, a Washington, D.C., newspaper, which chronicled the progress of African Americans in the United States. The newspaper gave him the opportunities to further his beliefs on the individual rights of his people, but the newspaper closed in 1874. He then served as police commissioner of the **District of Columbia** and was appointed to its territorial legislature by President **Rutherford B. Hayes**. In 1872, he served as a presidential elector at large for New York. Because of his support of presidential candidate Benjamin Harrison, who won the election, Douglass became consul general to the Republic of Haiti; however, he resigned the post a year later in protest of American businessmen who engaged in dishonest industry. Finally, in 1880, President **James Garfield** appointed Douglass to the Washington, D.C., post of recorder of deeds, which managed property sales records in the capital.

Frederick Douglass, c. 1885. (Courtesy of the Library of Congress.)

In 1881, he wrote his final autobiography, *The Life and Times of Frederick Douglass*, which accounted for his postslavery experiences. In 1884, Douglass married Helen Pitts after his wife Anna's death, and they were married nine years. Douglass died in 1895 from a heart attack at his home in Washington, D.C. *See also* Abolition of Slavery; Black Suffrage; Black Troops (U.S.C.T.) in the Occupied South; Emancipation; Military Reconstruction Acts; Presidential Reconstruction; U.S. Army and Reconstruction.

Further Reading: Andrews, William L. "Frederick Douglass, Preacher." *American Literature* 54, no. 4 (1982): 592–97; Dillon, Merton L. *The Abolitionists: The Growth of a Dissenting Minority*. DeKalb: Northern Illinois University Press, 1974; Howard-Pitney, David. "The Enduring Black Jeremiad: The American Jeremiad and Black Protest Rhetoric, from Frederick Douglass to W.E.B. Du Bois, 1881–1919." *American Quarterly* 38, no. 3 (1986): 481–92; Martin, Waldo E., Jr. *The Mind of Frederick Douglass*. Chapel Hill: University of North Carolina Press, 1985; Ray, Angela G. "Frederick Douglass on the Lyceum Circuit: Social Assimilation, Social Transformation?" *Rhetoric and Public Affairs* 5, no. 4 (2002): 625–47.

Mary J. Sloat

Dunn, Oscar James (c. 1821–1871)

Oscar J. Dunn was a black political leader in **Louisiana** and lieutenant governor of the state from 1868 until his death in 1871. Born in New Orleans to a free woman of color who ran a boardinghouse, he learned to read, write, and play the violin from her lodgers, and before the Civil War he taught music, worked as a barber, and was apprenticed as a plasterer. After the federal capture of New Orleans in 1862, he joined the first regiment of black Union troops raised in Louisiana and achieved the rank of captain, but he resigned in protest in 1863, after having been passed over for promotion.

Toward the end of the war, Dunn became active with a group of fellow free black men and white **Radical Republicans** who advocated **black suffrage**, and he served as delegate to a state convention in September 1865 that marked the founding of the Republican Party in Louisiana. He also participated in **freedmen's relief** efforts and worked with both the **Freedmen's Bureau** and the **Freedman's Savings and Trust Company**. Dunn was appointed to various New Orleans city offices in 1867, and in early 1868, he was considered a possible candidate for governor. The Republican nomination, however, went to **Henry Clay Warmoth**, whom Dunn came to support, and Dunn was nominated lieutenant governor and elected in April 1868, the first black in U.S. history to hold that office.

Although a member of Warmoth's administration, Dunn, along with other Louisiana Republicans, clashed with the governor during the next two years over a number of issues, including Warmoth's appointing of white conservatives to office and his lukewarm support for black **civil rights**, state **patronage** and contracts, appointments at the U.S. Custom House in New Orleans, and both men's future political aspirations. By 1870, the Louisiana Republican Party had become bitterly divided, and Dunn emerged as a leading figure in the anti-Warmoth or "Custom House" faction, which eventually gained control of the party. When Warmoth temporarily left the state to recuperate from an injury in early 1871, Dunn seized the opportunity as acting governor to remove a number of Warmoth loyalists from office, and he was a leader in the convention later that year that ejected Warmoth and his supporters from the Republican Party. By late 1871, Custom House Republicans considered uniting with Democrats to impeach Warmoth, but this plan was temporarily sidetracked when Dunn died unexpectedly on November 22 from what was called congestion of the brain. His sudden death sparked rumors that he had been poisoned, but no evidence has ever surfaced to substantiate this allegation.

A strong proponent of black political, legal, and economic rights, Dunn had a profound influence among black Louisianans, and his personal integrity in a state known for corruption earned him even his opponents' grudging respect. His funeral was said to be one of the largest ever held in New Orleans, and so deeply was his death felt that it brought a temporary truce to the political warfare in Louisiana. Even Warmoth, who was eventually impeached, was among the pallbearers. Dunn was buried in New Orleans. *See also* African Americans; Black Politicians; Bureau of Refugees, Freedmen, and Abandoned Lands; Congressional Reconstruction; Democratic Party; Freedmen's Relief Societies; Pinchback, Pinckney Benton Stewart; Presidential Reconstruction; Suffrage; Wells, James M.

Further Reading: Foner, Eric. *Freedom's Lawmakers: A Directory of Black Office-holders during Reconstruction*. Rev. ed. Baton Rouge: Louisiana State University Press, 1996; Perkins, A. E. "Oscar James Dunn." *Phylon* 4 (1943): 105–21; Taylor, Joe Gray. *Louisiana Reconstructed: 1863–1877*. Baton Rouge: Louisiana State University Press, 1974.

John C. Rodrigue

E

Eaton, John (1829–1906)

John Eaton, educator, officer of **African American** troops in the Civil War, Freedmen's Bureau agent, and college president, was born in Sutton, New Hampshire, on December 5, 1829. Although his father owned a substantial 2,000-acre farm, young John preferred teaching to **agriculture**. Beginning his pedagogical career at the age of sixteen, he recognized his need for more formal **education** and attended Thetford Academy in Vermont and later Dartmouth College, where he graduated in 1854. In the years before the Civil War, he served as principal of schools in Cleveland and Toledo, Ohio. In 1859, he began his study of theology at Andover Theological Seminary.

Ordained in 1861, he became the chaplain of the Twenty-seventh Ohio Volunteer Infantry, and served with troops as they fought in Missouri and **Tennessee**. Twice he was captured by Confederates. After the Battle of Corinth (1862), General **Ulysses S. Grant** appointed him superintendent of freedmen for **Mississippi**, northern **Louisiana**, **Arkansas**, and western Tennessee, and charged him with organizing freedmen into camps, providing for their physical and educational needs, and using them to work on abandoned plantations. While there, the African Americans' poverty and sickness stunned him. He requisitioned doctors to help the former slaves and stopped the previous practice of burying horses, mules, and humans in common pits.

A master at public relations, he persuaded northern benevolent associations to send much-needed aid and money. He used black workers on rented plantations or he leased black workers to planters, where males received wages of seven dollars a month and females five dollars a month. New arrivals to **contraband** camps served in hospitals, city residents worked in more professional occupations, and the most physically fit chopped wood. Pushing education, he established schools and orphanages for young blacks. By 1864, more than 13,000 blacks received instruction in these schools.

Beginning in 1863, he supervised camps outside Memphis, Tennessee, Helena, Arkansas, Natchez, and Vicksburg, Mississippi, and monitored agents working throughout the state. Wanting blacks to begin to understand the dynamics of the free **labor system**, he mediated **contracts** between blacks and white landowners. Hoping to instill his views of marriage on the newly freed, he performed hundreds of black marriages. Alice Eugenia Shirley, the daughter of a Vicksburg, Mississippi, Unionist, became his wife on September 29, 1864. Constant harassment by guerrillas pushed him to form and lead the Seventh Regiment of Louisiana Volunteers of African Descent.

Appointed a brigadier general as he left the army, he received both praise and criticism for his work with the newly freed people. Some applauded his creativity and sympathy for blacks, while others condemned his paternalism and pro-planter policies.

Appointed an assistant commissioner of the **Bureau of Refugees, Freedmen, and Abandoned Lands** (Freedmen's Bureau) in May 1865, his work during the war had prepared him for the difficulties of Reconstruction. He often offered suggestions to Freedmen's Bureau chief **Oliver Otis Howard**. Sensing that the problems faced were intractable, he resigned in December 1865.

After the war, he and his new bride moved to Memphis, Tennessee, where he edited an anti–President **Andrew Johnson** newspaper, the *Memphis Post*. In 1870, he became the U.S. commissioner of education, a position in which he amassed mountains of statistics to encourage Congress and state legislatures to fund better schools. He presented pedagogical workshops that exposed the newest teaching techniques to educators throughout the United States. In his later career, he served as president of Marietta College (1886–1891) at Marietta, Ohio, and Sheldon Jackson College at Salt Lake City, Utah (1895–1899). At the end of the Spanish-American War he organized the schools of Puerto Rico. He died in Washington, D.C., in 1906. *See also* Emancipation; Freedmen's Relief Societies; U.S. Army and Reconstruction.

Further Reading: Berlin, Ira, ed.: *Freedom: The Destruction of Slavery.* Series I, Volume 1. New York: Oxford University Press, 1985; *Freedom: The Wartime Genesis of Free Labor: The Lower South.* Series I, Volume 3. New York: Oxford University Press, 1990; Bigelow, Martha. "Freedmen of the Mississippi Valley." *Civil War History* 8 (1962): 38–47; Eaton, John. *Grant, Lincoln, and the Freedmen: Reminiscences of the Civil* War. 1907; reprint, New York: Negro Universities Press, 1969; Gerteis, Louis S. *From Contraband to Freedman: Federal Policy toward Southern Blacks, 1861–1865.* Westport, CT: Greenwood Press, 1973; Ross, Steven Joseph. "Freed Soil, Freed Labor, Freed Men." *Journal of Southern History* 44 (1978): 213–32.

Randy Finley

Edisto Island, South Carolina

Located between Charleston and Beaufort on the **South Carolina** coast, Edisto Island became a focal point for the distribution of land to freedmen following the Civil War. Responding to a request by **African American** leaders in Savannah, **Georgia**, General **William T. Sherman** issued Special **Field Order No. 15** in January 1865. This order set aside a thirty-mile-wide strip of land along the Atlantic coast from Charleston to **Florida**'s St. Johns River for settlement by former slaves. Abandoned by white owners during the war, assistant Freedmen's Bureau commissioner, General **Rufus Saxton** began distribution of the land in forty-acre tracts. Freedmen would be given a possessory title to the land, and in some cases, they received mules and horses that had been seized by Sherman's troops.

Saxton recognized the determination of black people to acquire land. Their love of the soil and desire to own farms amounted to a passion. By June 1865, 40,000 freed people had settled on land that included James Island, Edisto Island, and Hilton Head in South Carolina, and Sapelo and St. Simon's Islands in Georgia.

However, white owners of the land appealed successfully to President **Andrew Johnson** for the return of the land. In September, Johnson ordered the commissioner of the **Bureau of Refugees, Freedmen, and Abandoned Lands**, General **Oliver Otis Howard**, to issue Circular 15, which effectively restored lands occupied by freedmen to the original owners.

Howard traveled to Edisto Island in October to appeal to freedmen to relinquish lands they worked, occupied, and believed that they would own. Speaking to a discontented crowd of perhaps 1,000, Howard insisted that they had to abandon the land, but that he would try to see that they would have the opportunity to work that land. Not placated in the least, a three-man committee—Henry Brown, Ishmael Moultrie, and Yates Sampson—told Howard that they must have land if they were to be truly free.

> We were promised homesteads by the government. . . . We are left at the mercy of those who are combined to prevent us from getting land enough. . . . You will see this is not the condition of really free men. You ask us to forgive the landowners of this island. You only lost your right arm in the war and might forgive them [Howard had lost his arm at the Battle of Fair Oaks]. The man who tied me to a tree and gave me 39 lashes, who stripped and flogged my mother & sister & and who will not let me stay in his empty hut except I will do his planting & be satisfied with his price & who combines with others to keep land away from men. (Oubre, 53)

In a petition to Johnson, the freedmen reminded the president that they had "always [been] true to the Union" and that they had every right to the land and were prepared to pay for it. They asked: "And now after what has been done will the good and just government take from us this right and make us subject to the will of those who cheated and oppressed us for many years? God forbid!" (Oubre, 56). Johnson, a Unionist who concurred with **abolition** and the **Thirteenth Amendment**, was nonetheless a former slaveholder who opposed any radical or racial modifications to the South. At a time when even most Republicans rejected the idea of land confiscation, President Johnson was far too racist and conservative to entertain the notion of giving white land to blacks. As a result, the president issued scores of **pardons** to former Confederates, which restored their political rights and their property—including land.

Only those freedmen who possessed valid titles or warrants to the land were permitted to remain on that land, and there was considerable controversy over what constituted a legitimate warrant. Although the precise number is not known, most freedmen on Edisto Island—and elsewhere on the coast—did not retain their land. *See also* Agriculture; Amnesty Proclamations; Congressional Reconstruction; Contraband, Slaves as; Labor Systems; Port Royal Experiment; Presidential Reconstruction; Republicans, Radical; Stevens, Thaddeus.

Further Reading: McFeely, William S. *Yankee Stepfather: General O. O. Howard and the Freedmen.* New York: W. W. Norton, 1968; Oubre, Claude F. *Forty Acres and a Mule: The Freedmen's Bureau and Black Land Ownership.* Baton Rouge: Louisiana State University Press, 1978.

William C. Hine

Education

Universal education was one of the most significant and permanent achievements of Reconstruction. This was made possible by government and military intervention, and a profusion of individuals, **churches** and religious organizations, and benevolent societies. **African Americans** themselves lent a considerable hand to these efforts. Advancements, such as the establishment of a never-before-seen southern public school system for blacks and poor whites, private schools, and black colleges and universities, permanently altered the southern landscape. The creation of a viable educational system for blacks proved to be a challenging task, but despite the high hopes of the philanthropists, education did not remedy the social, economic, and political ills of postslavery life.

Prior to the Civil War, education in the South was a luxury enjoyed by affluent landowners and their families. These landowners believed education was a private affair and the exclusive privilege of the wealthy ruling class. Education generally included private tutoring, music and dance lessons, English history, and instruction in plantation management. Extensive libraries located within planters' palatial homes supplemented this individual schooling. Many of their sons attended colleges or universities, followed by one- or two-year tours in Europe. Deprived of schools, the majority of yeomen (small farmers) and poor whites, who lived isolated in hilly or mountainous regions, were illiterate. Most southern states had laws that forbade slaves from receiving an education. In rare cases, sympathetic whites or Free Blacks taught slaves how to read, write, and even do arithmetic. Some slaves taught themselves. Preexisting free black communities, which established their own schools or followed a form of education similar to the wealthy landowners, were other, minor, exceptions. Consequently, education was another way that the great landed communities maintained their dominance over the lower levels (black and white) in this caste system.

During the Civil War, a vast number of individuals and groups swarmed into the South to educate blacks. In 1861, Mary Chase, a free black woman from **Virginia**, opened a school for blacks. Soon after, Mary Peake, another black woman, set up a school near Fortress Monroe in Virginia. The **American Missionary Association (AMA)** later funded both teachers' salaries. Also in 1861, a black cabinetmaker opened a formerly clandestine school on **South Carolina**'s Sea Islands. By the end of the decade, free blacks owned and financed ninety-six schools in **Georgia** alone. Blacks often preferred to establish private schools rather than attend public schools. Parents, mostly impoverished, eagerly paid the tuition to support schools taught and owned by blacks and well known for providing for the specific needs of their students. Moreover, blacks themselves raised significant funds in order to build schools and pay teacher salaries.

Numerous churches and benevolent aid societies (both secular and religious) from the North and South were instrumental in the establishment of new schools. These groups often cooperated with the government and the military. In 1865, Congress created the **Bureau of Refugees, Freedmen, and Abandoned Lands**, also known as the Freedmen's Bureau. The Bureau helped supply buildings using monies acquired from the rental of lands abandoned by their former owners, while private individuals and organizations paid for teaching supplies and teacher's salaries. In 1867, Congress endorsed legislation to provide for universal common schools. The Morrill Act of 1890 provided funds from the sale of federal lands to states willing to establish separate land-grant colleges for blacks. Alcorn A&M in **Mississippi**, **Florida** A&M, Southern University in **Louisiana**, and Tuskegee Institute in **Tennessee** were among those schools created. Within Congress, black and white politicians also campaigned for more and better schools, colleges, and universities for blacks.

Religious organizations, both black and white, produced more black colleges and universities during Reconstruction than in any other period in America's history. The AMA founded Atlanta University in Georgia, Fisk University in Tennessee, Talladega College in **Alabama**, Tougalloo College in Mississippi, and Hampton Institute in Virginia, which also accepted **American Indians**. White Methodists set up Clark College in Georgia, and Clafflin University in South Carolina, and white Baptists funded such schools as Atlanta Baptist College, later known as Morehouse College, in Georgia, and Shaw University in **North Carolina**. The Colored Methodists Episcopal Church opened Lane College in Tennessee, and the African Methodist Episcopal Church established both Allen University in South Carolina and Morris Brown College in Georgia. Many of the elite black men and women of this period attended these schools. More than 100 thriving black colleges and universities exist today.

Despite the proliferation of schools in the South, education was not without its obstacles and problems. Blacks were forced to attend segregated schools and subjected to **violence**, rioting, beatings, and killings. Other obstacles included a lack of funding and permanent support. However, blacks were enthusiastic learners despite inferior school buildings and classrooms, inadequate supplies, and outdated books. Moreover, white teachers at black schools were paid less than at white schools, and black teachers in general were paid even less. Black schools received another blow when the Freedman's Bureau ended most of its operations in 1870. National interest in black education waned

A primary schoolroom in Mississippi. (Courtesy of the Library of Congress.)

thereafter. Moreover, when conservative southern whites regained political power following Reconstruction, they withheld funding to black schools. Without federal and state assistance, schools suffered tremendously.

Many of the problems faced by blacks in society at large were reflected in the new educational system. Believing blacks unfit to govern themselves, whites insisted on controlling, funding, and teaching black schools themselves. On the other hand, blacks—both freedpeople and, to an extent, later generations—desired autonomy. Another issue was that the whites, and some blacks, controlling the schools reinforced black inferiority and stressed the status quo. The popular curriculum of the period promoted middle-class ethics based upon racist ideas geared toward limiting blacks to occupations in **agriculture**, industry, and service rather than empowering blacks to transcend the constraints of southern society. Some southern whites used education as a means of controlling and manipulating blacks.

Despite these significant shortcomings, a burgeoning population of black scholars, inventors, doctors, and professionals appeared. Yet, education did not alleviate the social, economic, and political problems confronting blacks. Southern whites—indeed, most white Americans—did not change their racist views. In fact, they kept blacks in a state not far from slavery by taking away their **civil rights** and liberties through **Jim Crow laws**, hoarding wealth and positions of power, and maintaining dominance through political control, racist court systems and law enforcement, violence, and intimidation. During the years after Reconstruction, white supremacists ousted blacks from arenas not designated for blacks only. Regardless of these difficult circumstances, education did enable blacks to govern themselves, to maintain self-sustaining communities, to stimulate positive change, and to make contributions to the nation. *See also* Black Politicians; Bourbons; Disfranchisement; Douglass, Frederick; Edisto Island, South Carolina; Freedmen's Relief Societies; Morrill, Justin Smith; Port Royal Experiment; Redemption; U.S. Army and Reconstruction.

Further Reading: Anderson, James D.: *The Education of Blacks in the South, 1860–1935.* Chapel Hill: University of North Carolina Press, 1988; "Historically Black Colleges and Universities." Online at PBS, http://www.pbs.org/itvs/fromswasticato jimcrow/blackcolleges.html. Accessed August 2005; Barnard, John, and Burner, David. *The American Experience in Education.* New York: Viewpoints, 1975; Butchart, Ronald E. *Northern Schools, Southern Black Schools, and Reconstruction.* Westport, CT: Greenwood Press, 1980; Gatewood, Willard B. *Aristocrats of Color: The Black Elite, 1880–1920.* Bloomington: Indiana University Press, 1990; Richardson, Joe M. *Christian Reconstruction: The American Missionary Association and Southern Blacks, 1861–1890.* Athens: University of Georgia Press, 1986.

Gladys L. Knight

Elections of 1864

The presidential election of 1864 took place amid a destructive and frustrating war, which substantially affected everything about the contest and shaped the nation's political agenda for years afterward.

The Democratic Party and Its Options

Both **Democratic** and Republican parties were beset by internal divisions as the election approached. In 1861, a small group of War Democrats had all but unreservedly thrown their support to the administration and its policies in order to preserve the Union. Other Democrats were less willing to do so. They were appalled by President **Abraham Lincoln**'s unremitting reach for more extensive powers and increased control over American citizens, both necessary, the administration argued, to meet the national emergency. But Democratic leaders disagreed over how far they should go in resisting the Republican onslaught. A large number believed that the party should clearly support the war as being necessary to restore the Union, but once having publicly legitimated themselves in this way, they should also challenge any attempt to enlarge the scope of federal power under the **U.S. Constitution** or to use the war as an excuse to overthrow the nation's existing social arrangements, particularly in respect to slavery. Their mantra was strict construction and no home front social revolution: "The Constitution as it is, the Union as it was." So-called Peace Democrats turned their faces resolutely against any pragmatic concessions on the war. They believed that continuing it was a mistake, it would not restore the Union, and it would inevitably cause dangerous challenges to the nation's deepest-held values and unacceptable changes to existing political institutions.

Lincoln's issuance of the **Emancipation** Proclamation in the fall of 1862, his "executive usurpation," and suppression of civil liberties (including the **U.S. Army**'s arrest of Peace Democratic leaders), confirmed fears of the dangers the country faced if the war was not ended.

The two main party wings argued it out from the early days of the war and into the 1864 national convention in Chicago in late August. They came to an uneasy compromise, adopting a so-called peace platform which, while calling for the Union to be restored and lauding the nation's soldiers for their bravery, branded the war a failure, and severely condemned the administration's actions on the home front. This message was accompanied by the nomination of a candidate, General George McClellan, who actually supported the war, but opposed the extremism that seemed to be gaining momentum in its prosecution. The vice presidential candidate, **George Hunt Pendleton**, came from the party's peace wing.

Republican-Turned-Union Party

The Republicans also had their problems. A vocal bloc, of which the Radicals composed the nucleus, believed that Lincoln was too moderate and hesitant. These politicians and generals had pushed the administration to embrace emancipation, and implement social and economic policies designed to aid former slaves in their transition to self-sufficiency. Lincoln did not totally disagree, and felt it prudent to follow a more restrained course in the hopes of maintaining national unity and winning support from outside the Republican Party. At Lincoln's prodding, party leaders actually changed the name of their organization to the **National Union Party** for the campaign. The Radicals strongly resisted Lincoln's tactics, and, for a time, there was a threat of a split in the party and an independent, Radical-led campaign behind a candidate and a platform more to their liking. That threat ultimately petered out as party members fell into line behind the administration, some of them, to be sure, in a grudging manner. At their national convention in Baltimore in early June, Lincoln's support proved much too strong for the dissidents and he was easily renominated. The delegates selected a War Democrat, **Andrew Johnson** of **Tennessee**, as the Union Party's vice presidential nominee, but the internal disagreements continued to trouble the party as the contest got under way.

The Campaign of 1864

Once the campaign began, internal party divisions dissipated out of necessity: the need to win. Their campaign organizations, the **Union League** Clubs for the Republicans, and the Society for the Diffusion of Political Knowledge for the Democrats, organized rallies and speeches and published pamphlets and partisan newspapers, all of which became the center of a national dialogue— argued in the harshest, most frightening terms possible. At the outset, the Democrats seemed to have the edge, for the campaign was taking place at the bleakest moment of the war. The Union's failure to defeat the rebellion on the battlefield led to growing war weariness and deepening resentment against such policies as emancipation and conscription—conditions that clearly invigorated the Democrats despite their failures in state-level elections the year before. And no end to the war was in sight. **Ulysses S. Grant**'s overland campaign in **Virginia**, begun with high hopes in the spring, seemed to be going nowhere despite enormous casualties to the Union armies. McClellan and his allies constantly played on the administration's failures as well as its submission to Radical demands. They reiterated what they had been saying since early in the war, the administration's "usurpation" of the Constitution for base purposes overlaid by heavy emphasis on racist themes. More than anything else, Democratic leaders believed that the country would reject emancipation and the uplifting of the freed blacks through federal actions, at the expense (they argued) of white Americans. The war had to be won, but that would never happen under Republican leadership and its promotion of social revolution.

The Republicans had their potent electoral weapons, as well, whatever their disagreements. Lincoln's political managers played down the administration's controversial policies on the home front in regard to slavery and individual freedom. They found it useful, instead, to focus on the Democrats' ambiguity about the war. Whatever Democratic support there was, they argued, was grudging and deceptive of the party's true aims. McClellan, who had supported the war in his acceptance letter, was at best a tool of the peace wing of the party, which clearly controlled the Democracy. The "Copperheads" conspired with southern sympathizers to undermine the war effort, not only provoking resistance to the draft, but even working with Confederate agents to undercut morale and damage efforts to mobilize the Union's strength. In short, Democrats belonged to the party of "Dixie, Davis and the Devil" (*New York Evening Post*, September 2, 1864), a subversive, treasonous, element at a time of the greatest danger to the republic. The only way to save the Union was the reelection of President Lincoln and the continuing leadership of the Republican Party.

For a time, all looked bleak for the administration. Even Lincoln believed in the summer that he would lose, but as the campaign developed, the Democrats' apparent edge faded. First, the war news grew better, culminating in Admiral Farragut's seizure of Mobile Bay, General **Philip H. Sheridan**'s successful campaign in the Shenandoah Valley, and General **William T. Sherman**'s capture of Atlanta. Suddenly there was light at the end of the tunnel, energizing Republican support and bringing wavering voters over to them. By early fall, Democrats' claims of failure no longer seemed as convincing as they had been. Further, Republican leaders were quite successful in mobilizing the soldier vote (several states permitted soldiers to vote in the field) behind their patriotic call for support. October elections in several key states, often an indicator of the public mood, offered little hope for the Democrats, a fact confirmed in early November. Almost four million votes were cast (including the soldiers, who went overwhelmingly for Lincoln), with the Republicans winning 2.2 million of them, about 55 percent of the total, and 212 electoral votes from twenty-two states. The Democrats had substantial popular support: 1.8 million had chosen them, about 45 percent of the electorate, but they remained a minority, winning only three states and twenty-one electoral votes. The Republicans, waving the banner of the Union and denouncing Democratic treason, had proved to be too much for them. *See also* Abolition, of

Slavery; Annual Messages of the President; Confiscation Acts; Contraband, Slaves as; Presidential Reconstruction; Republicans, Moderate; Wade, Benjamin Franklin.

Further Reading: Donald, David. *Lincoln*. New York: Simon and Schuster, 1995; Hyman, Harold M. "Election of 1864." In Arthur M. Schlesinger, Jr., ed., *History of American Presidential Elections, 1789-1968*. New York: Chelsea House, 1971; Silbey, Joel H. *A Respectable Minority: The Democratic Party in the Civil War Era*. New York: Norton, 1977; Waugh, John. *Reelecting Lincoln: The Battle for the 1864 Presidency*. New York: Crown, 1997.

Joel H. Silbey

Elections of 1866

The fall elections in 1866 marked a watershed in the history of Reconstruction. The elections pitted the name, policy, and party of the president, **Andrew Johnson**, against the **Moderate** and **Radical Republicans**. At stake was control of the U.S. Congress, and quite possibly the entire Reconstruction program. Republicans scored overwhelming successes across the northern states, assuring that the next Congress that convened would tolerate no opposition from the executive.

The Political Atmosphere: Summer 1866

Reconstruction occurred all across the country, in households and courtrooms, in the planter's fields and in the state legislatures. But regardless of one's interpretation of the process, the federal government would play perhaps the pivotal role in this drama. Its resources, its vision, its power and authority could make or unmake the future. Of utmost importance, then, are two issues: which branch of the federal government controlled Reconstruction, and which party controlled that branch.

The first question had been in play since **Abraham Lincoln** first broached the restoration issue in 1863. With the accession of Johnson to the presidency, at a time when Congress was not in session, it seemed that Reconstruction would be in the hands of the president. But Johnson's program was fraught with problems, for his liberal approach to former slaveholders and indifferent approach to former slaves led to a state of affairs in the South inconsistent with freedom for the latter and defeat for the former. Johnson, a Unionist War Democrat who had supported **emancipation** as a war measure, believed in a rigid **U.S. Constitution** that seemed under assault by radical manipulators bent on bringing racial conflict and federal despotism. When, in 1866, Moderate Republicans sought compromise via such proposals as the **Civil Rights** bill, **Freedmen's Bureau bill**, and **Fourteenth Amendment**, Johnson's hostile rejections drove more conservative Republicans into the Radical camp. Johnson's acerbic speeches, his antagonistic veto messages, and growing **violence** in the South—including the **Memphis riot** and capped by the **New Orleans riot** on July 30—convinced many northerners that the president was beyond cooperation. **Presidential Reconstruction** had failed to assist the freedpeople, had failed to bring peace, had failed to energize the Republican Party, and had failed to instill and reinforce loyalty in the white South.

So, by the summer of 1866, the two questions above had become linked for many northern voters: The president should not control Reconstruction, and his party should not control the federal government. This set the stage for the 1866 fall elections, which would determine which party controlled Congress and therefore the Reconstruction of the Union.

The 1866 Campaigns

Andrew Johnson understood the stakes, and realized a need to build political momentum. In order to defend his program and stave off Republican assaults, he had to develop a solid base in Congress. His vehicle for this was a new political party. Taking the name of the broad-based party Abraham Lincoln fostered in his successful bid for reelection in 1864, Johnson and his advisors announced their National Union Party in the summer of 1866. President Johnson hoped that the **National Union Movement** would gather all those disaffected with the radical nature of the Republican agenda. Certainly, his base was with the **Democratic Party** and other conservatives, but his appeal had to capture the North. At a convention in Philadelphia in August, pro-Johnson conservatives from around the nation gathered to applaud the Union veterans, criticize the Radical Republicans, and cheer on the program of Andrew John- son. The so-called "arm-and-arm" convention (because of wartime rivals ar- riving with arms linked as a show of unity) did its best to promote presidential Reconstruction and Johnson's message of reconciliation, peace, and stability.

The Republicans countered with two conventions, one in Philadelphia in September and the other later in Pittsburgh. These showed divisions in the party, in particular over **black suffrage**, but did little to either bolster the Republican effort or hamper it. Most Republicans walked a middle road, endorsing certain black civil rights but eschewing dangerous proposals for **suffrage** or land con- fiscation. In the end, the president, his program, and white southerners were their own worst enemies. Johnson's ill-fated "**Swing Around the Circle**" speaking tour made more enemies than friends, and even cost him some allies: **James Bennett** and his *New York Herald*, formerly staunch supporters, began to distance themselves from the president after the embarrassing saga. Johnson's obstinate behavior, and continuous reports of violence in the South, were proof enough that the president and his program had failed.

The Elections and Their Significance

The fall elections began in September and ended in November. With many of the southern states still out of the Union, the elections were primarily a northern and border-state contest. Along with the elections for national office, many states also had state seats up for grabs. As shown by historian Michael Les Benedict, usually in "off-year" nineteenth-century elections (non- presidential years), Democrats running for national office did very well since the focus tended to be on local and social issues. Although an "off-year," Johnson had turned 1866 into a referendum on Reconstruction, an issue firmly at center stage of a national drama.

Unfortunately for the president and his National Union Movement, election reports brought only disappointment. Turnout was high—the highest of a congressional off-year election between 1858 and 1874—and this too helped the Republicans. In the end, the contest for control of Congress proved to be no contest at all, as Republican candidates swept the field and increased their number in both houses of the national legislature. Johnson candidates suffered terrible losses, and the balance of power in Congress—and the federal government—shifted dramatically. The 40th Congress would be in effect "veto-proof" if members voted by party block, since the Republican Party now constituted more than two-thirds of the House and the Senate; it could in theory pass legislation at will, for it had the requisite numbers to override a presidential veto.

To prevent presidential interference and gather the momentum necessary for a full-fledged Reconstruction program, the sitting Congress called the new Congress-elect into session in March 1867, immediately after the 39th had closed. This would prevent Johnson from acting on his own when Congress was not in session (as he had done in 1865). Therefore, Reconstruction, in many respects, began anew in the spring of 1867, with a Republican-dominated Congress dictating policy. *See also* African Americans; Amnesty Proclamations; Black Codes; Bureau of Refugees, Freedmen, and Abandoned Lands; Cabinets, Executive; Civil Rights Act of 1866; Command of the Army Act; Congressional Reconstruction; Elections of 1864; Joint Committee on Reconstruction; Loyalty Oaths; Military Reconstruction Acts; Pardons; Provisional Governors; Race Riots; Readmission; Recusants; U.S. Army and Reconstruction.

Further Reading: Benedict, Michael Les. "The Politics of Reconstruction." In John F. Marszalek and Wilson D. Miscamble, eds., *American Political History: Essays on the State of the Discipline*. Notre Dame, IN: University of Notre Dame Press, 1997; Schroeder-Lein, Glenna, and Richard Zuczek. *Andrew Johnson: A Biographical Companion*. Santa Barbara, CA: ABC-CLIO, 2001; Trefousse, Hans L. *Andrew Johnson: A Biography*. New York: W. W. Norton and Co., 1989.

Richard Zuczek

Elections of 1867

Beginning in September and stretching into November, the fall elections of 1867 presented some of the most complex, and even contradictory, lessons for politicians during Reconstruction. Unlike the rather straightforward congressional **elections of 1866**, or the presidential years of 1868 and 1872, the elections of 1867 occurred at the state level, and involved a wider variety of players, issues, stages—and even results. In general, however, the effect was to embolden the **Democratic Party**, and confuse the **Radical Republicans**.

The elections of 1867 differed from other Reconstruction campaigns in another way as well: there were really two separate sets of elections under way—one in the North and one in the South. Although the central issues for both regions were related to Reconstruction, the elections themselves—who participated, what was at stake, and what resulted—differed tremendously.

Southern Elections

In the South, the former Confederate states were going through the process imposed by Congress via the **Military Reconstruction Acts** of the previous March. These acts called for the **U.S. Army** to oversee voter registration, including **African American** males and excluding many former Confederates, to hold a vote for a **constitutional convention**, and then to supervise the election of delegates for this convention.

It is difficult to neatly summarize the details of the southern state elections; these are covered in state entries elsewhere in this encyclopedia. Taken as a whole, however, some observations can be made. First, the fall elections did represent a real political revolution. For the first time, on a large scale, black men voted in the United States. The Military Reconstruction Act enfranchised black males, and they executed their voting rights in the calls for state constitutional conventions and the selection of delegates to the same.

Not surprising, the nascent Republican Party scored overwhelming triumphs in all former Confederate states. Attempts by white conservatives to stop the conventions by abstaining from voting (to deny the requirement for a majority-voter turnout to validate the election) failed, and actually resulted in Congress passing a new Reconstruction Act to close that loophole. Even President **Andrew Johnson**'s **Amnesty Proclamation** of September 7, which removed political disabilities from many (but not all) former Confederates, could not deny Republican victory. The combination of Confederate **disfranchisement**, black voters, progressive local whites and Unionists (who earned the epithet **scalawags**) and **carpetbaggers** from the North meant nearly every state of the former Confederacy would undergo a complete constitutional revision (**Tennessee** had been readmitted and was not operating under the acts). From the perspective of black and white members of the southern Republican Party, Reconstruction seemed to be steaming along.

Elections in the North

Things were different in the North. Again, these were state elections, without federal seats or positions at risk, but voters in the North went to the polls to vote for municipal, county, and state offices, including their legislatures and governors.

Unlike the previous year, when the congressional elections presented a cut-and-dry issue and a straightforward choice, northern voters in 1867 faced a multitude of topics and agendas. According to historian Michael Les Benedict, this fact by itself foretold woes for the Republicans: During the nineteenth century, in federal election years that did not involve presidential campaigns, Democrats proved victorious. Of course, 1867 did not involve a federal/national election, but the reasons for the Democratic success can be the same: Republicans did better on major, national issues that drew solid party voting, whereas Democrats did better when the topics were local and diverse, without an overriding national theme. Such was the case in 1867.

Of course, no election could completely ignore Reconstruction, and such was true in 1867, but the topics that related to Congress's Reconstruction program took on state characteristics and more local meaning (therefore, by extrapolating from Benedict's theory, played into Democratic hands). For instance, **black suffrage** was on the ballot in Ohio, Kansas (along with women's suffrage), and Minnesota; the proposals failed in all three states, as did many Republicans advocating them. In other states, issues of **disfranchisement** lost the party votes, as did talk of black equality and land confiscation. The exact reasons for the backlash are unclear. In some cases, moderate voters recoiled from extremist proposals. In other states, Republican intraparty dissension over such topics cost unity; for instance, many Republicans believed an alliance with white conservatives was the only long-term political solution for the southern Republican Party, a solution impossible if land **confiscation** and disfranchisement remained viable.

However, other topics crowded in with Reconstruction, especially since this election lacked a national focus, and for many—after the passage of the Reconstruction Acts—Reconstruction seemed old news. These certainly provided a boost to the Democratic Party. For example, ethnic demographics played a large role in many state elections, pitting the "Yankees" of the Republican Party against the growing number of Irish and Germans who held solidly to the Democratic fold. In Massachusetts and New York, the item of chief concern seemed to be prohibition and liquor laws. In some developing states, it was agitation for—or against—government aid to large **railroad** companies. In the West, which still formed the **agricultural** backbone of an agricultural nation, finances and monetary policy struck a cord. Western farmers supported inflationary policies, quite the opposite from the treasury's contraction program that was retiring greenbacks in preparation for a return to specie. Although the Johnson administration, and in particular his treasury secretary **Hugh McCulloch**, supported the contraction, voters considered it a Republican plot because of the party's hard-money policies and control of Congress. Similarly, many western voters viewed the national debt as a Republican problem, and backed the "Ohio Plan." The brainchild of **George H. Pendleton** of Ohio, this initiative called for the immediate repayment of government war bonds using greenbacks. Again, this cut across party lines, but as a mobilizing issue favored soft-money Democrats over the hard-money Republicans.

Across the North, Democrats did to Republicans at the state level what the latter had done to them at the federal level the year before. The party of **Lincoln** suffered its worst losses since before the Civil War, with Democrats taking possession of most state legislatures, most governors' offices, and a high percentage of judicial, county, and local positions. The next few years saw an interesting political dynamic at work, with the federal government securely in the hands of Republicans, while Democrats controlled the northern states.

Differing Interpretations

Although historians can carefully evaluate the northern elections in a cold, methodical way, contemporaries had less information, and less tendency to avoid rashness. Therefore, the northern results seemed to offer an array of lessons. Democrats took the results as a true reflection of the American electorate (unlike in the South, where "military tyranny" imposed Republican rule), and encouraged the party to continue stressing items that seemed to be working: anti-disfranchisement, anti–black suffrage, and proinflation. At the national level, no one was more pleased than the president, and some argue it was electoral success that convinced him the Radicals were on the run—and could be exposed completely by a grand act of defiance, such as the removal of **Edwin Stanton** as secretary of war. Many in the Democratic Party (including Johnson) saw the elections as a positive omen, forecasting presidential success in 1868. Not for the first time, Johnson and his party would misread and miscalculate, to their own detriment.

For Republicans, the meaning was more mixed. To be sure, the northern defeats were a shock and meant the party was doing something wrong, but what? Certain state returns clearly indicated opposition to black suffrage, but did that extend to black **civil rights** in general? Democrats loudly exclaimed that this was a warning, that the fall **impeachment** crisis was now surely dead. Was it? Were voters attacking Republicans for trying to impeach the president—or for failing to do it earlier? Was the message a turning away from radicalism, or a demand for more? Many Radical Republicans believed the latter, that the agenda had been too cautious and needed to more directly embrace the controversial issues.

By and large, however, Republicans saw the Democratic resurgence as a rebuke, a warning against going too far too fast. **Moderate Republicans**, the bulk of the party and the real driving force behind **Congressional Reconstruction**, moved more toward the political center, and became wary of political experiments. Although Johnson forced their hand into impeachment, one sees their conservatism in his acquittal. Certainly the choice of a lukewarm **Ulysses S. Grant** for the Republican nomination in 1868 reflected this also. Even in framing the capstone to the Reconstruction program, the **Fifteenth Amendment**, Republicans remembered this election; they made sure it was written as a negative presentation that banned certain discrimination, rather than a positive conferring of **suffrage**. *See also* Alabama; Annual Messages of the President; Arkansas; Black Politicians; Edisto Island, South Carolina; Elections of 1868; Field Order No. 15; Florida; Fourteenth Amendment; Georgia; House Judiciary Committee; Louisiana; Loyalty Oaths; Mississippi; National Union Movement; North Carolina; Pardons; Port Royal Experiment; Presidential Reconstruction; Readmission; South Carolina; Southern Homestead Act; Stevens, Thaddeus; Sumner, Charles; Tenure of Office Act; Texas; Union League of America; Virginia; Women's Movement.

Further Reading: Benedict, Michael Les: "The Politics of Reconstruction." In John F. Marszalek and Wilson D. Miscamble, eds., *American Political History: Essays on the State of the Discipline*. Notre Dame, IN: University of Notre Dame Press, 1997; "The Rout of Radicalism: Republicans and the Election of 1867." *Civil War History* 18 (December 1972): 334–44; Foner, Eric. *Reconstruction: America's Unfinished Revolution, 1863–1877*. New York: Harper and Row, 1988; Leppner, Paul. *The Third Electoral System, 1853–1892: Parties, Voters, and Political Cultures*. Chapel Hill: University of North Carolina Press, 1979.

Richard Zuczek

Elections of 1868

The first presidential election since the Civil War, the election of 1868 nonetheless continued many of the same debates seen four years earlier. In particular, arguments swirled over the expansion of the national government and the racial initiatives of the Republican Party, controversies that had been aired since the outbreak of the Civil War in 1861.

The Status of the Parties

Republican leaders were split over their strategy. Some accepted that they had pushed too far, that the 1867 results clearly indicated that they should pull back on their Reconstruction policies; certainly they had to avoid the **black suffrage** issue. The Radical wing of the party strongly demurred: the needed Reconstruction of the South was not yet finished, whites remained defiant and blacks still remained in thrall and under threat. The freedpeople needed protection, economic assistance, and the right to vote, but the more moderate party elements won out. At the Republican national convention in Chicago in May, the delegates unanimously chose **Ulysses S. Grant** as their candidate on a platform that, among other things, declared that black suffrage was a state-level question, not one for the federal government, at least in the states that had not seceded from the Union. Grant's mantra, "let us have peace," seemed to sum up the mood of the country. The Radicals were angry and resistant, but had no choice except to give way before Grant's popularity. Speaker of the House **Schuyler Colfax** of Indiana became his running mate, defeating his Radical opponent, Senator **Ben Wade**, in a close vote.

Despite the **Democratic Party**'s resistance to their wartime actions, the Republicans had maintained their political control in the presidential **election of 1864** and the congressional **elections of 1866**. As a result, the Democrats were in a chastened mood. They had been hurt by Republican assaults on their apparently less-than-full commitment to the war effort, their wavering in the face of the nation's determination to defend itself even at the cost of much bloodshed. In 1867, however, the party came bouncing back, at least partway, in a number of state-level victories and other, unexpectedly close run, contests. A combination of internal Republican divisions over **Congressional Reconstruction**, and the potency of the anti-**African American** sentiment as played on by the Democrats, had helped the latter make striking gains. The **impeachment of President Andrew Johnson** added to the party's determination and their hopes. The country seemed tired of heavily contested policies for reconstructing the South and was brutally racist in its response to postemancipation government attempts to aid the freedpeople. The **readmission** of southern states to the Union under President Johnson's lenient Reconstruction policies promised to add to the national Democratic vote as well. The party came into the election season in better shape than it had been for some time. Party leaders intended, therefore, to push ahead on the themes of restoration, excessive Republican radicalism, and resistance to black-centered policy initiatives. At the same time, they were determined not to let their opponents continue to brush them with the charge of treasonous behavior during the war.

Unfortunately for their hopes, the Democrats were also divided. The battles between Peace Democrats and the rest of the party had ebbed but had been replaced with sharp divisions over federal monetary policy. One group, particularly strong in the West, demanded the continuation of wartime federal policies concerning the national banknotes that had been issued during the emergency to help finance the conflict. These monetary radicals wanted the notes to remain in circulation and expanded in number rather than being withdrawn, as a necessary way of boosting a faltering economy. Fiscally conservative Democrats, particularly in the eastern states, committed to specie (metallic money) as the only legal circulating medium, resisted such financial heresy as dangerous, sure to disrupt and weaken confidence in the American economy, and warned their colleagues that they would lose once more unless they gave up such wild ideas and kept their focus on Republican Reconstruction failures.

At the Democratic convention in New York, which convened in the newly completed Tammany Hall on July 4, the soft money leader, **George Hunt Pendleton** of Ohio, took the early lead for the nomination but fell before the resistance to him from the more conservative wing who, while divided over a candidate, were determined not to let Pendleton, a peace leader four years before, and now a wild money man as they saw it, get the nod. (They were helped by the convention once more adopting the two-thirds rule—the number of votes a candidate needed to win the nomination.) For a time, some favored Chief Justice **Salmon P. Chase**, who had once been a Democrat, helped found the Republican Party, and sat in **Lincoln**'s **cabinet**, but then broke with his radical friends and handled the impeachment trial of Andrew Johnson with unexpected fairness. He could perhaps have been the best vote getter the party could put forward, but that was more than most party loyalists could accept. The conservatives finally fixed on **Horatio Seymour**, wartime governor of New York who had strongly challenged the Lincoln administration's "despotic" policies, while at the same time supporting the war.

After a long struggle, Seymour was finally nominated on the twenty-second ballot. **Frank Blair, Jr.**, of Missouri, a former Republican, Civil War general, and scion of a once-prominent Democratic family, was easily nominated for vice president.

The Campaign Opens

In the campaign that followed, both parties articulated their familiar themes through the usual run of speeches, pamphlets, and newspaper editorials, all circulated as widely as possible. Seymour and his colleagues reiterated their well-established constitutional and social conservatism. Their focus remained fixed on the failure of, and revolutionary tumult caused by, Republican southern policies despite their leaders' efforts to hide behind Grant's popularity. The Democrats' stance was, in the words of the April 14, 1868 issue of the *New York World*, "1. Opposition to Congressional usurpation. 2. Opposition to Negro supremacy. 3. Immediate restoration of the unity and peace of the nation."

The Republicans predictably counterattacked by waving the "**bloody shirt**," emphasizing the violent actions by southern whites determined to reverse the results of the war, the involvement of the Democrats in aiding and abetting

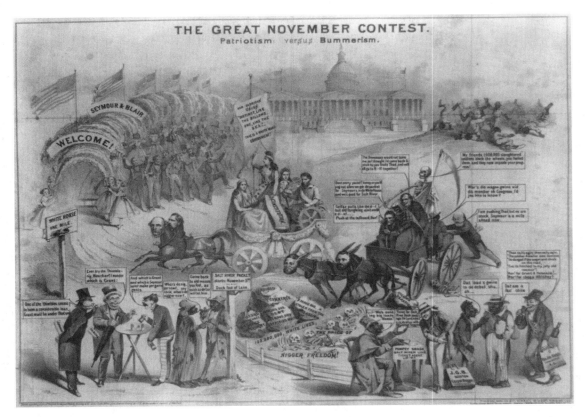

The strongly racist character of the Democratic presidential campaign of 1868 is displayed in this elaborate attack on Reconstruction and Republican support of Negro rights. (Courtesy of the Library of Congress.)

southern treason, and Seymour's support of the draft riots in New York City in 1863. (In trying to calm a violent crowd of rioters, he had allegedly addressed them as "my friends.") In Republican rhetoric, Seymour was "a traitor at heart." They also went after Blair for his strong statements that were not only pro-southern, but which seemed to call on former Confederates to resist Republican efforts in the South, even violently. In short, the contest was between Radicals and Copperheads, despotism and freedom, and—when economics came up—stability versus revolution, that is, hard money versus paper.

In the end, Republicans won their third straight presidential election, albeit with reduced margins. They captured twenty-six states with 214 electors, and 52.7 percent of the popular vote, to the Democrats' 80 electors and just over 47 percent of the votes cast. Eight (of eleven) reconstructed states of the former Confederacy participated in the election, with the Republicans winning six of them. However, the Democrats gained forty-two seats in the House of Representatives, rebounding from their disastrous totals of two years before. They hadn't won the presidency, nor regained control of Congress, but the results still gratified many Democrats and startled Republican leaders. The mood of the country seemed to be changing in the Democrats' favor. Nevertheless, the Republican Party was still in command, if in reduced circumstances. The potency of wartime memories, and charges of treasonable behavior, continued to favor the party of Lincoln. *See also* Presidential Reconstruction; Recusants; Republicans, Moderate; Republicans, Radical; Violence.

Further Reading: Coleman, Charles H. *The Election of 1868: The Democratic Effort to Regain Control.* New York: Columbia, 1933; Franklin, John Hope. "Election of 1868." In Arthur M. Schlesinger, Jr., ed., *History of American Presidential Elections, 1789–1968.* New York: Chelsea House, 1971; Mitchell, Stewart. *Horatio Seymour of New York.* Cambridge, MA: Harvard University Press, 1938; Simpson, Brooks. *Let Us Have Peace: Ulysses S. Grant and the Politics of War and Reconstruction.* Chapel Hill: University of North Carolina Press, 1991; Unger, Irwin. *The Greenback Era: A Social and Political History of American Finance, 1865–1879.* Princeton, NJ: Princeton University Press, 1964.

Joel H. Silbey

Elections of 1876

Many regard the U.S. presidential election of 1876 as the most disputed and controversial in American history. The **Democratic Party** nominee, **Samuel J. Tilden**, prevailed over Republican Party nominee **Rutherford B. Hayes** in the popular vote, but ran neck and neck in the Electoral College. The situation escalated when twenty electoral votes were disputed in Oregon, **Florida**, **Louisiana**, and **South Carolina**. Congress was compelled to create an unprecedented **Electoral Commission** to address the deadlock. After a long and intense standoff and a secret negotiation between opposing party leaders, Rutherford B. Hayes emerged as the nineteenth president of the United States.

Conditions Prior to the Election

Americans were anxious to replace President **Ulysses S. Grant**. Many blamed him for the **Panic of 1873** and the ensuing depression that had engulfed the nation, and his administration was notorious for its **scandals** and corruption. The Democrats, who had been out of power since 1861, were hungry to reclaim the presidency. They resented the Republicans, faulting them for instigating the Civil War and enforcing Reconstruction. By 1876, the Democrats had regained political power in all but three southern states—Louisiana, South Carolina, and Florida—by ruthlessly subduing Republican opposition and **black suffrage**. Thus, the Democrats represented a formidable challenge to the Republicans. For their part, the Republicans were desperate to keep the Democrats out of the presidency. Both parties were prepared to win at any cost.

The Nominees

Ohio Governor Rutherford B. Hayes narrowly won the Republican Party nomination over **James G. Blaine**. His running mate was William Almon Wheeler of New York. Hayes was an attorney and Civil War hero who had served three terms as governor of Ohio. The Republicans were particularly interested in Hayes because he was a well-known reformer. Although Hayes was a prominent leader, he did not necessarily outshine his rivals.

The Democratic Party was nearly unanimously in favor of New York governor Samuel J. Tilden, an eminent lawyer with many **railroad** companies as clients. Tilden had gained renown by challenging the powerful Tammany Hall organization and prosecuting **William M. "Boss" Tweed**. His running mate was Thomas Andrews Hendricks of Indiana.

The Greenback Labor Party nominated New York's Peter Fennimore Cooper for president and Ohio's Samuel F. Cary for vice president. Cooper had a striking background. He was a philanthropist and proponent of the **American Indian** reform movement. He also manufactured "Tom Thumb," the first steam-powered railroad locomotive made in America. The other parties, too small to pose a significant challenge, included the Prohibition Party, the American National Party, and the Communist Party.

General Election

The election of 1876 was a hotly contested race. Both the Democratic and Republican nominees promoted reform and the end of Reconstruction; both rallied an equally large number of supporters. Tilden garnered 4,288,546 votes. Hayes lagged behind him with 4,034,311 votes, and Cooper was third with 75,973. Thus, Tilden was the decisive winner of the popular votes, but the situation was far from clear in terms of the Electoral College votes. By the end of election day, Tilden had 184 electoral votes to Hayes's 165. The twenty remaining votes were in dispute. Outraged by the outcome, the Republicans argued that the Democrats had intimidated and bribed blacks, thereby taking votes that should have gone to Hayes. The Democrats retorted by accusing the Republicans of tampering with ballots in Florida. Evidence indicates, in fact, that both parties bought votes in Florida, Louisiana, and South Carolina.

Electoral Disputes

Congress was faced with a serious problem. One of Oregon's three electors, John Watts, could not be counted since he was a postman, and no federal officeholders were allowed to participate in the Electoral College. Oregon's Democratic governor Lafayette Grover tried to replace Watts with a Democratic elector, but Watts resigned his job, thereby legitimatizing his vote for Hayes. This left the nineteen contested votes in the three southern states.

Congress faced a unique challenge. Florida had four electoral votes, Louisiana eight, and South Carolina seven, just enough to put Hayes over the top if he had them all. All three states presented dual electoral votes to Congress, one from the official election supervisory agency and the other from the **carpetbag** Republicans. The supervisory agency showed Tilden ahead in the popular vote, but the Republicans nullified many Democratic ballots, claiming that the Democrats had committed fraud and used **violence** to steal votes. During the several months it took for Congress to reach a solution, tensions mounted.

The Electoral Commission of 1877

The Electoral Commission of 1877 was Congress's response to the election crisis. Its objective was to decide each of the nineteen disputed votes. The commission comprised five senators, five representatives, and five members of the **Supreme Court**. There were supposed to be seven Democrats, seven

Republicans, and one independent, but Justice **David Davis**, who was originally chosen as the independent, resigned from the Supreme Court for a Senate seat. Since all of the remaining justices on the Supreme Court were Republicans, it appeared that Hayes would be a sure winner. The day before the final vote, Justice Joseph Bradley announced his support for Tilden, the Democratic nominee, but he changed his vote after several Republicans met with him.

The next day, Bradley produced the definitive vote that gave the presidency to Rutherford B. Hayes, but Congress still had to approve the commission's decision. The Senate was dominated by the Republicans, but the House of Representatives, as a result of the 1874 election, was controlled by the Democrats. Enraged by the commission's decision, House Democrats threatened to filibuster the official Electoral College vote. The Republicans were just as determined to uphold Hayes's win. Without a resolution in sight—and with the inauguration day fixed—many feared that a second Civil War was imminent.

The Compromise of 1877 and the Results of the Election

Representatives from the Democratic and Republican Parties met in secret in the late winter of 1876 to negotiate what came to be known as the **Compromise of 1877**. They reached an agreement that brought an end to the presidential impasse. Democrats agreed to support the commission's decision in exchange for several promises. The specifics of those promises remain in dispute, but historians do know that the Republicans agreed to withdraw federal troops from the South, end Reconstruction, and provide support for southern railroads and internal improvements.

Two days prior to inauguration day, Congress awarded the nineteen remaining disputed votes to Hayes, giving him a total of 185 electoral votes, one more than Tilden. To obviate Democratic backlash, Hayes was sworn in as president in the Red Room of the White House on March 3, 1877. Two days later, Grant again swore in Hayes in a peaceful public ceremony.

In general, Hayes had a successful term. He attacked corruption in the federal government, grappled with civil-service reform, and brought about an end to the depression caused by the Panic of 1873. His presidency saw Herculean progress in America's economy, industry, and technological advancements. However, the withdrawal of federal support and law enforcement in the South left **African Americans** and their southern Republican allies unable to defend themselves against the heinous crimes of **disfranchisement**, discriminatory laws, and violence. Thus, the election marked the end of any serious, federally sponsored reconstruction efforts for nearly a century. *See also* Gary, Martin Witherspoon; Gun Clubs; Hampton, Wade, III; Kellogg, William Pitt; New South; Nicholls, Francis Redding Tillou; Packard, Stephen B.; Redemption; Red Shirts; Scandals; Shotgun Plan; Supreme Court; U.S. Army and Reconstruction; U.S. Constitution; Wells, James M.; White League.

Further Reading: Dickerson, Donna L. *The Reconstruction Era: Primary Documents on Events from 1865 to 1877*. Westport, CT: Greenwood Press, 2003; Haworth, Paul Leland. *The Hayes-Tilden Disputed Presidential Election of 1876*. Cleveland

and Detroit: Burrows Brothers Company, 1906; Morris, Roy. *Fraud of the Century: Rutherford B. Hayes, Samuel Tilden, and the Stolen Election of 1876*. New York: Simon & Schuster, 2003; Polakoff, Keith Ian. *The Politics of Inertia: The Election of 1876 and the End of Reconstruction*. Baton Rouge: Louisiana State University Press, 1973.

Gladys L. Knight

Electoral Commission of 1877

After more than a month of intense wrangling, the Republican-controlled Senate and the Democratic-controlled House of Representatives created the Electoral Commission of 1877 to settle the disputed presidential **election of 1876** between Republican **Rutherford B. Hayes** of Ohio and Democrat **Samuel J. Tilden** of New York. Although this unprecedented tribunal did little to quiet the highly charged political atmosphere both inside and outside Washington, D.C., it did ultimately resolve the crisis and bring closure to Reconstruction. It also made evident the necessity of a statutory procedure for counting the vote and resolving disputes, which was finally established in the Electoral Count Act of 1887.

The Election of 1876

In the November election, Tilden, the popular vote winner, came up one vote shy of the 185 electoral votes necessary to put him in the White House. Hayes had 165, but both parties claimed twenty disputed electoral votes. Although Hayes was able to claim one of these, a questionable Oregon elector, nineteen contested votes came from **South Carolina**, **Florida**, and **Louisiana**—the last three states where lingering Republican Reconstruction regimes still controlled the governor's office and the election machinery. In each of these southern states, Democratic intimidation of black voters produced majorities and a set of electoral returns for Tilden, but Republican returning boards threw out what they determined to be fraudulent votes and created a second set of returns favoring Hayes. If Congress accepted the Republican returns, Hayes could then claim victory in the Electoral College.

Convening in December, the lame-duck 44th Congress faced a partisan deadlock over which set of electoral returns from the three states should be deemed legitimate and who should do the counting. The terse Constitutional guidelines in the Twelfth Amendment stipulated only that "the President of the Senate shall, in the presence of the Senate and House of Representatives, open all the [electoral vote] certificates and the votes shall then be counted." Republicans clearly preferred that Thomas W. Ferry, president of the Senate, be allowed to count the disputed electoral votes—accepting those favoring Hayes, of course, yet they had previously denied such a power and the Senate president had never counted the votes under comparable circumstances. Democrats, with a majority in the House, argued that only the two houses acting concurrently had the power to determine which votes should be judged valid.

Creation of the Commission

To deal with the impasse, in mid-December, the Senate and House created select committees, which began to meet jointly in early January 1877 to consider possible compromise solutions. Headed by Republican senator George F. Edmunds of Vermont and Democratic representative Henry B. Payne of Ohio, the joint select committee worked through various proposals from both sides and recommended an Electoral Commission to be composed of five senators, five representatives, and five members of the **Supreme Court**. Given the Republicans' Senate majority, three of those five commission seats went to Republicans—**Oliver P. Morton** (Indiana), Frederick T. Frelinghuysen (New Jersey), and Edmunds—who were joined by Democrats Thomas F. Bayard (Delaware) and Allan G. Thurman (Ohio). Because the Democrats controlled the House, they had the same three-to-two advantage and selected Representatives Eppa Hunton (Virginia), Josiah G. Abbott (Massachusetts), and Payne, while Republicans chose **James A. Garfield** (Ohio) and George F. Hoar (Massachusetts). Although the five members of the Supreme Court were supposedly nonpartisan, the joint select committee chose two known Republicans (Justices Samuel F. Miller and William Strong) and two Democrats (Justices Nathan Clifford and Stephen J. Field) and charged them with selection of the final justice and ultimately deciding vote—which figured to be **David B. Davis** of Illinois, an Independent. The tribunal was to hear legal arguments from each side and was empowered, if it thought necessary, to go behind the returns and investigate each contested election. Only the concurrence of *both* the Senate and House could overturn the commission's decision in the disputed cases.

Senate and House Republicans actually opposed the Electoral Commission bill 57 to 84, but Democrats, thinking that the Independent Davis would endorse some of Tilden's claims, provided overwhelming support (181 to 19) in both houses. However, on January 25, a day before the final vote was taken, the Illinois legislature, ironically with full Democratic backing, elected Davis to the U.S. Senate. Even though he remained on the Court until March 5, he refused to join the commission, and the final seat went to Republican appointee Joseph P. Bradley, in Democratic eyes the least objectionable of the remaining justices.

Counting the Votes

On February 1, the electoral count began, and when the dual returns from Florida were reached, the joint session of Congress stopped the count and sent the case to the Electoral Commission. For the next ten days, the tribunal heard opposing arguments from a distinguished battery of Republican and Democratic lawyers, but decided not to go behind the returns signed by the Republican governor to examine the circumstances of the election, and awarded Florida to Hayes by a partisan margin of eight to seven. Tilden's supporters denounced Bradley's partisanship and the Democratic House rejected the commission's finding, but the Republican Senate approved it, so Hayes won Florida on February 10. Distressed House Democrats engaged in dilatory behavior such as recessing and periodically threatening a filibuster to delay the count as the eight-seven margin of the commission and Senate approval enabled Hayes to gain Louisiana's vote on February 16 and South Carolina's on February 28, giving him the necessary 185 votes. In the end, Democratic leaders had little stomach for the uncertainties of an interregnum and only delayed completion of the count until March 2, the eve of Hayes's inauguration.

Meanwhile, some southern Democrats sought Republican economic support for internal improvements and **patronage** influence in exchange for not supporting the Democratic filibuster, but primarily they worked behind the scenes extracting pledges from Hayes's supporters that he would not continue to endorse Republican administrations in Louisiana and South Carolina (Florida was already under Democratic control). When Hayes removed the troops supporting the Republican regimes after his inauguration, they collapsed, thus returning the entire South to "home rule." *See also* Chamberlain, Daniel Henry; Compromise of 1877; Disfranchisement; Gary, Martin Witherspoon; Gun Clubs; Hampton, Wade, III; Kellogg, William Pitt; Nicholls, Francis Redding Tillou; Packard, Stephen B.; Redemption; Red Shirts; Scandals; Shotgun Plan; Supreme Court; U.S. Army and Reconstruction; U.S. Constitution; Violence; Wells, James M.; White League.

Further Reading: Benedict, Michael Les. "Southern Democrats in the Crisis of 1876–1877: A Reconsideration of *Reunion and Reaction*." *Journal of Southern History* 46 (1980): 489–524; Peskin, Allan. "Was There a Compromise of 1877?" and C. Vann Woodward, "Yes, There Was a Compromise of 1877." *Journal of American History* 60 (1973): 63–75 and 215–23, respectively; Polakoff, Keith Ian. *The Politics of Inertia: The Election of 1876 and the End of Reconstruction*. Baton Rouge: Louisiana State University Press, 1973; Woodward, C. Vann. *Reunion and Reaction: The Compromise of 1877 and the End of Reconstruction*. Boston: Little, Brown and Company, 1951.

Terry L. Seip

Elliott, Robert B. (1842–1884)

Robert Brown Elliott is as clear an example as Reconstruction provides of a talented **African American** who rose from obscurity to positions of considerable political power as one of the leading Republicans in **South Carolina**. Although Elliott claimed to have been born in Boston on August 11, 1842, to parents from the West Indies, his biographer concludes that he was more likely born in Liverpool and arrived in Boston shortly after the Civil War. Somewhere, though probably not Eton College as he claimed, Elliott received a first-rate classical **education**, as his political speeches demonstrated. What does appear certain about his early years is that by 1867, he was working as a typesetter in Boston when he heard of an opportunity to move to Charleston, South Carolina, to join **Richard H. Cain** on the staff of a Republican newspaper, the *South Carolina Leader*.

Arriving as a black **carpetbagger** in South Carolina in March 1867, Elliott threw himself into political activity in response to the **Military Reconstruction Acts**, helping to organize the **Union League of America** and then serving as a delegate to the 1868 **Constitutional Convention** from Edgefield

County. In the convention, Elliott opposed **poll taxes** and literacy tests for voting. He was elected to the South Carolina House of Representatives later that year and served through 1870. Elliott also served as president of a state-wide labor convention in 1869. Elliott held several other positions and quickly became one of the most powerful Republicans in the state. He served as assistant adjutant general in 1869 and was largely responsible for organizing the controversial state **militia**. By 1872, Elliott was a member of the state executive committee of the Republican Party in South Carolina. During this period, he was admitted to the South Carolina bar, and he formed a law partnership with Macon B. Allen and **William. J. Whipper** in 1868.

In 1870, Elliott was elected to the U.S. House of Representatives, where he served two terms and was widely noted for his speaking ability and his determination to protect African Americans from **violence** and discrimination. Elliott's first major speech was in support of the **Enforcement Act**, but his most celebrated speech was delivered on January 6, 1874, in support of the bill that became the **Civil Rights Act** in 1875.

Elliott chose to resign his seat in Congress in 1874 and return to South Carolina to fight the corruption that was weakening the Republican Party. In cooperation with **Daniel H. Chamberlain**, Elliott succeeded in pushing the corrupt governor of South Carolina, **Franklin J. Moses, Jr.**, out of political life. He also formed a new law partnership with Daniel Augustus Straker and T. McCants Stewart. Elliott was elected to the South Carolina House of Representatives in 1874 and became the Speaker. In the chaotic **election of 1876**, he ran unsuccessfully for attorney general. By this time, the white conservative backlash in South Carolina was beyond control, and **Redemption** took its toll. With his law practice in tatters because of his Republican politics, Elliott accepted a federal **patronage** job as a customs official in Charleston. In 1881, Elliott was transferred to a customs post in New Orleans, but he soon found himself out of work. He died of malarial fever in New Orleans on August 9, 1884. *See also* Bourbons; Congressional Reconstruction; Disfranchisement; Scalawags; Scandals.

Further Reading: Lamson, Peggy. *The Glorious Failure: Black Congressman Robert Brown Elliott and the Reconstruction in South Carolina*. New York: W. W. Norton, 1973.

Bruce E. Baker

Emancipation

From the earliest days of colonization, blacks in America resisted enslavement through flight, appeals for reform, refusal to labor, and open rebellion. Determined to hold them in bondage, whites responded with the oppressive power of law, prejudice, and custom; appeals to property rights; paramilitary terror; and the military might of state and nation. After 1800, the spread of paternalist ideology only broadened the terrain of struggle. By 1860, slavery was firmly entrenched in American law and economic life, and seemed likely to expand its influence, yet **African Americans** and a handful of committed

abolitionists were more unreconciled to the peculiar institution than ever. The election of Republican **Abraham Lincoln** to the presidency that year brought the question of emancipation to crisis.

Secession and Slavery

Undeniably, the promulgation of the Emancipation Proclamation on January 1, 1863, marks a watershed in American historical development. It changed the meaning of the Civil War and led to the reconstruction of the United States under the contested terms of the **Thirteenth Amendment**. Yet the South, not the North put the question of emancipation on the table at the moment of secession. For all their talk about state's rights, it was the fear that Republicans would weaken, restrict, and eventually overthrow slavery, which drove white southerners toward disunion. The belief that a powerful coalition of intransigent African Americans, moralizing Yankees, and white southern "traitors" would subvert bondage formed the core of secessionist arguments.

The notion seemed absurd. America's slave population had quadrupled to four million souls across three generations, with no prospect of tailing off, and no sign that anyone had a viable plan of emancipation that would not wreck the national economy. More than this, racist whites could conjure up no realistic ideas for how to live with African Americans after emancipation, no workable scheme of segregation, or return to Africa. Britain's compensated emancipation program (1834) was derided as a softhearted disaster, offering powerful arguments against change. By 1860, too, there was little legal foundation for tinkering. Slavery was well protected in the nation by state and federal law. The 1857 **Supreme Court** decision in *Dred Scott v. Sanford* had ruled firmly that slaves were property, not persons, and that government could not interfere with owners' rights to these chattels. Implicitly, then, territorial governments could not restrict slavery without falling afoul of constitutional imperatives. For all moderates' concerns that a nation "half-slave, half-free" could not endure, America on the eve of secession was anything but "a house divided" in legal terms. Lincoln himself declared that he possessed neither power nor inclination as president to promote emancipation. Two days before his inauguration, Congress sent to the states an amendment to the **U.S. Constitution** intended to unite the country and end antislavery agitation once and for all. Henceforth, no law could be made to "abolish or interfere" with slavery in states where it now existed. To save the Union, American leaders were content to write a Thirteenth Amendment that would have rooted African Americans in bondage forever. Who could have imagined that, just five years later, slavery would be utterly destroyed, and that African Americans would be soldiers, property holders, voters, and even legislators?

Beginning of the End: The Civil War

It was, fundamentally, the intractability of masters and slaves themselves which propelled emancipation. Slaveholders, first, refused to be dissuaded from disunion by Lincoln's denials of abolitionist purpose and Congress's sweetheart deal. Slaves, meanwhile, grasped almost instantly that war between whites might mean freedom for African Americans. They did not break their chains through mass rebellion—politically and militarily, such a course was impossible. With powerful restricting ties to kin and community and the military firepower of whites, most enslaved peoples bided their time and watched carefully. As the war progressed and more and more white men left rural southern communities, in some instances, slaves were running the plantations and although they were still technically enslaved, freedoms increased for African Americans.

In other instances, direct resistance grew. As white southerners went off to fight Yankees, and mobilized slave labor to support that task, the steady trickle of runaways swelled, particularly in border areas. That put pressure on local Union commanders: Should fleeing slaves be returned to rebel masters, potentially to strengthen Confederate resistance? Six weeks after the fall of Fort Sumter, General **Benjamin F. Butler** said no, with delicious irony. Since *Dred Scott* had declared slaves property, he asserted, fugitive slaves at **Virginia**'s Fortress Monroe were actually "**contraband** of war," rebel property to be confiscated and put to work against the southern cause. The notion was almost whimsical, but at the beginning of August 1861, Congress backed him up with the **Confiscation Act**, denying owners' claims to fugitive slaves who had been employed in Confederate war efforts. Although worded via the property loophole, the move was in contradiction to the War Aims Resolution passed in the spring at the outset of war, when Congress openly declared that preserving the Union was the purpose of the war; the government, the resolution affirmed, had no intention of interfering with the "domestic affairs" of the states—meaning slavery.

However, with the failure of Union troops to crush the rebellion at Bull Run in July, northern feeling mounted that southerners should suffer for their intransigence. Led by **Frederick Douglass**, African American leaders agitated for immediate emancipation. Lincoln, however, strove to rein in radical sentiment, hoping a moderate course would win back the border South. When General John C. Frémont freed the slaves of Missouri rebels at the end of August, Lincoln warned him to go no farther than the Confiscation Act allowed. Four months later, he toned down Secretary of War Simon Cameron's annual report to Congress. Passages favoring emancipation and the use of contrabands as soldiers and military laborers were struck out, and soon afterward Cameron himself was gone, replaced by a more politically adept (and honest) **Edwin Stanton**. Facing the racism of the North, and the fact that four Union states allowed slavery—the "border states" of **Maryland**, Delaware, **Kentucky**, and Missouri—Lincoln was understandably hesitant to move too quickly.

Throughout 1862, runaway slaves, local military commanders, intransigent abolitionists, **Radical Republicans** in Congress, and Confederate victories all conspired to push emancipation upon Lincoln. In mid-March, Congress forbade military leaders from returning fugitive slaves to their owners, implicitly rebuking the president's order to Fremont. Emboldened—and plagued by thousands of contrabands—General David Hunter wrote the War Department from his post in the **South Carolina** Sea Islands two weeks later, seeking permission to enlist the African Americans whose masters had fled. While Washington dithered, he began mustering in. When Stanton refused pay or equipment for **black troops**, he disbanded grudgingly—then unilaterally declared all slaves in South Carolina, **Georgia**, and **Florida** free on May 9. Lincoln nullified Hunter's order ten days later, pushing harder the program of voluntary, gradual, compensated emancipation he sponsored. Congress had guaranteed funding for the program on April 10, and one week later abolished slavery in the **District of Columbia**, paying off loyal owners and appropriating funds for voluntary expatriation. By mid-June, Congress had solved the territorial question that split North and South, henceforth prohibiting slavery. For loyal border-state slaveholders, the handwriting was now on the wall. If they did not endorse gradualism and take cash for slaves, Lincoln warned, the war would leave them nothing at all. When border-state congressmen balked again, Radicals drove through sweeping changes with the passage of the Second Confiscation Act on July 17, 1862.

The act lashed out at all the temporizing Lincoln, Stanton, and the moderates had done for the past year. It allowed military officials to seize the slaves of persons engaged in or assisting the Confederate cause, ordered the seizure and sale of rebel property, and forbade the army from surrendering runaways to any claimant. Coupled with a new **Militia** Act, it authorized the president to enlist African Americans for any military service "for which they may be found competent." Slave volunteers would be granted freedom, and this award extended to other family members in cases where their owner was disloyal. In the North, in the Sea Islands, and in **Louisiana** (again, thanks to Benjamin Butler), regiments of "U.S. Colored Troops" began recruiting within weeks of this new legislation. Five days later, a hard-pressed Lincoln informed his **cabinet** that he was now determined to emancipate all slaves in rebel states. Pending a significant military victory, however, the president agreed to withhold his announcement.

No Turning Back: The Emancipation Proclamation

The bloodbath at Antietam was nothing like the breakthrough Lincoln hoped for, but it would have to do. The preliminary Emancipation Proclamation of September 22, 1862, announced that slaves held in rebel areas would be declared free on January 1, 1863. Simultaneously, it promised compensation once again for gradual or immediate emancipation programs any state would undertake; colonization would likewise be funded. Confederates and abolitionists alike scourged the plan, but it took effect at the beginning of 1863, backed up by new language promising to enlist African American troops for the Union cause. The peculiar institution was not outlawed by Lincoln's edict—slavery continued inviolate for loyal masters in loyal states—but there could be little prospect of its long-term survival.

Over the next two years, fully 200,000 African American men mustered into federal service. Many more than this refused to labor for the Confederate cause and made their way to Union lines in what has rightly been called the greatest strike in American labor history. Though only a few black regiments saw combat before Appomattox, they demonstrated courage and discipline in every instance. By June 1864, African American soldiers earned the same pay and enjoyed the same protections as whites. In upper South states such as

Tennessee and Kentucky, slave enlistment (with compensation for masters) provided a key for advancing emancipation. Eventually, even the slaveocracy hoped to muster in African American troops. By March 1865, dwindling manpower forced Confederate congressmen to allow slaves to enlist under the Stars and Bars, offering freedom in return for service. This was interesting as a gesture of desperation, but it was far too little, far too late.

Ending slavery in the Confederacy established little with regard to what freedom would mean for former bondmen, or who should decide how to proceed. For the moment, it remained a military question. On March 16, 1863, Stanton created the American Freedmen's Inquiry Commission to recommend what to do with former slaves. He and Lincoln met African American leaders and their allies periodically to puzzle over the question. As seen earlier, sometimes local military commanders shaped freedmen's fortunes. Most radical was General **William T. Sherman**'s Special **Field Order No. 15**, issued January 16, 1865, and quickly overruled, which set aside large areas of coastal South Carolina, Georgia, and Florida for exclusive black settlement. Finally, in March 1865, Congress created a **Bureau of Refugees, Freedmen, and Abandoned Lands** to establish uniform policy. It would prove chronically conservative, understaffed, and halfhearted.

Lincoln, meanwhile, pondered how to deal with ex-rebels and avoid turning civil war into race war. While it is important to recognize that Lincoln became "the Great Emancipator" thanks to a host of disparate local pressures and political actors—from Congress down to the humble runaway, as Ira Berlin and many others have shown—clearly he grew into and embraced that role. As James McPherson has argued, he steadfastly refused to modify or rescind the Emancipation Proclamation for political or military advantage, making it an integral part of his plans for national reconciliation. On December 8, 1863, his Proclamation of **Amnesty** and Reconstruction offered **pardon** and return of nonslave property to Confederates who swore allegiance to the Union and accepted emancipation. By April 1865, Louisiana, Missouri, Maryland, and Tennessee had all written slavery out of their states with new constitutions.

But emancipation—the freeing of slaves—was not **abolition**, the elimination of the institution itself. For a while longer, abolitionists in Congress encountered stiff resistance, even up to Lincoln's reelection in 1864. Not until January 31, 1865, did a Constitutional Amendment outlawing slavery finally pass; ratification by the states was achieved on December 18, 1865, and the Thirteenth Amendment became part of the U.S. Constitution. *See also* Congressional Reconstruction; Constitutional Conventions; Davis Bend, Mississippi; Democratic Party; Edisto Island, South Carolina; Elections of 1864; Garrison, William Lloyd; Johnson, Andrew; Joint Select Committee on the Conduct of the War; Loyalty Oaths; Phillips, Wendell; Port Royal Experiment; Presidential Reconstruction; Readmission.

Further Reading: Belz, Herman. *Emancipation and Equal Rights: Politics and Constitutionalism in the Civil War Era.* New York: W. W. Norton, 1978; Berlin, Ira, Leslie Rowland, et al., eds. *Freedom: A Documentary History of Emancipation, 1861–1867, Selected from the Holdings of the National Archives of the United States.* New York: Cambridge University Press, 1982–continuing; Berry, Mary F. *Military*

Necessity and Civil Rights Policy: Black Citizenship and the Constitution, 1861–1868. Port Washington, NY: Kennikat Press, 1977; Cox, LaWanda. *Lincoln and Black Freedom: A Study in Presidential Leadership*. Columbia: University of South Carolina Press, 1981; Gerteis, Louis S. *From Contraband to Freedmen: Federal Policy toward Southern Blacks, 1861–1865*. Westport, CT: Greenwood Press, 1973; Hahn, Steven. *A Nation under Our Feet: Black Political Struggles in the Rural South from Slavery to the Great Migration*. Cambridge, MA: Belknap, 2003; Litwack, Leon F. *Been in the Storm So Long: The Aftermath of Slavery*. New York: Alfred A. Knopf, 1979; McPherson, James. *Battle Cry of Freedom: The Civil War Era*. New York: Oxford University Press, 1988; Mohr, Clarence L. *On the Threshold of Freedom: Masters and Slaves in Civil War Georgia*. Athens: University of Georgia Press, 1986.

Vernon Burton

Enforcement Act (1875)

In an effort to safeguard and fortify Reconstruction, Congress passed a great deal of legislation in the years between 1867 and 1875. Certainly, the **Fourteenth** and **Fifteenth Amendments** represent capstones to this effort, but these laws met with considerable opposition in the South, so additional legislation sought to enforce and guarantee **civil rights** for **African Americans**. Among these laws were a series of measures called **Enforcement Acts**, three of which were passed in 1870 and 1871. For many historians, the 1875 attempt to pass a fourth enforcement act represented the closing congressional act of Reconstruction.

Earlier Precedents and the 1875 Act

The laws passed between 1870 and 1871 were criminal codes designed to protect blacks' rights to vote, serve on juries, hold political office, and receive equal protection under the law. These acts permitted federal intervention in cases where individual states were unable, or unwilling, to act. The third act, of April 1871, even allowed the president to suspend the writ of habeas corpus if necessary to facilitate criminal investigations and prosecutions. One chief reason for passing these laws was to protect black and white Republicans targeted by terrorist elements of the southern **Democratic Party**, such as the **Ku Klux Klan**.

Similar to the 1870 and 1871 legislation, the Enforcement Act of 1875 was designed to ensure blacks' rights and protect what remained of Reconstruction. With several southern states already back in the hands of white conservatives, Republicans in Congress recognized that **Redemption** would sweep away many of the positive changes. Furthermore, the national elections of 1874 marked a watershed, for the Democratic Party had regained control of Congress. Thus, the lame-duck Republican Congress recognized this might be their last opportunity to provide federal oversight on southern affairs.

Long advocated by **Radical Republican** Massachusetts senator **Charles Sumner** (1811–1874)—who had recently passed away—and proposed by **Benjamin Butler** (1818–1893) and other **Stalwarts**, the attempt to pass a new enforcement act followed the recent passage of the **Civil Rights Act of 1875** in March. Designed to protect equal rights and freedom of access to many public facilities, such as hotels, **railroads**, restaurants, and theaters, the Civil Rights Act included all persons, regardless of race. The law also prohibited the exclusion of blacks from jury duty, and allowed those denied equal access the right to sue for damages in a court of law.

A clause in this act opened the door for the new enforcement act, by stipulating that it was a criminal offense (albeit a misdemeanor) to deny entrance at public places to any person, regardless of race. A section also provided that fines could be levied upon those who violated this law. As a result, another enforcement act seemed a natural. The enforcement bill provided additional resources and authority for supervising elections, and even allowed the president to suspend the writ of habeas corpus, not seen since that provision of the 1871 act was revoked by Congress in 1872. Some certainly believed this act was vital to Republicans surviving the upcoming **elections of 1876**.

Waning Enforcement Vigor

Unfortunately, the environment that made for pushing these two acts also undercut the enthusiasm for them. Republicans had already begun to drift from their party and their agenda, and many were exasperated and tired of the Reconstruction muddle. The Civil Rights Act itself was a mere shadow of what Sumner had wanted, and in fact, some argued it was only passed as a eulogy to him. Thus, there was even less enthusiasm for an additional act to enforce existing legislation. Sensing that the fervor over protecting southern Republicans had burnt out, longtime Republican congressman and Speaker of the House **James G. Blaine** offered that it might be better to "lose the South and save the North," than end up losing both. Oddly, against his advice, the House did pass the measure, but it failed in the Senate. The last effort in the nineteenth century to provide federal enforcement was dead, and for blacks in particular, and Reconstruction in general, it seemed clear that congressional interest was as well.

Had it passed, the enforcement bill's impact would have been minimal. White opposition in the South, and apathy in the North, were too strong to admit of any serious enforcement. Moreover, the very next year, the **Supreme Court** delivered two landmark decisions that stopped federal enforcement in its tracks: In *United States v. Reese* and ***United States v. Cruikshank***, the Court severely curtailed the scope of the Fourteenth and Fifteenth Amendments and the federal government's jurisdiction. Later in *United States v. Harris* and the *Civil Rights Cases*, decisions delivered in 1883, the Court largely overturned the government's entire enforcement foundation. Just as it had expanded, the federal government's authority retracted, and left millions unsupported in the face of hostile state governments, businesses, and private individuals. *See also* American Indians; Black Suffrage; Bourbons; Congressional Reconstruction; Disfranchisement; Grant, Ulysses S.; Gun Clubs; Jim Crow Laws; Republicans, Liberal; Scandals; Suffrage; U.S. Army and Reconstruction; Violence.

Further Reading: Foner, Eric. *Reconstruction: America's Unfinished Revolution, 1863–1877.* New York: Harper and Row, 1988; Ford, Lacey K., ed. *A Companion to the Civil War and Reconstruction.* Malden, MA: Blackwell Publishing, 2005; Kelly,

Alfred H., Winfred Harbison, and Herman Belz. *The American Constitution: Its Origins, Growth, and Development*. 6th ed. New York: W. W. Norton, 1983.

Heather Duerre Humann

Enforcement Acts (1870, 1871)

Terrorist organizations such as the **Ku Klux Klan** and the Knights of the White Camellia appeared and spread during the late 1860s, especially in response to **Congressional Reconstruction** and its linchpin, **black suffrage**. Inadequate state responses to the **violence** and intimidation prompted the national government to pass four Enforcement Acts. Also known as Force Acts, these statutes were based on Congress's authority to enforce the new **Fourteenth** and **Fifteenth Amendments**. In all, Congress passed four such measures, and Republicans tried unsuccessfully to pass a fifth and sixth in 1875 and 1890.

The first act, passed on May 31, 1870, was entitled "An act to enforce the Right of Citizens of the United States to vote in the several States of this Union, and for other purposes." Focusing on the Fifteenth Amendment, it targeted private and public actions. It prohibited state election officials from enforcing discriminatory laws and from using force, intimidation, or bribery to prevent men from voting because of their race. It prohibited private citizens from combining and using force, intimidation, or violence to deny others their right to vote. Violators faced fine and imprisonment. The statute also reenacted the **Civil Rights Act of 1866** using both the Fourteenth and the Fifteenth Amendments as its constitutional base. In a path-breaking step, it also applied federal penalties to private individuals. Violations of the law were to be handled by the Department of Justice, newly created in 1870, and tried in federal courts.

The next two acts, of July 14, 1870, and February 28, 1871, expanded the number of federal election supervisors, especially for cities with more than 20,000 in population, an indication that Republican concerns extended to Democratic-dominated northern cities as well as to southern rural areas.

Passed on April 20, 1871, the fourth act, also known as the Ku Klux Klan Act, once again addressed discrimination within state laws as well as private conspiracies. Its title reveals its constitutional base: "An act to enforce the Provisions of the Fourteenth Amendment to the Constitution of the United States and for other Purposes." The act made it a federal crime to conspire and to disguise one's self in order to deny others the equal protection of the laws. Such restrictions on private action provoked debate in Congress over the intent and reach of all three Reconstruction amendments. The statute authorized the president to suspend the writ of habeas corpus, declare martial law, and employ federal troops in affected areas. Under its authority, in October 1871, President **Ulysses S. Grant** suspended the writ in nine counties of **South Carolina**. Use of the statute to attack Klan activity in that state, as well as **Mississippi**, **North Carolina**, and **Tennessee**, was undermined by many problems, including a lack of funds and federal troops, intimidation of officials, and uncertain commitment by federal enforcement and judicial officers.

Nevertheless, the federal troops, investigations, and trials were sufficient to temporarily restore law and order in South Carolina.

In early judicial challenges to the Enforcement Acts, courts supported their constitutionality in such rulings as *United States v. Hall* (1871). Soon, however, these early cases found themselves in conflict with **Supreme Court** rulings in *United States v. Reese* (1876), ***United States v. Cruikshank*** (1876), and *United States v. Harris* (1882). The Court invalidated sections of the Enforcement Acts as applying too broadly the Fourteenth and the **Thirteenth Amendments**.

In addition, as early as 1873, prosecutions under the statutes began to decrease, and by 1880, little effort was made to enforce them. Northerners, skeptical of strong federal power despite the new amendments, were increasingly uninterested in southern issues, especially ones involving black rights and dishonest and unstable governments. An 1875 effort to pass yet another Enforcement Act, one that gave the president the power to suspend the writ of habeas corpus in **Alabama**, **Arkansas**, **Louisiana**, and **Mississippi** and to put down conspiracies aimed at intimidating voters, succeeded in the House but received no action from the Senate. Opposition to continued federal involvement in state affairs, even from within the Republican Party, doomed the measure even as Congress finally passed a diluted version of the late senator **Charles Sumner**'s controversial **civil rights** act. Then, well over a decade later, Henry Cabot Lodge of Massachusetts proposed a final "Force Bill." In response to restrictions on black suffrage through such mechanisms as literacy tests, the 1890 bill once again sought to increase federal reach into the southern states. It too failed to receive congressional support; the time had long passed to raise substantial national interest in using federal power for black rights.

The nation's overall lack of interest, however, was not matched by a decline in violence and intimidation against blacks and white Republicans in the Democratic South. In a strategy known as the Mississippi Plan that began in the later years of Reconstruction, irregular **militia** units openly and publicly drilled and marched in black-populated areas, broke up Republican meetings, and prevented freedmen from registering to vote. Some groups went so far as to assault and murder Republicans. Despite the existence of such enforcement measures, the failure of will doomed the southern Republican governments. *See also* Civil Rights Act of 1866; Civil Rights Act of 1875; Democratic Party; Gun Clubs; Redemption; Republicans, Radical; Shotgun Plan; U.S. Constitution; White League.

Further Reading: Hyman, Harold M., and William M. Wiecek. *Equal Justice under Law: Constitutional Development, 1835–1875*. New York: Harper & Row, 1982; Nieman, Donald G. *Promises to Keep: African-Americans and the Constitutional Order, 1776 to the Present*. New York: Oxford University Press, 1991; Swinney, Everette. *Suppressing the Ku Klux Klan: Enforcement of the Reconstruction Amendments, 1870–1877*. New York: Garland, 1986; Williams, Lou Falkner. *The Great South Carolina Ku Klux Klan Trials, 1871–1872*. Athens: University of Georgia Press, 1996.

Claudine L. Ferrell

Executive Cabinets. *See* Cabinets, Executive.

F

Fessenden, William Pitt (1806–1869)

Congressman, senator, and leader of the **Moderate Republicans** in the Senate, William Pitt Fessenden remained a Whig to the end of his days. Fessenden was born in Boscawen, New Hampshire, but came to practice the law in Portland, Maine. He became one of the most reliable of the Whigs—in contrast to the passionate antislavery and anti-liquor enthusiasms of his relatives, themselves prominent Maine politicians—a state legislator, and in 1841 a one-term congressman. In so ruggedly Democratic a state, he could not have expected to rise higher, and, indeed, was defeated in later efforts to win the congressional seat. Then, in the early 1850s, the quarrels over liquor prohibition and the expansion of slavery into Kansas ripped the **Democratic Party** apart. In the political confusion, Whigs and anti-Nebraska Democrats had the votes to put Fessenden into the Senate in 1854. They were not disappointed; switching to the Republican Party almost at once, he held the seat until his death in 1869.

A cool, reserved man with poor digestion and a brittle temper, Fessenden won universal respect for his integrity and readiness to do hard work. His speeches had a lawyerly bent rather than an evangelical flair, but from his first address, a denunciation of the Kansas-Nebraska bill, he became a senator that colleagues listened to and admired. Supporters even mounted a small presidential boom before the 1860 convention. A strong antislavery voice, he could not hope to rival **Charles Sumner** of Massachusetts in that respect. And, partly from jealousy, partly from a stark difference in temperament, he came to hate Sumner to the point of fantasizing about cutting his throat. However, his skill on the Finance Committee made him a leader in writing banking and tax legislation in wartime. When he was appointed to succeed **Salmon P. Chase** as President **Abraham Lincoln**'s secretary of the treasury in 1864, there was universal relief in the financial community. Fessenden held on only into early 1865, when he could resign and win reelection to the Senate. There, he took front rank among the architects of **Congressional Reconstruction**. More conservative than most of his colleagues, he chaired the **Joint Committee on Reconstruction** that formulated the essential Republican response to **Andrew Johnson**'s southern policy. That made his disaffection all the worse in 1868 in the presidential **impeachment** trial. Worried at the diminution of executive authority that conviction would bring, alarmed that Johnson's deposition would bring a wild-eyed radical like **Benjamin Wade** of Ohio into the presidency, and concerned that the **Radical Republicans** would unsettle the conservative financial policy of Johnson's Treasury Department, he cast one of the decisive votes for acquittal. Legend has it that the act finished his career. On the contrary, Fessenden found financiers and Moderate Republicans rallying to the defense, if not of his vote, then of his right to follow where his conscience led. By his death in the fall of 1869, the chances of unseating him at the next election had gone glimmering. *See also* Presidential Reconstruction; Recusants.

Further Reading: Jellison, C. A. *Fessenden of Maine: Civil War Senator.* Syracuse, NY: Syracuse University Press, 1962.

Mark W. Summers

Field Order No. 15

Since Reconstruction, debates over the meaning of General **William T. Sherman**'s Field Order No. 15 have fueled demands for reparations by blacks and their white friends. Repeatedly, reparationists have cited Sherman's order as the origin of the U.S. government's promise of "forty acres and a mule." Proponents of reparations have argued that the government reneged on its wartime pledge to compensate the ex-slaves with land and farm animals. Reparationists continue to cite "forty acres and a mule" as justification for their appeals for a broad range of compensation—from cash payments to tax credits—for the descendants of America's 4 million black slaves.

On January 16, 1865, three months before Appomattox, Sherman issued his famous Special Field Order No. 15. This order set aside "the islands from Charleston south, the abandoned rice-fields along the rivers for thirty miles back from the sea, and the country bordering the St. John's River, **Florida**," for the exclusive settlement of slave refugees. Sherman instructed General **Rufus Saxton** to grant each head of a black family not more than forty acres of land and to "furnish...subject to the approval of the President of the United States, a possessory title."

By June 1865, Saxton reported that approximately 40,000 blacks had settled on about 400,000 acres of land on what became known as the Sherman Reservation. Sherman authorized Saxton to loan the black families farm animals—decrepit creatures too broken down for military service. These presumably were the "mules" intended to work the proverbial "forty acres." As the freedmen and women moved to occupy the land, in the summer and fall of 1865, President **Andrew Johnson** reversed the government's policy. Johnson pardoned former Confederates and ordered the restoration of all property except that sold under a court decree.

Subsequent events—creation of the **Bureau of Refugees, Freedmen, and Abandoned Lands** (the Freedmen's Bureau) in March 1865 and the passage of the **Southern Homestead Act** in June 1866—further complicated the role of the federal government in distributing land and farm animals to the freedpeople. In fact, the Freedmen's Bureau was authorized to lease, not to grant outright, "not more than forty acres" of abandoned or confiscated lands to freedmen with the option to "purchase the land and receive such titles thereto as to the United States can convey." The Homestead Act set aside public land in **Alabama**, **Arkansas**, Florida, **Louisiana**, and **Mississippi**, for purchase by the freedpeople for a five-dollar fee. The available land, however, was generally of inferior quality and the freedmen lacked sufficient capital to purchase implements and to farm the land properly. When, in 1876, Congress repealed the Homestead Act, blacks cultivated only several thousands acres, mostly in Florida.

Denying any role in misleading the freedmen and women in the Field Order No. 15, Sherman later recalled that "the military authorities at that day . . . had a perfect right to grant the possession of any vacant land to which they could extend military protection, but we did not undertake to give a fee-simple title; and all that was designed by these special field orders was to make temporary provisions for the freedmen and their families during the rest of the war, or until Congress should take action in the premises." Sherman added that Secretary of War **Edwin M. Stanton** approved his field order before it was announced.

Though some **Radical Republicans**, including **Thaddeus Stevens** and **George W. Julian**, supported **confiscation** of southern plantations with hopes of reforming the South's social and economic system, most nineteenth-century Americans held private property too sacred to endorse wide-scale land redistribution. Nonetheless, the slogan "forty acres and a mule" remains a rallying cry for reparationists, a symbol of the heartfelt hopes and dreams of many **African Americans**. *See also* Amnesty Proclamations; Contraband, Slaves as; Pardons.

Further Reading: Bentley, George R. *A History of the Freedmen's Bureau.* Philadelphia: University of Pennsylvania Press, 1955; Oubre, Claude F. *Forty Acres and a Mule: The Freedmen's Bureau and Black Land Ownership.* Baton Rouge: Louisiana State University Press, 1978; Sherman, William T. *Memoirs of General William T. Sherman. By Himself. In Two Volumes.* New York: D. Appleton and Company, 1875; Westley, Robert. "Many Billions Gone: Is It Time to Reconsider the Case for Black Reparations?" *Boston College Law Review* 40 (1998): 429–76.

John David Smith

Fifteenth Amendment (1870)

The Fifteenth Amendment was proposed in 1869 and ratified in 1870. It consists of two sections: The first section prohibits federal and state governments from denying or abridging U.S. citizens the right to vote "on account of race, color, or previous condition of servitude." The second section empowers Congress to enforce the amendment. Simply put, the amendment removed race as voting barrier for American citizens and enabled **African Americans**, including both ex-slaves in the South and **disfranchised** free blacks in the North, to participate in the American political process. Together with the **Thirteenth Amendment** (which **abolished slavery**) and **Fourteenth Amendment** (which established birthright citizenship and national protection of **civil rights**), the Fifteenth Amendment is now seen by historians as part of America's constitutional reinventions of the Reconstruction era that profoundly transformed the meaning and practice of American democracy.

By nationalizing black men's right to vote after the Civil War, the Fifteenth Amendment appeared to be the most revolutionary out of the three Reconstruction Constitutional Amendments. The amendment, however, was the first federal law that directly enfranchised former slaves. It simply nationalized the practice of black enfranchisement that had already been in place in the South since 1867. The amendment enfranchised northern blacks who were still denied voting rights and, perhaps more important, made **black suffrage** a constitutional right recognized and enforced by the national government.

In spite of African Americans' demands and agitation for equal **suffrage** during and after the Civil War, black suffrage was not included on the agenda of the phase of **Presidential Reconstruction** (1863–1866). Both Presidents **Abraham Lincoln** and **Andrew Johnson**, in their Reconstruction plans, limited the participation in reconstructing the postwar state governments to the whites. It was not until March 1867, when Congress passed the Reconstruction Act (enacted on March 2, 1867, over President Johnson's veto), that the freedmen in the South received the right to vote. The Reconstruction Act was a response to the political arrogance of the southern states, which under Johnson's encouragement, refused to ratify the Fourteenth Amendment. The first section of the Fourteenth Amendment conferred citizenship upon all freed slaves, and the second section threatened to reduce a state's representation in the House in proportion if it barred its qualified citizens from voting. By the Reconstruction Act of 1867, Congress required delegates of southern state **constitutional conventions** to be elected by universal manhood suffrage regardless of race or color and made it clear that equal suffrage be included as a permanent fixture of new state constitutions. As a result, freedmen in all ten ex-Confederate states received the right to vote (**Tennessee** was not affected). In 1867–1868, about 750,000 black men cast their votes for the first time. Black delegates were a majority in **Louisiana** and **South Carolina** state constitutional conventions. With their new state constitutions guaranteeing black men equal rights to vote and their ratifications of the Fourteenth Amendment, most southern states were readmitted into the Union by 1869.

Black enfranchisement in the South challenged black disfranchisement in the North and West, where twenty-one states still excluded free black citizens from voting. To rid the party of its ideological awkwardness and moral hypocrisy and to secure black suffrage on a more permanent constitutional basis, Republicans, who were a majority in both houses of Congress, proposed to nationalize black suffrage, but the party again was divided on how to construct the amendment. Several proposals were advanced, varying from an affirmative pronouncement of voting rights being conferred to all adult male American citizens to simply prohibiting denying citizens voting rights on a racial basis. Eventually, the prohibition version—the most conservative version—was chosen and agreed upon. The rationale for this version had to do with preserving the original separation of powers between federal and state governments. States had retained the power to prescribe qualifications for voters. And that power, in the understanding of many Moderate Republicans should not be completely removed.

Thus, the final wording of the Fifteenth Amendment did not directly confer voting rights to any U.S. citizens; it did prevent federal or state governments from denying voting rights to citizens on a racial basis. In other words, the amendment conferred upon U.S. citizens the right not to be denied the right to vote because of race. States could still use other mechanisms or qualifications to deprive citizens the right to vote. During the period of black disfranchisement in the 1880s and 1890s, southern states had indeed used such devices as **poll tax**, literacy test, and white primary to virtually disfranchise African Americans. The ratification of the Fifteenth Amendment went relatively quickly, compared with the ratification processes of the other two Reconstruction amendments. Western states like Nevada ratified the amendment only after they were assured that they could continue to use nativity to exclude undesirable groups like the Chinese from voting.

One of several large commemorative prints marking the enactment of the Fifteenth Amendment and showing the parade celebrating it in Baltimore. (Courtesy of the Library of Congress.)

Radical Republicans had attempted to write in the amendment the right for blacks to hold offices, but the issue was set aside. Women's suffrage also became a subject of debate. Although a few Radical Republicans were willing to eliminate gender as a voting barrier, the majority of the party refused to even consider the women's right to vote. (Unorganized federal territories like Wyoming allowed women to vote in the late 1860s, but nationalization of women's suffrage still had to wait until the ratification of the Nineteenth Amendment in 1920.)

The meaning and applications of the Fifteenth Amendment were subjects of constitutional debates in the late nineteenth and early twentieth centuries. In the early 1870s, the federal government had vigorously enforced the amendment and made, for instance, nearly 1,000 arrests under the laws enforcing the amendment in 1876. Women suffragettes like Susan B. Anthony and others had ventured to test the applicability of the amendment in cases of women's suffrage. The **Supreme Court** ruled that the amendment was not made for everyone to have the right to vote, but to make sure that no one would be denied voting rights simply because of his color or race. The Supreme Court's early interpretations, as expressed in *United States v. Cruikshank* (1876) and *United States v. Reese* (1876), were rather restrictive, rendering that the amendment did not give federal government a free hand to punish any act obstructing a citizen's right to vote without evidence to prove its racial motives. In the early 1880s, the Court in *Ex parte Siebold* (1880), *Ex parte Clarke* (1880), and *Ex parte Yarbrough* (1884) recognized that the amendment did confer on African Americans the right to vote. However, in *Williams v. Mississippi* (1898), the Court ruled that the grandfather clause—a device to require all blacks to take a literacy test before registering to vote—was not a violation of the Fifteenth Amendment. Not until 1915 did the Supreme Court, in its ruling on *Guinn*, outlaw such disfranchisement scheme, deeming it a violation of the Fifteenth Amendment.

After federal enforcement declined and the South redeemed in 1877, black disfranchisement emerged in the South and became the norm in the 1890s and throughout the 1950s. The Fifteenth Amendment was sparsely enforced during the period and yet remained a constitutional principle. It became the starting point for such African American political and intellectual leaders as W.E.B. Du Bois to initiate projects like the Niagara Movement, which asked for reinforcement of the amendment in 1905. It served as the constitutional source for African American reenfranchisement in the second half of the twentieth century.

Further Reading: Foner, Eric. *Reconstruction: America's Unfinished Revolution, 1863-1877.* New York: Harper and Row, 1988; Gillette, William. *The Right to Vote: Politics and the Passage of the Fifteenth Amendment.* Baltimore, MD: Johns Hopkins University Press, 1965; Goldman, Robert M. *Reconstruction and Black Suffrage: Losing the Vote in Reese & Cruikshank.* Lawrence: University Press of Kansas, 2001; Kaczorowski, Robert J. *The Politics of Judicial Interpretation: The Federal Courts, Department of Justice, and Civil Rights, 1866-1876.* 1985; reprint, New York: Fordham University Press, 2005; Keyssar, Alexander. *The Right to Vote: The Contested History of Democracy in the United States.* New York: Basic Books, 2000; Wang, Xi.

The Trial of Democracy: Black Suffrage and Northern Republicans, 1860–1910. Athens: University of Georgia Press, 1997.

Xi Wang

Fish, Hamilton (1808–1893)

Secretary of state in the **Ulysses S. Grant** administration, Fish was an American aristocrat who remained untainted by the decline in the public and political morals of the Reconstruction era and Gilded Age times. Born in New York City, Fish's father was Nicholas Fish, a leading military figure in the Revolutionary War and later a leading Federalist. His mother was Elizabeth Stuyvesant, a member of one of New York's first families. He did not rebel against this heritage. After graduating from Columbia University in 1827, he studied law with Peter Jay. Admitted to the bar in 1830, his practice dealt mainly with real estate. Inheritance from his mother's family made him a wealthy man. He married Julia Kean; they had eight children.

Politics became his vocation. As a Whig, he endorsed the active role of the state in economic development, but he rejected any "democratic" attempts at reducing the rights of property, and, of course, radical social change was totally rejected. In 1834, he lost in a race for the New York legislature. Eight years later, he was in the U.S. House of Representatives, but only for one term. He was successful on his second try for the office of lieutenant governor, which led to his election as governor in 1848. Three years later, he was the U.S. senator from New York.

Fish's record as senator was poor. He only watched from his Senate seat, the rapidity of events that led to the Civil War. Only slowly did he join the Republican Party, and remained uneasy with the party's antislavery position. The Republicans looked elsewhere for a candidate for his seat, and he retired from electoral politics and went to Europe for the next two years. He did, however, support **Abraham Lincoln** in 1860.

As secession became a reality, Fish supported compromise. When the fighting began, he led the New York Union Defense Committee. He supervised the treatment and exchange of prisoners of war. As the war ended, he welcomed **Andrew Johnson** as president of the United States and his modest plan for Reconstruction. He also became a close friend of Ulysses S. Grant and provided money to the general's family, but by 1867, he came to oppose President Johnson's policies, and rejected the **Democratic Party** as a meaningful alternative.

Instead, Fish looked to General Grant as his alternative. With money and influence, Fish worked hard for the general's candidacy for the **election of 1868**. In the Grant administration, Fish became secretary of state. He provided a constancy to a presidency racked by **scandal** and corruption, but Fish the aristocrat did his duty and did not abandon President Grant.

His record as secretary of state was one of success in dealing with the *Alabama* claims with Great Britain. He demonstrated great tact and skill in solving a complex diplomatic and political problem. The result was the Treaty of Washington, which solved several issues and concerns between the United

States and Great Britain. Fish also pushed for American commercial expansion around the globe, as seen in his commercial agreement with Hawaii and his support for a canal across Central America. Senator **Charles Sumner** from Massachusetts, chairman of the Foreign Relations Committee, opposed Fish's expansionism. Their stiffest confrontations occurred when Fish wanted the United States to annex several Caribbean islands, either as protectorates or under complete American ownership.

In domestic affairs, Fish was not so bold. He urged a moderate policy toward the rebel states, and his fiscal policy avoided inflationary programs. As an array of gentlemen and knaves passed through the Grant administration, Fish remained at his post, yet despite his aloofness and social distinction, he apparently never publicly denounced the spoilsmen.

When Grant left the White House in 1877, Fish retired from politics but remained active in city affairs appropriate for a gentleman. Such activities and organizations as the New York Historical Society, the Society of Cincinnati, the St. Nicholas Society, and the **Union League** filled his days. He remained a defender of Grant's reputation as both a president and military leader. He died and is buried at his estate on the Hudson River, where his grave overlooks New York.

Further Reading: Chapin, James B. "Hamilton Fish and American Expansion." Ph.D. dissertation, Cornell University, 1971; Donald, David H. *Charles Sumner and the Rights of Man.* New York: Knopf, 1970; Nevins, Allan. *Hamilton Fish: The Inner History of the Grant Administration.* Rev. ed. New York: F. Ungar, 1957.

Donald K. Pickens

Florida

Florida's Reconstruction officially began on May 20, 1865, when its Confederate officials surrendered to the Union army at the state capital of Tallahassee. The state and its 140,000 residents managed to emerge from the Civil War without witnessing the destruction of property and the great loss of life that her sisters in the Confederacy endured. At the end of hostilities, approximately 15,000 Floridians lost their lives on the battlefield and Tallahassee was the only southern capital to escape invasion during the war. Unfortunately, the state would not be as fortunate during Reconstruction, and struggled with the same socioeconomic and political problems as the rest of the South.

Florida's first effort at Reconstruction began with **Andrew Johnson**'s May 29, 1865, proclamation. In accordance with the proclamation, **William Marvin**, Johnson's appointed **provisional governor** for Florida, called for statewide elections for the purpose for selecting delegates for a **constitutional convention**. This election, which was limited to white males twenty-one years and older, occurred on October 10, 1865. Florida's voters selected fifty-four delegates who then converged on Tallahassee fifteen days later prepared to draft the state's first postwar constitution. The new document drafted by these men abided by the requirements of Johnson's proclamation by nullifying its ordinances of secession, repudiating the Confederate debt, and **abolishing slavery**, but in all other aspects, it mirrored the states previous constitution. It did not allow for **black suffrage**, and continued to count **African Americans** as three-fifths of a white person for the purpose of representation in the state assembly. Nevertheless, by December 1865, Florida had met all of the federal requirements to reassume its position as a state in the Union, having held elections for seats in its state assembly, selected representatives to Congress, and elected one of the state's former **Supreme Court** justices and Whig, David S. Walker, as governor. However, Walker's election coincided with Congress's initial efforts to dismantle **Presidential Reconstruction**. Consequently, frenzied political organization by Republicans and Democrats, episodes of racial **violence**, and efforts to restrict the newfound freedom of the state's African American population marked the state's first efforts at Reconstruction.

Ironically, many of the problems that Walker and the state faced during his brief two-year term as Florida's chief executive resulted from his efforts to pass laws he believed would ensure tranquility in the state. These laws, later known in Florida and in other southern states as **Black Codes**, not only relegated blacks to a second-class position in society, but also alienated citizens who had remained loyal to the Union during the war. By the spring of 1866, laws were in place providing severe penalties for crimes usually associated with the black community. These included **vagrancy**, possession of firearms, stealing, and breaking of labor **contracts**. Similar statutes provided for the involuntary apprenticeship of African American children and limitations on the ex-slaves' ability to seek redress for grievances in the state court system. This new manifestation of slavery, as well as the appearance that the Florida's former Confederate leaders were consolidating their power in the state, caused many Floridians to become more sympathetic to **Radical Republican** calls for a more stringent Reconstruction of the South.

Despite the many obstacles preventing Florida's freedmen from enjoying the full measure of American citizenship, they continued to live as though the government's granting of their political rights was imminent. With the assistance of Thomas W. Osborn and William J. Purman, two agents of the **Bureau of Refugees, Freedmen, and Abandoned Lands**, the state's African American population began to take an active interest in politics. They also joined groups such as the **Union League** and Lincoln Brotherhood that began appearing in the state after the war. In addition to introducing the freedmen to the electoral process, these organizations served as political training grounds for many of Florida's future African American leaders.

The opportunity of these leaders to participate in the political process came quickly. After Congress passed the **Military Reconstruction Act** in March 1867, Florida held an election to select delegates for the purpose of drafting a new constitution. This historic election, held in November 1867, was the first statewide election open to the state's African American population. However, the extending of the **suffrage** to many men who had been former slaves initiated much of the political turmoil and charges of corruption that plagued Florida during the Reconstruction. Many Democrats, refusing to acknowledge the legitimacy of any convention that had the participation of former slaves, stayed away from the polls on election day. In addition, the unity enjoyed by

Florida Republicans from the end of the war to the onset of **Congressional Reconstruction** disintegrated into two factions, the radicals or "Mule Team" and a group of moderates and conservatives known in some circles as Union Republicans.

The "Mule Team" earned its name because of the two mules that pulled their wagon as they campaigned throughout the state. Their uncompromising message of political and social equality appealed greatly to the state's African American population, but at the same time, frightened many native Floridians and Republicans alike. In response to this fear, Union Republicans, led by future governor **Harrison Reed**, hoped to create a coalition of Republicans and Democrats by placing emphasis on the economic reconstruction of the state rather than its social issues; an approach that enjoyed the support of many of Florida's wealthier citizens as well as the approval of President Johnson. Nevertheless, the Union Republicans were unable to arrest the momentum of the Mule Team. Their candidates prevailed during the election and the faction acquired enough seats to hold a slim majority in the convention.

When the **constitutional convention** convened in Tallahassee on January 20, 1868, African Americans were a well-represented minority, making up eighteen out of the forty-three delegates sent to Tallahassee. The radicals in the hall moved quickly to control the assembly and on the convention's opening day, elected its leader, Daniel Richards, to preside over the proceedings. However, the radicals' control was short-lived. Before they could submit their constitution to Congress for approval, more than half of the convention's delegates under the direction of Harrison Reed, met in a rump convention in an adjacent town where they drafted a more conservative document. Likewise, this new assembly drafted new rules that resulted in the dismissal of Richards and other radical delegates for not being Florida residents. Ultimately, Congress accepted the constitution drafted by the rump convention, despite the fierce debate by the radicals over the legitimacy of the process that created it.

Although Florida's new constitution was one of the most progressive in the history of the state, it differed from the Radicals' document in very significant ways and had a negative effect on Florida's African American population. Whereas the Radicals' constitution required all officeholders to take a **loyalty oath** and prohibited ex-Confederates from holding state office, the ratified constitution placed no such restrictions on former supporters of the Confederacy. In addition, the radicals favored making most state and local officials elected. However, the new document gave the governor the power to appoint individuals to fill these offices. Last, the new constitution limited the number of representatives each county could have in the state assembly to four, regardless of its population. The last provision had the most dramatic effect on the state's African Americans because it diminished their voting strength in counties where they were the most populous. This allowed, in effect, a third of the state's actual population to control the entire state legislature.

With the ratification of the new constitution, the tenuous bond between **Moderate Republicans** and Democrats quickly disintegrated. Harrison Reed, who had been instrumental in the drafting and ratification of the document, served as Florida's first governor under Congressional Reconstruction. However, political infighting, **violence**, and rumors of **scandal** marked his tenure as governor. By the time Reed's term in office expired in 1872, the state legislature had initiated impeachment proceedings against him on four different occasions. Fortunately for the besieged governor, all but one of the attempts fell apart before reaching the state senate. In the final attempt, occurring in 1872, the senate acquitted Reed by a vote of 10 to 7.

Despite losing much of their political power because of the constitution, Florida's African Americans made some gains during the Reed administration. Two of the most notable include Josiah T. Walls, an ex-slave and Union soldier who became Florida's first African American congressman in 1870, and Dartmouth graduate Jonathan C. Gibbs, who became secretary of state during the legislature's first attempt to impeach Reed in 1868. Similarly, African Americans made up a very active part of the state house, with men such as African Methodist Episcopal ministers Charles H. Pearce and Robert Meacham. However, most of their political gains occurred in the cities and towns, where they served in positions that lay outside of the governor's considerable power of **patronage**. Throughout the state, African Americans served as city aldermen, in law enforcement, and on city councils.

Not all Floridians welcomed these political gains, and some responded violently toward African Americans and Republicans throughout the state. Jonathan C. Gibbs, himself the target of several assassination plots, attributed more than 1,800 deaths to violence from groups such as the **Ku Klux Klan** during his first three years as secretary of state. The violence finally subsided after Congress passed the first of the **Enforcement Acts** in 1870; however, by this time, many African Americans had become reluctant to seek political office, vote, and some like Emanuel Fortune, father of the prominent African American newspaper editor T. Thomas Fortune, chose to flee the state altogether.

Outbreaks of violence, in concert with Republican factionalism and persistent charges of corruption, did much to return the control of the state back to the **Democratic Party**. The Republican Party retained control of the executive branch in 1872 with the election of Ossian B. Hart, a Florida Unionist and former slave owner, as governor. However, the Democrats made gains during the election that would continue to increase until they recaptured the state four years later. As early as 1870, the Democrats had a strong presence in both of the state houses and by 1873, were outnumbered by only two senators in the state senate and six representatives in the lower house. By 1875, the party's strength was sufficient to maintain segregation in public schools, despite the best efforts of the radicals in the legislature.

The party's momentum from the two previous elections carried on to the presidential **election of 1876**. In a highly contested election that had national as well as state ramifications, the Democrats successfully elected George F. Drew, a northerner, as governor. The voting irregularities that caused Florida to be one of the centers of controversy also affected Drew's election and made it appear that the Republican candidate, Marcellus Stearns, had won the election. Florida Democrats, in a decision that had national implications, chose to challenge the returns of the gubernatorial, but not the presidential, election.

Consequently, when the state ruled Drew the victor of the 1876 election, its decision not to recount presidential returns all but surrendered the state's coveted four electoral votes to **Rutherford B. Hayes**.

The inauguration of George F. Drew marked Florida's "**redemption**," the end of Republican control of the state and of the Reconstruction process. Although Florida suffered from many of the problems that plagued other southern states during the period, including economic hardship, election fraud, and violence, many positive changes occurred under Republican rule. The 1868 constitution, in addition to ushering the state back into the Union, extended democracy to both whites and African Americans and gave the state the responsibility for educating its citizens. Similarly, the Reconstruction in the state marked the beginning of its transition from being a territorial to a modern southern state. *See also* Black Politicians; Compromise of 1877; Shotgun Plan; White Leagues.

Further Reading: Richardson, Joe M. *The Negro in the Reconstruction of Florida, 1865–1877*. Tallahassee: Florida State University, 1965; Shofner, Jerrell H. *Nor Is It Over Yet: Florida in the Era of Reconstruction, 1863–1877*. Gainesville: University Presses of Florida, 1974.

Learotha Williams, Jr.

Forrest, Nathan Bedford (1821–1877)

Born in **Tennessee**, Forrest moved with his family to **Mississippi** in 1834, and there became responsible for the entire family after his father's death. Retaining his estates there, he later relocated back to Memphis, where he became quite wealthy as a planter and slave trader.

Forrest enlisted in the Confederate army in June 1861, and soon climbed the ranks, partly due to a natural military ability (he had no formal military training or **education**) and partly due to wealth—he could equip and supply entire cavalry units, and so became an officer automatically. At the head of mounted troops, Forrest saw extensive service in the western theater, and his simple-if-mythical slogan, "Get there first with the most" accurately summed his audacity and primitive cunning. Unfortunately, these are often overshadowed by the controversy surrounding the attack on Fort Pillow, which was followed by the massacre of black soldiers who had been taken as prisoners of war. To this day, his role in the alleged atrocity remains unclear.

In the closing days of the Civil War, now a lieutenant general, Forrest confronted the most difficult decision of his military career. He faced a number of options that ranged from continuing resistance to Union forces, accepting exile or, of course, surrendering. Forrest confounded the worst fears of his military opponents by opting to surrender his command. With his role in the conflict ended, he returned to his plantation property in Mississippi and vowed to be as loyal to the U.S. government in defeat as he had been determined once to triumph over it on the battlefield.

Immediately, the ex-Confederate cavalry commander undertook the difficult task of resurrecting his livelihood, including restoring a fortune that had stood at a million and a half dollars before the war. Demonstrating an acceptance of the verdict of the war, he employed several former Union officers as partners in his plantation enterprises and offered favorable **contracts** to former slaves as inducements for them to work for him. The federal soldiers helped him to obtain the laborers he required. His goal was to revive his plantation in Coahoma County, Mississippi, and he did this in part by repairing a steam-powered saw mill that also offered lumber to a public anxious to rebuild. Forrest focused his activities in this period on peaceful pursuits and thereby became the model of reconciliation.

A shrewd businessman, Forrest created a system for his workers that not only promised them relatively high wages, but bound them to himself through the contracts they signed with him. A report from an official of the **Bureau of Refugees, Freedmen, and Abandoned Lands** found that nearly all of his hands were indebted to him to one extent or another and the workers themselves hailed from distant as well as local sources. Thus, the former slave trader and cavalryman exhibited the same resourcefulness he had demonstrated in his prewar business activities and his wartime career.

Nevertheless, Forrest continued to struggle with financial instability and personal uncertainty. His wartime association with the "massacre" at Fort Pillow in April 1864 that had left 231 **African Americans** dead remained fresh in the minds of many. Threats of arrest for treason also hung over him. Worried friends and associates urged him to travel to Europe for refuge, but Forrest demurred vigorously, arguing that he was adhering to his parole by working peaceably at his plantation and adamant that he would continue to do so. In the meantime, he posted a $10,000 bond for a treason trial that never took place and sought a presidential **pardon** that he eventually received in 1868 from President **Andrew Johnson**.

Forrest enjoyed some success in his agricultural endeavors, but the persistence of economic difficulties compelled him to seek relief through other avenues. Employing the fame he had established for himself as a soldier, Forrest allowed his name to be used by Tate, Gill, Able & Company, a "Commission, Grocery & Cotton Factorage Business." This was the first of numerous ventures with which he associated himself, including a brief effort to pave the streets of Memphis and a stint as president of the Planters' Insurance Company. He also supervised the construction of the Memphis and Little Rock **Railroad**, the first of two major commitments he made to this type of endeavor in the postwar period.

Although he had vowed to remain peaceful, Forrest kept a wary eye on developing political affairs in his state and region. Seeing what he believed to be an increasing abuse of power on the part of **Radical Republicans**, particularly in Tennessee on the part of Governor **William G. "Parson" Brownlow**, he determined to act to combat it. As part of his effort to restore home rule to the **Democratic Party** and challenge these excesses, Forrest became involved in an organization known as the Pale Faces and then with the budding **Ku Klux Klan**.

Publicly, Forrest denied being a member of the secret society much less its leader, but he expressed intimate knowledge of its operations. One of the Klan's original cofounders confirmed that when the organization grew sufficiently large, it required a strong leader and the members turned to the cavalry

A searing, election-year indictment of four prominent figures in the Democratic Party. Nathan Bedford Forrest, the founder of the Ku Klux Klan, and infamous for his role in the massacre of surrendered Union troops at Fort Pillow, is called "The Butcher Forrest." (Courtesy of the Library of Congress.)

chieftain as grand wizard. This likely happened officially at a meeting in Nashville in April 1867.

Under Forrest's leadership, the Klan grew and expanded dramatically. Whenever his business associations took him into neighboring states, it was more than coincidental that the first public notices for the organization would appear in local newspapers. The Klan's expansion and the nature of its activities, however, worked against a central authority. The rigidly demanding ex-soldier found that he could not exert his full control over the wide-ranging secret society. In addition, the departure of his Tennessee nemesis, "Parson" Brownlow, to the U.S. Senate, and the advancement to the governorship of a more malleable DeWitt Clinton Senter, bode well for Democrats and ex-Confederates in the state. For such reasons as these, Forrest ordered the Klan to disband and the membership to destroy their regalia in early 1869.

Despite these instructions, Klan activity continued and the organization came under greater scrutiny. Forrest's one-time prominence in it prompted the U.S. Congress to summon him to appear before an investigative committee in 1871. His testimony alternately demonstrated in-depth knowledge and deliberate obfuscation as the ex-Confederate responded in detail or dodged questions he did not wish to answer.

Part of the reason for his loss of interest in the Klan may well have been his growing involvement in railroading. Forrest spent the greater part of his resources attempting to generate financing for the Selma, Marion and Memphis Railroad. Struggling through investment challenges and economic crises, Forrest poured himself fully into the effort as the line's president. The strenuous work met with some small successes, but even larger failures. Finally and reluctantly, he relinquished the railroad presidency on April 1, 1877, and refocused his energies on farming, leasing President's Island near Memphis.

Even in his declining years, Forrest found that old habits were hard to break. He continued to demonstrate the temper for which he was famous and a propensity for gambling that his wife, Mary Ann Montgomery Forrest, deplored, but could not make him forsake. He attended reunions and continued to run his landholdings, now with the aid of a convict-lease program from Shelby County that provided him with laborers. He also embraced religion, again under the powerful influence of his long-suffering wife. In 1875, he experienced a religious conversion. However, Forrest began to wear out, suffering breakdowns in his health (he may have been suffering from diabetes) as well as his finances. By 1877, he was facing the end, an emaciated shadow of his former robust stature. He discharged his debts and moved to his brother Jesse's house in Memphis, where he died on October 29, 1877.

In many ways, Nathan Bedford Forrest symbolized the Reconstruction era that framed his postwar years. He worked to restore his citizenship, plantation property, and personal fortune rather than continue a conflict that he recognized had been lost on the battlefield. Yet, he refused to remain idle to the threats he felt existed to former Confederates and Democrats in Tennessee and the South. He joined the Klan to battle those excesses, but disbanded the organization when it demonstrated excesses of its own that he could not control. Popularly, if erroneously, considered the founder of the Klan, Forrest worked for the reestablishment of home rule in his state and region. As he faced his own final battle, he must have derived some sense of satisfaction that he had helped to win that larger engagement. *See also* Abolition of Slavery; Agriculture; Amnesty Proclamations; Bourbons; Congressional Reconstruction; Emancipation; Enforcement Acts (1870, 1871); Redemption; Sharecropping; Violence; White Leagues.

Further Reading: Henry, Robert Selph. *"First with the Most" Forrest*. Indianapolis, IN: Bobbs-Merrill, 1944; Hurst, Jack. *Nathan Bedford Forrest: A Biography*. New York: Alfred A. Knopf, 1993; Wills, Brian Steel. *A Battle from the Start: Life of Nathan Bedford Forrest*. New York: HarperCollins Publishers, 1992.

Brian S. Wills

Fortieth Congress, Extra Session of (1867)

The extra session of the 40th Congress was a special session convened as the 39th Congress was going out of session. The **Radical Republicans** and **Andrew Johnson** were at a crossroads over how to handle folding the former rebel states of the South back into the Union. After the **assassination of Abraham Lincoln**, Radicals believed Johnson would follow a hard Reconstruction program, but he followed in the footsteps of **Lincoln**, passing a proclamation that called for only an **amnesty oath** that dealt with future loyalty to the Union. The Radicals and others in the North felt that this was too lenient and favored the white former Confederates at the expense of the freedpeople. However, Congress was not in session, so without being called by the executive (which Johnson had no intention of doing), the president had a free hand to determine Reconstruction policy. Northern politicians saw Johnson's southern state legislatures pass **Black Codes**, witnessed the electing of former Confederates to positions of power and importance, and were aghast that President Johnson did nothing.

Congressional elections in the fall of 1867 guaranteed that anti-Johnson forces would control the next Congress—the 40th Congress—set to convene in December 1867. By spring 1867, however, so many problems had erupted when Johnson dictated policy that Republicans in Congress moved to have the 40th Congress meet immediately, denying Johnson any opportunity to act without Congress in session. As a result, the 40th Congress convened the same day the 39th ended, March 4, 1867.

To restrict Johnson's power and move forward their Reconstruction agenda, the Republicans passed three resolutions. The first bill, the **Military Reconstruction Act, disfranchised** men qualified for office by the **Fourteenth Amendment** and stated that southern state governments were provisional and subject to the power of the federal government. The **Command of the Army Act** was a rider attached to the Army Appropriation Act, which made sure that General **Ulysses S. Grant** remained commanding general of the army, could not be removed from Washington, and that he issued all orders concerning military operations. The act also forbade the organization of **militias** in the southern states until authorized by Congress. The **Tenure of Office Act** required the consent of the Senate for the removal of any office whose appointment required Senate approval. This 40th Congress swiftly and successfully secured control of Reconstruction, and would eventually be the body to first impeach an American president. *See also* Amnesty Proclamations; Black Suffrage; Civil Rights; Congressional Reconstruction; Constitutional Conventions; Elections of 1866; House Judiciary Committee; Impeachment of Andrew Johnson; Presidential Reconstruction; Republicans, Moderate; Republicans, Radical; U.S. Army and Reconstruction.

Further Reading: Belz, Herman. *Reconstructing the Union: Theory and Policy during the Civil War*. Ithaca, NY: Cornell University Press, 1969; Hyman, Harold Melvin. *Era of the Oath: Northern Loyalty Tests during the Civil War and Reconstruction*. Philadelphia: University of Pennsylvania Press, 1954.

Catherine Anyaso

Fourteenth Amendment (1868)

With the **abolition of slavery** by the **Thirteenth Amendment** in 1865, questions immediately appeared regarding the status of the freedpeople in the South. Legal and extralegal restrictions in the southern states severely limited freedmen's economic rights and gave the former slaves few if any social or political rights. The former Confederate states were also indifferent to **violence** against blacks. In addition, with the abolition of slavery ending the Three-Fifths Compromise, southern strength in the House of Representatives and the Electoral College was even stronger after the Civil War than before.

Purpose Guiding the Amendment

In response to the changes wrought by war, Republicans in Congress moved to define the freedom created by the Thirteenth Amendment. Some hoped to enfranchise blacks and deny political rights to former Confederates. Within the Republican Party, Radicals hoped to define the rights, liberties, and status of all Americans, protecting them through federal power while maintaining state-based federalism. Along with many other northerners, they expected to secure the war's results (preservation of the Union and abolition of slavery) from southern modification or rejection.

President **Andrew Johnson**'s veto on March 27, 1866, of the **Civil Rights Act of 1866** prompted congressional Republicans to support a constitutional amendment that would make the act's definition of black civil equality (largely economic) safe from presidential reach and from reversal by a later Congress. It would also define the Republicans' plan for Reconstruction, just as the approaching 1866 congressional elections gave them the opportunity to challenge Johnson and the plan he initiated in May 1865.

Even before Johnson's veto, the **Joint Committee on Reconstruction** had discussed a proposal from committee member **John Bingham**. In January 1866, it had reported two amendments. One gave Congress power "to make all laws necessary and proper to secure to all citizens the same political rights and privileges" and to provide "to all persons . . . equal protection in the enjoyment of life, liberty, and property." The other required the reduction of a state's representation if the state limited voting rights "on account of race, creed or color." The first proposal, with "privileges and immunities" substituted for "political rights and privileges," died in the House; the Senate killed the second proposal.

The proposals' fate was the result of opposition from Democrats and from conservatives in the Republican Party to giving Congress new powers. Even some Radicals found reason for concern in the delegation of power to Congress to insure "equal protection" in states. All knew, for example, of women's lack of equality. Bingham emphasized that he sought not a transfer of power from states to Congress but only "an amendment which would arm Congress with the power to compel obedience to the [states' constitutional] oaths."

In April 1866, the Joint Committee on Reconstruction took its next step by considering a five-part proposal from Robert Dale Owen, a reformer who had served in the House in the 1840s. Including provisions on black **civil rights**, enfranchisement of blacks after 1876, penalties for restricting **black suffrage**, repudiation of Confederate debts, and congressional power to enforce the amendment, Owen's proposal also sought to define Reconstruction terms. For example, it required ratification of the amendment in order for the **readmission** of the former Confederate states to Congress. His proposal made the guarantee of rights self-executing through phrasing that acknowledged their existence within states. New York representative Giles W. Hotchkiss had suggested this approach as a substitute for a direct grant of power to Congress "to make all laws."

A Compromise Amendment

As passed by Congress, the **Fourteenth Amendment** was a compromise measure that followed the general structure of Owen's plan. It added to the Constitution the **Radical Republicans**' vision of a nation centered on equal rights protected by national power. However, the Radical desire for black suffrage and for **disfranchisement** of former Confederates was tempered by the widely held belief that **suffrage** was a privilege, not a right of citizenship, and by **Moderate Republican** support for a limited and speedy Reconstruction of the South that did little harm to state-based federalism. In addition, states remained responsible for regulating personal liberty and civil rights, but the national government gained supervisory oversight.

The first section's vague and general language that never mentions race was the result of the Joint Committee's concerns about federalism and desire to protect the rights of all Americans. Numerous committee votes on various versions of the provision ended with approval of a proposal submitted by Bingham and modeled after Hotchkiss's suggestion. First, however, section 1 began by providing the **U.S. Constitution**'s first definition of national citizenship: All born or naturalized in the United States were citizens. State citizenship would no longer determine national citizenship, and Chief Justice Roger Taney's denial of black citizenship in *Dred Scott v. Sanford* no longer carried constitutional weight, if it ever had. Supported by conservative and moderate members of the Joint Committee, as well as by Radicals to various degrees, section 1 next announced that a "State" could not "abridge the privileges and immunities of citizens," rights that it left undefined. The section also prohibited a "State" from depriving any "person" (as distinct from citizens and undoubtedly meant to include aliens) "life, liberty, or property without due process of law." It concluded by prohibiting denial of the "equal protection of the law" to any "person within its jurisdiction." Whether all congressional framers and backers of these provisions viewed them as prohibiting discrimination against blacks in all aspects of life (political, economic, and social), some Radicals with **abolitionist** backgrounds certainly did.

If section 1 generally satisfied Radicals, section 2 fell far short of their goals. Many Radical Republicans saw voting as a requirement for functional citizenship (and not just as a tool for use by freedmen to protect their rights), but the amendment made only a half-step in an area that was constitutionally and traditionally under state control. Republican awareness of northern whites' objections to black suffrage undoubtedly led Radical **Thaddeus Stevens**, a representative from Pennsylvania, to move to eliminate a suffrage provision during the Joint Committee's considerations. As a result, section 2 of the amendment stipulated that states that denied suffrage to any of its adult male citizens faced a proportional loss of representation in Congress. The threat would turn out to be a hollow one as, by the end of the century and well into the 1900s, adult black males were consistently denied suffrage through various state and private practices.

Section 3 was a response to the South's election in 1865 of antebellum and wartime leaders to fill state and national offices under President Johnson's Reconstruction plan. It also reflected the view that men responsible for a destructive civil war should not be allowed positions of political leadership after it. Therefore, the amendment provided that anyone who had held political or military office before the Civil War and who had sworn to support the Constitution could not hold a federal or state office ("civil or military") afterward if they had then fought for or aided the Confederacy. No restriction on suffrage rights was included, and Congress could remove the restriction through a two-thirds vote, which it soon did for most former Confederates.

Section 4 answered a question linked both to the war's impact on the nation's economy and to views of the South's secession. It stipulated that debts or other financial obligations resulting from support of the South's secessionist effort would not be honored by the national or state governments.

In addition, slave owners could not receive compensation for slaves lost through the war or through **emancipation**. All such claims were "illegal and void."

Finally, section 5 gave Congress "the power to enforce" the preceding four provisions by "appropriate legislation." This expansion of the national government's power, along with a parallel provision in section 2 of the Thirteenth Amendment, was the first increase in Congress's power in the Constitution's seventy-seven years of existence. Committee and congressional debate suggested, however, that the extent of the increase was problematic. While Democrat George S. Shanklin asserted that section 5 would end "State rights and invest all power in the national government," John Bingham defended it as "tak[ing] from no State any right that ever pertained to it."

Passage, Ratification, and the Fate of the South

In the view of many observers and many later historians, the final version of the Fourteenth Amendment was the best possible for the times. The Republican Party in general was satisfied with the amendment as a response to the South's and President Johnson's lack of concern for the status and rights of **African Americans** and as a means of securing the results of the Civil War. The views of the Radical wing, however, ranged from an "imperfect . . . proposition" (Thaddeus Stevens) to "a wanton betrayal of justice and humanity" (Representative **George Julian** of Indiana).

Congressional passage of the Fourteenth Amendment came on June 11, 1866. On June 13, Congress sent the amendment to the states. Less than two weeks later on June 25, Connecticut became the first state to vote for ratification.

Ratification, which required approval by three-quarters of the states, was tied to the debate over Reconstruction between the president and Congress. Which branch of the national government would set the final requirements for the "readmission" of the former Confederate states? And what changes would those requirements make in southern political and social structure? One answer came with **Tennessee**'s ratification of the amendment in July 1866. Congress quickly seated the state's eight representatives and senators, but a specific pledge to readmit seceded states that ratified the amendment was tabled by Congress that same month. The remaining ten seceded states shared Andrew Johnson's opposition to the Fourteenth Amendment and refused to ratify it, much of their opposition centering on the third section's restriction on white office holding and on the hope that northern public opinion would demand a more moderate policy.

To the white South's disappointment, the **elections of 1866** did not bring to power a conservative Congress or a retraction of the Fourteenth Amendment. With the amendment as their platform, Republicans came out of the elections with control of both houses of Congress. As a result, Radical and Moderate Republicans took control of Reconstruction. Their determination to revise Johnson's Reconstruction requirements was fueled by the **race riots** in Memphis and New Orleans in the summer of 1866 and by the president's opposition to any federal civil rights protection.

Congress's **Military Reconstruction Act** of March 2, 1867, voided the governments established under Johnson and temporarily arranged the ten former Confederate states into five military districts. The act also mandated black suffrage in those states (and only those states), a partial remedy for the amendment's indirect directive in section 2. In addition, the act required the states to ratify the Fourteenth Amendment or remain in constitutional limbo, unrepresented in Congress.

Black suffrage was not the only controversial matter. The requirement of ratification itself raised questions about the amendment's constitutionality and, if ratified, when it would go into effect. According to Article V of the Constitution, ratification is a state's decision, yet ratification was a requirement under the Reconstruction Act. Some supporters of this condition for readmission saw ratification as an important step in reconstructing southern thinking; some were concerned about any variance in the constitutional requirement of three-quarters of the states, and some thought southern votes might be necessary to secure the necessary numbers for approval of the amendment.

A year after being submitted to the states, the amendment had the approval of twenty-two states. Initially, the former Confederate states (minus Tennessee), as well as Delaware, **Maryland**, and **Kentucky**, rejected the amendment, and after votes for ratification, Ohio and New Jersey decided to rescind their approval.

On July 20, 1868, Secretary of State **William Henry Seward** announced the amendment's ratification if Congress did not accept the two rescissions. When Congress did not, Seward promulgated the amendment on July 28. By then the issue was moot, as eight former Confederate states had ratified the Fourteenth Amendment (in this order): Tennessee, **Arkansas**, **Florida**, **North Carolina**, **Louisiana**, **South Carolina**, **Alabama**, and **Georgia**. **Mississippi**, **Texas**, and **Virginia** soon added their approval. (Interestingly, Kentucky did not approve the amendment until a century later, in 1976.)

The Amendment's Limited Impact

The Fourteenth Amendment's impact during Reconstruction was limited because of the growing disinterest in the status of blacks and the continuing preference for a limited national government in a state-based federal system. Nevertheless, the amendment (as well as the **Fifteenth Amendment**, added to the Constitution in 1870) provided the basis for the **Enforcement Acts** of 1870–1871, which authorized the use of federal force to end, at least temporarily and in some sections of the South, violence against blacks and their white allies. In addition, in 1875, the lame-duck Republican Congress passed a modified version of Senator **Charles Sumner**'s public-accommodations bill, the **Civil Rights Act of 1875**. Based on the amendment, it prohibited discrimination in such "social" areas as eating, sleeping, traveling, and schooling.

Radicals' hopes for the law and the Fourteenth Amendment rested in Americans' often-conflicting belief in equality and in government's need to make distinctions when necessary for the public good. The U.S. **Supreme Court** interpreted the amendment with these beliefs as their guide. Decisions in the *Slaughterhouse Cases* (1873) and *United States v. Cruikshank* (1876) left most rights under state definition and control and limited the reach of the amendment to the actions of states unless denial of rights was motivated by racial hostility. This narrowed reach was confirmed in *United States v. Harris* and the *Civil Rights Cases*, both in 1883. More in tune with Radical thinking were three decisions in 1880, which ruled against state action that limited black service on juries, although in yet another case that year, the mere absence of blacks on juries was defined as insufficient to prove a denial of rights under the Fourteenth Amendment.

As the nineteenth century ended, a final Supreme Court ruling confirmed the earlier interpretative limitations on the reach of the Fourteenth Amendment. If its framers had intended that social equality be covered by section 1, *Plessy v. Ferguson* (1896) cancelled that application for more than half a century. The eight-man majority explained the need for and tradition of state regulations that distinguished between groups (such as whites and blacks). As a result, the regrettable doctrine of "separate but equal" entered the Fourteenth Amendment's history. *See also* Amnesty Proclamations; Black Codes; Congressional Reconstruction; Jim Crow Laws; Ku Klux Klan; New South; Pardons; Presidential Reconstruction; Trumbull, Lyman; Women's Movement.

Further Reading: James, Joseph B. *The Ratification of the Fourteenth Amendment*. Macon, GA: Mercer University Press, 1984; Maltz, Earl M. *Civil Rights, the Constitution, and Congress, 1863–1869*. Lawrence: University Press of Kansas, 1990; Meyer, Howard N. *The Amendment that Refused to Die: Equality and Justice Deferred: A History of the Fourteenth Amendment*. Updated ed. Lanham, MD: Madison Books, 2000; Nelson, William E. *The Fourteenth Amendment: From Political Principle to Judicial Doctrine*. Cambridge, MA: Harvard University Press, 1988.

Claudine L. Ferrell

Freedman's Bank. *See* Freedman's Savings and Trust Company.

Freedman's Savings and Trust Company

The Freedman's Savings and Trust Company, known as the Freedman's Bank, was a private savings bank chartered by Congress in 1865 primarily for the benefit of **African Americans**. After initial success, it was forced to close in 1874 as a result of questionable business practices, careless oversight, outright fraud, and the financial **Panic of 1873**. The bank's collapse, and the consequent losses suffered by thousands of small depositors, came to symbolize the nation's betrayal of the freedmen and the larger failure of Reconstruction.

Background and Establishment

The bank was born of the Civil War and **emancipation**. Freedmen working under free labor arrangements in Union-held areas had lacked a place to secure their earnings, while various military departments had created agencies for black veterans to deposit their bounties and pay. Recognizing the need for an interstate branch banking system to provide these services after the war,

Congress chartered The Freedman's Savings and Trust Company on March 3, 1865, the same day it established the **Bureau of Refugees, Freedmen, and Abandoned Lands** (the Freedmen's Bureau). The Freedman's Bank was the first interstate branch bank since Andrew Jackson killed the Second Bank of the United States during the 1830s.

The charter named fifty citizens to a board of trustees. Mainly New Yorkers, the trustees included some of the nation's most prominent businessmen, a number of whom also served on the boards of various **Freedmen's Relief Societies**. In fact, however, many trustees were listed as figureheads, and most had little involvement in bank affairs. Moreover, while the charter seemed to detail the bank's operations, it made insufficient provisions to guarantee that the bank would be run on sound business and banking principles.

The charter originally specified a minimum-risk investment strategy, since the Freedman's Bank was intended as a nonprofit, mutual savings bank owned by the depositors. There were no stockholders, initial capitalization, or authorization to make loans. Upon receiving deposits, the bank would retain as much as one-third for operating expenses and invest the rest in safe government securities. Profits were to be returned to the depositors as interest. The bank was envisioned as part of the larger mission to remake the South upon a free-labor basis and to inculcate in former slaves the values necessary to compete within capitalist society. By encouraging freedmen to save their earnings, reformers believed, the bank would help instill in them thrift, industry, and frugality, enabling them to acquire property and enter the American economic mainstream.

Growth and Development

Originally headquartered in New York City, the Freedman's Bank started small but grew quickly. There were ten branches by the end of 1865 and twenty-two by 1867. Eventually, the bank operated thirty-four branches in every southern state, Washington, D.C., and several northern states that had cities with significant black populations. It also received applications for branches from many other southern cities and towns that it could not accommodate. Although such rapid expansion contributed to some organizational and operational difficulties, the bank proved popular among former slaves and even attracted a small number of white clients. By 1870, the bank held some 23,000 active accounts and $1.6 million in deposits, and by 1874, more than 61,000 accounts and almost $4 million had been deposited. During its nine-year life, the bank handled a total of more than 100,000 accounts and more than $50 million in deposits.

The large majority of depositors were individuals with small accounts. The bank accepted deposits of as little as five cents to encourage freedmen to save. Larger individual accounts, though uncommon, were held in such cities as New Orleans and Charleston, which hosted an antebellum free-black elite. Black **churches**, schools, businesses, and mutual-aid and benevolent associations also accounted for an important part of the bank's business. Hundreds if not thousands of individual depositors, representing thousands more freedmen, purchased land, homes, or businesses with the money they had saved at the bank, while many others used their savings for religious or **educational** purposes.

The bank actively sought deposits from freedmen. Its advertisements and circulars—which included the image of **Abraham Lincoln** as well as those of **Ulysses S. Grant**, **William T. Sherman**, and other Union generals—gave the impression that the federal government stood behind the bank. Moreover, although there was no official connection between the bank and the Freedmen's Bureau, the two organizations overlapped considerably. Local bureau offices and branch banks often shared the same building, bureau agents served as bank cashiers and on branch advisory boards, and higher-ranking bureau officials sat on the board of trustees. John W. Alvord, a congregationalist minister who had been active in wartime freedmen's aid efforts and who was instrumental in establishing the bank, was an original trustee and served first as the bank's corresponding secretary and then as president, while also serving as the bureau's superintendent of education. Although the Freedmen's Bureau commissioner, General **Oliver Otis Howard**, played no official role in the bank and was not directly involved in its affairs, he nonetheless envisioned the bank as one among a host of organizations and institutions, including schools, hospitals, and freedmen's aid associations, that were centered around the bureau and worked for the freedmen's advancement. Bank passbooks (deposit books) even included an endorsement from Howard assuring depositors that the bank was "an auxiliary to the Freedmen's Bureau."

Speculation, Collapse, and Failure

Despite the bank's growth, heavy operating expenses and the desire to produce larger dividends prompted bank officials—who were always overwhelmingly white, although some blacks served as trustees or on branch advisory boards—to seek other sources of revenue. In 1870, they persuaded Congress to amend the charter to permit the bank to lend money. Although limited to investing in real estate securities, bank officials soon began to make large, unsecured loans and to speculate in a number of unauthorized ventures, thus transforming the bank's mission from philanthropy and racial uplift to the pursuit of profit. With its headquarters having been relocated to Washington, D.C., the bank now fell under the control of Henry Cooke, brother of Civil War financier Jay Cooke, and William S. Huntington of its finance committee. Cooke was a full partner in, and the Washington agent of, the financial house of Jay Cooke and Company. The Freedman's Bank began investing heavily in Washington real estate and construction companies, as the city was experiencing a population boom, and it even undertook selling the bonds of Jay Cooke's Northern Pacific Railroad. Moreover, the bank loaned large sums—without sufficient collateral—to companies in which bank officials or trustees held financial interests. By 1873, a major part of the bank's assets were invested not in government securities but in real estate and unsecured loans to **railroads** and other companies.

The inability of Jay Cooke and Company to market its Northern Pacific Railroad bonds brought about the house's collapse, precipitating the Panic of

1873 that caused hundreds of businesses nationwide to fail. Facing bankruptcy, bank officials undertook a number of measures in late 1873 and early 1874 to reassure nervous depositors, including naming **Frederick Douglass** as president in March. Douglass was not involved in daily bank affairs, however, and he failed to prevent the bank from continuing to make unwise loans. Congress passed a bill in June to keep the bank alive, but confidence in it had been lost, as depositors continued to withdraw funds. On July 2, 1874, the board of trustees voted to close the bank for good.

When the bank closed, it owed just under $3 million on 61,144 accounts, about half of which were for less than $50. The main office had only $400 in U.S. bonds, and the branches only $31,689 in cash. Freedmen throughout the South received the news of the bank's closing first with alarm and then resignation. An initial announcement that the bank would pay 93 percent of its indebtedness proved to be unfounded. Before closing the bank, the trustees appointed a committee to collect the bank's assets and repay depositors. It did so until 1881, when Congress, finding further mismanagement, abolished the commission and transferred the bank's affairs to the federal comptroller of the currency. Between 1875 and 1883, five dividends were paid totaling 62 percent of the bank's indebtedness. Of 61,131 eligible depositors, only 29,996—fewer than half—sent their passbooks as required to receive the first dividend. They received a total of $555,360.08, or an average of $18.51. With each subsequent dividend, the number of claimants declined, so that by the time the last formal dividend was paid, only 17,893 of the more than 61,000 original depositors received the full 62 percent.

The failure of the Freedman's Bank provided political ammunition to the **Democratic Party** and other opponents of governmental assistance to former slaves, and it contributed to disillusionment and a sense of betrayal among the freedmen. For years afterward, individual members of Congress argued, to no avail, that the federal government had an obligation to repay the depositors in full. The comptroller of the currency continued to recoup the bank's assets, and between 1899 and 1919, under congressional authority, dividends were paid to depositors and their descendants who could prove that they had not received the full 62 percent of their deposits. In 1919, the affairs of the bank were closed for good. *See also* Abolition of Slavery; American Missionary Association; Black Troops (U.S.C.T.) in the Occupied South; Bruce, Blanche Kelso; Scandals.

Further Reading: Fleming, Walter L. *The Freedmen's Savings Bank: A Chapter in the Economic History of the Negro Race.* Chapel Hill: University of North Carolina Press, 1927; McFeely, William S. *Yankee Stepfather: General O. O. Howard and the Freedmen.* New Haven, CT: Yale University Press, 1968; Osthaus, Carl R. *Freedmen, Philanthropy, and Fraud: A History of the Freedman's Savings Bank.* Urbana: University of Illinois Press, 1976.

John C. Rodrigue

Freedmen's Bureau. *See* Bureau of Refugees, Freedmen, and Abandoned Lands.

Freedmen's Bureau Bills

Between 1865 and 1872, Congress passed five bills, four of which were enacted, directly pertaining to the War Department's **Bureau of Refugees, Freedmen, and Abandoned Lands** (the Freedmen's Bureau), in addition to other legislation affecting the bureau.

Background

The federal government created the Freedmen's Bureau in response to the disruption of southern civilian life resulting from the Civil War. During the war, several **Freedmen's Relief Societies** and other benevolent groups provided assistance to former slaves, while various federal agencies, in particular the War Department and Treasury Department, assumed responsibility for implementing systems of free labor, administering abandoned and confiscated plantations, and providing relief to freedmen and loyal white refugees. Even before Union victory had been assured, Congress considered the need for a federal agency to handle these matters and to oversee the transition from slavery to freedom upon Confederate defeat.

The Freedmen's Bureau originated in a December 1863 bill introduced by House Republican Thomas D. Eliot of Massachusetts. This bill passed the House in March 1864, but stalled for a year in the Senate over whether the proposed agency should be part of the War Department or Treasury Department. Not until March 1865, with Union victory imminent, did Congress agree to locate the bureau within the War Department. On March 3, the last day of the 38th Congress, a bill entitled "An Act to establish a Bureau for the Relief of Freedmen and Refugees" was passed and signed by President **Abraham Lincoln**.

The 1865 Act

This act formally established within the War Department, for the remainder of the war and for one year thereafter, a "bureau of refugees, freedmen, and abandoned lands," which was charged with the supervision and management of abandoned lands and "the control of all subjects relating to refugees and freedmen from rebel states." The bureau was to be headed by a commissioner, appointed by the president with Senate consent, who would establish rules and regulations subject to presidential approval. The president was also authorized, with Senate approval, to appoint up to ten assistant commissioners to head the bureau in the insurrectionary states. Military officers could be assigned to bureau duty with no increase in pay. The commissioner was required to make an annual report to the president and any special reports as needed by the president or Congress; assistant commissioners were to make quarterly reports to the commissioner and special reports as necessary. The legislation authorized the secretary of war to issue provisions, clothing, and fuel for the relief of destitute refugees and freedmen. Finally, the act authorized the commissioner, under the president's direction, "to set apart, for the use of loyal refugees and freedmen," abandoned and confiscated land within the insurrectionary states. It stipulated that "every male citizen" could rent up to forty acres of such land and be protected in its use for three years with an option to purchase at any time during this period.

Beyond signing the act establishing the Freedmen's Bureau, Lincoln devoted little attention to it. His successor, **Andrew Johnson**, demonstrated no initial opposition to the bureau, but soon became hostile to it. Envisioning a limited Reconstruction, Johnson wanted to readmit the ex-Confederate states quickly and did not advocate overturning southern society. In particular, he objected to a program of land redistribution, and in September 1865, he ordered the bureau to restore land to pardoned owners. Throughout the rest of 1865 and into 1866, Johnson established southern state governments that enacted discriminatory **Black Codes**, while freedmen endured widespread **violence** and received no redress in southern courts. By February 1866, congressional Republicans concluded that Johnson's policy required modification, and they passed two bills toward that end: a **Civil Rights Act** and a second Freedmen's Bureau bill.

The 1866 Bills

The February 1866 Freedmen's Bureau bill was written by **Lyman Trumbull**, a **Moderate Republican** and U.S. senator from Illinois. It continued the bureau's existence indefinitely and provided for its first direct funding. The number of assistant commissioners could be increased to twelve, and a local bureau agent could be appointed for every county. The secretary of war was again charged with providing assistance—including medical care and transportation—to the needy, and the commissioner was directed to build schools and asylums. Possession of land under General **William T. Sherman**'s Special **Field Order No. 15**—a January 1865 directive that had conditionally granted freedmen land in coastal **South Carolina** and **Georgia**—was confirmed for a period of three years. Additionally, the president was to make available three million acres of public land in the South for freedmen and loyal refugees to rent in forty-acre plots with the option to purchase. The legislation also assigned to the bureau a law enforcement role in the southern states, authorizing the president, through the commissioner, to "extend military protection and jurisdiction over all cases" in which freedmen were denied equal protection of the law, and empowering bureau officials to assume jurisdiction over and prosecute such cases.

Although the bill passed both houses of Congress with overwhelming majorities, Johnson vetoed it and issued a scathing veto message. An attempt to override the veto failed when six senators who had voted for the bill reversed themselves and sustained Johnson. The veto marked a major turning point in relations between Johnson and congressional Republicans over Reconstruction. (Johnson also vetoed the Civil Rights bill, but was overridden in April 1866.) Following Johnson's action, congressional Republicans focused on drafting another Freedmen's Bureau bill that could survive a veto. By late June, a new bill had passed both houses of Congress. Johnson returned it with his veto on July 16, 1866, but Congress immediately overrode him.

The July 1866 act was narrower than the previous bill, but in conjunction with the Civil Rights Act, the June 1866 **Southern Homestead Act**, and the July 1866 Army Appropriation Act, it significantly strengthened the Freedmen's Bureau. The new bill continued the bureau's operations for an additional two years and extended its jurisdiction to loyal refugees and freedmen throughout the country. It required the president to appoint two additional assistant commissioners (for **Kentucky** and **Maryland**), and it authorized continuing the service of army officers on bureau duty whose regiments were mustered out. The act empowered the bureau commissioner to use ex-Confederate public property for freedmen's **education**. It also required the commissioner to provide schoolhouses for teachers employed by private benevolent associations and to furnish protection "for the safe conduct of such schools." These activities were financed through the Army Appropriation Act, which allocated almost seven million dollars for the bureau (for the fiscal year) and represented its first separate appropriation.

Six of the act's fifteen sections addressed land in coastal South Carolina that had either been confiscated under provisions of wartime direct-tax acts or fell within Sherman's special field order. The act "confirmed and established" previous direct-tax sales to freedmen, and it spelled out procedures for the disposition of land still controlled by U.S. tax commissioners. It also provided that when lands to which freedmen held valid titles under Sherman's order were returned to their original owners, dispossessed freedmen would be permitted to lease twenty-acre plots elsewhere with a six-year option to purchase. It further stipulated that Sherman lands still held by freedmen were not to be returned until the year's crops were gathered and until freedmen were reimbursed for improvements made to the land. The previous bill's provision requiring the president to reserve public lands in the South for freedmen and refugees was excluded, owing to passage of the Southern Homestead Act.

The new bill reiterated the bureau's broad judicial powers. It directed that the president, through the Freedmen's Bureau, would "extend military protection and have military jurisdiction over all cases" in which freedmen were denied equality before the law. The Civil Rights Act already permitted use of the federal district courts to prosecute racial discrimination, but now military tribunals were also available. This provision of the bureau law did not extend to states where insurrection had not interrupted civilian courts, and it would no longer apply upon an ex-Confederate state's **readmission** to the Union.

The Final Acts

Passage of the 1867 **Military Reconstruction Acts** and the 1868 readmission of several states resulted in the bureau relinquishing many of its responsibilities. Nonetheless, because of the unsettled state of affairs throughout the South, in July 1868, Congress enacted two laws concerning the bureau. The July 6 law (upon which Johnson took no action) extended the bureau for one year while also requiring the secretary of war to discontinue the bureau in any readmitted state—unless, upon consultation with the commissioner, he deemed its continuance necessary. This law excluded the bureau's education division, which was to continue until the southern states made sufficient provisions for freedmen's education. The second law, enacted over Johnson's veto on July 25, specified that the "present commissioner" would continue in his position and would nominate all his subordinates (to prevent Johnson from interfering with the bureau); it also decreed that the bureau would cease all operations on January 1, 1869, except for its education division and the collection and payment of veterans' claims. In an appropriation bill passed on June 10, 1872, Congress discontinued the bureau entirely as of the end of that month. *See also* Abolition of Slavery; African Americans; Agriculture; American Missionary Association (AMA); Amnesty Proclamations; Civil Rights; Confiscation Acts; Congressional Reconstruction; Contracts; Democratic Party; Edisto Island, South Carolina; Education; Elections of 1866; Emancipation; Fourteenth Amendment; Freedman's Savings and Trust Company; Howard, Oliver Otis; Joint Committee on Reconstruction; Labor Systems; *Milligan, Ex parte*; Pardons; Port Royal Experiment; Presidential Reconstruction; Republicans, Radical; Saxton, Rufus; Sharecropping; Stanton, Edwin M.; Stevens, Thaddeus; Sumner, Charles; Thirteenth Amendment; U.S. Army and Reconstruction; U.S. Constitution; Vagrancy; Washington's Birthday Speech.

Further Reading: Bentley, George R. *A History of the Freedmen's Bureau*. Philadelphia: University of Pennsylvania Press, 1955; Carpenter, John A. *Sword and Olive Branch: Oliver Otis Howard*. Pittsburgh: University of Pittsburgh Press, 1964; Howard, Oliver Otis. *Autobiography of Oliver Otis Howard*. 2 vols. New York: The Baker & Taylor Company, 1908; Hyman, Harold M. *A More Perfect Union: The Impact of the Civil War and Reconstruction on the Constitution*. New York: Alfred A. Knopf, 1973; McFeely, William S. *Yankee Stepfather: General O. O. Howard and the Freedmen*. New Haven, CT: Yale University Press, 1968; Nieman, Donald G. *To Set the Law in Motion: The Freedmen's Bureau and the Legal Rights of Blacks, 1865–1868*. Millwood, NY: KTO Press, 1979.

John C. Rodrigue

Freedmen's Relief Societies

During Reconstruction, a network of charitable organizations known as Freedmen's Relief Societies sought to guide and assist former slaves in the transition to freedom. These groups provided food and other material aid, helped build schools and **churches**, and worked to facilitate freedpeople in finding a meaningful place in the political and economic order that arose in the U.S. South following the Civil War.

Many relief workers came from religious backgrounds and had been active in **abolitionism** before the war, but the movement was not limited to such people. Soldiers, businessmen, politicians, and other interested people also participated. These men and women did much to help the freed **African Americans**, especially in terms of alleviating their worst suffering and establishing the beginnings of an **education** system for blacks in the South. They proved less successful in helping former slaves acquire land and in establishing true equality in the Reconstruction South.

Origins

The beginnings of the Freedmen's Relief Societies can be found during the Civil War. Early in the conflict, areas of the South with large concentrations of slaves came under Union control. The most famous such place was the Sea Islands region of coastal **South Carolina** and **Georgia**. Owners fled the arrival of Union forces, leaving behind thousands of slaves. **Abolitionists** in the North proved eager to travel south to assist these **contraband** slaves. A contingent of fifty plantation agents, as well as teachers, clergy, and doctors, under the leadership of Edward L. Pierce, a Boston lawyer appointed by Treasury secretary **Salmon P. Chase**, came to the Sea Islands in spring 1862. These "Gideonites" were the vanguard of an aid movement directed at former slaves whose activities would continue into Reconstruction and in some forms, especially education, for decades thereafter.

Education

After the war, education became the dominant activity of the Freedmen's Relief Societies. The **Bureau of Refugees, Freedmen, and Abandoned Lands**, a federal agency established in March 1865, took over the massive task of providing material relief for former slaves and war refugees. The bureau encouraged private organizations, such as the **American Missionary Association**, and numerous other religious and secular groups to channel their relief efforts into building schools and providing teachers for former slaves. Within four years, these groups had established thousands of schools in the southern states, serving hundreds of thousands of students.

The operation of the schools reflected the philosophy of aid organizations that sponsored them. Both secular and religious groups sought not merely to teach former slaves reading, writing, and arithmetic, but also such qualities as self discipline and self-reliance, traits relief workers saw their charges lacking as a result of the degradation of slavery. That is, middle-class Victorian values were an integral part of the curriculum, and teachers were expected to instill their students with these principles outside as well as inside their classroom through personal example, founding organizations such as temperance groups, and intervening if necessary in their students' private lives.

In other words, the schools tried to instruct freedpeople in basic academic skills, while also insuring they would become moral, productive, and law abiding. As such, they proved as paternalistic, if more benevolent, than the former master class. Their approach could be racist, reflecting notions of moral superiority and insensitivity to the culture of former slaves. Nonetheless, the former slaves of the South eagerly embraced the educational opportunities provided, so desperate were they for the learning that had been denied them in the days of bondage.

Women

While the leadership of the Freedmen's Relief Societies was almost invariably men, the service providers on the ground during Reconstruction often were women. Indeed, a classic image of this period in the South is the

Yankee schoolmarm, gently but energetically instructing and guiding her black pupils. While there is much truth to this picture, it conceals the fact that many of the women in the aid movement were activists as well as teachers, and their efforts involved more than simply education. Indeed, some women saw assisting freedpeople as a vehicle by which they might advance reform more generally and improve the status of women in American society by giving them a voice in the formulation of public policy. Hence, women served not only as teachers, but worked as lobbyists, fundraisers, organizers, agents of the Freedmen's Bureau, and helped former slaves obtain land, as well as encouraged the migration of ex-slaves to the North. Without the contribution of women, the efforts of the Freedmen's Relief Societies in the South during Reconstruction, especially in terms of education, would not have been possible. They provided much of the personnel on the ground, translating the good intentions of northern philanthropic groups into actual results.

Blacks

Blacks were not only beneficiaries of the Freedmen's Relief Societies, but also significant contributors. Free blacks in the North, starting during the Civil War, hastened to assist their brethren in the South. Elizabeth Keckley, seamstress to Mary Todd Lincoln, founded the Contraband Relief Association in 1862 to provide aid for slaves seeking refuge in Washington, D.C. Black northerners, such as Charlotte Forten, worked as part of the **Port Royal Experiment** in South Carolina as teachers.

Illustration showing freedmen's school at St. Helena Island, South Carolina, c. 1868. (Courtesy of the Library of Congress.)

Not surprisingly, the efforts of these northern blacks in the South extended into Reconstruction. The African Civilization Society, led by **Richard H. Cain**, a clergyman in the African Methodist Episcopal Church, sought to educate former slaves and encourage racial pride. Cain and his organization believed that blacks from the North were better teachers for blacks in the South since they had greater cultural affinity than white northerners and were less judgmental. Their approach and beliefs put them somewhat at odds with white-run organizations, especially those with more racist inclinations. While there was much cooperation between white and black aid workers, they tended to distrust each others' motives and priorities. Nonetheless, they were joined in the notion that the former slaves needed a helping hand and did much to lend positive assistance to that end.

After Reconstruction

The activities of these aid groups continued on a smaller scale after the end of Reconstruction, mostly centered in the field of education. White southerners had resented greatly the activities of the Freedmen's Relief Societies in the South, correctly seeing them as undermining white supremacy. Likewise, in the 1870s, northern interest in the plight of former slaves waned as support for **Congressional Reconstruction** declined. Hence, it was necessary for aid organizations to scale back their efforts and to demonstrate to the resurgent white southerners that they posed no threat. This goal accounts for the rise of the industrial education for blacks in the South, emphasizing practical skills and moral rectitude over classical education and political activism. By the end of the nineteenth century, the radical abolitionism of the Gideonites that had characterized the Freedmen's Relief Societies at their beginning had given way to the racial accommodation of the Tuskegee Institute and Booker T. Washington. *See also* Contracts; Edisto Island, South Carolina; Howard, Oliver Otis; Labor Systems; Redemption; Republicans, Radical; U.S. Army and Reconstruction; Women's Movement.

Further Reading: Butchart, Ronald E. *Northern Schools, Southern Blacks, and Reconstruction: Freedmen's Education, 1862–1875*. Westport, CT: Greenwood Press, 1980; Faulkner, Carol. *Women's Radical Reconstruction: The Freedmen's Aid Movement*. Philadelphia: University of Pennsylvania Press, 2004; Richardson, Joe M. *Christian Reconstruction: The American Missionary Association and Southern Blacks, 1861–1890*. Athens: University of Georgia Press, 1986.

Donald R. Shaffer

G

Garfield, James Abram (1831–1881)

Sometimes referred to as the last of the so-called "log cabin" presidents, Garfield was a native of Cuyahoga County, Ohio. He traveled to Massachusetts for school, graduating from the Williams Academy in 1856. He returned to Ohio, taught and became a college president, and ran for—and won—a seat in the Ohio Senate in 1859, as a Republican. Garfield drew a commission when the Civil War began, and by age thirty-one was a brigadier general. In 1862, he was nominated for Congress by his district, and allegedly persuaded by President **Abraham Lincoln** to leave the army and accept the seat.

As a congressman in the 1860s and 1870s, James A. Garfield reflected the evolution of the Republican Party as it moved from Radicalism to reconciliation in regard to reconstructing the Union. Entering the House of Representatives in 1863, still wearing his general's uniform, he breathed a soldier's defiance against his rebel foes, urging the **abolition of slavery**, equal rights for freedmen, the confiscation of rebel estates, and the exile of Confederate leaders. Impatient with halfway measures, he criticized that "second-rate Illinois lawyer," Abraham Lincoln, for his seeming timidity, supported the **Wade-Davis Bill** and Manifesto, and allied himself with such kindred anti-Lincoln Republicans as Henry Winter Davis, Robert C. Schenck, and Garfield's Ohio mentor, **Salmon P. Chase**. Such views were applauded by his constituents of the Nineteenth Congressional District in Ohio's Western Reserve. These were the voters who had repeatedly sent Joshua Giddings to Congress, earning a reputation as the most **abolitionist** district in the nation.

Yet Garfield himself was not completely comfortable with extremist views. A man of essentially moderate, reflective instincts, he preferred to occupy the middle ground. "I am trying to do two things," he confessed, "viz. be a radical and not be a fool." Pulled one way by his temperament, another by his constituents, he veered from one position to another. Once the Civil War ended, however, his moderate instincts, for a time, gained the upper hand.

The most striking example of this tendency came not in Congress but before the U.S. **Supreme Court** in the 1866 landmark case of *Ex parte Milligan*. In this case, his very first appearance in any courtroom, he defended a group of Indiana "copperheads" (Peace Democrats) who had been convicted of treason by a military tribunal. He successfully argued that such trials were unconstitutional if civil courts were available. Later generations would hail the decision as a victory for civil liberties, but at the time, Garfield was assailed by Radicals for defending traitors and for impeding **Congressional Reconstruction** and the execution of the **Military Reconstruction Acts** in the South.

Yet, not long afterward, Garfield was back in the Radical camp, driven there by President **Andrew Johnson**'s stubborn behavior and political overtures to former rebels. He enthusiastically supported the president's **impeachment** in the House and was disappointed by the Senate's failure to convict.

Garfield's flirtation with Radicalism was only temporary and with the passage of the **Fifteenth Amendment** in 1870, he regarded the work of Reconstruction as completed. Like so many other northerners, he turned his attention from southern affairs and devoted his energies to his new passion—financial legislation, particularly a crusade on behalf of "sound money." His occasional forays into matters southern were infrequent and inconsistent. On the one hand, he attacked the 1871 attempt to put down the **Ku Klux Klan** as a violation of the civil liberties he had defended in the *Milligan* case. On the other hand, he shamelessly waved the "**bloody shirt**" during the political season. Nonetheless, he was a key figure in negotiating the so-called **Compromise of 1877**, which, in effect, ratified white political control of the southern states in return for the peaceful inauguration of President **Rutherford B. Hayes**.

Four years later, Garfield himself was sworn in as president. In his inaugural address he deplored the **disfranchisement** of southern blacks by the white regimes he had helped install, but his only concrete proposal was a promise to encourage public **education** in the southern states. He was discussing this very matter with Secretary of State **James G. Blaine** on July 2, 1881, when two bullets from assassin Charles J. Guiteau interrupted the conversation and ended the Republican general's life and his administration. *See also* Black Suffrage; Enforcement Acts; Grant, Ulysses S.; Presidential Reconstruction; Redemption; U.S. Constitution; Violence.

Further Reading: Garfield, James A. *Works.* 2 vols. Boston: n.p., 1883; Peskin, Allan: *Garfield.* Kent, OH: Kent State University Press, 1978; "President Garfield and the Southern Question." *Southern Quarterly* 16, no. 4 (1978): 375–86.

Allan Peskin

Garrison, William Lloyd (1805–1879)

William Lloyd Garrison, white **abolitionist**, journalist, and social reformer, was born on December 10, 1805, in Newburyport, Massachusetts. The circumstances of his youth, a religiously inspired reform culture, and increasing black opposition to slavery shaped his life. A radical on issues of slavery and race during most of his career, Garrison became more conservative during the Civil War and Reconstruction.

Early Years

Garrison was the third of four children born to Abijah Garrison, a heavy-drinking seaman, and Frances (Lloyd) Garrison, an evangelical Baptist. Abijah abandoned the family in 1808, plunging it into poverty and stiffening Frances's resolve to instill a Christian conscience in each of her children. Her two daughters died before reaching adulthood, her elder son resisted her influence, and Lloyd—as he was called—became the recipient of her intense moralism.

In 1818, he became an apprentice in the office of the *Newburyport Herald*. There he learned to set type, gained a liberal **education**, and studied the writings of New England Federalists, whose condemnation of immorality reinforced his mother's. Between 1826 and 1828, Garrison edited reformist newspapers in Newburyport and Boston. Regarding himself as a "universal reformer," he wrote against the consumption of alcoholic beverages, Sunday mail delivery, lotteries, war, and racial oppression, but he failed to attract subscribers and the newspapers either failed or let him go.

In mid-1828, Garrison met Benjamin Lundy, a white Quaker abolitionist who published the *Genius of Universal Emancipation* in the slaveholding city of Baltimore. Inspired by Lundy, Garrison began his abolitionist career as editor of the *Journal of the Times* in Burlington, Vermont. Like Lundy and other abolitionists of the time, Garrison advocated gradual abolition and supported the American Colonization Society (ACS), which advocated transporting former slaves to Africa. By April 1829, when he moved to Baltimore to become coeditor of the *Genius of Universal Emancipation*, Garrison had begun to advocate immediate **emancipation** without expatriation.

Immediatism

In Baltimore, Garrison observed the brutality of slavery, lived and worked with black abolitionists, and read black abolitionist David Walker's *Appeal*. Although Garrison rejected Walker's endorsement of antislavery **violence**, he became a more determined advocate of **African American** rights. Garrison's denunciation of a slave trader led to a libel suit and, when he could not pay a $100 fine, to his imprisonment in a Baltimore jail. He remained there for forty-nine days, until wealthy New York City abolitionists Arthur and Lewis Tappan paid the fine.

The notoriety Garrison gained from his imprisonment prompted him to undertake a speaking tour in the Northeast to promote immediate abolitionism. He also raised money to finance his weekly *Liberator*, which began publication in Boston during January 1831. He declared in the first issue, "I am in earnest—I will not equivocate—I will not excuse—I will not retreat a single inch, and *I will be heard*." Dependent on black financial contributions and subscribers, *The Liberator* became the leading American abolitionist newspaper of the 1830s.

During the early years of that decade, Garrison promoted immediatist organizations and denounced the ACS as proslavery and racist. In December 1832, he helped establish the biracial New England Anti-Slavery Society. In 1833, he toured Great Britain ostensibly to raise money for a black manual labor school, but also to ally himself with British immediatists. At the end of the year at a meeting in Philadelphia, he led in the formation of the American Anti-Slavery Society (AASS). Garrison's moral views and Nat Turner's 1831 **Virginia** slave revolt shaped the society's rejection of violent means and its tactic of appealing to the conscience of slaveholders and other Americans. It contended that slaveholding was a sin and a crime and African Americans had a right to equality in the United States.

By 1835, the AASS, which represented a tiny minority of northerners, had undertaken massive efforts to petition Congress for the **abolition of slavery** in the **District of Columbia**, to send antislavery propaganda into the South, and promote the discussion of slavery in the North. These efforts produced an antiabolitionist and antiblack reaction. Congress refused to receive petitions related to slavery. Southern states banned the postal delivery of antislavery publications. All across the North, rioters attacked abolitionists and invaded black neighborhoods. In October 1835, a Boston mob captured Garrison and he barely escaped death.

A year earlier, Garrison had married Helen Benson, the daughter of one of his abolitionist allies. The couple had seven children and their home in Roxbury, Massachusetts, became a center for visiting abolitionists of both races. Helen also made their home a haven that provided Garrison with insulation from his hectic and dangerous career. The intensity of the reaction nevertheless convinced him that slavery had so corrupted American society that abolition alone could not redeem it. To avoid God's wrath, the nation required fundamental reform. Influenced by Christian perfectionism, Garrison embraced nonresistance, a philosophy that rejected all violence, including that exercised by government. Since government rested on force, Garrison and his closest associates became anarchists, refusing to vote or hold elective office. They maintained that the **U.S. Constitution** was a proslavery document. Garrison also opposed organized religion as superstitious, proslavery, and corrupting. Decrying patriarchal oppression, he supported the fledgling **women's movement**.

Most immediatists objected to Garrison's radical reform vision. They believed it kept potential recruits from joining the antislavery movement. Many black abolitionists regarded Garrison's rhetoric as impractical. Nearly all but his New England associates assumed that for moral suasion to succeed, it had to be allied with an independent abolitionist political party. Antiabolitionist violence in the North and signs of slave unrest in the South led relentlessly toward rejection of Garrison's pacifism. After several years of turmoil, the AASS shattered in 1840. While he and his associates retained control of the "old organization," most abolitionists—black and white—departed. Garrison's relations with the new **church**-oriented American and Foreign Anti-Slavery Society and Liberty Party remained bitter into the 1850s.

Starting in 1842, Garrison maintained that only dissolution of the Union could save northerners from the sin of slavery and promote abolition in the

South. On July 4, 1854, he burned a copy of the U.S. Constitution. Yet, he was not impractical. He understood that, as a radical, he had to influence the nation's politics. Therefore, while he condemned the tiny Liberty Party, he regarded the Free Soil Party, formed in 1848, and the Republican Party, formed between 1854 and 1856, as indications that nonabolitionist northerners were becoming more antagonistic to slavery. Although these mass political parties officially opposed only the expansion of slavery and slaveholder control of the U.S. government, Garrison encouraged them to take more advanced antislavery stands.

In the Civil War and Reconstruction

Proslavery leaders charged that Garrison, despite his pacifism, favored slave revolt and war between the sections. Nevertheless he was one of the few immediatists who remained committed to nonresistance at the time of John Brown's 1859 raid at Harpers Ferry, Virginia. Not until the Civil War began in April 1861 did Garrison contradict his earlier views and become a strong supporter of President **Abraham Lincoln**'s forceful effort to preserve the Union.

The Civil War made Garrison popular in the North, and his new status greatly gratified him. Like other immediatists, he urged Lincoln to make general emancipation a goal of the war and to enlist **black troops** on an equal basis with white troops. Garrison favored a constitutional amendment to permanently abolish slavery, but he withdrew from his role as an agitator and supported Lincoln's cautious approach to changing the South. Strangely, he defended Lincoln and the conservative and **Moderate Republicans** against those who advocated more rapid progress toward emancipation and black rights. In 1863 and 1864, he disagreed when his immediatist colleague **Wendell Phillips** and some **Radical Republicans** advocated providing land to former slaves, **black suffrage**, a constitutional amendment to prohibit racial discrimination, and an extended postwar military occupation of the former Confederacy.

In April 1865, shortly after the war ended but before the **assassination of Lincoln**, Garrison visited Charleston, **South Carolina**, where he addressed former slaves, declaring that they had the same "inalienable rights" as white people. The following month, believing that he and other abolitionists had achieved their goal, he called on the AASS to disband. When the great majority of members rejected his proposal, he and most of his Massachusetts colleagues withdrew from the organization. Following the ratification of the **Thirteenth Amendment** in December 1865, he ceased publication of the *Liberator*.

Garrison assumed that former slaves could advance themselves without national intervention to force white southerners to recognizing black rights. As it became clear in 1866 that white southerners would return most African Americans to slavery in all but name, he became more supportive of national government action to protect the freedpeople. By then, however, he was no longer a prominent figure in the debate over Reconstruction. He longed to retire, although he continued to speak in favor of prohibition, women's rights, a more enlightened policy toward **American Indians**, and black **civil**

rights. He died in New York City on May 24, 1879. *See also* Black Codes; Congressional Reconstruction; Disfranchisement; Presidential Reconstruction.

Further Reading: Mayer, Henry. *All on Fire: William Lloyd Garrison and the Abolition of Slavery*. New York: St. Martin's Press, 1998; Merrill, Walter M. *Against Wind and Tide: A Biography of William Lloyd Garrison*. Cambridge, MA: Harvard University Press, 1965; Stewart, James Brewer. *William Lloyd Garrison and the Challenge of Emancipation*. Arlington Heights, IL: Harlan Davidson, 1992; Thomas, John L. *The Liberator: William Lloyd Garrison, A Biography*. Boston: Little, Brown, 1963.

Stanley Harrold

Gary, Martin Witherspoon (1831–1881)

Known as the "Bald Eagle of Edgefield" because of his personality and appearance, Martin Witherspoon Gary played a primary role in helping the **South Carolina Democratic Party** reassert political control during Reconstruction.

Born on March 25, 1831, in Cokesbury, South Carolina, Gary attended South Carolina College from 1850 to 1852. Because of his participation in a student uprising (the Biscuit Rebellion), he withdrew from the college and enrolled at Harvard University, graduating in 1854. Gary returned to western South Carolina, where he studied law under Edgefield lawyer James Parsons Carroll. Admitted to the bar in 1855, he established a law practice in Edgefield and, in 1860, won election to the state legislature, where he strongly favored secession. Already a cavalry colonel in the South Carolina **militia**, Gary enlisted in the Confederate army as an infantry captain in Hampton's Legion. He participated in major battles including First and Second Manassas, Antietam, Fredericksburg, and Chickamauga. Gary was promoted to lieutenant colonel of infantry in June 1862, colonel in August 1862, and brigadier general in May 1864, whereupon he assumed command of all cavalry in and around Richmond, Virginia. In early April 1865, Gary received the rank of major general. Refusing to surrender at Appomattox, Gary and a small contingent of his forces joined with **Jefferson Davis** in Greensboro, **North Carolina**, and escorted the fleeing Confederate president as far as Cokesbury, South Carolina.

After the war, Gary resumed his legal practice in Edgefield. He became heavily involved in Democratic politics, crafting the "Edgefield Plan" to support Democratic candidates through fraud, voter intimidation, and vigilante action. Adamantly refusing fusion with **carpetbag**, **scalawag**, and **African American** Republicans, Gary led the "Straight-out" faction of the Democratic Party in support of **Wade Hampton III**'s successful 1876 gubernatorial election. That same year, Gary was also elected senator to the Fifty-second South Carolina General Assembly (1876–1878), although Republicans contested his victory and he was not officially seated until federal troops were removed from the state in April 1877. In 1878, Gary was reelected to a second term in the state senate (1878–1880) but some Democrats, including conservative Democrats, aligned behind Wade Hampton, and began to distance themselves from Gary's racial extremism and agrarian politics. He lost elections to the U.S.

Senate in 1877 and 1879, and became increasingly vitriolic toward his Democratic opponents. After losing the gubernatorial election of 1880 to one of Hampton's successors, Johnson Hagood, Gary returned to Edgefield. He died in 1881 after a brief illness. *See also* Chamberlain, Daniel Henry; Compromise of 1877; Congressional Reconstruction; Elections of 1876; Grant, Ulysses S.; Gun Clubs; Redemption; Shotgun Plan; U.S. Army and Reconstruction; Violence.

Further Reading: Bailey, N. Louise, Mary L. Morgan, and Carolyn R. Taylor. *Biographical Dictionary of the South Carolina Senate, 1776-1985.* Vol. 1. Columbia: University of South Carolina Press, 1986, pp. 552-54; Zuczek, Richard. *State of Rebellion: Reconstruction in South Carolina.* Columbia: University of South Carolina Press, 1996.

Kimberly R. Kellison

Georgia

The Reconstruction of Georgia (1865–1871) began in May 1865, with the end of the Civil War and the surrender of Georgia's Confederate governor, **Joseph E. Brown**. Much of the South was destroyed by the economic disruption of **agriculture**, the lack of social order, and the political overhaul inspired by the war. The Reconstruction of the South involved a three-pronged plan: restoring the South to the Union, reorganizing the structure of its society, and implementing legislation to address the rights of former slaves. President **Abraham Lincoln** issued a Proclamation of **Amnesty** and Reconstruction in 1863 that would allow southern states to be readmitted to the Union following certain steps. After President Lincoln's **assassination**, President **Andrew Johnson** adopted his plans and began to implement many of his strategies for bringing the South back into the Union.

Georgia and Johnson's Reconstruction

Georgia's road to Reconstruction began with President Johnson's appointment of a **provisional governor** to manage the difficult process of transforming the state economically, politically, and socially. On June 17, 1865, President Andrew Johnson appointed James Johnson provisional governor of Georgia. Governor Johnson had been a respected lawyer in Columbus, Georgia, and later became a member of Congress who opposed secession in 1861. Provisional Governor Johnson called for the election of delegates to a convention in Milledgeville, which took place in October 1865. The purpose of this convention was to restore Georgia to the Union, a goal Governor Johnson accepted when he accepted the president's appointment.

On October 3, 1865, the Georgia delegates met for the first time and were led by two men at the convention as they worked to frame a state constitution. **Charles Jones Jenkins** was the presiding officer and Herschel V. Johnson was chairman of the committee on business. Although both men were antisecessionists, their selection would create controversy among **Radical Republicans**, who later criticized Governor Johnson's handling of the state.

The convention's delegates developed a new constitution that repealed the Ordinance of Secession and declared the **abolition of slavery**. Another primary task for the conventions' delegates was the repudiation of the state's war debt. This was a hotly debated topic that became the most difficult issue to resolve. A bone of contention for many delegates, this issue raised such ire among committee participants that on November 6, Jenkins reported in the *Journal of the Constitutional Convention* that the committee was not able to agree on the resolution of this debt. Jenkins asked for a discharge, but the issue was finally resolved because committee members became convinced that repudiation was necessary for Georgia's restoration. There were not many differences between the state's early constitution in 1861 and this new one, under which the state applied for **readmission** to the Union.

A state election occurred on November 15, 1865, with Charles J. Jenkins as the only candidate for governorship. Jenkins was a conservative who seemed to rally the support of Georgians comfortable with his record of service in the government of Georgia. On December 5–6, 1865, the Georgia General Assembly ratified the **Thirteenth Amendment** to the **U.S. Constitution**, which abolished slavery. The new Georgia Assembly also enacted legislation concerning freedmen, which included a series of eleven laws for the regulation of freedmen's rights that were reported to Governor Charles Jenkins on December 19, 1865.

Freedmen's Bureau and Freed Blacks in Georgia

The **Bureau of Refugees, Freedmen, and Abandoned Lands** (the Freedmen's Bureau) was created in 1865 by Congress to provide food and supplies, establish schools, and redistribute land to former slaves and poor whites throughout the South. Through this initiative, any person who pledged loyalty to the Union could lease and later have the option to purchase forty acres of land from the Freedmen's Bureau. This concept was problematic for many southerners, and represented the problems inherent in the development of the bureau. White southerners often viewed the bureau as a means to enfranchise blacks and give away land that had formerly belonged to whites. This led to abuses against blacks that in some cases forced them to give up their land rather than risk being beaten or killed by irate whites who felt that the blacks should not own this land. The Freedmen's Bureau failed in its efforts to distribute land en masse to blacks, but was successful in setting up schools throughout the South for more than 200,000 free blacks.

The bureau faced many obstacles. In many of the former Confederate states, a backlash occurred among whites who believed that blacks were benefiting to the detriment of whites. As a result, the establishment of **Black Codes** in many southern states led to the highly regulated postwar position for **African Americans**. Although Georgia is noted as a state that did not create official Black Codes, its laws did deny blacks many rights, including the right to serve as jurors or to vote.

The work of the Freedmen's Bureau was understood differently by various groups of people. The organization primarily focused on issues that were educational, political, judicial, industrial, and social. Henry M. Turner joined the African Methodist Episcopal **Church** in Georgia in 1864, after resigning a commission within the Freedmen's Bureau that had been assigned to him by

President Andrew Johnson. Later, under **Congressional Reconstruction**, Turner encouraged black political independence and became a powerful **black politician** in the state of Georgia. Even before this, in January 1866, more than forty black delegates met in convention to discuss the issue of **education** for blacks. Supported by the Freedmen's Bureau's head, General Davis Tillson, the delegates established the Georgia Equal Rights and Educational Association to educate freedmen and secure equal rights for all citizens, regardless of race or color.

Radical Republicans and a New Reconstruction, 1865–1868

By the end of 1865, the former Confederate states had established new constitutions and elected new state and federal officers. With this, President Johnson declared Reconstruction completed in December 1865. However, the 39th Congress, which convened at the end of 1865, believed differently, and firmly blocked the restoration of these states. Republicans in Congress argued that the states had not been penalized for seceding from the Union and, more important, would not be inspired to change until forced to do so. Congress then began to put in place certain safeguards for the freedpeople and certain constraints on the former Confederates, embodied in **civil rights** bills, new **Freedmen's Bureau bills**, and eventually the **Fourteenth Amendment**. Conservative Johnson vetoed the Civil Rights Bill and Congress's attempt to renew the charter of the Freedmen's Bureau. Congress later successfully overrode Johnson's veto, and the Freedmen Bureau's charter was renewed. After several months of reviewing the conditions of the former Confederate states, Congress began to consider further reconstructing the South through a variety of means.

The ratification of a proposed Fourteenth Amendment was almost unanimously rejected in Georgia's legislature in November 1866. In spite of Johnson's views, Congress successfully passed the **Civil Rights Act of 1866** and later passed the Fourteenth Amendment. In March 1867, Congress passed the **Military Reconstruction Act**, which divided the South into five districts, each governed by an Army general who supervised the execution of the acts. Georgia was part of the Third Military District, governed by General **John Pope**, who registered eligible black and white voters according to the new constitution. To protest the changes that were occurring as a result of the new acts, in April 1867, Governor Charles Jenkins traveled to Washington and filed a petition before the **Supreme Court** for an injunction against the enforcement of the Reconstruction Act. The courts dismissed his petition in May of that year.

Jenkins conceded the loss and issued an Address to the People of Georgia that advised them not to act under the Act to avoid tensions and **violence** in the state. Georgia blacks, including Henry Turner and others, organized a black Republican Party in May 1867 that focused on forming alliances with white Republicans. The black-white Republican alliance in Georgia was instrumental in organizing mass meetings of blacks in rallies to support the registration of black voters and encourage celebrations of the congressional Reconstruction Acts.

In October and November 1867, an election was held for delegates to a **constitutional convention** that would meet from December 1867 to March

1868. A new state constitution was framed that included **black suffrage**, the establishment of free public schools, the move of the seat of state government from Milledgeville to Atlanta, and numerous other changes. The constitution was ratified in April and the new governor, Republican candidate **Rufus Bullock**, was elected.

In July 1868, the Georgia Assembly ratified the Fourteenth Amendment, inaugurated Governor Bullock to a four-year term, and at this point, the Reconstruction of Georgia was complete when the state was readmitted to the Union. However, it was also during this period that Georgia Democrats began to pressure the Georgia Assembly to reconsider Congressional Reconstruction. White Republicans who worked with blacks were labeled as **carpetbaggers** or **scalawags** based upon their affiliations with the South. Carpetbaggers were people who came from the North after the war and attempted to benefit from the South's political changes by becoming active under provisions that allowed one-year residents to hold office. Carpetbaggers were often viewed as greedy northerners who wanted to gain financially through their work in the South. Scalawags were whites born in the South or who had lived in the South before the war and were part of the Republican Party. These terms were important because they typically influenced the political agenda of an individual. Scalawags became extremely powerful in the Georgia Assembly and began to influence other whites to oust black legislators who had recently gained political status. Although scalawags by definition were Republicans, they often held more conservative views rooted in their southern upbringing.

Another major influence on the political evolution of Georgia during this period was the creation of an organization called the **Ku Klux Klan**. This organization was instrumental in organizing brutal, violent attacks against blacks who sought political or social enfranchisement. The Klan was blamed for the murder of Georgia Radical George W. Ashburn, a staunch Republican and advocate for blacks' civil rights. Several men were brought to trial but never convicted in spite of eyewitness accounts of the shooting. The Klan was also instrumental in further thwarting activities by blacks to gain economic, political, and social equality.

In September 1868, the black Republican Party planned to hold a rally in a small Georgia town known as Camilla. Prior to the scheduled event, there was a confrontation between blacks and whites that led to the killing of twelve blacks and the injuring of several whites. Known as the Camilla Massacre, this was one of many incidents during this period that was indicative of the precarious nature of blacks' political strivings. White Republicans also suffered at the hands of organized efforts by whites to curtail the efforts to secure civil rights for blacks. This period also began to signal the decline of black political agency and power and signify the ushering in of a new era that would signal the demise of Reconstruction.

Democratic Resurgence and the End of Georgia Reconstruction, 1869–1872

In an effort to finance public education, Republican politicians worked to implement a **poll tax**. Soon, it became evident that the poll tax would have negative consequences for black voters. Governor **Rufus Bullock** suspended the poll tax in November 1868 because he and others recognized that it would **disfranchise** black voters, but it was too late because once this tax had been introduced, Democrats recognized its value at controlling the ballot box.

In 1869, Congress passed the **Fifteenth Amendment**, which prohibited voting discrimination based on race. This amendment was ratified in 1870, but allowed a great many loopholes, including the poll tax. In December 1870, Georgia conservatives won back many seats in the General Assembly election for the November 1871 convening. The poll tax was reinstated, which, along with reports of intimidation by the Ku Klux Klan, reduced the black vote significantly.

Governor Rufus Bullock was castigated by Democrats and poorly perceived by many Republicans because of his views on military occupation and his personal affiliations. Bullock's activities were troubling to those who viewed him as a polarizing force within the Republican Party. His advocacy for blacks garnered him much of the black Republican support, but it did not secure his position as Georgia's governor. In fact, many Republicans began to recognize that Bullock had lost his political power and was likely to be impeached due to the political current of the state. As a result, blacks began to seriously consider how they would seek political redress under the circumstances. Some considered joining forces with sympathetic Democrats in hopes of retaining some of their political power.

Governor Bullock resigned in October 1871, recognizing that he would soon be impeached by Democrats who had retaken control of the legislature. Upon his resignation, Bullock warned Georgians that if they voted for leaders who ignored the Fourteenth and Fifteenth Amendments, then they risked never being able to incorporate the South into the mainstream of the United States. White conservative Democrats were called the Redeemers, and they were back in office with a stringent political agenda by 1872. Although Reconstruction in some southern states did not end until 1877, Reconstruction ended for Georgians with the election of both a Democratic governor (James Smith) and a Democratic legislature in January 1872. *See also* Presidential Reconstruction; Race Riots; Redemption; Union League of America.

Further Reading: Cimbala, Paul. *Under the Guardianship of the Nation: The Freedmen's Bureau and the Reconstruction of Georgia, 1865–1870.* Athens: University of Georgia Press, 1997; Drago, Edmund. *Black Politicians and Reconstruction in Georgia.* Baton Rouge: Louisiana State University Press, 1982; Thompson, Mildred. *Reconstruction in Georgia.* New York: Books for Library Press, 1915; reprinted 1971; Wetherington, Mark. *Plain Folks Fight: Civil War and Reconstruction in Piney Woods, Georgia.* Chapel Hill: University of North Carolina Press, 2005.

Kijua Sanders-McMurtry

Godkin, Edwin Lawrence (1831–1902)

A critical journalist regarding most events and policies during Reconstruction, Godkin was born in Ireland of English parents. He received a first-rate education at the Royal Institute and Queen's College in Belfast. He began his career in journalism covering the Crimean War for the *London Daily News*. During the American Civil War, Godkin supported the Union cause.

In 1865, he became the editor in chief of *The Nation*, an **abolitionist** journal of opinion, politics, and culture. Given that abolitionists had established the magazine, Godkin quickly redirected it into the safe ideological harbor of social conservatism. He disliked all forms of radicalism and reform, and the magazine reflected Godkin's opinion (and prejudices) until his retirement. He was a nineteenth-century liberal, which included a laissez-faire policy regarding politics and public policy. His conception of liberty meant a limited government operating within strict constitutional limits. In that way, Godkin was a pioneer critic of modern liberals and the future twentieth-century welfare state. His opposition to an activist government was consistent, and led to his rejection of many elements of the **Radical Republicans'** Reconstruction policy.

Godkin was a strong critic of democracy, desiring a very restrictive franchise and opposing women's and **black suffrage**. It logically followed that he endorsed immigration restriction. His social thought had a strong nativist hue. Organized labor according to him had a baneful effect on public policy. The rise of democratic values in the popular culture was the death toll of artistic taste and discernment. In brief, Godkin opposed "chromo-civilization," which constituted a culture of gossip, **scandal**, and sensationalism.

Always conservative, he supported the gold standard and civil service reform because both solutions kept the great unwashed away from the center of power. After 1881, when *The Nation* and the *New York Evening Post* merged, he attacked all forms of imperialism, including the Spanish-American War. Only an educated elite of taste and conservative sensibilities could save the Republic. He was a leading spokesman for anti-Democratic Anglo-American intellectuals. He thought democracy was a sham and a fake. While he saw Tammany Hall as corrupt, he supported Grover Cleveland in 1884, despite subscribers' protests and boycotts.

He remained a vocal advocate for an aristocratic liberalism. He rejected political parties, which delighted some intellectuals. Soon after his retirement, he died in Brixham, England. *See also* Congressional Reconstruction; Johnson, Andrew; Republicans, Liberal; U.S. Constitution; Women's Movement.

Further Reading: Armstrong, William M.: *E. L. Godkin: A Biography*. Albany: State University of New York Press, 1987; *E. L. Godkin and American Foreign Policy*. New York: Bookman Associates, 1957; Armstrong, William M., ed. *The Gilded Age Letters of E. L. Godkin*. Albany: State University of New York Press, 1974; Pringle, Henry F. "Great American Editor: E. L. Godkin." *Scribner's Magazine* 96 (December 1934): 327–34.

Donald K. Pickens

Gordon, John B. (1832–1904)

John Brown Gordon, Confederate major general and postwar politician, was born in **Georgia** on February 6, 1832. He attended the University of Georgia, but left that institution early to study law. At the outbreak of the Civil War, he was engaged in mining operations in northwest Georgia in partnership with his father.

Gordon entered the Civil War as a captain and rose in the ranks through arduous service that included a severe wounding at Sharpsburg (Antietam) in September 1862. His duties with the Army of Northern **Virginia** encompassed the major campaigns of the Eastern Theater in the war. On March 25, 1865, General Robert E. Lee chose Gordon's command for an assault on Fort Stedman in an attempt to lift the Union stranglehold on the Confederates at Petersburg. At Appomattox, when General Lee surrendered the army, Gordon poignantly offered a return salute to one given the defeated southerners by Joshua Lawrence Chamberlain.

Following the conflict, Gordon returned to Atlanta to resume the practice of law. Later, when law failed to provide him with sufficient financial support, he became president of the Atlanta branch of the Southern Life Insurance Company of Memphis. During this period, Gordon also became increasingly active in politics, supporting the **Democratic Party**. In 1868, he ran unsuccessfully for the governorship of Georgia against Republican **Rufus B. Bullock**, and was one of a number of prominent ex-Confederates to attend the **Democratic National Convention** in New York City, including **Nathan Bedford Forrest** and **Wade Hampton**.

At the same time, coinciding with a visit to Georgia by General Forrest, Gordon became involved with the **Ku Klux Klan** in the state, reputedly holding the post of Grand Dragon. Both Forrest and Gordon touted the organization—to which each denied actual membership—as existing solely for self-protection and made up only of the best sort of leading citizens and ex-Confederates. Both men also testified about the secret society before a congressional committee investigating Klan activity in 1871.

In 1873, the Georgia legislature selected Gordon for the U.S. Senate. He held that seat until 1880 and again in 1891–1897, playing a key role in helping to break the political impasse created by the disputed presidential **election of 1876**. Gordon interspersed his time in the Senate with work in the private sector and two terms as governor of Georgia (1886–1890). He was considered part of a powerful set of Democratic leaders in the state that represented a commercializing and industrializing **New South**. He also became active in the United Confederate Veterans, serving as that organization's commander until his death. Gordon completed his wartime memoirs, *Reminiscences of the Civil War* in 1903, shortly before dying in Miami, **Florida**, on January 9, 1904. *See also* Compromise of 1877; Congressional Reconstruction; Enforcement Acts; Grant, Ulysses S.; Redemption; Violence.

Further Reading: Bartley, Numan V. *The Creation of Modern Georgia*. Athens: University of Georgia Press, 1983; Eckert, Ralph Lowell. *John Brown Gordon: Soldier, Southerner, American*. Baton Rouge: Louisiana State University Press, 1989; Tankersley, Allen P. *John B. Gordon: A Study in Gallantry*. Atlanta: Whitehall Press, 1955.

Brian S. Wills

Gould, Jay (1836–1892)

Jay Gould, a financier and securities trader who first rose to national prominence during early Reconstruction, was perhaps the most notorious of the powerful businessmen sometimes known as "robber barons." Born to a poor farm family in Roxbury, New York, Gould displayed an early knack for real estate speculation as a teenager. By his early twenties, Gould was part-owner of a profitable Pennsylvania leathery tannery, and his partner's suicide in the wake of the Panic of 1857 left the first taint of **scandal** around Gould's name. It would not be the last.

Three Reconstruction-era episodes epitomized Gould's career and served to define his character in the public eye. First, in 1867–1868, Gould, along with James Fisk, aligned himself with Daniel Drew in stock speculations on the Erie **Railroad** (one of the four major trunk lines to lucrative midwestern markets) in order to contest its takeover by the aging Cornelius Vanderbilt. During the widely reported legal clash that ensued, Gould and Fisk stole across the Hudson River in the dead of night from New York City to New Jersey in March 1868 with the Erie's account books to prevent the Vanderbilt faction from assuming control of the railroad, which Gould was finally compelled to relinquish in 1872. Second, and even more damaging to Gould's reputation (if not his growing fortune), were his subsequent machinations to corner the U.S. gold market, which resulted in a major financial panic known as "Black Friday" on September 24, 1869. It soon came to light that Gould's efforts to influence federal fiscal policy in favor of his scheme had involved the brother-in-law of President **Ulysses S. Grant**, thus helping lend an early aura of corruption to that administration.

Finally, during the 1870s, the so-called "Mephistopheles of Wall Street" turned his attention further west, to the emergent transcontinental railroad systems and the communications network that paralleled them. His battles for control of the Union Pacific railroad and the Western Union telegraph company, among others, cemented his reputation as a ruthless if effective corporate speculator. Yet, critics charged that, under his ownership, properties were usually mismanaged and poorly maintained. Gould would gain further notoriety because of his hostility to the growing organized-labor movement, especially during the southwestern railroad strike of 1886.

During the Reconstruction era, individual businessmen fully emerged onto the national stage as celebrities, but even his recent champions admit that Gould was a terrible performer in this respect. An intensely private man, he had little talent for justifying himself to the public, and as his career progressed, he became increasingly ill-tempered in the face of the relentless attacks on his ethics and character. Anti-Semitism likely played a role in the tenor of these assaults, since Gould was long mistakenly identified as Jewish. Still, his reputation was not helped by the miserly philanthropic contributions he made during his lifetime; and upon his death in 1892, Gould bequeathed all of his $72 million estate to his family. It is perhaps testament to the ephemeral nature of the speculations in which Gould engaged so successfully that he proved unable to leave behind a self-sustaining fortune that far outlived him, as did his contemporaries like the Vanderbilts, Carnegies, and Rockefellers. *See also* Democratic Party; Elections of 1876; Panic of 1873.

Further Reading: Grodinsky, Julius. *Jay Gould: His Business Career, 1867–1892.* Philadelphia: University of Pennsylvania Press, 1957; Josephson, Matthew. *The Robber Barons.* New York: Harcourt, 1934; Klein, Maury. *The Life and Legend of Jay Gould.* Baltimore, MD: Johns Hopkins University Press, 1986.

Scott P. Marler

Grant, Ulysses S. (1822–1885)

Ulysses S. Grant, Union army general who rose to command of all federal armies by the end of the American Civil War, and became president of the United States from 1869 to 1877, based his fame as the architect of Union military victory over the Confederacy. Grant's still-controversial role in the politics of Reconstruction cannot be understood apart from his role in the winning of the Civil War.

Career before the Civil War

Born Hiram Ulysses Grant in Point Pleasant, Ohio, on April 27, 1822, Grant was the son of Jesse Root Grant and Hannah Simpson Grant. Grant's father was a farmer and tanner in frontier Ohio. Jesse Grant's activism in local Whig Party politics, where he acquired a reputation for antislavery opinions, permitted him to obtain an appointment for his son to the U.S. Military Academy at West Point, New York. Upon entry to the Military Academy in 1839, he permitted his name to be changed to Ulysses Simpson Grant, for reasons that have never been entirely clear. It was partly a clerical error attributable to the congressman who nominated him as a cadet, but Grant's own fear of being identified by the initials of his given name, "H.U.G.," appear to have contributed to his refusal to correct the error. Whatever the true reason, for the rest of his life, he went by the name of Ulysses Simpson Grant, giving rise to his famous nicknames—"U.S." Grant, or "Sam" Grant, which associated him in the minds of his many supporters with the ideas of Unconditional Surrender, Uncle Sam, and the United States.

As a cadet, Grant gave little indication that he would become the most dominant general of nineteenth-century America. He excelled in no subject in the classroom, finishing a mediocre twenty-first out of thirty-nine graduating cadets in the class of 1843. Among his fellow cadets, he was amiably regarded by many, but distinguished only by his sure grasp of horsemanship, a talent he had brought with him from Ohio. Upon graduation in June 1843, he was commissioned as a second lieutenant in the infantry and assigned to duty at Jefferson Barracks, outside of St. Louis, Missouri, where he met his future wife, Julia Dent.

In the spring of 1845, Grant, along with most of the **U.S. Army**, was assigned to duty under the command of General Zachary Taylor on the disputed border between **Texas** and Mexico. Taylor had been ordered to the border by President

James K. Polk, who had been elected on a platform calling for the annexation of Texas and an aggressive expansion of U.S. territory. After Mexican troops attacked a detachment of Taylor's soldiers on the American side of the Rio Grande River, Congress declared war on Mexico. In the campaigns that followed, Grant distinguished himself as a combat leader. Following American victories at Palo Alto and Resaca de la Palma, Grant accompanied Taylor's army to Monterey, where he fought in the brief siege in September 1846. He then transferred with his regiment, the Fourth Infantry, to the command of General Winfield Scott, who had been preparing a campaign against Mexico City commencing in the coastal port of Vera Cruz. Again, Grant distinguished himself in the sharp fighting that characterized Scott's campaign. At the battle at Molino del Rey on September 8, 1847, and the battle of Chapaultepec on September 13, 1847, which effectively ended the resistance of the Mexican army, Grant exhibited the great coolness under fire and stubborn determination to prevail that would characterize his generalship in the Civil War.

After the war, Grant returned to the United States, where his first order of business was to marry Julia. The Grants' marriage was a happy one, which produced four children, and Julia remained a stabilizing influence on Grant throughout his life. The peacetime army, however, brought scant satisfaction to Grant. With the end of the war with Mexico came the return of the monotonous routines of an army in garrison and the temptations of alcohol that went with it. Rumors and legends of Grant's drinking habits and alleged alcoholism date from this period. What is certain is that Grant was sent to the Oregon frontier in 1852 without his family and in 1854, he resigned from the army, almost certainly under the threat of dishonor and court-martial for drunkenness.

What followed was the lowest period of Grant's life. Stripped of the only profession he had ever known, he found himself compelled to return to St. Louis to a small plot of land he dubbed "Hardscrabble," which his father-in-law had deeded to him. For the next five years, he struggled to support his family by farming and engaging in a variety of petty commerce. All of these ventures failed, increasing both Grant's indebtedness and his sense of despair. In the spring of 1860, he moved his family to Galena, Illinois, where his father and brother had established a leather store. There, he heard the news that war had broken out between the North and the South.

Union General and Strategist

Once hostilities began, Grant's rise was meteoric, and the qualities he had displayed during the Mexican War returned to the fore. In Galena, he quickly organized a volunteer company of infantry in the first rush of outrage sweeping across the North after the firing on Ft. Sumter in Charleston, **South Carolina**, in April 1861. By early summer, he had been called to the capital at Springfield, Illinois, where he gained command of the Twenty-first Illinois Infantry Regiment and a commission as a colonel in the Union army. By August 1861, after a successful skirmish across the Mississippi River into Missouri, the U.S. Army appointed him brigadier general and he continued to show great skill in turning green farmhands and mechanics into competent soldiers. On

November 7, 1861, he launched an attack on the Confederates at Belmont, Missouri, and despite a determined Confederate counterattack, Grant's troops fought well under fire.

After Belmont, a strategy of seizing control of the vast river system of the American heartland crystallized in Grant's mind. Grant reasoned that the Union could use a combination of naval and land power to seize key points along the tributaries of the Mississippi River, enter deep into Confederate territory, cutting it into pieces and weakening its resistance to the point of defeat. In February 1862, he captured Forts Henry and Donelson on the Tennessee and Cumberland Rivers and forced the "unconditional surrender" of Confederate general Simon B. Buckner. In April 1862, at Shiloh Landing, he turned back the army of Confederate general Albert Sidney Johnston in a horrific two-day bloodbath that caused 13,000 Union casualties, and then marched upriver to Corinth, **Mississippi**. Grant's forces successfully defended Corinth against a Confederate attack in October 1862, and he then began a long but ultimately fruitful struggle to seize Vicksburg, the key to the Confederate defense of the entire lower Mississippi valley. On July 4, 1863, after a siege of six weeks, Confederate general John C. Pemberton surrendered his entire command of 30,000 troops, the largest Confederate surrender up to that point in the war.

After the fall of Vicksburg and the securing of the Mississippi, Grant turned his attention eastward. Following a buildup of forces at Chattanooga, **Tennessee**, he ordered an assault on the Confederate position at Missionary Ridge in November 1863, which threw the Confederate Army of Tennessee back into **Georgia** and forced Confederate president **Jefferson Davis** to fire its commander, General Braxton Bragg. Grant's victories at Vicksburg and Missionary Ridge paved the way for President **Abraham Lincoln** to name Grant as commanding general of the Union army and earned him a promotion to lieutenant general. Leaving his favorite subordinate, General **William T. Sherman**, in charge of the campaign in Georgia, Grant moved east in the spring of 1864 to take command of all Union armies and personally supervise a new campaign against Robert E. Lee's Army of Northern **Virginia**, which stood between the federal capital in Washington and the Confederate capital in Richmond, Virginia.

In a series of spectacular and costly battles in the spring and summer of 1864, Grant and Lee fought the final great act of the Civil War. At the Wilderness, Spotsylvania, Cold Harbor, and Petersburg, Grant drove relentlessly south while Lee parried his every move with great skill and mounting casualties on both sides. In the end, however, Grant forced Lee into a siege along a thirty-mile-long series of trench lines stretching from Richmond to Petersburg, similar to what he had done at Vicksburg the year before. In April 1865, Confederate defenses finally cracked, and Grant's forces pursued the remnants of Lee's army to its final surrender at Appomattox Court House.

Grant, Political Tumult, and Early Reconstruction

Confederate defeat, followed by the **assassination of Abraham Lincoln**, made Grant the most popular and heroic figure in the country. This, in turn, made Grant a natural candidate for president, but strained his relationship with Lincoln's successor, **Andrew Johnson**. In late 1865, Grant made an inspection tour across the defeated South at Johnson's urging. His public report emphasized his belief that ex-Confederates accepted defeat and the finality of the **emancipation** of their slaves. Johnson promptly used Grant's report to support his program of **pardon** and **amnesty**, which most Republicans in Congress opposed. At the time, many congressmen felt betrayed by what they interpreted as Grant's support for Johnson, a prewar southern Democrat, because Grant had been known to actively support Lincoln's decision to arm **black troops** and use army resources and personnel to run the **contraband** camps that were the forerunners of the **Bureau of Refugees, Freedmen, and Abandoned Lands**. Despite the fact that Johnson nominated Grant for the unprecedented rank of four-star general, Grant turned against Johnson in the summer and fall of 1866, fearing that Johnson's policies would ultimately rob the Union of what he termed "the fruits of victory."

After Republicans won a landslide in November 1866 that gave them veto-proof majorities in both houses of Congress, Grant increasingly had to contend with a commander in chief intent on thwarting the majority will in Congress. In August 1867, Grant accepted the position of interim secretary of war after Johnson removed **Edwin M. Stanton** in deliberate violation of the **Tenure of Office Act**. This action caused an enraged Republican Congress to vote for Johnson's **impeachment**. When the Senate refused to acquiesce in Stanton's relief in early 1868, Grant returned Stanton's office in the War Department. Johnson felt betrayed and tried to humiliate Grant in a full **cabinet** meeting at the White House, but Grant refused to relent, which again made him a heroic figure to Republicans and sealed his nomination for president. In November 1868, he won election against former New York governor **Horatio Seymour** on the campaign slogan, "Let Us Have Peace."

Republican President

Grant's record as president from 1869 to 1877 has been as fiercely disputed as the history of Reconstruction itself, and for nearly the same reasons. To many Americans at the time, particularly northerners who supported the war and **African Americans**, his ascent to the highest office of the land heralded an era of just and lasting civil peace to match a previous era of strife and civil war. To others, particularly white southerners who had fought for the Confederacy, his election represented a hated Yankee determination to oppress a prostrate South and establish the humiliations of "negro domination" and "bayonet rule" over southern states.

Using an unprecedented array of federal powers enacted in the wake of the Civil War, Grant made the greatest effort of any American president before the 1960s to enforce **civil rights** and political opportunity for African Americans. Ratification of the **Fifteenth Amendment** in 1870 outlawed voting discrimination on the basis of race. Passage of the **Enforcement Acts** of 1871 and 1872 put legislative teeth into the promise of the amendment, by making it a federal crime to conspire to prevent the exercise of the franchise and authorizing the suspension of the writ of habeas corpus in extreme cases of lawlessness. The creation of the Department of Justice during his administration gave the federal government the means to pursue legal cases against widespread white supremacist efforts to impede black voting in the South. In 1871–1872, Grant combined these powers in what became, in effect, a counterinsurgency campaign to break the power of the **Ku Klux Klan** across the states of the former Confederacy. The most extensive of these campaigns occurred in **South Carolina**, where he ordered the suspension of the writ and deployed the U.S. Army's Seventh Cavalry in nine upcountry counties when the Klan inaugurated a reign of terror. While the Department of Justice ultimately convicted fewer than 100 on federal felony charges, the wholesale arrest of thousands of suspected Klan members, in the view of most historians, broke the momentum of the Klan's secretive power and drove its membership into quiescence for several years.

Grant's success in ensuring free access to the ballot for blacks paid political dividends in his 1872 landslide reelection campaign against the New York newspaper editor **Horace Greeley**. Greeley's own ineptness as a politician, however, concealed a number of underlying problems that ultimately caused Reconstruction to unravel. In part, members of the **Democratic Party** nominated Greeley because he had been a Republican during the Civil War who ran on a platform of sectional reconciliation, made famous in his appeal to "clasp hands across the bloody chasm." In part, though, Democrats embraced Greeley because he had already been chosen as the candidate of the **Liberal Republicans**, a faction within the Republican Party that split with Grant over a number of issues, including his ill-considered scheme to annex Santo Domingo, civil service reform, and his use of the military in the South. This factional infighting among Republicans emerged in a byzantine struggle for power within **Louisiana**, where electoral fraud and **violence** caused Congress to refuse to certify the state's electoral votes from 1872 and led to repeated attempts to overthrow the black-supported Republican state government in New Orleans. In response, Grant sent federal troops, which created a national controversy when army commanders escorted disputed legislative candidates out of the chambers of the Louisiana House using armed soldiers. The uproar was so great that when Mississippi governor **Adelbert Ames** requested that Grant send federal troops to help supervise elections in his state in the fall of 1875, Grant's **cabinet** warned him against it. Without federal aid, Mississippi Republicans lost the state elections in November, and white supremacists seized the state legislature, impeached the black lieutenant governor, and forced Governor Ames to resign the following year under the threat of similar action. Across the South, black and white Republicans found themselves losing ground everywhere.

By 1876, Grant found his administration on the defensive on every front. In a series of decisions from the *Slaughterhouse Cases* in 1873 to the *Cruikshank* decision in 1876, the **Supreme Court** repeatedly ruled against expansive readings of federal power in the Fourteenth and Fifteenth Amendments, narrowing the prosecutorial authority of the Justice Department. A spreading series of corruption **scandals** undercut the Grant administration's reputation for integrity. While Grant himself was never personally implicated, his secretary of war, William W. Belknap, resigned under the cloud of a scandal involving kickback payments for sutler contracts at army posts, and his own personal secretary resigned after being implicated in the "Whiskey Ring" scandal, which involved large-scale tax evasion and bribery between liquor distillers and federal revenue agents. In 1873, a bank **panic** led to a stock market collapse and a run on banks that produced a five-year depression and led to the Democrats regaining control of the House in the mid-term elections of 1874.

Despite all of these difficulties, Grant's personal popularity remained enormous. Many Republicans wanted him to run for an unprecedented third term in 1876. Grant refused, and devoted his remaining time in office to ensure that the disputed presidential election between **Samuel Tilden** and **Rutherford B. Hayes** that year did not spill over into another civil war. After overseeing the secret inauguration of Hayes, the eventual Republican winner, at the White House in March 1877, he and Julia departed Washington for a two-year-long trip around the world that kept the Grants constantly in the public eye. Grant's triumphant return, and Hayes's decision not to seek a second term, made him a popular if not universal choice for president again in 1880. The campaign reached a climax on the thirty-sixth ballot of the Republican National Convention, when **James Garfield**, who had also served as a volunteer general during the Civil War, won the nomination.

Waning Years: Desperation and Victory

Grant's return to private life looked similar to his private life before the Civil War. He moved his family to New York and invested his life savings in a brokerage partnership with Frederick Ward, who eventually bankrupted the firm of Grant and Ward through speculative investments that crashed in the Wall Street panic of 1884. Desperate to pay his debts and support his family, and having learned that he had contracted cancer of the throat brought on by years of inveterate cigar smoking, Grant turned to writing the book that ultimately vindicated his public life. The two-volume *Personal Memoirs of Ulysses S. Grant* has been critically acclaimed as the finest military memoir in American letters. Sadly, it contains virtually no commentary about his trying years as president, other than a valedictory profession that the promise of freedom and American unity would prevail and make the nation great and whole again in time. Written with a bluntness and clarity that remain attractive to this day, it proved so popular and spellbinding that some believed it must have been ghostwritten by Mark Twain, who was a close personal friend of Grant's, or Adam Badeau, an aide who helped Grant gather documents. Those familiar with Grant's pithy dispatches during the war, however, immediately recognized that at the end of his life, Grant had regained that certainty of expression that had characterized his triumphant conduct of Union strategy in the Civil War. Grant did not live to see this last vindication, dying just days after finishing the final chapter at the summer resort of Mount McGregor in upstate New York on July 23, 1885. *See also* Black Suffrage; Command of the Army Act; Congressional Reconstruction; Elections of 1866; Elections of 1868; Elections of 1876; Presidential Reconstruction; Redemption; Republicans, Radical; Violence.

Further Reading: Gillette, William. *Retreat from Reconstruction, 1868–1879*. Baton Rouge: Louisiana State University Press, 1979; Simon, John Y. *The Papers of Ulysses S. Grant*. 26 vols. Carbondale: University of Southern Illinois Press, 1967–ongoing; Simpson, Brooks D. *Let Us Have Peace: Ulysses S. Grant and the Politics of War and Reconstruction, 1861–1868*. Chapel Hill: University of North Carolina Press, 1991.

James K. Hogue

Greeley, Horace (1811–1872)

Born in 1811 in Amherst, New Hampshire, to a poor family, Horace Greeley became one of the most powerful American figures of the nineteenth century. A small, eccentric man with a moon face and a fringe of white whiskers, who embraced a wide variety of reforming causes, Greeley was easy to lampoon, but anyone who underestimated him made a mistake. From his position as editor of the enormously powerful *New York Tribune*, Greeley became an important voice in American politics from the accession of John Tyler to the presidency after the death of William Henry Harrison to the anti-**Grant** campaign of 1872, in which Greeley himself was a presidential candidate.

Reform Spirit: Antebellum and Civil War

Trained as a printer as a boy, Greeley moved to New York City in 1831, and ten years later, started publication of the *New York Tribune*, which he designed to promote moral, intellectual, and political knowledge. Refusing to print police reports and unscrupulous advertisements, Greeley dedicated his paper to Whig policies and a reform agenda that included Fourierism, labor cooperatives, support for women's rights, and antislavery. While his utopian dreams ultimately had little affect on American policies, Greeley's staunch support for both the Whig policies of internal improvements and tariff walls and his antislavery position framed the direction of national politics in the mid-nineteenth century.

In his determination to stop the spread of slavery and develop the country with northern labor, Greeley was an early and vocal opponent of the 1854 Kansas-Nebraska Act that repealed the Missouri Compromise. He demanded that northerners hold the line against southern attempts to control the nation, and he hailed the birth of the Republican Party with enthusiasm. Although not a strong supporter of **Abraham Lincoln** in 1860, he helped to throw the Republican nomination to the Illinois lawyer out of a determination to make sure front-runner **William Henry Seward**, whom he considered unelectable, did not get the nomination. Although pleased to see a Republican in the White House, Greeley was continually frustrated with what he considered to be Lincoln's lackluster prosecution of the war. In August 1862, Greeley published "The Prayer of Twenty Millions," accusing the Lincoln administration of weakness and demanding that the president bolster the Union cause by embracing **emancipation**. Obliged to answer an attack from such a prominent Republican, Lincoln responded to Greeley directly. The president's now-famous reply defended his determination to save the Union, and to make his policy toward slaves serve that ultimate priority.

Postwar Disillusionment

With the end of the war, Greeley believed the nation was now free to move forward economically without the hampering weight of slavery. As soon as General Lee surrendered to Grant at Appomattox, Greeley called for "Magnanimity in Triumph," urging the country forward to a triumphant future. Greeley held to this course even after the **assassination of Abraham Lincoln**, and ultimately joined others in protesting the continued imprisonment of **Jefferson Davis** without trial. In 1867, Greeley was one of twenty men who guaranteed Davis's bail.

Greeley's willingness to sign a bond to free Jefferson Davis indicated his growing disillusionment with postwar Republicanism. Not surprisingly, Greeley had initially supported **Andrew Johnson**'s conciliatory policy, but had broken with him over his willingness to accept southern circumscription of black rights. However, he could not side unreservedly with **Radical Republicans** in Congress, either. As congressional party members increasingly consolidated their power to resist President Johnson's attempts to monopolize Reconstruction policy, Greeley chafed at Republicans' apparent willingness to appeal to voters' worst instincts to gain votes. Disgusted with the Republicans' apparent inability to find a true statesman as a leader, Greeley was a lukewarm supporter of Grant in the **election of 1868**, and quickly lost whatever enthusiasm he had for the president as the **scandals** of his administration began to come to light. Grant's attempt to force the annexation of Santo Domingo in 1869 and revelations that administration supporters demanded absolute political loyalty as well as kickbacks for political **patronage** appointments directly affronted Greeley's belief in an honest government that fairly developed the national interest.

Greeley's anger at Grant translated into a devastating blow for Reconstruction measures designed to protect black rights in the South. In spring 1871, Democrats in **South Carolina** charged that the Republican legislature—elected by black voters, although most of the legislators were white—was confiscating property through taxation in order to redistribute wealth to poor blacks. This sort of southern rhetoric was not new, but Greeley made it a national story in May 1871, with an opening salvo in an attack on Grant. His "Political Problems in South Carolina" suggested that the black voters the Grant administration was protecting were receiving federal protection solely to keep the Republicans in power, and that Republicans bought their votes with promises of government jobs. Only Greeley, with his long history of agitation for black rights, could have made this story valid in the North, and stick it did. He continued to reiterate

Undated portrait of Horace Greeley. (Courtesy of the Library of Congress.)

this argument to weaken Grant, and northern support for the protection of black Americans and their southern Republican allies faltered.

The Liberal Republican Movement

Greeley's attacks on the Republican administration played into the hands of reformers concerned about Republican corruption and apparent attempts to lock up the political system in Republicans' favor. When opponents of the administration organized as the **Liberal Republicans** for the election of 1872, Greeley was a hopeful supporter of their attempt to purify government. The Liberal Republicans insisted on the southern acceptance of the Reconstruction amendments to the **U.S. Constitution**, called for **pardons** for former Confederates who had been **disfranchised**, and demanded civil service reform and an end to government corruption. The bolters harnessed their hopes to protariff forces, and at their **Cincinnati Convention** they gave their presidential nomination to Greeley. In what would be a mixed blessing for the movement, the following month, the **Democratic Party** endorsed the platform and candidates of the Liberal Republicans.

Opponents of Greeley in the campaign attacked the editor so harshly that he mused that he sometimes could not tell if he was running "for the Presidency or the penitentiary." When Grant won the election handily, an exhausted Greeley fell into a despondency that was compounded by the death of his wife during the campaign. He died on November 29, even before the vote count had been completed. Greeley was buried in Brooklyn, New York. *See also* Abolitionists; Abolition of Slavery; African Americans; Amnesty Proclamations; Congressional Reconstruction; Fifteenth Amendment; Fourteenth Amendment; Labor Systems; Moses, Franklin J., Jr.; New Departure; Presidential Reconstruction; Republicans, Radical; Thirteenth Amendment; Women's Movement.

Further Reading: Greeley, Horace. *Recollections of a Busy Life.* New York: J. B. Ford, 1868; Richardson, Heather Cox. *The Death of Reconstruction: Race, Labor, and Politics in the Post–Civil War North.* Cambridge, MA: Harvard University Press, 2001; Stoddard, Henry Luther. *Horace Greeley: Printer, Editor, Crusader.* New York: G. P. Putnam's Sons, 1946; Van Deusen, Glyndon. *Horace Greeley: Nineteenth-Century Crusader.* Philadelphia: University of Pennsylvania Press, 1953.

Heather Cox Richardson

Grimes, James W. (1816–1872)

Republican senator James Wilson Grimes was born in Deering, New Hampshire, on October 20, 1816, the youngest of eight children. He graduated from Dartmouth College in 1836, and moved west to practice law in an area known as the "Black Hawk Purchase"—land that would eventually become Michigan, Wisconsin, the Dakotas, and Iowa.

Grimes set up his law practice in Burlington. When the Iowa territory was formed in 1838, he served as the librarian for a year and as a delegate on the territorial assembly from 1838 to 1839 and 1843 to 1844. He also served as the Burlington City solicitor, the justice of the peace, and worked in private law firms. In 1846, he married Sarah Elizabeth Neally, and they had one adopted child.

Once Iowa became a state in 1846, Grimes served in the legislature, and was eventually elected to serve as governor from 1854 to 1858. He was elected to the U.S. Senate in 1859, and served through the entire war. Although the **Democratic Party** had controlled Iowa, Grimes was elected governor from the Whig Party. Considered a moderate politician, he was an advocate of "free soil" issues (opposing the spread of slavery) and actually entered the Senate as a Republican. At the height of the sectional crisis, Grimes participated in the convention held in Washington, D.C., in 1861 in an effort to prevent the impending Civil War. In 1865, as a Republican, he ran again for the Senate and was reelected.

As a **Moderate Republican** and potential swing voter, Grimes was one of the power brokers in the Senate, often wooed by the **Radical Republicans**. He was an early supporter of President **Andrew Johnson**, and was especially shaken by Johnson's veto of the **Civil Rights Bill** in 1866. Thereafter, as Congress began to challenge the president for control of Reconstruction, he sat on the **Joint Committee on Reconstruction**. As with many Moderates, he felt betrayed by Johnson and became a harsh critic of his Reconstruction policy. He supported, with reservations, the **Military Reconstruction Acts**, but openly claimed that the **Tenure of Office Act** did not cover Secretary of War **Edwin Stanton**.

Grimes's outspoken moderation worried Radicals during the **impeachment** trial, as they knew the vote for conviction would be close. In May 1868, as the party pressure for conviction grew, Grimes suffered an attack of paralysis, and Radicals and their newspapers rejoiced, hoping this would keep him from voting. On May 16, when the Senate convened for its first vote, Grimes was carried in on a stretcher, and Chief Justice **Salmon P. Chase** even waived the rules so he could vote without standing. He became one of the seven so-called Republican "**recusants**" who voted not guilty, and allowed Johnson to stay in office.

His motives are fairly clear. There were personal issues involved—as everyone knew, Grimes hated **Benjamin Wade**, Johnson's successor should the latter be removed—but his sincere belief in fairness and moderation drove his vote. Grimes, interviewed soon after the Senate adjourned as High Court of Impeachment, placed the matter in perspective, saying,

> I can not agree to destroy the harmonious working of the Constitution for the sake of getting rid of an unacceptable President. Whatever may be my opinion of the incumbent, I can not consent to trifle with the high office he holds.... However widely, therefore, I may and do differ with the President respecting his political views and measure, and however deeply I have regretted, and do regret the differences between himself and the Congress of the United States, I am not able to record my vote that he is guilty of high crimes and misdemeanors by reason of those differences. (*Harper's Weekly*, June 6, 1868)

An immediate target of Republican retribution, Grimes's health never recovered. He suffered a more debilitating stroke in 1869, and resigned his

Senate seat. He moved abroad for two years, but not long after returning to the United States his heart developed problems, and he died on February 7, 1872. Grimes is buried in Aspen Grove Cemetery in Burlington, Iowa. *See also* Civil Rights; Congressional Reconstruction; Elections of 1866; Fessenden, William Pitt; Presidential Reconstruction; Ross, Edmund G.

Further Reading: "Biographical Directory of the United States Congress, 1774–Present," accessed at http://bioguide.congress.gov/scripts/biodisplay.pl?index= G000475; Foner, Eric. *Reconstruction: America's Unfinished Revolution, 1863–1877*. New York: Harper & Row, 1988; "The Iowa Official Register, Iowa History Project: The Nativity of the Pioneers of Iowa," accessed at http://iagenweb.org/history/ Pioneer%20Nativity.htm; Roske, Ralph J. "The Seven Martyrs?" *American Historical Review* 64 (January 1959): 323–30; "Virtual American Biographies: James Wilson Grimes," accessed at http://www.famousamericans.net/jameswilsongrimes/.

Michelle Mellon

Gun Clubs

Gun clubs, also known as "rifle clubs" or "sabre clubs," were an important link in the chain of Democratic paramilitary organizations active during Reconstruction, primarily in **South Carolina**. The history of the gun clubs illustrates the conflicts over who could legitimately use force. When the Republicans in Congress passed the **Military Reconstruction Act** in March 1867, it put the South under military supervision, and disbanded all existing state **militias**. When Governor **Robert K. Scott** reorganized South Carolina's militia in 1869 on an integrated basis, some all-white companies such as the Carolina Rifles of Charleston formed, but were not accepted. Several of these nominally changed from militia units to social clubs. The gun clubs tended to be led by prominent white citizens, including Andrew Pickens Butler and C. Irvine Walker, and held a variety of public social functions such as picnics, parades, and medieval-style tournaments. Despite this peaceful façade, the gun clubs were typically armed with rifles, shotguns, and even bayonets. A few more gun clubs formed in the cities over the next three years, but the proliferation of gun clubs across the state began in earnest in 1874, as conservatives responding to corruption in state government became determined to regain political control. Some clubs in rural areas, such as the Palmetto Sabre Club, were merely the latest incarnation of antebellum agricultural clubs that had monitored slave behavior.

When the 1876 campaign began in South Carolina, the **Democratic Party** already had an extensive network of gun clubs that could turn their hands to electioneering. These organizations were the basis of the **Red Shirts**, who harassed and intimidated Republican voters and candidates. Governor **Daniel H. Chamberlain** issued an order to disband all gun clubs in October 1876, but the gun clubs simply fell back on the fiction of their purely social purpose. The Allendale Rifle Club renamed itself the Allendale Mounted Baseball Club and continued its activities without a pause. Taking its cue from the so-called "**Mississippi** Plan" in the neighboring state, these private military forces staged parades and rallies, and often appeared at Republican functions to intimidate their political adversaries. Most contemporaries and historians agree that the armed presence of these large organizations had a powerful effect on the Republican turnout at the election.

Their impact did not end with the election. While the Democrats and Republicans, in South Carolina and Washington, D.C., argued over who had won, thousands of rifle club members converged on the state capital in Columbia. These groups claimed to be protecting Democrats who were contesting the election results, but they also served to pressure white and black Carolina Republicans. Since black militia units could not contend with former Confederate soldiers, only the **U.S. Army** protected Chamberlain and his government. Once the **election of 1876** was decided, and President **Hayes** removed federal troops from the southern capitals, the Republican administration had no choice but to capitulate. *See also* Carpetbaggers; Compromise of 1877; Congressional Reconstruction; Elections of 1876; Hampton, Wade, III; Ku Klux Klan; Redemption; Red Shirts; Violence.

Further Reading: Zuczek, Richard. *State of Rebellion: South Carolina during Reconstruction.* Columbia: University of South Carolina Press, 1996.

Bruce E. Baker

H

Hahn, Georg Michael Decker (1830–1886)

Michael Hahn, U.S. congressman and governor of unionist **Louisiana** during the Civil War, played a prominent role among Unionists in wartime New Orleans and within Louisiana's Republican Party during Reconstruction. Born in Germany on November 24, 1830, he emigrated as a small child with his widowed mother and siblings to the United States, eventually settling in New Orleans around 1840. Orphaned in 1841, he attended local schools and received his law degree in 1851 from what is today Tulane University. A Democrat before the war, he opposed secession, and, after New Orleans fell to federal forces in 1862, he helped organize Unionists and worked closely with federal military officials. He became a Republican, vigorously endorsing **emancipation** and the policies of President **Abraham Lincoln**, and in 1863, briefly represented Louisiana in the U.S. Congress. Returning to New Orleans, he purchased a pro-Confederate newspaper and used it to promote the Unionist cause. He played a key role in writing the state's 1864 constitution **abolishing slavery**, and that same year, he was elected governor under Lincoln's Ten Percent Plan. He resigned in early 1865 upon his election to the U.S. Senate, but, owing to congressional Republicans' misgivings over Lincoln's plan, he was never seated.

Following Lincoln's **assassination**, Hahn opposed the Reconstruction policies of President **Andrew Johnson**. He supported the attempt to reconvene the 1864 **constitutional convention** for the purpose of enacting **black suffrage**, and he almost died from a grievous gunshot wound suffered at the infamous **New Orleans riot** of July 30, 1866, that resulted when the convention tried to meet. Undeterred, he became manager and editor of the *New Orleans Republican* in 1867 and continued in these positions until 1871.

In 1872, Hahn moved to his sugar plantation in St. Charles Parish, where he founded the town of Hahnville, established the *St. Charles Herald*, and actively supported public **education**. Although Hahn was not as prominent in the Louisiana Republican Party during the 1870s as he had been, he held various public offices for the rest of his life. He was elected to the state legislature in 1872, 1874, and 1876, serving for a time as chairman of the Judiciary Committee and as Speaker of the House. He was appointed state registrar of voters in 1876; in 1878, he became superintendent of the U.S. Mint at New Orleans; and from 1879 to 1885, he served as a federal district judge in Louisiana. In 1880, he founded the *New Orleans Ledger* to support Republican candidates, and, after having initially declined the nomination, he was elected to Congress in 1884 by a large majority from Louisiana's heavily Democratic Second Congressional District. Hahn died in Washington, D.C., on March 15, 1886, before completing his term, and he was buried in Metairie, Louisiana.

Although considered a **Moderate Republican**, Hahn was nonetheless a principled defender of black **civil rights**. Even his political opponents came to admire his physical courage, strength of conviction, and personal integrity. Despite his long career in the law and politics, Hahn died financially impoverished. *See also* Amnesty Proclamations; Banks, Nathaniel P.; Butler, Benjamin Franklin; Presidential Reconstruction; Race Riots; Suffrage; Wells, James M.

Further Reading: McCrary, Peyton. *Abraham Lincoln and Reconstruction: The Louisiana Experiment*. Princeton, NJ: Princeton University Press, 1978; Simpson, Amos E., and Vaughan B. Baker. "Michael Hahn, Steady Patriot." *Louisiana History* 13 (1972): 229-52; Taylor, Joe Gray. *Louisiana Reconstructed: 1863-1877*. Baton Rouge: Louisiana State University Press, 1974.

John C. Rodrigue

Hampton, Wade, III (1818–1902)

Hampton was a former Confederate general who dominated **South Carolina** politics in the 1870s, ultimately leading the forces of "**Redemption**," which overthrew Republican rule in 1876.

Born into one of the wealthiest planter clans in the South, Hampton turned his attention to managing extensive family estates in South Carolina and **Mississippi** after graduating from South Carolina College in 1836. Like his father and grandfather, Hampton came to act as a conservative political power broker from his base at Millwood plantation, on the outskirts of Columbia. Elected to South Carolina's General Assembly in 1852 and 1858–1861, Hampton spoke out consistently against radical measures, opposing the movement to reopen the transatlantic slave trade and even the independent secession of his state in 1860. Once his state voted for disunion, however, he accepted a colonel's commission, raising and largely financing "Hampton's Legion," a unit comprising six companies of infantry, four companies of cavalry, and a battery of artillery. During the Civil War, he distinguished himself as a brave and skillful cavalry commander, rising to the rank of lieutenant general. When J.E.B. Stuart was killed in action, Hampton assumed command of Lee's cavalry forces. He and his unit were sent to South Carolina to shore up morale when Union general **William T. Sherman** invaded the state. By the time the Confederacy fell, he had lost his wealth and his slaves, seen Millwood burned, and been wounded five times. Still, he surrendered only reluctantly and soon became one of the progenitors of the "**Lost Cause**" movement.

Hampton returned to South Carolina in 1865 the gallant and beloved hero, a leader who had given his all for his home state. He could easily have been elected governor in that year (as he might well have been earlier on, had secession and war not intervened), but deferred to the like-minded **James L. Orr**, in the belief that the selection of an ex-Confederate general would inflame northern hostility. Conservatives put him on the ballot anyway, and more than 48 percent of voters supported him, demonstrating the power of his name and hinting at the strength and stridency of white intransigence. In the immediate postwar period, however, Hampton had his hands full settling up the legal wreckage of his family's agricultural empire. In 1868, with debts topping one million dollars, he declared bankruptcy and consigned his shattered property to creditors. By this time, Hampton's hesitant support for President **Andrew Johnson**'s Reconstruction plans had fully faded, as **African American** troops enforced federal control across the state and white and black Republicans dominated the statehouse. "If we had known you were going to back with bayonets the **carpetbagger**, the **scalawag**, and the negro in their infamous acts," he later told President **Ulysses S. Grant**, "we would never have given up our arms!"

Thousands of other white Carolinians felt likewise, engulfing the state in a reign of **Ku Klux Klan** terror. Responding to an appeal from Republican governor **Robert K. Scott**, Hampton issued a public call for the "preservation of order" in the fall of 1868. The fact that night-rider activity virtually disappeared for the next eighteen months again demonstrated his strength and popularity. It is important to remember, however, that Hampton—a once-wealthy, well-educated, stoical Episcopalian conservative—always put moderation and order at the forefront, and held faith in "fair treatment" from Washington long after **Radical Republicans** had dashed most other white southerners' hopes for a restoration of the old order. His 1872 call for "the Redemption of the South," culminating in the end of Reconstruction in South Carolina four years later, should be seen in that light.

Given the bloody vengefulness of the **Red Shirt** campaign during the **election of 1876**, it is easy to forget Hampton's moderating mission. Unlike Edgefield, South Carolina's **Martin W. Gary**, who served under Hampton in the Civil War and who masterminded the paramilitary strategy that put Hampton in the governor's chair that year, Hampton's **Bourbon**ism still held room for restraint—"force without **violence**," in his phrase—and for racial accommodation, if nothing like political or social equality. Such rhetoric drew some **African Americans** to the conservative cause, while doing little to restrain white **gun clubs** eager to settle scores and reassert dominance. Still, Hampton was the veteran, the glorious war hero, and the Democratic candidate for governor, making him responsible for the violence and terrorism that murdered and intimidated African American citizens in the state. The former officers of his Confederate Hampton Legion led and directed the Red Shirt campaign across the state. Republican dedication and willpower, devoid of support from Washington, were no match for the planning, brutality, and thoroughness of Hampton's campaign. Carpetbag governor **Daniel H. Chamberlain** disputed the state's election results, but his cries fell on deaf ears. With the so-called **Compromise of 1877** taking effect, Hampton and his ilk regained power in the spring of 1877.

Once in power, Hampton and his cronies (many of whom were high-ranking Confederate veterans and landholders) displayed little in the way of political vision. They threw Republican appointees out of state offices, began opulent prosecutions of Republican officials, developed a more onerous crop lien law in 1878, and established provisions for more restrictive fence laws. By the time Hampton was sent to the U.S. Senate in 1879, he had done much to reestablish planter hegemony in South Carolina and turn back the clock on race relations. For the state's black and white agricultural working class, Hampton's success set the stage for much meaner times ahead. *See also* Agriculture; Black Troops (U.S.C.T.) in the Occupied South; Bourbons; Civil Rights; Congressional Reconstruction; Disfranchisement; Jim Crow Laws; Military Reconstruction Acts; Presidential Reconstruction; Race Riots; Scandals; Sharecropping; U.S. Army and Reconstruction.

Further Reading: Drago, Edmund L. *Hurrah for Hampton! Black Red Shirts in South Carolina during Reconstruction.* Fayetteville: University of Arkansas Press, 1998; Jarrell, Hampton M. *Wade Hampton and the Negro: The Road Not Taken.* Columbia: University of South Carolina Press, 1949; Wellman, Manly W. *Giant in Gray: A Biography of Wade Hampton of South Carolina.* New York: Charles Scribners' Sons, 1949; Williams, Alfred B. *Hampton and His Red Shirts: South Carolina's Deliverance in 1876.* Charleston, SC: Walker, Evans, and Cogswell, 1935.

Vernon Burton

Hancock, Winfield Scott (1824–1886)

A professional army officer, Hancock commanded troops in **Louisiana** during Reconstruction. A native of Pennsylvania, Hancock was born in Montgomery Square to a respected attorney and his wife. He graduated from the U.S. Military Academy at West Point, New York, in 1844, ranking eighteenth of twenty-five cadets. Serving in the infantry, Hancock saw frontier service, fought in the Mexican War, and subsequently returned to duties in the West.

In the Civil War, Hancock clearly enunciated his devotion to the Union, supported the **Democratic Party**, and established an excellent record as a leader in battle. He fought at the battle of Antietam (1862) and was especially notable for his gallant stand against "Pickett's Charge" at the battle of Gettysburg (1863), where he was badly wounded. By the end of the war, he was accorded a hero's status in the North and was one of only five major generals in the regular army in 1866.

When Congress passed the **Military Reconstruction Acts** over the president's veto in 1867, President **Andrew Johnson** sought innovative ways to oppose the **Radical Republicans**' program. Following Hancock's lackluster showing in an Indian campaign in Kansas, President Johnson assigned him to command the Fifth Military District (Louisiana and **Texas**) in November 1867. Johnson knew that Hancock openly identified with the Democrats, and preferred that to some officers who had held command before him, such as **Philip H. Sheridan** and Joseph A. Mower, who had been linked to the Republicans.

As Johnson had hoped, Hancock seized the opportunity in Louisiana to try to reverse the policies of Sheridan and Mower, in the process highlighting his affiliation with the Democrats. Seeking to improve their personal, political, or economic standing, Louisiana politicians entered and left political office at a dizzying rate, giving Hancock numerous opportunities to appoint replacements to vacant positions; most of his appointees were Democrats. He also eased out some Republican officeholders put in by his predecessors. Mindful that Sheridan and Mower had favored Republican policy by putting **African American** men on juries, Hancock set aside the policy. Knowing that Republicans favored voter registration for black males, Hancock discouraged them. President Johnson was pleased with Hancock's service in the Fifth District.

On November 20, 1867, Hancock issued his hallmark political statement, embodied in his General Order No. 40. Announcing that whenever possible civilian officials' decisions should take priority over military rulings, Hancock's General Order No. 40 undercut military government authorized in the congressional Military Reconstruction Acts and his own authority in supervising the operation of local, county (parish), and state governments. Democrats had castigated federal generals who carried out the Military Reconstruction Acts and tilted to the Republicans; now they sang the praises of Hancock and his General Order No. 40.

Hancock's actions naturally came to the attention of General **Ulysses S. Grant** in Washington, D.C. Determined to halt how Hancock had undercut the process of Reconstruction, Grant drew an imaginary protective line around the Republican city council of New Orleans, headquarters of the Fifth District. When Hancock wanted to replace some of the councilmen, Grant blocked the move, prompting Hancock to seek a transfer out of Louisiana. Grant gladly accommodated his request.

Hancock was significant as a Reconstruction commander for several reasons. The general spoke or acted for many conservative army officers (such as George Meade) who opposed Republican Reconstruction policies. Hancock's heroic status and his steps to slow or turn back Reconstruction in Louisiana even earned him some discussion as the Democratic nominee for president in 1868. Despite his evident opposition to the national policy embodied in the congressional Military Reconstruction Acts, Hancock was not punished, demoted in rank, or sent to isolated outposts because of his actions in Louisiana. To the contrary, he remained in the army for the rest of his life as a major general, and commanded military departments appropriate for an officer of his rank.

In the postwar years, Hancock made no secret of his presidential aspirations. He might have made a good choice for the Democrats to counter the Republicans' nomination of General Grant for the **election of 1868**, and likewise could have pitted his creditable military record against the incumbent in 1872. Instead, the Democrats eschewed the war hero and placed their hopes on New York governor **Horatio Seymour** and newspaperman **Horace Greeley**, respectively, neither of whom had served in the military during the war. Hancock was again passed over in 1876, this time for New York governor **Samuel Tilden**, who was also not a veteran. Hancock was finally nominated for president by the Democrats in 1880, narrowly losing the election to the Republican nominee, **James A. Garfield**, a former Union volunteer general. Hancock remained on active duty until his death at Governors Island, New York. *See also* Black Suffrage; Congressional Reconstruction; Elections of 1876; Republicans, Liberal; U.S. Army and Reconstruction.

Further Reading: Dawson, Joseph G., III. *Army Generals and Reconstruction: Louisiana, 1862–1877*. Baton Rouge: Louisiana State University Press, 1982; Jordan, David M. *Winfield Scott Hancock: A Soldier's Life*. Bloomington: Indiana University Press, 1988; Richter, William L. *The Army in Texas during Reconstruction*. College Station: Texas A&M University Press, 1987.

Joseph G. Dawson III

Hayes, Rutherford Birchard (1822–1893)

Rutherford B. Hayes, nineteenth president of the United States, was born in Delaware, Ohio, the posthumous son of Rutherford Hayes and Sarah Birchard Hayes. Brought up by his mother and wealthy uncle, Sardis Birchard, he was educated at Kenyon College and Harvard Law School. After practicing law with his uncle in what is now Fremont, Ohio, he moved to Cincinnati where he became a successful attorney and served as city solicitor from 1858 to 1861. In politics, he was an antislavery Whig who defended fugitive slaves.

In 1852, Hayes married Lucy Ware Webb of Chillicothe, with whom he had eight children, seven boys and one girl, of whom five survived. The marriage could not have been happier, and for some forty years, she was the mainstay of his life and furthered his temperance views.

During the Civil War, Hayes established an estimable record, particularly as colonel of the Twenty-third Ohio Volunteer Infantry Regiment, both in **West Virginia** and the Shenandoah Valley. Wounded several times, he rose to the rank of major general. Elected as a Republican to Congress in 1864, he refused to give up his military service while the war was still going on; he did not take his seat in the House of Representatives until late in 1865. A Republican but not an extremist, he opposed President **Andrew Johnson**, and in 1867, was elected governor of Ohio, though the legislature fell to the **Democratic Party**. Reelected two years later, he sought to retire in 1872, but was prevailed upon to try again for Congress that fall, and suffered his only electoral defeat. In 1875, however, he managed to defeat the inflationist William Allan for governor, thus winning an unprecedented third term.

At the 1876 Cincinnati Republican National Convention, the leading candidates—**James G. Blaine**, **Oliver Morton**, and **Roscoe Conkling**—because of their rivalries, were unable to muster majorities. Hayes became the compromise candidate for the Republicans in the **election of 1876**. William

Wheeler of New York was his running mate on a platform pledging equal rights for all, including women, speedy resumption of specie payments, and the separation of powers, while accusing the Democrats of sympathy for rebellion. Because of the corruption during General **Ulysses S. Grant**'s presidency, Hayes's reputation for honesty made him an attractive candidate.

Hayes's opponent was New York governor **Samuel J. Tilden**, who had established a record as a reformer by smashing the notorious **Tweed** Ring in his state. With two such candidates, the election was bound to be close, and the result was one of the most disputed elections in American history. Although most of the southern states had already been "redeemed" by the conservatives and Democrats, in **Florida**, **South Carolina**, and **Louisiana**, there were still Republican claimants. Visiting statesmen from both parties descended upon these states to influence the returning boards that had power to annul dubious votes, and these commonwealths sent in two returns, so that Hayes had 165 undisputed electoral votes, and Tilden had 184. For election, 185 were necessary so that 20 disputed votes (one was disputed in Oregon because of a technicality) would decide the outcome. The Republicans, who controlled the Senate, maintained that the presiding officer of that body ought to decide which votes were legitimate, but the Democrats, in control of the House, demurred. The result was the appointment of a Joint **Electoral Commission**, consisting of three Republican and two Democratic senators, three Democratic and two Republican representatives, and one Republican and one Democratic **Supreme Court** justice, with an independent justice, presumably **David Davis**. Davis, however, was elected a Democratic senator from Illinois and thus refused to serve. His substitute was Justice Joseph P. Bradley of New Jersey, a Republican, who sided with his party, so that the commission, by a party vote of 8 to 7, decided for Hayes, with 185–184 electoral votes.

The Democrats were naturally dissatisfied with this decision and threatened to filibuster to prevent the inauguration of their opponent. This outcome was prevented by a series of deals involving Republican promises to southern ex-Whigs of economic aid, especially to the Texas Pacific **Railroad**, as well as agreements to withdraw the remaining federal troops from southern state houses. Thus, Hayes was inaugurated on March 5, although he lacked a popular majority (4,300,590 were cast for Tilden, and 4,036,298 for Hayes). Yet, he always believed he had been honestly elected because any number of black voters were denied the vote in the three states and would have given him **Mississippi** as well.

The Hayes presidency was controversial from the beginning—opponents called him "your fraudulency" or "Rutherfraud." Instead of appointing any of his rival candidates to the **cabinet**, he chose reformers such as William Evarts, who had defended Andrew Johnson, and **Carl Schurz**, who had bolted in 1872 with the formation of the **Liberal Republicans**, as well as a southerner, David M. Key. This annoyed the **Stalwarts** without winning over their opponents, the Half Breeds. Hayes's most controversial action was his withdrawal of the federal troops from the southern state houses. Accused of thereby ending **Congressional Reconstruction**, he actually had little choice in the matter, as President Grant had already made the first moves. Personally devoted to black welfare and **civil rights**, he sought promises from southerners to treat **African Americans** well, a promise that was soon forgotten after **Daniel H. Chamberlain** had to give up the governorship of **South Carolina** and **Stephen B. Packard** that of **Louisiana**. To the end of his life, however, Hayes actively supported black **education** by work with the Slater Fund and the Peabody Foundation. In addition, he vetoed several Democratic attempts to repeal the **Enforcement Acts** by riders to appropriation bills.

His other problem was civil service reform. Bitterly opposed by regular Republicans, this change was introduced in some departments, particularly in Carl Schurz's Department of the Interior, but it encountered real difficulty in New York, where **Roscoe Conkling**'s machine sought to resist efforts to remove its supporters in the Customs House. For more than a year, the Senate refused to confirm Hayes's appointment of successors to Collector Chester A. Arthur and naval officer Alonzo B. Cornell, until Hayes finally prevailed.

His final difficulty was the economic problem created by the **Panic of 1873**. Confronted with railroad strikes in the summer of 1877, Hayes finally sent federal troops upon the request of various state governors. These did not have to go into action, but the measure has been criticized as an antilabor policy by the administration. At the time, however, it was considered perfectly justified, and not until the turn of the century did the Theodore Roosevelt government adopt a more equitable attitude toward strikes. Always opposed to inflation, in 1878, the president unsuccessfully vetoed the Bland-Allison Act for the coinage of silver, but kept the purchase at a minimum and was gratified by the resumption of specie payments in 1879. The panic lifted during the later years of his administration.

Always having advocated a one-term presidency, Hayes was not a candidate for reelection, but his administration had been successful enough to make possible the victory of **James A. Garfield** as his successor. Hayes enjoyed a lengthy retirement devoted to his favorite causes, such as help for black education. He died at Fremont in 1893. *See also* Compromise of 1877; Redemption; Scandals.

Further Reading: Barnard, Harry. *Rutherford B. Hayes and His America*. Indianapolis, IN: Bobbs-Merrill, 1954; Davison, Kenneth E. *The Presidency of Rutherford B. Hayes*. Westport, CT: Greenwood Press, 1972; Hoogenboom, Ari. *Rutherford B. Hayes: Warrior and President*. Lawrence: University Press of Kansas, 1995; Trefousse, Hans L. *Rutherford B. Hayes*. New York: Henry Holt, 2002.

Hans L. Trefousse

Holden, William Woods (1818–1892)

William Woods Holden was **North Carolina provisional governor** under President **Andrew Johnson**'s plan of Reconstruction and Republican governor during **Congressional Reconstruction**. Holden was the illegitimate son of Thomas Holden and Priscilla Woods; he lived with his father and his wife until at age seventeen he became a typesetter on a Raleigh newspaper. In 1843, with the aid of friends, he became editor and proprietor of the *North Carolina Standard*, the organ of the state **Democratic Party**. Holden quickly

developed the *Standard* into a powerful statewide newspaper, and his political influence grew in the same proportion. As the Democratic Party consolidated its power in North Carolina during the 1850s, Holden became its
dominant figure and supported the southern rights cause. In 1858, he sought
his party's nomination for governor but was defeated by John W. Ellis, which
created a division in the party. After **Abraham Lincoln**'s election in 1860,
Holden led the constitutional Union or moderate party that advocated a "wait
and watch" policy toward the antislavery president. The Union party in February 1861 checked the secessionist effort to take the state out of the Union,
but after Fort Sumter and Lincoln's call for troops to suppress the rebellion,
Holden reversed his position and called on North Carolinians to resist the
president's "gross usurpation" of power. He served as a delegate to the state
convention in May that took North Carolina out of the Union and into the
Confederate states.

The Civil War

Holden soon violated his own plea that the state's citizens declare a holiday
on political divisions until southern independence had been won. By 1862, he
was bitterly criticizing the state Democratic and Confederate administrations
for discriminating against old Union men in their military appointments and
other policies. The adoption of conscription by the **Jefferson Davis** government gave Holden additional cause for denouncing Confederate authorities. Holden organized the Conservative Party in 1862, and secured the
nomination and election of young Zebulon B. Vance as governor. When
Holden organized a peace movement in the state in mid-1863, staunch Confederates charged that he was giving aid and comfort to their enemies and
encouraging desertions from the army, charges that he denied. In early 1864,
he proposed that a state convention meet to seek peace in cooperation with
other southern states. He also announced his candidacy for governor against
Vance, who had broken with Holden over war issues. Vance easily won the
election.

As Provisional Governor

One month after the war, President Andrew Johnson appointed Holden
provisional governor of the state to launch the process of civil reorganization
under his lenient plan of Reconstruction. As required by Johnson, Holden
called a state convention to invalidate the secession ordinance, abolish slavery,
and repudiate the Confederate debt. He achieved these tasks, but he used his
office to deny presidential **pardons** to his old political enemies, including
former governors Zebulon B. Vance and William A. Graham. When elections
were held in the fall of 1865 for the new state government, Holden ran
for governor against **Jonathan Worth**, the candidate of the Vance-Graham
faction. After he lost in a close election, Holden became upset when Johnson
failed to sustain him against those whom he characterized as unrepentant
rebels. Though still professing support for the president, by late 1866, Holden
could see that the Republican Congress had prevailed in the struggle over
Reconstruction policy.

Holden and Congressional Reconstruction

When Congress passed the **Military Reconstruction Acts** in early 1867, Holden cast his lot with the Republicans and, through the columns of the *Raleigh North Carolina Standard*, assisted in the organization of the party in the state. He argued that North Carolinians must put the Civil War behind them, accept the new political reality in the nation, and save the state from further ruin. Holden announced his acceptance of black **civil rights** and **suffrage**, the promulgation of a new state constitution recognizing the changes, and the ratification of the **Fourteenth Amendment** to the **U.S. Constitution**—all requirements by Congress before North Carolina could be readmitted to the Union. In April 1868, Holden, with a large number of blacks and white dissidents voting for him, was elected governor by a vote of 92,235 to 73,593 over his Conservative (Democratic) Party opponent; Republicans also won control of the General Assembly and the other state offices.

Republican Governor and White Resistance

In July, Holden took the oath of office as governor and military rule was ended, but the efforts of the Republican administration to advance progressive policies like a comprehensive system of public **education** for both races soon went awry. A large majority of the white citizens, encouraged by Vance and Graham, never accepted the legitimacy of the new biracial political order headed by Holden. Conservatives seized every opportunity to discredit the Republicans. The overextension of state aid to complete the statewide **railroad** system and the **scandals** associated with it offered a fertile field for their attacks, though Holden was never directly implicated in the wrongdoing. However, it was the threat that Republicans posed to white supremacy that aroused white North Carolinians to employ intimidation and **violence** against the Holden regime.

By 1869, violent bands known generically as the **Ku Klux Klan** had emerged in the state. Governor Holden's first response to the threat was to issue proclamations calling on the people to assert themselves and suppress Klan activity. This approach did not work. In late 1869 and early 1870, Klan violence intensified, and Holden secured the passage of a bill that gave him the authority to proclaim a state of insurrection and call out the **militia** whenever local authorities were unable to protect the citizens. Holden, however, drew back from using the poorly organized militia, consisting primarily of blacks. In February 1870, Wyatt Outlaw, the leading black Republican in Alamance County, was murdered by the Klan. Holden declared the county in a state of insurrection and asked President **Ulysses S. Grant** for troops. Grant refused to intervene and advised the governor to use his own resources to put down the lawless elements. The approaching election in August for seats in the General Assembly and for the state's attorney general insured that the violence would not abate.

The final straw for Holden occurred in May, when John W. Stephens, a Republican state senator, was killed in the Caswell County courthouse while a meeting was going on upstairs. The governor raised a force of 670 men in western North Carolina under the command of Colonel George W. Kirk, who had commanded a Union regiment in the area during the Civil War, and dispatched it to Alamance and Caswell Counties with orders to suppress the Klan. Not a shot was fired in the so-called **Kirk-Holden War**, though minor incidents occurred, including the partial hanging of three suspected Klansmen in an attempt to extract information. More than one hundred Klansmen were arrested and confined pending military trials. Holden refused to honor writs of habeas corpus issued by state chief justice Richmond M. Pearson, though the constitution of 1868 drawn up by the Republicans provided that this right could not be suspended. The Klan attorneys appealed to the federal district court, which stunned Holden by issuing the writs. The governor then appealed to President Grant, who advised him to honor the decision and deliver the prisoners to the regular courts for trials, which he did.

Defeat of Holden and the Republicans

The reaction to the Kirk-Holden War and the military arrests helped defeat the Republicans in the August 1870 election. With a two to one majority in the General Assembly, during the late fall, the Conservatives moved to impeach and remove Holden from office. In his annual message to the General Assembly, Holden, assuming a conciliatory tone, indicated that "peace and good order" had been restored, and he was therefore revoking his insurrection proclamations for Alamance and Caswell Counties. He promised to cooperate with the legislature in measures "to promote the prosperity and happiness of our people." The time for conciliation, however, had passed. On December 19, the House of Representatives voted eight articles of **impeachment** against the governor, most of which charged him with raising an illegal military force and wrongfully directing it to arrest and hold suspected Klansmen. Holden answered the charges by claiming that he had acted to protect the citizens of the state from "insurgents," and he had intended to surrender the Klansmen to the regular courts after order had been restored. On March 22, 1871, the North Carolina Senate rendered its verdict: Holden was found guilty and removed from office, the first governor in American history to suffer this indignity.

After a brief period of "exile" in Washington to escape possible court action against him, Holden returned to Raleigh in 1872. The next year, President Grant appointed him postmaster of Raleigh, but his support of Grant for the Republican nomination in 1880 led to his removal from office in 1881 by President **James A. Garfield**. Although he made peace with many of his old political foes, including Vance, Holden spent his post-Reconstruction years attempting in vain to obtain a reversal of the impeachment verdict. In North Carolina historical lore, he is the villain of the Reconstruction era. *See also* Amnesty Proclamations; Black Suffrage; Readmission; Redemption.

Further Reading: Harris, William C. *William Woods Holden: Firebrand of North Carolina Politics*. Baton Rouge: Louisiana State University Press, 1987; Raper, Horace W., and Thornton W. Mitchell, eds. *The Papers of William Woods Holden*. Raleigh: North Carolina Division of Archives and History, 2000; Trelease, Allen W. *White Terror: The Ku Klux Klan Conspiracy and Southern Reconstruction*. New York: Harper and Row, 1971.

William C. Harris

House Judiciary Committee

The U.S. House of Representatives has the constitutional responsibility to impeach federal officials if necessary. During Reconstruction, many people wanted President **Andrew Johnson** impeached because they disagreed with his policies. The House of Representatives referred all resolutions pertaining to the **impeachment of Andrew Johnson** to its Judiciary Committee, whose members were to conduct investigations to determine whether Johnson had actually done the things of which he was accused. If he had, the committee was to determine whether these were in fact impeachable offenses.

The Judiciary Committee, as of January 1867, consisted of nine lawyers. Four of them were **Moderate Republicans**, including committee chairman James F. Wilson (Iowa), Frederick E. Woodbridge (Vermont), Daniel Morris (New York), and Francis Thomas (Maryland). **George S. Boutwell** (Massachusetts), Thomas Williams (Pennsylvania), Burton C. Cook (Illinois), and William Lawrence (Ohio) were **Radical Republicans**, while Andrew J. Rogers (New Jersey) was the only member of the **Democratic Party**.

Although there had been considerable talk about impeachment previously, on January 7, 1867, Republican **James M. Ashley** (Ohio) was the first to introduce a resolution to impeach the president. The committee began secret investigations immediately. The issues under investigation included whether Johnson had improperly corresponded with former Confederate president **Jefferson Davis**, had sold offices, had made illegal appointments of **provisional governors** in the South, had improperly taken money from the U.S. Treasury, and had illegal dealings with some **railroads**. Several **cabinet** members and Judge Advocate General Joseph Holt answered the committee's summons to serve as witnesses, as did the controversial detective Lafayette Baker, and several disappointed office seekers. However, none of these witnesses produced much relevant information and the committee reported that the investigation should be continued.

Because the new Congress took their seats on March 4, 1867, several members of the Judiciary Committee changed. Republican John C. Churchill (New York), and Democrats Charles A. Eldredge (Wisconsin) and Samuel S. Marshall (Illinois) replaced Morris, Rogers, and Cook. The reorganized committee continued fishing for some impeachable private or political offense that Johnson might have committed. Witnesses testified about Johnson's veto messages, **pardons**, appointments, the **New Orleans riot**, the government's failure to try Jefferson Davis, and other issues. However, the committee still could find no impeachable offense and voted to adjourn on June 3, 1867. Although they soon met again, on June 26, the committee had to report that they could not have an impeachment charge ready before the next congressional session. Johnson added fuel to the impeachment fire in August when he suspended Secretary of War **Edwin M. Stanton** and removed army district commanders **Philip H. Sheridan** and **Daniel E. Sickles**. When the committee met, for a fourth time, in November 1867, they finally recommended impeachment by a narrow 5 to 4 vote. Wilson, Woodbridge, Eldredge, and Marshall opposed impeachment. Williams, who wrote the majority report, charged Johnson with a number of offenses, including pardoning traitors, causing the New Orleans riot, and defying Congress. Although Wilson and Woodbridge believed that Johnson had done the things charged, they did not agree that these were impeachable offenses.

On December 5, 1867, Boutwell introduced the impeachment resolution in the House. Many of the members believed that Johnson could not be impeached unless he had committed an indictable crime. Because there was no evidence that Johnson had done so, the members defeated the resolution by a vote of 108 to 57.

Johnson soon did something else to provoke impeachment sentiment. In February 1868, he removed Stanton from being secretary of war, allegedly in violation of the **Tenure of Office Act**. John Covode (Pennsylvania) quickly presented an impeachment resolution to the House. This time, however, the House bypassed the Judiciary Committee and referred the resolution to the **Joint Committee on Reconstruction**, chaired by Radical Republican **Thaddeus Stevens**. When presented by the committee to the House, this resolution to impeach Johnson passed on February 24, 1868, and the impeachment proceedings began. The Judiciary Committee as a whole had no further involvement with Johnson's impeachment and trial, although Wilson, Boutwell, and Williams served as **impeachment managers**. *See also* Amnesty Proclamations; Congressional Reconstruction; Presidential Reconstruction; Recusants; U.S. Constitution.

Further Reading: Trefousse, Hans L. *Impeachment of a President: Andrew Johnson, the Blacks, and Reconstruction.* Knoxville: University of Tennessee Press, 1975.

Glenna R. Schroeder-Lein

Howard, Oliver Otis (1830–1909)

A Union general during and after the Civil War, Oliver Otis Howard served during Reconstruction as commissioner of the War Department's **Bureau of Refugees, Freedmen, and Abandoned Lands**, commonly known as the Freedmen's Bureau. Although Howard was genuinely committed to black **education** and to the economic advancement and **civil rights** of **African Americans**, his record as Freedmen's Bureau commissioner was one of mixed success.

Background and Civil War Years

Howard was born on November 8, 1830, in Leeds, Maine. His father died when Howard was young, and his mother, who remarried, encouraged his education. He attended Bowdoin College during the late 1840s and graduated in 1850. Lacking immediate career prospects, Howard received an appointment to the U.S. Military Academy at West Point, secured for him by an uncle in Congress, despite Howard's initial lack of enthusiasm for a military career. He graduated in 1854, and decided to remain in the military. After fighting the Seminoles in **Florida**, Howard returned to West Point as an instructor in 1857. While in Florida, Howard had undergone a religious conversion experience and became an avowed Christian, and he served as an informal chaplain at

West Point. By 1860, he contemplated leaving the military for the ministry, but the outbreak of the Civil War convinced him to stay in the army. During the war, Howard earned the sobriquet "Christian General" for his religious zeal.

In spring 1861, Howard was commissioned a colonel of Maine volunteers, and he resigned his regular army commission. By that autumn, he had achieved the rank of brigadier general, and during the next two years he participated in nearly all the major battles of the Army of the Potomac. He lost his right arm during the Peninsula Campaign of spring 1862, but soon returned to command and fought at Antietam, Fredericksburg, Chancellorsville, and Gettysburg. Howard was promoted to major general of volunteers in November 1862, but he was largely responsible for the disastrous Union defeat at Chancellorsville in May 1863. The following fall, Howard was transferred to the western theater, and he participated in the 1864 Atlanta campaign. Union general **William T. Sherman** subsequently named Howard to command the Army of the Tennessee in Sherman's campaign through **Georgia** and the Carolinas, and at the end of the war, Howard was made a brigadier general in the regular army.

Howard and the Freedmen's Bureau

Also following the Confederate surrender, Secretary of War **Edwin M. Stanton** offered Howard the position of commissioner of the recently created Freedmen's Bureau. Building upon wartime relief and freedmen's aid efforts, and recognizing the need for a federal agency to oversee the South's transition from slavery to freedom, in March 1865, Congress had created the Freedmen's Bureau as a branch of the War Department. Howard's missionary sense of purpose, antislavery credentials, and distinguished combat record, along with the fact that the Freedmen's Bureau would be staffed largely by army personnel, made Howard a leading candidate for the commissioner's job. Further strengthening his prospects was Stanton's belief that Howard would be able to work with both religious and secular reformers in reconstructing the South. President **Abraham Lincoln** had not indicated his choice for bureau commissioner before his **assassination**, but Stanton believed Howard's qualifications made him acceptable to President **Andrew Johnson**, who approved the appointment. Choosing again to remain in the military, Howard became Freedmen's Bureau commissioner in May 1865.

Howard faced a number of challenges in his position. Congress had bestowed upon the bureau a daunting task. It was responsible for implementing free labor in the South, distributing federally controlled land to the freedmen, establishing schools, providing aid and relief to wartime refugees and to the destitute of both races, maintaining systems of public health, adjudicating disputes and securing justice, and providing many other essential services in the war-ravaged South. To fulfill these tasks, the bureau initially received no fiscal appropriation of its own and was chronically understaffed. Despite its broad mandate, moreover, the bureau was generally regarded as temporary, causing many white southerners and other opponents to resist its authority.

Howard himself reflected the contradictions of the bureau's mission to remake southern society. Recognizing that the former slaves required some form of assistance while emerging from centuries of servitude, he also subscribed to nineteenth-century free-labor ideology, which emphasized individual initiative and the supremacy of the capitalist marketplace, and he feared the creation of a class of permanent dependents. Howard also displayed an almost naive faith in human nature, and he often seemed oblivious to the machinations of Reconstruction politics, in which he, as head of the controversial Freedmen's Bureau, was inevitably embroiled.

Struggles with President Johnson

Perhaps Howard's greatest challenge was President Johnson's opposition to the Freedmen's Bureau. Subscribing to an essentially conservative vision of Reconstruction, Johnson did not foresee a fundamental overturning of southern society, and he believed that the Freedmen's Bureau represented an unconstitutional expansion of federal authority. In particular, Johnson objected to the bureau's mandate, as defined by Congress, to make available to freedmen the abandoned and confiscated land that various federal agencies had controlled at the end of war and that had been transferred to the Freedmen's Bureau. Although Johnson's **Amnesty Proclamation** of May 1865 restored almost all property rights to pardoned ex-Confederates, the legal status of bureau-held land remained unclear, and in late July, Howard drafted an order instructing bureau agents not to return such land to its former owners, even to those who had secured presidential **pardons**. This order was never officially promulgated, but Johnson objected to it and directed Howard in September to issue a second order rescinding the first and specifying that bureau-controlled land be returned to pardoned former Confederates. Although some freedmen gained title to a portion of this land, most of it was eventually restored to its former owners.

Johnson also resorted to other tactics, both overt and subtle, in his war on the Freedmen's Bureau. He pressured Howard to dismiss assistant commissioners (heads of the bureau in the southern states), such as **Rufus Saxton** of **South Carolina**, who were too radical in their political views and who advocated too strongly the interests of the freedmen. In a move that contributed to the break between Johnson and congressional Republicans, in February 1866, Johnson vetoed the **Freedmen's Bureau Bill**, which authorized extending the bureau's existence beyond the originally imposed one-year time limit (after the end of hostilities). That spring, Johnson also ordered an official investigation clearly intended to discredit the bureau. Congress subsequently passed two laws in July continuing the bureau for another two years (overriding a second veto) and providing it a separate appropriation. Despite these difficulties, and despite his beliefs that Johnson had subverted the will of Congress and had undermined the mission of the Freedmen's Bureau, especially on land restoration, Howard never offered his resignation as bureau commissioner in protest.

End of the Freedmen's Bureau and Post-Bureau Years

Notwithstanding the many challenges it faced and the numerous disadvantages it suffered, the Freedmen's Bureau under Howard dramatically improved the lives of thousands of freedmen and indigent whites during the immediate postwar years. With passage of the **Military Reconstruction Acts** in 1867, however, the bureau lost much of its independent identity within the War Department, and Howard relinquished most of his authority to the military district commanders. As southern states gained **readmission** to the Union, the bureau surrendered most of its responsibilities to the civilian governments, although Congress enacted one final law extending the bureau until after the **elections of 1868**. At the end of that year, the bureau ceased all operations except for its educational work and the securing of black veterans' bounty claims, which continued until 1872, when the bureau was finally closed.

Education had been of particular importance to Howard, and he was instrumental in Congress's 1867 chartering of historically black Howard University in Washington, D.C., which was named after him. He served as president of the school from 1869 until 1873 (while still bureau commissioner) and continued to be involved in its affairs for the rest of his life. Although the school was not affiliated with the Freedmen's Bureau, an accident during its construction resulted in an 1870 congressional investigation that exonerated Howard but found much inefficiency and misappropriation of funds within the bureau. Moreover, irregularities surrounding the paying of veterans' bounties led to a military court of inquiry in 1874 that again absolved Howard of wrongdoing. That same year, the **Freedman's Savings and Trust Company** (the Freedman's Bank) failed, a victim of poor oversight and the financial **Panic of 1873**. Although not officially part of the Freedmen's Bureau, the bank was closely identified with it, and the bank's demise further clouded Howard's and the bureau's reputations.

In 1874, Howard returned to active duty in the Pacific Northwest, and he led the 1877 campaign that captured Chief Joseph and the Nez Perce Indians. He served briefly as superintendent of West Point during the early 1880s, was promoted to major general in 1886, and held several other commands until his retirement in 1894. Howard settled in Burlington, Vermont, and remained active in religious and educational endeavors. He published his autobiography in 1908, and he died on October 26, 1909, in Burlington, where he was buried. *See also* Agriculture; American Indians; American Missionary Association (AMA); Black Codes; Black Troops (U.S.C.T.) in the Occupied South; Cabinets, Executive; Churches; Civil Rights Act of 1866; Congressional Reconstruction; Contracts; Democratic Party; Eaton, John; Edisto Island, South Carolina; Field Order No. 15; Freedmen's Relief Societies; Grant, Ulysses S.; Labor Systems; Port Royal Experiment; Presidential Reconstruction; Republicans, Moderate; Republicans, Radical; Sharecropping; Southern Homestead Act; Trumbull, Lyman; U.S. Army and Reconstruction; Vagrancy.

Further Reading: Bentley, George R. *A History of the Freedmen's Bureau*. Philadelphia: University of Pennsylvania Press, 1955; Carpenter, John A. *Sword and Olive Branch: Oliver Otis Howard*. Pittsburgh: University of Pittsburgh Press, 1964; Howard, Oliver Otis. *Autobiography of Oliver Otis Howard*. 2 vols. New York: The Baker & Taylor Company, 1908; McFeely, William S. *Yankee Stepfather: General O. O. Howard and the Freedmen*. New Haven, CT: Yale University Press, 1968.

John C. Rodrigue

Humphreys, Benjamin Grubb (1808–1882)

Born on August 26, 1808, in Claiborne County, **Mississippi**, Benjamin Grubb Humphreys was one of thirteen children. He attended preparatory schools in both **Kentucky** and New Jersey. He was admitted to West Point in 1825, but after a Christmas frolic that turned into a student riot, he was expelled in May 1827.

Back in Mississippi, Humphreys studied law and assisted his father in managing the family's home plantation, the Hermitage. He married his first wife, Mary McLaughlin, in 1832, and together they established a home on the Big Black River. Three years later, his wife died and Humphreys and his children (Mary and Thomas) returned to his father's plantation.

An antebellum Whig, Humphreys was elected as an "Independent" to the lower house of the state legislature in 1837. Two years later, he served a term as state senator. After that, he retired from politics and devoted himself to his agricultural interests, his second wife, and their growing family. Reentering politics in the crisis atmosphere of 1860, he ran unsuccessfully as an outspoken Unionist candidate for Mississippi's secessionist convention. Once the state had cast its lot with the Confederacy, however, Humphreys raised a company of volunteers and entered the Confederate service.

First, as a captain and later as regimental commander, Humphreys's Twenty-first Mississippi Infantry served in **Virginia** as part of William Barksdale's Mississippi brigade. Compiling a distinguished record in the field, he replaced Barksdale in command of the brigade after the latter's death at Gettysburg. Humphreys was promoted to brigadier general the following month. His command, then, accompanied **James Longstreet** to **Georgia** and **Tennessee** and was under Jubal A. Early in the Shenandoah Valley in 1864. Wounded at Berryville in 1864, he spent the remainder of the year recovering, but just before the war's end, he was appointed to the command of a new, experimental unit composed exclusively of slaves. The conflict concluded, however, before his command was tested under fire.

Returning to Mississippi, Humphreys quickly involved himself in the postwar politics of the state. Following under President **Andrew Johnson**'s restoration system, he was elected governor on October 2, 1865, with a vote of 19,036. Other antebellum Whigs won all of Mississippi's congressional elections, as well as the majority in the state legislature. He received a presidential **pardon** from Andrew Johnson three days later. Humphreys saw himself as a voice of moderation and reunion. However, he was forced to defend the state's newly enacted **Black Codes** in public as well as the state's growing reputation for racial **violence**. Conditions in Mississippi, conflict with the military governor, and the emergence of **Congressional Reconstruction** resulted in the physical removal of Humphreys from the governor's office by federal soldiers.

Humphreys essentially retired from elective politics after 1868, but he became a respected leader in Mississippi's new Conservative Party. He returned to his plantation, Lucknow, outside Port Gibson, where he practiced law and dabbled in the insurance business. He died there in 1882. *See also* Military Reconstruction Acts; Presidential Reconstruction; U.S. Army and Reconstruction.

Further Reading: Harris, William. *Presidential Reconstruction in Mississippi.* Baton Rouge: Louisiana State University Press, 1967; Rainwater, Percy L., ed. "The Autobiography of Benjamin Grubb Humphreys." *Mississippi Valley Historical Review* 21 (1934): 231–54; Warner, Ezra. *Generals in Gray: Lives of Confederate Commanders.* Baton Rouge: Louisiana State University Press, 1959.

Martin J. Hardeman

Hunnicutt, James W. (1814–1880)

James Walter Hunnicutt, Baptist minister, newspaper editor, Unionist, and **Radical Republican**, was born in **South Carolina** in 1814. Despite his South Carolina birth, Hunnicutt called **Virginia** home for most of his life. In 1848, Hunnicutt launched the *Christian Banner* newspaper in Fredericksburg, Virginia. As its editor, he exhibited an acerbic temperament and a penchant for controversy that made his paper a popular read in his adopted community. During the secession crisis and Civil War, however, Hunnicutt's opinions clashed with the town's pro-Confederate majority. His outspoken unionism ultimately forced Hunnicutt to flee Fredericksburg in the summer of 1862. Confederate defeat brought Hunnicutt home, and he quickly became the state's leading Radical Republican.

The Civil War halted publication of the *Christian Banner*, but failed to silence its editor. In October 1865, he launched the Richmond *New Nation* newspaper, which he used to criticize President **Andrew Johnson**'s conciliatory Reconstruction policy. Early the following year, he was among the southern Unionists who testified before Congress's **Joint Committee on Reconstruction**. Hunnicutt's testimony reaffirmed his disdain for the Confederacy and its leaders. Such testimony showed Congress the depth of opposition to Johnson's policy. Hunnicutt believed the president's strategy placed Virginia's restoration in the hands of former Confederates who mistreated blacks and white southern Unionists.

His defense of blacks' **civil rights** defined Hunnicutt's Reconstruction career. Through the *New Nation*, Hunnicutt advocated **black suffrage** as well as the redistribution of occupied lands to blacks. His commitment to these issues distinguished the editor as the most radical Republican in Virginia, and strained his relationship with his **Moderate Republican** colleagues. As the party worked to establish a solid organization in Virginia, it had to shift its focus from cultivating northern support to seeking local backing. Hunnicutt had strong support among the **African American** population and more urban areas where many northern migrants congregated, but in the countryside, white Virginians viewed his ideas with little enthusiasm.

The conflict within the party came to a head in 1867. Drawing upon his broad support among black Virginians, Hunnicutt sought the Republican nomination for governor in the 1868 election. In April, a convention dominated by Hunnicutt and his black supporters drafted a radical platform that shocked Moderate Republicans. A second convention in August undermined Republican unity, leading the moderates to do whatever they could to undermine Hunnicutt's candidacy. His failure to secure the party's nomination began a steady decline of Hunnicutt's political influence. The editor's efforts to include a provision **disfranchising** former Confederates in the state's new constitution later that year sealed his political fate.

In 1868, Hunnicutt's opponents strove to silence him publicly for good. Months of pressure forced the *New Nation* out of business. Renewed factional fighting among the Republicans in the early 1870s sparked a brief comeback and one last run for public office, but Hunnicutt failed in what became his final bid for public office. Smarting from that defeat, Hunnicutt retired to Stafford County to live out his final years peacefully at home. He died in 1880. *See also* Congressional Reconstruction; Presidential Reconstruction; Republicans, Liberal; Scalawags.

Further Reading: Eckenrode, Hamilton James. *The Political History of Virginia during the Reconstruction*. Baltimore, MD: Johns Hopkins Press, 1904; Fessenden, William Pitt, James W. Grimes, et al., eds. *Report of the Joint Committee on Reconstruction, at the First Session, Thirty-Ninth Congress*. Washington, DC: Government Printing Office, 1866; Hunnicutt, James W. *The Conspiracy Unveiled: The South Sacrificed, or the Horrors of Secession*. Philadelphia: J. B. Lippincott & Co., 1863; Lowe, Richard. *Republicans and Reconstruction in Virginia, 1856–1870*. Charlottesville: University Press of Virginia, 1991; Olsen, Otto H., ed. *Reconstruction and Redemption in the South*. Baton Rouge: Louisiana State University Press, 1980; Taylor, Alrutheus A. *The Negro in the Reconstruction of Virginia*. Washington, DC: The Association for the Study of Negro Life and History, 1926.

Steven E. Nash

I

Impeachment Managers

The impeachment managers were, in effect, the prosecution at the Senate trial of President **Andrew Johnson.** Chosen from their peers in the House of Representatives, these men were expected to take the eleven Articles of Impeachment and convince the U.S. Senate that these offenses warranted conviction and removal from office.

The House selected seven Republicans to serve as managers. The chair was **John A. Bingham** of Ohio. The most vocal and extreme of the mangers were **Thaddeus Stevens** of Pennsylvania and **Benjamin F. Butler** of Massachusetts. Other members were former general John A. Logan of Illinois, **George Boutwell** of Massachusetts, Thomas Williams of Pennsylvania, and James F. Wilson of Iowa. All presented solid Republican credentials, as there was no need for neutrality here; although charges of partisanship will forever taint the impeachment vote and the Senate vote, the impeachment managers were deliberately selected to present a powerful, convincing case against Johnson.

This they did not do. The trial, which began on March 30 and lasted until May 26, 1868, represented an unprecedented event in American political history, so the managers had no training or guidelines to follow. Although every manager was in fact a lawyer, questions and disagreements over how to proceed led to dissension in the team, and a poor showing at the trial. Stevens, the most forceful and famous of the seven, had become seriously ill (he never did recover) and this deprived the committee of his contribution; most orations and arguments were left to Representative Butler, who many found as antagonistic as Stevens, but without his talent or passion. Newspapers spoofed his performance almost daily, and even pro-Republican presses called for a replacement. The managers also called witnesses, although the nature of the charges left little of fact unknown and provided no real rationale for witnesses.

The managers frequently called for changes in rules and objected to various components of Johnson's defense counsel's tactics.

Many forces converged to undercut the manager's case against Johnson: The articles of impeachment were themselves weak, especially those hinging upon the dubious **Tenure of Office Act**. The Senate trial was presided over by Chief Justice **Salmon P. Chase**, who accommodated no horseplay or antics; he was neutral, or even pro-Johnson, in his interpretations of the rules of order, so the managers received no assistance from him. Johnson's five-man defense counsel was exceptional, boasting two former attorneys general (**Reverdy Johnson** and Henry Stanbery) and a former **Supreme Court** justice (Benjamin R. Curtis).

Managers and defense counsel presented their final statements in the last week of April and first week of May. Voting was scheduled for May 12, 1868, but was postponed until May 16. Managers and other Republicans watched in horror as the Senate acquitted Johnson of Article XI by a vote of 35 to 19, one vote shy of the two-thirds necessary for conviction. Voting commenced on Article II on May 26, with exactly the same result. The managers had failed to convince the Senate that President Johnson was guilty of "high crimes and misdemeanors." The Senate as high court adjourned, and the position of impeachment manager evaporated.

Benjamin Butler, however, was not finished. Butler, and perhaps other managers, thought the result impossible and the margin too curious. Certain that Johnson was acquitted as a result of foul play, Butler convinced the House to allow the managers to act as an impromptu investigating committee. They charged that Republican senators had been bribed for their votes, and especially targeted **Edmund Ross** of Kansas (even though his moderate leaning was well documented). Butler issued subpoenas, called witnesses, interviewed scores of people, and even confiscated bank records, telegrams, and mail. In the end, he was unable to find any evidence of bribery. *See also* Black, Jeremiah Sullivan; Congressional Reconstruction; Democratic Party; House Judiciary Committee; Joint Committee on Reconstruction; Presidential Reconstruction; Recusants; Republicans, Radical; Schofield, John M.; Stanton, Edwin M.; Thomas, Lorenzo; U.S. Constitution.

Further Reading: Benedict, Michael Les. *The Impeachment and Trial of Andrew Johnson*. New York: W. W. Norton and Co., 1973; Schroeder-Lein, Glenna, and Richard Zuczek. *Andrew Johnson: A Biographical Companion*. Santa Barbara, CA: ABC-CLIO, 2001; Trefousse, Hans L. *Impeachment of a President: Andrew Johnson, the Blacks, and Reconstruction*. Knoxville: University of Tennessee Press, 1975.

Richard Zuczek

Impeachment of Andrew Johnson (1868)

A three-year struggle between President **Andrew Johnson** and the **Moderate** and **Radical Republicans** in Congress over the extent and direction of Reconstruction culminated in 1868 with the impeachment of the president. The Republican Party was dedicated to protecting the **civil rights** of the newly freed **African Americans** and preventing the ex-Confederates from reassuming power in the South. Johnson's strict constructionist view of the **U.S. Constitution**, his determination to prevent a social revolution in his native South, and his desire to build a new Conservative Party from a coalition of white southerners, northern Democrats, and Conservative Republicans led to a clash with Congress.

Conflicting Reconstruction Policies

In May 1865, Johnson announced his plan for restoring the southern states to the Union. Like his predecessor **Abraham Lincoln**, he wanted a lenient peace, and, also like his predecessor, he offered a blanket **pardon** for virtually all former rebels. The ex-Confederate states then needed only to organize **constitutional conventions** where they would renounce secession, repudiate all debts incurred during the war, and **abolish slavery**. Elections for state and national offices would follow, the new legislatures would ratify the **Thirteenth Amendment**, and the restoration process would end with the **readmission** of the states.

Initially, many conservative Republicans in Congress supported the president's plan. However, when the former Confederate states established restrictive laws known as the **Black Codes** to hold the former slaves in subordinate economic and social positions and elected former Confederate military and civilian leaders to Congress, the Radical wing of the party convinced other Republicans that the president's plan had to be modified.

Congress refused to seat the former rebels sent to Washington and established a **Joint Committee on Reconstruction** to study the situation in the South. Wanting to play an active role in reconstructing the South, Congress passed two bills in 1866 to support the freedpeople. The **Freedmen's Bureau Bill** expanded the agency's operations, and the **Civil Rights** bill extended citizenship to blacks and essentially nullified the Black Codes. Not only were these measures resisted by white southerners, they were resisted by Johnson as well. He viewed them as unnecessary and unconstitutional, and he vetoed both. Congress overrode his veto of the civil rights bill and subsequently passed another Freedmen's Bureau bill. Johnson, however, was determined that the chief executive would control the restoration of the South. When Congress passed the **Fourteenth Amendment** granting black citizenship, nullifying the Black Codes, and restricting the political influence of ex-Confederates, he urged the southern states to not ratify the measure. Johnson and Congress pleaded their cases to the northern public in the **elections of 1866**. The Republicans won a huge majority in both houses of Congress and assumed control of the Reconstruction process.

Stunned by the white South's obstinacy, Congress passed the **Military Reconstruction Act** in March 1867. It organized loyal governments in all former Confederate states except **Tennessee**, which, having ratified the Fourteenth Amendment in 1866, was regarded as reconstructed. The ten remaining states were divided into five military districts, each headed by a major general in the **U.S. Army**. The major general supervised the registration of voters, including blacks. These voters would select delegates to participate in constitutional conventions where they would write new constitutions providing for **black suffrage** and barring ex-Confederates from holding state and federal offices. Only when a state had ratified its new constitution and the Fourteenth Amendment would the process of political reorganization be complete. Johnson vetoed this Military Reconstruction Act and also two subsequent acts designed to clarify and strengthen it. The Republican majority in Congress overrode his vetoes easily. However, under his authority as commander in chief and in an effort to slow or redirect the congressional intent, Johnson appointed conservative officers, such as **Winfield Scott Hancock**, to command the military districts.

Congress versus the President

While many Radical Republicans called for Johnson's removal, their conservative and moderate colleagues sought to curtail his power through two laws of questionable constitutionality. A provision of the Army Appropriations Act of 1867 required the president to issue all orders to army commanders through the general in chief of the army, **Ulysses S. Grant**. The Radicals hoped Grant could exercise a controlling influence over Johnson, but the most direct challenge to presidential authority was the **Tenure of Office Act**, which authorized an official appointed with the Senate's consent to remain in office until that body approved a successor. Ostensibly intended to protect **patronage** offices, the law, in reality, was designed to prevent the removal of Secretary of War **Edwin M. Stanton**, a Radical in Johnson's inherited **Cabinet**. Johnson vetoed the Tenure of Office Act, but signed the Military Appropriations bill in order to fund the army, despite its command provisions.

Even with these attempts to restrict Johnson's impact on Reconstruction, the president retained a considerable capacity to obstruct congressional efforts. As commander in chief, he appointed conservative generals to administer the five military districts, and as chief executive he could interpret the Reconstruction Act narrowly in terms of its enforcement. Radicals recognized Johnson's intent and advocated his removal from office. Their first **impeachment** effort occurred in January 1867, when the House passed a resolution authorizing the **House Judiciary Committee** to investigate the possibility. However, Moderates dominated the committee and saw no reason for such an extreme step. While Radicals claimed that the president's thwarting of congressional legislation constituted a misuse of power and was, therefore, grounds for impeachment, Moderates insisted that the president could only be removed from office for committing indictable crimes.

Perhaps encouraged by this, Johnson took advantage of a loophole in the Tenure of Office Act, which permitted the president to remove and appoint officials while the Senate was in recess. Once reconvened, the Senate would then decide to support or reject the president's actions. Johnson waited until Congress adjourned and suspended Stanton in August 1867. He then persuaded Ulysses S. Grant to assume the position of interim secretary of war. Johnson surmised that Grant's status as a war hero would prevent the Radicals from forcing the general's removal. Grant had urged the president not to suspend Stanton, but he accepted the appointment, perhaps hoping to curb Johnson's influence with the military. However, Grant could not prevent

Johnson from removing generals sympathetic to the Radical agenda and replacing them with conservatives or Democrats who would stymie their efforts. According to Republicans in the press, in Congress, and across the South, these moves encouraged white southern resistance to **Congressional Reconstruction**. This time, the Radicals in the House were able to force a vote on impeachment. In December 1867, the House defeated the measure 108 to 57.

Johnson's Overt Challenge

Congress had reconvened, and now the Senate had to decide to reject or uphold Johnson's suspension of Stanton. If the Senate opposed the president's action, then Johnson planned to challenge the constitutionality of the Tenure of Office Act in the courts. To do this, however, he needed Grant's cooperation. Johnson believed he had secured Grant's word to remain as interim secretary regardless of the Senate decision; yet when the Senate rejected Johnson's rationale for Stanton's suspension, Grant vacated the office, and turned it back to its former occupant. Johnson charged the general with bad faith. A bitter exchange of letters between the men headlined the front pages of newspapers as Grant proclaimed he would not violate the act.

Foiled in his attempt to use Grant's prestige to rid himself of Stanton, the president challenged Congress headlong by *removing* Stanton (not suspending him), this time while the Senate *was in session*. He nominated Adjutant General **Lorenzo Thomas** as interim secretary of war. An uproar erupted in Congress, and when Republican senators urged Stanton to ignore the order, he barricaded himself in the War Department and refused to leave.

Cartoon from *Frank Leslie's Newspaper* of the formal notice of the impeachment of Andrew Johnson, 1868. (Courtesy of the Library of Congress.)

1868: Impeachment and Trial

Johnson's obvious disregard of the terms of the Tenure of Office Act convinced even Moderate Republicans that he would oppose all congressional requirements in the Reconstruction process. Therefore, on February 24, 1868, the House voted to impeach the president along a strict party-line vote of 126 to 47. So eager were the Republicans to remove Johnson that they voted to impeach the president before drawing up formal charges. The House then created a committee of prosecutors known as **impeachment managers** that included Radicals such as **Thaddeus Stevens**, **George Julian**, **Benjamin Butler**, John Logan, and **George Boutwell**.

The House promptly produced eleven articles of impeachment. The first eight dealt with Johnson's attempt, in violation of the Tenure of Office Act, to remove Stanton and to appoint a successor without the Senate's consent. The ninth article charged Johnson with trying to persuade the army commander in the **District of Columbia** to violate the command provisions of the 1867 Army Appropriations bill (**Command of the Army Act**) by accepting orders directly from the president. The tenth article accused the president of harboring resentment against Congress, and the final "omnibus" article essentially drew together all the charges of the previous ten.

The Senate trial began March 30, 1868, and continued with interruptions for two months. This protracted process worked in the president's favor by cooling the passions that had climaxed with his attempted removal of Stanton. Johnson's defense counsel included some of the leading lawyers in the country: **Henry Stanbery**, the attorney general; William M. Evarts, a future attorney general under Johnson and secretary of state under President **Rutherford B. Hayes**; and Benjamin R. Curtis, a former justice of the **Supreme Court**. During the trial, these men demonstrated a good deal more legal acumen than did the House's **impeachment managers**. Johnson's team based its defense on three arguments: that a government official can be impeached only for criminal offenses that would be indictable in ordinary court; that Johnson had committed no crime by seeking to remove Stanton and testing the constitutionality of the Tenure of Office Act; and that because the act applied only to cabinet officers "during the term of the president by whom they may have been appointed," it did not apply to Stanton, who had been appointed by Lincoln.

The impeachment managers challenged this line of defense, asserting that because Johnson was serving out Lincoln's term, the Tenure of Office Act did cover Stanton. To allow the president to disobey a law to test it in court would set a dangerous precedent. Finally, whether or not Johnson was guilty of any crime, impeachment was a political rather than criminal process. Regardless of the charges, everyone understood that Johnson was being tried for his three years of relentless opposition to the Republican Reconstruction program.

Although Moderate Republicans abhorred Johnson, many feared his removal would pave the way for future parties with a two-thirds congressional majority to remove any president who disagreed with their proposals. The constitutional balance of power would be destroyed. Moderates also distrusted radical **Benjamin Wade**, president pro tem of the Senate and next in line for the presidency. Using intermediaries, Johnson and the Moderates worked toward an understanding. The president gave no more speeches or interviews denouncing Congress, and he promised to enforce the Military Reconstruction Acts. Johnson also appointed the highly respected general **John M. Schofield** as secretary of war.

On May 16, 1868, the Senate voted on the eleventh article of impeachment, 35–19. All twelve Democrats and seven Moderate Republicans voted against conviction and removal. With a two-thirds majority needed to remove the president from office, Johnson had been saved by one single vote. Votes on articles 2 and 3 on May 26 ended in the same result, forcing the impeachment managers to concede defeat. As these were the most legitimate and valid articles, failure to reach conviction on these left the others irrelevant.

Nonetheless, Johnson continued to defy Congress by vetoing Reconstruction bills and criticizing congressional Reconstruction efforts. Congress continued to pass the acts over his objections, and while the process frustrated both parties, the constitutional balance between the president and Congress had been preserved. The nation had survived a serious challenge to the stability of its government. *See also* Bureau of Refugees, Freedmen, and Abandoned Lands; Canby, Edward Richard Sprigg; Disfranchisement; Elections of 1868; Pope, John M.; Presidential Reconstruction; Recusants; Ross, Edmund G.; Sheridan, Philip H.; Sickles, Daniel E.

Further Reading: Benedict, Michael Les. *The Impeachment and Trial of Andrew Johnson*. New York: W. W. Norton and Co., 1973; McKitrick, Eric L. *Andrew Johnson and Reconstruction*. Chicago: University of Chicago Press, 1960; reprint, New York: Oxford University Press, 1988; Trefousse, Hans L. *Impeachment of a President: Andrew Johnson, the Blacks, and Reconstruction*. Knoxville: University of Tennessee Press, 1975; reprint, New York: Fordham University Press, 1999.

John D. Fowler

Indians. *See* American Indians.

J

Jenkins, Charles J. (1807–1883)

Best known as the first elected governor of **Georgia** after the Civil War, Charles Jones Jenkins was also the last governor to take residence in the governor's mansion in Milledgeville, Georgia.

Antebellum Georgian

Charles Jones Jenkins was born on January 6, 1805, in Beauford District, **South Carolina**. He moved with his family to Jefferson County, Georgia, in 1816. Jenkins completed his undergraduate education at Union College in New York and later studied law with John Berrien of Savannah, Georgia. He was elected to the Georgia House of Representatives in 1830. The following year in 1831, he became attorney general of the state of Georgia. Jenkins was often the Speaker of the House when the **Democratic Party** was in the majority in the legislature and remained active in the legislature during the period between 1836 and 1850.

He also became well known in political circles in Georgia as the author of "The Georgia Platform," a proclamation issued by a special state convention that supported the Compromise of 1850 and was particularly opposed to acts of Congress that would abolish slavery. The Compromise of 1850 included legislation by Congress that addressed issues including slavery and territorial boundaries that developed after the Mexican-American War (1846–1848). Jenkins became a state senator in 1856 and later, during the Civil War, he was appointed by Governor **Joseph E. Brown** as a justice of the Georgian Supreme Court.

Conservative Reconstruction Governor

In June 1865, President **Andrew Johnson** appointed James Johnson **provisional governor** of Georgia. The Reconstruction of Georgia was initiated by a convention held in Milledgeville, Georgia, in October 1865. Charles Jones Jenkins worked with Herschel V. Johnson to manage this convention of nearly 300 delegates. Johnson acted as the presiding officer while Jenkins held the office of chairman of the committee on business. Jenkins's active participation in this body of legislation and in the efforts to restore Georgia to the Union allowed him to be viewed as the only viable candidate for the governorship of Georgia.

Jenkins was unanimously supported by the convention and on December 14, 1865, was inaugurated as governor-elect. The provisional governor, James Johnson, was not officially removed until five days later. Jenkins immediately began working to resolve the state budget crisis and address other issues of restoration including the ratification of the **Thirteenth Amendment** to the **U.S. Constitution**. Jenkins's tenure as governor of Georgia was between 1865 and 1868. During this time, he was able to resolve the state budget and restore the Western and Atlantic **Railroad**. Jenkins also persuaded the Georgia legislature not to ratify the **Fourteenth Amendment** in November 1866, which Republicans required for **readmission** to the Union. The rejection of this amendment by every former Confederate state except **Tennessee** was the beginning of the end of Andrew Johnson's program, and with it Georgia's conservative efforts toward Reconstruction.

In 1867, the U.S. Congress revoked the legitimacy of the governments in most of the southern states under the **Military Reconstruction Acts**. The southern states were divided into five military districts. **Alabama**, **Florida**, and Georgia were all placed in the Third Military District. Southern states were expected to pay various debts of the war and this caused uproar among many of the legislative bodies in these states. Governor Jenkins traveled to Washington, D.C., to enter a petition before the **Supreme Court** for an injunction against the enforcement of the Reconstruction Act that authorized military control in his state. Jenkins also refused to have Georgia pay the state funds that were ordered by the federal government for a **constitutional convention**. He protested the federal government's mandate that $40,000 in state funds be used to pay for this convention. Some accounts report that Jenkins protested payment for this convention because it was racially integrated; other accounts note that Jenkins believed that the proceedings were illegal and was concerned about Georgia's recently stabilized budget.

With his refusal to pay for this convention, Jenkins was removed from office in January 1868. The military reconstruction of Georgia was supervised by General **John M. Pope**, who installed General Thomas H. Ruger as military governor in 1868. **Rufus B. Bullock** was appointed provisional governor of Georgia in January 1868 and was inaugurated as the official governor in July of the same year. Jenkins fled the state, and took records of the governor's office along with the seal of the executive department. He also removed state funds and deposited the funds into a New York bank account. Jenkins toured Europe and later fled to Nova Scotia until Reconstruction fervor died down in Georgia, in 1872. He returned to Augusta, Georgia, in the early 1870s, and gave all of the state property in his possession to then governor James M. Smith.

Post-Gubernatorial Career

Jenkins was a popular governor because of his resistance to **Congressional Reconstruction** during his tenure. In 1872, he received two Electoral College votes for the vice presidency of the United States because of the death of the **Liberal Republican** candidate, **Horace Greeley**, who had been endorsed by the **Democratic party**. For a while, Jenkins retired to private life and did not reenter politics until 1877, when he became the chair/president of the Georgia Constitutional Convention that year. Jenkins also became president of the Board of Trustees of the University of Georgia. Charles Jones Jenkins died on June 14, 1883. Jenkins County, Georgia, was named in his honor in 1905. *See also* Amnesty Proclamations; Black Codes; Disfranchisement; Presidential Reconstruction.

Further Reading: Cimbala, Paul. "The Terms of Freedom: The Freedmen's Bureau and Reconstruction in Georgia, 1865–1870." Ph.D. dissertation, Emory University, 1983; James, Joseph. "Southern Reaction to the Proposal of the Fourteenth Amendment." *Journal of Southern History* 22, no. 4 (November 1956): 477–97; McCrary, Royce, ed. "The Authorship of the Georgia Platform of 1850: A Letter by Charles J. Jenkins." *Georgia Historical Quarterly* 54 (Winter 1970): 585–90; Thompson, Mildred. *Reconstruction in Georgia*. Freeport, NY: Books for Library Press, 1915, reprinted 1971.

Kijua Sanders-McMurtry

Jim Crow Laws

Following the Civil War, and with it the **abolition of slavery**, a large body of custom and law developed across the South that was meant to regulate relations between **African Americans** and whites. They were collectively referred to as Jim Crow, a term taken from the name of a popular prewar minstrel character that appeared in blackface. While their main aim was to enforce racial segregation, Jim Crow also represented a pervasive—and invasive—system designed to remind black southerners of their inferiority. It prevented them from marrying across racial lines, attending the same schools as whites, and accessing on an equal basis all manner of public services and facilities. These codes placed humiliating restrictions on blacks throughout their lives, and even after their deaths, as southern cemeteries were segregated as well.

Origins

While precursors to Jim Crow can be found in the prewar North and in the treatment of free blacks in the South before the Civil War, the postwar system's origins lay in Reconstruction. It was in the tumult and confusion of this period that its early outlines are visible, as the people of the South struggled to establish a new racial order to replace slavery. White southerners greatly resented slavery's end and during **Presidential Reconstruction**, when they controlled the South, sought to return blacks as close to slave status as possible through the **Black Codes**. These laws restricted blacks to working as agricultural laborers or domestic servants, and even permitted their arrest if they refused to work for whites. Both blacks and their white supporters in the North, especially **Radical Republicans** in the U.S. Congress, vigorously opposed the Black Codes. The Radicals worked to guarantee blacks citizenship and equality through the **Civil Rights Act of 1866** and soon thereafter through the **Fourteenth Amendment** to the **U.S. Constitution**, which Congress required the southern states to ratify before they would be allowed to reenter the Union.

Informal Segregation

Despite the activities of Congress aimed at insuring racial equality in the South, informal segregation appeared in the region from the earliest days following the Civil War. In part, this de facto or customary segregation merely reflected the very real divide between the two races that had existed even under slavery, and persisted and even grew under freedom. During Reconstruction, many blacks proved eager to carve out for themselves an existence independent of whites. Most notably, blacks broke away from white-controlled denominations and established their own **churches**. They reunited their families, resisting attempts to keep black children under the control of former owners through forced apprenticeships. Many would have also established an independent black economy, with former slaves farming for themselves, except for their failure to obtain land during Reconstruction. Indeed, the priority of blacks during Reconstruction seems less to insist on racial integration, but simply on obtaining access to the public facilities and formal equality under the law.

A good example of informal segregation during Reconstruction was in **education**. Most places in the South did not have public schools prior to the Civil War. Hence, the priority of state and local governments during this period was to establish public school systems, and the main concern of black parents was to win their children access to public education. The integration of such schools did not appear to have been a significant concern. Both white and black parents seemed to have assumed their children would attend separate schools. In fact, of all the school systems that appeared in the South during Reconstruction, only the one in New Orleans is known to have integrated schools, and its experiment in interracial education came to an abrupt end in 1874, when the schools' operations were disrupted by white rioters.

Formal Segregation

Despite the widespread existence of informal segregation, a formal—legally mandated—Jim Crow system did not appear until after Reconstruction. While black southerners apparently acquiesced to many forms of informal segregation during Reconstruction, as long as they had access to the public facilities and services they desired, they and their white allies during Reconstruction opposed formalizing segregation as a part of the law. Indeed, they fought for formal equality. The **Civil Rights Act of 1875** outlawed racial discrimination under federal law in the access and use of trains, hotels, and other public facilities. Yet, to get this act through Congress, its supporters had to remove any effective enforcement provisions from the law. So it was never truly implemented and became invalid in 1883, when the **Supreme Court** ruled it unconstitutional.

So formal segregation—characterized by laws formally distinguishing between the races—started after the end of Reconstruction. The first state to enact such a statute was **Tennessee**, which segregated its railway cars in 1882. Under its **railroad** law, blacks were prohibited from riding in the first-class railroad cars even if they purchased a first-class ticket. Instead, they were forced to ride in the second-class car, which lacked comfortable amenities and where smoking was permitted. Other southern states quickly followed Tennessee's lead and through the 1880s and the decades that followed, enacted their own laws segregating railroads and other public facilities. These laws would be given the blessing of the Supreme Court in *Plessy v. Ferguson* (1896), where all but one justice ruled that racial segregation was constitutional as long as the facilities for whites and blacks were equal. The "separate but equal" doctrine provided a legal fiction that continued to justify

Undated cartoon of Jim Crow. (Courtesy of the Library of Congress.)

the very real inequalities of Jim Crow in the U.S. South for the next six decades, until a reversal started in 1954 with the decision in *Brown v. Topeka Board of Education*.

Extralegal Violence

It should be noted that one other significant aspect of Jim Crow was established during Reconstruction. Racial segregation in the South ultimately was made possible not only by the law but also the willingness of white southerners to use extralegal **violence** to enforce it. The law and economic pressure kept most blacks subordinated, but for serious transgressions, beatings and even murder became the all-too-common response. Lynching, or extralegal execution, was the most extreme sanction meted out to those persons who violated Jim Crow. In the heyday of the practice, between 1889 and 1946, almost 4,000 black southerners met their end in lynching at the hands of white mobs. Although many of these resulted from alleged rape accusations, the horrible practice of lynching was a community's reaction to perceived violations of the larger context of Jim Crow—racial subordination and obedience.

Racial violence was nothing new in the South by the late 1880s. Indeed, it had been integral to the collapse of Reconstruction, when the **Ku Klux Klan** and other violent groups terrorized blacks and their white allies in the South. Indeed, as tragic as these lynchings were in the Jim Crow South, they paled in comparison to incidents such as 1874's Colfax Massacre when nearly 300 black men defending the government seat of Grant Parish, **Louisiana**, were killed by a force of white paramilitaries, many after they had attempted to surrender. The only real difference in the violence was that during Reconstruction, it was used to destroy the experiment in biracial democracy, while afterward it was used to bolster white supremacy and the racist regimes that depended on it for their survival. So, in other words, extralegal violence was just another, if particularly gruesome, aspect of Jim Crow, which is first identifiable during Reconstruction. *See also* Disfranchisement; Enforcement Acts; Race Riots; Redemption; Tourgee, Albion Winegar; *United States v. Cruikshank*.

Further Reading: Litwack, Leon F. *Trouble in Mind: Black Southerners in the Age of Jim Crow*. New York: Alfred A. Knopf, 1998; Williamson, Joel: *The Crucible of Race: Black-White Relations in the American South since Emancipation*. New York: Oxford University Press, 1984; *A Rage for Order: Black-White Relations in the American South since Emancipation*. New York: Oxford University Press, 1986; Wormser, Richard. *The Rise and Fall of Jim Crow*. New York: St. Martin's Press, 2003.

Donald R. Shaffer

Johnson, Andrew (1808–1875)

Andrew Johnson became the seventeenth president of the United States (1865–1869) following John Wilkes Booth's **assassination of Abraham Lincoln** on April 14, 1865. Johnson faced the immediate challenge of restoring the former Confederate states to the Union. His constitutional and social conservatism and ambition led to an immediate clash with congressional Republicans, and a savage political struggle over the Reconstruction process erupted. As a result, Johnson became the first U.S. president to be impeached, escaping conviction in his Senate trial when Republicans failed by one vote to garner the required two-thirds majority.

Early Life

Andrew Johnson was born in Raleigh, **North Carolina**, on December 29, 1808, the second son of Jacob and Mary McDonough Johnson. Andrew's parents were poor, illiterate, and landless laborers who worked for a local inn. When Jacob died shortly after Andrew's third birthday, Mary was left to eke out a living for the family as a seamstress and washerwoman. Unable to provide a future for her son, she apprenticed Andrew to James J. Selby, a tailor. It was in Selby's shop that the future president learned to sew and also to read. After five years with Selby, Andrew abruptly fled the community because an adolescent prank landed him in trouble with the law. He drifted about for several years before settling in Greeneville, **Tennessee**, in 1827. There, Johnson opened a tailor shop and shortly thereafter married Eliza McCardle. He earned a comfortable living, and eventually purchased a farm and a few slaves. Andrew and Eliza had five children—two daughters, Martha and Mary, and three sons, Charles, Robert, and Andrew, Jr. ("Frank").

Early Political Career

Johnson's burning ambition steered him into politics. In 1829, the twenty-year-old ran successfully for alderman, an office he won several times before being elected mayor of Greeneville in 1834 and several times afterward. Such early successes whetted Johnson's appetite for higher offices. His local popularity and skillful campaigning gained him a seat in the Tennessee general assembly in 1835. Although at first an independent, Johnson was drawn to the **Democratic Party** by its support of the laboring classes and anti-elite ideology. He served as a representative from 1835 to 1837 and again from 1839 to 1841 before moving to the state senate. In 1843, he made the leap to national office when he was elected to the first of five consecutive terms in the U.S. House of Representatives. As a southern Democrat, he backed the party's stance on limited federal spending, low tariffs, the annexation of **Texas**, and the subsequent Mexican War. Johnson also supported the institution of slavery. Although he owned a few slaves, most people in his home region of East Tennessee did not. Therefore, slavery was not a major issue to his constituents or to him, but, like many whites in his adopted region of Appalachia, Johnson resented the wealth and political power of the planter class. Always the champion of the lower classes, he sponsored a homestead bill granting poor white farmers free public lands. Although he guided the resolution through the House, it failed to attract enough support in the Senate.

In 1851, the Whig Party gained control of the Tennessee general assembly and subsequently gerrymandered Johnson's old congressional district so that it contained a majority of Whig voters. Facing certain defeat in another bid for Congress, Johnson shrewdly opted to vie for the Tennessee governorship. In 1853, he won the first of two consecutive terms as the Volunteer State's chief executive. As governor, he established a state library and a state-supported public school system. In 1857, the Tennessee general assembly selected him for the U.S. Senate. As a senator, Johnson directed most of his energy to securing his beloved homestead act. This time, he shepherded the bill through Congress only to have President James Buchanan veto the measure in 1860.

That year, the Democratic National Convention met in Charleston, **South Carolina**, to choose a presidential candidate. The Tennessee delegation offered Johnson's name, but he could not muster enough votes for the nomination. Northern and southern Democrats divided over slave expansion in the territories and split into rival factions. While northern Democrats nominated Senator Stephen A. Douglas of Illinois for president, southern Democrats rallied behind Buchanan's vice president, John C. Breckinridge of **Kentucky**. Fearful of disunion, Upper South states such as Tennessee supported the Constitutional Union Party's candidate, John Bell. Bell's appeal to Border State voters, coupled with the Democratic split, allowed the Republican candidate, Abraham Lincoln, to win the election handily.

In the wake of Lincoln's victory, the Deep South threatened secession. Johnson delivered a powerful speech in the Senate on December 18, 1860, denouncing disunion and declaring himself loyal to the United States. Two days later, his beloved Union dissolved as South Carolina seceded, quickly followed by the rest of the Deep South. In February 1861, Johnson gave another impassioned address against secession, and in the spring of that year, he returned to East Tennessee determined to prevent his home state from joining the exodus. He and other Unionists, including old political enemies such as Thomas A. R. Nelson and **William G. Brownlow**, rallied the state behind the Union. However, their efforts failed. In a June 1861 referendum, Tennessee joined the Confederacy, and Johnson fled his home to avoid capture by rebel authorities. He defiantly remained in the U.S. Senate, refusing to acknowledge Tennessee's decision. His devotion to the Union made him a northern celebrity and the chief spokesman for the so-called War Democrats who supported Lincoln.

By early 1862, federal forces had regained control of much of Middle and West Tennessee, and in March, President Lincoln appointed Johnson **military governor** of the state with the rank of brigadier general of volunteers. Lincoln hoped that Johnson's old popularity would enable him to restore civil government and hasten a return to the Union. Johnson believed that a handful of ardent rebels had coaxed the majority of the state's populace into seceding. In reality, however, the majority of Tennesseans actually supported the Confederacy and considered Johnson a traitor. For the next three years, the governor alternately punished and cajoled the state's rebels in an attempt to root out secessionist support.

Prior to the **election of 1864**, Republicans and War Democrats united to form the **National Union Party**. The fused party nominated Lincoln for president and Johnson as his running mate. Johnson was an expedient choice. He was a southerner, a leading War Democrat, and a devout Unionist. In November, the Lincoln-Johnson slate was elected in a huge Electoral College victory. Only six weeks after the inauguration, however, John Wilkes Booth assassinated Lincoln, thrusting Johnson into the presidency.

President Johnson's Program of Restoration

Andrew Johnson brought a wealth of experience to the office of the presidency, and he needed all his acumen to tackle the monumental tasks of restoring the Union, rebuilding the South, and determining the place of the former **African American** slaves in American society. Like Lincoln before him, Johnson favored a quick restoration with lenient terms. He formally recognized the Lincoln-sponsored governments of **Arkansas**, **Louisiana**, **Tennessee**, and **Virginia**, reconstructed under Lincoln's so-called Ten Percent Plan. Then, in May 1865, he issued two proclamations that outlined his Reconstruction plan. The first granted **amnesty** to most former Confederates, except certain groups such as prominent political and military leaders and those with more than $20,000 in taxable property. Johnson required these men to apply to him directly for a presidential **pardon**.

The second proclamation dealt specifically with the restoration of **North Carolina** but became the model for the remaining unreconstructed states. Johnson appointed **provisional governors**—often native Unionists, such as himself—and required that they organize state **constitutional conventions** where delegates would draft new constitutions to **abolish slavery**, repudiate state debts incurred under the Confederacy, and nullify ordinances of secession. Elections could then be held for state and federal officials. Once the new state legislatures ratified the **Thirteenth Amendment**, martial law would end, federal troops would be withdrawn, and the states could resume their place in the Union.

From the outset, white southerners attempted to manipulate Johnson's program. Some states refused to ratify the Thirteenth Amendment, others repealed rather than nullified their secession ordinances, and many balked at repudiating the Confederate debt. The new state legislatures also passed a series of laws known as the **Black Codes** to restrict black **civil rights**. Perhaps most brazen, the states elected high-ranking ex-Confederate civil and military leaders to political offices. Frustrated, Johnson decided to ignore such actions because he hoped to merge white southerners, northern Democrats, and conservative Republicans into a new national conservative party, led by him.

In December 1865, Congress refused to seat the new southern congressmen and created a **Joint Committee on Reconstruction** to study the situation in the South. Although Congress insisted on playing a role in the Reconstruction process, deep divisions riddled the Republican Party. **Radical Republicans**, the minority wing, advocated reducing the former Confederate states to territories to be administered by Congress. Additionally, they called for long-term **disfranchisement** of former Confederates, the imposition of **black suffrage**, the confiscation and redistribution of land to the freedpeople, and a federally supported **educational** system for the ex-slaves. The party majority, **Moderate Republicans** who wanted to secure basic civil rights for the blacks and prevent prominent ex-rebels from reasserting control of the South, stopped shy of political rights or land redistribution. Hoping to cooperate with the president, in 1866, the Moderates proposed two bills, one extending the life of the **Bureau of Refugees, Freedmen, and Abandoned Lands**, and the other voiding the Black Codes and providing civil protection and support southern blacks needed. Although both the **Freedmen's Bureau Bill** and the civil rights bill passed easily, the president shocked and angered Moderate Republicans by vetoing both. They responded by using their two-thirds congressional majority eventually to override Johnson's vetoes and formulate their own plans for Reconstruction.

A Growing Rift with Congress

Republicans acknowledged that Johnson would never support their two goals of protecting the rights of southern blacks and preventing the ex-Confederates from returning to power in the South. Therefore, the Joint Committee on Reconstruction proposed the **Fourteenth Amendment** to the **U.S. Constitution**, which passed both houses of Congress in June 1866 and essentially became the Republican peace terms for the defeated Confederacy. To protect blacks, the amendment defined all native-born and naturalized persons as citizens and prohibited states from denying any person equal protection under

Cartoon showing Andrew Johnson as the deceitful Iago who betrayed Othello, portrayed here as an African American Civil War veteran. Includes scenes of slave auction, whites attacking African Americans in Memphis and New Orleans, and "Copperhead" and "C.S.A." snakes wrapped around an African American man while Andrew Johnson and others watch, 1866. (Courtesy of the Library of Congress.)

the law. Also, while blacks were not granted **suffrage**, any state that withheld the vote from its adult male citizens would have its congressional representation reduced proportionally. This allowed the Republicans to prevent the former confederate states from increasing their congressional representation in the absence of the Three-Fifths Compromise. The Confederate debt was voided, and the amendment stipulated that any person who had taken an oath to uphold the Constitution and then supported the rebellion was now disqualified from federal and state offices (although a two-thirds vote by Congress could remove the disability).

For the amendment to become part of the Constitution, it needed a three-fourths vote of approval from the states, including some former Confederate states. Although white southerners knew implicitly that any southern state that ratified the Fourteenth Amendment would be restored to the Union, they resisted it. Johnson even discouraged the southern states from approving the amendment, claiming that it was unconstitutional because Congress had no right to demand ratification without the southern states being represented in Congress. To Johnson's dismay, his home state of Tennessee ratified it in July 1866 and became the first Confederate state to reenter the Union.

Undaunted, Johnson embarked on a speaking tour of the northeastern and midwestern states to drum up support for his policies, influence the 1866 elections, and promote his new, conservative, **National Union Movement** and party. Although this **Swing Around the Circle**, as he called it, began favorably, he quickly encountered unruly and hostile crowds. The president made matters worse by engaging in arguments with hecklers and denouncing certain Republicans as traitors. Newspapers and cartoonists lambasted the president, while Radicals attacked both Johnson and his Democratic supporters as the true traitors to the Union.

Johnson found it impossible to convince the northern public that the ex-rebels were now eager to support the Union. Major race riots in **Memphis** (May) and **New Orleans** (July), coupled with the former Confederate states' resistance to the Fourteenth Amendment, persuaded northern voters that Johnson's policies could not be trusted to guarantee what many called the "fruits of victory." As a result, Republicans achieved overwhelming victories in the **elections of 1866**.

As Johnson's bid for a new conservative coalition collapsed, **Congressional Reconstruction** entered a more radical phase in which the Republicans prepared to force the recalcitrant South into submission. The first step would be to coerce at least four of the unreconstructed states to adopt the Fourteenth Amendment. This would give Congress the needed number of votes to ratify the Amendment. However, since only Tennessee's legislature would cooperate, Congress debated measures to compel compliance.

Intense deliberation and compromise produced the **Military Reconstruction Act** in February 1867. Passed over the president's veto, the law declared that the ten Johnson-supported state governments were provisional and divided them into five military districts, each commanded by a major general. Congress granted the army authority to supervise the registration of all male voters, including blacks, but excluding whites who were barred under the Fourteenth Amendment. Once registered, voters would elect delegates to participate in state conventions where they would frame new constitutions providing for black suffrage. Once Congress approved the new constitutions, elections for state and national office would follow, and the new legislatures would be required to ratify the Fourteenth Amendment. Reconstruction would then end. Although the provisions of the Military Reconstruction Act fell far short of the restructuring of southern society sought by the Radicals, they did secure the Moderates' two key requirements of protecting black rights and preventing the former Confederates from returning to power.

Congressional Republicans Take the Offensive

President Johnson remained obstinate, and used his constitutional authority as commander in chief of the armed forces to interfere with the Republican program. To curtail the president's power, Congress passed two statutes of questionable constitutionality. The **Command of the Army Act**, a provision of the 1867 Army Appropriations Act, required Johnson to issue all orders to subordinate army commanders through the general-in-chief of the army, **Ulysses S. Grant**. The Radicals hoped Grant could serve as a controlling force over Johnson's actions. The most direct challenge to presidential authority, however, was the **Tenure of Office Act**, which authorized an official appointed with the Senate's consent to remain in office until that body approved a successor. Ostensibly intended to protect **patronage** offices, in reality, the law was designed to prevent the removal of Secretary of War **Edwin Stanton**, a Radical in Johnson's inherited **cabinet**. Johnson vetoed the Tenure of Office Act and considered vetoing the Army Appropriations Act. However, he signed this bill, allowing the army to receive its funding, yet sent in a formal written protest to the Command of the Army provision.

Meanwhile, white southerners refused to succumb to congressional demands and fought to delay the registration of voters indefinitely. Congress passed the subsequent additions to the Reconstruction Act to close loopholes and strengthen the military's control of the process. Johnson was appalled at congressional efforts to enfranchise blacks while disfranchising the very southern whites he hoped to entice into a conservative coalition for the **election of 1868**. Becoming more and more unrealistic, he continued to maneuver around the congressional program. Despite Republicans' attempts to restrict Johnson's authority and power, as commander in chief he could appoint conservative generals to administer the five military districts, and as chief executive he could interpret the Reconstruction Act narrowly in terms of its enforcement.

Johnson's Impeachment and Trial

Radicals recognized Johnson's intent and advocated his removal from office. Their first attempt occurred in January 1867, when the **House Judiciary Committee** was authorized to investigate the possibility of **impeachment**. However, Moderates saw no reason to take such an extreme step. The Radicals launched another impeachment effort after Johnson suspended Secretary of War Edwin Stanton in August 1867 and replaced generals such as **Philip H. Sheridan** and **Daniel E. Sickles**, who energetically enforced the Reconstruction Acts. However, Moderates still balked on openly challenging the president and the constitutional balance of power. Since Johnson's suspension of Stanton occurred when Congress was in recess, it did not technically violate the Tenure of Office Act. Of course, Congress had to approve the suspension when it reconvened. In December 1867, the Radicals forced a House vote on impeachment, but without Moderate support, the resolution failed, 108 to 57. Johnson's subsequent actions, however, resurrected the specter of impeachment one last time.

The president was determined to rid himself of Stanton, test the Tenure of Office Act, and challenge congressional authority, and so removed the secretary of war completely in February 1868. Since the House and Senate were now in session, Johnson's actions violated the Tenure of Office Act and prompted another outcry for his impeachment. This time, the Moderates voted with the Radicals, and the House impeached Johnson by a party-line vote of 126 to 47 on February 24, 1868. House prosecutors, known as **impeachment managers** subsequently proffered eleven charges against the president, called "articles of impeachment." Eight dealt with his apparent violation of the Tenure of Office Act, while one accused the president of attempting to circumvent the army's chain of command in violation of the rider to the Army Appropriations bill of 1867. The tenth article accused Johnson of bringing Congress into disrepute with his public pronouncements, while the final article drew together charges from the previous ten. Johnson's able legal team claimed that he had committed no crime in testing the constitutionality of the Tenure of Office Act. They argued that even if the act was constitutional, it did not apply to Stanton, who had been appointed by Lincoln, not Johnson.

Once impeached, the issue then passed to the Senate for a formal trial, with the chief justice, **Salmon P. Chase**, presiding. If convicted, the president would be removed from office. Although Moderate Republicans abhorred Johnson, many feared a dangerous precedent: His removal could pave the way for future parties with a two-thirds congressional majority to remove any president who disagreed with them. The constitutional system of checks and balances could be destroyed. Moderates also distrusted radical **Benjamin Wade**, president pro tem of the Senate and next in line to the presidency (no one had replaced Johnson as vice president). Using intermediaries, Johnson and the Moderates worked toward an understanding. The president gave no more speeches or interviews denouncing Congress, promised to enforce Reconstruction Acts, appointed the well-respected General **John M. Schofield** as the new secretary of war. On May 16, 1868, the Senate voted on the eleventh article of impeachment, 35 guilty to 19 not guilty. All twelve Democrats and seven Moderate Republicans voted against conviction and removal. With a two-thirds majority needed to remove the president from office, Johnson had been saved by a single vote. Votes on articles 2 and 3 on May 26 had the same result, leading the managers to concede defeat and adjourn the proceedings.

During his final months in office, Johnson did not adhere to the spirit of the accommodation, and continued to defy Congress by vetoing Reconstruction bills and delivering speeches critical of the Radicals. Congress, in return, largely ignored him, and routinely passed legislation over his vetoes. Politically crippled, Johnson naively clung to the hope that the **Democratic Party** would nominate him for president in 1868. While some northern Democrats supported Johnson's struggle against the Radicals, they accurately surmised he could not win the election. After twenty-two ballots, the party finally threw its support behind New York governor **Horatio Seymour**, leaving Johnson as a lame-duck president without a party or any real influence on national policy. The man who had won election to nearly every position in American democracy would never be elected to its highest office.

Postpresidency: The Elder Statesman

After leaving the White House in the hands of his successor, Republican Ulysses S. Grant (Johnson did not attend the inauguration), Johnson returned to Tennessee where he remained obsessed with politics. Unsuccessful attempts to land a congressional seat in 1869 and 1872 did not deter this lifelong politician. Finally elected to the U.S. Senate in 1875, Johnson became the only president to serve in the Senate after leaving the presidency. On March 5, 1875, during a special session of the Senate, he took his seat to the applause of many conservative senators. When the Senate recessed, Johnson returned to Tennessee and suffered a paralytic stroke four months later. He died on July 31, 1875, and was buried in Greeneville. Befitting his devotion to the Union, mourners wrapped Johnson in an American flag and placed a copy of the Constitution in his hand.

Johnson remains as enigmatic today as during his lifetime. A southern slaveholder, he risked his career, all his possessions, and even his life in support of the Union. A savvy and successful career politician, his skills and cleverness failed him when he needed them the most. Clearly racist and stubbornly conservative, it has been argued that his opposition directly contributed to Republican unity—and as a result, a much broader and more progressive Reconstruction program. Certainly a product of nineteenth-century southern mores, he was a man of principle who was blindly devoted to his definition of constitutional, democratic government. His ultimate legacy is yet to be determined. *See also* Democratic National Convention; Presidential Reconstruction; Race Riots; Recusants; U.S. Army and Reconstruction; Violence.

Further Reading: Benedict, Michael Les. *The Impeachment and Trial of Andrew Johnson.* New York: Norton, 1973; Castel, Albert E. *The Presidency of Andrew*

Johnson. Lawrence: Regents Press of Kansas, 1979; Graf, LeRoy P., Ralph W. Haskins, and Paul H. Bergeron, eds. *The Papers of Andrew Johnson.* 16 vols. Knoxville: University of Tennessee Press, 1967–2000; McKitrick, Eric L. *Andrew Johnson and Reconstruction.* Chicago: University of Chicago Press, 1960; reprint, New York: Oxford University Press, 1988; Sefton, James E. *Andrew Johnson and the Uses of Constitutional Power.* Boston: Little, Brown, 1980; Trefousse, Hans L.: *Andrew Johnson: A Biography.* New York: Norton, 1989; *Impeachment of a President: Andrew Johnson, the Blacks, and Reconstruction.* Knoxville: University of Tennessee Press, 1975; reprint, New York: Fordham University Press, 1999.

John D. Fowler

Johnson, Andrew, Impeachment of. *See* Impeachment of Andrew Johnson (1868).

Johnson, Reverdy (1796–1876)

Reverdy Johnson, a respected constitutional lawyer and defender of President **Andrew Johnson** during the latter's **impeachment** trial in the U.S. Senate in 1868, also served as minister to Great Britain from 1868 to 1869. Born in Annapolis, **Maryland**, Johnson was educated at St. John's College and studied law with his father. Admitted to the bar in 1815, he moved to Baltimore where he married, had fifteen children, and soon became a well-known lawyer. His political career began with his election to the Maryland state senate in 1821, and briefly included his service as President Zachary Taylor's attorney general. In 1845, Johnson was elected to the U.S. Senate where he served intermittently until 1869.

Johnson supported the Union during the Civil War, but he was also sympathetic toward the South. When the war ended, he urged the immediate **readmission** of the former Confederate states. During the war, he had at first opposed the bill creating the **Bureau of Refugees, Freedmen, and Abandoned Lands**, yet he later supported the **Fourteenth Amendment**. His most significant service during Reconstruction involved his role in the impeachment trial of Andrew Johnson, whose removal from office he opposed. Reverdy Johnson was a member of the committee that formulated the rules used by the Senate, and he opposed Senator **Benjamin Wade**'s presiding in a case from which Wade, as the president of the Senate, stood to gain; Were President Johnson removed, since there was no sitting vice president, Wade would become chief executive. An astute lawyer, Johnson also argued that removal from office only pertained if the president's acts were of a sort that would bring criminal prosecution in civilian courts. Moreover, he insisted that bills for impeachment and removal could never be based on speeches. The latter were protected by the First Amendment, assuring freedom of speech. Nor did Johnson think the **Tenure of Office Act**, which denied the president's right to remove Secretary of War **Edwin Stanton**, was valid. On these grounds, Reverdy Johnson was crucial in persuading several key senators to vote against the president's removal from office in the close vote that took place on May 16, 1868, and that led to Johnson's acquittal.

In 1868, President Johnson appointed Reverdy Johnson minister to Great Britain, where he negotiated the American claims against the British for their role in the building of warships made in their shipyards during the Civil War and then transferred to the Confederacy. This Anglo-American disagreement had escalated beyond the claims of individuals to the argument that the British were responsible for prolonging the war. While Johnson was able to secure a treaty, he was unable to secure an apology or any expression of regret from a stubborn British government. The Senate rejected the treaty and only later in the administration of **Ulysses S. Grant** were these so-called "Alabama claims" (named for the most infamous British-built raider) satisfactorily resolved.

In 1869, Johnson returned to Baltimore, where he continued to practice law and argue cases before the **Supreme Court** until his death in 1876. *See also* Cabinets, Executive; Congressional Reconstruction; House Judiciary Committee; Impeachment Managers; Presidential Reconstruction.

Further Reading: Benedict, Michael Les. *The Impeachment and Trial of Andrew Johnson.* New York: Norton, 1973; Steiner, Bernard. *Life of Reverdy Johnson.* Baltimore, MD: The Norman, Remington Co., 1914.

Jean H. Baker

Joint Committee on Reconstruction

By a 133 to 36 vote in December 1865, Congress asserted its constitutional role in and responsibility for Reconstruction through the establishment of the Joint Committee on Reconstruction. The committee's task was to investigate and report on conditions in the former Confederate states. Since May of that year, the eleven southern states had been under the authority of President **Andrew Johnson**'s proclamations defining his Reconstruction program. Congress had not been in session since March, but even before it convened in December, many Republican members had decided to challenge if Johnson's approach was the proper way to "reconstruct" the Union—and how such could happen without a congressional voice.

In December, Congress faced a choice. It could accept the president's verdict that the states were ready to resume their place in the federal system, and thus that the southern states' congressional representatives should take their seats in the House of Representatives and the Senate. This step would end federal power over the states and place southern states' internal affairs off-limits to Congress. Congress's other option—one employed earlier during **Abraham Lincoln**'s attempt at **Presidential Reconstruction**—was to re-fuse to seat the southerners under Article I, Section 5 of the Constitution. That provision gave Congress power to rule on the qualifications of its own members. Congress chose the latter, and excluded the representatives of the former Confederate states when the clerk of the House, Edward McPherson, called roll on December 4, 1865. Then, the two houses of the national legislature took their first active step to formulating a counterprogram to Johnson's, by forming the Joint Committee of Fifteen on Reconstruction.

The committee, proposed by Pennsylvania representative **Thaddeus Stevens**, a member of the **Radical Republican** faction in the party, was created by concurrent resolution. It was composed of nine members from the House and six from the Senate. Three were from the **Democratic Party**, and the rest were Republicans. The majority of the committee were **Moderate Republicans**, including its chair, the respected Maine senator **William Pitt Fessenden**. Other Republican members included **John Bingham** of Ohio, **Roscoe Conkling** of New York, and **George Boutwell** of Massachusetts; among the Democrats was **Reverdy Johnson** of **Maryland**.

During the early months of 1866, the committee listened to witnesses who spoke both of the postwar problems and successes in the South, especially those related to the newly freed **African Americans** and their northern supporters and to southern whites who had opposed the war or who now cooperated with the federal government after the conflict. Most testimony pointed to harassment and mistreatment by southern whites who opposed federal authority, black freedom, and any form of equal **civil rights**. With exceptions, testimony painted a picture of an unrepentant South, a place still obsessed with slavery and secession.

The committee's final report, issued in June 1866, reflected this picture as it reviewed the situation in each of the eleven states and made recommendations. Despite Johnson's December 18, 1865, speech announcing the readiness of the states to reestablish themselves in the Union, the multipart report argued the need for further and more thoroughgoing reconstruction. It found civil rights to be unsecured and stable government and equal representation to be missing; those who had led the rebellion had been elected to lead the South once again, while loyal southerners were denied their **suffrage** (the right to vote). The report accepted the idea of "forfeited rights," that is, the southern states had never left the Union but through their actions, they had forfeited their political rights in it. These rights could be restored only through congressional, not presidential, action.

The testimony the committee heard motivated it to do more than report. It framed the **Fourteenth Amendment** in the spring of 1866 as relations between Congress and the president and, in particular, between Radicals and Johnson deteriorated. The president alienated Moderates when he vetoed both the **Civil Rights Act** and the **Freedmen's Bureau Bill** proposed by the Senate Judiciary Committee, chaired by Moderate **Lyman Trumbull** of Illinois. Through significant compromise, a final version of the amendment was framed to address the problem of black citizenship and rights and to settle other issues troubling congressional Republicans, including status of the Confederate debt, the growth of southern political strength following the demise of slavery and its three-fifths clause, and the selection of ex-Confederates for political office in the South. The amendment was submitted to the states that summer. Committee member John Bingham proposed making ratification a guarantee of **readmission**; Radicals, hesitant about limiting their opportunity for remaking the South and protecting blacks and the party, prevented the expression of this or any other explicit formula for readmission.

The committee was reconstituted in late 1866, but Stevens's efforts to have it continue even longer failed in the next session. Overwhelming Republican victories in the **elections of 1866**, and growing party unity brought on by President Johnson's obstinacy, made the committee superfluous. Congress itself would assume directly the responsibility for Reconstruction. *See also* Amnesty Proclamations; Congressional Reconstruction.

Further Reading: Foner, Eric. *Reconstruction: America's Unfinished Revolution, 1863–1877*. New York: Harper & Row, 1988; Kendrick, Benjamin B. *The Journal of the Joint Committee of Fifteen on Reconstruction, Thirty-Ninth Congress, 1865–1867*. New York: Columbia University and Longmans, Green, 1914; Trefousse, Hans L. *Reconstruction: America's First Effort at Racial Democracy*. Malabar, FL: Krieger, 1999.

Claudine L. Ferrell

Joint Select Committee on the Conduct of the War

The Joint Select Committee on the Conduct of the War was a technically bipartisan though heavily **Radical Republican** committee, made up of three senators and four members of the House of Representatives. Congress established the committee in December 1861 in response to Union military failures, especially the recent defeat at Ball's Bluff. The original committee members were Senators **Benjamin F. Wade** (Ohio, Republican), the chairman, **Zachariah Chandler** (Michigan, Republican), and **Andrew Johnson (Tennessee**, Democrat), as well as Representatives **George W. Julian** (Indiana, Republican), John Covode (Pennsylvania, Republican), Daniel Gooch (Massachusetts, Republican), and Moses Odell (New York, Democrat). When Johnson became **military governor** of Tennessee in March 1862, he resigned from the Senate and was replaced on the committee by Joseph Wright (Indiana), who was succeeded by Benjamin F. Harding (Oregon), and finally, Charles R. Buckalew (Pennsylvania), all Democrats. Later, when Covode ran for governor rather than for reelection to the House, he was succeeded by Benjamin F. Loan (Missouri, Republican) in January 1864.

Over the course of the war, the committee investigated many things, such as the causes of certain battle defeats, the behavior and competence of particular generals, alleged rebel atrocities after First Manassas (Bull Run) and Fort Pillow, and potential corruption in military supply contracts. A particular problem of the committee seemed to be zeal without knowledge. None of the committee members (with the exception of Loan at the end) had any military background whatsoever, nor did they think that they needed to learn anything about military realities. They believed that military success depended upon common sense and proper politics, so they opposed West Point–trained generals, particularly harassed generals who were members of the **Democratic Party**, such as George B. McClellan, and pushed the careers of Republican generals like John C. Fremont and **Benjamin F. Butler**, even after they had proved their incompetence. The committee also continually gave advice to President **Abraham Lincoln**, who followed their counsels only if they already suited his purposes.

While several of the committee's investigations were useful and may have improved the morale of the northern civilians and soldiers, the committee generally had a more negative effect. Their failure to understand the realities of warfare encouraged unrealistic ideas among the population about what a general and an army might accomplish in a single battle. The committee's political emphasis encouraged factions rather than cooperation and unfairly damaged the reputation of several generals.

When Andrew Johnson became president following Lincoln's **assassination** in April 1865, Johnson's former committee colleagues were pleased because they expected him to be tougher about reconstructing the South than Lincoln seemed to be. Wade, Julian, and Chandler promptly visited Johnson, hoping to become his political advisors. However, when it became evident that Johnson would be even more lenient toward the South than Lincoln, Wade, Julian, and Chandler became some of his most outspoken enemies during Reconstruction. The Committee on the Conduct of the War permanently adjourned on May 22, 1865. The **Joint Committee on Reconstruction** was established on the same model in December 1865. *See also* Congressional Reconstruction; Presidential Reconstruction; U.S. Army and Reconstruction.

Further Reading: Tap, Bruce. *Over Lincoln's Shoulder: The Committee on the Conduct of the War*. Lawrence: University Press of Kansas, 1998.

Glenna R. Schroeder-Lein

Julian, George Washington (1817–1899)

A leading Radical in the Republican Party, George Washington Julian was a constant reformer his entire life, championing many causes. Born in Centerville, Indiana, Julian was the fourth of six children of Rebecca Hoover and Isaac Julian, a county official. His father died in 1823, and Julian was raised by his devout Quaker mother. By eighteen, Julian began his legal studies and developed his interest in politics. In 1845, as a Whig, he was elected to the Indiana legislature. In the same year, he married Anne Elizabeth Finch; they had three children. Anne died in 1860, and three years later, Julian married the daughter of Joshua Giddings, Laura. They had two children. Laura died in 1884.

George W. Julian was a deeply religious man. William Channing's (1780–1842) writings led Julian to **abolitionism** and a host of other reforms. He believed that slavery was a moral evil and its existence retarded the civil liberties of speech and thought for all men. Julian's political pilgrimage was quite long. It was instructive of how theology and politics combined to influence the reforming attitudes of this Radical and his contemporaries.

His first destination after leaving the Whigs was the Free Soil Party. Julian endorsed the party's free soil, free labor, free men creed, which remained with him his complete life. Martin Van Buren as a Free Soiler was his presidential candidate in 1848. The next year, Julian was elected to the House of Representatives, where he opposed the measures collectively known as the Compromise of 1850, and especially the components related to the Fugitive Slave Act. This measure was a horror to him, and he even represented runaway slaves in the Indiana courts in the 1850s.

Early during the Civil War, Julian urged President **Abraham Lincoln** to see the conflict as an issue of slavery verus freedom. As a member of the powerful **Joint Select Committee on the Conduct of the War**, Julian worked for the removal of General George McClellan from any leadership position. He welcomed the **Emancipation** Proclamation, which for him meant abolitionism had become a firm part of the Union war effort.

Julian's commitment to abolitionism was part of a larger vision of reform and social justice. His other foe was land monopoly and the preservation of the rural way of life. To that end, as chair of the Committee on Public Land, he pushed for the Homestead Act, which passed in 1862. He also wanted to confiscate the planter's land for the freed **African Americans**, who could work their own land. Displeased with President Lincoln's cautious policies, Julian nevertheless supported him for reelection in 1864.

From Julian's perspective, President **Andrew Johnson**'s accession to the presidency was a disaster of major scope. Pressing for land and **suffrage** for the freedmen, Julian served on the House Committee on **Impeachment**. Greatly disappointed by failure to remove President Andrew Johnson from the White House, Julian took comfort in his leadership role in the passage of the **Southern Homestead Act (1866)**.

Defeated for Congress, Julian turned to the **Liberal Republican** crusade in the election of 1872. He supported **Horace Greeley**. Later, he campaigned on behalf of **Samuel J. Tilden** in the disputed **election of 1876**. After practicing law for several years, Julian became surveyor general for New Mexico under President Grover Cleveland. There, he fought against the land interests of **railroads** and speculators. Always crusading for a good cause, Julian's last one was for the "Gold Democrats" against the populists and similar advocates of free silver. On the eve of the twentieth century, Julian died in Irvington, Indiana, his hometown. *See also* Abolition of Slavery; African Americans; Civil Rights; Emancipation; Presidential Reconstruction; Republicans, Radical; Suffrage.

Further Reading: Stampp, Kenneth M. *Indiana Politics during the Civil War.* Indianapolis: Indiana Historical Bureau, 1949; Trefousse, Hans L. *The Radical Republicans, Lincoln's Vanguard for Racial Justice.* Baton Rouge: Louisiana State University Press, 1968; Unger, Irwin. *The Greenback Era: A Social and Political History of American Finance, 1865–1879.* Princeton, NJ: Princeton University Press, 1965.

Donald K. Pickens

K

Kellogg, William Pitt (1830–1918)

William Pitt Kellogg was a **carpetbagger** who served as U.S. senator (1868–1872) and as governor (1873–1877) of **Louisiana** during **Congressional Reconstruction**, though his gubernatorial election was mired in controversy. A native of Vermont, Kellogg moved with his family in the 1840s to Illinois, where he taught school and read law. He was admitted to the bar in 1853, and in 1856, he helped found the Illinois Republican Party. Appointed by President **Abraham Lincoln** as chief justice of the Nebraska Territory, he resigned to fight in the Civil War and eventually commanded a cavalry brigade before ill health forced him out of the service. Kellogg initially resumed his Nebraska duties, but in April 1865, Lincoln named him collector of customs in New Orleans (Lincoln's last appointment), a position he used to build the Louisiana Republican Party. Kellogg held this post until July 1868, when the Louisiana legislature, upon the state's **readmission** to the Union, elected him to the U.S. Senate. Kellogg resigned from the Senate in November 1872, having been nominated Republican candidate for governor of Louisiana.

The election of 1872 in Louisiana was among the most controversial in the state's history. Intimidation and **violence**, especially against blacks, characterized the campaign, and fraud marred the election. Both Kellogg and Democratic gubernatorial candidate John D. McEnery claimed victory. In January 1873, separate inaugurations were held, and Democratic- and Republican-majority legislatures convened. Louisiana endured the spectacle of rival state governments until May 1873, when President **Ulysses S. Grant** recognized Kellogg as governor.

The Kellogg administration never overcame the circumstances of its birth, and the large majority of white Louisianians vilified Kellogg. Democrats and other white conservatives engaged in tax strikes; civil insurrection and violence increased, as white vigilantes massacred black and white Republicans at Colfax (April 1873) and Coushatta (August 1874); the paramilitary **White League** ousted Kellogg in September 1874, necessitating intervention by federal troops; Kellogg survived an assassination attempt; and a Democratic legislature impeached Kellogg in early 1876, though the Republican state senate refused to convict. Kellogg did not run for reelection in 1876, but he was elected to the U.S. Senate as part of the **Compromise of 1877**. In 1883, he won election to the U.S. House of Representatives. When his term expired in 1885, Kellogg retired from public office and moved to Washington, D.C., where he died on August 10, 1918. He is buried in Arlington National Cemetery.

As governor, Kellogg implemented a number of reforms, including lowering taxes and public expenditures, funding and reducing the state debt, and making government more efficient, all important measures during the economic depression of the 1870s. Yet his term was hampered by fierce white opposition, owing to the circumstances surrounding his election, his appointing of blacks to key offices and his support for black **civil rights**, his extended summer absences from the state, and his party affiliation. Kellogg also harmed the Republican cause by engaging in bribery and other corrupt practices associated with nineteenth-century Louisiana politics—a luxury that he and his party could ill afford. *See also* Black Suffrage; Democratic Party; Elections of 1876; Electoral Commission of 1877; Longstreet, James; Nicholls, Francis Redding Tillou; Packard, Stephen B.; Panic of 1873; Pinchback, Pinckney Benton Stewart; Race Riots; Railroads; Redemption; Scandals; Taxpayers' Conventions; Twitchell, Marshall H.; U.S. Army and Reconstruction; *United States v. Cruikshank*; Warmoth, Henry Clay.

Further Reading: Gonzales, John E. "William Pitt Kellogg, Reconstruction Governor of Louisiana, 1873-1877." *Louisiana Historical Quarterly* 29 (1946): 394–495; Lonn, Ella. *Reconstruction in Louisiana after 1868.* New York: G. P. Putnam's Sons, 1918; Taylor, Joe Gray. *Louisiana Reconstructed: 1863-1877.* Baton Rouge: Louisiana State University Press, 1974.

John C. Rodrigue

Kentucky

When Confederate armies surrendered in spring 1865, Kentucky officially stood as a "border state," a loyal state—albeit one with slavery—that had never left the Union. As a full member of that Union, it did not anticipate undergoing the Reconstruction process affecting the former Confederate states. So instead, it found itself in a nebulous, confusing, and uncertain status after Appomattox. Oddly, both northerners and southerners viewed it more as a former Confederate state than a Union one—and with much justification. Kentucky had representatives at the Confederate Congress, and a star on the Confederate flag. In an oft-quoted statement written six decades after the conflict's end, one historian concluded that Kentucky "waited until after the war was over to secede from the Union" (Coulter, 439). If the state did not experience full Reconstruction, it certainly went through what could be termed "readjustment." The South, under full Reconstruction, viewed unfettered Kentucky as the spokesman for its interests. In turn, Kentucky's actions and reactions to postwar events suggest how the South might have reacted without Reconstruction. A very different Kentucky emerged from that era than had existed at the start of the Civil War.

A Victor Embracing Defeat

One of the largest slave states in population, wealth, and importance, and with a natural defense line at the Ohio River, Kentucky had been a sought-after prize for both governments at the start of the Civil War. Legend has it that early in the conflict, **Abraham Lincoln** (who was born in Kentucky) told his **cabinet**, "I certainly hope God is on our side. But I must have Kentucky!" Badly divided—for it would be truly "The Brothers' War" in Kentucky—the state first chose neutrality for a period of four months. Devoted to both the Union and slavery, Kentucky abandoned neutrality and indicated its intention to remain part of the United States. Disgruntled Confederate supporters organized their own rump government, and the state became a star in both flags, but the state's initial Unionist sympathies eroded as the war raged. The **Emancipation** Proclamation did not affect loyal state Kentucky, but it did signal that the **abolition of slavery** had become a wartime aim. Many angry, proslavery Unionists changed in sentiment. Thus, as the Union won battle after battle, it continued to lose the fight for the minds of Kentuckians. Historians would later note that the South's distinctiveness came about partially as a result of being the only section of the American nation to experience defeat. Yet Kentucky had fought on the winning side, but in a sense it *chose* defeat, by supporting the *postwar South*, heart and soul. As a result, the less numerous former Confederates and Confederate sympathizers dominated politics, winning the next six governorships. In a sense, the vanquished ruled the victors.

Those leaders faced the harsh reality of rebuilding after the war. A good prewar educational system stood in shambles, and the commonwealth's economy remained crippled. Kentucky numbered 90,000 fewer horses, 170,000 fewer cattle, and almost 50,000 fewer mules than it had five years earlier. Thousands of young lives had ended; many of its best and brightest had died. Across the state, the **violence** of the virulent guerrilla warfare that had raged almost unchecked for the last three years of the conflict continued on, making rural areas dangerous for white and black alike. By the 1870s, mountain feuds brought a different kind of violence to the commonwealth.

Not all places had suffered. Louisville, in particular, had prospered as a supply center for Union forces and as a transportation hub for rivers and **railroads** southward. After the war, it eagerly sent its drummers to supply the devastated South. Meanwhile, the merger of three city newspapers in 1868 produced the Louisville *Courier-Journal*, which, for a time, would have the largest circulation of any paper in the South. Its editor, "Marse Henry" Watterson, used its pages to thunder his denunciations of **Radical Republicans** and **Congressional Reconstruction**; the northern press, in turn, would caricature him as the personification of the Kentucky—and southern—colonel. But Watterson's toast that "a union of pork, tobacco, and whisky will make us all wealthy, healthy, and frisky" (Tapp and Klotter, 307) emphasized the state's relative recovery from the war. By 1877, Kentucky's per capita wealth of $533 led the South (although that figure badly trailed the national average of $870).

Race Relations

The greatest change in postwar Kentucky concerned not economics but rather race relations. Almost one in every five Kentuckians had been an enslaved person in 1861. In fact, the state had furnished some 23,000 black soldiers to the Union cause—the second highest number of any state. Various federal laws and general orders had declared those soldiers and their families to be free, an action Kentucky refused to recognize. The state's highest court declared such actions unconstitutional in December 1865, and the legislature refused to ratify any of the Reconstruction amendments. By the time of the ratification of the **Thirteenth Amendment** in December 1865, only Kentucky and Delaware still retained slavery. The system died hard in the state.

Newspapers soon filled with dire concerns of racial revolution, black control, and military rule. Some warned of a restarting of the war. Resulting **Ku Klux Klan** and Regulator violence matched or exceeded similar acts in Deep South states, and at least 100 lynchings occurred in a four-year period. Some blacks formed protective hamlets in rural areas, while others migrated to the relative safety of Kentucky's more urban areas or to other states. Such opposition to black rights caused martial law to be continued until October 1865. As late as 1873, George A. Custer and the Seventh Cavalry served in the state to help control rampant Klan activity.

Opposition to black rights resulted in legal actions as well. While several 1866 legislative actions, similar to the **Black Codes** passed by the former Confederate states, placed former slaves under the same laws and penalties as whites, they also made exceptions regarding rape and racial intermarriage. Nor could blacks testify in cases against whites, until federal actions forced passage of an 1872 black testimony act. The state also set up a separate, racially segregated school system, but not until 1874 would it really function, and not until eight years after that would the funds from both white and black taxes be merged into a common pool for redistribution. A rare exception to the growing segregation was Berea College, which offered biracial **education** (this ended in 1908, when the U.S. **Supreme Court**, in *Berea College v. Kentucky*, forced the school to expel its black students).

The racial violence, restrictive rights, and educational deficiencies brought limited federal involvement in Kentucky, in the form of the Freedman's Bureau. It started in the state in December 1865 and continued operations in some form until 1871. Kentucky vigorously protested that the agency could only operate in states formerly in rebellion, but to no avail. Underfunded, understaffed, and often overwhelmed, the bureau still did much good. Its 369 schools, staffed mostly by black teachers, educated nearly 19,000 students, despite opposition that in a one-year period included 20 murders, 18 other shootings, 11 rapes, and 270 further acts of violence. Yet, despite all the opposition, blacks won several victories, including a successful fight to resist the segregation of streetcars in Louisville. They had already won the greater battle of developing strong communities as free people.

Women, white and black, faced resistance in their struggle for further rights as well, but legal barriers were slowly crumbling. Widows with school-age children could vote for school trustees, for example, and in 1867, women organized a **suffrage** organization in Hardin County. Most legal gains for women, however, awaited the decades after Reconstruction.

Kentucky Politics

Change did occur in Kentucky politics. The chaos of the conflict left uncertainty about several questions as peacetime elections began. What role would former Confederate supporters play? How would the once-dominant ex-Whigs go? Which party would control the postwar political world? A wartime **loyalty oath** remained in force in 1865, but in the next year, legislative actions pardoned all ex-Confederates with wartime restrictions against them. The first major test of the political scene came in the 1867 gubernatorial and legislative elections. Since Kentucky had never left the Union, the **Military Reconstruction Acts** did not apply, so the black male population was not enfranchised as it was in ten former Confederate states. In the campaign, three groups vied for votes. All sought to win over the old ex-Whigs and the ex-Unionists from both prewar parties. The Union Party (Radical Republicans) openly supported the congressional Reconstruction program and the federal amendments, and stressed their Union ties. Opponents tried to tar them with radicalism and supporting black rights. The **Democratic Party**, in turn, openly rejected further support for blacks. Opponents termed them unrepentant rebels, and the party's candidate was an ex-Whig whose son had been killed fighting for the Confederate army. A third group, the Conservative Union Party, tried to take a more moderate stance and unite the Unionist ex-Whigs under its banner. That attempt to re-form a new alliance failed, the third party died, and the democracy dominated for the next three decades. In 1867, they won 113 of 138 legislative seats; in a special governor's race the next year, the party won 80 percent of the popular vote. The Democrats had forged a fragile coalition of former Confederates, some ex-Whigs, a few old Unionists angered by racial issues, and of course the more conservative prewar Democrats. Republicans got the rest, including the black male voters who cast their ballots after the ratification of the **Fifteenth Amendment** in 1870.

Within the Democracy, various sectional and philosophical rivalries split the party into factions. **New Departure** Democrats, led by Watterson, called for recognition of black rights, an end to sectional controversy, and a **New South** industrial order. The more numerous **Bourbon** Democrats more commonly resisted actions aiding blacks and looked more wistfully to an Old South ideal. Commercial and other differences between the central Bluegrass, Louisville, and west Kentucky exacerbated the differences, as did later agrarian unrest, reflected in a strong 1870s Granger movement. Yet, in the end, Democrats united enough to win, over a Republican Party shackled by memories of the war and race. Even when the Republicans put forth their best candidate, John

Marshall Harlan, he lost out in 1871 to ex-Whig Preston Leslie, 126,455 to 89,299 (Harlan later became a progressive Supreme Court justice, offering brilliant dissents in the *Civil Rights Cases* (1883) and *Plessy v. Ferguson* (1896). Four years later Harlan lost to former Confederate colonel James B. McCreary, 130,026 to 94,236. The lack of a large black population, combined with the cultural alliance with the former Confederate states, drove Kentucky toward becoming part of the Solid South.

Yet, despite all the postwar changes, people of both races and both sexes went on with their lives, growing the new burley tobacco, making a hard living on farms, and seeking education for their children. They viewed a state unencumbered by debt, but one that devoted too little support for social and public services. They observed a commonwealth that displayed wealth in its cities and horse farms, but more commonly presented a people suffering from a poverty of the spirit. They saw a Kentucky in change, yet unchanging. *See also* African Americans; Agriculture; Black Suffrage; Bureau of Refugees, Freedmen, and Abandoned Lands; Civil Rights; Disfranchisement; Fourteenth Amendment; Freedmen's Relief Societies; U.S. Army and Reconstruction.

Further Reading: Coulter, E. Merton. *The Civil War and Readjustment in Kentucky.* Chapel Hill: University of North Carolina Press, 1926; Harrison, Lowell H., and James C. Klotter. *A New History of Kentucky.* Lexington: University Press of Kentucky, 1997; Lucas, Marion B. *A History of Blacks in Kentucky: From Slavery to Segregation, 1760-1891.* Frankfort: Kentucky Historical Society, 1992; Tapp, Hambleton, and James C. Klotter. *Kentucky: Decades of Discord, 1865-1900.* Frankfort: Kentucky Historical Society, 1977; Webb, Ross. *Kentucky in the Reconstruction Era.* Lexington: University Press of Kentucky, 1979.

James C. Klotter

Kirk-Holden War (1869–1870)

Named for George W. Kirk, a Civil War colonel who commanded Union troops in east **Tennessee** and western **North Carolina**, and **William W. Holden**, the Republican governor of North Carolina, the Kirk-Holden War represented a desperate state effort to end a reign of terror that had cost the lives of leading Republicans and intimidated countless white and black voters between 1869 and 1870. Although successful in ending Klan activity in central North Carolina, the Kirk-Holden War represented the high water mark of Republican rule in North Carolina during Reconstruction. While the Kirk-Holden War helped destroy the **Ku Klux Klan** in central North Carolina, it also resulted in the impeachment of Governor William W. Holden.

Emergence of the Ku Klux Klan

Founded in Tennessee following the Civil War, the Ku Klux Klan became the extralegal political arm of the **Democratic Party** in many of the former Confederate states. In 1867, following the passage of the **Military Reconstruction Act** and the advent of **Congressional Reconstruction**, the combination of **black suffrage** and political activity by native **scalawags** and northern **carpetbaggers** completely ousted white Democrats from political power. As a result, the Ku Klux Klan evolved into a terrorist organization, aimed at wresting political control away from the infant southern Republican Party. In general, the Klan was most active in counties where a fairly even numerical split existed between blacks and whites. It was in those counties that the organization's violent tactics could deter enough Republicans from the polls to tip the balance in the Democrats' favor.

The political **violence** troubled state Republicans, and Holden tried to curtail it with persuasion. In October 1869, he threatened to declare a state of insurrection in Lenoir and Jones Counties. Local Klan operations effectively ceased after that. Similar tactics achieved comparable results elsewhere. The Republican-controlled legislature followed the governor's lead, and passed a law making it illegal to appear disguised in public for the purpose of violence or intimidation. However, such measures meant little if local law enforcement ignored them, so Holden cultivated support within troubled communities. He appealed to white conservatives' desire for stability and beseeched them to convince Klansmen to disband. These efforts helped restore peace in several troubled counties.

Alamance and Caswell Counties, however, defied the governor's attempts to negotiate peace. White Republicans went out of their way to appease the Democrats in each county, hoping that they could bring an end to the night riding. In fact, many of the local political and law enforcement officers in Alamance County were Democrats, but local control failed to placate the Klansmen. In both counties, night riders tormented white and black Republicans continuously.

Conciliation's failure in Alamance and Caswell forced Holden to confront the Ku Klux Klan directly. In late 1869, state senator T. M. Shoffner, a Republican from Alamance County, introduced legislation to expand the state's ability to deal with the violence. The proposed legislation authorized the governor to suspend the writ of habeas corpus and to employ state **militia** against the Klan in counties where the civil authorities were ineffective. The so-called Shoffner Act proved a mixed blessing. Despite giving the governor greater control over the militia, the provision for the suspension of habeas corpus clashed with the state constitution and was removed from the final act. For Senator Shoffner, the legislation's impact was personal. If not for a warning delivered by a disaffected Klan leader, Shoffner might have found himself at the wrong end of a gun rather than in a new home in Indiana.

Murder Galvanizes the Republicans

Matters in Alamance and Caswell came to a head following the murder of two high-profile Republicans. The first was Wyatt Outlaw, an **African American** leader from Alamance County. Despite a reputation for personal integrity, Outlaw's status as a town councilman and president of the local **Union League** raised the Klan's ire. In the early hours of February 26, 1870, night riders broke into Outlaw's home and dragged the black leader away from his family. Residents awoke the following morning to find Outlaw's body hanging from a rope in the public square.

Republicans could not understand how conservative men could countenance such blatant disregard for the law. However, a more immediate concern for Holden and his colleagues was the state elections scheduled for August. If Klan violence continued unabated, it might sufficiently deter blacks from voting and cost the Republicans' political control. Still, Holden hesitated to take decisive action against the Ku Klux. The Shoffner Act allowed him to call out the militia, but the blunting of the legislation's provisions pertaining to the writ of habeas corpus weakened the chances of bringing offenders to justice. As was the case with many southern administrations, the beleaguered governor turned to the federal government. Told that no federal troops were forthcoming, Holden again sought conciliation. He pressured local law enforcement officials to act, sent detectives to troubled counties, and tried to find local whites who could successfully negotiate an end to the violence.

Holden's moderate approach collapsed in the wake of another political murder. On the night of May 21, 1870, John W. Stephens, a native white Republican, attended a Democratic Party convention in the Caswell County courthouse. Stephens supported Holden's efforts to end the violence in the state, going so far as to endorse a local conservative for sheriff in an effort to placate local Klansmen. While the speakers took turns denouncing the Republican in their midst, the man Stephens promoted as the candidate of law and order invited the Republican into the basement. Once out of the crowd's sight, Klansmen dragged Stephens into a small room, where they choked and stabbed him. They then locked the door and left Stephens to die.

Stephens's murder was the last straw for Holden. Under a tremendous amount of pressure to restore order, the governor issued a proclamation offering rewards for the capture of Outlaw and Stephens's killers. Holden also made a final plea for federal assistance. President **Ulysses S. Grant**, however, felt that North Carolina's problems were its own and offered Holden no support. Since conciliation had failed and the federal government would not help, the governor and his advisors decided it was time Holden called out the militia.

Rally to Your Old Commander

Deciding to employ the militia was only the first step, since Holden had to find reliable men to fill its ranks. Realizing that forces drawn from the counties surrounding Alamance and Caswell would probably include many of the Klansmen he sought to defeat, Holden turned to the western counties. He hoped that many of the former Unionists in the state's mountain counties would rally once again to suppress rebellious elements in the state. Although initial command over state forces was given to Colonel William J. Clarke, a northerner living in New Bern, it passed to George W. Kirk after Clarke left to secure supplies in the nation's capital. The east Tennessean commanded troops in the Carolina mountains during the Civil War and Holden hoped that his presence would lure his former soldiers into the ranks again. Kirk's popularity, coupled with the promise of regular army pay, brought 670 men between the ages of fifteen and seventy into the ranks in late June and early July 1870.

Once Holden declared Alamance and Caswell in a state of insurrection, Kirk's militia began arresting suspected Klansmen in the troubled counties almost immediately. The men arrested reflected the membership of the Klan in the state. Some were white men of respectability and wealth, but the majority of those arrested were younger men from the ranks of small or middling farmers. Despite the lower class status of most of the suspects, the most publicized arrest was that of Democratic newspaper editor Josiah Turner, Jr., near his home in Orange County. The fact that Turner lived in a county not under martial law proved troublesome for Holden. While an outspoken proponent of the Klan's activities, no evidence linked Turner directly to any violence, and Holden's political opponents decried his arrest as an act of tyranny.

The arrest of Turner and nearly 100 other suspected Klansmen had the effect Holden intended. Night riding in Alamance and Caswell halted, allowing Holden to resume negotiations to end the violence. Conservative residents, frustrated by violence but afraid to speak out against the terror organization, seized the opportunity to work for the Klan's demise.

Nevertheless, success failed to ease the pressure on the governor and his militia. Both found themselves in trouble with the law. The state Supreme Court's issuance of writs of habeas corpus for Kirk's prisoners presented Holden with a dilemma. Turning over his prisoners threatened to undermine the success already achieved, but refusing would give credence to the charges that he abused his authority. Adding to the governor's woes was the fact that Kirk was busy collecting confessions, but was unprepared to present that evidence in court. Trapped in a predicament of his own making, Holden chose to ignore the court and move forward with his plan to try the prisoners before a military tribunal.

Most of the detainees never made it to a military court. With their appeals to the state judicial system stymied by the governor, the alleged Klansmen appealed to a federal judge in Salisbury. Although sympathetic to Holden's efforts, the federal judge issued a writ of habeas corpus for the accused men, who ironically had claimed that their rights to due process guaranteed by the **Fourteenth Amendment** had been violated. Using an amendment to free the Klansmen—which Holden himself supported as a guarantee of blacks' political and **civil rights**—made it painfully clear that the governor had overplayed his hand. His militia disbanded on September 21, 1870.

Impeachment of a Governor

Holden's opponents refused to let the matter dissipate with the militia. Klan violence and intimidation kept hundreds of Republican voters from the polls on August 4, 1870, allowing Holden's opponents to capture a majority in the state legislature. Not long after taking office, the new legislators—many of whom had ties to the Ku Klux Klan—filed eight charges of impropriety against Governor Holden and initiated impeachment proceedings. Holden responded to charges of violating the state constitution by mobilizing the militia and declaring a state of insurrection by presenting Kirk's evidence of the danger posed by the Klan. Holden's antagonists were unimpressed. The legislature voted 36 to 13 for impeachment on March 22, 1871. Their action removed Holden from office, and also barred him from holding state political office again. More important, their political revenge against Holden marked the fall of the Republicans and the "**redemption**" of North Carolina as Democrats took control—virtually ending Republican influence in the state for the next generation. *See also* Black Suffrage; Bloody Shirt; Disfranchisement; Enforcement Acts; Race Riots; U.S. Army and Reconstruction; White League.

Further Reading: Escott, Paul D. *Many Excellent People: Power and Privilege in North Carolina, 1850–1900.* Chapel Hill: University of North Carolina Press, 1985; Hamilton, J. G. de Roulhac. *Reconstruction in North Carolina.* New York: Columbia University Press, 1914; Harris, William C. *William Woods Holden: Firebrand of North Carolina Politics.* Baton Rouge: Louisiana State University Press, 1987; Trelease, Allen. *White Terror: The Ku Klux Klan Conspiracy and Southern Reconstruction.* Baton Rouge: Louisiana State University Press, 1971; Zuber, Richard L. *North Carolina during Reconstruction.* Raleigh, NC: State Department of Archives and History, 1969.

Steven E. Nash

KKK. *See* Ku Klux Klan.

Ku Klux Klan (KKK)

The Ku Klux Klan was an organization dedicated to restoring political and social power to white Conservative Democrats in the South after the Civil War. It became the counterrevolutionary vehicle for the **Democratic Party**, through which extralegal means could be employed to thwart the Reconstruction agenda of **Radical Republicans**, Unionist **scalawags**, **carpetbaggers**, and their **African American** allies. It grew into a multifaceted organization that appealed to a wide range of southern white citizenry based upon the premise of white supremacy and employing methods that included persuasion as well as coercion to accomplish its goals. At its height, the Klan served as the military manifestation of the struggle for "home rule," as well as a breeding ground for intimidation and **violence**, having transformed from a largely fraternal organization with limited numbers and goals into a secret society that spanned the South and demonstrated the willingness to employ all the weapons at its disposal to achieve its ends.

Genesis and Structure of the Organization

Begun in Pulaski, **Tennessee**, in early 1866, by six former Confederate officers, the organization at first served as a source of amusement and an opportunity to recall wartime connections for the ex-soldiers. The first order of business was to decide upon a name and establish the rules and rituals. The early members settled on a hybrid of Greek (kuklos or circle) and English (clan). The rules and rituals took some time to compose and reflected the relatively innocuous nature of the organization at this point in its existence.

The initial practices of the Klan amounted to little more than harmless pranks, but success in mild forms of intimidation became infectious and Klan activities grew more audacious and aggressive. Nevertheless, the founders and early leaders touted the secret society as essentially benevolent in nature, providing assistance to whites in need and serving a self-anointed local, as well as internal, policing role. In this way, it harkened back to the slave patrols and other community-sponsored outfits that enforced black subordination before the war. Proponents of the organization insisted that its membership consisted of former Confederates who had served honorably, and other leading citizens.

The Klan's military heritage was unmistakable in its chain of command and structural hierarchy. The "Invisible Empire," commanded by a Grand Wizard was subdivided into realms (statewide organizations led by a Grand Dragon), dominions (congressional districts under a Grand Titan), provinces (counties commanded by a Grand Giant), and local dens (headed by a Grand Cyclops). Since the founders and most of the members were veterans, it made sense that these descending units and offices corresponded to those found in the military. It also reflected a cultural propensity and tradition of secret order and rites, such as those found in the popular Masonic Order of the time. A "Prescript" or constitution established the nature and purposes of the organization, its authorship attributed to former Confederate general George W. Gordon, an attorney in Pulaski who also served as a key Klan leader.

The Klan thrived in secrecy. Members sent messages in code and carried out recruitment in stealth. Willingness to obtain membership was evident in

Early Klan members depicted wearing the precursor to the white hood. (Courtesy of the Library of Congress.)

the interest shown outside of Pulaski. By the end of 1866, the Ku Klux Klan in Tennessee had spread statewide. In April 1867, the leadership met in Nashville at the Maxwell House hotel to give the organization greater cohesion. At about the same time, it received its most famous recruit—and future leader—when former Confederate cavalry general **Nathan Bedford Forrest** joined its ranks and, according to some, assumed the office of grand wizard. Forrest had vowed to remain quietly at home when the war ended until he felt the actions of wartime Unionist and postwar governor **William G. "Parson" Brownlow** against former Confederates and Democrats in the state prompted him to become active in response.

The Klan Expands in Size and Purpose

Under Forrest's leadership, the Klan grew exponentially. Using his contacts in his **railroad** construction and insurance ventures, Forrest worked to expand the organization into neighboring states and throughout the South. Often he met on business matters with ex-Confederate colleagues such as **John B. Gordon**, who then subsequently became central figures in establishing and leading Klan activities in their states. Forrest also benefited from friendly newspapers that included notices or editorialized favorably on the secret society's behalf.

In 1867, as the Republican Reconstruction program implemented **black suffrage**, the Ku Klux Klan turned its attention to the political arena. At first, the organization employed mostly nonviolent tactics in an attempt to persuade African Americans to vote Democratic, largely on the antebellum assumption that they would view their former masters as most closely associated with their best interests. When this did not occur, frustrated whites turned increasingly to force, or at least the threat of force, to obtain the same result—prevent blacks from participating in the political process. Thus, the Ku Klux Klan sought to influence political affairs and restore the social order to something approximating the prewar status quo. To this end, Klan members targeted the people and organizations they identified as active challengers to their conservative aims, especially the secret Republican clubs known as **Union Leagues** (also called Loyal Leagues), whose membership included blacks and Unionists.

The Klan played an important but as it turned out not very decisive role in the presidential **election of 1868** between Democrat **Horatio Seymour** and Republican **Ulysses S. Grant**. In **Georgia**, Klan forces also failed to elect Democrat and Klan leader John B. Gordon over Republican **Rufus Bullock**. At the same time, **William W. Holden**, originally appointed as **provisional governor** by President **Andrew Johnson**, became **North Carolina**'s first Republican governor. Yet, the organization enjoyed some successes in its home state of Tennessee when Governor Brownlow left the statehouse to take up a seat in the U.S. Senate and his successor, DeWitt Clinton Senter, proved more amenable to the former Confederates and Democrats there. In North Carolina, Governor Holden employed the **militia** under Colonel George W. Kirk to battle continuously with Klan forces in his state, before finally being impeached and removed from that office in 1871.

Yet, by this point in its development, the Ku Klux Klan was also becoming an organization that no central authority, even one as determined and dynamic as Nathan Bedford Forrest, could control. Although this became a common and convenient subterfuge—such as when Klan members wanted to deny violence and intimidation in their ranks by attributing such activities to renegade elements—it was sufficient to encourage Forrest to dissociate himself from the organization. Consequently, in early 1869, the grand wizard sent out an edict for members to destroy their regalia. Although the Klan officially disbanded, it by no means disappeared and in some areas became even more pronounced in its abusive methods.

Continuing Klan violence prompted the U.S. Congress to pass **Enforcement Acts** in 1870 and 1871 to combat these excesses and counteract the organization's effectiveness in threatening the southern Republican Party. Congress also called prominent leaders felt to be associated with the organization, including Nathan Bedford Forrest and John B. Gordon, to testify in Washington. In their descriptions of the secret society, offered despite their denial of membership in the Klan, such leaders demonstrated considerable knowledge and detail concerning it. Their testimonies also presented numerous examples of evasion and false or misleading statements, but, by this point, they could repudiate the violence in an organization that no longer existed, officially, at least. This sort of politically motivated violence would subside after **Redemption** as **Bourbon** governments returned Democrats to power. Then, legal **disfranchisement** measures were developed to eliminate the political roles and opportunities for blacks.

Despite the celebratory images, the stereotypes, and the heated rhetoric of "**Lost Cause**" adherents, the Ku Klux Klan was not solely responsible for the undoing of Reconstruction, but it clearly aided in the endeavors of white southern conservative Democrats to return to power and helped to reestablish a social system of white supremacy in the South. The Klan returned to public attention in the 1910s and 1920s (the cross-burning, anti-Semitic, xenophobic Klan developed here) and again in the 1960s, but the Reconstruction Klan clearly remained an inspiration for these later versions, as evidenced by Thomas Dixon's novel *The Clansman*, which served as the source for D. W. Griffith's silent film, *The Birth of a Nation* (1915), and the words and actions of the **Jim Crow** segregationists of the Civil Rights era. *See also* Bloody Shirt; Congressional Reconstruction; Kirk-Holden War; Race Riots; U.S. Army and Reconstruction; White League.

Further Reading: Chalmers, David M. *Hooded Americanism: The History of the Ku Klux Klan.* New York: Doubleday & Company, 1965; Foner, Eric. *Reconstruction: America's Unfinished Revolution, 1863–1877.* New York: Harper & Row, 1988; Horn, Stanley F. *Invisible Empire: The Story of the Ku Klux Klan, 1866–1871.* Boston: Houghton Mifflin, Co., 1939; Trelease, Allen W. *White Terror: The Ku Klux Klan Conspiracy and Southern Reconstruction.* New York: Harper & Row, 1971; Wade, Wyn Craig. *The Fiery Cross: The Ku Klux Klan in America.* New York: Simon & Schuster, 1987.

Brian S. Wills

L

Labor Systems

One might expect that Union victory in the Civil War would have presented a fait accompli with regard to the labor system of the former Confederate states. **Emancipation** meant that the slaves of the South were now, ipso facto, free laborers, a condition codified by the **Thirteenth Amendment** (1865), which **abolished slavery** entirely and prohibited labor systems based on "slavery or involuntary servitude."

But matters were not so simple. Southern whites, especially former slave owners, were reluctant to treat blacks with even the modicum of equality necessary to forming **contracts** between mutually consenting parties; more common were racist attitudes that viewed the **African American** freedpeople as naturally inferior. On the other hand, among the freedpeople, the habits and work discipline of a modern wage-labor force could not be inculcated under decades of slavery, and unsurprisingly, most former slaves preferred self-sufficiency for themselves and their families rather than entering into market-oriented relationships, which struck them as merely their old bosses in new clothes. Finally, among the federal representatives who presided over the reconstruction of southern labor systems, as in the North more generally, the practical aspects and very meaning of "free labor" were erratically understood, vaguely defined, and often bitterly contested.

Transition: From Slavery to Free Labor

The basis of the southern economy both before and after the Civil War was the production of agricultural commodities, chiefly cotton. Before the war, most cotton was produced on farms or plantations by black slaves working under the supervision of white owners. As a labor system, slavery had meant that workers toiled only because of the constant threat—and often, reality—of

violence; that is, a form of extraeconomic compulsion. Slaves were a form of property, and as such, black workers in the antebellum South had no rights, remunerative or otherwise, that their owners were legally obligated to respect. By contrast, in the systems of production then in place in the northern and western states, laborers were "free," which is to say that the work they performed was part of a reciprocal exchange (for example, tasks for wages) governed mainly by market incentives and the laws of **contract**.

During the early years of Reconstruction, military officers working under the auspices of the federal **Bureau of Refugees, Freedmen, and Abandoned Lands** (BRFAL), or the Freedmen's Bureau, were the immediate adjudicators of the labor arrangements that emerged in various southern localities. During the war, the army had been responsible for dealing with slaves defined as **contraband**, so this seemed a logical outgrowth of that policy. Early on, however, the army interfered only minimally, and the arrangements presented by southern whites had much of the compulsory character of slavery, especially under the short-lived **Black Codes** of 1865–1866, which sought to limit freedpeople's movement through harsh penalties for **vagrancy** and lack of employment. Though these codes were soon nullified by federal action, the attitudes that undergirded them persisted for years to come, profoundly delimiting the development of a true free labor system for the post-emancipation South.

There was no escaping a simple reality: White landowners needed labor, and the freedpeople needed jobs. At first, the most common means of reaching labor agreements with the former slaves was to contract with them as groups, often in "squads" composed of loosely allied families and individuals. Attempts were made to pay these squads cash wages on a semiregular basis—weekly or monthly—but the lack of capital among white landowners made such wage payments nearly impossible to sustain. In their place, a variety of arrangements emerged across the South by the late 1860s, whose crux was the deferral of cash wages in favor of a portion of the crop to be produced and sold at prevailing market prices. This was the genesis of the **sharecropping** system that was to dominate southern **agriculture** through the Great Depression.

Sharecropping Takes Hold

Though not a uniquely American form of labor system—sharecropping had many global and historical antecedents—its form in the postwar South had particular features that were well adapted to the regional context. As a substitute for a system of cash wages, the advantages of sharecropping were superior for both parties. The deferral of compensation meant that white planters could productively employ the only capital they had left—the land—without the need for monetary reserves, and as freedpeople impelled the further evolution of sharecropping away from the gang labor common to the squad system toward contracts with individual households, they grew reconciled to sharecropping's ability to approximate the ideal of independent farming that most held dear. Still, sharecropping fully satisfied no one: Landowning capitalists would have preferred more leeway for regulating and disciplining "their" laborers; freedpeople would have preferred to own their own land on which to produce as they saw fit.

If this was "free labor," then it was a most peculiar form of it at best. Sharecropping's main shortcomings were to be found in the need for seasonal agricultural credit that could provide for the day-to-day needs of workers until the annual harvesting and marketing of the crop. Although some planters took an active role in provisioning their tenants over the course of the year, the same lack of liquid capital that kept them from paying regular cash wages made it difficult for most to obtain goods from northern markets for distribution to their workforces. As a result, a third party, the independent furnishing merchant with ties to outside capital, arose during Reconstruction, when the numbers of so-called country stores (many were actually located in or served as the basis of small towns) grew tremendously throughout the South. Though white landowners greatly resented the intrusion of these merchants into their customary positions of community power (many of them were northern migrants, and often Jewish as well), the situation proved even worse for the sharecropping farmers themselves. Many found themselves forced into long-term debt to the furnishing merchant as a result of high interest rates, as well as shortfalls due to poor harvests, low crop prices, or both. The consequent restrictions on freedpeoples' mobility and choice of crop mix were soon widely perceived as a form of debt peonage—restoring them to a condition disturbingly similar to slavery.

This makeshift, inefficient labor system, gestated and born during Reconstruction, plagued the southern economy for decades to come. Like slavery, sharecropping was never the exclusive labor system of the South—it coexisted with other steps on the "agricultural ladder," from cash renting to farm ownership. It did, however, constitute the dominant mode of production, and as such, it exerted a determinant influence on the relationships in those around it. There were other forms of labor control in the postwar South: Perhaps the most authoritarian was the notorious convict-lease system, which was gaining wide popularity by the late 1860s. Also, similarities to other labor systems then arising in the mining towns of the West could be found in the new cotton-mill villages of the lower Atlantic seaboard, where displaced white rural workers—men, women, and children—were transformed into factory operatives under conditions of company paternalism.

Labor Movements in the North

In the North, the workforce still remained surprisingly rurally dispersed immediately after the war, but the trend was clearly toward its increasing concentration in urban areas, especially after labor's ranks were augmented by the waves of immigration that picked up steam during the late Reconstruction era. As the manufacturing sector grew in importance during the postwar years, there were crucial efforts to further institutionalize the nascent organized labor movement, but with mixed results. Partisan politics intruded on attempts to build and sustain the National Labor Union led by William H. Sylvis; the Knights of Labor, founded in 1869, would enjoy greater success beginning in the late 1870s. The clearest harbinger of the future of the

American labor movement were the attempts to organize craft unions by particular trades during Reconstruction, though most of these were wiped out by the **Panic of 1873**. However, throughout the many strikes of the 1870s, which culminated in the great strike wave of 1877, community-oriented, mutualist forms of consciousness continued to predominate among workers, who were also often divided by ethnoreligious conflicts, and Union actions thus tended to remain spontaneous, unfocused, and vulnerable to disruption. *See also* Freedmen's Relief Societies; Southern Homestead Act; Stevens, Thaddeus; U.S. Army and Reconstruction.

Further Reading: Jaynes, Gerald David. *Branches without Roots: The Genesis of the Black Working Class in the American South, 1862–1882*. New York: Oxford University Press, 1986; Marler, Scott P. "Fables of the Reconstruction: Reconstruction of the Fables." *Journal of the Historical Society* 4 (Winter 2004): 113–37; Montgomery, David. *Beyond Equality: Labor and the Radical Republicans, 1862–1872*. New York: Alfred A. Knopf, 1967; Ransom, Roger L., and Richard Sutch. *One Kind of Freedom: The Economic Consequences of Emancipation*. 2nd ed. New York: Cambridge University Press, 2001.

Scott P. Marler

Liberal Republicans. *See* Republicans, Liberal.

Lincoln, Abraham (1809–1865)

Abraham Lincoln, sixteenth president of the United States, in his first inaugural address on March 4, 1861, announced his intention to preserve the government and to restore the seceded states to the Union. The reconstruction of these states—or, as he preferred, restoration—was his duty as president under the **U.S. Constitution**. Lincoln never recognized the legitimacy of secession or the government of the Confederate states. He reasoned that individuals, not states, had rebelled and thereby had overturned republican forms of government in the South as guaranteed by the Constitution. When the war began in April 1861, Lincoln believed that it was his supreme constitutional responsibility as commander in chief to suppress the armed rebellion and restore legitimate, loyal governments in the southern states. In his mind, the states were indestructible and their prewar constitutions and laws should remain unchanged unless amended or replaced by the normal state processes. Throughout the war, Lincoln insisted that his aim was to return the southern states and their people to their "proper practical relation with the Union."

Lincoln's Plan of Restoration

Lincoln favored a large measure of self-reconstruction that would be led by a nucleus of southern Unionists as federal armies penetrated the rebel areas. He had faith in the "good sense" of the southern people to want reunion once they understood that he was no threat to slavery or their rights. Until late in the war, he consistently overestimated the strength of southern Unionism and, conversely, underestimated the support of the southern people for the war.

Lincoln's first effort toward Reconstruction occurred in western **Virginia**. With his encouragement, Unionists in this area met at Wheeling in June 1861, and created the Restored Government of Virginia. They selected as governor **Francis H. Pierpont**, elected two U.S. senators, and called for the popular elections of three congressmen under the laws of Virginia. Lincoln gave his approval to the work, and Congress seated the senators and representatives from the Pierpont government. When this government gave its approval in 1862 to the formation of the state of **West Virginia**, Lincoln reluctantly agreed and Congress approved the division. The Restored Government of Virginia then moved to Alexandria within Union lines where it maintained only a skeleton government until the end of the war. After Robert E. Lee's surrender, Governor Pierpont assumed control in Richmond. In 1868, he was removed by General **John M. Schofield** under **Congressional Reconstruction**.

Early in the war, Lincoln sought to liberate the Unionists of East **Tennessee** from rebel rule and establish the foundation for the restoration of the state to the Union. He pressed his military commanders to launch campaigns into the area. The effort to penetrate East Tennessee through Cumberland Gap failed, but in early 1862, Nashville fell to federal forces, and Lincoln dispatched Senator **Andrew Johnson** to Middle Tennessee to begin the process of Reconstruction. Appointed **military governor** of the state, Johnson refused to hold state elections until Unionists in East Tennessee were liberated and could prevent rebels from overwhelming the new government. Lincoln also had to placate Johnson and East Tennessee Unionists by exempting all of the state from the **Emancipation** Proclamation. However, these Unionists, including Johnson, later supported emancipation. By early 1865, the federal army had finally succeeded in redeeming East Tennessee, and a state convention of Unionists abolished slavery and formed a government under **William G. "Parson" Brownlow**. It was not until after the war that Tennessee sent representatives to Congress.

Also in 1862, Lincoln appointed military governors for **North Carolina**, **Louisiana**, and **Texas**. After federal forces occupied northeastern North Carolina in March, Lincoln sent Edward Stanly, a former congressman, to New Bern to begin the process of civil reorganization in the state. Stanly, however, made little progress toward Reconstruction, and when the president issued his Emancipation Proclamation, he resigned. Lincoln did not appoint a replacement. After New Orleans fell to federal forces in May 1862, Lincoln appointed Colonel George F. Shepley, under the overall command of General **Benjamin F. Butler**, as military governor of the city and directed him to seek the restoration of civil government and hold elections for two congressmen in the occupied districts. Only after much prodding on the president's part were two representatives elected, and in early 1863, they were seated to serve out the remaining days of the congressional term. Lincoln's appointment of Andrew Jackson Hamilton for Texas proved fruitless, mainly because the Union controlled only a coastal sliver of the state. However, after the war, President Andrew Johnson appointed Hamilton **provisional governor** of Texas.

Lincoln and Amnesty

The federal military successes at Gettysburg, Vicksburg, Chattanooga, and elsewhere during the summer and fall of 1863 encouraged Lincoln to launch a new initiative on Reconstruction while maintaining the substance of his southern Unionist–controlled policy. On December 8, 1863, he issued what has been called the Proclamation of **Amnesty** and Reconstruction. Lincoln declared that he was issuing the proclamation because "in some states the elements for resumption" of Union governments "seem ready for action, but remain inactive, apparently for want of a rallying point—a plan of action." He also said that circumstances in a state might dictate a variance on his plan, though certain general requirements had to be met. His plan granted amnesty to the great majority of southerners who would take a simple oath of future loyalty to the Union, the Constitution, and the proclamations and laws regarding slavery. Certain classes of Confederate officials and those who had mistreated prisoners of war would be excluded from amnesty for the time being. Later, Lincoln said that he did not intend to withhold **pardons** from members of the excluded classes; and indeed, he did not.

In the second part of his proclamation, Lincoln outlined a method to restore the state governments to the Union. He indicated that whenever one-tenth of those eligible to vote in the 1860 presidential election had taken the oath of allegiance, they could "re-establish a State government which shall be republican" in character. The president did not explain why the Ten Percent Plan was chosen, but, eager to get the process under way, he probably believed that while the war raged, this percentage of the 1860 voters would constitute a "tangible nucleus" to launch loyal state governments. He required that the restored governments affirm the **abolition of slavery**, though as a "temporary arrangement" they could adopt measures that recognized the freedpeople's "present condition as a laboring, landless, and homeless class." However, they must acknowledge their permanent freedom and provide for the **education** of young blacks.

Lincoln's December 8, 1863, proclamation resulted in a flurry of Reconstruction activity in federal-occupied areas, though the process was not completed in any state until after the war. Louisiana became the centerpiece of the president's new initiative. There, in early 1864, a loyal government was elected, mainly representative of the federal-occupied New Orleans area, and it provided for an election of delegates for a state **constitutional convention**. One month before the assembling of the convention, a delegation of prominent New Orleans blacks traveled to Washington and presented a petition to President Lincoln asking for the right to vote for members of their race. Lincoln told the delegation that he could not impose a **suffrage** requirement upon the people of Louisiana. However, ten days later, he raised the issue with the new governor, Michael Hahn, in a letter marked "Private." "I barely suggest for your private consideration," he wrote, "whether some of the colored people may not be let in—as, for instance, the very intelligent, and [soldiers]. . . . But this is only a suggestion, not to the public, but to you alone." When the convention met, Hahn showed the letter to leading delegates, but they rejected the president's plea. However, as required by Lincoln, they ended slavery in the new state constitution.

When the war became stalemated during the summer of 1864, Lincoln's political stock plummeted not only in the nation but also within his party. **Radical Republicans**, joined by other Lincoln opponents, secured the passage of the **Wade-Davis** Reconstruction bill designed to substitute a stringent Reconstruction policy for the president's lenient plan. Lincoln pocket vetoed the measure. After Lincoln won reelection, he directed his efforts toward securing an early peace on his mild terms—the surrender of the rebel armies, restoration of the Union, and emancipation. At the Hampton Roads Peace Conference with Confederate commissioners on February 3, 1865, he realized that **Jefferson Davis**'s administration was determined to continue the fight. One month later, in his classic second inaugural address, Lincoln ended with the plea,

> With malice toward none; with charity for all; with firmness in the right, as God gives us to see the right, let us strive on to finish the work we are in; to bind up the nation's wounds; to care for him who shall have borne the battle, and for his widow, and his orphan—to do all which may achieve . . . a lasting peace.

The End of the Civil War

On April 11, three days before his tragic death, Lincoln made his final public statement on Reconstruction. It was also his last speech. Though some historians disagree, it seems probable that Lincoln had not changed his fundamental policy of self-Reconstruction controlled by southern Unionists and not by the federal government. He announced that the differences among the loyal people regarding "the mode, manner, and means of reconstruction" had caused "additional embarrassment," and, with Louisiana in mind, Lincoln admitted that he would have preferred that "the elective franchise" were "conferred on the very intelligent [blacks], and on those who serve our cause as soldiers." Nowhere in this address, however, did he suggest that he would impose **black suffrage** or **civil rights** upon Louisiana or any southern state. He did indicate that "it may be my duty to make some new announcement to the people of the South." With the war ending, Lincoln probably was thinking about a declaration extending temporary military control to states where no loyal governments existed, a purpose that became clearer when he met with his **cabinet** three days later. A second meeting on a proposal along this line by Secretary of War **Edwin M. Stanton** was scheduled for April 18. Lincoln was dead, and the meeting was never held. *See also* Assassination of Abraham Lincoln; Black Codes; Disfranchisement; Elections of 1864; Presidential Reconstruction; Readmission.

Further Reading: Belz, Herman. *Reconstructing the Union: Theory and Policy during the Civil War.* Ithaca, NY: Cornell University Press, 1969; Cox, LaWanda. *Lincoln and Black Freedom: A Study in Presidential Leadership.* Columbia: University of South Carolina Press, 1981; Harris, William C. *With Charity for All: Lincoln and the Restoration of the Union.* Lexington: University Press of Kentucky, 1997.

William C. Harris

Lincoln, Abraham, Assassination of. *See* Assassination of Abraham Lincoln (1865).

Lindsay, Robert B. (1824–1902)

Robert Burns Lindsay was one of the more troubled Democratic governors of the Reconstruction era, perhaps most famous for presiding over the unraveling of **Alabama**'s ambitious **railroad** subsidy program.

Lindsay, born in Scotland in 1824, entered politics as a Democratic legislator from the **Tennessee** Valley in the 1850s. He was the son-in-law of Governor John Winston, known for his opposition to railroad subsidies, an association that aided his political career. In the presidential campaign of 1860, Lindsay supported Stephen Douglas and opposed secession. He took "a slight part in the rebellion" and was "never much of a soldier." In reluctantly Confederate north Alabama, this political profile was popular, and after a brief dalliance with Reconstruction, he emerged as a moderate leader in the **Democratic Party**, relatively untainted with sectional extremism.

Governor Lindsay

The Republican Party ascended to power under the **Military Reconstruction Acts**, and was readmitted to the Union in 1868. Republican **William H. Smith** was the first governor elected under **Congressional Reconstruction**, and ran again in 1870. In November 1870, Democrat Lindsay challenged Smith, and claimed a narrow victory over the incumbent. After several weeks of tension and near-violence, a court decision in Lindsay's favor placed the Democrat in office.

As Lindsay assumed office, a fiscal crisis immediately ensued. In January 1871, the Alabama & Chattanooga Railroad defaulted on its state-endorsed bonds, and Lindsay discovered that his predecessor had signed some half a million dollars in unauthorized securities. Lindsay refused to honor the extralegal bonds, and he declined to pay anything for months without full investigation. The upright course paralyzed the largest railroad in the state before its completion, leading to its bankruptcy, and it also undermined the financing of all the other projects under construction in the state. With the coming of the **Panic of 1873**, most of the endorsed lines went bankrupt, taking the state government with them.

The railroad imbroglio also damaged the governor's personal reputation. When the state government took over the failing Alabama & Chattanooga line, the previous management lavishly bribed Lindsay's best friend in an attempt to regain control of the company. The governor may or may not have been involved, but his reputation was compromised, and militant Democrats pressed for more wholesale repudiation of the tainted company's bonds. Furthermore, Alabama's financial crisis closed the public schools for a year, further damaging an educational system just trying to regain its footing. As a result of these difficulties, the party rejected Governor Lindsay's bid for renomination; the Democrats went on to lose the governorship in the next election by a substantial margin.

Despite his difficulties, Lindsay's administration was not without positive features. Lindsay thought it was important that the Democrats discourage **Ku Klux Klan** terrorism, for fear the federal government would intervene (rather, apparently, than for reasons of morality). He was less committed to the rule of law than to the elimination of the Republican Party, but still, he publicly denounced "crime and lawlessness," arguing that it was "condemned by the leading and influential citizens of the country." He was less than candid about the prevalence of terrorist activity, but these avowals may have contributed to the decline in Klan activity over the course of his administration.

Soon after leaving office, Lindsay suffered an attack of paralysis. He resumed law practice at a limited level, but he took no further interest in politics. He remained an invalid until his death in Tuscumbia, Alabama, in 1902. *See also* African Americans; Amnesty Proclamations; Carpetbaggers; Education; Fourteenth Amendment; Johnson, Andrew; Parsons, Lewis E.; Readmission; Republicans, Radical; Scandals; Violence.

Further Reading: Fitzgerald, Michael W. "Wager Swayne, the Freedmen's Bureau, and the Politics of Reconstruction in Alabama." *Alabama Review* (July 1995): 188–218; Owen, Thomas M. *History of Alabama and Dictionary of Alabama Biography*. 4 vols. Chicago: S. J. Clark, 1921; Summers, Mark W. *Railroads, Reconstruction, and the Gospel of Prosperity: Aid under the Radical Republicans, 1865–1877*. Princeton, NJ: Princeton University Press, 1984; Webb, Samuel L. "A Jacksonian Democrat in Postbellum Alabama: The Ideology and Influence of Journalist Robert McKee, 1869–1896." *Journal of Southern History* 62 (May 1996): 239-74.

Michael W. Fitzgerald

Longstreet, James (1821–1904)

James Longstreet distinguished himself as one of the highest-ranking Confederates to join the Republican Party during Reconstruction. He was born in Edgefield District, **South Carolina**, but grew up in **Georgia**. He graduated from the U.S. Military Academy in 1842, ranking fifty-fourth of sixty-two cadets. During the war, Longstreet led the First Corps of Robert E. Lee's Army of Northern Virginia, and Lee designated Longstreet to take over the army should Lee be killed or incapacitated. Due to Longstreet's high rank and a position close to Lee, it was a shock to former Confederates when he announced in the spring of 1867 that he was joining the Republican Party. At one stroke, Longstreet cast himself out of the Confederate pantheon of heroes and made himself vulnerable to critics of his generalship and his postwar politics.

Longstreet did not accept all of the political and social tenets offered by the Republicans during Reconstruction. He did not follow the Radical wing of the party, and found fault with the **Military Reconstruction Acts** that formed the basis of **Congressional Reconstruction** policy. Still, he recognized that Republicans, not Democrats, controlled Reconstruction. When his antebellum friend, **Ulysses S. Grant**, won the presidency in 1868, Longstreet hoped to help guide Reconstruction as well as improve his financial standing. However, affiliating with the Republicans turned away many Democrats and former

Confederates from Longstreet's insurance company and his cotton marketing business. In April 1869, Grant gave Longstreet a political plum, making him surveyor of the port of New Orleans, where Longstreet resided. For many, becoming a Republican and accepting Grant's **patronage** made Longstreet a "**scalawag**" and a traitor to the **Lost Cause**.

As a former general (and now Republican), Longstreet seemed a logical choice in 1873 to head the New Orleans Metropolitan Police. This force was controversial and especially galling to former Confederates because it contained so many **African Americans**. They formed the main line of defense for **Louisiana**'s Republican governor, **William P. Kellogg**. He also appointed Longstreet to serve on the Louisiana Levee Commission, another patronage job.

Longstreet commanded police units in New Orleans when former Confederates tried to overthrow Kellogg in September 1874. Members of the Louisiana **White League** (similar to the **Ku Klux Klan**) fought against Longstreet's policemen in urban warfare—the so-called "Battle of Liberty Place." Longstreet reportedly blanched when he heard Kellogg's opponents shouting the Rebel Yell. The Metropolitan Police could not subdue the rioting, and **U.S. Army** troops were sent in to quell the disorder.

Abandoning the bayous, Longstreet returned to Georgia and bought a farm. A request for a political favor from President **Rutherford B. Hayes** gained him the post of U.S. minister (ambassador) to Turkey, and subsequently he took the appointment of U.S. marshal for Georgia, 1881–1883. In later years, apologists for the Lost Cause, led by Jubal Early, heaped criticism on Longstreet, blaming him for the southern defeat at Gettysburg and undermining the chance for Confederate independence. Longstreet defended himself in his memoir, *From Manassas to Appomattox* (1896), and in magazine articles, but his opponents had succeeded in permanently tarnishing his reputation. *See also* Democratic Party; Elections of 1868; Race Riots; Violence.

Further Reading: Piston, William G. *Lee's Tarnished Lieutenant: James Longstreet and His Place in Southern History*. Athens: University of Georgia Press, 1987; Richter, William L. "James Longstreet: From Rebel to Scalawag." *Louisiana History* 11 (Summer 1970): 215–30; Wert, Jeffrey D. *General James Longstreet: The Confederacy's Most Controversial Soldier*. New York: Simon and Schuster, 1993.

Joseph G. Dawson III

Lost Cause

The Lost Cause is the name given to a romanticized interpretation of the Civil War and Reconstruction periods that seeks to salve the southern conscience at the expense of both historical accuracy and **African Americans**. The movement gained definitive shape in the 1880s, mostly through the writings of Civil War veterans, especially former Confederate general Jubal Early. The interpretation, or memory, consists of a set of beliefs that justified the southern side of Civil War. Over the late nineteenth and early twentieth centuries, this memory became ritualized, institutionalized, and was often expressed in quasi-religious terms in the South.

The Old South and the Confederacy

The cult of Lost Cause is characterized by an intense focus on the past and is closely connected in time to the creation of historically minded institutions like the Southern Historical Association, the United Daughters of the Confederacy, and the United Confederate Veterans. The Lost Cause consists of four central tenets. First, white southerners fought the Civil War as a defense of the political philosophy of state's rights. This offers an elegant philosophical justification for the **violence** committed during the war. Second, the results of the war can be explained with reference to the North's overwhelming numerical advantage, both in terms of supplies and soldiers. This explanation denies all historical contingency during the war and offers a reassuring vision (to its adherents) of the antebellum South as an innocent rural region and the antebellum North as an avaricious industrial giant. Third, the Confederacy is portrayed as the true Christian society. In this account, Robert E. Lee, Stonewall Jackson, and Confederate women's undying sacrifices stand as testimony to the dedication and faith of white southerners. In contrast, northerners are represented as money-worshipping Yankees whose greed blinds them to the necessity of spiritual humility, and ultimately, salvation. Last, the Lost Cause treats slavery as a benevolent institution. African slaves were lucky to have had the opportunity to be brought to America where they were introduced to Christianity and kindly masters instead of dwelling in pagan barbarism in Africa. The antebellum South is presented as a lost time of near perfection—a utopia for white people, and, when black people are considered at all, a decided improvement over their fortunes had they remained in Africa. The centrality of slavery to the Civil War, and the institution's obvious inhumane and repressive aspects, are left out entirely.

Postwar America: Reconstruction and Reconciliation

Although the Lost Cause is typically identified with the constellation of issues described above and related to the Civil War, it extends easily to explain the period of Reconstruction. The interpretation of Reconstruction continues the picture of blameless southern whites and incompetent blacks upon which so much of the wartime story rests. The rise of Republican governments in the South is regarded as an unholy alliance between greedy northern **carpetbaggers**, debased white southern **scalawags**, and gullible freedmen. The policies of these governments are portrayed as uniformly disastrous and the governments themselves as hopelessly corrupt. **Redemption** by white conservatives—not accidentally a term with religious overtones—is thus regarded as an improvement for both the white southerners whose rights were denied by **Radical Republicans** and, ultimately, a boon to the South, because with men of good character returned to office, the future of the South would be safe once again.

The Lost Cause emerged at a time—the 1880s—when white southerners continued to decry northern economic dominance of their region, but when both regions sought actual reunion. In its time, the Lost Cause helped perform much of the work of reconciliation by explaining the war as a test of wills among honorable white men. Both sides could take pride in their heroism without disagreeing over the causes or outcomes. Once Reconstruction had ended, the nation began to look toward issues capable of unifying whites, North and South. These included **American Indian** wars, westward expansion, and even overseas imperialism via the war with Spain. At the same time, Civil War veterans' reunions were becoming more and more popular; both former Yankees and Rebels, wittingly or not, embraced the Lost Cause just as they embraced each other, former enemies, now all Americans.

The Lost Cause received its most dramatic articulation in *The Birth of a Nation*, D. W. Griffith's 1915 film about the effects of black rule on the South. Based upon the Thomas Dixon novel *The Clansman*, the film's characterization of rapacious ignorant blacks, deceitful northern whites, and aggrieved but dignified southern whites typifies the racist and villanizing treatment that Lost Cause adherents attributed to Reconstruction. The film's popularity around the country demonstrated the eagerness with which northern whites constructed and consumed the same myths. For anxious white northerners contending with the rise of corporations and labor unions, the influx of immigrants, and the instability of rapid urban growth, the idyllic vision of the plantation South represented the tranquility and control they desperately sought in their own lives.

From its inception, the Lost Cause interpretation was vigorously contested by African Americans like **Frederick Douglass** and later W.E.B. Du Bois. Douglass campaigned throughout the remainder of his life, as did many black veterans, insisting on the centrality of slavery as a cause of the war and on **emancipation** as its most important outcome. In 1935, Du Bois published his *Black Reconstruction*, which represented both a rebuttal to the Lost Cause and its demeaning characterizations of black people, and an alternative reading of the whole experience of Reconstruction. In Du Bois's view, the lower classes of the South, white and black, missed a crucial opportunity to build a more equitable society in the wake of war.

The work of Douglass and Du Bois continues to this day. Despite the outpouring of scholarship on the Civil War era, a few dominant ideas continue to influence popular conceptions of the period. Among these are the importance of state's rights as the prime justification of the war, the inevitable superiority of a modern urban-industrial North, and a blameless, honorable white South. Modern incarnations of the Lost Cause take care not to portray slavery as the positive good that most postbellum southern scholars did. They do this primarily by removing the whole issue from view. The importance of slavery to the antebellum southern economy is denied or ignored, as is its relevance to the war. The centrality of race to the experience of Reconstruction is thus lost as well, leading students back into a curiously truncated and inaccurate interpretation of the period as one of a noble lost cause. *See also* Bourbons; Congressional Reconstruction; Ku Klux Klan; New South; Scandals; Violence.

Further Reading: Foster, Gaines. *Ghosts of the Confederacy: Defeat, The Lost Cause, and the Emergence of the New South.* New York: Oxford University Press, 1987; Gallagher, Gary W., and Alan T. Nolan, eds. *The Myth of the Lost Cause and Civil War History.* Bloomington: Indiana University Press, 2000; Wilson, Charles R.

Baptized in Blood: The Religion of the Lost Cause, 1865–1920. Athens: University of Georgia Press, 1980.

Aaron Sheehan-Dean

Louisiana

President **Abraham Lincoln** implemented some of Reconstruction's earliest steps in Louisiana, and the state was one of the last in the American South to have a Republican governor in the nineteenth century.

The Civil War and Wartime Reconstruction

Louisiana, home to the South's largest city and gateway to its largest river, was an early target for Union forces during the Civil War. In April 1862, General **Benjamin F. Butler** led the federal military expedition that occupied New Orleans, and under his controversial guidance, Louisiana began renewing its ties to the Union. Lincoln had high hopes that Louisiana would provide a positive example of his **Presidential Reconstruction** policy, one that might be applied to the rest of the Confederacy. Lincoln's plan of restoration looked to a policy that would shorten the war by inviting southern states back to the Union under the most lenient of terms.

Although Butler and a sequence of other officers, notably General **Nathaniel P. Banks**, compiled administrative accomplishments, it was extremely difficult to reconstruct Louisiana as long as the Civil War continued and more than half of Louisiana was outside federal control. Despite these handicaps, **military governors** and Unionists put through some reforms, including drafting a new state constitution that abolished slavery, holding elections for the U.S. Congress, and setting up a new system of public **education** open to black as well as white students in New Orleans.

From 1862 to 1877, Louisiana served as a laboratory for political, social, and military experiments. The state demonstrated bitter partisanship and factionalism within its Republican and Democratic parties and various contributions to the process of Reconstruction made by so-called **scalawags** and **carpetbaggers**. In 1860, Louisiana's population was about 49 percent **African American**. Therefore, it was logical for blacks to hold office during Reconstruction on the local, parish (county), and state levels, indicating that the status of African Americans would change in the South and the nation. Louisiana also displayed a distressing amount of violence, as former Confederates responded to the new society produced by defeat and Reconstruction.

A Diverse and Divided State Republican Party

From 1862 on, Louisiana's Republican factions seldom agreed on a unified course of action. These disagreements meant that their opponents (including Democrats, conservative Unionists, ex-Confederates, and some disaffected Republicans) gained their political footing and sometimes exploited openings created by the Republicans' factionalism. The strongest faction was the so-called "Custom House Ring." In the building on Canal Street in New Orleans where the federal government collected the customs duties (tariffs), the Ring dominated the city, then serving as the state capital. The Ring consolidated behind the regular wing of the national Republican Party and supported President **Ulysses S. Grant**. Leaders of the Ring included U.S. marshal **Stephen B. Packard**, U.S. senator **William P. Kellogg**, U.S. customs official James F. Casey, brother-in-law of Grant's wife, and **Oscar J. Dunn**, a leading black politician.

Both Lincoln and Grant depended partly upon southern state leaders who had opposed secession and remained loyal to the Union—men stigmatized by the Democrats as being scalawags. Most scalawags were not Louisiana natives, but the most prominent had resided in the state for twenty years or more and established themselves in respectable professions and **agricultural** pursuits. They included Joshua Baker, an engineer and judge born in **Kentucky** and residing in Louisiana since 1822; Michael J. Hahn, born in the German state of Bavaria and residing in Louisiana since 1840; and Benjamin F. Flanders, **a railroad** executive born in New Hampshire and a Louisiana resident since 1843. Another was Louisiana native **James Madison Wells**, one of the state's controversial politicians of the postwar period. All of them held the office of governor during Reconstruction and three held other offices: Flanders was mayor of New Orleans; Hahn was a state legislator; and Wells was federal surveyor of customs at New Orleans. James G. Taliaferro, a native of **Virginia**, settled in Louisiana in the 1820s; and Thomas J. Durant, born in Pennsylvania, came to Louisiana in the 1830s. Taliaferro and Durant provided leadership to the fledgling Union-Republican Party and advocated civil and political reforms. As a **Radical Republican**, Taliaferro later sought the governorship in opposition to a fellow Republican in 1868. Within a few years, peer pressure from other southern whites and bitter politics undercut some scalawags' careers. Republicans began to turn to leaders from outside the state.

Carpetbaggers were northern men who moved to the South during or after the war, sometimes bringing their families with them. Opponents of Reconstruction not only condemned and vilified the carpetbaggers; they created a derisive negative label that smeared them during Reconstruction and ever since. However, detailed research by historians demonstrates a variety of motives, backgrounds, and actions by these settlers from the North. For example, originally from Vermont, William Pitt Kellogg entered politics in Illinois and served in an Illinois regiment during the war. Kellogg was elected U.S. senator and then Louisiana governor, and anti-Reconstruction forces attempted to overthrow his administration in street fighting in 1874. Stephen Packard, a Union army veteran from Maine, held the **patronage** post of U.S. marshal for Louisiana. He wielded considerable political influence and was nominated as the Republican candidate for governor in the contested **election of 1876**.

Because they were from out of state, politicians like Kellogg and Packard were easy targets for Democrats to stigmatize as carpetbaggers, but **Marshall H. Twitchell** was another type. A heroic soldier with the Vermont brigade during the war, Twitchell encouraged several members of his family to settle with him in north Louisiana. There, the Twitchells not only entered into business enterprises, but they also crusaded for black civil, political, and economic rights. Twitchell tried to indicate his attachment to his new state by marrying the daughter of a local dignitary, but his enemies realized that Twitchell personified Reconstruction's social, political, and economic changes. Unknown assailants murdered seven members of Twitchell's family and severely wounded him, shooting him down in broad daylight and leaving him for dead. Distraught and crippled, he returned to Vermont.

Among the most significant carpetbaggers was **Henry Clay Warmoth**, a former Union officer from Missouri who was elected Louisiana governor, serving from 1868 to 1872. A flamboyant and powerful politician, Warmoth proposed a list of expensive state construction projects, appeared to foster an integrated public school system, worked with African American politicians, and seemed to support **black suffrage**. On the other hand, he let black **civil rights** slide and slipped over toward the Democrats, opposing President Grant and the Custom House faction. Consequently, Warmoth failed to unify Louisiana's Republican Party and opponents in the state house of representatives impeached him in 1872, but he remained a Louisiana resident until his death in 1931. Warmoth's impeachment suspended him from office and opened the way for an African American governor.

Louisiana had one of the largest pools of educated free and enslaved blacks in the United States before the Civil War. Born free in New Orleans, **Oscar J. Dunn**, gained recognition and gradually moved up in the Republican Party. Nominated as lieutenant governor, Dunn ran on Warmoth's ticket in 1868. Upon his election, Dunn became Louisiana's most influential African American political official. Suddenly, however, on November 22, 1871, Dunn died of an uncertain physical ailment. Promptly, replacements lined up, and Republican leaders decided that Dunn's office had to be filled by another African American. One possibility was state senator Caesar C. Antoine, a former barber from Caddo Parish and member of the state **constitutional convention** of 1867–1868. Antoine later served as Kellogg's lieutenant governor. Another prospect was Dunn's sharpest competitor, **Pinckney Benton Stewart Pinchback**. Born a slave in **Georgia**, Pinchback had worked as a riverboat steward and served in two federal military units, including as a captain in one. In politics, Pinchback also had held a seat in the 1867–1868 constitutional convention with Antoine and then was elected state senator. In December 1871, his senate colleagues picked Pinchback to complete Dunn's term. A year later, Pinchback understood that Warmoth was suspended from office while awaiting trial in the state senate, and thus for thirty-five days, he became the only African American governor of a state during Reconstruction (and the only black governor in the United States until Douglas Wilder was elected governor of Virginia in the late twentieth century).

Democratic Opposition and Violence

Although they tried, Democrats neither persuaded high-profile African American leaders to leave the Republican Party nor rallied the black vote—in part, at least, because of the Democrats' consistent use of **violence** during Reconstruction. By 1876, a few blacks had been intimidated or bribed into announcing that they would vote for Democrats, but employing violence and threats of violence against white and black Republicans offset the claims by ex-Confederates that they would provide the best political home for freedmen and their families. Indeed, the prospect of violence hung like a pall over Louisiana and other southern states throughout the Reconstruction era. The threat of violence could not be offset or removed by either federal officials, such as U.S. marshals, federal attorneys, and the **U.S. Army**, or by state or local officers, including the Metropolitan Police (actually, what amounted to the Louisiana state **militia**), district attorneys, or county sheriffs. Violent acts by anti-Reconstruction forces, such as those perpetrated against the Twitchells, meant that unless federal or state officials happened to be nearby, ex-Confederates and their supporters could strike almost any time against Republican businessmen and their investments, schoolteachers and their schools (including ones enrolling black pupils), **church** leaders and houses of worship, and politicians, including mayors, town councilmen, sheriffs, judges, and state legislators. All Republicans, including businessmen, teachers, ministers, officeholders, and independent-minded farmers who were African Americans, became symbols of Reconstruction's new social, economic, and political order.

Not even the soldiers and officers of the U.S. Army could protect all Republicans all the time across Louisiana. Wartime volunteer "political generals" such as Butler and Banks were succeeded by professional officers educated at West Point, including Generals **E.R.S. Canby**, **Philip H. Sheridan**, **Winfield S. Hancock**, and William H. Emory. Each of them carried out duties as commander of army units in Louisiana in their own way, but all found their assignment difficult, especially when the scale of violence increased. The army's influence was strongest in Louisiana while the state was under the **Military Reconstruction Act** as part of the Fifth Military District in 1867–1868, but anti-Reconstruction forces harped on the assertion that because the army enforced *congressional* acts—guiding the drafting of Louisiana's new constitution, and protecting the new state government—the gubernatorial administrations of Warmoth and Kellogg were illegitimate. This assertion dismissed the fact that the Republicans brought together a majority of voters—native white Louisianans who had supported the Union or opposed the Confederacy, northern settlers, and African Americans.

Spectacular incidents of violence undermined the whole process of Reconstruction, and added the terrifying specter of mass violence to the menace of individual brutal acts. Such spectacular incidents occurred in other former Confederate states (such as the riot in **Memphis**, Tennessee, on April 30, 1866), but Louisiana tallied a terrible toll of killed and injured in civil disorders; most of those casualties were black and white Republicans. One of the worst was the **New Orleans riot** of July 30, 1866, in which dozens of people were killed and injured. Although the situation was ominous before the riot, the U.S. Army failed to take steps to prevent violence. City policemen failed to suppress the riot and instead became rioters themselves. Ironically, when combined with other factors, such as the opposition by President **Andrew Johnson** to rechartering the **Bureau of Refugees, Freedmen, and Abandoned Lands** (Freedmen's Bureau) and the proposed **Fourteenth**

Amendment to the **U.S. Constitution**, the New Orleans riot contributed to the willingness of congressional Republicans to pass the Military Reconstruction Acts of 1867.

Numerous other violent incidents marred Louisiana's record, some carried out by vigilantes belonging to the **White League** and the Knights of the White Camellia, groups similar to the **Ku Klux Klan**. Among them were the actions of armed whites who murdered several black leaders in St. Landry Parish in October 1868. In April 1873, at the town of Colfax, named for **Schuyler Colfax**, Grant's vice president, in Grant Parish, named for the president himself, an organized group of whites attacked the parish courthouse, resulting in more than 100 deaths or injuries, mostly to black men. In the town of Coushatta in Red River Parish in August 1874, as many as 1,000 White Leaguers detained several Republicans, including a deputy U.S. marshal. Although they let the marshal go, the Leaguers murdered their other unarmed captives, including Homer Twitchell.

Perhaps the most spectacular and well-organized violence occurred in September 1874 in New Orleans. Ex-Confederates and supporters of the defeated Democratic candidates in the gubernatorial election of 1872 sought to overthrow Governor Kellogg, and nearly succeeded. Rejecting the certified results of the election, Democratic candidate John D. McEnery arranged an inauguration ceremony at the time that Kellogg officially took the oath of office. Louisiana suffered the spectacle of dual governors. General Emory of the U.S. Army hoped that violence would not flare up, but decided against posting troops at key locations in the city. When street fighting occurred, he had no option but to send army units to assist Kellogg's Metropolitan Police. The Metropolitans, about half of whom were African Americans, were led by former Confederate general **James Longstreet**. One of the riot's leaders was David B. Penn, a former Confederate colonel and the defeated Democratic candidate for lieutenant governor. Penn led McEnery's shadow state militia—the White League. When the Leaguers heard that the U.S. Army was marching to assist the Metropolitans, the violence ended, leaving dozens dead and injured. Thereafter, Kellogg found it difficult to administer the state outside of New Orleans and some southern parishes.

Commentators in the nineteenth century and in later years tried to point to local or parish (county) tensions, rivalries, or antagonisms to explain these and other violent episodes. Taken together, however, such events showed the willingness of former Confederates and their supporters to employ domestic disorder on a large scale to block or cancel out the reforms of Reconstruction, including black male **suffrage**, holding office, serving in the militia, owning land, and serving on juries, as well as black children attending public schools. In violent clashes, blacks were the targets of white vigilantes, and blacks suffered the highest casualties. As a result of the violence, by the mid-1870s, some black and white Louisiana Republicans had decreased or ended their reform activities, left elective or appointive office, or moved out of the state.

During Reconstruction, violence in Louisiana produced notable cases before the U.S. **Supreme Court**. The ***Slaughterhouse Cases*** (1873) grew out of a dispute over the operation of a monopoly granted to a New Orleans meat-processing business, but the real issue related to the Fourteenth Amendment's vital citizenship rights clauses. The Supreme Court ruled in a manner that restricted the reach of federal authorities to protect citizens' rights under the amendment, placing the burden of that protection back on the states. In another case, after white vigilantes attacked the courthouse in Colfax, several of them were arrested, including William Cruikshank. He was one of four whites convicted of murder. He appealed. In ***United States* v. *Cruikshank*** (1876), anti-Reconstruction forces gained further unexpected help from the Supreme Court. It concluded that Cruikshank had been improperly indicted: He should have been indicted for violating the rights of black citizens, but the case focused on the murders, which should have been handled in state rather than federal court. The ruling in *Cruikshank* further restricted the capability of the federal government to uphold the terms of the Fourteenth Amendment and the congressional **Enforcement Acts**.

In the presidential **election of 1876**, the Democrats' methodical applications of threats and violence in Louisiana and elsewhere in the South distorted the result of the canvass. It was dangerous in several Louisiana parishes for Republicans (white and black) to vote. Some towns or parishes that had recorded heavy votes for President Grant in 1868 and 1872 recorded few or no votes for **Rutherford B. Hayes**, the Republican presidential candidate in 1876. Democrats referred to their combined threats and applications of violence as "bulldozing." Bulldozing produced an election so close that Louisiana's Democrats and Republicans claimed victory. **James Madison Wells** and Louisiana's Republican returning board (the state election commission) certified the victory of Packard, with Caesar Antoine planning to continue serving as lieutenant governor. They were inaugurated. The Democrats again rejected the certified results. Democrats arranged for another returning board to claim a win for their candidate, former Confederate general **Francis R. T. Nicholls**, and inaugurated him. Again, Louisiana had dual governments. The outcome of the presidential vote bore directly on the state election. Deciding the outcome required establishing a special federal Election Commission, which declared Hayes the winner. However, Hayes indicated that he would withhold the army's support for Packard, placing the Democratic gubernatorial candidate, Nicholls, in office, and brought the traditional period of Reconstruction to a stunning conclusion.

For a decade after 1877, vestiges remained of the changes brought by Reconstruction. William Kellogg was elected to another term in the U.S. Senate in 1876, held his seat against a challenge, and then won election to the U.S. House of Representatives from 1883 to 1885. Louisiana voters elected four other Republicans to the U.S. House between 1877 and 1891, including Michael Hahn, who died in office in 1886. Scattered across the state, a handful of Republicans held office. Because African Americans appeared recalcitrant after 1877, Democrat "Redeemers" (who had "redeemed" the state for their party) sometimes employed violence against blacks—including lynching—as a means of repression or to channel the black vote to Democratic candidates. *See also* Amnesty Proclamations; Compromise of 1877; Congressional Reconstruction; Freedmen's Bureau Bills; Race Riots; Redemption.

Further Reading: Current, Richard N. *Those Terrible Carpetbaggers*. New York: Oxford University Press, 1988; Dawson, Joseph G., III. *Army Generals and Reconstruction: Louisiana, 1862–1877*. Baton Rouge: Louisiana State University Press, 1982; Foner, Eric. *Reconstruction: America's Unfinished Revolution, 1863–1877*. New York: Harper & Row, 1988; Taylor, Joe Gray. *Louisiana Reconstructed, 1863–1877*. Baton Rouge: Louisiana State University Press, 1974; Tunnell, Ted: *Crucible of Reconstruction: War, Radicalism, and Race in Louisiana, 1862–1877*. Baton Rouge: Louisiana State University Press, 1984; *Edge of the Sword: The Ordeal of Carpetbagger Marshall H. Twitchell in the Civil War and Reconstruction*. Baton Rouge: Louisiana State University Press, 2001; Vandal, Gilles. *Rethinking Southern Violence: Homicides in Post-Civil War Louisiana, 1866–1884*. Columbus: Ohio State University Press, 2000; Vincent, Charles. *Black Legislators in Louisiana during Reconstruction*. Baton Rouge: Louisiana State University Press, 1986.

Joseph G. Dawson III

Loyal League. *See* Union League of America.

Loyalty Oaths

Loyalty oaths were created during the Civil War to ensure that members of the Union were still loyal and as a way to usher the rebel states back into the Union once the war was over.

Abraham Lincoln's attorney general, Edward Bates, suggested that all employees of the departments take oaths of allegiance and by the second week of the Civil War loyalty tests began. Led by a Republican congressman, John F. Potter, a five-member committee was created to investigate which federal employees refused to take the oath. On August 6, 1861, Lincoln made it an official law that a loyalty oath was required of all federal and prospective federal employees. The oath affirmed future loyalty to the government and Constitution of the United States. Although not federally mandated, loyalty oaths swept across the nation in local forms based on the situation. Newspaper correspondents had to take oaths before they were allowed to accompany any federal expedition. Americans in European cities had to take oaths in order to renew visas and passports. In 1862, Lincoln signed into law the ironclad oath test. This required that all appointed or elected persons—except the president and vice president—to any U.S. government office, be it civil, military, or naval, take an oath attesting to past loyalty, meaning they never bore arms against the Union, and pledging future loyalty to the Union.

In December 1863, Lincoln presented his program of Reconstruction, which included an amnesty oath pardoning those former Confederates who pledged future loyalty to the Union. His so-called Ten Percent Plan also authorized the creation of state and local governments in those states, once 10 percent of the white male population (who had voted in 1860) took the oath and pledged to support the Constitution and all federal laws regarding slavery—including **emancipation** and the institution's impending **abolition**.

A growing sect of **Radical Republicans** in Congress opposed the leniency and minimal requirements put forth by the president. As an alternative to Lincoln's proposal, in 1864, congressional Republicans introduced the **Wade-Davis bill**, which required use of an "ironclad oath" that not only required *future* support of the Constitution (as under Lincoln's plan) but also a profession of *past* support. In other words, anyone who had supported the Confederacy, resigned a commission in the U.S. government or its military, or in any way aided the rebellion was automatically disqualified from voting or holding office. Lincoln, seeking a speedy reconciliation, pocket-vetoed the bill.

Following the **assassination of Abraham Lincoln**, **Andrew Johnson** seemed to offer hope to the more radical elements in the party. Although a southern Democrat, Johnson's position as a War Democrat since 1864 and his unswerving loyalty to the Union encouraged other Republicans. As **military governor** of **Tennessee** during the war, Johnson followed a hard line toward Confederates, so Radicals believed Johnson would support them in using the ironclad oath test to keep former rebels away from the polls and out of office. However, the war was over and the Union preserved, so the emergency had passed. Johnson, in his approach to Reconstruction, was at least as lenient as Lincoln, and in effect folded something very much like Lincoln's amnesty oath in his own program. From 1865 through 1867, the president and Congress battled over issues of amnesty, **disfranchisement**, and civil and political rights.

Following the **election of 1866**, Republicans in Congress gained the upper hand. With the passage of the **Military Reconstruction Acts** in 1867, most former Confederates found themselves swept aside by the **U.S. Army**, which was charged with enforcing these new Reconstruction measures—and using severe oaths to eliminate former rebels from the political arena. As a result, Republican **carpetbaggers**, **scalawags**, and newly enfranchised **African American** males seized control of most southern states. In 1868, the ratification of the **Fourteenth Amendment** nationalized the issue and softened the blow. The amendment largely removed the oath from the scene and replaced it with a carrot-and-stick approach, as former Confederates would be disqualified at a rate equal to the disqualification of black males. Finally, upon southern states' **readmission** to the Union, the issue of loyalty was subsumed back into the local sphere. Congress did not dictate that a readmitted state needed to measure the loyalty of its citizens, and so most states dropped the issue altogether. *See also* Amnesty Proclamations; Black Suffrage; Cabinets, Executive; Civil Rights; Congressional Reconstruction; Constitutional Conventions; Democratic Party; Joint Committee on Reconstruction; Pardons; Presidential Reconstruction; Republicans, Liberal; Republicans, Moderate; Stalwarts; Suffrage; Supreme Court; *Texas v. White*; U.S. Constitution.

Further Reading: Hyman, Harold M. *Era of the Oath: Northern Loyalty Tests during the Civil War and Reconstruction*. Philadelphia: University of Pennsylvania Press, 1954.

Catherine Anyaso

Lynch, James D. (1839–1872)

James D. Lynch was among the throng of black leaders from the North who migrated to the South during Reconstruction. In **Mississippi**, Lynch established himself as an influential educator, speaker, minister, editor, and politician. He worked diligently to advance the issues he believed were seminal to black advancement—spiritual well-being, **education**, political rights, and economic empowerment. His early death, at the age of 33, deprived black Mississippians of one of their greatest advocates.

Antebellum and War Years

Lynch was born on January 8, 1839, in Baltimore, **Maryland**. He was raised in relative freedom. His mother was a former slave, but her husband had purchased her freedom. Lynch's father made his living as a merchant and a minister. Lynch attended an elementary school operated by the reverend Daniel A. Payne of the Bethel African Methodist Episcopal (A.M.E.) **Church**. When he was 13, Lynch's parents sent him to Kimball Union Academy in Meriden, New Hampshire, one of the few schools in the region that accepted blacks at that time. Two years later, his father's business struggling to survive, Lynch was forced to leave due to financial hardship. Uncertain what to do with his life, Lynch moved to New York, where he taught for a time in Long Island, and studied for the ministry in Brooklyn.

Lynch's ministerial aspirations led him to train under Elisha Weaver, an A.M.E. minister, in Indianapolis, Indiana. After receiving his preacher's license, Lynch served at a small church in Galena, Illinois. He later moved to the **District of Columbia**, where he was ordained and preached at another church. In 1862, Lynch moved to Baltimore, where he ministered at Waters Chapel Church and married Eugenia Rice. In the same year, Bishop Payne challenged blacks to go to the mission fields of the South. Bitter war had erupted between the North and the South the previous year, and thousands of slaves had been freed as a result. Those thousands of slaves, Lynch and others believed, desperately needed guidance and assistance. Lynch responded to Payne's challenge.

In **South Carolina** and **Georgia**, Lynch ministered to several black regiments and helped establish schools for black children. In Savannah, Georgia, he delivered a moving speech at a meeting attended by black leaders, Secretary of War **Edwin Stanton**, and General **William T. Sherman**. He spoke boldly in support of racial integration. This was only the first of Lynch's many renowned political speeches. He was later elected secretary of the A.M.E.'s first southern conference. This was followed by a busy period of traveling, preaching, and teaching. Bewildered and unequipped for life in liberty, blacks flocked to Lynch, who was himself a symbol of what they could attain. He captivated them with his oratorical style and exhorted them with messages of hope and optimism. He delivered his sermons and speeches with passion, speaking to the hearts of the former slaves. He spoke of their sorrows and showed his understanding of their culture, their concerns, and their innermost desires.

In 1866, Lynch and his family moved to Philadelphia, Pennsylvania, where he edited the *Christian Reader*, a publication for the A.M.E. Church. After sixteen months, he left the Methodist Episcopal (M.E.) Church South and the A.M.E. Church, and lent his services to the M.E. Church North. Longing to recommit to his previous work with the former slaves in the South, Lynch and his family relocated to **Mississippi**. By moving back to the South, Lynch gave up a promising ministerial career in the North.

A Black Carpetbagger with a Cause

Lynch quickly became a political and spiritual giant in Mississippi. Within a year of his return to the South, he had acquired 6,000 black members and established twenty meeting houses. His popularity grew as he further perfected his oratorical skills. Blacks walked for miles to hear him speak. Lynch used his influence to emphasize the need for **education** and to cultivate black voting power. He believed the Republican Party was the best advocate for blacks. He actively worked to help organize the Mississippi Republican Party, contributing greatly to its mass black support. With the coming of **Congressional Reconstruction**, white Republicans took notice and elected him vice president of the first state party convention in the fall of 1867. Lynch's political career gained momentum when he established the *Colored Citizen Monthly*, which he used to promote his views and kept blacks well informed. By the end of 1869, Lynch was one of the most prominent **black politicians** in the state, though he also maintained his commitment to the church.

In politics, Lynch held moderate views. As a result, he was more inclusive than his radical colleagues. Whereas the **Radical Republicans** wanted to exclude the former Confederates from voting and political power, Lynch endorsed **black suffrage** but did not support Confederate **disfranchisement**; indeed, he believed all males should vote. Whereas the local white conservatives wanted to limit black freedom and political power, Lynch espoused black rights and equality. As a result, he toiled to win not only black support but to convert Democrats. Although Lynch desired to integrate schools, he moved charily around this subject. He believed that an immediate radical approach could avert any chances of winning universal support. Lynch also endorsed black economic power. He believed that wealth and landownership would ultimately give blacks control of their lives. Thus, he opposed the **sharecropping** and crop-lien systems that many conservatives supported.

Uncommon Accomplishments

A young, black outsider, Lynch accomplished an extraordinary amount in a short period. He helped manage public lands, enabling Mississippi to allocate lands for schools, and in other ways, helped move Mississippi toward its first free public school system. Lynch held numerous positions as well, including Freedmen's Bureau state assistant, superintendent for education, a member of the Mississippi Board of Education, and secretary of state for Mississippi in 1869 and 1871. He also edited *The Field Hand*, and founded and served as president of the Laboring Man's Association. Following his second stint as secretary of state, he served as a delegate to the National Republican

Convention in 1868. Although he did not obtain his party's nomination for Congress, he campaigned in Indiana for the Grant-Wilson ticket. Upon his return to Mississippi in late 1872, Lynch died unexpectedly from a bronchial infection and Bright's disease.

Lynch was the first known black leader in Mississippi to be buried alongside other state dignitaries in the all-white Greenwood Cemetery in Jackson, Mississippi. The Republican-dominated state legislature appropriated $1,000 toward a monument in his honor. During the **Jim Crow** era, whites challenged the presence of Lynch's remains in the segregated cemetery. Members of the Ladies Auxiliary Cemetery Association were granted permission to remove his remains and the monument erected in his honor. However, the organization never followed through, and James D. Lynch and his monument remain at Greenwood Cemetery today. *See also* African Americans; Black Politicians; Bureau of Refugees, Freedmen, and Abandoned Lands; Carpetbaggers; Contraband, slaves as; Contracts; Democratic Party; Edisto Island, South Carolina; Elections of 1868; Emancipation; Field Order No. 15; Freedmen's Relief Societies; Labor Systems; Military Reconstruction Acts; Port Royal Experiment; Republicans, Moderate; Revels, Hiram R.

Further Reading: Gravely, William. *Gilbert Haven, Methodist Abolitionist: A Study in Race, Religion, and Reform, 1850–1880.* Nashville, TN: Abingdon Press, 1973; Harris, William C. *The Day of the Carpetbagger: Republican Reconstruction in Mississippi.* Baton Rouge: Louisiana State University Press, 1979; Morris, Robert C. *Reading, 'Riting, and Reconstruction: The Education of Freedmen in the South, 1861–1870.* Urbana: University of Chicago Press, 1981; Walker, Clarence. *A Rock in a Weary Land: The African Methodist Episcopal Church during the Civil War and Reconstruction.* Baton Rouge: Louisiana State University Press, 1982. Wharton, Vernon Lane. *The Negro in Mississippi.* Chapel Hill: University of North Carolina Press, 1947.

Gladys L. Knight

Lynch, John R. (1847–1939)

John Roy Lynch, first black congressman from **Mississippi**, Reconstruction historian, lawyer, soldier, and businessman, was one of the most distinguished leaders of the Reconstruction and post-Reconstruction eras.

Humble Slave Beginnings

Born near Vidalia, **Louisiana**, on September 10, 1847, on his father's plantation, Lynch remained a slave until the Civil War. His white father and slave mother also had at least two other children. Although Lynch's father had promised to free Lynch's mother and children, he died before he had completed the official paperwork. A trusted friend failed to carry out his charge, and instead sold Lynch and the rest of his family to a prominent Natchez, Mississippian, Alfred V. Davis. Lynch served as Davis's body servant until 1863, when the young slave escaped to Union lines as northern troops approached Natchez. Lynch then worked in the Union camp and later as a waiter on a naval vessel. After the war, with Natchez occupied by Union troops, he was

John R. Lynch. (Courtesy of the Library of Congress.)

able to get his only formal **education**, attending night school for four months until the school closed. He furthered his education by reading on his own and listening to the lessons at the white school across the alley from the photographic studio where he worked and eventually managed.

Reconstruction Politician

With the coming of the Republican Party to the South—following the passage of the **Military Reconstruction Acts** in 1867—Lynch began to move into politics. It seemed a logical progression: Aristocratic in appearance, slender, with a light complexion and impressive oratorical skills, Lynch seemed a natural **African American** leader. As Mississippi crafted its new government under **Congressional Reconstruction**, Lynch joined the Republican Party and campaigned for black **civil rights** and the new state constitution. Impressed with the young man's abilities, Governor **Adelbert Ames** appointed Lynch a Natchez justice of the peace. After serving for a year, Lynch entered the Mississippi legislature in 1870 as the representative from Adams County, where he served for three terms. Although blacks represented a minority in the state house of representatives and Lynch was only in his mid-twenties, he was elected speaker in 1873. Democrats and Republicans, whites and blacks, praised his intelligence, his speaking abilities, and his impartiality. Indeed, one **Democratic Party** member admitted that there were few who could exceed Lynch's skills as a stump speaker. As a state legislator, Lynch introduced legislation attempting to declare the **Ku Klux Klan** illegal, to establish a university for blacks, and to provide for integrated seating in public transportation. He also fought the convict-lease system and urged the governor to request federal troops to counter **violence** in Mississippi.

In November 1872, citizens of Mississippi's Sixth Congressional District elected Lynch to the U.S. Congress, choosing him over the white Republican incumbent, L. W. Pearce and then over his Democratic opponent, Judge Hiram Cassidy. Taking his seat in December 1873, Lynch entered as the youngest member of the 43rd Congress, the first black congressman from Mississippi, and only one of twenty-two blacks to serve in Congress between 1870 and 1901. Reelected to the 44th Congress, Lynch was the only Republican to win a congressional seat from Mississippi for that term, narrowly defeating Democrat Roderick Seal, a prominent antebellum politician and Confederate war hero. While in Congress, Lynch worked in many ways to ensure fair elections and a life for all free of intimidation. For example, he spoke forcefully for the enactment of stronger **enforcement** legislation to protect equal rights in the South and worked energetically for the passage of the **Civil Rights Act of 1875**, which banned discrimination in public accommodations (later declared unconstitutional by the U.S. **Supreme Court** in the *Civil Rights Cases* of 1883).

After Redemption

However, Lynch could not survive the white Mississippians' "**redemption**" techniques of violence, intimidation, and corruption; he lost in November 1876 by 4,000 votes to Confederate general James R. Chalmers, who had commanded the troops at the Fort Pillow massacre. Although he appealed to Congress, charging the Democrats with fraud, the Democratic majority on the House Committee on Elections refused to consider his case.

In November 1880, Lynch again ran for Congress against Chalmers. In another close contest, Lynch was declared the loser, only after the Democratically-controlled election board threw out thousands of votes. This time, the Republican majority in Congress listened to Lynch's charges of fraud and, on April 27, 1882, voted to seat him. In this, his last term in Congress, he introduced bills attempting to ensure honest elections, to provide relief for orphans, and to reimburse depositors who had lost money in the **Freedman's Savings and Trust Company**. After losing by narrow majorities in his 1882 and 1884 bids for Congress, Lynch retired from elective politics. Throughout his congressional career, he had been one of the most influential blacks in the country, frequently consulting with Presidents **Ulysses S. Grant** and **James A. Garfield**.

Returning to Natchez as a private citizen, Lynch engaged in agricultural and real estate ventures, eventually owning several plantations and other property in the Natchez area. He also invested in a black-owned bank and, in 1897, became its president. Politically, he served as chair of the Republican State Executive Committee from 1881 to 1892, advocating fusion of Mississippi's Republicans with Independent-Populists, and as a delegate from Mississippi to five Republican national conventions. In 1884, as the first black to serve as the temporary chairman of a party convention, Lynch delivered the convention's keynote address, urging party unity and attacking the Democrats' fraudulent election practices. At the 1888 Republican National Convention, Lynch served on the most important committees—the committee on resolutions and the subcommittee that prepared the platform. He also served as fourth auditor of the Treasury Department during President Benjamin Harrison's administration.

After resigning the auditor position in 1893, Lynch returned to Mississippi, read law, and passed the Mississippi bar in 1896. He then returned to Washington, D.C., where he practiced law and wrote articles advocating black rights. In 1898, at the age of fifty-one, he embarked on a new career as an officer in the **U.S. Army**, answering President William McKinley's call for black officers at the start of the Spanish-American War. Serving as a paymaster, Lynch traveled to Cuba, Haiti, other Caribbean islands, and the Philippines. Lynch had married Ella W. Somerville in 1884, with whom he had a daughter, but that marriage ended in divorce in 1900. Upon his retirement from the army in 1911 with the rank of major, Lynch married Cora E. Williamson of Chicago and moved to Chicago, resuming his law practice.

Reconstruction Historian

More important, Lynch took up the task of correcting what he saw as the errors historians of Reconstruction were making. In 1913, he published *The Facts of Reconstruction*, attacking the histories of James Ford Rhodes, William A. Dunning, and their many students. Writing that his goal was "to bring to public notice those things that were commendable and meritorious" during Reconstruction, Lynch denied the Dunning school's story of greedy **carpetbaggers**, corrupt **scalawags**, and ignorant blacks. Rather, he detailed his experiences in Mississippi, contending that the southern Reconstruction governments accomplished a great deal of good, broadened democracy, and were neither corrupt nor inept. He continued this fight against historical distortion when he published articles in the *Journal of Negro History* in 1917 and 1918, later published in 1922 as a book entitled *Some Historical Errors of James F. Rhodes*. Arguing against Rhodes's claim that illegal election methods were needed to overthrow "Negro domination," Lynch demonstrated that Republicans, not blacks, dominated. Further, he contended, the Reconstruction governments were the only governments in the South to ever have a truly Republican form of government. At his death, he was writing his *Reminiscences of an Active Life*; in 1970, this was edited and published by John Hope Franklin and the University of Chicago Press. Those reminiscences detail Lynch's life, including his struggles to win elections in the face of white hostility and fraud and his role in Reconstruction politics. Lynch died in Chicago on November 2, 1939, at the age of ninety-two. He was buried in Arlington National Cemetery with full military honors. *See also* Black Politicians; Constitutional Conventions; Contraband, Slaves as; White League. Also consult the Introduction for coverage of the various trends in Reconstruction history.

Further Reading: Franklin, John Hope. "John Roy Lynch: Republican Stalwart from Mississippi." In *Race and History: Selected Essays, 1938–1988*. Baton Rouge: Louisiana University Press, 1989, pp. 250–66; Lynch, John R.: *The Facts of Reconstruction*. New York: The Neale Publishing Company, 1913; *Reminiscences of an Active Life*. Edited with an introduction by John Hope Franklin. Chicago: University of Chicago Press, 1970; *Some Historical Errors of James Ford Rhodes*. Boston: The Cornhill Publishing Co., 1922; McLaughlin, James H. "John R. Lynch the Reconstruction Politician: A Historical Perspective." Ph.D. dissertation, Ball State University, 1981.

Roberta Sue Alexander